American History for Children and Young Adults

Libraries Unlimited Data Books

American History for Children and Young Adults: An Annotated Bibliographic Index. By Vandelia VanMeter.

The Best: High/Low Books for Reluctant Readers. By Marianne Laino Pilla.

CD-ROM: An Annotated Bibliography. By Ahmed M. Elshami.

Science Experiments Index for Young People. By Mary Anne Pilger.

AMERICAN HISTORY

An Annotated
Bibliographic
Index

FOR

CHILDREN

AND

YOUNG

ADULTS

Vandelia
VanMeter

A Libraries Unlimited Data Book

1990
LIBRARIES UNLIMITED, INC.
Englewood, Colorado

LIBRARIES UNLIMITED, INC.
P.O. Box 3988
Englewood, CO 80155-3988

Library of Congress Cataloging-in-Publication Data

VanMeter, Vandelia.
   American history for children and young adults : an annotated
bibliographic index / Vandelia VanMeter.
      xv, 324p. 22x28 cm. -- (Libraries Unlimited data books)
      ISBN 0-87287-731-0
      1. United States--History--Indexes.   2. United States--History--Juvenile
literature--Indexes.   I. Title.   II. Series.
Z1236.V35   1990
[E178]
016.973--dc20   90-5815
                                                                             CIP

Contents

Libraries Unlimited Data Books

The Libraries Unlimited Data Book series consists of bibliographies and indexes that are issued simultaneously in traditional print format and in one or several computerized databases. Unlike most CD-ROM products, data books are designed as inexpensive in-house resources to be used with popular database managers used by most libraries, such as Microsoft Works, AppleWorks, or dBase.

Indexes presented in the series provide an innovative idea in indexing for the individual library. Purchasers can tailor the index to their own collections. For example, if the database indexes 300 books and the library owns only 200 of those titles, the 100 titles not owned by the library can be deleted from the database, thus producing an index that matches the library's collection. Titles owned by the library but not indexed can be added to the database as needed. The database can be printed out or consulted by computer as needed by library patrons.

Bibliographies in the series have the advantage of being searched in ways not possible with the printed version. The limitations of these searches are those of the database manager that the librarian uses, that is, the limitations are those of dBase III + , PC File + , Microsoft Works, or any other package used to search the data. The advantage of the bibliography on disk is that it can be modified to suit the needs of local patrons. Local call numbers may be added, new entries may be added by the library, and the publisher can keep the bibliography current between editions of the printed version. Versions for IBM, Macintosh, and the Apple II family are available. Write or call the publisher for details.

Special Needs

Libraries or individuals needing the data in a special computer format or needing parts of the databases are invited to write to the editorial department of Libraries Unlimited for assistance. Include a description of your needs and the format in which you wish the data to be arranged. A price quotation will be provided by return mail.

Users who find errors in the data or who could provide updates to the data are invited to correspond with the editorial department.

Write:

Head,
Editorial Department
Libraries Unlimited, Inc.
P.O. Box 3988
Englewood, CO 80155-3988
Phone: (303) 770-1220

Acknowledgments

From inception to publication, *American History for Children and Young Adults* has been two years in development. During that time many persons at the University of Southern Mississippi have contributed work and encouragement to its completion. They include my graduate assistants over that time, Sandra Shaw, Robert Strauss, and Jamie Elston. Each of them has been meticulous in the work and unstinting in enthusiasm and support. Other graduate students who have assisted include Elyse McCrory, Shu Hua (Diana) Yang, Lisa DeKruif, and Pollyanne S. Frantz. They have photocopied, alphabetized, entered records on the database, checked *OCLC, Book Review Index,* and *Book Review Digest*, and proofread. Secretary Mary Wade contributed greatly by photocopying and alphabetizing thousands of reviews.

My colleagues have unfailingly provided moral support. Professors Glenn Wittig and Julia Young have each been a sounding board and have helped me think through problems, and Julia's editing suggestions were very helpful. My friend, Dr. James L. Thomas, of Texas Woman's University, convinced me that I really could do this.

Without Vic, my husband of 35 years, this book could never have been begun, let alone completed. He provided moral support, entered hundreds of records, taught me how to be an effective user of a database, and generally kept me sane.

Thanks to all of you, here it is.

Introduction

American History for Children and Young Adults has three purposes: to provide an annotated bibliography of recently recommended nonfiction and fiction trade books relating to U.S. history for students grades K-12, arranged chronologically and by subject; to provide a guide to reviews of these books; and to include annotations and a guide to reviews of "old standbys" still in print.

The recent titles listed were reviewed between 1980 and 1988 in standard reviewing tools commonly used by school and public libraries. The old standbys are those works found in Seymour Metzner's *American History in Juvenile Books* (H. W. Wilson, 1966), which have remained so popular that they are still in print. In-print items listed in the Metzner bibliography are included because Metzner is still in print in spite of its age, and it is referenced in such standard works as *Elementary School Library Collection* and *Children's Catalog*. Since those individual titles are still in print (usually in new editions), it is assumed that they have been found to be of value and therefore warrant inclusion in this work. It is regretted that titles published 1966-1979 are not included here. If demand makes it worthwhile to publish a supplement that covers those dates, it will be considered and suggestions are welcome.

Criteria for Selection

All books selected are related to American history in a broad sense. They include works on immigrants, inventors, and the growth of labor unions, along with more traditional works on explorers, wars, and presidents. Also included are works on the social life and customs of each time period since this type of work has proven valuable in stimulating the interest of students into the investigation of the events of the time. Works on the history of the Indians of North America are included; works primarily on Indian culture are omitted, since this material is adequate in quantity to justify another volume. Basically, works that treat persons, events, or movements that might reasonably be considered as having influenced the development of American history or that provide insight into the times are included.

The old standbys included were listed in the Metzner bibliography and in the 1986-1987 issue of *Books in Print*. Where possible, one review of the original work or the new edition is listed for the Metzner items. Of the items reviewed 1980-1988, each title included received a favorable or mixed review in at least one of the review sources examined, and a search was made to find and include reference to all the other reviews on that title from the following review journals. The journals chosen as the basis for the search for recently recommended titles are journals in common use in school and public libraries. The journals searched are:

Book Report
Booklist
Bulletin for the Center of Children's Books
History Teacher
Horn Book
Library Journal
School Library Journal
Social Education
Voice of Youth Advocates

Scope

The nine periodicals listed above, dated 1980-1988, were searched for appropriate reviews. *American History* lists 2,901 titles, including fiction, nonfiction, and biography, with reference to over 6,000 reviews. The list includes works on particular historical and political events and movements as well as works of a more general nature. These may examine a time period from a particular point of view or provide a feeling for the time through a work of fiction.

Fiction that has a historic setting is included only when it appears from the reviews that the time and setting are an integral part of, and influence, the action. If the setting appears incidental to the story, the title is omitted. Materials on wars that involve the U.S. and other nations will be found here if the review indicates that coverage of U.S. involvement is a major part of the work. Books dealing with the history of agriculture, airplanes, medicine, etc., are not included unless it appears from the review that the work relates this specialized history to its impact on the historical development of the nation.

The arrangement of the titles is intended to be of maximum usefulness to the following groups:

1. School and public librarians for collection development

2. Teachers conducting individualized reading programs

3. Teachers, parents, and librarians wishing to provide guidance to students seeking reading materials for personal enjoyment or for school assignments

4. Librarians, teachers, or parents of gifted or remedial students who need materials above or below grade level

5. Authors and publishers who need a ready reference to the availability of literature in specific areas of American history

The inclusion of fiction and nonfiction make this a valuable tool for librarians and teachers assisting readers, who, whether for personal enjoyment or for an assignment, need to find books set in a particular period. The subdivisions under each period provide quick access to more specialized materials.

The inclusion of both old and new titles broadens the usefulness of *American History*. In addition to the old titles found in Metzner, there are other old titles that were listed in the 1980-1988 journals. These may be new editions or they may have been included in a retrospective subject listing. Their inclusion will make this book helpful to librarians as an additional tool for collection analysis and weeding as well as in selection of new purchases.

A certain ethnocentric bias is seen in the selection of titles for inclusion in this work. In all cases the compiler attempted to keep in mind the manner in which these topics are approached in a normal U.S. history class. For example, a book about World War I, World War II, the Korean War, or the Vietnamese War, will be included here if it contains information about American involvement. A biography of the Marquis de Lafayette is included in the division pertaining to the Revolutionary War since that is where American students usually become acquainted with him.

The general heading of History, which precedes all other chronologic divisions, includes materials too broad to place in other divisions. In many cases the divisions in this book do not precisely match those of the book reviewed, and a judgment was made on whether to place that title in the broad category of History or in the nearest chronologic division possible. For this reason, users are encouraged to check the obvious chronologic divisions, the divisions on either side of that, the History division, and the proper indexes.

General biographies of presidents are found in the chronologic division of their presidency, regardless of their other notable activities. If, however, a work deals exclusively with one portion of a president's life, it will be found in the appropriate chronology, e.g., a work on Eisenhower's leadership during World War II, excluding any other aspect of his life, would be found in the 1939-1945 division.

Arrangement

Entries are arranged under the appropriate chronologic divisions and subdivisions. The subdivisions are coordinated with *Sears List of Subject Headings* (13th edition, 1986). In some cases subdivisions were combined, e.g., Espionage and Spies; Inventions and Inventors. Subdivisions were occasionally subdivided again if the quantity and subject matter made this seem appropriate, e.g., Reformers, Reformers — Black, Reformers — Women.

A typical entry includes the following information:

Title and subtitle.

Author/Editor. Restrictions of space in the database allowed the entry of the first named author/editor only. The absence of the names of other contributors is regretted.

Series. The name of the series is included in parentheses if it is available through the reviews. Unfortunately, review journals have differing policies on the inclusion of series information, so it is possible that some series names may be omitted.

The reviews of some items published by *Congressional Quarterly* show this as a series entry also. For the convenience of those who may wish to locate easily all items by *Congressional Quarterly*, a series entry under that name has been made for all their publications. The many publications of the Opposing Viewpoints series also required special consideration. These are generally on current political rather than historic topics. If, however, the review indicates that in a particular title the treatment of the topic under discussion includes a historical perspective, the title is included.

Publisher/Distributor. All publishers and distributors are given in a recognizable abbreviated form. In the case of small presses whose addresses may not appear in the usual publishers' directories, the user is referred to the reviews where that information may be found.

Date. For items republished at a much later date than the original, both dates are provided where they are reasonably available through reviews, *OCLC, Book Review Digest*, or other standard sources. The dates are presented in this format: 1961, 1987.

Cost. All costs are rounded up to the nearest dollar. The price listed is for the trade edition unless specified as paperback (*Pb*) or library edition (*Lib. ed.*), insofar as this information could be determined from the reviews. Users are cautioned that the prices listed here can be used only as a general guide, since they change rapidly. Even so, it is felt that the price listed in the review would be useful as an indication of what the purchaser might expect to pay.

Physical Description. This includes information on paging, volumes, and illustrations. All illustrations, drawings, photographs, lithographs, maps, and other illustrative matter are listed under the abbreviation *ill.* unless the review indicates that the only illustrative matter is maps, in which case the word *Maps* appears.

Grade Level. If a work received multiple reviews, and if the reviewers recommend varied grade levels, the inclusive range is provided, with ages interpolated as grades. In the event that the reviews do not indicate grade or age, *Books in Print* was consulted. The user will note that on some titles the inclusive grade range given in the reviews is very broad. Those selecting titles for purchase are encouraged to consider this, to check the reviews in their favorite sources, and to make grade level judgments based on their experiences with that particular journal. Some items, particularly from *Booklist* and *Library Journal*, have been recommended for public libraries, but appear to be suitable for advanced or gifted students or for collections more highly developed than the norm. These items are included with the designation *Adult*.

Abbreviations to review sources. The titles of the review sources are abbreviated in this way:

B	*Booklist*
BC	*Bulletin for the Center of Children's Books*
BR	*Book Report*
HB	*Horn Book*
HT	*History Teacher*
LJ	*Library Journal*
SE	*Social Education*
SLJ	*School Library Journal*
VOYA	*Voice of Youth Advocates*

Following the abbreviation for the title of the journal, the volume number and date are given. A symbol may appear before the abbreviation for the title of the journal to indicate a ranking, e.g., * for highly recommended, + - for mixed recommendation, - for a negative review. The absence of a symbol indicates a normal recommendation. Items reviewed in *Voice of Youth Advocates* (*VOYA*) are given an * if *VOYA* rates an item 5Q or 4Q5P.

All titles included received at least a mixed review in at least one of the journals searched, or appeared in Metzner. As many reviews as possible from the list of review journals are included. If an item is listed in Metzner this is noted as *Metzner* in the description. If the review sources used published reviews to the titles listed in Metzner, these reviews are included in brackets following Metzner, e.g., Metzner [B 52: Oct 15 1955. HB 31: Dec 1955].

The design of the database limits the number of reviews to seven. In some cases a mixed review shows serious reservations, but in others it may be based on illustrations or some editorial decision that does not negate the value of the content. Thus users interested in the subject matter of an item are encouraged to read the reviews to determine whether it may have value for them. Users are urged to read as many reviews as possible before purchase, especially where mixed or unfavorable reviews are listed.

Annotations

Brief annotations have been provided to clarify subject matter. All annotations are based on an examination of the reviews listed for each title. Unfavorable comments are not included in annotations since all the reviewers may not agree, but they are indicated by the evaluative symbols mentioned above. If there is a consensus of excellence concerning organization, photographs, or similar features, this is mentioned as space allows. Once again, users of this book are urged to use it as a reference to the original reviews whenever possible.

Sample Entry

Pioneers–Biographies–Fiction

1381. McCall, Edith. Message from the Mountains. (Walker's American History Series for Young People). Walker, 1985. 122 p. map. $12.
Gr 6-9. BC 39: Dec 1985. SLJ 32: Nov 1985. VOYA 8: Dec 1985. A fictionalized but accurate account of young Kit Carson and his friend Jim, growing up in Franklin, Missouri in 1826.

Alphabetization

Because *American History* was done on a database, users will note that the manner in which the subdivisions are alphabetized does not follow standard practice. Commas precede dashes, achieving the following result: Immigration; Immigration, Chinese; Immigration, Swedish; Immigration—Children; Immigration—Fiction.

Indexes

Under the appropriate chronological division and subject subdivision, entries are arranged by author. Indexes are provided to authors, titles, subjects, series, and grade levels. Entries in all the indexes refer the user back to the master item number, not the page number.

Supplements

The compiler and Libraries Unlimited plan supplements to this book. These supplements will follow the same format and will be announced in Libraries Unlimited's catalogs.

Related Work

Soon after the publication of this title, a related work entitled *World History for Children and Young Adults: An Annotated Bibliographic Index* is scheduled for release. *World History* will be useful for K-12 classes in social studies and world history, and both books will be helpful in covering topics of international interest, such as wars, foreign policy, and exploration.

General History

1. Concise Dictionary of American History. Scribner, 1983. 1140 p. $60.
Gr 9+. B 80: May 15 1984. LJ 108: Jul 1983. A rich one-volume version of the eight-volume Dictionary of American History (1976) with articles abridged, bibliographies and index omitted.

2. Scribner Desk Dictionary of American History. Scribner, 1984. 631 p. $25.
Gr 9+. +- B 81: May 15 1985. Provides brief identification of events, places, and movements.

3. Sense of History: The Best Writing from the Pages of American Heritage. American Heritage; dist. by Houghton, 1985. 832 p. $30.
Gr 9+. B 82: Nov 15 1985. Fifty articles gleaned from the first 30 years of American Heritage.

4. Agel, Jerome. America At Random: Q & A. Priam: Arbor House, 1983. 254 p. ill. Pb. $7.
Gr 9+. LJ 108: Aug 1983. Questions and answers on all aspects of U.S. history suitable for trivia collections.

5. Anno, Mitsumasa. Anno's U.S.A. Philomel, 1983. 49 p. ill. $11.
Gr K+. +- B 80: Feb 1 1984. B 83: Sep 15 1986; Mar 1 1987. * BC 37: Dec 1983. HB 60: Feb 1984. * SE 48: May 1984. SLJ 30: Jan 1984. A lone oarsman makes his way east from California through the countryside and the cities, enjoying nature and U.S. history in this wordless picture book for all ages.

6. Appel, David H. Album for Americans, An. Crown, 1983. 268 p. ill. $25.
Gr 9+. LJ 108: Oct 15 1983. SLJ 30: Nov 1983. The American story told through prose, poems, songs, ballads, and documents. Well indexed.

7. Boardman, Barrington. Isaac Asimov Presents from Harding to Hiroshima. Dembner Books; dist. by Norton, 1988. 336 p. $20.
Gr 9+. LJ 113: Mar 1 1988. Chronologically and topically arranged anecdotes and trivia on U.S. history, 1921-1945.

8. Brogan, Hugh. Longman History of the United States of America, The. Morrow, 1986. 740 p. ill. $25.
Gr 10+. LJ 111: Jul 1986. A lively history of the United States as seen from the British point of view.

9. Brownstone, Douglas. Field Guide to America's History, A. Facts on File, 1984. 320 p. ill. $18. Pb $10.
Gr 9+. B 81: Dec 15 1984. This guide to natural and manmade features in our history covers canals, inns, railroads, millstones, noted architecture, and important agricultural implements. Indexed.

10. Burns, James MacGregor. Vineyard of Liberty, The. (American Experiment). Knopf, 1982. 703 p. $23.
Gr 9+. B 78: Nov 1 1981. * LJ 106: Dec 15 1981. Reconstructs the life of the Republic from the ratification of the Constitution through the Emancipation Proclamation. The first of three planned volumes.

11. Burns, James MacGregor. Workshop of Democracy, The. (American Experiment). Knopf, 1985. 672 p. $25.
Gr 9+. B 82: Sep 1 1985. * LJ 110: Aug 1985. Covers social, political and cultural issues and trends, and significant persons from the Civil War to the Depression. Volume two of the series.

12. Carpenter, Allan. Far-Flung America. (New Enchantment of America Series). Rev. ed. Childrens Press, 1979. 96 p. ill. $7.
Gr 5-7. SLJ 26: Mar 1980. An overview of U.S. history, geography, economy, resources, culture, and people. Updated, with full-color photos and large type.

13. Carruth, Gorton. Encyclopedia of American Facts and Dates. 7th ed. Crowell, 1979. 1015 p. $15.
Gr 9+. B 76: Jul 1 1980. A chronological look at political and social events, 986 A.D.-1977. Provides facts, dates, and noteworthy events. Excellent index.

14. Carruth, Gorton. Encyclopedia of American Facts and Dates. 8th ed. Harper, 1987. 1006 p. $30.
Gr 9+. B 83: Apr 15 1987. Four parallel columns list events chronologically from 986 to 1986 on such topics as politics and war, the arts, social events, business, science, education, and religion.

15. Chafe, William. Unfinished Journey: America since World War II. Oxford University Press, 1986. 516 p. $25. Pb $15.
Gr 9+. HT 21: Aug 1988. An overview of American economics, foreign policy, politics and social trends from 1945 through the mid 1980s. Chafe examines the effects of these changes on all races, classes, and genders with useful detail.

16. Cross, R. W. 20th Century. Rev. ed. Purnell, 1979. 20 vol. ill. $300.
Gr 9+. +- B 77: Jan 15 1981. A comprehensive survey, with emphasis on political, economic, social, and military history, including over 5000 illustrations. Current to 1978.

17. Divine, Robert A. America: Past and Present. Scott, Foresman, 1983. 2 vol. ill. $27 single vol.; $17 ea. for splits.
Gr 11+. HT 18: Nov 1984. For advanced placement students, a colorful political, military, and diplomatic history.

18. Dollar, Charles M. American Issues: A Documentary Reader. Random House, 1988. 478 p. ill. $11.
Gr 11+. SE 52: Sep 1988. The full range of American history is covered in this sourcebook of readings for advanced placement students. Includes photos, graphs, and charts.

19. Goldberg, M. Hirsh. Blunder Book: Gigantic Slipups, Minor Mistakes, and Colossal Errors That Have Changed the Course of History. Morrow, 1984. 233 p. $13.
Gr 9+. B 80: Aug 1984. LJ 109: Aug 1984. A delightful survey of Murphy's Law in action in U.S. history.

20. Hanmer, Trudy J. Advancing Frontier, The. (Issues in American History). Watts, 1986. 144 p. ill. $11.
Gr 8+. B 83: Feb 15 1987. +- SLJ 33: Jan 1987. VOYA 9: Feb 1987. Examines how the ideals of democracy were influenced by Jefferson, Lincoln, and other leaders and by the expanding frontier. Also makes it clear that many groups did not benefit from their ideas.

21. Hochman, Stanley. Yesterday and Today: A Dictionary of Recent American History. McGraw-Hill, 1979. 407 p. ill. $20.
Gr 9+. +- B 77: Sep 1 1980. LJ 105: Jan 1 1980, Apr 15 1980. Defines and describes major and minor events in national political and cultural life since 1945. Includes cultural allusions and quotations.

22. Lee, R. Alton. Encyclopedia USA: The Encyclopedia of the United States of America Past and Present. Academic International Press, 1983-. 7 Vols. $32/Vol.
Gr 9+. +- B 82: Aug 1986. The first seven volumes of an "open-ended project to create the most comprehensive encyclopedia of American history and life yet printed."

23. Morison, Samuel Eliot. Growth of the American Republic, The. 7th ed. Oxford University Press, 1980. 2 vol. ill. $17 ea., $50 set.
Gr 9+. * B 76: May 1 1980. An updated edition of a lucid and objective work that has been a standard in the field for 50 years.

24. National Archives Trust Fund Board. American Image: Photographs from the National Archives, 1860-1960. Pantheon; dist by Random, 1979. 191 p. ill. $20. Pb $10.
Gr 9+. B 76: Feb 1 1980. LJ 105: Feb 15 1980. This sample of over 200 photos from the Archives covers a fascinating mix of historical and cultural topics, including war, exploration and expansion, urbanization and technology, immigration, and racial conflict.

25. Phillips, John. It Happened in Our Lifetime: A Memoir in Words and Pictures. Little, Brown, 1985. 279 p. ill. $25.
Gr 10+. B 82: Dec 15 1985. LJ 111: Jan 1986. Algerian-born Phillips was a pioneering photographer for Life magazine. His photos of events since the 1930s are enhanced by fascinating anecdotes.

26. Schlesinger, Arthur M., Jr. Almanac of American History, The. Putnam, 1983. 623 p. ill. $25.
Gr 9+. +- B 80: Aug 1984. LJ 109: Jan 1984. This illustrated chronology of American history A.D. 986 to 1986 includes mini-essays on people and events.

27. Scott, John Anthony. Story of America: A National Geographic Picture Atlas. National Geographic Society, 1984. 324 p. col. ill. $20. Lib. ed. $22.
Gr 5-9. B 81: Jan 1 1985. BC 38: Mar 1985. SLJ 31: Feb 1985, May 1985. From the Paleo-Indians through the Vietnam War, this is a lavishly illustrated social history of the area now known as the United States.

28. Swanson, June. Spice of America, The. (Good Time Library). Carolrhoda, 1983. 92 p. ill. $8.
Gr 3-7. HB 60: Apr 1984. SE 48: May 1984. SLJ 30: Feb 1984. Brief stories about little known events in U.S. history. Recommended for browsing, trivia buffs, or those who think history must be dull.

29. Tindall, George Brown. America: A Narrative History. Norton, 1984. 2 vol. ill. $35.
Gr 9+. B 80: Feb 15 1984. LJ 109: Feb 15 1984. Social and economic considerations are taken into account in this detailed history that permits each time period to stand alone.

30. Urdang, Laurence. Timetables of American History, The. Simon & Schuster, 1981. 470 p. ill. $25.
Gr 9+. B 78: Mar 1 1982. LJ 107: Mar 15 1982. VOYA 5: Jun 1982. Juxtaposes events in U.S. history with concurrent events in world history, under a variety of topics. Extensive indexing.

31. Youngs, J. William T. American Realities: Historical Episodes from Reconstruction to the Present. Little, Brown, 1981. 286 p. $15.
Adult. +- HT 17: Nov 1983. Essays to help students feel their common humanity with people of the past.

32. Youngs, J. William T. American Realities: Historical Episodes From the First Settlement to the Civil War. Little, Brown, 1981. 270 p. $15.
Adult. +- HT 17: Nov 1983. Essays to help students feel their common humanity with people of the past.

33. Zinn, Howard. People's History of the United States, A. Harper, 1980. 512 p. $18.
Gr 9+. B 76: Jan 15 1980. LJ 105: Jan 1 1980. U.S. history from the perspective of ordinary powerless people.

General History–Bibliographies

34. Wiltz, John E. Books in American History: A Basic List for High Schools and Junior Colleges. 2nd rev. ed. Indiana University Press, 1981. 128 p. $13. Pb $6.
Gr 9+. B 78: Sep 1 1981. LJ 106: Apr 1 1981. Covers fiction, nonfiction, and nonprint materials from early days through the Nixon years. Annotated and arranged by subject.

General History–Maps

35. Ferrell, Robert H. Atlas of American History. Facts on File, 1987. 192 p. ill. $25.
Gr 9+. B 84: Mar 1 1988. BR 7: May/Jun 1988. +- LJ 113: Jan 1988. Two hundred maps accompanied by essays provide an overview of our history through 1984 in this totally new one-volume historical atlas that emphasizes military activity.

36. Moore, R. I. Rand McNally Atlas of World History. Rev. and updated ed. Rand McNally, 1987. 192 p. maps. $18.
Gr 7+. B 84: Jun 15 1988. Includes maps on U.S. and world history.

37. Portinaro, Pierluigi. Cartography of North America: 1500-1800. Facts on File, 1987. 320 p. ill. $60.

Gr 11+. +- BR 7: May/Jun 1988. Includes maps from Columbus' time to the late 18th century, with commentaries and numerous illustrations.

General History–Songs

38. Forcucci, Samuel L. Folk Song History of America: America through Its Songs. Prentice-Hall/Reward, 1984. 256 p. $23. Pb $13.
Gr 9+. B 80: May 15 1984. LJ 109: Jun 1 1984. A chronological and regional arrangement of folk songs from the Revolution to the 20th century. Includes music, lyrics, and guitar chords.

39. Scott, John Anthony. Ballad of America, The. Southern Illinois University Press, 1983. 439 p. $13.
Adult. HT 17: Aug 1984. Approximately 150 folkballads are arranged chronologically, representing diverse groups of people in society. Introductory essays and discographies are useful.

Agriculture

40. Bellville, Cheryl Walsh. Farming Today: Yesterday's Way. Carolrhoda, 1984. 40 p. ill. $9.
Gr 1-3. B 81: Oct 1 1984. HB 60: Nov/Dec 1984. * SLJ 31: Nov 1984. Covers one year of work on a Wisconsin farm where work is still done with draft horses as the pioneers worked. Excellent photos.

41. Ebeling, Walter. Fruited Plain: Story of American Agriculture. University of California Press, 1980. 433 p. ill. $23.
Gr 9+. B 76: May 1 1980. LJ 104: Nov 15 1979. This comprehensive overview includes a chapter on the roots of agricultural history, detailed studies of the development of seven U.S. geographical regions, an aerial survey, and current farming methods.

42. Horwitz, Elinor Lander. On the Land: American Agriculture from Past to Present. Atheneum, 1980. 132 p. ill. $9.
Gr 7+. * B 76: Jul 1 1980. BC 34: Nov 1980. * SLJ 27: Oct 1980. A succinct overview of agricultural history, including the roles of indentured servants, slaves, tenant farmers, migrant workers, and how governmental policy affects agriculture. Includes photos.

Airplanes and Pilots

43. Bryan, C. D. B. National Air and Space Museum: Volume One: Air, Volume Two: Space. Peacock Press/Bantam, 1979, 1982. 2 vol. ill. $13 ea.
Gr 7+. BR 1: Jan/Feb 1983. Presents the details of man's attempt to fly and information on his flying machines. Numerous colored photos are included.

44. Delear, Frank J. Famous First Flights across the Atlantic. Dodd, 1979. 204 p. ill. $9.
Gr 6-9. B 76: Jan 1 1980. +- SLJ 26: Nov 1979. The events of 10 early transatlantic air crossings, including those by Lindbergh, Earhart, and Balbo, plus dirigible and balloon crossings, are related.

45. Hayman, LeRoy. Aces, Heroes, and Daredevils of the Air. Messner, 1981. 189 p. ill. $10.

Gr 5-9. B 78: Sep 15 1981. Individual chapters on fliers who dominated aeronautical history from 1903 to 1945 provide an introduction to aviation history.

46. Jefferis, David. Epic Flights. (Wings: The Conquest of the Air). Watts, 1988. 32 p. ill. Lib. ed. $11.
Gr 4-8. B 84: May 1 1988. +- BR 7: Sep/Oct 1988. Covers history-making flights and flyers. Easy-to-read, with many illustrations and maps.

47. Oliver, Carl R. Plane Talk: Aviators' and Astronauts' Own Stories. Houghton, 1980. 179 p. ill. $8.
Gr 6+. B 77: Dec 1 1980. HB 56: Dec 1980. SLJ 27: Jan 1981. Nineteen first-person accounts, with photos from Orville Wright through Buzz Aldrin.

48. Parfit, Michael. Chasing the Glory: Travels across America. Macmillan, 1988. 288 p. $18.
Gr 9+. B 85: Oct 1 1988. As Parfit retraces Lindbergh's 1927 tour of the U.S. he tells how aviation and the nation have changed in the past 60 years.

49. Rosenblum, Richard. Wings: The Early Years of Aviation. Four Winds, 1980. 64 p. ill. $8.
Gr 3-7. B 76: Jul 1 1980. HB 56: Aug 1980. This history of aviation from the earliest days through World War I includes numerous line drawings.

50. Sullivan, George. Famous U.S. Spy Planes. Dodd, 1987. 64 p. ill. $11.
Gr 3-8. B 83: Jul 1987. BC 41: Sep 1987. * BR 6: Nov/Dec 1987. A photo essay on U.S. spy planes since World War I that provides background and technical data.

51. Sullivan, George. Thunderbirds, The. Dodd, 1986. 64 p. ill. $13.
Gr 4-7. B 83: Nov 1 1986. BR 5: Jan/Feb 1987. SLJ 33: Oct 1986. Relates the history and development of a crack aerial demonstration team.

52. Taylor, Michael J. H. Milestones of Flight. Janes; dist. by Van Nostrand, 1983. 288 p. $18.
Gr 9+. B 80: May 15 1984. B 81: Nov 1 1984. Presents a brief account of many significant events in aviation since 863 B.C.

53. Zisfein, Melvin B. Flight, a Panorama of Aviation. Pantheon, 1981. 119 p. ill. $12.
Gr 4+. BC 35: Mar 1982. SLJ 28: Nov 1981. VOYA 5: Jun 1982. An attractive, highly illustrated, oversized history of human flight from the beginning to space vehicles. Suitable for all ages.

Airplanes and Pilots–Women

54. Hodgman, Ann. Skystars: The History of Women in Aviation. Atheneum, 1981. 186 p. ill. $12.
Gr 7+. B 78: Nov 1 1981. BC 35: Dec 1981. HB 57: Dec 1981. * SE 46: Apr 1982. SLJ 28: Dec 1981. VOYA 4: Feb 1982. This chronological history of women in aviation since the days of ballooning covers their motivations, personal lives, sacrifices, and dress.

55. Lomax, Judy. Women of the Air. Dodd, 1987. 224 p. ill. $16.

Gr 9+. B 83: May 1 1987. LJ 112: Jun 1 1987. SLJ 34: Oct 1987. These profiles of forgotten women who were pioneer pilots include the first black woman pilot, the first woman commercial pilot, and sisters who were stunt pilots.

Alabama

56. Fradin, Dennis B. Alabama: In Words and Pictures. (Young People's Stories of Our States Series). Childrens Press, 1980. 48 p. ill. $7.
Gr 2-5. +- SLJ 27: Mar 1981. Covers the political and economic history, geography, people, and trivia of Alabama.

57. Thompson, Kathleen. Alabama. (Portrait of America). Raintree, 1988. 48 p. ill. $16. Pb $12.
Gr 3-5. B 84: May 15 1988. Alabama history, economy, culture, and notable persons are discussed. Includes informal interviews and photos.

Alaska

58. Cheney, Cora. Alaska: Indians, Eskimos, Russians, and the Rest. Dodd, 1980. 143 p. ill. $7.
Gr 4-8. +- BC 34: Dec 1980. HB 56: Oct 1980. * SE 45: Apr 1981. - SLJ 27: Nov 1980. A partly fictionalized coverage of some of Alaska's more interesting historical episodes.

59. Dunnahoo, Terry. Alaska. (First Book). Watts, 1987. 72 p. ill. $10.
Gr 5-8. +- B 84: Nov 15 1987. BR 6: Jan/Feb 1988. SLJ 34: Dec 1987. Covers the history, geography, resources, development of industry, and noted persons of Alaska. Includes photos.

60. Nach, James. Alaska in Pictures. (Visual Geography Series). Rev. ed. Sterling, 1980. 64 p. ill. $5. Pb $3.
Gr 5-7. SLJ 27: Feb 1981. Covers the history, geography, culture, and government of Alaska in this revised edition.

61. Stefansson, Evelyn. Here is Alaska. 4th ed. Scribner, 1983. 178 p. ill. $13.
Gr 5+. B 80: Jan 1 1984. +- SLJ 30: Jan 1984. VOYA 7: Jun 1984. An overview of the 49th state which puts into perspective the historic, geographic, political, and environmental issues which shape it. Updates the 1973 edition.

62. Thompson, Kathleen. Alaska. (Portrait of America). Raintree, 1988. 48 p. ill. $16. Pb $12.
Gr 3-5. B 84: May 15 1988. Alaskan history, economy, culture, and notable persons are discussed. Includes informal interviews and photos.

Alaska–Fiction

63. Dailey, Janet. Great Alone, The. Poseidon Press, 1986. 768 p. $19.
Gr 10+. +- B 82: May 1 1986. LJ 111: Jun 15 1986. The history of Alaska told in an epic story of the Tarakanov family.

64. Reiser, Joanne. Hannah's Alaska. Raintree/Carnival Press, 1983. 31 p. ill. $11.
Gr 1-3. B 80: Jan 1 1984. The appeal of the Alaskan wilderness comes through in this story of Hannah and her new neighbors who came to Alaska from California and only slowly discover the beauty of their new home.

Appalachia

65. Hoffman, Edwin D. Fighting Mountaineers: The Struggle for Justice in the Appalachians. Houghton, 1979. 224 p. $9.
Gr 7+. B 67: Jan 1 1980. HB 56: Feb 1980. * SE 44: Apr 1980. SLJ 26: Dec 1979. These seven episodes that demonstrate how Appalachians have worked cooperatively for common causes since the 1830s are based on primary sources.

Arizona

66. Carpenter, Allan. Arizona. (New Enchantment of America Series). Rev. ed. Childrens Press, 1979. 96 p. ill. $7.
Gr 5-7. SLJ 26: Mar 1980. Covers history, geography, culture, economy, resources, attractions, and people of Arizona. This updated edition uses full-color photos and large type.

67. Fireman, Bert M. Arizona: Historic Land. Knopf, 1982. 305 p. ill. $15.
Gr 9+. B 79: Sep 1 1982. +- LJ 107: Oct 1 1982. An overview of Arizona history from prehistoric times to 1980.

68. Fradin, Dennis B. Arizona: In Words and Pictures. (Young People's Stories of Our States Series). Childrens Press, 1980. 48 p. ill. $7.
Gr 2-5. +- B 76: May 15 1980. +- SLJ 26: Aug 1980. Covers Arizona's political and economic history, geography, people, and trivia.

69. Morgan, Anne Hodges. Arizona Memories. University of Arizona Press, 1984. 384 p. $30.
Gr 10+. LJ 109: Oct 15 1984. Reminiscences of people who helped shape Arizona–tales of mining, ranching, and old-time celebrations.

Arkansas

70. Fountain, Sarah M. Authentic Voices: Arkansas Culture, 1541-1860. University of Central Arkansas Press, 1986. 321 p. ill. $29.
Gr 9+. BR 5: Nov/Dec 1986. These primary materials on Arkansas, 1541-1860 include letters, reports, and diaries with introductions to provide the setting.

71. Fradin, Dennis B. Arkansas: In Words and Pictures. (Young People's Stories of Our States Series). Childrens Press, 1980. 48 p. ill. $7.
Gr 2-4. +- SLJ 27: Mar 1981. A brief introduction to the history, geography, people, and trivia of Arkansas.

Asian Americans

72. Kim, Hyung-Chan. Dictionary of Asian American History. Greenwood, 1986. 627 p. $65.

Gr 9+. B 83: May 15 1987. Covers all aspects of the history of Asian Americans. Includes biographies, a chronology, a bibliography, and an extensive index.

Attorneys

73. Kornstein, Daniel. Thinking under Fire. Dodd, 1987. 243 p. $19.
Gr 9+. VOYA 10: Oct 1987. Introduces 10 outstanding lawyers who have been instrumental in shaping the current interpretation of the Constitution.

Biographies

74. American Leaders, 1789-1987: A Biographical Summary. (Congressional Quarterly). Congressional Quarterly, 1987. 453 p. $20.
Gr 9+. B 84: Dec 15 1987. A handy one-volume collection of biographies of presidents, members of Congress, justices of the Supreme Court, and governors 1789-1987.

75. Concise Dictionary of American Biography. 3rd ed. Scribner, 1980. 1333 p. $75.
Gr 9+. B 80: Jun 15 1984. This condensed version of the Dictionary of American Biography includes abridged versions of all entries in the parent set and six supplements.

76. Dictionary of American Biography. American Council of Learned Societies/Scribner, 1981. 17 Vol. $1100.
Gr 9+. B 80: Jun 15 1984. These scholarly biographies on noteworthy Americans since colonial times do not include living persons. Includes several indexes. Price includes 17 vols. and seven 5-year supplements.

77. Benet, Rosemary. Book of Americans, A. Holt, 1933, 1987. 114 p. ill. $13. Pb $5.
Gr 4-8. B 83: Apr 15 1987. * BR 6: Nov/Dec 1987. This spirited collection of poetry provides a humorous introduction to 56 national figures from Columbus to Woodrow Wilson. Illustrated.

78. Boughton, Simon. Great Lives. Doubleday, 1988. 279 p. ill. $18.
Gr 4+. B 85: Oct 1 1988. +- BC 42: Oct 1988. * BR 7: Nov/Dec 1988. +- SLJ 35: Sep 1988. Photos, a chronological table, subject index, and glossary enhance these brief biographies of persons from all fields, from ancient to modern times.

79. Bramhall, William. Great American Misfits. Potter, 1982. 78 p. $8.
Gr 7-9. B 79: Jan 1 1983. BR 2: May/Jun 1983. SLJ 29: Apr 1983. VOYA 6: Apr 1983. Covers 26 eccentric or incompetent Americans, including George Custer, Warren G. Harding, and many others—a witch hunter, a miser, and a man who believes the earth is flat. Strictly for fun.

80. Dickerson, Robert B. Final Placement: A Guide to the Deaths, Funerals, and Burials of Notable Americans. Reference Publications, 1982. 250 p. ill. $20.

Gr 9+. B 79: Mar 1 1983. LJ 107: Dec 1 1982. Brief biographies of the famous and infamous, with details on their deaths and burial places.

81. Downs, Robert B. Memorable Americans, 1750-1950. Libraries Unlimited, 1983. 379 p. $24.
Gr 7+. B 80: Jun 15 1984. Biographies of 150 deceased "genuine achievers," indexed by subject, with lists by occupation and birth date.

82. Downs, Robert B. More Memorable Americans, 1750-1950. Libraries Unlimited, 1985. 397 p. $30.
Gr 7+. B 82: Jan 15 1986. BR 4: Sep/Oct 1985. VOYA 8: Dec 1985. Short biographies of deceased Americans from all fields.

83. Eastman, John. Who Lived Where: A Biographical Guide to Homes and Museums. Facts on File, 1983. 513 p. ill. $30.
Gr 9+. B 81: Nov 1 1984. LJ 108: May 15 1983. Covers 600 persons whose lives affected U.S. political and cultural history.

84. Felton, Bruce. Famous Americans You Never Knew Existed. Stein & Day, 1981. 293 p. ill. Pb $7.
Gr 9+. B 80: Jun 15 1984. Covers 400 living and deceased Americans, arranged by topics.

85. Garraty, John A. Dictionary of American Biography: Supplement Seven, 1961-1965. Scribner, 1981. 854 p. $55.
Gr 9+. B 78: Jul 1982. Biographies of noted Americans from all fields. Each supplement covers persons who died 15-20 years before its publication.

86. Garraty, John A. Dictionary of American Biography: Supplement Six, 1956-1960. Scribner, 1980. 769 p. $53.
Gr 9+. B 77: Nov 1 1980. Biographies of noted Americans from all fields. Each supplement covers persons who died 15-20 years before its publication.

87. Holloway, Charles M. Profiles in Achievement. College Entrance Examination Board, 1987. 173 p. ill. $16. Pb $10.
Gr 9+. B 84: Feb 1 1988. +- BR 6: Mar/Apr 1988. SLJ 34: Feb 1988. SLJ 34: Mar 1988. Eight short biographies of minority persons who succeeded in spite of poverty and prejudice.

88. Hubbard, Linda S. Notable Americans: What They Did, from 1620 to the Present. 4th ed. Gale, 1988. 733 p. $150.
Gr 9+. B 84: May 15 1988. BR 7: May/Jun 1988. Contains over 50,000 names, arranged chronologically, under such headings as government, military, business, labor, religion, and culture. Includes an index to awards.

89. Lukacs, John. Philadelphia: Patricians and Philistines, 1900-1950. Farrar, 1981. 375 p. $18.
Gr 9+. BR 1: May/Jun 1982. LJ 106: May 15 1981. Covers noted Philadelphians, including ambassador William C. Bullitt, immigrant reformer/journalist Edward W. Bok, authors Owen Wister and Agnes Repplier, and others. For regional collections.

90. Magill, Frank N. Great Lives from History: American Series. Salem, 1987. 5 vol. $325.
Gr 7+. B 84: Oct 15 1987. LJ 112: Jun 1 1987. Persons in politics, business, technology, entertainment, sports, and the arts are covered in these brief biographies that include women and minorities. Most of the biographees are deceased.

91. Sifakis, Carl. American Eccentrics: 150 of the Greatest Human Interest Stories Ever Told. Facts on File, 1984. 320 p. $18.
Gr 9+. B 81: Nov 1 1984, Nov 15 1984. Includes coverage on unusual, sensational, and amusing American eccentrics. Good for browsing and as a supplement to the biography collection.

92. Smith, C. Carter. Faces of America, The. Facts on File, 1988. 366 p. ill. $125.
Gr 7+. B 85: Oct 1 1988. * BR 7: Sep/Oct 1988. This balanced collection of 311 copyright-free portraits is suitable for students to reproduce to accompany reports. It includes minorities and represents a wide range of occupations.

93. Voss, Frederick. Man of the Year: A Time Honored Tradition. Smithsonian Institution Press, 1987. 64 p. ill. Pb $13.
Gr 9+. BR 7: May/Jun 1988. Each two-page spread includes a one-page text on the honoree and a full-size reproduction of the Time magazine Man of the Year cover since the tradition began in 1928.

94. Wintle, Justin. Makers of Nineteenth Century Culture, 1800-1914: A Biographical Dictionary. Routledge & Kegan Paul, 1982. 709 p. $38.
Gr 9+. B 80: Jun 15 1984. Includes writers, artists, scientists, philosophers, musicians, and others.

Biographies–Bibliographies

95. Briscoe, Mary Louise. American Autobiography 1945-1980: A Bibliography. University of Wisconsin Press, 1982. 365 p. $30.
Adult. B 80: Sep 15 1983. LJ 108: Mar 1 1983. Lists 5008 books, memoirs, diaries, collections of letters, and similar items by Americans and by foreigners who have resided here for a long time. Includes subject index.

Blacks

96. Social and Economic Status of the Black Population in the United States: A Historical View, 1790-1978. (Current Population Reports). U.S. Department of Commerce, Bureau of Census, 1980. 271 p. Pb $5.
Gr 9+. B 77: Oct 15 1980. Covers changes in population distribution, income, employment, education, housing, voting, and many other topics. Not indexed. Series P-23; Special Studies number 80 of the Current Population Reports.

97. Berry, Mary F. Long Memory: The Black Experience in America. Oxford University Press, 1982. 544 p. ill. $20. Pb $12.
Adult. * LJ 106: Dec 15 1981. An interpretive essay which examines the literary, cultural, and social history of blacks in America.

98. Corbin, Raymond M. 1999 Facts about Blacks: A Sourcebook of African-American Accomplishment. Beckham House; dist. by Talman, 1987. 288 p. ill. Pb $11.
Gr 9+. LJ 112: Aug 1987. SLJ 34: Jun/Jul 1987. Entertaining information in a question and answer format, arranged under broad topics such as history, art, sports, and entertainment.

99. Harding, Vincent. There Is a River: The Black Struggle for Freedom in America. Harcourt Brace Jovanovich, 1981. 416 p. ill. $20.
Gr 9+. * B 78: Dec 1 1981. +- LJ 106: Oct 15 1981. VOYA 9: Feb 1987. Chronicles black opposition to white tyranny in the U.S. from the beginning of the slave trade through the Thirteenth Amendment. The first of a planned three-volume work.

100. Lamon, Lester C. Blacks in Tennessee, 1791-1970. (Tennessee Three Star Series). University of Tennessee Press, 1982. 124 p. Lib. ed. $9. Pb $4.
Gr 9+. HT 16: Feb 1983. The black experience in Tennessee through the eyes of five persons, a slave, an entrepreneur, a feminist, a Bookerite, and a civil rights leader.

101. Meltzer, Milton. Black Americans: A History in Their Own Words. Crowell, 1984. 306 p. ill. $14. Lib. ed. $13.
Gr 7+. B 81: Nov 1 1984. BC 38: Jan 1985. * BR 3: Mar/Apr 1985. HB 61: Jan/Feb 1985. * SE 49: Apr 1985. SLJ 31: Dec 1984. * VOYA 7: Feb 1985. This black history 1619-1983 is based on excerpts from primary sources.

102. Ploski, Harry A. Negro Almanac: A Reference Work on the Afro-American. 4th ed. Wiley, 1983. 1550 p. $97.
Gr 9+. B 80: Oct 1 1983. LJ 108: Jun 1 1983. VOYA 9: Feb 1987. A comprehensive source of brief articles covering the events and people that contributed to the black experience in the U.S. and the world.

103. Redford, Dorothy. Somerset Homecoming. Doubleday/Anchor, 1988. 312 p. $19.
Gr 9+. * B 84: Aug 1988. LJ 113: Oct 1 1988. Redford's genealogical search resulted in a reunion of over 2000 relatives. This chronicle of her family since the days of slavery is an affirmation of black family life.

Blacks–Bibliographies

104. McGee, Leo. Education of the Black Adult in the United States: An Annotated Bibliography. (Bibliographies and Indexes in Afro-American and African Studies). Greenwood, 1985. 108 p. $30.
Gr 9+. B 82: Sep 15 1985. A chronological bibliography of works since 1619 dealing with the efforts of blacks to obtain their rights through education. Compiled for use by high school and college students. Number four of the series.

Blacks–Biographies

105. Adams, Russell L. Great Negroes, Past and Present. 3rd ed. Afro-Am, 1981. 212 p. ill. $15. Pb $10.

Gr 10+. B 80: Jun 15 1984. Easy-to-read biographies, arranged by categories: African heroes, early Americans, science and industry, business pioneers, religion, education, literature, the theater, music, and art.

106. Blackett, R. J. M. Beating against the Barriers: Biographical Essays in 19th Century Afro-American History. Louisiana State University Press, 1986. 412 p. ill. $38.
Gr 9+. B 82: Aug 1986. LJ 111: Sep 1 1986. A vivid cross-sectional view of the struggle for emancipation and equality in the 19th century, focusing on the lives of six little-known black Americans.

107. Bontemps, Arna. 100 Years of Negro Freedom. Dodd; Greenwood, 1961, 1980. 276 p. Pb $3.
Gr 9+. * B 57: Jul 1 1961. VOYA 9: Feb 1987. Glimpses of the lives of black leaders from Reconstruction to the work of Martin Luther King in moving and dramatic essays.

108. Franklin, John Hope. Black Leaders of the Twentieth Century. (Blacks in the New World). University of Illinois Press, 1982. 387 p. ill. $20.
Gr 9+. B 78: Apr 1 1982. Concise and discerning presentations of fifteen 20th-century black men and women who led the struggle to overcome racism.

109. Haley, Alex. Roots. Doubleday; Dell, 1976. 587 p. $18. Pb $5.
Gr 7+. B 83: Sept 1 1986. This family history begins with Kunta Kinte who was kidnapped in Africa and brought to the U.S. as a slave in the mid-1770s.

110. Hancock, Sibyl. Famous Firsts of Black Americans. Pelican, 1983. 128 p. ill. $10.
Gr 4-7. SLJ 30: Jan 1984. Brief biographies, chronologically arranged, of familiar and lesser known black scientists, politicians, sports figures, and artists.

111. Hughes, Langston. Pictorial History of Black Americans, A. 5th rev. ed. Crown, 1983. 380 p. ill. $20.
Gr 6+. B 81: Nov 15 1984; Dec 1 1984. LJ 109: Jun 1 1984. SLJ 31: May 1985. VOYA 7: Feb 1 1985. An overview, highlighting history, religion, economics, education, and social, cultural, and political achievements. Indexed.

112. King, Martin Luther. Daddy King: An Autobiography. Morrow, 1980. 215 p. ill. $11.
Gr 9+. B 76: Jul 1 1980. LJ 105: Sep 15 1980. SLJ 27: Mar 1981. King's reminiscences of his life, and of 80 years of the black struggle for civil rights, reflect his pride in his people's progress and his determination that the struggle continue.

113. Litwack, Leon F. Black Leaders of the Nineteenth Century. (Blacks in the New World). University of Illinois Press, 1988. 360 p. ill. $25.
Gr 9+. B 84: Apr 1 1988. LJ 113: May 15 1988. These essays on 17 black leaders, some famous, others lesser known but influential, were all written by specialists.

114. Logan, Rayford W. Dictionary of American Negro Biography. Norton, 1982. 680 p. $50.
Gr 9+. B 80: Sep 15 1983, Jun 15 1984. LJ 108: Mar 1 1983. More than 700 biographical sketches of blacks who were "major influences in their region or local community." Restricted to persons who died before January 1, 1970.

115. Marable, Manning. W. E. B. Du Bois: Black Radical Democrat. (Twayne's Twentieth Century American Biography Series). Twayne, 1986. 312 p. ill. $19. Pb $10.
Gr 9+. B 83: Nov 1 1986. LJ 111: Dec 1986. For advanced students, a biography of the founder of the NAACP.

116. Rollins, C. H. They Showed the Way: Forty American Negro Leaders. Crowell, 1964. 196 p. $12.
Gr 5-7. Metzner [+- LJ 89: Oct 15 1964]. These biographies of 40 black leaders emphasize the overwhelming difficulties they overcame in achieving success. Alphabetically arranged.

117. Stuart, Karlton. Black History and Achievement in America. Phoenix, 1982. 227 p. $25.
Gr 7+. +- BR 2: Sep/Oct 1983. Topically arranged biographies that cover black achievements in the military, the arts, science, religion, law, invention, education, sports, and other fields.

Blacks–Fiction

118. Abrahams, Peter. View from Coyaba, The. Faber & Faber, 1985. 440 p. $20. Pb $9.
Adult. B 81: May 1 1985. LJ 110: Apr 1 1985. This story, the struggle for autonomy of four generations of a black family, is set in the Caribbean, Africa, and America.

119. Gaines, Ernest. Autobiography of Miss Jane Pittman, The. Doubleday; Bantam, 1971. 256 p. $13. Pb $3.
Gr 9+. B 81: Jul 1985. A courageous black woman began life as a slave and lived to take part in the civil rights demonstrations of the 1960s.

120. Lester, Julius. Do Lord Remember Me. Holt, 1985. 210 p. $14.
Gr 9+. B 81: Dec 15 1984. LJ 109: Dec 1984. * VOYA 8: Aug 1985. As 80 year-old Rev. Joshua Smith writes his own obituary, he looks back over family hardships since slavery, and links past to present.

121. Lester, Julius. Long Journey Home: Stories from Black History. Dial, 1972. 176 p. $8.
Gr 7+. SE 44: Oct 1980. Six short stories tell of the search for freedom and dignity by ordinary people. The time span is from slave days to the 1920s.

122. Tate, Eleanora E. Secret of Gumbo Grove, The. Watts, 1987. 266 p. $12. Lib. ed. $13.
Gr 5-8. B 83: May 1 1987. BC 40: Jun 1987. SLJ 33: Mar 1987. VOYA 10: Aug/Sep 1987. In an effort to trace the history of her South Carolina community, Raisen interviews elderly Miz Effie and hears stories of slavery and segregation that many of the adults would rather not recall.

123. Yarbrough, Camille. Cornrows. Coward, 1979. 44 p. ill. $8.

Gr 3-8. HB 56: Apr 1980. * SE 44: Apr 1980. SLJ 26: Dec 1979. In telling the story of cornrow hair styles, Great Grammaw tells of the history, strength, and wisdom of the African people. A warm, positive, and poetic story.

Blacks–Quotations

124. King, Anita. Quotations in Black. Greenwood, 1981. 320 p. $35.
Gr 9+. LJ 106: Jun 15 1981. VOYA 9: Feb 1987. Over 1100 quotes by blacks from all times and places. Arranged chronologically and includes brief biographies and proverbs.

Blacks–Women

125. Davis, Angela Yvonne. Women, Race, and Class. Random House, 1982. 240 p. $14.
Gr 9+. B 78: Dec 15 1981. LJ 107: Jan 15 1982. The black militant spokeswoman addresses the effects of racism on black women.

126. Giddings, Paula. When and Where I Enter: The Impact of Black Women on Race and Sex in America. Morrow, 1984. 408 p. $16.
Gr 9+. B 80: May 1 1984. LJ 109: May 1 1984. SLJ 31: Jan 1985. A powerful and well-documented social and political history of black women since the 17th century.

127. Greenfield, Eloise. Childtimes: A Three-Generation Memoir. Crowell, 1979. 160 p. ill. $8.
Gr 4-8. HB 55: Dec 1979. * SE 44: Apr 1980. SLJ 26: Dec 1979. A memorable book about the childhood of three generations of black women.

128. Jones, Jacqueline. Labor of Love, Labor of Sorrow: Black Women, and the Family From Slavery to the Present. Basic Books, 1985. 386 p. $27.
Gr 9+. B 81: Mar 1 1985. * LJ 110: Mar 1 1985. This history of black women since the days of slavery shows the effects of double prejudice, against both blacks and women, and the unending labor of these woman who work to make a living and provide a home for the family.

Business and Business People

129. Collier, Peter. Fords: An American Epic. Summit, 1987. 406 p. ill. $23.
Adult. B 84: Sep 1 1987. LJ 112: Nov 15 1987. Covers the development of the Ford empire and the lifestyles of the wealthy Ford family.

130. Cowles, Virginia Spencer. Astors, The. Knopf; dist. by Random, 1979. 256 p. ill. $18.
Gr 9+. B 76: Mar 15 1980. John Jacob Astor was a poor German immigrant who became the richest man in the country through the fur trade and real estate. This traces seven generations of Astors. Numerous photos.

131. Hambleton, Ronald. Branding of America: From Levi Strauss to Chrysler, from Westinghouse to Gillette, the Forgotten Fathers of America's Best-Known Brand Names. Yankee Books, 1987. 247 p. ill. $20.
Gr 9+. B 83: Mar 1 1987. A delightful social history that reveals the successes and failures of U.S. inventors and entrepreneurs and the personalities behind famous brand names.

132. Harr, John Ensor. Rockefeller Century, The. Scribner, 1988. 598 p. ill. $30.
Gr 9+. B 84: Jun 15 1988. * LJ 113: May 1 1988. An authoritative coverage of the private and public accomplishments of the three John D. Rockefellers that emphasizes the development of their philanthropies.

133. Hart, William B. United States and World Trade, The. (Economics Impact Book). Watts, 1985. 103 p. ill. $10.
Gr 7+. B 82: Jan 15 1986. BR 4: Mar/Apr 1986. +- SLJ 32: Feb 1986. A history of U.S. trade relations, including examples to illustrate basic concepts.

134. Robertson, James Oliver. America's Business. Hill and Wang; Farrar, 1985. 258 p. $17.
Gr 9+. B 81: Jan 15 1985. LJ 110: Jan 1985. Explores the history of the American people as primarily a "business" people.

135. Taylor, Peter. Smoke Ring: Tobacco, Money, and Multinational Politics, The. Pantheon, 1984. 329 p. $19.
Gr 9+. * B 80: Aug 1984. LJ 110: Jan 1985. A history of the tobacco industry that clarifies its economic and political power in the U.S. and in Third World countries.

California

136. Arnold, Caroline. Golden Gate Bridge, The. (First Book). Watts, 1986. 72 p. ill. $10.
Gr 4-9. B 83: Dec 15 1986. SLJ 33: Jan 1987. VOYA 10: Apr 1987. Discusses the planning, design, construction, gala opening, and maintenance of the bridge.

137. Batman, Richard. Outer Coast, The. Harcourt Brace Jovanovich, 1985. 364 p. ill. $19.
Adult. B 82: Nov 1 1985. LJ 110: Oct 15 1985. A survey of the early history of California and the Pacific Coastal area.

138. Dolan, Edward F. Famous Builders of California. Dodd, 1987. 126 p. ill. $11.
Gr 4-7. B 83: Aug 1987. SLJ 33: Jun/Jul 1987. An introduction to Fr. Junipero Serra, John Charles Fremont, John Sutter, John Muir, Luther Burbank, Henry Wells, and William Fargo.

139. Hart, James D. Companion to California. University of California Press, 1987. 591 p. ill. $38.
Gr 9+. B 84: Aug 1988. Covers history, politics, social life, agriculture, industry, geography, literature, sports, and entertainment. Entries are alphabetically arranged. Includes maps and photos.

140. Henstell, Bruce. Los Angeles: An Illustrated History. Knopf, 1980. 224 p. ill. $25. Pb. 6.
Gr 9+. B 77: Feb 15 1981. LJ 105: Dec 15 1980. An illustrated essay of the people, places, topography, and events that characterize the history of Los Angeles. Includes over 400 photos, drawings, and maps.

141. Morrison, Faye Brown. Golden Poppies: California History and Contemporary Life in Books and Other Media for Yound Readers. Rev. ed. Shoe String, 1986. 285 p. $30. Pb $19.
Gr 1+. B 83: Jan 1 1987. An annotated bibliography of print and non-print materials about California for grades 1-12.

142. Pack, Janet. California. (First Book). Watts, 1987. 95 p. ill. $10.
Gr 5-7. B 84: Jan 1 1988. +- SLJ 34: Feb 1988. Covers the history, geography, industry, resources, immigration, pollution, economic problems, and notable persons of California.

143. Starr, Kevin. Inventing the Dream: California through the Progressive Era. Oxford University Press, 1985. 364 p. ill. $20.
Adult. B 81: Feb 15 1985. LJ 110: May 1 1985. This study of the growth of California from 1850-1920 is a sequel to the author's Americans and the California Dream (1973).

144. Stein, R. Conrad. California. (America the Beautiful Series). Childrens Press, 1988. 144 p. ill. $24.
Gr 4-6. B 84: Aug 1988. Outstanding photos, biographical sketches, and numerous statistics enhance this introduction to the history, geography, and economy of California.

145. Wollenberg, Charles. Golden Gate Metropolis: Perspectives on Bay Area History. University of California Press, 1985. 350 p. ill. $15.
Adult. LJ 110: Jun 1 1985. These essays on the geography, history, and political and social influence of California are highly illustrated.

Census

146. Anderson, Madelyn Klein. Counting on You: The United States Census. Vanguard, 1980. 96 p. ill. $8.
Gr 6-9. BC 33: Jul/Aug 1980. The history of census-taking and the uses of these figures.

147. Halacy, Daniel Stephen. Census: 190 Years of Counting America. Elsevier/Nelson, 1980. 240 p. ill. $10.
Gr 9+. B 76: Apr 15 1980. BC 34: Nov 1980. +- LJ 105: Apr 15 1980. SLJ 27: Feb 1981. Covers censuses of the past, the census process, and the uses made of the information gathered.

Chinese Americans

148. Dicker, Laverne Mau. Chinese in San Francisco: A Pictorial History. Dover, 1980. 134 p. ill. Pb $6.
Gr 9+. LJ 105: Jun 1 1980. Traces the Chinese experience in California since the early days. Photos show all aspects of Chinese-American life.

149. Kingston, Maxine Hong. China Men. Knopf, 1980. 308 p. $11.
Gr 9+. B 76: Jun 15 1980. HB 56: Oct 1980. LJ 105: Jun 15 1980. VOYA 3: Dec 1980. This tapestry of the author's male family members, interspersed with fas-cinating historical data, presents a unique view of the Chinese in America and is suitable for advanced readers.

150. Tsai, Shih-shan Henry. Chinese Experience in America. (Minorities in Modern America). Indiana University Press, 1986. 256 p. ill. $30. Pb $9.
Adult. LJ 112: Jan 1987. A solid history that traces the changing relationships of the Chinese in America to the homeland of their ancestors as the relationships between China and the United States have changed over the years.

151. Yung, Judy. Chinese Women of America: A Pictorial History. University of Washington/Chinese Culture Fooundation, 1986. 128 p. ill. $25. Pb $13.
Gr 9+. B 83: Dec 15 1986. An introductory overview of the experience of Chinese women in America. Chronologically arranged, the 132 photos and text clearly show the error of stereotypic perceptions.

Cities

152. Beekman, Dan. Forest, Village, Town, City. Crowell, 1982. 32 p. ill. $12.
Gr K-6. B 78: May 15 1982. +- BC 35: Apr 1982. * SE 47: Apr 1983. A beautifully illustrated history of our country, highlighting the evolution of American cities.

153. Hanmer, Trudy J. Growth of Cities, The. (Issues in American History). Watts, 1985. 120 p. ill. $11.
Gr 6+. B 82: Dec 1 1985. BR 5: May/Jun 1986. SLJ 32: Feb 1986. Traces the growth of the American city and the influences of immigration and industrialization.

154. Jackson, Kenneth T. Crabgrass Frontier: The Suburbanization of the United States. Oxford Univeristy Press, 1985. 352 p. ill. $22.
Adult. LJ 110: Sep 1 1985. Covers suburban growth over three centuries including the influence of transportation, government policy, housing and racism.

Cities–Fiction

155. Von Tscharner, Renata. New Providence: A Changing Cityscape. Harcourt Brace Jovanovich/Gulliver, 1987. 32 p. ill. $11.
Gr 3-8. * B 83: Apr 15 1987. BC 40: Mar 1987. HB 63: Jul/Aug 1987. * SE 52: Apr/May 1988. * SLJ 33: Mar 1987. In picture book format, with double-page spreads, the physical, economic, political, and cultural development of a fictional, but typical, American city is seen.

Civil Rights

156. Haskins, James. Quiet Revolution: The Struggle for the Rights of Disabled Americans. Crowell, 1979. 147 p. ill. $8.
Gr 5+. BC 33: Apr 1980. SLJ 26: Jan 1980. VOYA 3: Aug 1980. A history of the effort since the 1950s to achieve the rights of the disabled.

157. Mannetti, Lisa. Equality. (American Values First Book). Watts, 1985. 64 p. ill. $10.
Gr 5-8. B 82: Feb 15 1986. * BR 5: May/Jun 1986. SLJ 32: Feb 1986. Discusses the place of the concept of equality in our system and the struggle of minorities,

including blacks, women, the handicapped, the elderly, and Native Americans.

158. McKissack, Patricia. Civil Rights Movement in America from 1865 to the Present, The. Childrens Press, 1987. 320 p. ill. $35.
Gr 5-9. * B 83: Jun 1 1987. SLJ 33: Aug 1987. An extensive history of the struggles of all American minorities for their rights since the Civil War. Includes numerous photos, time lines of major events, and cameos of noted persons.

159. Norrell, Robert J. Reaping the Whirlwind: The Civil Rights Movement in Tuskegee. Knopf, 1985. 250 p. ill. $20.
Adult. B 81: Aug 1985. LJ 110: Sep 1 1985. A study of the civil rights movement at Tuskegee since the 1940s.

Colorado

160. Fradin, Dennis B. Colorado: In Words and Pictures. (Young People's Stories of Our States Series). Childrens Press, 1980. 48 p. ill. $7.
Gr 2-5. +- SLJ 27: Mar 1981. Covers the political and economic history, geography, people, and trivia of Colorado.

Congress and the Legislative Branch

161. Capitol: A Pictorial History of the Capitol and of the Congress. 7th ed. Congress. House. Doc. no. 95-260, 1979. 192 p. ill. Pb $5.
Gr 9+. B 76: May 15 1980. A photo history of the capitol and Congress, and a view of Congress at work.

162. Capitol: A Pictorial History of the Capitol and the Congress. 8th ed. Congress. House. Doc. no. 96-374, 1981. 192 p. ill. Pb $7.
Gr 9+. B 78: May 15 1982. A brief history of Congress, its leaders, and the vice-presidents that includes many color photos.

163. How Congress Works. (Congressional Quarterly). Congressional Quarterly, 1983. 219 p. Pb $10.
Gr 6+. B 79: Aug 1983. BR 2: Mar/Apr 1984. Essays on the history of Congress, its leaders, lobbying, committees, pay, "perks," and impeachment.

164. Fisher, Louis. Politics of Shared Power: Congress and the Executive. (Congressional Quarterly). Congressional Quarterly, 1987. 241 p. Pb $11.
Gr 10+. BR 6: Nov/Dec 1987. For advanced students an analysis of the complex relationships between the legislative and executive branches throughout U.S. history.

165. Goode, Stephen. New Congress, The. Messner, 1980. 221 p. Lib. ed. $10.
Gr 7+. * B 77: Dec 15 1980. SLJ 27: Feb 1981. Examines the role of Congress as established by the Constitution, the character of the House and Senate, and explains how each have dealt with the changes and complexities of our government.

166. Mikva, Abner J. American Congress: The First Branch. Watts, 1983. 434 p. ill. $20.

Gr 9+. B 79: Aug 1983. Explains the evolution of the processes and powers of Congress. Appendixes include lists of committees, subcommittees, and House Speakers.

167. Stein, R. Conrad. Story of the Powers of Congress, The. (Cornerstones of Freedom). Childrens Press, 1985. 30 p. ill. $10.
Gr 3-5. B 82: Mar 15 1986. +- SLJ 32: Mar 1986. This review of the development of the three governmental branches as they have jockeyed for power includes anecdotes and quotations.

Connecticut

168. Carpenter, Allan. Connecticut. (New Enchantment of America Series). Rev. ed. Childrens Press, 1979. 96 p. ill. $7.
Gr 5-7. SLJ 26: Mar 1980. Covers the history, geography, culture, economy, resources, attractions, and people of Connecticut. Updated, with full-color photos and large type.

169. Fradin, Dennis B. Connecticut: In Words and Pictures. (Young People's Stories of Our States Series). Childrens Press, 1980. 48 p. ill. $7.
Gr 2-5. +- B 76: May 15 1980. +- SLJ 26: Aug 1980. Covers Connecticut's political and economic history, geography, people, and trivia.

Constitution

170. Citizen's Guide to Individual Rights under the Constitution of the United States of America. 6th ed. Congress. Senate. Committee on the Judiciary, 1980. 47 p. Pb $4.
Gr 10+. B 77: Oct 15 1980. Explains individual rights as found in the Constitution and its amendments.

171. Constitution: Evolution of a Government. (Social Issues Resources Series). National Archives/Social Issues Resources Series, Inc., 1986. 34 documents. $35.
Gr 7+. BR 5: Sep/Oct 1986. A boxed set of primary sources useful for all students.

172. Right to Keep and Bear Arms, The. Congress. Senate. Committee on the Judiciary, 1982. 175 p. Pb $5.
Gr 9+. B 78: Jun 15 1982. Examines the controversy surrounding the Second Amendment.

173. Adler, Mortimer J. We Hold These Truths: Understanding the Ideas and Ideals of the Constitution. Macmillan, 1987. 278 p. $17.
Gr 9+. B 83: Jun 1 1987. LJ 112: Mar 1 1987. Analyzes the basis of the Constitution and its historical significance. Includes the texts of the Declaration of Independence, the Constitution, and the Gettysburg Address.

174. Bach, Julie S. Civil Liberties. (Opposing Viewpoints Series). Greenhaven, 1988. 230 p. ill. $7.
Gr 8+. +- B 84: Jun 15 1988. Covers historical and current arguments on separation of church and state, freedom of speech, privacy, and minority rights. Includes many quotes from notables.

175. Batchelor, John E. States' Rights. (First Book). Watts, 1986. 64 p. ill. $10.
Gr 5+. B 82: Jul 1986. * BR 5: Nov/Dec 1986. - SLJ 33: Jan 1987. VOYA 9: Dec 1986. Explores the conflicts between state and federal government since 1776.

176. Bender, David L. American Government. (Opposing Viewpoints Series). Greenhaven, 1987. 268 p. $14. Pb $7.
Gr 9+. B 84: Feb 15 1988. SLJ 34: Mar 1988. Presents conflicting viewpoints on constitutional questions since its inception, including the possibility of another constitutional convention.

177. Berger, Melvin. Censorship. (Impact Book). Watts, 1982. 84 p. ill. $8.
Gr 7+. B 79: Sep 15 1982. Examines both historic and contemporary court cases and principal positions concerning censorship of all types of materials.

178. Bosmajian, Haig A. Freedom of Religion. (First Amendment in the Classroom Series). Neal-Schuman, 1987. 163 p. $25.
Gr 7+. BR 6: Mar/Apr 1988. * VOYA 11: Apr 1988. A chronological presentation of cases that involve students' rights in cases of school prayer, Bible reading, evolution/creationism, and similar topics. Volume 2 of the series.

179. Bosmajian, Haig A. Freedom to Read, The. (First Amendment in the Classroom Series). Neal-Schuman, 1987. 205 p. $25.
Gr 6+. BR 6: Sep/Oct 1987. VOYA 10: Aug/Sep 1987. Covers the issue of student freedom to read through state and federal court cases.

180. Cantwell, Lois. Freedom. (American Values First Book). Watts, 1985. 64 p. ill. $10.
Gr 5-8. B 82: Feb 15 1986. * BR 5: May/Jun 1986. SLJ 32: Feb 1986. An examination of the First Amendment and the controversies that have surrounded it.

181. Chute, Marchette. Green Tree of Democracy, The. Dutton, 1971. 197 p. $10.
Gr 8+. B 81: Sep 15 1984. A history of the right to vote from colonial days to 1970.

182. Corbin, Carole Lynn. Right to Vote, The. (Issues in American History). Watts, 1985. 103 p. ill. $11.
Gr 6-9. B 81: Jun 15 1985. +- SLJ Aug 1985. VOYA 9: Apr 1986. This overview addresses the reasons why universal suffrage was omitted from the Constitution and the battle by blacks and women for the right to vote.

183. Dolan, Edward F. Gun Control: A Decision for Americans. (Impact Book). Rev. ed. Watts, 1982. 114 p. ill. $8.
Gr 7+. B 78: Jul 1982. Covers the historic basis for the Second Amendment and discusses the current controversy.

184. Dolan, Edward F. Insanity Plea, The. (Impact Book). Watts, 1984. 112 p. $10.
Gr 7-8. B 80: May 1 1984. BR 3: Sep/Oct 1984. * SE 49: Apr 1985. SLJ 30: Aug 1984. +- VOYA Dec 1984. Explains the problems engendered by the insanity plea as well as arguments for and against it, and alternatives.

185. Faber, Doris. We the People: The Story of the United States Constitution since 1787. Scribner, 1987. 256 p. ill. $14.
Gr 7+. B 83: May 15 1987. HB 63: Jul/Aug 1987. * SE 52: Apr/May 1988. * SLJ 33: May 1987. VOYA 10: Apr 1987. Traces the development of the Constitution from 1783 into the 1980s, including amendments and the role of the Supreme Court as its interpreter.

186. Friendly, Fred W. Constitution: That Delicate Balance. Random House, 1984. 352 p. ill. $18. Pb $9.
Gr 9+. B 81: Sep 1 1984. BR 4: May/Jun 1985. LJ 109: Nov 15 1984. SLJ 32: Oct 1985. This lively examination of court cases that were significant challenges to the Constitution makes the litigants and the issues come alive.

187. Garraty, John A. Quarrels That Have Shaped the Constitution. Rev. ed. Harper, 1987. 400 p. ill. $19. Pb $9.
Gr 9+. B 83: May 15 1987. Twenty essays on landmark cases, each written by a noted expert, explain the background and constitutional issues involved.

188. Gerberg, Mort. U.S. Constitution for Everyone, The. Putnam/Perigee, 1987. 64 p. ill. Pb $5.
Gr 8+. +- B 83: May 1 1987. The text of the Constitution and its amendments are amplified by anecdotes and commentary. The text and the commentary are printed on facing pages for easy use.

189. Goode, Stephen. Right to Privacy, The. Watts, 1983 149 p. $10.
Gr 6+. B 80: Nov 15 1983. * BR 2: Mar/Apr 1984. * SE 48: May 1984. SLJ 30: Jan 1984. VOYA 7: Jun 1984. Analyzes privacy as a human right, reasonable searches, eavesdropping, personality tests and polygraphs, the threat to privacy by computer, and related topics.

190. Hentoff, Nat. American Heroes: In and Out of School. Delacorte; dist. by Doubleday, 1987. 126 p. $15.
Gr 7+. B 84: Nov 1 1987. BC 40: Jul/Aug 1987. BR 6: Nov/Dec 1987. SLJ 34: Sep 1987. A book about Americans who fought for the Bill of Rights. The cases were chosen to be of special interest to teenagers.

191. Hentoff, Nat. First Freedom: The Tumultuous History of Free Speech in America. Delacorte, 1980. 340 p. ill. $10.
Gr 9+. B 76: Apr 15 1980. * BR 7: Nov/Dec 1988. LJ 105: Mar 1 1980. SLJ 26: Aug 1980. VOYA 4: Oct 1981. Reviews past threats to freedom including the dilemmas of censorship, separation of church and state, judicial gag orders, national security, libel, offensive speech, and the protection of journalists' sources.

192. Holder, Angela Roddey. Meaning of the Constitution, The. Rev. ed. Barron's, 1974, 1987. 144 p. $8.
Gr 10+. BR 6: Sep/Oct 1987. Presents the Constitution and the 26 amendments with explanations, citations from Supreme Court decisions, and an essay on the evolution

of constitutional interpretation under succeeding chief justices.

193. Hoobler, Dorothy. Your Right to Privacy. (First Book). Watts, 1986. 66 p. ill. $10.
Gr 5+. B 82: Jul 1986. * BR 5: Nov/Dec 1986. +- SLJ 33: Jan 1987. VOYA 9: Dec 1986. Traces the attitudes of private citizens and the Supreme Court toward the right to privacy.

194. Johnson, Joan. Justice. (American Values First Book). Watts, 1985. 64 p. ill. $10.
Gr 5-8. B 82: Feb 15 1986. * BR 5: May/Jun 1986. SLJ 32: Feb 1986. This discussion of the strengths and weaknesses of our judicial system emphasizes the rights of the accused.

195. Kammen, Michael. Machine That Would Go of Itself: The Constitution in American Culture. Knopf, 1986. 576 p. ill. $30.
Adult. B 83: Nov 15 1986. +- HT Nov 21: Nov 1987. * LJ 111: Oct 1 1986. +- SE 52: Mar 1988. A survey that shows how conflict and Supreme Court decisions have influenced the development of the Constitution.

196. Kleeberg, Irene Cumming. Separation of Church and State. (First Book). Watts, 1986. 64 p. ill. $10.
Gr 5+. B 82: Jul 1986. BC 40: Sep 1986. BR 5: Nov/Dec 1986. +- SLJ 33: Jan 1987. VOYA 9: Dec 1986. Traces the separation of church and state from colonial days through the 1980s.

197. Kronenwetter, Michael. Free Press Versus Fair Trial: Television and Other Media in the Courtroom. (Impact Book). Watts, 1986. 104 p. $11.
Gr 7+. B 82: May 1 1986. BC 39: May 1986. BR 5: Sep/Oct 1986. SLJ 32: Aug 1986. Explores constitutional issues affecting due process, the history of the press, the right of a defendant to a fair trial, and the question of media influence on the public.

198. Lawson, Don. Changing Face of the Constitution, The. Watts, 1979. 118 p. $7.
Gr 7-8. * SE 44: Apr 1980. Examines four issues which demonstrate the stable yet flexible nature of the Constitution, including Prohibition, universal suffrage, women's rights, and religious freedom.

199. Levy, Leonard W. Encyclopedia of the American Constitution. Macmillan, 1986. 4 Vols. $320.
Gr 9+. B 83: Mar 15 1987, Jun 1 1987. * BR 6: Sep/Oct 1987. * LJ 111: Dec 1986. This innovative celebration of Constitutional development is detailed and easy to use. It includes over 2000 articles on constitutional concepts, judicial decisions, historical periods, laws, and persons.

200. Lieberman, Jethro K. Enduring Constitution: A Bicentennial Perspective. West, 1987. 483 p. ill. $34.
Gr 9+. B 83: Jul 1987. A readable and lively work, with a wealth of incidental information covering longrange constitutional issues. Well organized and illustrated.

201. Lieberman, Jethro K. Free Speech, Free Press, and the Law. Lothrop, 1980. 160 p. $8. Lib. ed. $8.
Gr 7+. B 76: Feb 1 1980. SLJ 26: Mar 1980. * SE 45: Apr 1981. Examines fifty Supreme Court cases that tested the rights of Americans to enjoy free speech and free press. Concepts such as "clear and present danger," "prior restraint," and "non-verbal speech," are included.

202. Lieberman, Jethro K. Privacy and the Law. Lothrop, 1978. 160 p. $7.
Gr 7+. +- SE 44: Nov/Dec 1980. Examines the right to privacy in cases involving wiretapping, bugging, warrentless search, mail tampering, and other issues.

203. Lindop, Edmund. Birth of the Constitution. Enslow, 1987. 160 p. ill. $14. Pb $7.
Gr 6+. B 83: May 15 1987. BR 6: May/Jun 1987. HB 6: Jul/Aug 1987. SLJ 33: May 1987. VOYA 10: Apr 1987. An easy-to-read introduction to the writing of the Constitution and the events surrounding the amendments.

204. Mabie, Margot C. J. Constitution: Reflection of a Changing Nation. Holt, 1987. 138 p. ill. $13.
Gr 7+. B 83: May 1 1987. +- HB 63: Jul/Aug 1987. SLJ 34: Sep 1987. Explains constitutional origins and amendments, and its influence on U.S. history.

205. Maddox, Robert L. Separation of Church and State: Guarantor of Religious Freedom. Crossroad; dist. by Harper, 1987. 196 p. $17.
Gr 9+. B 84: Dec 1 1987. LJ 113: Mar 1 1988. Examines the history and significance of the principle of the separation of church and state.

206. Miller, William Lee. First Liberty: Religion and the American Republic. Knopf, 1986. 416 p. $25.
Adult. B 82: Jan 15 1986. * LJ 111: Feb 1 1986. Chronicles episodes that shaped our religious freedom, from the 1776 draft of the Declaration of Rights through modern court cases.

207. Mitchell, Ralph. Guide to the U.S. Constitution. (Congressional Quarterly). Congressional Quarterly, 1986. 108 p. ill. Pb $10.
Gr 7+. * BR 5: Nov/Dec 1986. Information on the writing of the Constitution, with study aids.

208. Phelan, Mary Kay. Our United States Constitution: Created in Convention. Perfection Form, 1987. 140 p. ill. $8. Pb $4.
Gr 5-8. B 84: Sep 1 1987. Using the writings of Madison, Washington, and Franklin, Phelan writes in the present tense, giving the reader a sense of being at the convention in this chronological account.

209. Sexton, John. How Free Are We? What the Constitution Says We Can and Cannot Do. Evans; dist. by Dutton, 1986. 324 p. $18. Pb $10.
Gr 9+. B 82: Jun 1 1986. LJ 111: Jun 15 1986. This overview, written in question-and-answer format, covers the history and development of the Constitution and the structure of the federal system.

210. Sgroi, Peter. Living Constitution, The. Messner, 1987. 127 p. ill. $10.
Gr 7+. B 83: May 1 1987. SLJ 33: Jun/Jul 1987. Uses national crises as the basis for studying constitutional issues, including the power of the Court, the Dred Scott decision, and the issue of executive privilege.

211. Spier, Peter. We the People: The Constitution of the United States of America. Doubleday, 1987. 43 p. ill. $14.
Gr K-3. * B 84: Oct 15 1987. * SE 52: Apr/May 1988. * SLJ 34: Oct 1987. Original and entertaining art work accompany the text of the Constitution and relate its development and its meaning for Americans today.

212. Taylor, C. L. Censorship. (First Book). Watts, 1986. 72 p. ill. $10.
Gr 5-9. B 83: Dec 1 1986. BC 40: Feb 1987. BR 5: Nov/Dec 1986. SLJ 33: Nov 1986. VOYA 9: Feb 1987. A brief history of world censorship is followed by a survey of censorship incidents in the U.S. The relationship of censorship to national security is also discussed.

213. Weiss, Ann E. God and Government: The Separation of Church and State. Houghton, 1982. 132 p. $9.
Gr 5-10. * B 78: Jun 15 1982. BC 36: Nov 1982. HB 58: Aug 1982. * SE 47: Apr 1983. * SLJ 28: Mar 1982. An objective examination of American religious freedom since colonial days.

214. Wilson, Reginald. Our Rights: Civil Liberties and the U.S. (Think Series). Walker, 1988. 123 p. ill. $15.
Gr 7+. SLJ 34: Aug 1988. * VOYA 11: Aug 1988. The development of American civil liberties is shown through the use of a timeline. Background material and recent court decisions of particular interest to teens are presented in a readable format.

215. Woods, Geraldine. Right to Bear Arms, The. (First Book). Watts, 1986. 66 p. ill. $10.
Gr 5+. B 82: Jul 1986. * BR 5: Nov/Dec 1986. SLJ 33: Jan 1987. VOYA 9: Dec 1986. A history of the issue of gun control.

216. Zerman, Melvyn Bernard. Taking On the Press: Constitutional Rights in Conflict. Harper/Crowell, 1986. 212 p. ill. $12. Lib. ed. $12.
Gr 8+. B 82: Apr 1 1986. BC 39: Jun 1986. * SLJ 33: Oct 1986. * VOYA 9: Dec 1986. Actual court cases are used to explore First Amendment conflicts between the government, individuals, and the press.

Cowhands

217. Dary, David. Cowboy Culture: A Saga of Five Centuries. Knopf, 1981. 416 p. ill. $18.
Gr 9+. B 77: Jun 15 1981. LJ 106: Jul 1981. Covers five centuries of raising cattle in North America.

Crime and Criminals

218. Browning, Frank. American Way of Crime, The. Putnam, 1980. 539 p. $15.
Gr 9+. LJ 105: Jul 1980. SLJ 27: Oct 1980. Includes causes and examples of crimes of violence and white collar crime throughout U.S. history. Sections may be used separately.

219. David, Andrew. Famous Criminal Trials. (On Trial Series). Lerner, 1979. 128 p. ill. Lib. ed. $7.
Gr 5-9. B 76: Jan 1 1980. SLJ 26: Apr 1980. Discusses eight familiar cases, including Sacco and Vanzetti, John T. Scopes, Bruno Hauptmann, the Rosenbergs, the Chicago Eight, Sirhan Sirhan, and James Earl Ray.

220. Kadish, Sanford H. Encyclopedia of Crime and Justice. Free Press/Macmillan, 1983. 4 Vol. $300.
Adult. B 81: Oct 1 1984. LJ 109: Jan 1984. For extensive collections. Covers crime, criminal behavior and law, and the criminal justice system.

221. Kohn, George C. Dictionary of Culprits and Criminals. Scarecrow, 1986. 447 p. $35.
Gr 9+. B 83: Nov 15 1986. Includes the unsavory and notorious, as well as those convicted of crime. Appendices categorize entries. Indexed.

222. Kosof, Anna. Prison Life in America. Watts, 1984. 104 p. $10.
Gr 6-10. B 81: Nov 15 1984, Feb 1 1985. +- SLJ 31: Mar 1985. * VOYA 8: Apr 1985. An introduction to the history of U.S. prisons and a plea for alternatives.

223. Mueller, G. O. W. Outlaws of the Ocean: Complete Book of Contemporary Crime on the High Seas. Hearst Marine Books, 1985. 370 p. ill. $16.
Gr 9+. B 81: Feb 1 1985. LJ 110: Feb 1 1985. A survey of maritime crime, including smuggling, piracy, terrorism, insurance fraud, and espionage.

224. Nash, Jay Robert. Bloodletters and Bad Men. Warner, 1982. 3 Vols. $5 each.
Gr 10+. VOYA 7: Feb 1985. Histories of the most notorious murderers, outlaws, robbers, gangsters, assassins and kidnappers since the 1800s. Each volume may be purchased separately.

225. Szumski, Bonnie. Criminal Justice. (Opposing Viewpoints Series). Rev. ed. Greenhaven, 1987. 216 p. ill. $13. Pb $7.
Gr 9+. B 83: Jun 1 1987. BR 6: May 1987. SLJ 33: Aug 1987. VOYA 10: Aug/Sep 1987. Examines both sides of controversies concerning the criminal justice system. Includes cartoons, quotations, and a bibliography.

226. Szumski, Bonnie. Death Penalty, The. (Opposing Viewpoints Series). Greenhaven, 1986. 175 p. ill. $12. Pb $7.
Gr 9+. B 82: May 15 1986. SLJ 32: Aug 1986. This history of capital punishment examines the issues and encourages critical thinking.

Delaware

227. Fradin, Dennis B. Delaware: In Words and Pictures. (Young People's Stories of Our States Series). Childrens Press, 1980. 48 p. ill. $7.
Gr 2-5. +- SLJ 27: Mar 1981. Covers the political and economic history, geography, people, and trivia of Delaware.

Disease

228. Simpson, Howard N. Invisible Armies: The Impact of Disease on American History. Bobbs-Merrill, 1980. 239 p. $13.

Gr 9+. B 77: Oct 15 1980. A realistic picture of the toll of disease on native Americans and on pioneers through the end of the 19th century.

Economics

229. Bruchey, Stuart. Wealth of the Nation: An Economic History of the United States. Harper, 1988. 256 p. $17. Pb $7.
Gr 9+. B 84: Jan 15 1988. A thoughtful history and analysis of the U.S. economic system as it has developed throughout our history.

230. Davis, Bertha. National Debt, The. (Impact Book). Watts, 1987. 128 p. ill. $12.
Gr 8+. B 84: Apr 15 1988. BR 6: Jan 1988. +- SLJ 34: Jan 1988. * VOYA 10: Feb 1988. Explains basic economic principles, the Federal Reserve System, and attempts to control the national debt. Includes graphs, tables, cartoons, and a glossary.

231. Kimmens, Andrew C. Federal Deficit, The. (Reference Shelf). Wilson, 1985. 250 p. Pb $8.
Gr 9+. BR 5: Sep/Oct 1986. Explains deficits in current terms and historical context. This item is number four of volume 57 in the series.

232. Kronenwetter, Michael. Capitalism vs. Socialism: Economic Policies of the USA and the USSR. (Economics Impact Book). Watts, 1986. 104 p. ill. $11.
Gr 7-9. B 82: Jul 1986. +- SLJ 32: Aug 1986. Explains the development of the two economic systems and examines them in practice.

233. Leone, Bruno. Capitalism: Opposing Viewpoints. (Isms: Modern Doctrines and Movements). 2nd. Rev. ed. Greenhaven, 1986. 150 p. ill. Lib. ed. $13. Pb $7.
Gr 8+. B 82: Aug 1986. SLJ 33: Oct 1986. A history of our economic system that compares several economic systems, presents opposing viewpoints, and helps students recognize facts, opinion, stereotypes, and ethnocentrism.

234. Sapinsley, Barbara. Taxes. (Issues in American History). Watts, 1986. 128 p. ill. $11.
Gr 7+. B 83: Feb 15 1987. BR 5: Mar/Apr 1987. * SE 51: Apr/May 1987. SLJ 33: Jan 1987. VOYA 10: Apr 1987. Recounts how the purposes of taxation have changed throughout our history, and the conflicts caused by taxation. Clearly written and well organized.

Espionage and Spies

235. Military Intelligence: Its Heroes and Legends. Army Intelligence and Security Command, 1987. 173 p. ill. Pb $6.
Gr 10+. B 85: Sep 15 1988. Features 13 stories about military intelligence from the Revolution through the Vietnamese War.

Fiction

236. Bethancourt, T. Ernesto. Tomorrow Connection, The. Holiday, 1984. 134 p. $11.
Gr 7+. B 81: Dec 1 1984. BC 38: May 1985. HB 61: Mar/Apr 1985. SLJ 31: Dec 1984. VOYA Apr 1985. A time-travel story that provides historical and social insights into the U.S. as it was in 1906, 1912, and 1942.

237. Merriman, John M. For Want of a Horse: Choice and Chance in History. Greene; dist. by Viking, 1985. 163 p. Pb $6.
Gr 9+. B 81: Jun 15 1985. Historians speculate on "what might have happened, if... ."

238. Michener, James A. Legacy. Random House, 1987. 176 p. $17.
Gr 11+. B 83: Aug 1987. * LJ 112: Sep 15 1987. Through the saga of the Starr family the reader follows the changing political attitudes of the nation since its beginning.

239. Moore, Ruth Nulton. In Search of Liberty. Herald Press, 1983. 173 p. Pb $7.
Gr 6-9. +- SLJ 30: Feb 1984. Beginning in 1794 the possessors of an American penny pursue freedom. They include a chimney sweep, an orphaned slave, an Oregon settler, a fugitive Indian, and a Vietnamese refugee.

Fiction–Bibliographies

240. Adamson, Lynda G. Reference Guide to Historical Fiction for Children and Young Adults, A. Greenwood, 1987. 401 p. $50.
Gr 4+. +- B 84: Feb 15 1988. Includes 80 award-winning authors and their works, with plot summaries and lists of characters. Useful for grades 4-12.

241. Gerhardstein, Virginia Brokaw. Dickinson's American Historical Fiction. 5th ed. Scarecrow, 1986. 352 p. $28.
Gr 9+. B 83: Oct 15 1986. An annotated list of over 3000 novels on American history published between 1917 and 1984.

242. Howard, Elizabeth F. America as Story: Historical Fiction for Secondary Schools. American Library Association, 1988. 137 p. Pb $15.
Gr 6+. B 85: Nov 15 1988. For 154 recommended fiction titles Howard provides a synopsis, grade levels, and suggested activities. Arranged by chronological divisions.

Firearms

243. Brown, M. L. Firearms in Colonial America: The Impact on History and Technology, 1492-1792. Smithsonian Institution Press, 1981. 448 p. ill. $45.
Adult. LJ 106: Apr 1 1981. Clarifies the role of firearms during our colonial period and the Revolutionary War, and discusses their impact on the American manufacturing system.

244. Rosa, Joseph G. Guns of the American West. Crown, 1985. 192 p. ill. $25.
Gr 9+. B 82: Jan 15 1986. Includes a mini-encyclopedia of guns used in the U.S., 1776-1866, and essays on such topics as violence in the West, buffalo hunters, and cowboys.

245. Walter, John. Handgun. David and Charles; dist. by Sterling, 1988. 160 p. ill. $20.

Gr 9+. B 85: Oct 15 1988. This highly illustrated history of handguns from the first matchlock to laser-sighted weapons also discusses the inventors and engineers who developed them.

Firefighting

246. Loeper, John J. By Hook & Ladder: The Story of Fire Fighting in America. Atheneum, 1981. 77 p. ill. $8.
Gr 4-6. B 78: Sep 15 1981. SLJ 28: Feb 1982. Both young children and illustrious statesmen are featured in these stories of heroic actions by the obscure and the famous. The growth of firefighting technology is also discussed. Slightly fictionalized.

Flags

247. Furlong, William Rea. So Proudly We Hail: The History of the United States Flag. Smithsonian Institution Press, 1981. 260 p. ill. $23. Pb. $10.
Gr 9+. B 78: Mar 15 1982. LJ 107: Jan 15 1982. SLJ 28: Apr 1982. A history of the flags associated with the exploration and settlement of North America, and information on laws and regulations. Includes the Pledge of Allegience and the American Creed.

248. Jones, Rebecca C. Biggest (and Best) Flag That Ever Flew, The. Cornell Maritime Press, 1988. 28 p. ill. $7.
Gr 5-8. B 84: Jun 15 1988. An illustrated story of the creation of the flag that flew over Fort McHenry and inspired the writing of the Star Spangled Banner.

249. Williams, Earl P. What You Should Know about the American Flag. Maryland Historical Press, 1987. 52 p. ill. Pb $6.
Gr 4-9. B 84: Nov 15 1987. This comprehensive history of the development of the U.S. flag includes proper display methods and colorful drawings.

Florida

250. Allman, T. D. Miami: City of the Future. Atlantic Monthly Press; dist. by Little, Brown, 1987. 424 p. $19.
Adult. B 83: Mar 15 1987. LJ 112: Apr 1 1987. This vivid history of Miami presents a picture of the turmoil in the development of one of America's most multi-ethnic cities.

251. Coil, Suzanne M. Florida. (First Book). Watts, 1987. 95 p. ill. $10.
Gr 4-7. +- B 84: Nov 1987. +- BR 6: Jan/Feb 1988. SLJ 34: Dec 1987. An overview of Florida history, geography, resources, industrial development, people, and major cities.

252. Fradin, Dennis B. Florida: In Words and Pictures. (Young People's Stories of Our States Series). Childrens Press, 1980. 48 p. ill. $7.
Gr 2-5. +- SLJ 27: Mar 1981. Covers Florida's political and economic history, geography, people, and trivia.

253. Stone, Lynn M. Florida. (America the Beautiful Series). Childrens Press, 1988. 144 p. ill. $24.

Gr 4-8. B 84: May 15 1988. Covers Florida history, geography, government, economy, industry, arts and leisure, and historic sites. Includes a reference section of statistics, maps, and biographic sketches.

Foreign Policy

254. What Citizens Need to Know about World Affairs. (Social Issues Resources Series). U.S. News & World Report, 1983. 212 p. ill. $13.
Gr 9+. B 80: Feb 15 1984. Historical overviews and current information provide a global perspective on population, the distribution of resources, religion, and other topics.

255. Barnet, Richard J. Alliance: America, Europe, Japan: A History of the Post-War World. Simon & Schuster, 1983. 544 p. $20.
Gr 11+. * LJ 108: Nov 15 1983. Traces U.S. foreign policy since World War II, shows the developing relationship of the U.S. with its former enemies, and explains why the Western alliance is a successful partnership.

256. Brune, Lester H. Chronological History of United States Foreign Relations, 1776-January 20, 1981. (Garland Reference Library of Social Science). Garland, 1985. 2 Vol. ill. $200.
Adult. B 82: Apr 15 1986. LJ 110: Sep 15 1985. Events and actions relating to U.S. foreign policy since 1776 are arranged chronologically and presented in a clear summary with reference to other relevant dates. Volume 196 in the series.

257. Chace, James. America Invulnerable: The Quest for Absolute Security from 1812 to Star Wars. Summit; dist. by Simon & Schuster, 1988. 316 p. ill. $20.
Adult. B 84: Mar 15 1988. LJ 113: Mar 15 1988. Examines U.S. foreign policy from 1812 through the mid-1980s and emphasizes efforts to be invulnerable to all enemies.

258. Cooney, James A. Think about Foreign Policy: The U.S. and the World. (Think Series). Walker, 1988. 172 p. ill. $15. Pb $6.
Gr 6+. * SLJ 35: May 1988. VOYA 11: Jun 1988. A thoughtful introduction to U.S. foreign policy throughout our history.

259. Divine, Robert A. Since 1945: Politics and Diplomacy in Recent American History. 3rd ed. Knopf, 1985. 285 p. $10.
Gr 10+. HT 20: Feb 1987. A balanced assessment of U.S. foreign policy since World War II. Suitable for advanced placement students.

260. Findling, John E. Dictionary of American Diplomatic History. Greenwood, 1980. 622 p. $40.
Gr 9+. B 78: Aug 1982. LJ 105: Mar 1 1980. Covers diplomats, journalists, historians, diplomatic terms, concepts, treaties, events, and organizations. Includes valuable cross references, appendices, and bibliographies.

261. Goode, Stephen. Foreign Policy Debate, The. (Impact Book). Watts, 1984. 120 p. $10.
Gr 9+. B 81: Oct 1 1984. * BR 4: May/Jun 1985. SLJ 31: Dec 1984. * VOYA 8: Apr 1985. Discusses historic

and current foreign policy and its relationship to the question of international human rights.

262.   Jones, Howard. Course of American Diplomacy: From the Revolution to the Present. Watts, 1985. 639 p. ill. $25.
Gr 9+. BR 5: May/Jun 1986. SLJ 32: Feb 1986. A balanced view of major diplomatic events, arranged chronologically. Includes photos, news clippings and maps. Indexed.

263.   Parker, Thomas. America's Foreign Policy 1945-1976: Its Creators and Critics. Facts on File, 1980. 246 p. $23.
Gr 10+. B 77: Mar 15 1981. B 78: Oct 15 1981. Includes an overview and a chronology of foreign policy events, biographical essays, a bibliography, and an index.

264.   Sharnik, John. Inside the Cold War: An Oral History. Arbor House, 1987. 352 p. ill. $20.
Gr 9+. B 83: Jun 15 1987. Presents interviews with public figures and private citizens discussing global events of the years since World War II.

265.   Spanier, John. American Foreign Policy since World War II. 11th ed. Congressional Quarterly, 1988. 410 p. Pb $19.
Gr 9+. +- BR 7: Sep/Oct 1988. Emphasizes U.S.-U.S.S.R. relations, 1945-1988. Covers critical events and shows how global events and changes in leadership influence foreign policy.

Foreign Policy–Canada

266.   Martin, Lawrence. Presidents and the Prime Ministers: Washington and Ottawa Face to Face: The Myth of Bilateral Bliss, 1867-1982. Doubleday, 1983. 300 p. ill. $20.
Adult. LJ 108: Mar 15 1983. An account of the relations between Canadian prime ministers and U.S. presidents who frequently ignored or bullied their counterparts.

Foreign Policy–Central America

267.   LaFeber, Walter. Inevitable Revolutions: The United States in Central America. Norton, 1983. 384 p. $19.
Gr 11+. LJ 108: Dec 1 1983. Traces 150 years of U.S.-Central American relations.

268.   Langley, Lester D. Central America: The Real Stakes. Crown, 1985. 288 p. $16.
Gr 9+. B 81: Jun 1 1985. LJ 110: May 1 1985. A historical overview of U.S. involvement in Central America.

Foreign Policy–China

269.   China: U.S. Policy since 1945. (Congressional Quarterly). Congressional Quarterly, 1980. 387 p. ill. Pb $11.
Gr 9+. * B 76: Jul 1 1980. LJ 105: Jun 1 1980. SLJ 27: Oct 1980. A chronology of U.S.-China relations since 1945, including documents, biographies, and maps.

270.   Hoobler, Dorothy. U.S.-China Relations since World War II. (Impact Book). Watts, 1981. 104 p. $8.
Gr 6-9. B 77: Jul 1 1981. Hoobler explores Chinese relations with the West and Japan prior to World War II in order to explain the Communist revolution and traces U.S.-Chinese relations since that time.

271.   Lawson, Don. Eagle and the Dragon: The History of U.S.-China Relations. Crowell, 1985. 213 p. ill. $12.
Gr 7+. B 82: Nov 15 1985. BC 39: Feb 1986. BR 5: May/Jun 1985. HB 62: Jan/Feb 1986. SLJ 32: Dec 1985. * VOYA 8: Dec 1985. This explanation of the ever-changing relationship between the U.S. and China also presents a history of China. Includes photos.

Foreign Policy–Cuba

272.   Dolan, Edward F. Cuba and the United States: Troubled Neighbors. (Impact Book). Watts, 1987. 128 p. ill. $12.
Gr 7-10. B 83: Apr 1 1987. * BR 6: May/Jun 1987. SLJ 33: May 1987. VOYA 10: Oct 1987. VOYA 11: Jun 1988. A concise history that covers both sides of controversial events.

Foreign Policy–Great Britain

273.   Dimbleby, David. Ocean Apart: The Relationship between Britain and America in the Twentieth Century. Random House, 1988. 320 p. ill. $25.
Gr 9+. B 84: Jun 15 1988. LJ 113: Jul 1988. Explores the changing relationship between Great Britain and the U.S. from the time of the Revolutionary War through the emergence of the U.S. as a world power and the decline of the British empire.

Foreign Policy–Latin America

274.   Szumski, Bonnie. Latin America and U.S. Foreign Policy. (Opposing Viewpoints Series). Greenhaven, 1987. 237 p. ill. $14. Pb $7.
Gr 9+. B 84: Jan 1 1988. SLJ 34: Mar 1988. A wide range of views are presented on the question of whether the U.S. has been a benefactor or the cause of the problems in Central and South America. Includes political cartoons.

275.   Weiss, Ann E. Good Neighbors? The United States and Latin America. Houghton, 1985. 167 p. $13.
Gr 7+. * B 82: Mar 15 1986. BR 5: May/Jun 1986. HB 62: Jan/Feb 1986. SE 50: Apr/May 1986. - SLJ 32: Dec 1985. VOYA 8: Dec 1985. Traces the history of the relations of nations in Central and South America with the United States.

Foreign Policy–Mexico

276.   Fincher, Ernest Barksdale. Mexico and the United States: Their Linked Destinies. Crowell, 1983. 213 p. ill. $11. Lib. ed. $11.
Gr 6+. B 79: Mar 15 1983. B 81: Jun 15 1985. * BR 2: Nov/Dec 1983. HB 59: Jun 1983. +- HT 19: Nov 1985. +- SLJ 30: Sep 1983. This history of Mexico clarifies U.S.-Mexican economic, political, and historical relationships. Topics covered include illegal immigration and bilingual education.

Foreign Policy–Middle East

277. Groisser, Philip L. United States and the Middle East, The. University of New York Press, 1982. 255 p. ill. $30. Pb $8.
Gr 9+. HT 16: May 1983. This introduction to the American role in the Middle East provides background on the history and culture of eight area nations. It emphasizes the period since World War II.

Foreign Policy–Nicaragua

278. Tessendorf, K. C. Uncle Sam in Nicaragua. Atheneum, 1987. 135 p. ill. $14.
Gr 7+. B 84: Jan 1 1988. +- BC 41: Sep 1987. SLJ 34: Dec 1987. VOYA 10: Dec 1987. Traces the relations of the U.S. and Nicaragua by highlighting the colorful persons who have led on both sides.

Foreign Policy–U.S.S.R.

279. Goode, Stephen. End of Detente? U.S.-Soviet Relations. (Impact Book). Watts, 1981. 92 p. $8.
Gr 7+. B 78: Dec 15 1981. SLJ 28: Feb 1982. Short, informative chapters explain U.S.-Soviet relationships since 1917. Each conflict is covered separately with quotes from world leaders.

280. Leone, Bruno. Opposing Viewpoints Sources: Soviet-American Debate, Vol. 1. (Opposing Viewpoints Series). Greenhaven, 1985. 382 p. $40.
Gr 9+. B 82: Aug 1986. HT 21: May 1988. A balanced and well-organized history of U.S.-Soviet relations over the past 40 years, preceding the administration of Mikhail Gorbachev.

Frontier and Pioneer Life

281. Alweis, Frank. Our Social and Cultural History: American Studies. Globe Book Company, 1977. 326 p. ill. $7.
Gr 10+. SE 46: May 1982. The chapters on schooling, religion, work, the family, women, and cities include graphs and tables and are followed by discussion questions.

282. Gragg, Rod. Old West Quiz and Fact Book, The. Harper/Perennial, 1986. 230 p. ill. $16. Pb $9.
Gr 9+. B 83: Nov 1 1986. In question-and-answer format, topically arranged, a factual and fun resource on topics such as outlaws, mountain men, pioneers, wranglers, Indians, and Hollywood cowboys.

283. L'Amour, Louis. Frontier. Bantam, 1984. 224 p. ill. $30.
Gr 10+. B 81: Nov 15 1984. LJ 109: Nov 1 1984. Essays on all the frontiers in our history.

284. Lyons, Grant. Mustangs, Six-Shooters and Barbed Wire: How the West Was Really Won. Messner, 1981. 96 p. ill. $9.
Gr 4-7. SLJ 28: Dec 1981. Clarifies the role of barbed wire, horses, and buffalo in the settlement of the West.

285. Slotkin, Richard. Fatal Environment: The Myth of the Frontier in the Age of Industrialization, 1800-1890. Atheneum, 1985. 688 p. $23.
Adult. B 81: Apr 1 1985. * LJ 110: Apr 15 1985. Slotkin explores the influence of the frontier tradition on American internal and foreign policy at the turn of the century.

Frontier and Pioneer Life–Bibliographies

286. Tuska, Jon. Encyclopedia of Frontier and Western Fiction. McGraw-Hill, 1983. 365 p. $30.
Gr 9+. B 81: Sep 1 1984. Bibliographies on "fiction of all kinds, set on the North American continent," plus subject essays and biographical sketches on authors.

287. Tuska, Jon. Frontier Experience: A Reader's Guide to the Life & Literature of the American West. McFarland, 1984. 434 p. $30.
Adult. B 81: Aug 1985. An annotated bibliography on 20 different aspects of the American West.

Frontier and Pioneer Life–Women

288. Exley, Jo Ella Powell. Texas Tears and Texas Sunshine: Voices of Frontier Women. (Centennial Series of the Association of Former Students). Texas A & M University Press, 1985. 264 p. ill. $15.
Adult. LJ 110: Jan 1985. A collection of informative and entertaining reminiscences that record the varied and demanding experiences of Texas women. Number 17 of the series.

289. Myers, Sandra L. Westering Women and the Frontier Experience, 1800-1915. University of New Mexico Press, 1982. 365 p. ill. $25. Pb $13.
Adult. HT 20: Nov 1986. Covers the broad range of women's experiences on the frontier, 1800-1915. Based on over 400 diaries and reminiscences.

Georgia

290. Carpenter, Allan. Georgia. (New Enchantment of America Series). Rev. ed. Childrens Press, 1979. 96 p. ill. $7.
Gr 5-7. SLJ 26: Mar 1980. Covers the history, geography, culture, economy, resources, attractions, and people of Georgia. Updated, using full-color photos and large type.

291. Fradin, Dennis B. Georgia: In Words and Pictures. (Young People's Stories of Our States Series). Childrens Press, 1981. 48 p. ill. $7.
Gr 2-5. +- SLJ 28: Oct 1981. Covers political and economic history, geography, people, and trivia.

292. Kent, Zachary A. Georgia. (America the Beautiful Series). Childrens Press, 1988. 144 p. ill. $24.
Gr 4-8. B 84: Aug 1988. SLJ 35: Oct 1988. This colorful and informative book covers Georgia history, geography, economics, and noted persons. Includes maps, photos, and lists of facts.

German Americans

293. Bittinger, Lucy F. Germans in Colonial Times, The. Heritage, 1901, 1986. 314 p. $20.
Gr 9+. BR 6: Sep/Oct 1987. Chronicles the many contributions made by German Americans to their new nation.

Great Lakes

294. Ashworth, William. Late, Great Lakes: An Environmental History. Knopf, 1986. 320 p. ill. $18.
Gr 9+. B 82: May 15 1986. * LJ 111: May 15 1986. A natural and human history of the area and a plea for environmental awareness.

Guam

295. Lutz, William. Guam. (Let's Visit Series). Chelsea House, 1987. 112 p. ill. $12.
Gr 6-9. SLJ 34: Jan 1988. The history and current status of Guam as a U.S. dependency are clearly presented through an easy-to-read text and well chosen photos.

Hawaii

296. Carpenter, Allan. Hawaii. (New Enchantment of America Series). Rev. ed. Childrens Press, 1979. 96 p. ill. $7.
Gr 5-7. SLJ 26: Mar 1980. Covers the history, geography, culture, economy, resources, attractions, and people of Hawaii. Updated, with full-color photos and large type.

297. Fradin, Dennis B. Hawaii: In Words and Pictures. (Young People's Stories of Our States Series). Childrens Press, 1980. 48 p. ill. $7.
Gr 2-5. +- B 76: May 15 1980. +- SLJ 26: Aug 1980. Covers the political and economic history, geography, people, and trivia of Hawaii.

298. Rayson, Ann. Modern Hawaiian History. Bess Press, 1984. 282 p. ill. $17. Pb $15.
Gr 5-9. B 81: Feb 1 1985. Covers the range of Hawaiian history plus geographical and cultural information.

Historic Sites

299. Independence: A Guide to Independence National Historical Park, Philadelphia, Pennsylvania. (National Park Service Handbook). National Park Service, 1982. 64 p. ill. $5.
Gr 9+. B 79: Mar 15 1983. A guide to the buildings and historic sites located at this National Park. This is item number 115 in the Handbook Series.

300. Lincoln Memorial: A Guide to the Lincoln Memorial, District of Columbia. (National Park Service Handbook). National Park Service, 1986. 48 p. ill. Pb $2.
Gr 9+. B 83: Nov 15 1986. This description of the planning and building of the Lincoln Memorial includes a brief biography and information on other historical sites associated with Lincoln. Report number 129 in the Handbook Series.

301. Preserving America's Past. National Geographic Society, 1983. 199 p. ill. $7. Lib. ed. $9.
Gr 7+. B 79: Jun 15 1983. Examines efforts to restore historic sites and recapture life-styles and crafts of the past. Color photos.

302. Bigler, Philip. In Honored Glory: Arlington National Cemetery: The Final Post. Vandamere Press, 1986. 144 p. ill. Pb $8.
Gr 9+. LJ 112: Mar 1 1987. As historian of Arlington, Bigler offers a history of the national cemetery in addition to an insider's view on the internments of the Kennedys and other recent national figures.

303. Boring, Mel. Incredible Constructions and the People Who Built Them. (Walker's American History Series for Young People). Walker, 1985. 90 p. $14.
Gr 4-7. B 81: Jun 1 1985. BR 4: Sep/Oct 1985. SLJ 31: Aug 1985. VOYA 8: Aug 1985. Includes the Mesa Verde Dwellings, National Road, Washington Monument, Panama Canal, Holland Tunnel, Hoover Dam, and other notable structures.

304. Diehl, Lorraine B. Late, Great Pennsylvania Station, The. American Heritage; dist. by Houghton, 1985. 168 p. ill. $20.
Adult. B 82: Oct 15 1985. LJ 110: Dec 1985. Photos, drawings, and text recapture the grandeur of the station that was the gateway to New York City for over 50 years.

305. Hilowitz, Beverly. Great Historic Places. (Fireside Book). Rev. ed. American Heritage/Simon & Schuster, 1980. 319 p. ill. Pb. $7.
Gr 9+. B 77: Oct 1 1980. Over 1000 sites prominent in early American history are listed, with information on hours open, location, and historic significance.

306. Kostof, Spiro. America by Design. Oxford University Press, 1987. 388 p. ill. $25.
Gr 9+. SLJ 34: Jan 1988. Hundreds of photos show the development of America's buildings, streets, highways, parks, and monuments across our history.

307. Peters, James Edward. Arlington National Cemetery: Shrine to America's Heroes. Woodbine House, 1986. 313 p. ill. Pb $10.
Gr 9+. * B 83: Dec 1 1986. LJ 111: Mar 1 1987. A history of the cemetery and profiles of 100 of the persons buried there.

308. Smith, Rex Alan. Carving of Mount Rushmore, The. Abbeville Press, 1985. 415 p. ill. $20.
Gr 9+. B 81: Jun 1 1985. This vivid account of how Mount Rushmore came to be carved details the controversies and the work behind its creation.

309. St. George, Judith. Mount Rushmore Story, The. Putnam, 1985. 128 p. ill. $14.
Gr 6+. * B 82: Sep 15 1985. HB 61: Nov/Dec 1985. * SE 50: Apr/May 1986. SLJ 32: Oct 1985. VOYA 8: Dec 1985. The story of the monument, its creation and its creator, who was a strong individualist. Includes excellent photos and a map.

310. Torres, Louis. To the Immortal Name and Memory of George Washington: The United States Army Corps of Engineers and the Construction of the Washington Monument. Army Corps of Engineers, 1985. 152 p. ill. Pb $5.
Gr 9+. B 82: May 15 1986. This official history discusses the plans, construction, and modern history of the world-famous Washington Monument that was nearly 100 years in the making. This is publication EP 870-1-21.

Holidays, Patriotic

311. Giblin, James Cross. Fireworks, Picnics, and Flags: The Story of the Fourth of July Symbols. Clarion, 1983. 96 p. ill. $11. Pb $4.
Gr 4-6. B 79: Aug 1983. BC 37: Oct 1983. HB 59: Aug 1983. * SE 48: May 1984. SLJ 30: Sep 1983. Explains some of the most prominent of our nation's patriotic symbols.

312. Scott, Geoffrey. Memorial Day. Carolrhoda, 1983. 48 p. ill. $7.
Gr 2-4. B 80: Nov 15 1983. +- BC 37: Apr 1984. SLJ 30: Mar 1984. A discussion of the development of the holiday that honors veterans and those who died in war, also describes a celebration held in 1878.

313. Shachtman, Tom. America's Birthday: The Fourth of July. Macmillan, 1986. 46 p. ill. $14.
Gr 3-7. B 82: Jul 1986. +- BC 39: Apr 1986. HB 62: May/Jun 1986. +- SLJ 33: Dec 1986. Spotlights the patriotic celebrations of New England.

Idaho

314. Carpenter, Allan. Idaho. (New Enchantment of America Series). Rev. ed. Childrens Press, 1979. 96 p. ill. $7.
Gr 5-7. SLJ 26: Mar 1980. Covers the history, geography, culture, economy, resources, attractions, and people of Idaho. Updated, with full-color photos and large type.

315. Fradin, Dennis B. Idaho: In Words and Pictures. (Young People's Stories of Our States Series). Childrens Press, 1980. 48 p. ill. $7.
Gr 2-5. +- SLJ 27: Mar 1981. Idaho's political and economic history, geography, people, and trivia are discussed.

Illinois

316. Carpenter, Allan. Illinois. (New Enchantment of America Series). Rev. ed. Childrens Press, 1979. 96 p. ill. $7.
Gr 5-7. SLJ 26: Mar 1980. Covers Illinois history, geography, culture, economy, resources, attractions, and people. Updated, with full-color photos and large type.

317. Carter, Alden R. Illinois. (First Book). Watts, 1987. 95 p. ill. $10.
Gr 4-7. +- B 84: Nov 15 1987. +- BC 41: Jan 1988. +- BR 6: Jan/Feb 1988. +- SLJ 34: Mar 1988. - VOYA 10: Feb 1988. An overview of Illinois history, geography,

resources, industrial development, people, and major cities.

318. Cromie, Robert. Short History of Chicago, A. Lexikos, 1984. 140 p. ill. Pb $10.
Adult. +- B 81: Jan 1 1985. LJ 110: Mar 1 1985. This anectodal history, with numerous quotes, covers Chicago from 1674 to the election of Harold Washington, the city's first black mayor, in 1983.

319. Granger, Bill. Lords of the Last Machine: The Story of Politics in Chicago. Random House, 1987. 222 p. ill. $19.
Adult. B 83: May 15 1987. LJ 112: Sep 1 1987. Examines the Chicago political machine, reveals how it worked for a hundred years, and how it was destroyed.

320. Stein, R. Conrad. Illinois. (America the Beautiful State Book). Childrens Press, 1987. 144 p. ill. $18.
Gr 4-7. B 83: Apr 1 1987. SLJ 34: Feb 1988. Includes Illinois history, geography, culture, economy, historic sites, famous people, a section entitled "Facts at a Glance," maps and photos.

321. Terkel, Studs. Chicago. Pantheon, 1986. 148 p. ill. $16.
Gr 10+. B 83: Sep 15 1986. +- LJ 112: Jan 1987. Terkel presents an entertaining and nostalgic personal view of the last 60 years of Chicago history.

Immigration

322. Review of U.S. Refugee Resettlement Programs and Policies. Congress. Senate. Committee on the Judiciary, 1980. 342 p. Pb $7.
Adult. B 77: Jan 15 1981. An overview of refugee admission programs and policies since 1945.

323. Anderson, Lydia. Immigration. (Impact Book). Watts, 1981. 88 p. ill. $8.
Gr 7-10. B 78: Oct 1 1981. SLJ 28: Mar 1982. This survey of immigration since colonial times covers legislative restrictions, the problems of agencies, and includes a discussion of recent refugees and illegal aliens.

324. Archdeacon, Thomas J. Becoming American: An Ethnic History. Free Press, 1983. 300 p. $18.
Gr 10+. LJ 108: Jun 1 1983. A blend of fact and analysis concerning immigration and the problems of assimilation since 1607.

325. Benton, Barbara. Ellis Island: A Pictorial History. Facts on File, 1985. 192 p. ill. $19.
Gr 7+. B 82: Mar 1 1986. BR 5: Nov/Dec 1986. A photo-history based on the writings of immigrants and officials.

326. Bentz, Thomas. New Immigrants: Portraits in Passage. Pilgrim, 1981. 209 p. Pb $8.
Gr 6+. LJ 106: Oct 1 1981. * VOYA 5: Aug 1982. The stories of 11 immigrant families, their hopes, achievements, and disappointments. Appendices list immigrants who became national treasures and other valuable information.

327. Billington, Ray Allen. Land of Savagery, Land of Promise: The European Image of the American Frontier. Norton, 1981. 364 p. ill. $19.
Gr 9+. B 77: Apr 1 1981. LJ 106: Jan 15 1981. SLJ 27: Mar 1981. Explains the complex and contradictory attitudes of Europeans toward America, which they see as both barbaric and the land of opportunity. For advanced students.

328. Bouvier, Leon F. Immigration: Diversity in the U.S. (Think Series). Walker, 1988. 167 p. ill. $15. Pb $6.
Gr 7+. * SLJ 35: May 1988. +- VOYA 11: Aug 1988. Presents a historical perspective on U.S. immigration patterns and policies as well as opposing ideas on current political and social problems related to immigration.

329. Fisher, Leonard Everett. Ellis Island: Gateway to the New World. Holiday, 1986. 64 p. ill. $13.
Gr 5-8. B 83: Nov 15 1986. BC 40: Dec 1986. HB 63: Mar/Apr 1987. * SLJ 33: Dec 1986. Fisher discusses the experiences of those who come to Ellis Island—those who became new Americans and those who came but could not stay.

330. Handlin, Oscar. Uprooted, The. Little, Brown, 1973. 333 p. $7.
Gr 7+. SE 46: Oct 1982. SE 50: Mar 1986. An update of a classic introduction to the history of U.S. immigration.

331. Hook, J. N. Family Names: How Our Surnames Came to America. Macmillan, 1982. 400 p. $17.
Gr 9+. B 78: Apr 15 1982. LJ 107: May 15 1982. This delightful tour of American ethnic variety discusses waves of immigration in terms of surnames and name changes.

332. Keely, Charles B. U.S. Immigration: A Policy Analysis. (Public Issues Paper of the Population Council). Population Council, 1979. 87 p. Free.
Adult. SE 50: Mar 1986. Examines immigration policies from 1790 to the present as well as current trends in immigration.

333. Kurelek, William. They Sought a New World: The Story of European Immigration to North America. Tundra, 1985. 45 p. ill. $15.
Gr 3-7. B 82: Dec 15 1985. BC 39: Jan 1986. SLJ 32: Jan/Feb 1986. An empathetic look at the European immigrant experience in the U.S. and Canada 1850-1950. Kuralek's vivid paintings highlight this work that covers the effect of immigration on men, women, and children

334. Loescher, Gil. Calculated Kindness: Refugees and America's Half-Open Door, 1945-Present. Free Press, 1986. 331 p. $20.
Gr 9+. B 82: Aug 1986. Emphasis is on immigration from Third World countries and the double standards which determine admission.

335. Morrison, Joan. American Mosaic: The Immigrant Experience in the Words of Those Who Lived It. Dutton, 1980. 512 p. $20.
Gr 9+. B 77: Sep 1 1980. LJ 105: Aug 1980. SE 45: Oct 1981. Inclues over 100 interviews with immigrants from many countries, some notable, but mostly ordinary people. Each is asked why and how they came, and what they found here.

336. Namias, June. First Generation: In the Words of Twentieth-century American Immigrants. Beacon Press, 1978. 234 p. $6.
Gr 10+. HT 13: May 1980. A collection of informative and well-edited interviews of immigrants since 1900. A preface places each interview in context.

337. Novotny, Ann. Strangers at the Door: Ellis Island, Castle Garden, & the Great Migration to America. Chatham Press; dist. by Viking, 1972. 160 p. ill. $13.
Gr 9+. LJ 97: Feb 15 1972, Mar 15 1972. SE 46: Oct 1982. Embraces the whole story of immigration, with abundant photos and drawings. Includes a chapter on famous immigrants and one on the economic conditions the immigrants found.

338. Reimers, David M. Still the Golden Door: The Third World Comes to America, 1943-1983. Columbia University Press, 1985. 320 p. $25.
Adult. LJ 110: Sep 1 1985. Explains how changes in immigration policy and international conditions have influenced recent immigration, and how Third World immigrants have fared in the U.S.

339. Rips, Gladys Nadler. Coming to America: Immigrants from Southern Europe. Delacorte, 1981. 143 p. ill. $10. Pb $3.
Gr 7+. B 77: Jun 1 1981. BC 35: Oct 1981. BR 2: May/Jun 1983. * SE 47: Apr 1983. SLJ 27: Aug 1981. Gives attention to immigrants from Italy, Spain, Portugal, and Greece, explains why they came, and what they found in the melting pot. Includes excerpts from letters and interviews.

340. Robbins, Albert. Coming to America: Immigrants from Northern Europe. Delacorte; Dell, 1981, 1982. 214 p. $10. Pb $3.
Gr 7+. B 77: Jun 15 1981. BC 34: Jun 1981. BR 2: May/Jun 1983. SLJ 27: Aug 1981. VOYA 4: Dec 1981. Excerpts from primary sources plus commentary cover the experiences of immigrants from the Netherlands, France, Germany, and Scandinavian countries from colonial times to the 1950s.

341. Siegel, Beatrice. Sam Ellis's Island. Four Winds, 1985. 128 p. $12.
Gr 4-6. B 82: Dec 15 1985, May 1 1986. BC 39: Nov 1985. +- SLJ 32: Jan 1986. The experiences of explorers, slaves, soldiers, colonists, and other immigrants who were involved in the history of Ellis Island are presented.

342. Sowell, Thomas. Ethnic America: A History. Basic Books, 1981. 353 p. $17.
Gr 9+. B 78: Oct 1 1981. LJ 106: Jun 1 1981. In his survey of the history of nine ethnic groups (Irish, Germans, Jews, Italians, Chinese, Japanese, blacks, Puerto Ricans, and Mexicans) Sowell emphasizes the importance of time and education in assimilation.

Immigration, Arabian

343. Naff, Alixa. Arab Americans, The. (Peoples of North America). Chelsea House, 1988. 109 p. ill. $17.

Gr 7-10. B 84: Mar 15 1988. SLJ 34: Aug 1988. Presents the reasons for immigration by Arabs, areas settled, their problems, and the skills and traditions of these immigrants, in a readable and well-researched volume. Color photos.

Immigration, Asian

344. Knoll, Tricia. Becoming Americans: Asian Sojourners, Immigrants, and Refugees in the Western United States. Coast to Coast Books, 1982. 356 p. ill. $23. Pb $15.
Gr 10+. B 79: Dec 15 1982. HT 16: May 1983. This comprehensive study of Asian Americans, from the first Chinese laborers in 1848 to the Vietnamese boat people, covers the circumstances of their emigration, their expectations, and their legal and social status.

345. Perrin, Linda. Coming to America: Immigrants from the Far East. Delacorte, 1980. 182 p. ill. $10.
Gr 7+. B 77: Oct 15 1980. B 83: Oct 1 1986. BC 34: Jan 1981. * SE 45: Apr 1981. SLJ 27: Jan 1981. Covers Chinese, Japanese, Filipino, and Vietnamese immigrants, why they came, and the problems they found here.

Immigration, Chinese

346. Daley, William. Chinese Americans, The. (Peoples of North America). Chelsea House, 1987. 93 p. ill. $16.
Gr 6-9. B 84: Jan 1 1988. Covers the problems that caused immigrants to come from China, the discrimination they encountered, their culture, and notable persons.

347. McCunn, Ruthanne Lum. Illustrated History of the Chinese in America, An. Design Enterprises of San Francisco, 1979. 136 p. ill. $12. Pb $7.
Gr 6-9. B 81: Feb 1 1985. SLJ 26: Oct 1979. An informative, topically arranged, and highly illustrated coverage of Chinese immigrants, explaining why they came, the prejudice they faced, their occupations, and how they organized for social stability.

348. Meltzer, Milton. Chinese Americans, The. Harper/Crowell, 1980. 182 p. ill. $11. Lib. ed. $11.
Gr 5-8. B 81: Feb 1 1985, Jul 1985. BC 34: Jan 1981. HB 57: Feb 1981. SLJ 27: Dec 1980. * SE 45: Apr 1981, May 1981. This introduction to the life of Chinese immigrants in cities, towns, and mining and railroad camps examines family and group relationships, prejudices, and persecution.

Immigration, Danish

349. Mussari, Mark. Danish Americans, The. (Peoples of North America). Chelsea House, 1988. 109 p. ill. $17.
Gr 7-10. B 84: Jun 1 1988. - BR 7: Nov/Dec 1988. This explanation of the reasons why immigrants came from Denmark and what they found here also highlights noted persons. Enriched by photos and illustrations.

350. Petersen, Peter L. Danes in America, The. (In America Series). Lerner, 1987. 95 p. ill. $8. Pb $4.
Gr 4-8. B 83: Jun 15 1987. SLJ 34: Sep 1987. Covers the reasons for Danish emigration, outlines the Danish experience in America, and introduces prominent Danish Americans. Includes photos and illustrations.

Immigration, French

351. Morrice, Polly. French Americans, The. (Peoples of North America). Chelsea House, 1988. 110 p. ill. $17.
Gr 7-10. B 84: Jun 1 1988. BR 7: Nov/Dec 1988. Explains why the French immigrants came, what they found here, and highlights noted persons. Enriched by photos and illustrations.

Immigration, Greek

352. Monos, Dimitris. Greek Americans, The. (Peoples of North America). Chelsea House, 1988. 110 p. ill. $17.
Gr 7-10. B 84: Jun 1 1988. BR 7: Nov/Dec 1988. Covers the reasons why the Greek immigrants came, what they found here, and profiles noted persons. Enriched by photos and illustrations.

Immigration, Hispanic

353. Garver, Susan. Coming to North America from Mexico, Cuba, and Puerto Rico. Delacorte; dist. by Doubleday, 1981. 224 p. ill. $12. Pb $4.
Gr 7+. B 78: Dec 1 1981. B 81: Jun 15 1985. BC 35: Mar 1982. * SE 46: Apr 1982. SLJ 29: Nov 1982. VOYA 6: Feb 1983. A frank discussion of the problems of adjustment, poverty, and discrimination encountered by Hispanic newcomers. Emphasis is on immigrants from Mexico.

354. Meltzer, Milton. Hispanic Americans, The. Harper/Crowell, 1982. 149 p. ill. $12. Lib. ed. $11.
Gr 4-9. B 78: Jul 1982. BC 36: Dec 1982. HB 58: Aug 1982. * SE 47: Apr 1983. +- SLJ 28: Apr 1982. +- VOYA 5: Aug 1982. Focuses on the Cubans, Puerto Ricans, and Mexicans who immigrated to the U.S. Includes many photos and quotes.

Immigration, Italian

355. di Franco, J. Philip. Italian Americans, The. (Peoples of North America). Chelsea House, 1987. 93 p. ill. $16.
Gr 6-9. B 84: Jan 1 1988. - SLJ 34: Feb 1988. Covers the history, culture, and religion of Italian immigrants, explains why they came, and what they contributed to the U.S.

356. Panella, Vincent. Other Side: Growing Up Italian in America. Doubleday, 1979. 189 p. ill. $13.
Gr 9+. SLJ 26: Mar 1980. The author's grandparents immigrated from Italy. Their retention of the Italian way of life caused conflict with later generations. Panella examines the cultural conflict within the Melting Pot.

Immigration, Japanese

357. Ichioka, Yuji. Issei: The World of the First Generation Japanese Immigrants, 1885-1924. Free Press, 1988. 309 p. $23.
Gr 10+. * LJ 113: Aug 1988. Covers the obstacles imposed by both the Japanese and U.S. governments, and the difficulties immigrants faced in getting jobs, finding housing, and dealing with prejudice.

Immigration, Jewish

358. Brownstone, David M. Jewish-American Heritage. (America's Ethnic Heritage). Facts on File, 1988. 134 p. ill. $16.
Gr 6+. B 84: Aug 1988. +- SLJ 35: May 1988. VOYA 11: Oct 1988. Covers Jewish immigration, anti-Semitism, religious revival, and the impact of Israel on Jewish Americans.

359. Howe, Irving. How We Lived: A Documentary History of Immigrant Jews in America 1880-1930. Marek, 1979. 360 p. ill. $23.
Gr 9+. SLJ 26: Feb 1980. These topically arranged photos and excerpts from newspapers, memoirs, records, and interviews cover social, political, and labor history.

360. Meltzer, Milton. Jewish Americans: A History in Their Own Words 1650-1950. Harper/Crowell, 1982. 192 p. ill. $11. Lib. ed. $11.
Gr 6+. B 79: Nov 1 1982. BC 36: Apr 1983. HB 58: Oct 1982. HT 16: Aug 1983. * SE 47: Apr 1983. * VOYA 6: Feb 1983. A first-hand account of the varied experiences of American Jews of all classes, based on excerpts from letters, journals, books, and other documents.

361. Muggamin, Howard. Jewish Americans, The. (Peoples of North America). Chelsea House, 1988. 125 p. ill. $17.
Gr 7-10. B 84: Jun 1 1988. BR 7: Nov/Dec 1988. SLJ 35: Nov 1988. Explains why the immigrants came, what they found here, and profiles noted persons. Enriched by photos and illustrations.

Immigration, Korean

362. Lehrer, Brian. Korean Americans, The. (Peoples of North America). Chelsea House, 1988. 108 p. ill. $17.
Gr 5-10. B 84: Mar 15 1988. SLJ 34: Apr 1988. Covers the background of Korean immigrants, what they found here, and their contributions to the U.S. The readable and well-researched text is accompanied by a section of full-color photos.

Immigration, Lebanese

363. Harik, Elsa Marston. Lebanese in America, The. (In America Series). Lerner, 1987. 95 p. ill. $8. Pb $4.
Gr 4-8. B 83: Aug 1987. +- SLJ 34: Jan 1988. Includes a brief history of Lebanon, reasons the Lebanese people emigrated to the U.S., the conditions they found, how they adapted to their new home, and information on noted persons.

Immigration, Mexican

364. Catalano, Julie. Mexican Americans, The. (Peoples of North America). Chelsea House, 1987. 95 p. ill. $16.
Gr 6-9. B 84: Jan 1 1988. BR 7: Nov/Dec 1988. SLJ 34: Feb 1988. Covers the history and culture of the immigrants, the reasons they left Mexico, and notable persons.

365. Vigil, James Diego. From Indians to Chicanos: A Sociological History. Mosby, 1980. 245 p. Pb $12.
Adult. HT 16: Nov 1982. For advanced students, an examination of Chicano history and culture.

Immigration, Norwegian

366. Lovoll, Odd S. Promise of America: A History of the Norwegian-American People. University of Minnesota Press, 1984. 240 p. ill. $35. Pb $16.
Gr 10+. LJ 109: Jul 1984. This well-written and lavishly illustrated history of Norwegian immigrants shows how early immigrants defended their culture and notes the contributions of Norwegians to their new country.

Immigration, Romanian

367. Diamond, Arthur. Romanian Americans, The. (Peoples of North America). Chelsea House, 1988. 109 p. ill. $17.
Gr 7-10. B 84: Jun 1 1988. BR 7: Nov/Dec 1988. VOYA 11: Oct 1988. Reliable coverage of the causes for immigration, the characteristics of Romanian Americans, and their contributions to their new nation.

Immigration, Scandinavian

368. Franck, Irene M. Scandinavian-American Heritage, The. (America's Ethnic Heritage). Facts on File, 1988. 123 p. ill. $16.
Gr 6+. B 84: Aug 1988. BR 7: Nov/Dec 1988. SLJ 35: May 1988. Covers immigrants from Denmark, Finland, Iceland, Norway, and Sweden, tells why they came and the difficulties they faced. A separate chapter covers each group. Includes photos and maps.

Immigration, Slovak

369. Stolarik, M. Mark. Slovak Americans, The. (Peoples of North America). Chelsea House, 1988. 109 p. ill. $17.
Gr 7-10. B 84: Mar 15 1988. Provides reasons for immigration from the Slovak nations, the contributions of the immigrants, and the problems of cultural assimilation. Includes photos.

Immigration, Swedish

370. Ljungmark, Lars. Swedish Exodus. Southern Illinois University Press, 1979. 165 p. ill. $12.
Adult. B 76: Feb 15 1980. LJ 105: Mar 1 1980. Biographies are used to illustrate major points in this concise account of why more than a million Swedes came to the U.S.

371. McGill, Allyson. Swedish Americans, The. (Peoples of North America). Chelsea House, 1988. 109 p. ill. $17.
Gr 7-10. B 84: Jun 1 1988. - BR 7: Nov/Dec 1988. Includes the reasons for immigration, what the new citizens found, Swedish American contributions to their new land, and the accomplishments of influential individuals.

Immigration–Women

372. Seller, Maxine S. Immigrant Women. Temple University Press, 1981. 347 p. $30. Pb $11.
Gr 9+. B 77: Apr 1 1981. SE 50: Mar 1986. A chronological anthology on the political, social, and work experience of immigrant women, and their clashes with their Americanized daughters and granddaughters. Based on primary and secondary sources.

373. Weatherford, Doris. Foreign and Female: Immigrant Women in America, 1840-1930. Schocken, 1987. 320 p. ill. $19.
Gr 9+. B 83: Jan 1 1987. LJ 112: Jan 1987. Presents the quality of life of immigrant women on the frontier and in cities. Covers courtship, family life, clothing, manners, work, food, and homes.

Indiana

374. Fradin, Dennis B. Indiana: In Words and Pictures. (Young People's Stories of Our States Series). Childrens Press, 1980. 48 p. ill. $7.
Gr 2-5. +- B 76: May 15 1980. +- SLJ 26: Aug 1980. Covers Indiana's political and economic history, geography, people, and trivia.

375. Gray, Ralph. Hoosier State: Readings in Indiana History. Eerdmans, 1980. 2 vol. Pb $17, $19.
Gr 10+. HT 16: Nov 1982. An extensive collection of primary sources which provides a rich picture of Indiana life, work, and culture, and highlights celebrities.

376. Hoover, Dwight W. Pictorial History of Indiana, A. Indiana University Press, 1981. 304 p. ill. $20.
Gr 9+. LJ 106: May 1 1981. A basic political, social, and economic history of Indiana.

Indians of North America

377. America's Fascinating Indian Heritage. Reader's Digest Association; dist. by Norton, 1978. 416 p. ill. $18.
Gr 7+. B 75: Mar 1 1979. HT 21: Aug 1988. LJ 104: Feb 1 1979. This well-illustrated broad overview of Indian history and culture since their arrival in the New World includes appendixes that list historic and archeological sites and museums.

378. World of the American Indian, The. (Story of Man Library). National Geographic Society, 1974. 399 p. ill. $11.
Gr 9+. B 71: Feb 1 1975. HT 21: Aug 1988. LJ 100: Jan 1 1975. A wide-ranging overview of Indian history on this continent since the crossing of the Bering Strait. Includes hundreds of illustrations, mostly in color.

379. Bancroft-Hunt, Norman. Indians of the Great Plains, The. Morrow, 1982. 128 p. ill. $25.
Gr 9+. B 79: Nov 15 1982. The history and traditions of the Plains Indians–Sioux, Blackfoot, Apache, Cheyenne, and Shoshone.

380. Brown, Virginia Pounds. World of the Southern Indians, The. Beechwood Books, 1983. 176 p. ill. $16.
Gr 6-9. B 80: Jan 1 1984. B 81: Apr 15 1985. Covers the history and contributions of the Cherokee, Chickasaw, Choctow, Creeks, and Seminoles.

381. Deur, Lynne. Nishwawbe: A Story of Indians in Michigan. River Road, 1981. 52 p. ill. $10. Pb $8.
Gr 4-6. SLJ 28: May 1982. Examines the early culture of the Michigan Indian tribes (Hopewells, Ojibwa, Ottawa, Potawatomie, and others), the changes brought by white men, and their contemporary life.

382. Edmunds, R. David. American Indian Leaders. University of Nebraska Press, 1980. 257 p. ill. $20. Pb $6.
Adult. LJ 105: Sep 15 1980. Edmunds focuses on the leadership attributes of 12 Indian leaders and each person's place in history. He also clarifies the reasons for continued misunderstanding between white and Indian cultures.

383. Galeano, Eduardo. Memory of Fire: Genesis, Part One of a Trilogy. Pantheon, 1985. 289 p. $19.
Gr 9+. B 82: Nov 15 1985. LJ 110: Oct 1 1985. A survey that examines Indian history from the arrival of the Indian people in North America to the triumph of the European colonists.

384. Grim, John A. Shaman: Patterns of Siberian & Ojibway Healing. (Civilization of American Indian Series). University of Oklahoma Press, 1984. 264 p. ill. $20.
Gr 9+. SE 49: Jan 1985. History, sociology, anthropology, psychology, and mythology contribute to this indepth treatment of Shamanism.

385. Harlan, Judith. American Indians Today: Issues and Conflicts. (Impact Book). Watts, 1987. 128 p. ill. $12.
Gr 7+. B 83: Jun 1 1987. * BR 6: Sep/Oct 1987. * SE 52: Apr/May 1988. +- SLJ 33: Aug 1987. VOYA 10: Sep 1987. A factual account of current Indian problems, including cultural conflicts, land claims, and health concerns, set in historic context.

386. Hirschfelder, Arlene. Happily May I Walk: American Indians and Alaska Natives Today. Scribner, 1986. 152 p. ill. $14.
Gr 5-8. * B 83: Dec 15 1986. BC 40: Jan 1987. * SE 51: Apr/May 1987. * SLJ 33: Jan 1987. Hirschfelder examines Indian history, explains how white society has influenced current cultural practices among Indian, Aleut, and Inuit tribes, and corrects popular misconceptions of Indian people and culture.

387. Hodgson, Pat. Growing Up with the North American Indians. (Growing Up). Batsford; dist. by David & Charles, 1980. 72 p. ill. $15.
Gr 6-8. B 77: Apr 15 1981. +- SLJ 27: Mar 1981. An overview of Native American culture and the impact of

white settlers. Includes a chronology, glossary, and quotes from both Indian and white leaders.

388. Hughes, Jill. Plains Indians. (Civilization Library). Rev. ed. Gloucester; dist. by Watts, 1984. 32 p. ill. $9.
Gr 4-6. B 81: Sep 1 1984. SLJ 31: Oct 1984. An overview of the life of the Plains Indians that contrasts various tribes, and explains customs and the importance of the buffalo in Indian history.

389. Jacobson, Daniel. Indians of North America. (Reference First Book). Watts, 1983. 88 p. ill. $9.
Gr 4-9. B 80: Jan 1 1984. +- SLJ 30: Jan 1984. An encyclopedic treatment of the histories, leaders, culture, demography, economy, and legal status of 30 tribes.

390. Josephy, Alvin M. American Heritage Book of Indians. American Heritage, 1961. 424 p. ill. $18.
Gr 9+. B 58: Dec 1 1961. HT 21: Aug 1988. +- LJ 86: Dec 1 1961. Following an introduction to the history of all Indians in the New World prior to the coming of the Europeans is a profusely illustrated history of the struggle of the Indians in the U.S. as the frontier moved west.

391. Katz, Jane. Let Me Be a Free Man: A Documentary History of Indian Resistance. (Voices of the American Indian). Lerner, 1975. 184 p. ill. $7.
Gr 7-9. B 72: Jan 15 1976. B 81: Apr 15 1985. SLJ 22: Jan 1976. An anthology of primary source material that reveals the dishonesty and brutality of white civilization as seen by such Indian leaders as Powhatan, King Philip, Tecumseh, Chief Joseph, and Geronimo.

392. Leitch, Barbara A. Concise Dictionary of Indian Tribes of North America, A. Reference Publications, 1980. 646 p. ill. $60.
Gr 9+. B 77: Mar 1 1981. +- LJ 105: Apr 1 1980. A concise, accurate history of each North American tribe, its religion, language, relationship with other tribes, and its past and current geographic locations.

393. Lyons, Grant. Pacific Coast Indians of North America. Messner, 1983. 128 p. ill. $9.
Gr 5-10. B 79: Aug 1983. +- BR 2: Nov/Dec 1983. SLJ 30: Sep 1983. An overview of several Northwest tribes, their history and the impact of the coming of the white man.

394. May, Robin. Plains Indians of North America. (Original Peoples). Rourke, 1987. 48 p. ill. $13.
Gr 4-6. B 84: Jan 15 1988. SLJ 34: Apr 1988. An accurate history that includes an explanation of the culture of the Plains Indians and the impact of white society. Numerous illustrations.

395. Poatgieter, Alice Hermina. Indian Legacy: Native American Influences on World Life and Culture. Messner, 1981. 191 p. ill. $11.
Gr 5-10. +- B 78: Feb 15 1982. SLJ 28: Apr 1982. An interesting and informative account of the contributions of North and South American Indians, ranging from agriculture to politics.

396. Prucha, Francis Paul. Indians in American Society: From the Revolutionary War to the Present. University of California Press, 1985. 127 p. $16.
Gr 9+. B 82: Apr 15 1986. LJ 110: Dec 1985. Traces the development of the policies that have regulated U.S. government treatment of Indians, its impact, and the recent Indian rights movement.

397. Ruby, Robert H. Guide to the Indian Tribes of the Pacific Northwest, A. University of Oklahoma Press, 1986. 304 p. ill. $30.
Adult. LJ 111: Jun 15 1986. A brief history of 150 tribes of the Pacific Northwest as seen through the eyes of missionaries, explorers, and government officials. Especially useful for information on lesser-known native groups.

398. Tannenbaum, Beulah. Science of the Early American Indians. (First Book). Watts, 1988. 96 p. ill. $10.
Gr 5-7. B 84: May 1 1988. BR 7: Sep/Oct 1988. Presents discoveries of North and South American Indians in astronomy, agriculture, medicine, weaving, and art. Includes photos, illustrations, and a glossary.

399. Waldman, Carl. Atlas of the North American Indian. Facts on File, 1985. 276 p. ill. $30.
Gr 9+. * B 82: Jan 15 1986. BR 5: Jan/Feb 1987. LJ 111: Jan 1986. SLJ 32: May 1986. This compact, wide-ranging account summarizes Indian origins, history, culture and contemporary conditions. Illustrations include 122 maps.

400. Waldman, Carl. Encyclopedia of Native American Tribes. Facts on File, 1987. 320 p. ill. $35.
Gr 6+. B 84: Mar 15 1988. BR 7: Sep/Oct 1988. LJ 112: Nov 15 1987. Covers the history and customs of individual North American Indian tribes from ancient times and explores how contact with whites affected them.

401. Weatherford, Jack. Indian Givers: How the Indians of the Americas Transformed the World. Crown, 1988. 288 p. $18.
Gr 9+. B 85: Oct 15 1988. Discusses the contributions of North American Indians to world culture, including the potato, gold and silver, many medicines, and many concepts of democracy.

402. Weeks, Philip. Subjugation and Dishonor: A Brief History of the Travail of the Native Americans. Krieger, 1981. 145 p. $13. Pb $6.
Gr 10+. HT 14: Aug 1981. A general history of the ethnocentric ways of non-Indians toward Indians that resulted in their relegation to a position of social inferiority.

403. Wheeler, M. J. First Came the Indians. Atheneum, 1983. 32 p. ill. $10.
Gr 2-4. B 79: Jun 1 1983. B 81: Apr 15 1985. An introduction to Indian history and customs.

404. Wolfson, Evelyn. From Abenaki to Zuni: A Dictionary of Native American Tribes. Walker, 1988. 215 p. ill. $18. Lib ed. $19.

Gr 4-9. B 84: Jun 1 1988. - BR 7: Nov 1988. +- SLJ 34: Jun/Jul 1988. An alphabetically arranged capsule treatment of 68 tribes, covering such topics as clothing, shelter, food, transportation, religion, relations with white men, and current status.

Indians of North America–Biographies

405. Dockstader, Frederick J. Great North American Indians: Profiles in Life and Leadership. Van Nostrand, 1977. 386 p. $23.
Gr 9+. B 80: Jun 15 1984. Provides biographical information on 300 deceased American Indian men and women from the 16th century to 1977 and places the individual in the context of the time. Includes lists by tribe and by birth date.

Indians of North America–Blackfeet

406. Farr, William E. Reservation Blackfeet, 1882-1945: A Photographic History of Cultural Survival. University of Washington Press, 1985. 210 p. maps. $20.
Gr 9+. HT 21: Aug 1988. LJ 110: Jan 1985. A photo-history that shows changes in reservation life, including such topics as education, economy, religion, and holidays.

Indians of North America–Cherokee

407. Bealer, Alex. Only the Names Remain: The Cherokees and the Trail of Tears. Little, Brown, 1972. 88 p. ill. $8.
Gr 4-6. B 81: Apr 15 1985. HB 48: Jun 1972. LJ 97: May 15 1972. Based on legend and primary sources, this is a lucid account of Cherokee efforts to synthesize their ancient customs and white traditions into a new culture, and the tragic events that culminated in the Trail of Tears.

408. Lepthien, Emilie U. Cherokee, The. (New True Book). Childrens Press, 1985. 45 p. ill. $8.
Gr 1-4. B 82: Dec 1 1985. SLJ 32: Mar 1986. Insights into the history and customs of the Cherokee.

Indians of North America–Cheyenne

409. Ashabranner, Brent. Morning Star, Black Sun: The Northern Cheyenne Indians and America's Energy Crisis. Dodd, 1982. 154 p. ill. $11.
Gr 6+. * B 79: Oct 1 1982. BC 36: Sep 1982. HB 58: Oct 1982. SLJ 29: Sep 1982. VOYA 4: Dec 1982. An account of the effort of the Northern Cheyenne Indians to protect their homeland and culture, first from settlers and the army, and more recently from mining corporations which threaten to destroy the land.

410. Fradin, Dennis B. Cheyenne, The. (New True Book). Childrens Press, 1988. 48 p. ill. $12.
Gr 1-4. +- B 84: Aug 1988. +- SLJ 35: Nov 1988. A simple large-type introduction to Cheyenne history and culture.

Indians of North America–Chippewa

411. Osinski, Alice. Chippewa, The. (New True Book). Childrens Press, 1987. 45 p. ill. $12.
Gr 2-5. B 84: Nov 1 1987. BC 41: Nov 1987. SLJ 34: Feb 1988. A clear and factual coverage of Chippewa history, culture, and relations with other tribes and with white men.

Indians of North America–Eskimo

412. Smith, J. H. Greg. Eskimos: The Inuit of the Arctic. (Original Peoples). Rourke, 1987. 48 p. ill. $13.
Gr 3-6. B 84: Jan 15 1988. SLJ 34: Apr 1988. Distinguishes between the Inuit of the past and present, and examines the problems they face because of cultural and economic pressures.

Indians of North America–Fiction

413. Brown, Dee Alexander. Creek Mary's Blood. Holt, 1980. 401 p. $13.
Gr 9+. B 76: Feb 15 1980. * LJ 105: Mar 1 1980. * SE 45: Feb 1981. SLJ 26: Mar 1980. VOYA 3: Aug 1980. This fictional biography of Creek Mary and her descendants is a microcosmic view of the destruction of the Indian people.

414. Kittleman, Laurence R. Canyons Beyond the Sky. Atheneum, 1985. 212 p. $14.
Gr 6-8. B 82: Feb 1 1986. BC 39: Feb 1986. In a taut adventure, a modern boy learns about the life of the early Native Americans.

415. Mayne, William. Drift. Delacorte, 1986. 160 p. $15.
Gr 5-9. B 82: May 1 1986. BC 39: Jun 1986. HB 62: Jul/Aug 1986. SLJ 32: Aug 1986. VOYA 9: Jun 1986. In a thought-provoking adventure a white boy and an Indian girl struggle to survive in the wilderness.

Indians of North America–Hopi

416. Tomcheck, Ann Heinrichs. Hopi, The. (New True Book). Childrens Press, 1987. 45 p. ill. $12.
Gr 2-5. B 84: Nov 1 1987. BC 41: Nov 1987. SLJ 34: Feb 1988. A well-rounded examination of the history, environment, and past and present culture of the Hopi. The easy-to-read text is accompanied by vivid photos and maps.

Indians of North America–Mixed Bloods

417. Katz, William Loren. Black Indians: A Hidden Heritage. Atheneum, 1986. 163 p. $14.
Gr 6-10. +- B 82: Jun 15 1986. +- BC 39: Apr 1986. LJ 111: Aug 1986. * SE 51: Apr/May 1987. SLJ 32: Aug 1986. Discusses the relations, mostly cooperative, between blacks and Indians.

Indians of North America–Modoc

418. Faulk, Odie B. Modoc, The. (Indians of North America). Chelsea House, 1988. 96 p. ill. $17.

Gr 7-10. B 84: Jun 1 1988. Discusses the history and changing fortunes of the Modoc who lived in Oregon and California. Decimated by war and disease, they now number around 200 persons.

Indians of North America–Nanticoke

419. Porter, Frank W. Nanticoke, The. (Indians of North America). Chelsea House, 1987. 96 p. ill. $17.
Gr 6-9. B 84: Sep 1 1987. SLJ 33: Jun/Jul 1987. Covers the history of the Nanticoke people of the Maryland and Delaware area, with emphasis on their struggle to retain their cultural identity after the coming of the white man. Includes illustrations and maps.

Indians of North America–Navaho

420. Boyce, George A. Some People Are Indians. Vanguard, 1974. 165 p. ill. $7.
Gr 7-9. B 71: Mar 1 1975. B 81: Apr 15 1985. Navaho history and custom based on the author's remembrance.

421. Osinski, Alice. Navaho, The. (New True Book). Childrens Press, 1987. 31 p. ill. $9.
Gr 2-5. B 84: Nov 1 1987. BC 41: Nov 1987. SLJ 34: Feb 1988. A clear and factual coverage of Navaho history and culture and their relations with other tribes and with white men.

422. Underhill, Ruth. Here Come the Navaho: A History of the Largest Indian Tribe in the U.S. Treasure Chest, 1983. 285 p. ill. $13.
Gr 9+. B 80: Dec 1 1983. A general history of the Navaho people and information on their culture and art. Abundant photos.

Indians of North America–Potawatomi

423. Clifton, James A. Potawatomi, The. (Indians of North America). Chelsea House, 1987. 98 p. ill. $17.
Gr 6-9. B 84: Nov 1 1987. SLJ 34: Jan 1988. Covers the history of the Potawatomi nation, their interaction with white men and with other Indian tribes, and their current problems. Includes numerous maps, photos, and drawings.

Indians of North America–Pueblo

424. Erdoes, Richard. Native Americans: The Pueblos. Sterling, 1984. 96 p. ill. $17. Lib. ed. $20.
Gr 4-9. B 79: Feb 1 1983. +- B 80: Apr 1 1984. SLJ 30: Aug 1984. This survey of the history and culture of the Pueblo people includes an abundance of photos.

425. Yue, Charlotte. Pueblo, The. Houghton, 1986. 117 p. ill. $13.
Gr 4-7. BC 39: Jun 1986. * SE 51: Apr/May 1987. SLJ 32: Aug 1986. VOYA 9: Dec 1986. This history of the Pueblo people emphasizes how Pueblo villages were built and the culture of the Pueblo people. The final chapter deals with their present-day life.

Indians of North America–Seminole

426. Lepthien, Emilie U. Seminole, The. (New True Book). Childrens Press, 1985. 45 p. ill. $8.

Gr 1-4. B 82: Dec 1 1985. SLJ 32: Mar 1986. Insights into Seminole history and customs.

Indians of North America–Sioux

427. Dyck, Paul. Brule: The Sioux People of the Rosebud. Northland Press, 1971. 365 p. ill. $20.
Gr 9+. HT 21: Aug 1988. LJ 96: Jul 1971. A photo-history of the Sioux on Rosebud reservation, based on photos taken by John Anderson who went there in 1880 and stayed for over 40 years.

428. Erdoes, Richard. Native Americans: The Sioux. Sterling, 1982. 96 p. ill. $15. Lib. ed. $14.
Gr 6-9. B 79: Feb 1 1983. BR 1: Jan/Feb 1983. This illustrated history of the Sioux from ancient to modern times also covers their culture, customs, and efforts to preserve their rights.

429. Osinski, Alice. Sioux, The. (New True Book). Childrens Press, 1984. 45 p. ill. $8.
Gr 1-4. B 81: Mar 1 1985. SLJ 31: Apr 1985. Full-color photos illustrate this readable introduction to Sioux history that covers tribal organization, their encounters with whites, customs, and religion.

Indians of North America–Wars

430. Dillon, Richard H. North American Indian Wars. Facts on File, 1983. 256 p. ill. $30.
Gr 9+. * B 80: Feb 15 1984. A definitive history of Indian war and conquest 1492-1891. Illustrations, maps, photos, anecdotal material, and an extensive index contribute to its value.

431. Morris, Richard B. Indian Wars, The. (American History Topic Books). Rev. ed. Lerner, 1985. 84 p. ill. $9.
Gr 4-6. B 82: Mar 1 1986. SLJ 33: Sep 1986. Presents the view of both Native Americans and white settlers concerning the reasons for their violent conflicts.

432. Schmitt, Martin Ferdinand. Fighting Indians of the West. Scribner, 1948. 362 p. ill. $10.
Gr 7+. B 45: Dec 15 1948. HT 21: Aug 1988. A simple, clear, and moving text accompanies this collection of over 250 photos, paintings, and drawings that illustrate the Indian wars. Included are dozens of full-page portraits of chiefs and warriors.

Indians of North America–Yankton

433. Hoover, Herbert T. Yankton Sioux, The. (Indians of North America). Chelsea House, 1987. 112 p. ill. $17.
Gr 7+. B 84: Jun 1 1988. SLJ 34: Mar 1988. Explores the historic and current problems of the Yankton, one of the major divisions of the Sioux nation. The Yankton tribe lives mainly in South Dakota and Iowa.

Inventions and Inventors

434. Small Inventions That Make a Big Difference. (Books For World Explorers). National Geographic Society, 1984. 104 p. ill. $7. Lib. ed. $9.

Gr 4-8. B 80: Aug 1984. This history of many inventions shows how they affect our lives. Brief biographies of famous inventors and the photos and drawings on each page enhance this work.

435. Cosner, Shaaron. Light Bulb, The. (Inventions That Changed Our Lives). Walker, 1984. 64 p. $11.
Gr 4-8. SLJ 31: Mar 1985. Discusses the invention of the light bulb and its social and economic impact.

436. Cosner, Shaaron. Rubber. (Inventions That Changed Our Lives). Walker, 1986. 56 p. ill. $11. Lib. ed. $11.
Gr 4-6. B 83: Oct 1 1986. BR 5: Mar/Apr 1987. The history of rubber and its impact on our society are introduced.

437. Murphy, Jim. Tractors: From Yesterday's Steam Wagons to Today's Turbocharged Giants. Lippincott; dist. by Harper, 1984. 60 p. ill. $11. Lib. ed. $11.
Gr 5-7. B 81: Sep 1 1984. Recounts the 300 year history of the tractor in a humorous and well-illustrated history.

438. Olney, Ross R. Farm Combine, The. (Inventions That Changed Our Lives). Walker, 1984. 64 p. ill. $11.
Gr 4-8. B 81: Feb 15 1985. SLJ 31: Mar 1985. Examines the development of the combine and its impact on crop yield and farm laborers.

439. Richards, Norman. Dreamers & Doers: Inventors Who Changed Our World. Atheneum, 1984. 153 p. ill. $11.
Gr 6-8. B 80: Aug 1984. SLJ 31: Sep 1984. Covers the lives and contributions of Robert Goddard, Charles Goodyear, Thomas Edison and George Eastman.

440. Siegel, Beatrice. Sewing Machine, The. (Inventions That Changed Our Lives). Walker, 1984. 56 p. ill. $11.
Gr 4-6. B 81: Sep 15 1984. SLJ 31: Sep 1984. Traces the history of the sewing machine and its impact on industry and individual lives. Includes biographies of Elias Howe and Isaac Singer.

441. Siegel, Beatrice. Steam Engine, The. (Inventions That Changed Our Lives). Walker, 1986. 51 p. ill. $11. Lib. ed. $11.
Gr 4-6. B 83: Nov 1 1986. Introduces the development of the steam engine and explains its effect on transportation, industry, and farming.

Iowa

442. Carpenter, Allan. Iowa. (New Enchantment of America Series). Rev. ed. Childrens Press, 1979. 96 p. ill. $7.
Gr 5-7. SLJ 26: Mar 1980. Covers the history, geography, culture, economy, resources, attractions, and people of Iowa. Updated, with full-color photos and large type.

443. Fradin, Dennis B. Iowa: In Words and Pictures. (Young People's Stories of Our States Series). Childrens Press, 1980. 48 p. ill. $7.

Gr 2-5. +- B 76: May 15 1980. +- SLJ 26: Aug 1980. Covers the political and economic history, geography, people, and trivia of Iowa.

Irish Americans

444. Watts, J. F. Irish Americans, The. (Peoples of North America). Chelsea House, 1987. 110 p. ill. $17.
Gr 6-9. B 84: Jan 1 1988. Discusses the history, culture, and religion of Irish Americans, with emphasis on their contributions to American life.

Japanese Americans

445. Endo, Takako. Japanese American Journey: The Story of a People. Japanese American Curriculum Project, 1985. 178 p. ill. $23. Pb $13.
Gr 6+. SLJ 32: Aug 1986. This celebration of Japanese American history and culture is highly illustrated. Its three sections include history, ten brief biographies, and three short stories on the Japanese American experience.

446. Kitano, Harry. Japanese Americans, The. (Peoples of North America). Chelsea House, 1987. 92 p. ill. $16.
Gr 5+. B 83: Jul 1987. BR 7: Nov/Dec 1988. +- SLJ 33: Jun/Jul 1987. Traces the lives of Japanese Americans since the 1860s, exploring the injustices they suffered and their many achievements.

447. Wilson, Robert Arden. East to America: A History of the Japanese in the United States. Morrow, 1980. 351 p. ill. $13.
Gr 9+. B 76: Jul 1 1980. LJ 105: Aug 1980. Exposes the prejudice, discrimination, and hostility faced by Japanese Americans and explains how they overcame this to join the mainstream of American life.

Jewish Americans

448. Libo, Kenneth. We Lived There Too: In Their Own Words and Pictures–Pioneer Jews and the Westward Movement of America, 1630-1930. St. Martin's/Marek, 1984. 352 p. ill. $25.
Gr 10+. B 81: Dec 1 1984. LJ 109: Dec 1984. Brings to life the everyday experiences and contributions of Jews who were pioneers in the movement west from the earliest days of our nation. Based on diaries, memoirs, personal letters and newspaper accounts.

449. Meltzer, Milton. Jews in America: A Picture Album. Jewish Publication Society, 1986. 169 p. ill. $13.
Gr 5+. SLJ 33: Oct 1986. This photo album includes a great deal of history. It is skillfully written and updates the author's 1974 work entitled Remember the Days.

450. Polacco, Patricia. Keeping Quilt, The. Simon & Schuster, 1988. 32 p. ill. $15.
Gr K-2. B 85: Dec 1 1988. * SLJ 35: Oct 1988. Follows a special quilt through four generations descended from Russian Jewish immigrants and shows that even though customs and fashions change the family remains constant.

451. Rochlin, Harriet. Pioneer Jews: A New Life in the Far West. Houghton, 1984. 519 p. ill. $18.
Gr 11+. +- LJ 109: Aug 1984. This lively story of Jewish life in the western U.S. from the early days to 1920 describes the lives of Jewish settlers, including business people, professionals, and religious leaders. Includes rare photos.

452. Simons, Howard. Jewish Times: Voices of the American Jewish Experience. Houghton, 1988. 418 p. $23.
Gr 9+. B 85: Sep 15 1988. +- LJ 113: Oct 15 1988. In this portrait of Jewish American life based on interviews, Simons seeks to discover why, for the past 200 years, so many Jews have succeeded in realizing the American dream.

Journalists

453. Ashley, Perry J. American Newspaper Journalists, 1690-1872. (Dictionary of Literary Biography). Gale, 1985. 527 p. ill. $88.
Gr 9+. B 82: Jul 1986. Biographical sketches of journalists (62 men and 4 women) who participated in and reported historic events from colonial days into the Reconstruction period. Volume number 43 of the series.

454. Schoenbrun, David. America Inside Out. McGraw-Hill, 1984. 512 p. ill. $18.
Gr 9+. B 80: Aug 1984. LJ 109: Aug 1984. A memoir of Schoenbrun's experiences as a radio and television journalist from World War II through Vietnam. He recounts his meetings with world leaders and how his professional creed was influenced by his experiences.

Judicial Branch and Judges

455. Guide to the U.S. Supreme Court. (Congressional Quarterly). Congressional Quarterly, 1979. 1022 p. ill. $65.
Gr 9+. B 77: May 1 1981. LJ 105: Jan 15 1980. A comprehensive guide to the historical development of the court, its major decisions, and how it works. Includes biographies of justices.

456. Supreme Court: Justice and the Law. (Congressional Quarterly). 3rd ed. Congressional Quarterly, 1983. 194 p. Pb $10.
Gr 6+. B 80: Sep 15 1983. * BR 2: Mar/Apr 1984. Covers key personalities, decisions, and relations of the court with the presidents and Congress.

457. Barnes, Catherine A. Men of the Supreme Court: Profiles of the Justices. Facts on File, 1978. 221 p. ill. $20.
Gr 10+. B 76: Feb 1 1980. Essays on the justices who served 1945-1976.

458. Baum, Lawrence. Supreme Court, The. (Congressional Quarterly). Congressional Quarterly, 1981. 248 p. Pb $8.
Gr 9+. B 77: Jun 1 1981. The history of the court, its place in the judicial and political systems, the operation of the court, and its role as a policy-making body.

459. Baum, Lawrence. Supreme Court, The. (Congressional Quarterly). 2nd ed. Congressional Quarterly, 1985. 270 p. Pb $13.
Gr 9+. BR 4: Jan/Feb 1986. The history and impact of the Supreme Court.

460. Carp, Robert A. Federal Courts, The. (Congressional Quarterly). Congressional Quarterly, 1985. 258 p. Pb $14.
Gr 9+. BR 5: May/Jun 1986. A history of the federal court system and an explanation of how it works.

461. David, Andrew. Famous Supreme Court Cases. (On Trial Series). Lerner, 1980. 120 p. ill. Lib. ed. $7.
Gr 6-9. B 76: Mar 1 1980. SLJ 26: Aug 1980. Includes coverage of many historic cases including the Scottsboro Nine, Korematsu, Brown, Mapp, Gideon, Seeger, Miranda, Gault, Berger, and Bakke.

462. Douglas, William Orville. Court Years, 1939-1975, The. Random House, 1980. 434 p. ill. $17.
Gr 9+. B 77: Nov 15 1980. LJ 105: Nov 15 1980. Douglas reviews his years on the Supreme Court, examines cases, feuds and friendships, and speaks his mind on many topics, including the press.

463. Friedman, Leon. Justices of the United States Supreme Court: Their Lives and Major Opinions. v. V: The Burger Court, 1969-1978. Chelsea House, 1978. 510 p. $45.
Gr 11+. B 76: Jul 1 1980. Essays on recent justices, including information on their legal philosophies, work on the court, and biography. This volume updates the 1969 set, but may be purchased separately. For extensive collections.

464. Gustafson, Anita. Guilty or Innocent. Holt, 1985. 150 p. $13.
Gr 8+. * B 82: Nov 15 1985. +- BC 39: Dec 1985. * BR 4: Mar/Apr 1986. SLJ 33: Sep 1986. Explores the basic tenets of our court system, those events which have influenced its development, and major criminal cases that have set precedents.

465. Harrell, Mary Ann. Equal Justice Under Law: The Supreme Court in American Life. 4th ed. Supreme Court Historical Society, 1982. 162 p. ill. $9.
Gr 11+. B 79: Mar 15 1983. Highlights the significant decisions of the court throughout its history.

466. Kay, Richard S. Reference Guide to the United States Supreme Court, A. Facts on File, 1986. 476 p. ill. $50.
Gr 9+. B 83: Jan 1 1987. Includes essays on landmark cases, individual rights, the changing role of the court, and its relation to the legislative and executive branches, in addition to extensive biographies of the justices.

467. Lawson, Don. Landmark Supreme Court Cases. Enslow, 1987. 128 p. ill. $14.
Gr 6+. B 83: Jun 1 1987. BR 6: Sep/Oct 1987. SLJ 33: Jun/Jul 1987. * VOYA 10: Oct 1987. From the details of individual cases, Lawson moves to the important issues involved in each. This readable book, full of fascinating detail, includes photos and a list of justices.

468. Rehnquist, William H. Supreme Court: How It Was, How It Is. Morrow, 1987. 354 p. ill. $20.
Gr 9+. B 84: Sep 15 1987. * LJ 112: Sep 15 1987. Covers the evolution of the court, its role in the political process, and the minutiae of everyday activity. Informative and timely.

469. Rembar, Charles. Law of the Land: The Evolution of Our Legal System. Simon & Schuster, 1980. 447 p. $15.
Gr 9+. B 76: Jun 15 1980. LJ 105: May 1 1980. An engrossing history of the U.S. legal system which traces the origins of terms and practice from feudal days.

470. Shnayerson, Robert. Illustrated History of the Supreme Court of the United States, The. Abrams, 1986. 304 p. ill. $60.
Gr 9+. B 83: Apr 15, 1987, Jun 1 1987. LJ 111: Dec 1986. The origin, evolution, personalities, and issues of the court enhanced by 380 photos and other illustrations of people, documents and the facility.

471. Weiss, Ann E. Supreme Court, The. Enslow, 1986. 128 p. $13.
Gr 7-10. B 83: Sep 1 1986. BC 40: Apr 1987. BR 6: Sep/Oct 1987. * SE 52: Apr/May 1988. SLJ 33: Mar 1987. The history and changing role of the court is explored through the examination of a case in which a New Jersey teenager carried a right to privacy case all the way to the Supreme Court.

472. Zerman, Melvyn Bernard. Beyond a Reasonable Doubt: Inside the American Jury System. Crowell, 1981. 217 p. ill. $10. Lib. ed. $10.
Gr 7+. B 77: Apr 15 1981. BC 34: Jul/Aug 1981. HB 57: Aug 1981. * SLJ 27: Apr 1981. This history of the jury system that examines how juries work, and the strengths and weaknesses of the system, uses historical and fictional reenactments for clarification.

Kansas

473. Carpenter, Allan. Kansas. (New Enchantment of America Series). Rev. ed. Childrens Press, 1979. 96 p. ill. $7.
Gr 5-7. SLJ 26: Mar 1980. Covers Kansas history, geography, culture, economy, resources, attractions, and people. Updated, with full-color photos and large type.

474. Fradin, Dennis B. Kansas: In Words and Pictures. (Young People's Stories of Our States Series). Childrens Press, 1980. 48 p. ill. $7.
Gr 2-5. +- SLJ 27: Mar 1981. Covers the political and economic history, geography, people, and trivia of Kansas.

Kentucky

475. Carpenter, Allan. Kentucky. (New Enchantment of America Series). Rev. ed. Childrens Press, 1979. 96 p. ill. $7.
Gr 5-7. SLJ 26: Mar 1980. Kentucky history, geography, culture, economy, resources, attractions, and people are covered in this updated edition that features full-color photos and large type.

476. Fradin, Dennis B. Kentucky: In Words and Pictures. (Young People's Stories of Our States Series). Childrens Press, 1981. 48 p. ill. $7.
Gr 2-5. +- SLJ 28: Oct 1981. Covers the political and economic history, geography, people, and trivia of Kentucky.

477. McNair, Sylvia. Kentucky. (America the Beautiful Series). Childrens Press, 1988. 144 p. ill. $24.
Gr 4-8. B 84: Aug 1988. SLJ 35: Oct 1988. Covers Kentucky history, geography, economics, government, arts and leisure, historic sites, and noted persons. Includes maps and colorful photos.

Ku Klux Klan

478. Cook, Fred J. Ku Klux Klan: America's Recurring Nightmare. Messner, 1980. 159 p. ill. $9.
Gr 7+. +- B 77: Dec 1 1980. BC 34: Apr 1981. * SE 45: Apr 1981. SLJ 28: Sep 1981. Examines the racial bigotry and religious intolerance which have resulted in Klan violence since 1865.

479. Katz, William Loren. Invisible Empire: The Ku Klux Klan Impact on History. Open Hand, 1986. 166 p. ill. $18.
Gr 9+. SLJ 33: Apr 1987. Covers the history of the Klan, shows how it has influenced U.S. history, and explores its resurgence in the 1980s.

480. Meltzer, Milton. Truth about the Ku Klux Klan, The. Watts, 1982. 120 p. ill. $9.
Gr 6+. B 79: Jan 1 1983. BC 36: Feb 1983. HB 59: Apr 1983. * SE 47: Apr 1983. SLJ 29: Nov 1982. Traces the horror and brutality of Klan activities from the 1880s to today. Based on newspaper accounts and interviews.

Ku Klux Klan–Bibliographies

481. Davis, Lenwood G. Ku Klux Klan: A Bibliography. Greenwood, 1984. 643 p. $50.
Adult. B 81: Nov 15 1984. A well-arranged bibliography of all types of materials by and about the Klan.

Labor Unions and Laborers

482. Bornstein, Jerry. Unions in Transition. Messner, 1981. 188 p. $10.
Gr 7+. B 78: Dec 1 1981. SLJ 28: Feb 1982. VOYA 5: Aug 1982. A history of unions and an analysis of current strengths and weaknesses.

483. Claypool, Jane. Worker in America, The. (Issues in American History). Watts, 1985. 120 p. ill. $11.
Gr 6-9. B 81: Aug 1985. SLJ 32: Oct 1985. VOYA 8: Dec 1985. Includes chapters on black, immigrant, and women workers and the development of labor unions.

484. Fisher, Leonard Everett. Unions, The. (Nineteenth Century America). Holiday, 1982. 62 p. ill. $10.
Gr 5-8. B 78: Jun 1 1982. BC 35: Jul/Aug 1982. Traces labor unions from 1648 to 1900.

485. Green, James R. World of the Worker: Labor in Twentieth-Century America. (American Century Series). Hill and Wang, 1981. 274 p. Pb $8.
Gr 9+. B 77: Feb 15 1981. LJ 106: Jan 15 1981. Emphasizes the struggle between management and labor to control working conditions, wages, and the private lives of workers. Attention is given to the role of women and blacks.

486. Lens, Sidney. Strikemakers and Strikebreakers. Dutton/Lodestar, 1985. 170 p. ill. $15.
Gr 7+. B 81: May 15 1985. BC 39: Dec 1985. * SE 50: Apr/May 1986. SLJ 32: Sep 1985. The development of the labor movement is explored by examining several famous strikes. Discusses causes for union development, violence, racketeering, racism, and various trade unions.

487. Marshall, Ray. Role of Unions in the American Economy, The. 2nd. ed. Joint Council on Economic Education, 1985. 172 p. Pb $9.
Gr 9+. SE 49: Nov/Dec 1985. Explores the history and function of labor unions.

488. Scott, Geoffrey. Labor Day. (On My Own Books). Carolrhoda, 1982. 48 p. ill. $6.
Gr 1-4. B 78: Aug 1982. SLJ 28: May 1982. Describes the working conditions that led to the "labor festival" in September 1882, and traces the labor movement for the next 100 years in a nonsexist presentation.

Labor Unions and Laborers–Songs

489. Seeger, Pete. Carry It On! A History in Song and Picture of the Working Men and Women of America. Simon & Schuster, 1985. 224 p. ill. $19. Pb $10.
Gr 9+. B 82: Nov 15 1985. LJ 110: Dec 1985. A chronicle of American labor history told through folksongs introduced with quotes and narrative to give the sense of time and place. Melodies, all verses, guitar chords, and pictures enhance the work.

Labor Unions and Laborers–Women

490. Biddle, Marcia McKenna. Labor: Contributions of Women. (Contributions of Women). Dillon Press, 1979. 126 p. ill. $8.
Gr 7+. B 76: Apr 15 1980. SLJ 27: Oct 1980. Profiles the accomplishments of five women who were leaders in the labor movement, Mary Harris Jones, Delores Huerta, Mary Heaton Vorse, Frances Perkins, and Addie Wyatt, and provides brief information on 10 others.

Local and Oral History

491. Carey, Helen H. How to Use Primary Sources. (Social Studies Skills Book). Watts, 1983. 81 p. ill. $10.
Gr 6-8. B 80: Jan 15 1984. BR 2: Mar 1984. SLJ 30: Mar 1984. Includes interviewing techniques and the use of photos, documents, etc.

492. Carey, Helen H. How to Use Your Community as a Resource. (Social Studies Skills Book). Watts, 1983. 86 p. ill. $10.

Gr 6-8. B 80: Jan 15 1984. BR 2: Mar 1984. SE 48: May 1984. SLJ 30: Jan 1984. Tips to help the student historian; suggests sources and techniques.

493. Fletcher, William P. Recording Your Family History: A Guide to Preserving Oral History with Videotape, Audiotape, Suggested Topics and Questions, Interview Techniques. Rev. ed. Dodd, 1986. 330 p. $19. Pb $10.
Gr 9+. B 83: Nov 15 1986. SLJ 33: Dec 1986. VOYA 10: Jun 1987. A revised and updated version of the 1985 "Talking Your Roots."

494. Fletcher, William P. Talking Your Roots: A Family Guide to Tape Recording and Videotaping Oral History. Talking Your Roots, 1985. 294 p. $22.
Gr 9+. B 81: Jun 15 1985. An excellent aid to individuals wanting to document reminiscences. Includes hundreds of suggested questions to ask so that the interview will be personal and meaningful.

495. Kyvig, David E. Your Family History: A Handbook for Research and Writing. AHM Publishers, 1978. 69 p. $3.
Gr 9+. HT 13: Feb 1980. SE 44: Oct 1980. A how-to guide with examples from family histories written by students.

496. Metcalf, Fay D. Using Local History in the Classroom. American Association for State and Local History, 1982. 274 p. $18.
Gr 9+. HT 16: Nov 1982, May 1983. HT 20: May 1987. SE 47: Jan 1983. A comprehensive guide, providing a sound theoretical base, a variety of practical exercises, specific suggestions, and examples, all useful to those doing research in local history.

Louisiana

497. Fradin, Dennis B. Louisiana: In Words and Pictures. (Young People's Stories of Our States Series). Childrens Press, 1981. 48 p. ill. $7.
Gr 2-5. +- SLJ 28: Oct 1981. Covers the political and economic history, geography, people, and trivia of Louisiana.

498. Garvey, Joan B. Beautiful Crescent: A History of New Orleans. Garmer, 1982. 249 p. $10.
Gr 6+. BR 2: Nov/Dec 1983. Tells the story of New Orleans through accounts of its many colorful inhabitants.

499. Kent, Deborah. Louisiana. (America the Beautiful Series). Childrens Press, 1988. 144 p. ill. $24.
Gr 4-8. B 84: Aug 1988. SLJ 35: Oct 1988. This colorful and informative book covers Louisiana history, geography, economics, and noted persons. Includes maps, photos, and lists of facts.

Maine

500. Carpenter, Allan. Maine. (New Enchantment of America Series). Rev. ed. Childrens Press, 1979. 96 p. ill. $7.

Gr 5-7. SLJ 26: Mar 1980. Covers Maine history, geography, culture, economy, resources, attractions, and people. Updated, using full-color photos and large type.

501. Fradin, Dennis B. Maine: In Words and Pictures. (Young People's Stories of Our States Series). Childrens Press, 1980. 48 p. ill. $7.
Gr 2-5. +- B 76: May 15 1980. +- SLJ 26: Aug 1980. The political and economic history, geography, people, and trivia of Maine are introduced.

Maryland

502. Fradin, Dennis B. Maryland: In Words and Pictures. (Young People's Stories of Our States Series). Childrens Press, 1980. 48 p. ill. $7.
Gr 2-5. +- SLJ 27: Mar 1981. The political and economic history of Maryland are introduced, along with its geography, people, and trivia items of interest.

Massachusetts

503. Fradin, Dennis B. Massachusetts: In Words and Pictures. (Young People's Stories of Our States Series). Childrens Press, 1981. 48 p. ill. $7.
Gr 2-5. +- SLJ 28: Oct 1981. Covers Massachusetts political and economic history, geography, people and trivia.

504. Kent, Deborah. Massachusetts. (America the Beautiful Series). Childrens Press, 1988. 144 p. ill. $24.
Gr 4-8. B 84: May 15 1988. Covers Massachusetts history, geography, government, economy, industry, arts and leisure, and historic sites. Includes a reference section of statistics, maps, and biographic sketches.

Mexican Americans

505. Callihan, D. Jeanne. Our Mexican Ancestors, Vol. I. Institute of Texan Cultures, 1981. 124 p. $9. Pb $6.
Gr 1-6. B 83: Jun 15 1987. An overview of the ancestry of Texas Mexican Americans since the time of the Aztecs.

506. De Leon, Arnoldo. They Called Them Greasers: Anglo Attitudes toward Mexicans in Texas, 1821-1900. University of Texas Press, 1983. 167 p. $20. Pb $9.
Gr 9+. HT 18: May 1985. Examines ethnic conflict in Texas as seen through the eyes of whites. Shows how racism is used to subjugate and control a minority group.

507. Hernandez, Jose Amaro. Mutual Aid for Survival: The Case of the Mexican American. Krieger, 1983. 160 p. $12.
Adult. HT 17: Feb 1984. Historical perspective on "mutualistas," which provide avenues for political action by Mexican Americans.

508. Steiner, Stan. Raza, La: The Mexican-Americans. Harper, 1980. 448 p. $8.
Gr 10+. B 66: May 1 1970. B 81: Jun 15 1985. LJ 94: Dec 15 1969. LJ 95: Dec 15 1970. LJ 96: Nov 15 1971. Delves into all aspects of Chicano life in migrant labor camps, on farms, and in cities, and dis-

closes the prejudice and exploitation that have been a part of the life of Mexican Americans.

Michigan

509. Fradin, Dennis B. Michigan: In Words and Pictures. (Young People's Stories of Our States Series). Childrens Press, 1980. 48 p. ill. $7.
Gr 2-5. +- B 76: May 15 1980. +- SLJ 26: Aug 1980. Introduces the political and economic history, geography, people, and trivia of Michigan.

510. Hintz, Martin. Michigan. (First Book). Watts, 1987. 95 p. ill. $10.
Gr 4-8. B 84: Jan 1 1988. +- SLJ 34: Feb 1988. An overview of the history, geography, industry, resources, and noted persons of Michigan.

511. Stein, R. Conrad. Michigan. (America the Beautiful Series). Childrens Press, 1988. 144 p. ill. $24.
Gr 4-8. B 84: May 15 1988. Covers Michigan history, geography, government, economy, industry, arts and leisure, and historic sites. Includes a reference section of statistics, maps, and biographic sketches.

Military History

512. Brown, Ashley. U.S. Marines in Action, The. (Villard Military Series). Villard/Random House, 1986. 96 p. ill. $5.
Gr 7+. BR 5: Jan 1987. VOYA 10: Apr 1987. A history of the Marine Corps from 1946 to 1985. Includes a chronology and many photos.

513. Buckner, David N. Brief History of the 10th Marines, A. Marine Corps, 1981. 131 p. ill. $6.
Gr 11+. B 78: Apr 15 1982. Emphasis is on the 10th division, but a general history of the Marine Corps since 1914 is also included.

514. David, Andrew. Famous Military Trials. (On Trial Series). Lerner, 1980. 120 p. ill. $7.
Gr 5-9. B 76: Mar 1 1980. SLJ 26: Aug 1980. This explanation of military law provides information on many critical cases.

515. Ferrara, Peter L. NATO: An Entangled Alliance. (Impact Book). Watts, 1984. 90 p. ill. $10.
Gr 8+. +- B 81: Feb 15 1985. BR 4: May/Jun 1985. SLJ 31: Feb 1985. A readable overview of the post-war relations of Europe and the U.S.

516. Halberstadt, Hans. Green Berets: Unconventional Warriors. Presidio, 1988. 134 p. ill. $13.
Gr 9+. B 85: Oct 15 1988. Covers the history, mission, selection, and training of the Green Beret elite fighting forces.

517. Halter, Jon C. Their Backs to the Wall: Famous Last Stands. Messner, 1980. 224 p. maps. $9.
Gr 7+. SLJ 28: Sep 1981. Examines six battles that would have changed the course of history had the other side won. Includes the battles of Trenton, Gettysburg, the Marne, Stalingrad, Midway, and the Battle of Britain.

518. Leckie, Robert. Wars of America, The. Rev. and updated ed. Harper, 1981. 1136 p. ill. $20.

Gr 9+. +- B 77: Mar 15 1981. A massive popular military history, complete through 1979.

519. Lewinski, Jorge. Camera at War: A History of War Photography from 1848 to the Present Day. Simon & Schuster, 1980. 240 p. ill. $18.
Gr 9+. B 76: Jun 1 1980. LJ 105: May 15 1980. SLJ 27: Sep 1980. This history of war as seen through the camera's eye traces the chronology of war photography and the experiences of the photographers.

520. Mets, David R. NATO: Alliance for Peace. Messner, 1981. 223 p. ill. $11.
Gr 9+. B 77: Jul 15/Aug 1981. SLJ 28: Feb 1982. Discusses the evolution, strategy, and future of the North Atlantic Treaty Organization. Analyzes the impact of NATO on the Korean conflict, the Cuban missile crisis, the SALT talks, and other Cold War events.

521. Millett, Allan R. For the Common Defense: A Military History of the United States of America. Free Press/Macmillan, 1984. 621 p. ill. $25.
Gr 9+. * B 81: Dec 1 1984. LJ 109: Nov 1 1984. SLJ 31: Aug 1985. For the layman, all aspects of military history, with emphasis on the Cold War and contemporary periods. Discusses the dilemma of the military in a democracy which distrusts centralized power.

522. Morris, Charles R. Iron Destinies, Lost Opportunities: The Arms Race Between the U.S. and the U.S.S.R., 1945-1987. Harper/Cornelia and Micheal Bessie, 1988. 533 p. $23.
Gr 9+. B 84: May 15 1988. * LJ 113: Aug 1988. A balanced examination of the strategic arms race.

523. Murphy, Jack. History of the U.S. Marines. Exeter Books; dist. by Bookthrift, 1984. 224 p. ill. $15.
Gr 9+. B 81: Jan 15 1985. This clear introduction to the history of the Marines includes numerous illustrations and maps and covers controversial events in which the Marines have played a prominent role.

524. Norman, C. J. Tanks. (Picture Library). Watts, 1986. 32 p. ill. $10.
Gr 3-8. B 83: Jan 15 1987. SLJ 33: Feb 1987. This good visual reference about tanks provides a nutshell history, a listing of facts, a glossary, and photos.

525. Olmos, David. National Defense Spending: How Much Is Enough? (Impact Book). Watts, 1984. 92 p. $10.
Gr 7+. * BR 3: Nov/Dec 1984. VOYA 7: Dec 1984. Discusses defense spending from a historical viewpoint, compares U.S. defense spending with that of other nations and as a part of the total budget. Presents both sides of the issue.

526. Palmer, Dave Richard. Early American Wars and Military Institutions. (West Point Military History). Avery, 1987. 104 p. ill. $25. Pb $18.
Gr 9+. B 83: Feb 1 1987. A clear and accurate coverage of U.S. armies, 1775-1861, including campaigns, battles, and relations with society. Includes maps.

527. Pangallo, Michelle. North American Forts and Fortifications. Cambridge University Press, 1986. 48 p. maps. $8. Pb $3.

Gr 4-8. BR 5: Jan/Feb 1987. Covers 13 forts, their significance in our history, and their current status.

528. Simpson, Charles M. Inside the Green Berets: The First Thirty Years. Presidio, 1983. 288 p. $16.
Gr 9+. B 79: Apr 15 1983. LJ 108: Jun 15 1983. The first book-length history of the U.S. Army Special Forces (Green Berets). For extensive military collections.

529. Taylor, L. B. Draft: A Necessary Evil? (Impact Book). Watts, 1981. 83 p. $8.
Gr 9+. B 77: Jun 1 1981. SLJ 28: Oct 1981. Places the draft in historic context, and examines changes since the Vietnam War.

530. Urwin, Gregory J. W. United States Cavalry: An Illustrated History. Blandford Press; dist. by Sterling, 1984. 192 p. ill. $18.
Gr 9+. B 80: Feb 1 1984. LJ 109: Feb 1 1984. Explains and analyzes the role of "pony soldiers" from the Revolution to W.W. II.

531. Williams, T. Harry. History of American Wars: From 1745 to 1918. Knopf; dist. by Random, 1981. 512 p. $20.
Gr 9+. B 77: May 1 1981. LJ 106: Jun 1 1981. An analysis of the causes, objectives, events, tactics, and weaponry of American wars from colonial days through World War I.

532. Willinger, Kurt. American Jeep in War and Peace, The. Crown, 1983. 144 p. ill. $18. Pb $9.
Gr 9+. B 79: Jun 15 1983. An oversized pictorial history of the jeep since W.W. II.

Military History–Aerial Operations and Aircraft

533. Doss, Helen Grigsby. U.S. Air Force: From Balloons to Spaceships. Messner, 1981. 64 p. ill. $9.
Gr 4-7. +- B 78: Sep 15 1981. SLJ 28: Feb 1982. Traces the history of aircraft from balloons through gliders and biplanes to the space shuttle. Emphasis is on planes in the world wars.

534. Heatley, C. J. Forged in Steel: U.S. Marine Corps Aviation. Howell, 1987. 207 p. ill. $37.
Gr 9+. B 84: Feb 15 1988. Includes a brief history of Marine aviation, but emphasizes recent aircraft, using excellent color photos with anecdotal captions.

535. Hoyt, Edwin P. Airborne: The History of American Parachute Forces. Stein & Day, 1980. 228 p. ill. $13.
Gr 9+. B 76: Apr 1 1980. LJ 105: Jan 1 1980. Covers American paratroop and glider activities from World War I through Vietnam, but focuses on World War II.

536. Jefferis, David. Jet Age, The. (Wings: the Conquest of the Air). Watts, 1988. 32 p. ill. $11.
Gr 4-6. B 84: May 1 1988. +- BR 7: Sep/Oct 1988. Traces the role of jet aircraft in combat since World War II and notes the development of new missiles and training techniques.

537. Norman, C. J. Combat Aircraft. (Picture Library). Watts, 1986. 32 p. ill. $10.

Gr 3-8. B 83: Jan 15 1987. SLJ 33: Feb 1987. A good
visual reference about combat aircraft. It provides a nutshell history, a listing of facts, a glossary, and photos.

538. Norman, C. J. Military Helicopters. (Picture
Library). Watts, 1986. 32 p. ill. $10.
Gr 3-8. B 83: Jan 15 1987. SLJ 33: Feb 1987. A good
visual reference about military helicopters. It provides
a nutshell history, a listing of facts, a glossary, and
photos.

539. Sullivan, George. Famous Navy Attack Planes.
Dodd, 1986. 63 p. ill. $11.
Gr 4-7. B 83: Nov 1 1986. BR 5: Jan/Feb 1987. SLJ
33: Feb 1987. Covers the development of naval attack
aircraft from W.W. I to the 1980s.

540. Sullivan, George. Famous Navy Fighter Planes.
Dodd, 1986. 64 p. ill. $11.
Gr 4-7. B 83: Nov 1 1986. SLJ 33: Feb 1987. Presents
the development of naval fighter aircraft from W.W. I to
the 1980s.

541. Thum, Marcella. Airlift! The Story of the Military
Airlift Command. Dodd, 1986. 143 p. ill. $13.
Gr 5-9. B 82: Jul 1986. SLJ 32: Aug 1986. Describes
the history and duties of the Military Airlift Command,
including air rescue, weather reconnaissance, and
humanitarian relief missions.

542. Yenne, Bill. History of the U.S. Air Force, The.
Exeter Books; dist. by Bookthrift, 1984. 234 p. ill. $15.
Gr 9+. B 81: Feb 15 1985. A highly illustrated general
history of the Air Force with capsule biographies of
chiefs of staff. Examines administration, aircraft,
weapons, bases, and personnel.

Military History–Bibliographies

543. Lane, Jack C. America's Military Past: A Guide
to Information Sources. (American Government and
History Information Guide Series). Gale, 1980. 280 p.
$28.
Gr 9+. B 77: Apr 15 1981. An annotated chronological
bibliography of books and articles on American land and
air forces. Volume number seven in the series.

Military History–Naval Operations and Ships

544. Conway's All the World's Fighting Ships 1947-
1982. Annapolis Marketing Dept., U.S. Naval Institute
Press, 1983. 2 Vol. ill. $70/$35 each vol.
Adult. B 81: Dec 1 1984. Part of a series in the history
of iron and steel warships. Part I covers the fighting
ships of NATO members. Part II covers those of the
Warsaw pact.

545. United States Naval Aviation, 1910-1980. 3rd ed.
Naval Air Systems Command NAVAIR 00-80P-1, 1981.
541 p. ill. $17.
Gr 10+. B 79: Mar 15 1983. A chronology of significant events in naval aviation. Appendices include
lists and statistical tables on aviators, aircraft carriers,
and related topics.

546. Hoyt, Edwin P. Submarines at War: The History
of the American Silent Service. Stein & Day, 1983.
368 p. ill. $20.
Adult. LJ 108: Feb 15 1983. An action-filled account
of U.S. undersea warfare, with good coverage of both
world wars.

547. Kirk, John. Ships of the U.S. Navy. Exeter
Books; dist. by Bookthrift, 1987. 192 p. ill. $15.
Gr 9+. B 84: Jan 1 1988. This background material on
the development of various types of ships is clarified by
many color and black-and-white photos.

548. Lovette, Leland Pearson. Naval Ceremonies, Customs, and Traditions. 5th ed. Naval Institute, 1980. 386
p. ill. $17.
Gr 9+. B 77: Jan 15 1981. The history, traditions, and
social customs of the U.S. Navy.

549. Morris, James M. History of the U.S. Navy. Exeter Books; dist. by Bookthrift, 1984. 224 p. ill. $15.
Gr 9+. B 81: Jan 15 1985. A profusely illustrated history that features an overview of important naval battles
and covers controversial events and practices that concerned the navy.

550. Norman, C. J. Aircraft Carriers. Watts, 1986. 32
p. ill. $10.
Gr 3-8. B 83: Jan 15 1987. SLJ 33: Feb 1987. A good
visual reference that provides a nutshell history of
aircraft carriers and a listing of facts, a glossary, and
photos.

551. Norman, C. J. Submarines. (Picture Library).
Watts, 1986. 32 p. ill. $10.
Gr 3-8. B 83: Jan 15 1987. SLJ 33: Feb 1987. This
good visual reference about submarines provides a nutshell history, a listing of facts, a glossary, and photos.

552. Norman, C. J. Warships. (Picture Library). Watts,
1986. 32 p. ill. $10.
Gr 3-8. B 83: Jan 15 1987. SLJ 33: Feb 1987. A good
visual reference that provides a nutshell history of warships, a listing of facts, a glossary, and photos.

553. Sullivan, George. Return of the Battleship.
Dodd, 1983. 127 p. $11.
Gr 5+. B 80: Feb 1 1984. +- BR 2: Mar/Apr 1984.
SLJ 30: Jan 1984. A chronological history of the bat-
tleship from early armored ships to modern times.

554. Van Orden, M. D. Book of United States Navy
Ships, The. 4th rev. ed. Dodd, 1985. 96 p. ill. $12.
Gr 5+. B 81: Aug 1985. SLJ 32: Nov 1985. Covers
terminology, ship names, ship types, and designations.
Outlines the role of each type of ship, and provides a
history for individual ships. Numerous photos.

Military Personnel

555. Above and Beyond: A History of the Medal of
Honor from the Civil War to Vietnam. Time/Life by
Boston Publishing Company; dist. by Little, 1985. 346
p. ill. $40.
Adult. B 82: Dec 15 1985. LJ 110: Dec 1985. Lavish
illustrations highlight the text that covers all military
medal winners since the Civil War and provides an ac-

count of the circumstances surrounding medal-winning feats. Also covers civilian medal winners.

556. Bowers, Michael. North American Fighting Uniforms: An Illustrated History since 1756. Blandford Press; dist. by Sterling, 1985. 128 p. ill. $15.
Gr 7+. BR 4: Jan/Feb 1986. SLJ 31: Apr 1985. A survey of uniforms since 1756, mostly from the Revolutionary and Civil Wars.

557. Elting, John Robert. American Army Life. Scribner, 1982. 328 p. ill. $35.
Gr 9+. B 79: Feb 1 1983. LJ 107: Dec 15 1982. A lavishly illustrated examination of the living and fighting conditions of U.S. soldiers from the Revolution to the 1970s.

558. Matloff, Maurice. American Wars and Heroes: Revolutionary War through Vietnam. Arco, 1985. 378 p. $20.
Gr 9+. BR 4: Sep/Oct 1985. - LJ 110: Feb 15 1985. Details the nine major wars fought by the U.S. For advanced students.

Military Personnel–Biographies

559. Frisbee, John L. Makers of the United States Air Force. (USAF Warrior Studies). Office of Air Force History, U.S. Air Force, 1987. 362 p. ill. $13.
Adult. B 84: Jan 15 1988. Biographical essays of 12 officers who were important in the development of the Air Force.

560. Spiller, Roger J. Dictionary of American Military Biography. Greenwood, 1984. 3 Vol. $145.
Gr 10+. B 81: Mar 15 1985. * LJ 109: Dec 1984. Includes military leaders, inventors, physicians, cabinet secretaries, and others who influenced the development of our military history.

Military Personnel–Blacks

561. Black Americans in Defense of our Nation. Department of Defense, 1985. 189 p. ill. Pb $6.
Adult. B 81: Jul 1985. Contributions of blacks in wars and conflicts from the colonial period to the post-Vietnam era.

562. Nalty, Bernard C. Strength for the Fight: A History of Black Americans in the Military. Free Press, 1986. 409 p. $23.
Gr 9+. B 82: May 15 1986. LJ 111: May 15 1986. Examines the history of race relations in the U.S. military, details the progress that has been made throughout our history, and explains how those changes came about.

Military Personnel–Women

563. Rogan, Helen. Mixed Company: Women in the Modern Army. Putnam, 1981. 333 p. $15.
Gr 9+. B 78: Feb 1 1982. LJ 106: Oct 15 1981. SLJ 28: Aug 1982. VOYA 5: Aug 1982. Puts the experiences of modern military women into the context of experiences of female warriors, partisans, and soldiers from antiquity through World War II.

564. Stremlow, Mary V. History of the Women Marines, 1946-1977, A. Marine Corps. History and Museums Division, 1986. 260 p. ill. Pb $14.
Gr 9+. B 83: Nov 15 1986. An official history of those events that led to the current status of women as an integrated part of the Marine Corps.

Minnesota

565. Fradin, Dennis B. Minnesota: In Words and Pictures. (Young People's Stories of Our States Series). Childrens Press, 1980. 48 p. ill. $7.
Gr 2-5. +- B 76: May 15 1980. +- SLJ 26: Aug 1980. Covers Minnesota political and economic history, geography, people, and trivia.

Mississippi

566. Fradin, Dennis B. Mississippi: In Words and Pictures. (Young People's Stories of Our States Series). Childrens Press, 1980. 48 p. ill. $7.
Gr 2-5. +- SLJ 27: Mar 1981. Mississippi political and economic history, geography, people, and trivia are introduced.

Mississippi River

567. Cooper, Kay. Journeys on the Mississippi. Messner, 1981. 96 p. ill. $9.
Gr 3-5. SLJ 38: Dec 1981. Takes readers on a journey down the Mississippi to show how the river and its valley have changed in the past four centuries.

568. Crisman, Ruth. Mississippi, The. (First Book). Watts, 1984. 64 p. ill. $9.
Gr 6-8. B 81: Dec 15 1984. SLJ 31: Dec 1984. This history of the Mississippi River introduces early explorers and examines the role of the river in frontier commerce.

Missouri

569. Fradin, Dennis B. Missouri: In Words and Pictures. (Young People's Stories of Our States Series). Childrens Press, 1980. 48 p. ill. $7.
Gr 2-5. +- SLJ 27: Mar 1981. The political and economic history, geography, people, and trivia of Missouri are introduced.

Montana

570. Carpenter, Allan. Montana. (New Enchantment of America Series). Rev. ed. Childrens Press, 1979. 96 p. ill. $7.
Gr 5-7. SLJ 26: Mar 1980. Covers Montana history, geography, culture, economy, resources, attractions and people. Updated, with full-color photos and large type.

571. Fradin, Dennis B. Montana: In Words and Pictures. (Young People's Stories of Our States Series). Childrens Press, 1981. 48 p. ill. $7.
Gr 2-5. +- SLJ 28: Oct 1981. Covers Montana political and economic history, geography, people, and trivia.

572. Swarthout, Robert R., Jr. Montana Vistas: Selected Historical Essays. University Press of America, 1981. 282 p. Pb $11.
Gr 11+. HT 16: Nov 1982. This collection of previously published articles emphasizes the importance of natural resources in the history of Montana and gives attention to the contributions of minorities and ethnic groups.

National Parks

573. Sanborn, Margaret. Yosemite: Its Discovery, Its Wonders, and Its People. Random House, 1981. 289 p. ill. $18.
Gr 9+. B 78: Jan 1 1982. LJ 106: Oct 15 1981. SLJ 28: Feb 1982. Stories of Yosemite and the people connected with it, including Tenaya, Grizzly Adams, and Theodore Roosevelt.

Nebraska

574. Fradin, Dennis B. Nebraska: In Words and Pictures. (Young People's Stories of Our States Series). Childrens Press, 1980. 48 p. ill. $7.
Gr 2-5. +- B 76: May 15 1980. - BC 33: Jun 1980. +- SLJ 26: Aug 1980. Covers the political and economic history, geography, people, and trivia of Nebraska.

575. Thompson, Kathleen. Nebraska. (Portrait of America). Raintree, 1988. 48 p. ill. $16. Pb $12.
Gr 3-5. B 84: May 15 1988. Nebraska history, economy, culture, and notable persons are discussed. Includes informal interviews and photos.

Nevada

576. Carpenter, Allan. Nevada. (New Enchantment of America Series). Rev. ed. Childrens Press, 1979. 96 p. ill. $7.
Gr 5-7. SLJ 26: Mar 1980. Covers Nevada history, geography, culture, economy, resources, attractions and people. Updated, with full-color photos and large type.

577. Fradin, Dennis B. Nevada: In Words and Pictures. (Young People's Stories of Our States Series). Childrens Press, 1981. 48 p. ill. $7.
Gr 2-5. +- SLJ 28: Oct 1981. Covers the political and economic history, geography, people, and trivia of Nevada.

New England

578. O'Brien, Robert. Encyclopedia of New England, The. Facts on File, 1985. 613 p. ill. $30.
Gr 9+. B 82: Jul 1986. An overview of the cultural, geographic, statistical, political and thematic aspects of the region, plus biographies.

New Hampshire

579. Carpenter, Allan. New Hampshire. (New Enchantment of America Series). Rev. ed. Childrens Press, 1979. 96 p. ill. $7.

Gr 5-7. SLJ 26: Mar 1980. Covers history, geography, culture, economy, resources, attractions and people. Updated, with full-color photos and large type.

580. Fradin, Dennis B. New Hampshire: In Words and Pictures. (Young People's Stories of Our States Series). Childrens Press, 1981. 48 p. ill. $7.
Gr 2-5. +- SLJ 28: Oct 1981. Introduces the political and economic history, geography, people, and trivia of New Hampshire.

New Jersey

581. Bain, Jeri. New Jersey. (First Book). Watts, 1987. 93 p. ill. $10.
Gr 4-8. +- B 84: Nov 15 1987. +- BR 6: Jan/Feb 1988. SLJ 34: Jan 1988. A general overview of the history, geography, resources, and industrial development of New Jersey.

582. Fradin, Dennis B. New Jersey: In Words and Pictures. (Young People's Stories of Our States Series). Childrens Press, 1980. 48 p. ill. $7.
Gr 2-5. +- SLJ 27: Mar 1981. The political and economic history, geography, people, and trivia of New Jersey are introduced.

583. Kent, Deborah. New Jersey. (America the Beautiful Series). Childrens Press, 1988. 144 p. ill. $24.
Gr 4-8. B 84: May 15 1988. Covers New Jersey history, geography, government, economy, industry, arts and leisure, and historic sites. Includes a reference section of statistics, maps, and biographic sketches.

New Mexico

584. Fradin, Dennis B. New Mexico: In Words and Pictures. (Young People's Stories of Our States Series). Childrens Press, 1981. 48 p. ill. $7.
Gr 2-5. +- SLJ 28: Oct 1981. Covers New Mexico political and economic history, geography, people, and trivia.

585. Stein, R. Conrad. New Mexico. (America the Beautiful Series). Childrens Press, 1988. 144 p. ill. $24.
Gr 4-6. B 84: Aug 1988. Covers New Mexico history, geography, government, economy, industry, arts and leisure, and historic sites. Includes a reference section of statistics, maps, and biographic sketches.

New York

586. Fradin, Dennis B. New York: In Words and Pictures. (Young People's Stories of Our States Series). Childrens Press, 1981. 48 p. ill. $7.
Gr 2-5. +- SLJ 28: Oct 1981. Introduces the political and economic history, geography, people, and trivia of New York state.

587. LeVert, Suzanne. New York. (First Book). Watts, 1987. 95 p. ill. $10.
Gr 4-8. B 84: Nov 15 1987. +- BR 6: Jan/Feb 1988. SLJ 34: Jan 1988. Covers New York history, geography, resources, industrial development, and prominent citizens.

588. Thompson, Kathleen. New York. (Portrait of America). Raintree, 1988. 48 p. ill. $16. Pb $12.
Gr 3-5. B 84: May 15 1988. New York history, economy, culture, and notable persons are discussed. Includes informal interviews and photos.

Newspapers

589. Fisher, Leonard Everett. Newspapers, The. (Nineteenth Century America). Holiday, 1981. 62 p. ill. $8.
Gr 5-7. B 77: May 1 1981. BC 35: Oct 1981. * SE 46: Apr 1982. SLJ 27: Aug 1981. Discusses the development of American newspapers and their impact on our society.

North Carolina

590. Carpenter, Allan. North Carolina. (New Enchantment of America Series). Rev. ed. Childrens Press, 1979. 96 p. ill. $7.
Gr 5-7. SLJ 26: Mar 1980. Covers the history, geography, culture, economy, resources, attractions, and people of North Carolina. Updated, with full-color photos and large type.

591. Fradin, Dennis B. North Carolina: In Words and Pictures. (Young People's Stories of Our States Series). Childrens Press, 1980. 48 p. ill. $7.
Gr 2-5. +- B 76: May 15 1980. +- SLJ 26: Aug 1980. North Carolina political and economic history, geography, people, and trivia are introduced.

North Dakota

592. Carpenter, Allan. North Dakota. (New Enchantment of America Series). Rev. ed. Childrens Press, 1979. 96 p. ill. $7.
Gr 5-7. SLJ 26: Mar 1980. Covers North Dakota history, geography, culture, economy, resources, attractions and people. Updated, with full-color photos and large type.

593. Fradin, Dennis B. North Dakota: In Words and Pictures. (Young People's Stories of Our States Series). Childrens Press, 1981. 48 p. ill. $7.
Gr 2-5. +- SLJ 28: Oct 1981. Introduces the political and economic history, geography, people, and trivia of North Dakota.

Nuclear Power

594. Haines, Gail Kay. Great Nuclear Power Debate, The. Dodd, 1985. 176 p. ill. $12.
Gr 6+. * B 82: Apr 1 1986. BC 39: Feb 1986. A brief history of the development of nuclear power including case studies of problems with nuclear power.

Nuclear Warfare

595. Bundy, William P. Nuclear Controversy: A "Foreign Affairs" Reader. New American Library-/Meridian, 1985. 300 p. Pb $10.
Gr 9+. SLJ 32: Dec 1985. Originally published in Foreign Affairs magazine, this collection of articles presents many different aspects of the nuclear defense controversy.

596. Cox, John. Overkill: Weapons of the Nuclear Age. Crowell, 1978. 208 p. ill. $10.
Gr 7-9. B 80: Mar 15 1984. An overview of the arms race up through 1978.

597. Feldbaum, Carl B. Looking the Tiger in the Eye: Confronting the Nuclear Threat. Harper, 1988. 320 p. ill. $15. Lib. ed. $15.
Gr 7+. +- B 84: Aug 1988. BC 42: Sep 1988. * SLJ 35: Sep 1988. This history of the arms race emphasizes the decisions of individual politicians and scientists and the circumstances that led to those decisions. Includes quotes and paraphrases from documents and memoirs.

598. Hawkes, Nigel. Nuclear Arms Race. (Issues-Issues-Issues). Gloucester, 1986. 32 p. ill. $11.
Gr 5-8. B 83: Nov 15 1986. * BR 6: Sep/Oct 1987. This history of the arms buildup includes statistics, maps, colorful photos, diagrams, and charts. Hawkes addresses the questions of balance of terror and nuclear deterrence.

599. Lens, Sidney. Bomb, The. Dutton/Lodestar, 1982. 160 p. ill. $12.
Gr 7+. B 78: Aug 1982. B 80: Mar 1 1984. * SLJ 28: Aug 1982. Explores the development of the atomic bomb and the escalation of the nuclear arms race.

600. McNamara, Robert. Blundering into Disaster: Surviving the First Century of the Nuclear Age. Pantheon, 1986. 194 p. $14. Pb $6.
Gr 9+. B 83: Nov 15 1986. LJ 111: Nov 1 1986. This history of nuclear arms strategy examines popular myths about nuclear armaments.

601. Pringle, Laurence. Nuclear War: From Hiroshima to Nuclear Winter. Enslow, 1985. 121 p. ill. $12.
Gr 7+. B 82: Nov 15 1985. BC 39: Feb 1986. * BR 4: Mar/Apr 1986. * SE 50: Apr/May 1986. SLJ 32: Dec 1985. +- VOYA 9: Jun 1986. An introduction to the effects of nuclear war based on research, government studies, and interviews with analysts.

602. Taylor, L. B. Nuclear Arms Race, The. (Impact Book). Watts, 1982. 102 p. ill. $9.
Gr 7-9. B 78: Jun 1 1982. B 80: Mar 15 1984. This well-researched and balanced examination of the history and controversy surrounding the buildup of nuclear arsenals compares U.S. and Soviet strengths and discusses disarmament treaties.

Nuclear Warfare–Bibliographies

603. Burns, Grant. Atomic Papers: A Citizen's Guide to Selected Books and Articles on the Bomb, the Arms Race, Nuclear Power, the Peace Movement, and Related Issues. Scarecrow, 1984. 309 p. $23.
Gr 9+. B 81: Apr 15 1985. LJ 109: Nov 15 1984. Includes over 1000 annotated citations of materials suitable for school, public, and academic libraries.

Ohio

604. Fox, Mary Virginia. Ohio. (First Book). Watts, 1987. 71 p. ill. $10.
Gr 5-8. +- B 84: Nov 15 1987. +- BR 6: Jan/Feb 1988. +- SLJ 34: Mar 1988. An overview of the history, geography, resources, industrial development, and noted persons of Ohio.

Oklahoma

605. Carpenter, Allan. Oklahoma. (New Enchantment of America Series). Rev. ed. Childrens Press, 1979. 96 p. ill. $7.
Gr 5-7. SLJ 26: Mar 1980. Covers Oklahoma history, geography, culture, economy, resources, attractions, and people. Updated, with full-color photos and large type.

606. Fradin, Dennis B. Oklahoma: In Words and Pictures. (Young People's Stories of Our States Series). Childrens Press, 1981. 48 p. ill. $7.
Gr 2-5. +- SLJ 28: Oct 1981. An introduction to the political and economic history, geography, people, and trivia of Oklahoma.

Oregon

607. Fradin, Dennis B. Oregon: In Words and Pictures. (Young People's Stories of Our States Series). Childrens Press, 1980. 48 p. ill. $7.
Gr 2-5. +- SLJ 27: Mar 1981. Oregon political and economic history, geography, people, and trivia are introduced.

Pacifists

608. DeBenedetti, Charles. Peace Heroes in Twentieth Century America. Indiana University Press, 1986. 276 p. ill. $23.
Gr 9+. B 82: Jun 15 1986. LJ 111: Jun 1 1986. Essays on Eugene V. Debs, Norman Thomas, A. J. Muste, Daniel and Philip Berrigan, Jane Addams, Norman Cousins, Albert Einstein, and Martin Luther King, Jr.

609. DeBenedetti, Charles. Peace Reform in American History, The. Indiana University Press, 1980. 245 p. $19.
Gr 9+. HT 15: May 1982. LJ 105: Mar 15 1980. Traces the efforts of those groups which have sought to eliminate violence and war since colonial days. For advanced students.

610. Josephson, Harold. Biographical Dictionary of Modern Peace Leaders. Greenwood, 1985. 864 p. $75.
Adult. * LJ 110: Aug 1985. A compilation of 750 biographical essays on peace leaders, 1800-1900.

611. Kohn, Stephen M. Jailed For Peace: The History of American Draft Law Violators, 1658-1985. (Contributions in Military Studies). Greenwood, 1986. 184 p. $30.
Gr 9+. B 82: Mar 1 1986. B 83: Sep 15 1986. A history of U.S. pacifism since the early Quakers. Number 49 of the series.

612. Meltzer, Milton. Ain't Gonna Study War No More: The Story of America's Peace Seekers. Harper, 1985. 282 p. ill. $14. Lib. ed. $12.
Gr 7+. B 81: May 1985. BC 38: Jul/Aug 1985. * BR 4: Jan/Feb 1986. HB 61: Sep/Oct 1985. * SLJ 32: Sep 1985. * VOYA 8: Aug 1985. A study of pacifism from the Revolution to Vietnam.

Pennsylvania

613. Fradin, Dennis B. Pennsylvania: In Words and Pictures. (Young People's Stories of Our States Series). Childrens Press, 1980. 48 p. ill. $7.
Gr 2-5. +- B 76: May 15 1980. +- SLJ 26: Aug 1980. Covers Pennsylvania political and economic history, geography, people, and trivia.

614. Kent, Deborah. Pennsylvania. (America the Beautiful Series). Childrens Press, 1988. 144 p. ill. $24.
Gr 4-6. B 84: Aug 1988. Covers Pennsylvania history, geography, government, economy, industry, arts and leisure, and historic sites. Includes a reference section of statistics, maps, and biographic sketches.

615. Shebar, Sharon Sigmond. Pennsylvania. (First Book). Watts, 1987. 95 p. ill. $10.
Gr 5-7. +- B 84: Nov 15 1987. - SLJ 34: Jan 1988. Covers Pennsylvania history, geography, resources, and the development of industry.

616. Smith, Philip Chadwick Foster. Philadelphia on the River. Philadelphia Maritime Museum; Univ. of Penn. Press, 1986. 176 p. ill. $29.
Adult. LJ 111: Jan 1986. A photographic survey of Philadelphia's role as a major international port.

Photographers

617. Moutoussamy-Ashe, Jeanne. Viewfinders: Black Women Photographers. Dodd, 1984. 224 p. ill. $20. Pb $13.
Gr 9+. LJ 111: Jun 1 1986. SLJ 33: Sep 1986. This photographic essay provides an overview of the lives of 34 black women photographers and the times in which they lived.

618. Sufrin, Mark. Focus on America: Profiles of Nine Photographers. Scribner, 1987. 176 p. ill. $13.
Gr 7+. B 83: Apr 15 1987. SLJ 33: Jun/Jul 1987. VOYA 10: Jun 1987. Profiles 9 photographers who have documented changes in our society since the 1860s and includes photos by M. Brady, W. H. Jackson, E. Curtis, L. Hine, D. Lange, B. Abbott, W. Evans, W. E. Smith and M. Bourke-White.

Polish Americans

619. Bukowczyk, John J. And My Children Did not Know Me: A History of the Polish-Americans. (Minorities in Modern America). Indiana University Press, 1986. 192 p. ill. $28. Pb $9.
Adult. LJ 111: Dec 1986. Explores the problems of Polish immigrants torn between the old culture and the new and forced to deal with anti-Polish prejudice.

Politics

620. Guide to U.S. Elections. (Congressional Quarterly). 2nd ed. Congressional Quarterly, 1985. 1308 p. ill. $100
Gr 9+. B 82: Jun 15 1986. A guide to elections for president, governors, senators and representatives, 1788-1984.

621. National Party Conventions 1831-1984. (Congressional Quarterly). Congressional Quarterly, 1987. 250 p. ill. Pb $13.
Gr 9+. SLJ 35: May 1988. Includes the history of American political parties and a detailed chronology and analysis of nominating conventions.

622. Presidential Elections Since 1789. (Congressional Quarterly). Rev. ed. Congressional Quarterly, 1987. 235 p. ill. Pb $13.
Gr 9+. SLJ 35: May 1988. Includes essays on the presidents and vice-presidents, a survey of primary returns, 1831-1984, descriptions of conventions, several appendices and a bibliography.

623. Washington Lobby, The. (Congressional Quarterly). 5th ed. Congressional Quarterly, 1987. 212 p. Pb $12.
Gr 12+. BR 6: Sep/Oct 1987. Covers the history of lobbying, and explains how presidential lobbying and that of political interest groups influence policy and legislation. Illustrated by case studies on topics such as contra aid and import taxes.

624. Archer, Jules. Winners and Losers: How Elections Work in America. Harcourt Brace Jovanovich, 1984. 240 p. ill. $14.
Gr 7+. B 80: Apr 15 1984. B 81: Sep 15 1984. HB 60: Jun 1984. * SE 49: Apr 1985. * SLJ 30: Aug 1984. * VOYA 7: Oct 1984. This lively explanation of the electoral process, campaigns, conventions, and voting fraud also compares the U.S. electoral system with others and assesses its strengths and weaknesses.

625. Barber, James David. Pulse of Politics: Electing Presidents in the Media Age. Norton, 1980. 342 p. $15.
Gr 9+. LJ 105: May 1 1980. SLJ 27: Sep 1980. Barber examines the cycles in presidential elections, 1900-1980, and the role of the media, which he contends is replacing traditional political parties.

626. Bender, David L. Political Spectrum, The. (Opposing Viewpoints Series). Greenhaven, 1986. 211 p. ill. $13. Pb $7.
Gr 9+. B 83: Dec 1 1986. BR 6: May 1987. SLJ 33: May 1987. An examination of the issues which have divided conservatives and liberals throughout our history.

627. Buchanan, Bruce. Citizen's Presidency, The. (Congressional Quarterly). Congressional Quarterly, 1987. 233 p. Pb $10.
Gr 12+. BR 6: Sep/Oct 1987. By comparing presidents Carter and Reagan, Buchanan examines criteria for evaluating candidates, interactions between candidates, and relations with the press.

628. Bush, Gregory. Campaign Speeches of American Presidential Campaigns, 1948-1984. Ungar, 1985. 343 p. $25.
Gr 9+. B 82: Dec 15 1985. Includes an introduction to each campaign, the nomination acceptance speech, one representative campaign speech for each of the two major-party candidates, and some speeches by minor-party candidates.

629. Cook, Fred J. Rise of American Political Parties, The. (First Book). Watts, 1971. 90 p. ill. $4.
Gr 5-9. B 81: Sep 15 1984. Traces the evolution of the two-party system.

630. Diamond, Edwin. Spot: The Rise of Political Advertising on Television. MIT Press, 1984. 416 p. ill. $18.
Gr 9+. B 80: Aug 1984. LJ 109: Jul 1984. This history of televised political advertising includes a wealth of verbal and photographic examples of political ads that have altered political advertising. Useful for reports and fun for browsers.

631. Fradin, Dennis B. Voting and Elections. (New True Book). Childrens Press, 1985. 45 p. ill. $8.
Gr K-4. SLJ 32: Apr 1986. Includes a history of voting, the struggle of minorities to gain voting rights, and a description of the election process.

632. Gardner, Gerald. Mocking of the President: A History of Campaign Humor from Ike to Ronnie. (Humor in Life and Letters). Wayne State University Press, 1988. 234 p. $18.
Gr 10+. B 84: Jun 15 1988. LJ 113: Aug 1988. Three decades of political humor based on the foibles of presidents and presidential hopefuls.

633. Gazourian, Ann. What Citizens Need To Know About Government. (Social Issues Resources Series). Rev. ed. U.S. News & World Report, 1983. 190 p. ill. $11.
Gr 9+. BR 3: May/Jun 1984. A profile of the American political system.

634. Goode, Stephen. New Federalism: States' Rights in American History. Watts, 1983. 160 p. ill. $10.
Gr 7+. B 79: Jun 15 1983. * SE 48: May 1984. SLJ 30: Sep 1983. A look at federalism from the Constitutional Convention to the Reagan administration.

635. Hargrove, Jim. Story of Presidential Elections, The. (Cornerstones of Freedom). Childrens Press, 1988. 32 p. ill. $12.
Gr 3-6. B 84: Aug 1988. SLJ 35: Sep 1988. Discusses all aspects of presidential elections, including primaries, conventions, funding, and strategies.

636. Jamieson, Kathleen Hall. Packaging the Presidency: A History and Criticism of Presidential Campaign Advertising. Oxford University Press, 1984. 505 p. ill. $20.
Gr 10+. B 81: Nov 1 1984. LJ 109: Oct 1 1984. For advanced students, an examination of the judgment, leadership style, and temperament of presidential candidates, 1952-1980, based on their political advertising campaigns.

637. Kronenwetter, Michael. Politics and the Press. (Issues in American History). Watts, 1987. 144 p. ill. $12.
Gr 6+. B 83: May 15 1987. BR 6: Sep/Oct 1987. SLJ 34: Sep 1987. VOYA 10: Aug/Sep 1987. Presents the history of the relations between national leaders and the press since the development of the printing press. Includes reproductions of front pages and numerous photos.

638. Kronenwetter, Michael. Threat from Within: Unethical Politics and Politicians. Watts, 1986. 128 p. ill. $12.
Gr 7+. B 83: Mar 15 1987. BR 5: Mar 1987. VOYA 9: Feb 1987. Covers vote fraud, bribery, dirty tricks, pressure groups, and other ethical issues in U.S. political history from Jefferson to Reagan. Includes photos and political cartoons.

639. Lurie, Leonard. Party Politics: Why We Have Poor Presidents. Stein & Day, 1980. 336 p. $13.
Gr 9+. B 77: Nov 1 1980. Examines presidential elections from Washington through Carter and the change in the method of choosing the candidates from congressional caucus to selection by party politics.

640. Modl, Tom. America's Elections: Opposing Viewpoints. (Opposing Viewpoints Series). Greenhaven, 1988. 173 p. ill. $13. Pb $7.
Gr 10+. SLJ 35: Aug 1988. Presents differing opinions on topics such as the electoral college, the Voting Rights Act, bilingual balloting, campaign financing, the media, and the presidential primary.

641. Nelson, Michael. Presidency and the Political System, The. (Congressional Quarterly). 2nd ed. Congressional Quarterly, 1988. 498 p. Pb $18.
Gr 11+. BR 6: Mar/Apr 1988. Covers the election process, political parties, interest groups, the media, lame ducks, the vice-presidency and presidential competence. Provides historical coverage, but emphasis is on recent decades.

642. Raynor, Thomas. Politics, Power, and People: Four Governments in Action. Watts, 1983. 128 p. $10.
Gr 7+. B 80: Oct 15 1983. * BR 2: Mar/Apr 1984. * SE 48: May 1984. +- VOYA 6: Feb 1984. +- VOYA 7: Apr 1984. Compares the governments of the U.S., Great Britain, the U.S.S.R., and Argentina.

643. Roseboom, Eugene Holloway. History of Presidential Elections, from George Washington to Jimmy Carter. 4th ed. Macmillan, 1980. 355 p. $18. Pb $10.
Gr 11+. B 76: Mar 1 1980. For each campaign through 1976, Roseboom re-creates the personalities, power struggles, campaign tactics, and the mood of the country.

644. Schlesinger, Arthur M., Jr. Cycles of American History, The. Houghton, 1986. 478 p. $19.
Adult. * LJ 111: Nov 1 1986. A noted historian expresses his opinions on such topics as the Cold War, politics, and the presidency.

645. Sheehy, Gail. Character: America's Search for Leadership. Morrow, 1988. 303 p. $18.
Adult. * LJ 113: Aug 1988. Intensive interviews with 1988 presidential candidates and their close associates provide insight into the leadership styles of Hart, Gore, Dukakis, Jackson, Bush, and Reagan.

646. Thompson, Margaret C. Presidential Elections since 1789. (Congressional Quarterly). 3rd ed. Congressional Quarterly, 1983. 211 p. ill. Pb $9.
Gr 9+. BR 2: Nov/Dec 1983. Primarily tables and maps that detail the voting history of presidential elections. Covers major and minor parties, primaries, and conventions. Includes brief biographies of all candidates who received electoral votes.

647. Watson, Richard. Presidential Contest, The. (Congressional Quarterly). Congressional Quarterly, 1988. 155 p. Pb $10.
Gr 9+. BR 7: May/Jun 1988. SLJ 35: May 1988. Explores the differences between the nomination and election processes, how voters make decisions, and how these decisions influence party policy.

648. Weiss, Ann E. Party Politics, Party Problems. Crowell, 1980. 135 p. $9.
Gr 7-9. B 77: Oct 15 1980. HT 15: May 1982. SLJ 27: Feb 1981. VOYA 4: Apr 1981. A brief history of the development of political parties followed by an analysis of the American party system.

649. White, Theodore H. America in Search of Itself: The Making of the President, 1956-1980. Harper, 1982. 456 p. $16.
Gr 10+. B 78: Apr 15 1982. HB 58: Aug 1982. LJ 107: Jun 1 1982. An analysis of the presidential candidates and campaigns, how politics has changed over the years, and the evolving role of the media.

Politics–Biographies

650. Cargill, Martha. Who's Who in American Politics. 9th ed. Bowker, 1983. 1704 p. ill. $98.
Adult. B 80: Jan 1 1984. Profiles of 22,000 men and women active in the political arena from the local through national levels.

Politics–Quotations

651. Green, Jonathon. Book of Political Quotes, The. McGraw-Hill, 1983. 246 p. ill. $9.
Gr 9+. B 79: Jun 15 1983. Topically arranged quotes, ranging from the humorous to the frightening, from American and world politicians.

Population

652. Nam, Charles B. Think about Our Population: The Changing Face of America. (Think Series). Walker, 1988. 117 p. $15.
Gr 6+. VOYA 11: Aug 1988. Frequent drawings and charts clarify the causes of population growth as well as the causes of shifts in population.

Presidency and the Executive Branch

653. Great Seal of the United States, The. Rev. ed. Department of State, 1986. 16 p. ill. Pb $1.

Gr 7+. B 83: Nov 15 1986. Discusses the design, meaning, and use of the seal.

654. Alotta, Robert I. Look at the Vice Presidency, A. Messner, 1981. 256 p. ill. $11.
Gr 7+. B 77: Jul 15/Aug 1981. SLJ 28: Feb 1982. Traces the evolution of the office of the vice-president through colorful narrative and lively descriptions. Includes statistics, bibliography, and unusual photos.

655. Armbruster, Maxim E. Presidents of the United States and Their Administrations from Washington to Reagan. 7th Rev. ed. Horizon, 1982. 409 p. ill. $16.
Gr 9+. B 80: Jun 15 1984. Lengthy essays on the 39 presidents arranged chronologically and illustrated.

656. Bailey, Thomas A. Presidential Saints and Sinners. Free Press, 1981. 291 p. $20.
Adult. LJ 106: Oct 1 1981. +- SLJ 28: Feb 1982. Details the good and bad in every administration from Washington through Carter, from the point of view of "presidential integrity."

657. Bailey, Thomas A. Pugnacious Presidents: White House Warriors on Parade. Free Press, 1980. 416 p. $16.
Adult. LJ 105: Aug 1980. A study of the militancy of each president in foreign and domestic affairs, according to Bailey's "pugnacity index."

658. Beard, Charles A. Charles A. Beard's The Presidents in American History. Rev. ed. Messner, 1985. 220 p. ill. $10.
Gr 5-9. B 82: Dec 15 1985. SLJ 32: Dec 1985. This standard tool covers the U.S. presidency through Reagan's first term. A brief biography and the highlights of each administration are included along with statistics, lists of cabinet members, and other facts.

659. Beard, Charles A. Charles A. Beard's The Presidents in American History: Brought Forward Since 1948. Rev. ed. Messner, 1981. 220 p. ill. $10.
Gr 5-9. B 78: Apr 15 1982. This basic handbook on the American presidency through 1981 includes information on each administration, a list of cabinet members, and a brief biography of the president.

660. Blassingame, Wyatt. Look It Up Book of Presidents, The. Random House, 1984. 154 p. ill. $9.
Gr 3-8. B 81: Oct 1 1984. BC 38: Jan 1985. * BR 3: Mar/Apr 1985. SLJ 30: Nov 1984. +- SLJ 31: May 1985. Includes facts, anecdotes, political analysis, photos, political cartoons, and information on presidential successes and failures.

661. Blum, John Morton. Progressive Presidents: Roosevelt, Wilson, Roosevelt, Johnson. Norton, 1980. 221 p. $12.
Gr 9+. B 76: Jul 1 1980. LJ 105: Apr 15 1980. Essays on four 20th-century presidents who expanded the power of the presidency to effect political and social reform.

662. Boller, Paul F. Presidential Anecdotes. Oxford Univeristy Press, 1981. 416 p. $15.
Gr 9+. B 77: Jul/Aug 1981. LJ 106: Sep 1 1981. Following a brief description of each president and his ad-ministration is a collection of witty sayings and revealing quotes.

663. Coy, Harold. First Book of Presidents, The. (First Book). Rev. ed. Watts, 1981. 68 p. ill. $7.
Gr 4-6. B 77: May 1981. SLJ 28: Oct 1981. Discusses the duties and responsibilities of the presidents, and provides information on each president's personal and political life, election, and administration. Complete through Reagan's first election.

664. Cronin, Thomas E. State of the Presidency, The. 2nd ed. Little, Brown, 1980. 402 p. $15.
Gr 9+. B 76: May 1 1980. Cronin examines the presidency and encourages electoral reform and presidential checks and balances.

665. Deakin, James. Straight Stuff: The Reporters, the Government, and the Truth. Morrow, 1984. 368 p. $18.
Gr 9+. B 80: Feb 15 1984. LJ 109: Mar 1 1984. Journalist Deakin comments on the relationships of presidents Eisenhower through Carter with the press in a humorous and perceptive book.

666. Donovan, Hedley. Roosevelt to Reagan: A Reporter's Encounters with Nine Presidents. Harper, 1985. 352 p. $25.
Adult. B 81: May 15 1985. LJ 110: May 15 1985. The author, a journalist, comments on how presidents FDR through Reagan handled responsibility, according to contemporary and later assessment, and comments on presidential job requirements.

667. Elliot, Jeffrey M. Presidential-Congressional Political Dictionary, The. (Clio Dictionaries in Political Science). ABC-Clio, 1984. 365 p. ill. $28.
Gr 9+. B 81: Jun 15 1985. Covers the historical significance of political terms, assessments of presidential administrations, and explanations of the functions of executive branch offices. Number nine of the series.

668. Ford, Gerald R. Humor and the Presidency. Arbor House, 1987. 130 p. ill. $17.
Gr 10+. B 84: Oct 1 1987. A light-hearted survey of anecdotes and political cartoons by and about former presidents.

669. Frost, Elizabeth. Bully Pulpit: Quotations from America's Presidents. Facts on File, 1988. 282 p. $24.
Gr 9+. B 84: Aug 1988. A collection of witty, inane, profound, emotional, and prophetic quotes from presidents Washington through Reagan.

670. Gilfond, Henry. Executive Branch of the United States Government, The. (First Book). Watts, 1981. 64 p. ill. $7.
Gr 6-8. B 77: May 1981. SLJ 28: Oct 1981. Traces the development of presidential power, the cabinet, and the support staff of the executive branch.

671. Graff, Henry F. Presidents: A Reference History. Scribner, 1984. 700 p. $65.
Adult. B 81: Jan 1 1985. LJ 109: Jul 1984. Essays examining the accomplishments and impact of all administrations through Carter.

372. Greenstein, Fred I. Leadership in the Modern Presidency. Harvard University Press, 1988. 430 p. $30.
Adult. LJ 113: Jul 1988. Examines the leadership performance of presidents from Franklin Delano Roosevelt through Reagan. Thoroughly researched and documented, and suitable for advanced secondary students.

673. Hirschhorn, Bernard. Perilous Presidency, The. Richards Rosen Press, 1979. 212 p. $8.
Gr 7+. SE 45: Feb 1981. Examples of presidential roles, situations, behaviors, and conflicts between the White House and Congress.

674. Hoopes, Roy. Changing Vice-Presidency, The. Harper/Crowell, 1981. 192 p. ill. $12. Lib. ed. $11.
Gr 6+. B 78: Nov 1 1981. B 81: Sep 15 1984. HT 16: May 1983. SLJ 28: Feb 1982. * SE 46: Apr 1982. VOYA 5: Apr 1982. Explores the changing role of the vice-presidency and includes brief biographies of former vice-presidents.

675. Kane, Joseph Nathan. Facts about the Presidents, Supplement. Wilson, 1985. 12 p. Pb $4.
Gr 9+. B 82: Jan 1 1986. Updates the 1981 fourth edition of Facts About the Presidents with information about the Reagan presidency.

676. Kane, Joseph Nathan. Facts about the Presidents: A Compilation of Biographical and Historical Information. 4th ed. Wilson, 1981. 456 p. ill. $25.
Gr 9+. B 78: Dec 1 1981, Jun 15 1982. One chapter per president, covering personal, political and administration information, and statistics. Current to Reagan.

677. Lyons, Thomas T. President: Preacher, Teacher, Salesman: Selected Presidential Speeches, 1933-1983. World Eagle, 1985. 206 p. ill. Lib. ed. $15. Pb $10.
Gr 9+. B 81: Jul 1985. Excerpts from speeches which show how presidents influence public opinion.

678. Miers, Earl Schenck. America and Its Presidents. Rev. ed. Grosset, 1982. 256 p. ill. $11.
Gr 4-6. +- BC 36: Sep 1982. An oversized book with color photos of each president through Reagan. Emphasizes the political career of each president and events in U.S. history during each administration.

679. Nelson, Michael. Presidency and the Political System, The. (Congressional Quarterly). Congressional Quarterly, 1984. 522 p. Pb $14.
Gr 10+. BR 3: Sep/Oct 1984. Analyzes the evolution and problems of the presidency and provides a comparison of presidents since FDR.

680. Parker, Nancy Winslow. President's Car, The. Crowell, 1981. 58 p. ill. $9. Lib. ed. $9.
Gr 3-6. B 77: Jul 1 1981. BC 35: Nov 1981. SLJ 28: Nov 1981. Provides descriptions and drawings of the official vehicles of each of the presidents.

681. Post, Robert C. Every Four Years. Smithsonian Institution Press; dist. by Norton, 1980. 228 p. ill. $22.
Gr 9+. B 76: Jul 15 1980. SLJ 27: Oct 1980. Traces the changes in the presidency caused by the times and by personalities. Includes copious illustrations from the Smithsonian collection.

682. Scriabine, Christine Brendel. Presidency, The. (Know Your Government). Chelsea House, 1988. 96 p. ill. $13.
Gr 5-8. B 84: Aug 1988. Covers the evolution of the presidency and the growth of presidential power.

683. Sobel, Robert. Biographical Directory of the United States Executive Branch, 1774-1977. Greenwood, 1977. 503 p. $45.
Gr 9+. B 80: Jun 15 1984. Covers presidents, vice-presidents, cabinet officers and other officials of the executive branch.

684. Sullivan, George. Mr. President: A Book of U.S. Presidents. Dodd, 1985. 158 p. ill. $9.
Gr 4-7. SLJ 32: Feb 1986. The key events of each administration and summaries of the lives of the presidents.

685. Tebbel, John. Press and the Presidency: From George Washington to Ronald Reagan. Oxford University Press, 1985. 564 p. $25.
Gr 9+. B 82: Sep 1 1985. LJ 110: Sep 1 1985. Covers the relationships of all the presidents with the press, shows the growing technological sophistication of the media, and the increase in the power of the presidency to control public opinion.

686. Watson, Richard. Politics of the Presidency. (Congressional Quarterly). 3rd ed. Congressional Quarterly, 1988. 547 p. Pb $18.
Gr 9+. * BR 6: Mar/Apr 1988. SLJ 35: May 1988. This overview of the presidency considers historical, constitutional, and psychological perspectives in examining the relationships of presidents with the public and the rest of the government.

Presidency and the Executive Branch–Bibliographies

687. Martin, Fenton S. American Presidency: A Bibliography. (Congressional Quarterly). Congressional Quarterly, 1987. 506 p. $75.
Gr 10+. B 84: Dec 1 1987. BR 6: Nov/Dec 1987. LJ 112: Dec 1987. A listing of books, articles, and other works on the office of the presidency. Covers the elections, media, law, and foreign affairs.

Presidency and the Executive Branch–Cabinet, Agencies, etc.

688. Brandt, Betty. Special Delivery. (On My Own Books). Carolrhoda, 1988. 40 p. ill. $9.
Gr 1-3. +- B 84: Apr 1 1988. +- SLJ 34: Aug 1988. An overview of the history and responsibilities of the U.S. postal service.

689. Cutrona, Cheryl. Internal Revenue Service, The. (Know Your Government). Chelsea House, 1988. 96 p. ill. $13.
Gr 6+. BR 7: Sep/Oct 1988. Covers the purpose, history, development, and organization of the IRS. Includes photos and glossary.

690. Ellis, Rafaela. Central Intelligence Agency, The. (Know Your Government). Chelsea House, 1987. 93 p. ill. $13.
Gr 5-9. B 84: Jan 1 1988. SLJ 34: Feb 1988. A straightforward account of the history of the CIA.

691. Fisch, Arnold G., Jr. Department of the Army. (Know Your Government). Chelsea House, 1987. 93 p. ill. $13.
Gr 8+. +- SLJ 34: Feb 1988. An overview of the history of the Department of the Army, with numerous large photos.

692. Fitzgerald, Merni Ingrassia. Voice of America, The. Dodd, 1987. 118 p. ill. $13.
Gr 4-9. B 83: Aug 1987. SLJ 33: Aug 1987. An introduction to the history, purpose, and value of the international radio broadcasts of the Voice of America since World War II.

693. Goode, Stephen. CIA, The. Watts, 1982. 152 p. $9.
Gr 7+. B 78: May 1 1982. Traces the CIA from its inception in 1947, and covers the U-2 incident, the Bay of Pigs, Vietnam involvement, through the Carter administration.

694. Hargrove, Jim. Story of the FBI, The. (Cornerstones of Freedom). Childrens Press, 1988. 32 p. ill. $12.
Gr 3-6. B 84: Aug 1988. A history of the Federal Bureau of Investigation, the investigative branch of the U.S. Justice Department.

695. Hoobler, Dorothy. Social Security System, The. (Impact Book). Watts, 1982. 84 p. ill. $8.
Gr 7-10. B 79: Feb 15 1983. The history of the Social Security system and its problems in the 1980s.

696. Hopson, Glover. Veterans Administration, The. (Know Your Government). Chelsea House, 1988. 96 p. ill. $13.
Gr 6+. BR 7: Sep/Oct 1988. Covers the history, development, organization, and departments of the Veterans Administration.

697. Israel, Fred L. FBI, The. (Know Your Government). Chelsea House, 1986. 96 p. ill. $13.
Gr 6-10. B 83: Feb 1 1987. SLJ 33: Dec 1986. Explains the function and history of the FBI and discusses some of its more controversial cases. Covers the Freedom of Information Act and the requirements for becoming an agent.

698. Law, Kevin. Environmental Protection Agency, The. (Know Your Government). Chelsea House, 1988. 93 p. $13.
Gr 6+. BR 7: Sep/Oct 1988. VOYA 11: Oct 1988. Covers the purpose, history, and organization of the Environmental Protection Agency.

699. Mackintosh, Barry. National Park Service, The. (Know Your Government). Chelsea House, 1987. 94 p. ill. $13.
Gr 5-9. B 84: Jan 1 1988. The organizational structure and the activities of the National Park Service are explained. Enhanced by photographs and a glossary.

700. Matusky, Gregory. U.S. Secret Service, The. (Know Your Government). Chelsea House, 1988. 89 p. ill. $15.
Gr 5+. B 84: Aug 1988. BR 7: Sep/Oct 1988. An introduction to the purpose, history, and organization of the Secret Service. Includes photos and a glossary.

701. McAfee, Cheryl Weant. United States Postal Service, The. (Know Your Government). Chelsea House, 1987. 92 p. ill. $13.
Gr 4-7. +- B 83: Jun 1 1987. BR 7: Sep/Oct 1988. SLJ 34: Sep 1987. Covers the history of the postal service, its current operation, and speculates about the future.

702. Ranelagh, John. Agency: The Rise and Decline of the CIA. Simon & Shuster, 1986. 845 p. $20.
Adult. B 82: Jun 1 1986. LJ 111: Jun 1 1986. A thorough and objective history of the CIA within the context of international events.

703. Sniegoski, Stephen J. Department of Education, The. (Know Your Government). Chelsea House, 1988. 93 p. ill. $13.
Gr 5+. SLJ 34: Aug 1988. A highly illustrated historic overview of the programs and problems of the Department of Education.

704. Stefany, Wallace. Department of Transportation, The. (Know Your Government). Chelsea House, 1988. 93 p. $13.
Gr 6+. BR 7: Sep/Oct 1988. Covers the history, purpose, and development of the agency.

705. Taylor, Jack. Internal Revenue Service, The. (Know Your Government). Chelsea House, 1986. 92 p. ill. $13.
Gr 5-9. B 83: Jun 15 1987. SLJ 33: Jun/Jul 1987. A well-organized presentation of the history, structure, and purpose of the IRS. Useful photos clarify the daily operation of the agency.

706. Van Fleet, Alanson A. Tennessee Valley Authority, The. (Know Your Government). Chelsea House, 1987. 92 p. ill. $13.
Gr 6-9. B 84: Sep 1 1987. +- SLJ 34: Dec 1987. An account of the controversial TVA, an experimental governmental agency intended to provide energy and improve the economy of the southeast.

707. Watts, J. F. Smithsonian, The. (Know Your Government). Chelsea House, 1987. 92 p. ill. $13.
Gr 4-7. B 83: Jun 1 1987. BR 7: Sep/Oct 1988. SLJ 34: Sep 1987. Describes the history of the Smithsonian, its current projects, and the research done there.

708. Wolman, Paul. U.S. Mint, The. (Know Your Government). Chelsea House, 1987. 92 p. ill. $13.
Gr 7-10. SLJ 34: Jan 1988. Wolman links the development of the responsibilities of the mint to historical events in a readable, well-researched, and highly illustrated volume.

Presidents and Their Families

709. First Ladies, The. White House Historical Association, 1981. 92 p. ill. $5. Pb $4.

Gr 9+. B 80: Jun 15 1984. Plentiful illustrations and approximately one page of text introduce each first lady.

710. Armour, Richard. Our Presidents. Norton, 1964. 81 p. ill. $10. Pb $6.
Gr 7+. Metzner [- LJ 89: Feb 15 1964]. Humorous biographies in verse.

711. Boller, Paul F. Presidential Wives. Oxford University Press, 1988. 471 p. $20.
Gr 9+. B 84: Apr 1 1988. LJ 113: Apr 1 1988 For each first lady, an essay on her life and accomplishments, plus anecdotes which illuminate events and personalities.

712. Bourne, Miriam Anne. White House Children. (Step-Up Books). Random House, 1979. 69 p. ill. $4.
Gr 2-3. +- SLJ 26: Feb 1980. Simple anecdotes about children who lived in the White House, through the time of Amy Carter.

713. Caroli, Betty Boyd. First Ladies. Oxford University Press, 1987. 398 p. ill. $20.
Gr 9+. B 84: Sep 1 1987. LJ 112: Sep 1 1987. Examines the 36 first ladies–how they performed that role, how it changed them and how they changed it. Also includes a ranking of first ladies by historians.

714. Cooke, D. E. Atlas of the Presidents. Hammond, 1962. 93 p. ill. $9.
Gr 5+. Metzner [LJ 90: Jan 15 1965]. Includes a portrait and two pages of biographical information on each president, plus maps that indicate important events and places for each, and voting patterns of the elections.

715. DeGregorio, William A. Complete Book of U.S. Presidents, The. Dembner Books; dist. by Norton, 1984. 691 p. ill. $23.
Gr 9+. B 81: Jan 1 1985. Personal and statistical information on the presidents informally presented and conveniently arranged.

716. Frank, Sid. Presidents: Tidbits and Trivia. Hammond, 1980. 160 p. ill. $7.
Gr 9+. SLJ 27: Dec 1980. Endless bits of fascinating trivia about the presidents–who was tallest, shortest, heaviest, who liked to skinny dip, who served hot dogs to the King of England?

717. Freidel, Frank. Our Country's Presidents. 9th ed. National Geographic Society, 1981. 288 p. ill. $7.
Gr 9+. B 80: Jun 15 1984. Essays on the first 39 presidents, Washington through Carter, in chronological order.

718. Freidel, Frank. Presidents of the United States of America, The. White House Historical Association, 1982. 88 p. ill. Pb $8.
Gr 9+. B 79: Jan 15 1983. B 80: Jun 15 1984. One page of text and a one-page illustration introduce each president.

719. Hay, Peter. All the Presidents' Ladies: Anecdotes of the Women Behind the Men in the White House. Viking, 1988. 303 p. $20.
Gr 9+. B 84: Aug 1988. Anecdotes, gossip, humor, and tales about the important women in the lives of the presidents, including wives, mothers, daughters, and mistresses.

720. Healy, Diana Dixon. America's First Ladies: Private Lives of the Presidential Wives. Atheneum, 1988. 177 p. ill. $19.
Gr 9+. B 84: May 15 1988. LJ 113: Apr 15 1988. Brief biographical sketches of each first lady, enlivened by anecdotes. Explains the influence of each first lady on the social life in the White House.

721. Kern, Ellyn R. Where the American Presidents Lived: Including a Guide to the Homes That Are Open. Cottontail Pub., 1982. 120 p. ill. $11.
Gr 9+. B 78: Aug 1982. A chronological listing of all presidential residences with descriptions, and tourist information on those homes open to the public. Includes maps, drawings, and photos.

722. McElroy, Richard L. American Presidents: Fascinating Facts, Stories, & Questions of Our Chief Executives and Their Families. Daring Press, 1984. 168 p. ill. Pb $4.
Gr 5-9. B 81: Sep 15 1984. Trivia about the presidents, including anecdotes, odd facts, nicknames, pets, and lists.

723. Montgomery-Massingberd, Hugh. Burke's Presidential Families of the United States of America. Burke's Peerage, 1981. 598 p. ill. $70.
Gr 9+. B 78: Apr 14 1982. B 80: Jun 15 1984. Biographical information on each president, with genealogies, plus brief information on the vice-presidents and on the elections.

724. Moses, John B. Presidential Courage. Norton, 1980. 214 p. $12.
Gr 9+. B 76: Apr 15 1980. LJ 105: Apr 1 1980. Examines the health problems of the presidents. Moses is a physician who has done some fascinating medical detection.

725. Nagel, Paul C. Descent from Glory. Oxford University Press, 1982. 400 p. $25.
Gr 10+. B 79: Oct 1 1982. +- BR 2: May/Jun 1983. LJ 107: Dec 1 1982. Concentrates on the private lives of four generations of the Adams family, 1735-1925. Appropriate for serious students of U.S. history.

726. Whitney, David C. American Presidents, The. Doubleday, 1978. 561 p. ill. $15.
Gr 9+. B 80: Jun 15 1984. Concise illustrated biographies of presidents through Gerald Ford, with a chronology for each. Includes lists of vice-presidents, first ladies, and cabinet officers.

Presidents and Their Families–Bibliographies

727. Martin, Fenton S. American Presidents: A Bibliography. (Congressional Quarterly). Congressional Quarterly, 1987. 756 p. $125.
Gr 10+. B 84: Dec 1 1987. BR 6: Nov/Dec 1987. LJ 112: Dec 1987. A listing of books, articles, and other works, mostly written between 1885 and 1986. Categories include: biographies, private life, presidency, other public careers, and writings.

Public Officials

728. Attorneys General of the United States, 1789-1979. Department of Justice, 1980. 147 p. ill. $6.
Gr 10+. B 77: Feb 15 1981. A brief biography and a portrait of each attorney general through 1980.

729. Attorneys General of the United States, 1789-1985. Department of Justice, 1985. 151 p. ill. Pb $6.
Gr 10+. B 81: Jul 1985. A brief biography and a portrait of each attorney general through 1985.

730. Members of Congress since 1789. (Congressional Quarterly). 2nd ed. Congressional Quarterly, 1981. 180 p. Pb $8.
Gr 9+. B 78: Apr 15 1982. B 80: Jun 15 1984. Biographical information on members of Congress since 1789, plus collective and statistical data.

731. Secretaries of State: Portraits and Biographical Sketches. (Department of State. Department and Foreign Service Series). Department of State, 1979. 125 p. Pb $4.
Gr 7+. B 76: Mar 15 1980. Includes portraits and biographical sketches of 56 secretaries of state plus two secretaries of foreign affairs under the Continental Congress. Report number 162 of the series.

732. Bell, William Gardner. Secretaries of War and Secretaries of the Army: Portraits and Biographical Sketches. Army Center of Military History, 1982. 175 p. ill. $12.
Gr 9+. B 78: Jun 15 1982. Full-page photos and short biographies of the secretaries from 1789 to 1981.

733. Cheney, Richard B. Kings of the Hill: Power and Personality in the House of Representatives. Continuum, 1983. 226 p. $15.
Gr 9+. * BR 3: May/Jun 1984. LJ 108: May 15 1983. Anecdotal portraits of eight men who rose to power in the House, including Henry Clay, James K. Polk, Thaddeus Stevens, and Samuel Rayburn.

734. Felt, W. Mark. FBI Pyramid from the Inside, The. Putnam, 1980. 351 p. ill. $13.
Gr 9+. B 76: Mar 1 1980. LJ 105: Apr 1 1980. Felt recalls his career as deputy associate director of the FBI under Hoover. He supports Hoover, explains the training and work of agents, and clarifies how political interference has weakened the agency.

735. Kennedy, John Fitzgerald. Profiles in Courage. Harper, 1964. 164 p. ill. Pb $4.
Gr 5+. Metzner. B 82: Jan 1 1986. An exploration of courageous turning points in the lives of U.S. statesmen.

736. Powers, Richard Gid. Secrecy and Power: The Life of J. Edgar Hoover. Free Press, 1987. 624 p. ill. $30.
Gr 9+. B 83: Apr 1 1987. LJ 112: Feb 1 1987. A detailed reconstruction of the 50-year career of the famous and feared head of the FBI.

737. Southwick, Leslie H. Presidential Also-Rans and Running Mates, 1788-1980. McFarland, 1984. 736 p. $50.
Gr 9+. B 81: May 1 1985. Brief biographies of losing presidential and vice-presidential candidates; information on all elections.

738. Theoharis, Athan G. Boss: J. Edgar Hoover and the Great American Inquisition. Temple University Press, 1988. 464 p. ill. $28.
Gr 10+. * LJ 113: Jun 1 1988. A highly documented biography of the head of the FBI who instituted illegal wiretaps and the collection of gossip.

Public Officials–Women

739. Whitney, Sharon. Women in Politics. Watts, 1986. 143 p. ill. $12.
Gr 8+. B 83: Mar 15 1987. BC 40: Mar 1987. BR 6: May/Jun 1987. SLJ 33: Jan 1987. * VOYA 10: Apr 1987. These sketches of pioneer women politicians include Jeanette Rankin and Frances Perkins from the 1940s, and Sandra Day O'Connor, Shirley Chisholm, Jane Byrne, and Geraldine Ferraro from the 1970s and 1980s.

Puerto Rico

740. Masters, Robert V. Puerto Rico in Pictures. (Visual Geography Series). Rev. ed. Sterling, 1980. 64 p. ill. $5. Pb $3.
Gr 5-7. SLJ 27: Feb 1981. Covers Puerto Rican history, geography, culture, and government.

Puerto Rico–Biographies

741. Tuck, Jay. Heroes of Puerto Rico. Fleet Press, 1969. 141 p. $9.
Gr 5-8. B 83: Jun 15 1987. Brief biographies of famous men of Puerto Rico from colonial days to the 1960s.

Puerto Rico–Fiction

742. Belpre, Pura. Once in Puerto Rico. Warne, 1973. 96 p. ill. $8.
Gr 2-6. B 82: Dec 1 1985. LJ 99: Apr 15 1974. Tales of early Puerto Rican history, customs and beliefs.

Quotations

743. Conlin, Joseph R. Morrow Book of Quotations in American History, The. Morrow, 1984. 336 p. $16.
Gr 9+. B 80: Aug 1984. LJ 109: Aug 1984. The political, social, and cultural evolution of U.S. history is seen in this collection of 2500 quotes and quips.

744. Edelhart, Mike. America the Quotable. Facts on File, 1983. 507 p. $30.
Gr 9+. B 81: Oct 1 1984. The nature of America is reflected in 7000 quotes on nation, people, way of life, politics, history, states, cities, and regions.

Racism

745. Drinnon, Richard. Keeper of Concentration Camps: Dillon S. Myer and American Racism. University of California Press, 1987. 384 p. ill. $25.

Gr 9+. B 83: Dec 1 1986. LJ 111: Dec 1986. As a product of a racist society Myer directed Japanese American internment and a policy of destruction of Indian culture.

746. Leone, Bruno. Racism: Opposing Viewpoints. (Isms: Modern Doctrines and Movements). Greenhaven, 1986. 233 p. ill. $12. Pb $7.
Gr 9+. B 82: Jul 1986. Includes a history of racist thought, historical debate over immigration policies, and information on the impact of racism on society today.

747. Pascoe, Elaine. Racial Prejudice. (Issues in American History). Watts, 1985. 118 p. ill. $11.
Gr 7+. * B 82: Dec 15 1985. BC 39: Feb 1986. BR 5: May/Jun 1986. SE 50: Apr/May 1986. SLJ 32: Apr 1986. * VOYA 9: Apr 1986. Details how prejudice arises, how it is perpetuated, how it affects its victims, and efforts to overcome it.

Reformers

748. Trattner, Walter I. Biographical Dictionary of Social Welfare in America. Greenwood, 1986. 897 p. $75.
Gr 9+. B 83: Sep 1 1986. Covers persons involved in the promotion of public welfare programs, social insurance, public and mental health, and child welfare throughout our history.

749. Whitman, Alden. American Reformers: A Biographical Dictionary. Wilson, 1985. 930 p. ill. $75.
Gr 9+. B 82: Jun 15 1986. Brief biographies with photos, covering U.S. reformers since the 17th century. A subject index provides access by area of interest.

Rhode Island

750. Fradin, Dennis B. Rhode Island: In Words and Pictures. (Young People's Stories of Our States Series). Childrens Press, 1981. 48 p. ill. $7.
Gr 2-5. +- SLJ 28: Oct 1981. Rhode Island political and economic history, geography, people, and trivia are introduced.

Ships and Shipping

751. Hartman, Tom. Guinness Book of Ships and Shipping Facts and Feats, The. Sterling, 1984. 265 p. ill. $20.
Gr 6+. B 80: Feb 1 1984. +- BR 3: Sep/Oct 1984. A book on ships and shipping for trivia fans.

Slaves and Slavery

752. Evitts, William J. Captive Bodies, Free Spirits: The Story of Southern Slavery. Messner, 1985. 144 p. ill. $10.
Gr 5-9. B 82: Feb 1 1986. BC 39: Mar 1986. SLJ 32: Mar 1986. +- VOYA 9: Jun 1986. A history of U.S. slavery, 1619-1865, made vivid by anecdotes and personal stories.

753. Meltzer, Milton. All Times, All Peoples: A World History of Slavery. Harper, 1980. 65 p. ill. $9.

Gr 6+. B 77: Sep 15 1980. HB 56: Oct 1980. * SLJ 27: Oct 1980. Examines U.S. and world slavery, its impact on the individual and on society.

754. Walvin, James. Slavery and the Slave Trade: A Short Illustrated History. University Press of Mississippi, 1983. 168 p. ill. $15. Pb $9.
Gr 9+. B 80: Nov 1 1983. An overview of slavery in world history, with emphasis on black slavery in the New World. Includes the operation of the slave trade, the work of slaves, their social activities, and their resistance to slavery.

Social Life and Customs

755. Life: The First Fifty Years, 1936-1986. Little, Brown, 1986. 317 p. ill. $50.
Gr 9+. B 83: Nov 15 1986. A capsule of America's fads, entertainment, fashions, science, and politics is seen in these b/w and colored photos from the pages of Life magazine. Arranged chronologically, with new captions and brief text.

756. Burns, Amy Stechler. Shakers: Hands to Work, Hearts to God: The History and Visions of the United Society of Believers in Christ's Second Appearing from 1774 to the Present. Aperture; dist. by Farrar, 1987. 127 p. ill. $40.
Gr 9+. B 84: Feb 15 1988. +- LJ 113: Apr 1 1988. A photo essay on the history of beliefs of the Shaker people.

757. Cohen, Hennig. Folklore of American Holidays. Gale, 1987. 431 p. $78.
Gr 7+. B 83: May 15 1987. * BR 6: Sep/Oct 1987. LJ 112: Apr 1 1987. SLJ 34: May 1988. This comprehensive volume covers familiar and obscure celebrations, their origins, development, and customs. Well indexed.

758. Dolan, Jay P. American Catholic Experience: History from Colonial Times to the Present. Doubleday, 1985. 492 p. $20.
Gr 9+. B 82: Dec 1 1985. LJ 110: Oct 15 1985. Covers the founding of missions, the role of Catholics in the founding of the nation, the influx of Catholic immigrants, the social position of Catholics, and the relationship of American Catholics to the Vatican.

759. Faber, Doris. Perfect Life: The Shakers in America. Farrar, 1974. 224 p. $11.
Gr 9+. SE 44: Oct 1980. Explains the attempts of the Shakers to live the perfect life, their successes and failures.

760. Fisher, Leonard Everett. Sports, The. (Nineteenth Century America). Holiday, 1980. 62 p. ill. $8.
Gr 5-8. B 77: Jan 15 1981. BC 34: Feb 1981. SLJ 27: Dec 1980. Covers several dozen 19th-century sports, how they were organized and played, and information on prominent players.

761. Foster, Sally. Where Time Stands Still. Dodd, 1987. 64 p. ill. $14.
Gr K-3. B 84: Jan 15 1988. +- BC 41: Jan 1988. * SE 52: Apr/May 1988. +- SLJ 34: Feb 1988. Photos and text follow the daily activities of Amish children and

clarify the Amish self-sufficient agricultural economy as well as their styles of clothing, educational values, and leisure activities.

762. Gilbo, Patrick. American Red Cross, The. (Know Your Government). Chelsea House, 1987. 92 p. ill. $13.
Gr 6+. B 83: Aug 1987. BR 7: Sep/Oct 1988. SLJ 34: Sep 1987. Explains the origin of the Red Cross, how it acquired semi-governmental status, and the involvement of the agency in disaster relief, blood collection, education, and other activities.

763. Gordon, Lois. American Chronicle: Six Decades in American Life, 1920-1980. Atheneum, 1987. 565 p. ill. $40. Pb $17.
Gr 9+. B 84: Feb 15 1988. A readable and highly illustrated social history, covering fashions, arts, science, and popular culture for each decade.

764. Huntington, Lee Pennock. Americans at Home: Four Hundred Years of American Houses. Coward, 1981. 80 p. ill. $10.
Gr 6+. B 78: Dec 15 1981. SLJ 28: Feb 1982. A chronological photographic survey of the homes of both ordinary and wealthy Americans.

765. Inge, M. Thomas. Concise Histories of American Popular Culture. Greenwood, 1982. 504 p. Pb $10.
Gr 10+. HT 17: Feb 1984. A mini-encyclopedia on all topics in American popular culture including advertising, dance, exercise, fashion, and the occult.

766. Issel, William. Social Change in the United States, 1945-1983. Schocken, 1985. 228 p. $24.
Adult. LJ 110: May 15 1985. Concise and enlightening examples that explain social changes, including the growing importance of the Sun Belt, and changes in the role of business. A helpful analysis of the implications of national trends.

767. Lipman, Jean. Young America: A Folk-Art History. Hudson Hills, 1986. 199 p. ill. $45.
Gr 9+. B 83: Dec 1 1986. LJ 111: Dec 1986. Folk art organized to show how ordinary people lived, 1783-1914.

768. Marling, Karal Ann. Colossus of Roads: Myth and Symbol Along the American Highway. University of Minnesota Press, 1984. 148 p. ill. $28. Pb $13.
Gr 10+. LJ 109: Sep 15 1984. Marling finds significance in oversized recreations of real and mythical figures as varied as Mt. Rushmore and the Jolly Green Giant.

769. Marty, Martin E. Christianity in the New World from 1500 to 1800. Winston, 1984. 127 p. ill. $13.
Gr 4-8. +- SLJ 30: Nov 1984. * VOYA 7: Feb 1985. This readable and highly illustrated introduction to the influence of religion in the New World does not gloss over the issues of slavery and intolerance.

770. Marum, Andrew. Follies and Foibles: A View of 20th Century Fads. Facts on File, 1984. 256 p. ill. $23. Pb $15.
Adult. +- B 81: Sep 1 1984. +- B 81: Nov 15 1984. A look at the wacky fads of the 20th century, arranged by decades.

771. Mendleson, Jack H. Alcohol Use and Abuse in America. Little, Brown, 1985. 416 p. ill. $25.
Gr 9+. B 81: Jul 1985. LJ 110: Jul 1985. This history of alcohol use in the U.S. puts current trends in perspective and concludes with current research on alcohol abuse.

772. Mintz, Steven. Domestic Revolutions: A Social History of American Family Life. Free Press, 1988. 316 p. ill. $23.
Gr 9+. SLJ 35: Sep 1988. Traces historic changes in the American family and clarifies the economic and social causes of those changes. Includes many ethnic groups.

773. Morgan, Hal. Symbols of America. Viking, 1986. 240 p. ill. $30.
Gr 9+. B 82: Jan 1 1986. LJ 111: Feb 1 1986. A collection of trademarks and other symbols used by American corporations, sports, and famous persons. Histories of the most noteworthy symbols are included.

774. Morse, Flo. Shakers and the World's People, The. Dodd, 1980. 378 p. ill. $18.
Gr 9+. B 77: Oct 1 1980. LJ 105: Oct 1 1980. SLJ 27: Apr 1981. A complete and coherent view of the Shakers as seen by themselves and others throughout their history.

775. Nash, Gary B. Private Side of American History: Readings in Everyday Life. Harcourt Brace Jovanovich, 1983. 2 vol. $13 ea.
Gr 10+. SE 46: May 1982. Two volumes of essays on everyday life, for able students. Volume 1 to 1877, volume 2 since 1865.

776. Noverr, Douglas A. Games They Played: Sports in American History, 1865-1980. Nelson-Hall, 1983. 423 p. $35.
Gr 9+. +- HT 19: Nov 1985. Covers baseball, basketball, football, track and field, boxing, golf, and tennis.

777. Peterson, Robert W. Boy Scouts, The. American Heritage; dist. by Houghton, 1985. 256 p. ill. $25.
Gr 9+. B 81: May 1 1985. LJ 110: Apr 15 1985. A collection of over 300 photos enhance this celebration of the 75th anniversary of the Boy Scouts. Included are paintings by Norman Rockwell.

778. Rollins, Peter C. Hollywood as Historian: American Film in a Cultural Context. University Press of Kentucky, 1983. 276 p. $16. Pb $10.
Adult. HT: 17 Feb 1984. Shows how motion pictures have influenced our society since their earliest days.

779. Seuling, Barbara. It Is Illegal to Quack Like a Duck and Other Freaky Laws. Dutton/Lodestar, 1988. 55 p. ill. $12. Pb $6.
Gr 3-6. B 85: Oct 15 1988. An amusing collection of strange laws, past and present, that shows the wide divergence of acceptable behavior.

780. Terkel, Studs. American Dreams: Lost and Found. Pantheon, 1980. 475 p. $15.
Gr 10+. B 76: Jul 15 1980. HB 57: Feb 1981. LJ 105: Nov 1 1980. SE 45: May 1981. A master interviewer

examines the aspirations, failures, disillusionments, and dreams of Americans of all types.

Social Life and Customs–Bibliographies

781. Ireland, Norma Olin. Index to America: Life and Customs, 19th Century, Vol. 3. Scarecrow, 1984. 350 p. $25.
Gr 9+. B 81: Apr 15 1985. An index to recent books about life and customs of the 19th century.

782. Landrum, Larry N. American Popular Culture: A Guide to Information Sources. Gale, 1982. 435 p. $40.
Gr 9+. B 80: Oct 15 1983. An annotated bibliography of materials on U.S. culture, selected for their appeal to students.

783. Mitterling, Philip. United States Cultural History: A Guide to Information Sources. (American Government and History Information Guide Series). Gale, 1980. 581 p. $28.
Gr 9+. B 77: Mar 1 1981. SE 45: Feb 1981. This guide to cultural and intellectual interaction in U.S. history is arranged in 11 topical chapters with chronological subdivisions and includes annotations and indexes. Volume number five in the series.

Social Life and Customs–Children

784. Cable, Mary. Little Darlings: A History of Child Rearing in America. Scribner, 1975. 214 p. ill. $9.
Adult. SE 50: Apr/May 1986. A history of American attitudes toward children.

785. Kett, Joseph F. Rites of Passage: Adolescence in America, 1790 to the Present. Basic Books, 1977. 327 p. ill. $17. Pb $10.
Adult. +- SE 50: Apr/May 1986. Kett maintains that adolescence was not recognized as a separate developmental stage until the late 19th century.

786. McCullough, David Willis. American Childhoods: An Anthology. Little, Brown, 1987. 416 p. ill. $23.
Gr 9+. B 83: Jun 15 1987. This anthology of excerpts from autobiographies relates childhood experiences. The writers include the famous and obscure and many ethnic groups from colonial and modern times.

787. Zelizer, Viviana A. Pricing the Priceless Child: The Changing Social Value of Children. Basic Books, 1985. 288 p. $19.
Adult. LJ 110: May 1 1985. Explores changes in United States culture that defined a child's value in the United States from 1870 to 1930.

Social Life and Customs–Fiction

788. Haynes, Mary. Pot Belly Tales. Lothrop, 1982. 74 p. ill. $9.
Gr 3-5. B 78: May 15 1982. BC 35: May 1982. SLJ 29: Sep 1982. Eleven vignettes show our changing culture through the story of a stove (cast in 1888) and its subsequent owners.

Social Life and Customs–Women

789. Banner, Lois W. American Beauty. Knopf, 1983. 352 p. ill. $25.
Adult. B 79: Jan 15 1983. LJ 108: Jan 1 1983. Relates the concept of American feminine beauty to social and cultural events throughout our history.

Social Policy

790. Katz, Michael B. In the Shadow of the Poorhouse: A Social History of Welfare in America. Basic Books, 1986. 321 p. $23.
Gr 9+. B 83: Sep 15 1986. LJ 111: Aug 1986. Explores the ways in which U.S. governments at all levels have dealt with poverty since the late 18th century.

791. Leinwand, Gerald. Hunger and Malnutrition in America. (Impact Book). Watts, 1985. 90 p. ill. $11.
Gr 7+. B 82: Dec 1 1985. BR 4: Mar 1986. SLJ 32: Dec 1985. +- VOYA 9: Apr 1986. Briefly discusses hunger and malnutrition in the U.S. in the 1930s and '60s. Examines current American problems of malnutrition among all classes and hunger among the poor, and the effects of government policy.

South Carolina

792. Carpenter, Allan. South Carolina. (New Enchantment of America Series). Rev. ed. Childrens Press, 1979. 96 p. ill. $7.
Gr 5-7. SLJ 26: Mar 1980. Introduces the history, geography, culture, economy, resources, attractions and people of South Carolina. Updated, with full-color photos and large type.

793. Fradin, Dennis B. South Carolina: In Words and Pictures. (Young People's Stories of Our States Series). Childrens Press, 1980. 48 p. ill. $7.
Gr 2-5. +- B 76: May 15 1980. +- SLJ 26: Aug 1980. Covers South Carolina political and economic history, geography, people, and trivia.

South Dakota

794. Fradin, Dennis B. South Dakota: In Words and Pictures. (Young People's Stories of Our States Series). Childrens Press, 1981. 48 p. ill. $7.
Gr 2-5. +- SLJ 28: Oct 1981. South Dakota's political and economic history, geography, and people are introduced.

States

795. Worldmark Encyclopedia of the States: A Practical Guide to the Geographic, Demographic, Historical, Political, Economic, and Social Development of the United States. 2nd ed. Worldmark Press; dist. by Wiley, 1986. 690 p. ill. $100.
Gr 7+. +- B 83: Sep 1 1986. For each state information on 50 headings, including history, geography, statistics, government, economy, culture, agriculture, taxation, tourism, and transportation.

796. Aylesworth, Thomas G. Atlantic: District of Columbia, Virginia, West Virginia. (Let's Discover the States). Chelsea House, 1988. 64 p. ill. $15.
Gr 3-6. B 84: Aug 1988. This well-organized series discusses area history, geography, culture, and noted persons. Also provided are factual information, a map, recent photos, and useful addresses.

797. Aylesworth, Thomas G. Eastern Great Lakes: Indiana, Michigan, Ohio. (Let's Discover the States). Chelsea House, 1988. 64 p. ill. $15.
Gr 3-6. B 84: Aug 1988. This well-organized series discusses area history, geography, culture, and noted persons. Also provided are factual information, a map, recent photos, and useful addresses.

798. Aylesworth, Thomas G. Great Plains: Montana, Nebraska, North Dakota, South Dakota, Wyoming. (Let's Discover the States). Chelsea House, 1988. 48 p. ill. $13.
Gr 3-8. B 84: Mar 15 1988. Each state has a section on history, geography, people and symbols. Includes photos and maps.

799. Aylesworth, Thomas G. Lower Atlantic: North Carolina, South Carolina. (Let's Discover the States). Chelsea House, 1987. 64 p. ill. $13.
Gr 3-8. B 84: Nov 1 1987. SLJ 34: Jun/Jul 1988. Surveys the history, geography, and culture of the area. Highlights distinguished persons and places of interest. Includes a map and photos.

800. Aylesworth, Thomas G. Mid-Atlantic: Delaware, Maryland, Pennsylvania. (Let's Discover the States). Chelsea House, 1988. 64 p. ill. $13.
Gr 3-8. B 84: Mar 15 1988. Each state has a section on history, geography, people, and symbols. Includes photos and maps.

801. Aylesworth, Thomas G. Northern New England: Maine, New Hampshire, Vermont. (Let's Discover the States). Chelsea House, 1988. 64 p. ill. $15.
Gr 3-6. B 84: Aug 1988. This well-organized series discusses area history, geography, culture, and noted persons. Also provided are factual information, a map, recent photos, and useful addresses.

802. Aylesworth, Thomas G. Northwest: Alaska, Idaho, Oregon, Washington. (Let's Discover the States). Chelsea House, 1988. 64 p. ill. $13.
Gr 3-8. B 84: Mar 15 1988. Each state has a section on history, geography, people and symbols. Includes photos and maps.

803. Aylesworth, Thomas G. Pacific: California, Hawaii. (Let's Discover the States). Chelsea House, 1987. 64 p. ill. $13.
Gr 3-8. B 84: Nov 1 1987. SLJ 34: Jun/Jul 1988. Surveys the history, geography, and culture of the area. Highlights distinguished persons and places of interest. Includes a map and photos.

804. Aylesworth, Thomas G. South Central: Arkansas, Kansas, Louisiana, Missouri, Oklahoma. (Let's Discover the States). Chelsea House, 1988. 64 p. ill. $15.
Gr 3-6. B 84: Aug 1988. This well-organized series discusses area history, geography, culture, and noted per-

sons. Also provided are factual information, a map, recent photos, and useful addresses.

805. Aylesworth, Thomas G. South: Alabama, Florida, Mississippi. (Let's Discover the States). Chelsea House, 1987. 64 p. ill. $13.
Gr 3-8. B 84: Nov 1 1987. SLJ 34: Nov 1987. Surveys the history, land, and culture of the area. Highlights distinguished persons and places of interest. Includes a map and photos.

806. Aylesworth, Thomas G. Southeast: Georgia, Kentucky, Tennessee. (Let's Discover the States). Chelsea House, 1987. 64 p. ill. $13.
Gr 3-8. B 84: Nov 1 1987. SLJ 34: Nov 1987. Surveys the history, land, and culture of the area. Highlights distinguished persons and places of interest. Includes a map and photos.

807. Aylesworth, Thomas G. Southern New England: Connecticut, Massachusetts, Rhode Island. (Let's Discover the States). Chelsea House, 1988. 64 p. ill. $13.
Gr 3-8. B 84: Mar 15 1988. Each state has a section on history, geography, people and symbols. Includes photos and maps.

808. Aylesworth, Thomas G. Southwest: Colorado, New Mexico, Texas. (Let's Discover the States). Chelsea House, 1988. 64 p. ill. $15.
Gr 3-8. B 84: Aug 1988. SLJ 35: Nov 1988. This well-organized series discusses area history, geography, culture, and noted persons. Also provided are factual information, a map, recent photos, and useful addresses.

809. Aylesworth, Thomas G. Upper Atlantic: New Jersey, New York. (Let's Discover the States). Chelsea House, 1987. 64 p. ill. $13.
Gr 3-8. B 84: Sep 1 1987. +- SLJ 34: Nov 1987. Chapters on each state cover history, geography, climate, people, and symbols. Includes photos and maps.

810. Aylesworth, Thomas G. West: Arizona, Nevada, and Utah. (Let's Discover the States). Chelsea House, 1988. 64 p. ill. $15.
Gr 3-8. B 84: Aug 1988. SLJ 35: Nov 1988. This well-organized series discusses area history, geography, culture, and noted persons. Also provided are factual information, a map, recent photos, and useful addresses.

811. Aylesworth, Thomas G. Western Great Lakes: Illinois, Iowa, Minnesota, Wisconsin. (Let's Discover the States). Chelsea House, 1987. 64 p. ill. $13.
Gr 3-8. B 84: Sep 1 1987. SLJ 34: Nov 1987. Surveys the history, land, and culture of the area. Highlights distinguished persons and places of interest. Includes a map and photos.

812. Berger, Gilda. Southeast States, The. (First Book). Watts, 1984. 88 p. ill. $9.
Gr 5-8. B 80: May 15 1984. SLJ 30: May 1984. Presents an introduction to the region and brief chapters on each state. Includes brief histories, geography, statistics, photos, and maps.

813. Bogue, Margaret Beattie. Around the Shores of Lake Michigan: A Guide to Historic Sites. University of Wisconsin Press, 1985. 382 p. ill. $35. Pb $20.

Adult. LJ 110: Aug 1985. The political, cultural, and commercial history of the Wisconsin/Illinois/ Michigan region.

814. Gilfond, Henry. Northeast States, The. (First Book). Watts, 1984. 88 p. ill. $9.
Gr 5-8. B 80: Apr 14 1984. +- SLJ 30: May 1984. Includes an introduction to the region and brief chapters on each state. Includes history, geography, economics, statistics, photos, and maps.

815. Jacobson, Daniel. North Central States, The. (First Book). Watts, 1984. 90 p. ill. $9.
Gr 4-8. +- B 80: Apr 14 1984. SLJ 30: Aug 1984. Explains how the westward movement led to growth in the region. Current problems are presented as well as information on individual states.

816. Krakel, Dean. Downriver: A Yellowstone Journey. Sierra Club; dist. by Random, 1987. 272 p. $17.
Gr 9+. LJ 112: Apr 1 1987. A composite anecdotal account of those persons and events, from Lewis and Clark through modern dams and oil drilling, that have had an impact on the Yellowstone River in Wyoming, Montana, and North Dakota.

817. Lavender, David Sievert. Southwest, The. (Regions of America). Harper, 1980. 384 p. maps. $15.
Gr 9+. B 76: Apr 1 1980. LJ 104: Dec 15 1979. This history of the Southwest, New Mexico, Arizona, and the surrounding states emphasizes the conflicts among the Indians, Hispanics, and Anglos and other events which have shaped today's culture.

818. Lawson, Don. Pacific States, The. (First Book). Watts, 1984. 92 p. ill. $9.
Gr 4-8. B 80: Apr 15 1984. SLJ 30: Aug 1984. The separate chapters on each state cover history, geography, growth, and current problems.

819. Peirce, Neal R. Book of America: Inside 50 States Today. Norton, 1983. 896 p. maps. $25.
Gr 10+. B 79: Jun 1 1983. LJ 108: Jun 1 1983. Examines the history, politics, economics, culture, and environment of each state, region, and major city, and describes the characteristics that make each unique.

820. Peirce, Neal R. Great Lakes States of America: People, Politics, and Power. Norton, 1980. 383 p. maps. $17.
Gr 9+. SLJ 27: Mar 1981. Detailed coverage of the political and economic histories of Illinois, Indiana, Ohio, Michigan, and Wisconsin.

821. Sachs, Moshe Y. Worldmark Encyclopedia of the States. Worldmark Press; dist. by Harper, 1981. 690 p. maps. $70.
Gr 7+. +- B 78: Dec 1 1981. LJ 106: Jun 15 1981. LJ 107: May 15 1982. SE 45: May 1981. SLJ 28: May 1982. Information on 50 topics, including agriculture, history, taxation, tourism, and transportation for all states, the District of Columbia, Puerto Rico and U.S. dependencies.

822. Shearer, Benjamin F. State Names, Seals, Flags, and Symbols: A Historical Guide. Greenwood, 1987. 239 p. ill. $40.

Gr 9+. B 84: Dec 1 1987. LJ 112: Oct 1 1987. Covers state names, nicknames, mottoes, seals, flags, capitols, flowers, trees, birds, songs, etc., with descriptions and explanations. Arranged by category.

823. Taylor, L. B. Rocky Mountain States, The. (First Book). Watts, 1984. 64 p. ill. $9.
Gr 4-6. B 80: Apr 15 1984. SLJ 30: Aug 1984. Regional information plus the history, geography, growth, and problems of each state.

824. Thompson, Ian. Four Corners Country. University of Arizona Press, 1986. 112 p. ill. $28.
Gr 10+. LJ 111: Nov 15 1986. A geological and social history of the area bounded by Utah, Colorado, New Mexico, and Arizona.

825. Vexler, Robert L. Chronology and Documentary Handbooks of the States. Oceana, 1978. 50 vol. $8 ea.
Gr 9+. B 76: May 15 1980. This series of 50 volumes, one for each state, provides ready-reference information, including lists of important persons. Volumes may be purchased separately.

826. Woods, Harold. South Central States, The. (First Book). Watts, 1984. 66 p. ill. $9.
Gr 4-6. B 80: Apr 15 1984. SLJ 30: Aug 1984. The historical growth, influences of geography, and current problems of each state are introduced.

Technology and Civilization

827. Fisher, Leonard Everett. Factories, The. Holiday, 1979. 62 p. ill. $7.
Gr 4-8. BC 33: Jan 1980. HB 55: Dec 1979. * SE 44: Apr 1980. SLJ 26: Nov 1979. Anecdotes about the first textile mill, the growth of factories, the lives of their workers, and the 1876 Exposition that highlighted the new era of consumer goods.

828. Hawke, David Freeman. Nuts and Bolts of the Past: A History of American Technology, 1776-1860. Harper, 1988. 288 p. $18.
Gr 9+. B 84: Aug 1988. Celebrates the inventors, technologists, and workers whose innovations launched the American industrial revolution.

829. Hindle, Brooke. Engines of Change: The American Industrial Revolution, 1790-1880. Smithsonian Institution Press, 1986. 309 p. $30.
Gr 11+. +- BR 6: May/Jun 1987. Illuminates major developments in technology, business, economics, and labor, and includes details about American life as it has been affected by technology.

830. Kiernan, Thomas. Road to Colossus: Invention, Technology, and the Machining of America. Morrow, 1985. 373 p. $17.
Gr 9+. B 81: Jan 1 1985. In a controversial treatment the author compares contemporary lives with those 200 years ago and concludes that higher technology is the way to better lives.

831. Pizer, Vernon. Shortchanged by History: America's Neglected Innovators. Putnam, 1979. 158 p. ill. $9.

Gr 7-8. BC 33: Dec 1979. * SE 44: Apr 1980. SLJ 26: Sep 1979. Explores the contributions of forgotten innovators, black and white, male and female, who improved our way of doing things.

Tennessee

832. Fradin, Dennis B. Tennessee: In Words and Pictures. (Young People's Stories of Our States Series). Childrens Press, 1980. 48 p. ill. $7.
Gr 2-5. +- B 76: May 15 1980. +- SLJ 26: Aug 1980. Introduces the political and economic history, geography, people, and trivia of Tennessee.

Territories

833. Aylesworth, Thomas G. Territories and Possessions: Puerto Rico; U.S. Virgin Islands; Guam; American Samoa; Wake; Midway and the Other Islands; and Micronesia. (Let's Discover the States). Chelsea House, 1988. 64 p. ill. $15.
Gr 3-8. B 84: Aug 1988. SLJ 35: Nov 1988. This well-organized series discusses area history, geography, culture, and noted persons. Also provided are factual information, a map, recent photos, and useful addresses.

Texas

834. Dingus, Anne. Book of Texas Lists, The. Texas Monthly Press, 1981. 300 p. $15.
Gr 9+. LJ 106: Oct 1 1981. All kinds of lists about Texas and Texans for trivia buffs.

835. Fradin, Dennis B. Texas: In Words and Pictures. (Young People's Stories of Our States Series). Childrens Press, 1980. 48 p. ill. $13. Pb $4.
Gr 2-4. +- SLJ 28: Oct 1981. Covers Texas political and economic history, geography, people, and trivia.

836. Hagler, Skeeter. Where Texas Meets the Sea: A Coastal Portrait. Pressworks, 1985. 95 p. ill. Pb $25.
Adult. LJ 110: Aug 1985. Geography, history, and contemporary coastal life are highlighted in this colorful, highly illustrated volume that presents the huge cities and sleepy fishing villages of the region.

837. Haley, James L. Texas: An Album of History. Doubleday, 1985. 292 p. ill. $25.
Gr 9+. B 82: Oct 1 1985. LJ 110: Sep 1 1985. Examines key events and people in Texas history.

838. McDonald, Archie P. Texas Experience, The. Texas A & M University Press, 1986. 119 p. ill. $20.
Gr 9+. B 83: Sep 1 1986. Essays on Texas historical and cultural development.

839. Peacock, Howard. Big Thicket of Texas, The. Little, Brown, 1984. 89 p. ill. $14.
Gr 6+. BC 38: Nov 1984. BR 4: May/Jun 1985. An introduction to the formation of the land, the wildlife, the original Indian tribes, and pioneer life in the Big Thicket region of southeast Texas.

840. Phillips, Betty Lou. Texas. (First Book). Watts, 1987. 95 p. ill. $10.

Gr 5-9. B 84: Nov 15 1987. BR 6: Jan 1988. SLJ 34: Dec 1987. Covers the history, geography, resources, government, economy, cities, and noted persons of Texas. Includes maps and photos.

841. Sitton, Thad. Loblolly Book, The. Texas Monthly Press, 1983. 250 p. Pb $11.
Gr 9+. * HT 20: Nov 1986. LJ 108: Nov 15 1983. First-hand stories of life in East and Central Texas.

Texas–Fiction

842. Michener, James A. Texas. Random House, 1985. 1096 p. $22.
Adult. B 82: Sep 15 1985. * LJ 110: Oct 15 1985. An extensive and dramatic history of Texas and its people.

Thanksgiving

843. Penner, Lucille Recht. Thanksgiving Book, The. Hastings, 1986. 160 p. ill. $15. Lib. ed. $15.
Gr 3-6. B 83: Jan 15 1987. HB 63: Jan/Feb 1987. Surveys customs of thanksgiving festivals all around the U.S. and the world throughout history. Includes numerous photos and illustrations.

Thanksgiving–Fiction

844. Bunting, Eve. How Many Days to America? A Thanksgiving Story. Clarion, 1988. Unp. ill. $15.
Gr 1-4. SLJ 35: Oct 1988. A simple and moving story about a refugee family that overcomes many obstacles and arrives in the land of freedom on Thanksgiving Day.

Transportation

845. Allen, G. Freeman. Railways: Past, Present & Future. Morrow, 1983. 303 p. ill. $40.
Gr 9+. B 79: Jan 1 1983. LJ 108: Jan 15 1983. Attractive photos enhance this overview of the evolution of the railroad.

846. Brown, Dee Alexander. Lonesome Whistle: The Story of the First Transcontinental Railroad. Holt, 1980. 144 p. ill. $9.
Gr 4-8. B 76: May 15 1980. SLJ 26: Mar 1980. * SE 45: Apr 1981. Depicts the development of the railroad and its influence on the settlement of the West. Adapted for young readers from the author's Hear That Lonesome Whistle Blow.

847. Cudahy, Brian J. Under the Sidewalks of New York: The Story of the Greatest Subway System in the World. Stephen Greene; dist. by Viking, 1988. 128 p. ill. $20.
Gr 9+. B 85: Oct 15 1988. This enthusiastic history of the New York subway system includes many photos and diagrams.

848. Fisher, Leonard Everett. Railroads, The. (Nineteenth Century America). Holiday, 1979. 62 p. ill. $7.
Gr 5-7. +- BC 33: Jan 1980. HB 55: Dec 1979. +- SLJ 26: Nov 1979. Covers the building of the railroads, the engineering of the trains, the attacks of desperadoes, and the making of fortunes.

849. Gibbons, Gail. From Path to Highway: The Story of the Boston Post Road. Crowell, 1986. 31 p. ill. $12. Lib. ed. $12.
Gr 1-7. B 82: Jun 15 1986. BC 39: Jun 1986. HB 62: Sep/Oct 1986. This informative, and occasionally humorous, examination of the development of New England paths into major highways would apply to similar systems throughout the nation.

850. Gunston, Bill. Railroads. (Topics). Watts/Bookwright Press, 1988. 32 p. ill. $11.
Gr 2-5. B 84: Apr 15 1988. Traces the development of the railway system and how it works today.

851. Hilton, Suzanne. Getting There: Frontier Travel without Power. Westminster, 1980. 192 p. ill. $10.
Gr 4-8. B 77: Sep 1 1980. SLJ 26: Apr 1980. Examines all types of 19th-century land and water travel, including travel across the ocean, by horseback, stagecoach, canal, river flatboat, and covered wagon.

852. Hubbard, Freeman H. Encyclopedia of North American Railroading: 150 Years of Railroading in the United States and Canada. McGraw-Hill, 1981. 377 p. ill. $40.
Gr 9+. * B 78: Oct 15 1981. B 79: Sep 1 1982. LJ 106: Oct 15 1981. Covers the major companies, biographies, wrecks, robberies, terminology, and related material. Subject index.

853. Leuthner, Stuart. Railroaders, The. Random House, 1983. 152 p. $20.
Gr 7+. BR 2: Mar/Apr 1984. LJ 108: Oct 1 1983. * VOYA 6: Feb 1984. This oral history presents an authentic picture of the experiences of 33 men and women who worked on the railroad from 1910 to 1970.

854. Miller, Marilyn. Transcontinental Railroad, The. (Turning Points in American History). Silver Burdett, 1987. 64 p. ill. $15.
Gr 4-8. B 83: Jul 1987. SLJ 34: Sep 1987. Presents the successes and tragedies of this massive effort to connect East to West by rail. Enriched by numerous maps and illustrations.

855. Pettifer, Julian. Automania: Man and the Motor Car. Little, Brown, 1985. 288 p. ill. $20.
Gr 9+. B 81: Apr 15 1985. LJ 110: May 1 1985. A history of the social change caused by the automobile.

856. Pizer, Vernon. Irrepressible Automobile: A Freewheeling Jaunt Through the Fascinating World of the Motorcar. Dodd, 1986. 128 p. $11.
Gr 5-8. B 82: Mar 15 1986. BR 5: Sep/Oct 1986. SLJ 32: Aug 1986. * VOYA 9: Aug/Oct 1986. A look at America's love affair with the automobile, and how it has influenced our economy, history, and culture.

857. Scarry, Huck. Aboard a Steam Locomotive: A Sketchbook. Prentice-Hall, 1987. 64 p. ill. $13.
Gr 3+. B 83: Jul 1987. SLJ 33: Aug 1987. A history of railroading along with a detailed and well-illustrated explanation of how steam engines work, the duties of the crew, and related topics. Suitable for all ages.

858. Spier, Peter. Tin Lizzie. Doubleday, 1975. 48 p. ill. $11. Pb $3.

Gr 3-5. B 85: Mar 1 1987. Through the life story of a Model T, vintage 1909, we see how U.S. society has changed because of developing transportation and technology.

859. Stilgoe, John R. Metropolitan Corridor: Railroads and the American Scene, 1880 to 1935. Yale University Press, 1983. 416 p. ill. $30.
Adult. LJ 108: Sep 1 1983. Examines the role of railroads in creating urban industrial districts and commuter suburbs, and other influences of railroad environment.

Utah

860. Carpenter, Allan. Utah. (New Enchantment of America Series). Rev. ed. Childrens Press, 1979. 96 p. ill. $7.
Gr 5-7. SLJ 26: Mar 1980. Utah history, geography, culture, economy, resources, attractions, and people are introduced. Updated, with full-color photos and large type.

861. Fradin, Dennis B. Utah: In Words and Pictures. (Young People's Stories of Our States Series). Childrens Press, 1980. 48 p. ill. $7.
Gr 2-5. +- SLJ 27: Mar 1981. Covers Utah political and economic history, geography, people, and trivia.

Vermont

862. Carpenter, Allan. Vermont. (New Enchantment of America Series). Rev. ed. Childrens Press, 1979. 96 p. ill. $7.
Gr 5-7. SLJ 26: Mar 1980. Covers Vermont history, geography, culture, economy, resources, attractions, and people. Updated, with full-color photos and large type.

863. Fradin, Dennis B. Vermont: In Words and Pictures. (Young People's Stories of Our States Series). Childrens Press, 1980. 48 p. ill. $7.
Gr 2-5. +- B 76: May 15 1980. +- SLJ 26: Aug 1980. Introduces the political and economic history, geography, people, and trivia of Vermont.

864. Strickland, Ron. Vermonters: Oral Histories from Down Country to the Northeast Kingdom. Chronicle, 1986. 186 p. ill. $13.
Gr 10+. LJ 112: Jan 1987. Reveals the independent character of Vermonters and the changes they have seen.

Violence

865. Goode, Stephen. Violence in America. Messner, 1984. 288 p. $17. Pb $10.
Gr 7+. B 80: Feb 15 1984. BC 37: Jun 1984. SE 49: Jan 1985. * SE 49: Apr 1985. SLJ 30: May 1984. VOYA 7: Feb 1985. A history of racially and criminally motivated violence in the United States.

866. Harris, Jonathan. New Terrorism: Politics of Violence. Messner, 1983. 197 p. ill. $10. Pb $5.
Gr 7+. B 79: Mar 15 1983. BC 37: Sep 1983. BR 2: Nov/Dec 1983. SLJ 29: Apr 1983. VOYA 6: Oct 1983. Examines the historical roots of terrorism, the motivation of terrorists, and contemporary terrorist groups and their activities.

867. Meltzer, Milton. Terrorists, The. Harper, 1983. 216 p. $11. Lib. ed. $11.
Gr 7+. B 80: Oct 15 1983. BC 37: Oct 1983. BR 3: May/Jun 1984. HB 60: Feb 1984. SLJ 30: Dec 1983. VOYA 6: Dec 1983. This history of international terrorism covers the activities of many current terrorist groups, their ideologies and training.

868. Raynor, Thomas. Terrorism: Past, Present, Future. Rev. ed. Watts, 1987. 176 p. $12.
Gr 7+. B 83: Apr 15 1987. BR 6: May/Jun 1987. SLJ 33: May 1987. Traces the history of international terrorism, with emphasis on terrorist activities since the 1960s and the influence of media coverage.

Washington

869. Carpenter, Allan. Washington. (New Enchantment of America Series). Rev. ed. Childrens Press, 1979. 96 p. ill. $7.
Gr 5-7. SLJ 26: Mar 1980. The history, geography, culture, economy, resources, attractions, and people of Washington state are introduced in this updated edition that uses full-color photos and large type.

870. Fradin, Dennis B. Washington: In Words and Pictures. (Young People's Stories of Our States Series). Childrens Press, 1980. 48 p. ill. $7.
Gr 2-5. +- SLJ 27: Mar 1981. The political and economic history, geography, people, and trivia of the state of Washington are introduced.

Washington D.C.

871. Carpenter, Allan. District of Columbia. (New Enchantment of America Series). Rev. ed. Childrens Press, 1979. 96 p. ill. $7.
Gr 5-7. SLJ 26: Mar 1980. Covers history, geography, culture, economy, resources, attractions, and people of the District of Columbia. Updated, with full-color photos and large type.

872. Epstein, Samuel. Washington, D.C.: The Nation's Capital. (First Book). Rev. ed. Watts, 1981. 86 p. $7.
Gr 4-6. B 77: May 1981. SLJ 28: Dec 1981. An up-to-date guide to the nation's capital, its history, landmarks, and statistics. Includes quizzes and puzzles.

873. Krementz, Jill. Visit to Washington, D.C., A. Scholastic, 1987. 48 p. ill. $14.
Gr K-4. B 83: May 15 1987. BC 40: Jul/Aug 1987. +- HB 63: Jul/Aug 1987. SLJ 33: May 1987. Six-year-old Matt is the narrator on this colorful tour that offers bits of history and shows children enjoying visits to many historic sites.

874. Lumley, Kathryn Wentzel. District of Columbia: In Words and Pictures. (Young People's Stories of Our States Series). Childrens Press, 1981. 47 p. ill. $7.
Gr 2-4. B 77: Jul 1 1981. +- SLJ 28: Oct 1981. Covers the history, geography, culture, economy, and noted individuals of the District of Columbia. Maps included.

875. Munro, Roxie. Inside-Outside Book of Washington, D.C., The. Dutton, 1987. 46 p. ill. $13.
Gr 1-3. +- B 83: May 15 1987. +- BC 40: Apr 1987. * HB 63: May/Jun 1987. * SE 52: Apr/May 1988. SLJ 33: May 1987. Watercolor glimpses of Washington's unique buildings and their contents.

West Virginia

876. Carpenter, Allan. West Virginia. (New Enchantment of America Series). Rev. ed. Childrens Press, 1979. 96 p. ill. $7.
Gr 5-7. SLJ 26: Mar 1980. Covers the history, geography, culture, economy, resources, attractions, and people of West Virginia. Updated, full-color photos and large type.

West, The

877. Adams, Alexander B. Disputed Lands: A History of the American West. Putnam, 1981. 480 p. $18.
Gr 11+. * LJ 106: Jan 15 1981. +- SLJ 27: Aug 1981. A factual history of the West, 1536-1886, packed with exciting adventure.

878. Barsness, Larry. Heads, Hides & Horns: The Complete Buffalo Book. Texas Christian University Press, 1986. 233 p. ill. $40. Pb $20.
Adult. B 82: May 1 1986. LJ 111: Jun 15 1986. Explores the relationship among the buffalo, the Indians, and the white settlers.

879. Bowman, John S. World Almanac of the American West, The. Pharos Books; dist. by Ballantine, 1986. 368 p. ill. $30.
Gr 10+. B 83: Jan 15 1987. LJ 111: Nov 1 1986. SLJ 33: May 1987. A chronology of westward movement from Columbus to 1985.

880. Chrisman, Harry. 1,001 Most Asked Questions About the American West. Ohio University Press, 1982. 349 p. ill. $26.
Gr 9+. B 79: Nov 1 1982. LJ 107: Oct 15 1982. Questions and answers organized in 12 chapters, covering such topics as cowboys, folklore, Indians, law enforcers, and pioneer life.

881. Freedman, Russell. Buffalo Hunt. Holiday, 1988. 52 p. ill. $17.
Gr 4-8. * B 85: Oct 1 1988. * BC 42: Oct 1988. * SLJ 35: Oct 1988. This discussion of the meaning of the buffalo to both Indian and white society includes colored reproductions of historical art of the Old West.

882. Howard, Helen Addison. American Frontier Tales. Mountain Press, 1982. 277 p. ill. $9.
Gr 9+. B 78: May 1 1982. Fifteen true frontier tales with new and interesting facts. Covered are stories about the very early Eastern tribes, Chief Joseph, the First Dragoons, the experimental U.S. Camel Corps, Sacagawea, and more.

883. May, Robin. History of the American West. Exeter Books; dist. by Bookthrift, 1984. 256 p. ill. $17.
Gr 9+. B 81: Mar 15 1985. An epic history of "The West" as it moved from the Atlantic Coast across the continent. Illustrated with over 100 color and b/w reproductions and photos.

884. McGaw, William C. Southwest Saga–The Way It Really Was! Golden West, 1988. 160 p. ill. Pb $5.
Gr 9+. B 85: Oct 1 1988. These vignettes on notable characters and events of the Old West from 1848 to the 1920s are based on interviews and archival records, and include rare photos.

885. Rossi, Paul A. Art of the Old West: The Collection of the Gilcrease Institute. Knopf, 1972. 335 p. ill. $35.
Gr 9+. B 68: Dec 15 1971. HT 21: Aug 1988. LJ 68: Dec 15 1971. Narrative, paintings, and sculpture record the changing face of the Old West from the time of the earliest explorations. Included are the Plains Indians, soldiers, cowboys, trappers, and freight handlers.

886. Tyler, Ron. American Frontier Life: Early Western Painting and Prints. Abbeville Press, 1987. 202 p. ill. $40.
Adult. B 83: Jul 1987. LJ 112: Aug 1987. Essays relate the influence of artworks about the west and compare the image they present with that in contemporary works. Includes works by white and Indian artists.

West, The–Fiction

887. Jekel, Pamela. Columbia. St. Martin's, 1986. 448 p. $19.
Adult. B 82: May 1 1986. LJ 111: Jun 1 1986. The saga of a family who settled the Columbia country of the Pacific Northwest.

White House

888. Living White House, The. 7th ed. White House Historical Association, 1982. 151 p. ill. Pb $10.
Gr 9+. B 79: May 15 1983. A colorfully illustrated guide to the White House lives of the presidents and their families.

889. White House: An Historic Guide. 15th ed. White House Historical Association, 1982. 160 p. ill. $10.
Gr 7+. B 79: Nov 15 1982, Mar 15 1983. Describes those rooms open to the public and some which are not, and traces the architectural history of the White House.

890. Sandak, Cass R. White House, The. (First Book). Watts, 1981. 62 p. $7.
Gr 5-7. B 77: May 1981. The history of the White House from its beginning, including its architecture and furnishings, plus anecdotes about first families.

891. Seale, William. President's House: A History. Abrams/White House Historical Association, 1987. 2 vol. ill. $40.
Gr 10+. * B 83: Apr 1 1987. LJ 112: Feb 15 1987. A scholarly study that includes anecdotes and tales of life in the White House. Numerous photos. Covers the presidents through Truman.

892. White House Historical Association. White House: An Historical Guide. Grosset, 1962. 143 p. ill. $6. Pb $4.
Gr 5-6. Metzner. A profusely illustrated tour of the White House, with information on its historic development.

Wisconsin

893. Stein, R. Conrad. Wisconsin. (America the Beautiful Series). Childrens Press, 1988. 144 p. ill. $24.
Gr 4-8. B 84: May 15 1988. Covers Wisconsin history, geography, government, economy, industry, arts and leisure, and historic sites. Includes a reference section of statistics, maps, and biographic sketches.

Women

894. Chambers-Schiller, Lee Virginia. Liberty, a Better Husband: Single Women in America: The Generations of 1780-1840. Yale University Press, 1984. 285 p. $23.
Adult. LJ 109: Sep 1 1984. Spinsterhood in ante-bellum America–reasons for remaining single and the importance of collegiality.

895. Clark, Judith Freeman. Almanac of American Women in the 20th Century. Prentice-Hall, 1987. 320 p. ill. $25. Pb $16.
Gr 9+. +- B 84: Oct 15 1987. LJ 112: Aug 1987. A broad overview of women's history in the 20th century. Each decade has a chapter with a chronology and "first events" along with biographies and essays on women's issues.

896. Degler, Carl N. At Odds: Women and the Family in America from the Revolution to the Present. Oxford University Press, 1980. 527 p. $30.
Gr 9+. B 76: Jul 1 1980. SE 50: Apr/May 1986. For advanced students, an examination of the relationship between family needs and social, political, and economic equality of women. Based on diaries, letters, and sociological studies.

897. DePauw, Linda Grant. Seafaring Women. Houghton, 1982. 246 p. $11.
Gr 7+. B 79: Nov 1 1982. BC 36: Jan 1983. +- BR 2: May/Jun 1983. HB 58: Dec 1982. VOYA 6: Apr 1983. Explores the sea adventures of brave women of all races from early times to our modern Merchant Marines.

898. Forster, Margaret. Significant Sisters: The Grassroots of Active Feminism 1839-1939. Knopf, 1985. 368 p. ill. $18.
Gr 9+. B 81: Feb 1 1985. * LJ 110: Feb 1 1985. Examines the history of feminism in the late 19th century and early 20th century through the lives of eight women who worked in the fields of law, employment, education, sexual morality and politics.

899. Franzen, Monika. Make Way! 200 years of American Women in Cartoons. Chicago Review Press, 1987. 144 p. ill. $10.
Gr 9+. B 84: Nov 15 1987. SLJ 34: Jan 1988. A collection of political cartoons concerning the struggle for women's rights since the early 19th century.

900. Goodfriend, Joyce D. Lives of American Women: A History with Documents. Little, Brown, 1981. 362 p. $10.
Gr 10+. HT 15: Aug 1982. In these writings 27 ordinary women of varied ethnic and social groups who lived

throughout our history speak of personal experiences, relationships, and choices. Each document is placed in historic context.

901. Hinding, Andrea. Feminism: Opposing Viewpoints. (Isms: Modern Doctrines and Movements). Greenhaven, 1986. 261 p. ill. $12. Pb $7.
Gr 9+. B 82: Jun 15 1986. B 84: Sep 1 1987. An anthology of readings on women's rights, beginning with women's right to vote and continuing through controversial topics of the 1980s.

902. Ingraham, Gloria D. Album of American Women: Their Changing Role. (Picture Album Series). Watts, 1987. 96 p. ill. $13.
Gr 4-8. B 84: Jan 1 1988. +- SLJ 34: Feb 1988. This highly illustrated history of the changing role of U.S. women includes thumbnail biographies of noted women.

903. Kerber, Linda K. Women's America: Refocusing the Past. Oxford University Press, 1982 448 p. ill. $22. Pb $13.
Gr 9+. B 78: Jan 1 1982. LJ 107: Feb 1 1982. SLJ 29: Sep 1982. A sampler of primary sources and historical essays tracing the experiences of ordinary American women.

904. LaBastille, Anne. Women and Wilderness. Sierra Club, 1980, 1984. 310 p. ill. $13. Pb $9.
Gr 10+. BR 3: Mar/Apr 1985. SLJ 27: Feb 1981. Begins with the experiences of early pioneer women as homesteaders, army wives, adventurers, and teachers, and concludes with biographies of modern outdoorswomen who have pioneered new fields for women.

905. McCullough, Joan. First of All: Significant "Firsts" by American Women. Holt, 1981. 128 p. ill. $11. Pb $6.
Gr 9+. +- LJ 105: Dec 15 1980. SE 46: Jan 1982. Introduces American women who broke convention to be "the first." Their records and achievements are in the arts, aviation, business, education, law, medicine, the military, politics, science, and sports.

906. Nicholas, Susan Cary. Rights and Wrongs: Women's Struggle for Legal Equality. McGraw-Hill, 1979. 89 p. Pb $5.
Gr 11+. B 76: Feb 15 1980. SE 45: Mar 1981. This overview of women's historic struggles for equal treatment and their efforts to change laws includes excerpts from trials and other case studies.

907. O'Neill, Lois Decker. Women's Book of World Records and Achievements, The. Anchor/Doubleday, 1979. 798 p. ill. $20. Pb $10.
Gr 9+. B 76: Feb 1 1980. LJ 105: Apr 15 1980. This useful survey of the changing role of women in society is grouped by topics such as agriculture, politics, sports, and the military.

908. Pleck, Elizabeth. Restoring Women to History: Materials for U.S. II. Organization of American Historians, 1984. 300 p. Pb $20.
Gr 10+. HT 20: Aug 1987. Covers women's role in U.S. history since Reconstruction. Essays and articles, tables, graphs, discussion questions, and other features supplement the text.

909. Riley, Glenda. Women and Indians on the Frontier, 1825-1915. University of New Mexico Press, 1984. 336 p. ill. $25. Pb $13.
Gr 10+. BR 4: May/Jun 1985. LJ 110: Mar 1 1985. An exploration of how white and Indian women saw themselves and each other, and how men perceived them. Includes photos. For advanced students.

910. Solomon, Barbara M. In the Company of Educated Women: A History of Women and Higher Education in America. Yale University Press, 1985. 308 p. ill. $25.
Adult. B 81: Mar 15 1985. LJ 110: Apr 15 1985. The history of education for women is examined in the social and economic context of the times from 1776-1985.

911. Tinling, Marion. Women Remembered: A Guide to Landmarks of Women's History in the U.S. Greenwood, 1986. 796 p. $75.
Gr 9+. B 83: Dec 15 1986. LJ 111: Oct 1 1986. A directory to more than 2000 statues, tablets, markers, and buildings which honor our nation's women.

912. Woloch, Nancy. Women and the American Experience. Knopf, 1984. 567 p. $25.
Adult. HT 20: Nov 1986. Emphasizes women's organizations and the roles of women in the public and private spheres from colonial days to the mid-1960s.

Women–Bibliographies

913. Loeb, Catherine R. Women's Studies: A Recommended Core Bibliography, 1980-1985. Libraries Unlimited, 1987. 538 p. $55.
Gr 9+. B 83: Aug 1987. Includes 1793 international books and periodicals recommended for inclusion in collections deficient in women-related scholarship. Provides coverage of history, anthropology, art, law, and literature.

914. Loeb, Catherine R. Women's Studies: A Recommended Core Bibliography, 1980-1985. Abridged ed. Libraries Unlimited., 1987. 222 p. $24.
Gr 9+. BR 6: Mar/Apr 1988. This abridgment of the original contains 645 titles considered essential for smaller collections. Coverage is over the same fields, but excludes items that are expensive, out of print, or from obscure presses.

Women–Biographies

915. American Mothers Committee. Mothers of Achievement in American History, 1776-1976. Charles E. Tuttle, 1976. 636 p. ill. $15.
Gr 9+. B 80: Jun 15 1984. Arranged by state. Includes women notable in all fields.

916. Peavy, Linda. Dreams into Deeds: Nine Women Who Dared. Scribner, 1985. 144 p. ill. $13.
Gr 6+. B 82: Nov 1 1985. SE 50: Apr/May 1986. SLJ 32: Feb 1986. VOYA 9: Jun 1986. Included: Jane Addams, Marian Anderson, Rachel Carson, Alice Hamilton, Mother Jones, Juliette Gordon Low, Margaret Mead, Elizabeth Cady Stanton, and Babe Didrikson Zacharias.

917. Reynolds, Moira. Nine American Women of the 19th Century: Leaders into the 20th. McFarland, 1988. 157 p. $21.
Gr 9+. BR 7: Nov/Dec 1988. +- VOYA 11: Dec 1988. Informal biographies of nine women, Mary Lyon, Emma Willard, Clara Barton, Harriet Beecher Stowe, Julia Ward Howe, Emma Lazarus, Helen Hunt Jackson, and Katherine Lee Bates, showing their influence on our society.

918. Sicherman, Barbara. Notable American Women: The Modern Period. Harvard University Press, 1980. 773 p. $35.
Gr 9+. B 78: Apr 15 1982. SLJ 27: Dec 1980. This supplements Notable American Women 1607-1950 and covers over 400 women who died between 1951 and 1975. The arrangement is alphabetic with added lists according to subject or activity.

Women–Fiction

919. Peck, Richard. This Family of Women. Delacorte, 1983. 393 p. $16.
Gr 9+. B 79: Feb 1 1983. BR 2: Nov/Dec 1983. LJ 108: Feb 15 1983. SLJ 29: May 1983. This saga of American women stretches from covered wagon days to W.W. II and is rich in historical detail.

Women–Quotations

920. Partnow, Elaine. Quotable Woman: 1800-1981. Facts on File, 1983. 608 p. $30. Pb $15.
Gr 9+. B 32: Nov 1 1985. A Bartlett's-style volume of quotes from women of all fields, including politics, literature, science, and entertainment.

921. Partnow, Elaine. Quotable Woman: Eve to 1799. Facts on File, 1986. 480 p. $25. Pb $15.
Gr 9+. B 82: Nov 1 1985. VOYA 8: Dec 1985. Quotations from women worldwide, chronologically arranged, with geographical and subject indexes, and brief information on the women quoted.

Wyoming

922. Carpenter, Allan. Wyoming. (New Enchantment of America Series). Rev. ed. Childrens Press, 1979. 96 p. ill. $7.
Gr 5-7. SLJ 26: Mar 1980. Wyoming history, geography, culture, economy, resources, attractions, and people are introduced. Updated, with full-color photos and large type.

923. Fradin, Dennis B. Wyoming: In Words and Pictures. (Young People's Stories of Our States Series). Childrens Press, 1980. 48 p. ill. Lib. ed. $7.
Gr 2-4. +- B 76: May 15 1980. Covers Wyoming political and economic history, geography, people, and trivia.

0-1600

Colonies

924. Durant, David N. Ralegh's Lost Colony. Atheneum, 1981. 320 p. ill. $13.
Adult. B 77: Apr 1 1981. LJ 106: Mar 1 1981. A lively rendition of the obscure story of the colony which disappeared. Durant explains how the English fear of the Spanish and their love of privateering doomed the colonists sent by Raleigh in the 1580s.

Explorers

925. Albornoz, Miguel. Hernando de Soto: Knight of the Americas. Watts, 1986. 389 p. $19.
Gr 7+. BR 5: Jan/Feb 1987. LJ 111: Sep 1 1986. VOYA 11: Jun 1988. The exciting, romantic, and adventurous life of the conquistador and explorer of the southeastern U.S. who exemplified the best qualities of Spanish knights.

926. Bains, Rae. Christopher Columbus. (Venture Into Reading Series). Troll, 1985. 30 p. ill. $8. Pb $2.
Gr 3-5. SLJ 32: Mar 1986. An appealing account of the familiar tale, enhanced by vigorous illustrations.

927. Ceserani, Gian Paolo. Christopher Columbus. Random House, 1979. 38 p. ill. $5.
Gr K-3. B 75: May 15 1979. BC 33: Sep 1979. * SE 44: Apr 1980. SLJ 25: May 1979. A concise but comprehensive biography of Columbus with information on his first voyage.

928. D'Aulaire, Ingri. Columbus. Doubleday, 1955. 56 p. ill. $10.
Gr 3-6. B 82: Sep 15 1985. Metzner [HB 31: Dec 1955.] A well-written text based on original sources with striking color and b/w lithographs.

929. Foster, Genevieve. Year of Columbus 1492. Scribner, 1949. 64 p. ill. $5.
Gr 9+. SE 44: Oct 1980 Relates world events at the time of Columbus' voyage.

930. Fradin, Dennis B. Explorers. (New True Book). Childrens Press, 1984. 45 p. ill. $8.
Gr 1-4. B 81: Mar 1 1985. SLJ 31: Apr 1985 Exploration from early civilization through the space program, with emphasis on the exploration of the New World.

931. Fritz, Jean. Where Do you Think You're Going, Christopher Columbus? Putnam, 1980. 80 p. ill. $8. Pb $4.
Gr 3-7. B 77: Mar 1 1981. BC 34: Feb 1981. HB 57: Feb 1981. * SLJ 27: Dec 1980. Fritz shows Columbus as obsessed with his vision, optimistic, vain, religious, sure of his destiny, a victim of his personality and the ignorance of his time.

932. Fuson, Robert Henderson. Log of Christopher Columbus, The. International Marine Publishing Co., 1987. 252 p. ill. $30.
Gr 9+. SLJ 35: Nov 1988. A prologue provides introduction to Columbus, his log, and the ships. The log chronicles daily events from August 1492 to March

1493. Seven appendices provide easy access to added information.

933. Gleiter, Jan. Christopher Columbus. Raintree, 1986. 32 p. ill. $11. Pb $7.
Gr 2-4. SLJ 33: May 1987. Tells the familiar story by means of a fictionalized conversation between Columbus and his son Fernando 10 years after the first voyage.

934. Goodnough, David. Christopher Columbus. (Adventures in the New World). Troll, 1979. 48 p. ill. $5. Pb $2.
Gr 5-8. SLJ 26: Jan 1980. This objective biography which captures the social and political climate of the time.

935. Goodnough, David. Francis Drake. (Adventures in Discovery). Troll, 1979. 48 p. ill. $5. Pb $2.
Gr 5-8. SLJ 26: Jan 1980. A factual representation of the times and the exploits of the noted explorer.

936. Graham-Campbell, James. Vikings, The. British Museum/Metro. Museum of Art; dist. by Morrow, 1980. 200 p. ill. $23.
Gr 9+. B 77: Sep 1 1980. Photographs and plates of a museum display are the reference points for a survey of Viking history, character, and treasure.

937. Granzotto, Gianni. Christopher Columbus. Doubleday, 1985. 287 p. ill. $19.
Adult. * LJ 110: Oct 15 1985. Insights into the personality of a fascinating man with a fanatical vision.

938. Harley, Ruth. Henry Hudson. (Adventures in the New World). Troll, 1979. 48 p. ill. $5. Pb $2.
Gr 5-8. SLJ 26: Jan 1980. An objective treatment, capturing the political and cultural climate that affected the decisions of the explorer.

939. Irwin, Constance H. Strange Footprints on the Land: Vikings in America. Harper, 1980. 182 p. ill. $9. Lib. ed. $9.
Gr 8-10. * B 76: Jul 15 1980. BC 33: Jun 1980. HB 56: Jun 1980. * SE 45: Apr 1981. * SLJ 26: Apr 1980. A detailed examination of the evidence of Viking settlements in North America ca. 900 A.D.

940. Janeway, Elizabeth. Vikings, The. (Landmark Books). Random House, 1951. 175 p. ill. Pb $3.
Gr 5-6. Metzner [+- LJ 76: Oct 15 1951]. The story of Eric the Red and Leif Ericson on Iceland and Greenland and the Vineland settlements.

941. Krensky, Stephen. Who Really Discovered America? Hastings, 1988. 60 p. ill. $11.
Gr 4-6. B 84: Jan 15 1988. SLJ 34: Apr 1988. Covers the arrival of Asian tribes from Siberia 40,000 years ago, the Vikings and other early European explorers, the discovery of Japanese pottery in Ecuador, and the possibility of ancient Chinese explorers.

942. Lillegard, Dee. My First Columbus Day Book. (My First Holiday Books). Childrens Press, 1988. 29 p. ill. $8.
Gr 1-2. +- SLJ 34: Aug 1988. The traditional story is simply told in verse. Watercolor illustrations.

943. Monchieri, Lino. Christopher Columbus. (Why They Became Famous). Silver Burdett, 1985. 62 p. ill. Lib. ed. $10. Pb $7.
Gr 4-7. +- BR 4: Jan/Feb 1986. - SLJ 32: Apr 1986. Emphasis is on Columbus' convictions, his efforts to find a royal patron, and on his first voyage.

944. Neal, Harry Edward. Before Columbus: Who Discovered America? Messner, 1981. 95 p. ill. $9.
Gr 4-6. B 78: Mar 1 1982. Includes information on the ancient ancestors of the American Indians, the probable Norse explorations, and the speculation about possible Israelite settlements.

945. Osborne, Mary Pope. Story of Christopher Columbus, Admiral of the Ocean Sea, The. Dell/Yearling, 1987. 90 p. ill. Pb $3.
Gr 3-5. B 84: Mar 1 1988. SLJ 37: Mar 1988. This objective biography recounts Columbus' successes and failures.

946. Weil, Lisl. I, Christopher Columbus. Atheneum, 1983. 48 p. ill. $11.
Gr K-3. B 79: Mar 15 1983. HB 59: Apr 1983. * SE 48: May 1984. +- SLJ 29: Aug 1983. This first-person picture-book biography shows the exploitation of the Indians and Columbus' belief that he had found the route to the Far East.

Explorers–Fiction

947. O'Dell, Scott. King's Fifth, The. Houghton, 1966. 264 p. ill. $15.
Gr 7-10. SE 47: Apr 1983. Esteban, a mapmaker, accompanied six members of Coronado's army who were looking for the cities of gold. A believable and dramatic story.

948. Steele, William O. Wilderness Tattoo, The. Harcourt Brace Jovanovich, 1972. 184 p. $5.
Gr 7+. SE 44: Oct 1980. Based on careful research, this novel concerns the adventures of Juan Ortiz who was with the DeSoto expedition.

Indians of North America

949. Batherman, Muriel. Before Columbus. Houghton, 1981. 32 p. ill. $9.
Gr 1-3. B 77: Apr 1 1981. BC 34: May 1981. HB 57: Apr 1981. SLJ 27: Mar 1981. A picture book history of the prehistoric Basket Makers. Key artifacts are described to clarify how scientists learn about vanished cultures.

950. Coe, Michael. Atlas of Ancient America. Facts on File, 1986. 240 p. ill. $35.
Gr 7+. B 83: Jan 1 1987. BR 6: Sep/Oct 1987. * LJ 112: Feb 1, Apr 15 1987. SLJ 33: Mar 1987. Emphasizes the prehistoric Indian people of North, Middle, and South America. Maps and text show how each tribe adapted to local conditions and how these ancient cultures have influenced modern Indian culture.

951. Fagan, Brian M. Great Journey: The Peopling of Ancient America. Thames and Hudson; dist. by Norton, 1987. 288 p. ill. $20.

Gr 9+. B 84: Sep 1 1987. LJ 112: Sep 15 1987. SLJ 34: Mar 1988. A highly readable work, explaining various views on how ancient people came to, and spread across, the Americas.

952. Frazier, Kendrick. People of Chaco: A Canyon and Its Culture. Norton, 1986. 224 p. ill. $20.
Adult. * LJ 111: Oct 15 1986. The story of the Chaco Canyon Indians who settled in New Mexico about 1000 years ago.

953. Lyttle, Richard B. People of the Dawn: Early Man in the Americas. Atheneum, 1980. 181 p. $11.
Gr 7+. B 76: Jul 15 1980. HB 56: Aug 1980. SLJ 27: Sep 1980. The author helps the reader discover the history and culture of ancient people through the use of archeological techniques.

Indians of North America–Fiction

954. Baker, Betty. Stranger and Afraid, A. Macmillan, 1971. 161 p. $5.
Gr 7+. SE 44: Oct 1980. A Plains Indian youth, captured by pueblo-dwellers, resents them as much as he does the conquistadors.

955. Bulla, Clyde. Conquista! Crowell, 1978. 35 p. ill. $7.
Gr 4-8. SE 44: Oct 1980. This brief but moving story of how the Indians may have acquired horses is followed by an explanation of the impact horses made on Indian life.

956. Deloria, Ella Cara. Waterlily. University of Nebraska Press, 1988. 244 p. $20.
Gr 9+. B 84: Apr 1 1988. LJ 113: Jun 1 1988. The role of women in Sioux society before the coming of the white man is clarified in this unusual and well-researched novel that includes information about women's duties, beliefs, skills, and relationships.

957. Shuler, Linda Lay. She Who Remembers. Arbor House, 1988. 394 p. $19.
Gr 9+. LJ 113: Feb 15 1988. SLJ 34: Aug 1988. This entertaining story of a young Pueblo Indian woman who is feared because she is believed to be a witch, is informative about ancient Pueblo customs and rituals.

1600-1775

Authors–Black

958. Jensen, Marilyn. Phyllis Wheatley. Lion, 1987. 233 p. $15.
Gr 7+. +- BC 41: Nov 1987. * BR 6: Nov/Dec 1987. SLJ 34: Dec 1987. Phyllis (1753?-1784) was a slave child raised by the affluent Wheatley family of Boston. She was a celebrated poet, but her master's death forced her to face the grim reality of the life of a freed slave.

959. Richmond, Merle. Phyllis Wheatley. (American Women of Achievement). Chelsea House, 1987. 111 p. ill. $17.
Gr 6-10. B 84: Feb 15 1988. SLJ 34: Apr 1988. As the new nation was moving toward independence, Phyllis Wheatley, a freed slave and internationally recognized poet, faced the racism of colonial Massachusetts.

Biographies

960. Risjord, Norman K. Representative Americans: The Colonists. Heath, 1981. 253 p. Pb $7.
Gr 10+. HT 15: Nov 1981. Biographies of thirteen colonists, including Anne Hutchinson, Cotton Mather, John Smith, William Bradford, Eliza Lucas Pinkney, and William Penn.

California–Fiction

961. Fisher, A. B. Bears, Pirates, and Silver Lace. Binfords, 1975. 158 p. $6.
Gr 5-6. Metzner. A romance of early California.

Explorers

962. Stein, R. Conrad. Story of Marquette and Joliet, The. (Cornerstones of Freedom). Childrens Press, 1981. 30 p. ill. $6.

Gr 3-5. +- B 78: Feb 15 1982. SLJ 28: Mar 1982. Anecdotes and quotes enliven the straightforward text. Slightly fictionalized.

Explorers–Fiction

963. Vernon, John. La Salle: A Novel. Viking, 1986. 240 p. $18.
Adult. LJ 111: Jun 1 1986. A realistic biographical novel of the eccentric explorer of the Mississippi Valley and of his mapmaker. Based on journals and letters.

Fiction

964. Ross, Bette M. Gennie, the Huguenot Woman. Revell, 1983. 189 p. $11.
Gr 7+. VOYA 6: Dec 1983. Gennie is an indentured servant. When her fiance is believed to be dead, she is forced into a cruel marriage from which she escapes into the wilderness. Provides good characterizations and historical detail.

965. Speare, Elizabeth G. Calico Captive. Houghton; Dell, 1957. 288 p. $13.
Gr 7-8. * SE 47: Apr 1983. Captured by the Indians, Miriam is sold to a wealthy French family in Montreal. Based on a real incident, this book sheds light on Indian-French relations and early Canadian history.

French and Indian War, 1755-1763

966. Marrin, Albert. Struggle for a Continent: The French and Indian Wars. Atheneum, 1987. 218 p. ill. $14.
Gr 5+. B 84: Jan 15 1988. HB 64: Jan/Feb 1988. * SLJ 34: Dec 1987. * VOYA 10: Oct 1987. A dramatic overview of the struggles among the French, English,

and the Indians for control of North America that explains the political and military maneuverings and their impact on the lives of the settlers.

French and Indian War, 1755-1763–Fiction

967. Cassel, Virginia C. Juniata Valley. Viking, 1981. 329 p. $15.
Gr 6+. VOYA 5: Jun 1982. A well-researched saga of five families. Following an Indian attack, the survivors hunt for those who were captured. Set during the French and Indian War.

968. Henty, G. A. With Wolfe in Canada: Winning of a Continent. Walker, 1886, 1963. 307 p. ill. $30.
Gr 7-8. Metzner. Exciting adventure during the French and Indian War.

969. Peck, Robert Newton. Fawn. Little; Dell, 1975. 143 p. maps. $6.
Gr 7-9. B 71: Mar 15 1975. +- BC 29: Nov 1975. SE 47: Apr 1983. Fawn is Mohawk and French. Through his story the reader sees the complexities of the French and Indian War.

Frontier and Pioneer Life–Fiction

970. Altsheler, J. A. Border Watch, The. Appleton, 1912, 1950. 370 p. $22.
Gr 7+. Metzner [B 9: Oct 1912]. The last of the Young Trailers series. Henry Ware joins George Rogers Clark in his expedition against the Indians.

971. Altsheler, J. A. Eyes of the Woods, The. Appleton, 1917, 1984. 318 p. $20.
Gr 7+. Metzner. More frontier adventures in the Kentucky and Ohio forests.

972. Altsheler, J. A. Forest Runners, The. Appleton, 1908, 1976. 362 p. $20.
Gr 7+. Metzner [* B 4: Dec 1908]. Sequel to The Young Trailers. Henry Ware and his friends save a band of settlers from massacre. A strong story that gives a good picture of the courage of the frontiersmen.

973. Altsheler, J. A. Free Rangers, The. Appleton, 1909, 1984. 364 p. $20.
Gr 7+. Metzner [B 4: Dec 1908]. Sequel to Forest Runners. Henry and his friends journey down the Mississippi to New Orleans to talk to the Spanish Governor-General about the mistreatment of American settlers by Spanish agents.

974. Altsheler, J. A. Keepers of the Trail, The. Appleton, 1916, 1950. 323 p. $18.
Gr 7+. Metzner. A young frontiersman's adventures in the Kentucky and Ohio forests.

975. Altsheler, J. A. Riflemen of the Ohio, The. Appleton, 1910, 1984. 354 p. $21.
Gr 7+. Metzner. Sequel to Young Trailers. Henry Ware is captured by Wyandot Indians.

976. Altsheler, J. A. Scouts of the Valley, The. Appleton, 1911, 1984. 362 p. $20.

Gr 7+. Metzner [B 8: Dec 1911]. Young scouts pit their skills against those of the natives in this story of Indian warfare set in the Pennsylvania wilderness.

977. Altsheler, J. A. Young Trailers: A Story of Early Kentucky. Appleton, 1907, 1976. 331 p. ill. $20.
Gr 7+. Metzner. Henry Ware, a young frontiersman, gains skill in wilderness survival and learns Indian ways in the Kentucky forest.

978. Cooper, James Fenimore. Deerslayer, The. Available in several editions, 1841. Paging varies. Price varies by edition.
Gr 7+. Metzner. The first of the five Leatherstocking Tales. Natty Bumpo, brought up among the Delaware Indians, rescues a pioneer family and makes lifelong friends among white men and Indians.

979. Cooper, James Fenimore. Last of the Mohicans, The. Available in several editions, 1826. Paging varies. Price varies by edition.
Gr 7+. Metzner. The second of the Leatherstocking tales, followed by The Pathfinder. The scout Hawkeye rescues Cora, Alice, and Major Heywood during the French and Indian War.

980. Cooper, James Fenimore. Pathfinder, The. Available in several editions, 1840. Paging varies. Price varies by edition.
Gr 7+. Metzner. Sequel to The Last of the Mohicans, and the third of the Leatherstocking tales. Exciting adventure at a small outpost on Lake Ontario.

981. Dalgliesh, Alice. Courage of Sarah Noble. Scribner, 1954. 147 p. ill. $7.
Gr 4-6. Metzner [B 50: June 15 1954. HB 30: Aug 1954. LJ 79: Jun 1 1954]. Eight-year-old Sarah makes a home with her father on the frontier and battles her fear of the Indians. Based on a true incident.

982. Edmonds, Walter D. Matchlock Gun. Dodd, 1941. 50 p. ill. $12.
Gr 4-6. Metzner [B 38: Nov 1 1941. HB 17: Nov 1941. LJ 66: Oct 15 1941]. Using a Spanish gun handed down from his ancestors, Edward prepares to defend his home against the Indians. Based on a true story.

983. Finlayson, Ann. Greenhorn on the Frontier. Warne, 1974. 209 p. ill. $5.
Gr 7-9. +- B 70: Jul 1 1974. BC 28: Oct 1974. +- LJ 99: Sep 15 1974. SE 44: Oct 1980. An orphaned brother and sister travel across the Alleghenies with a handcart.

984. Steele, William O. Trail through Danger. Harcourt, 1965. 192 p. ill. $5.
Gr 3-6. Metzner. A young boy faces danger in the wilderness.

985. Thom, James Alexander. Follow the River. Ballantine, 1981. 299 p. $7.
Gr 9+. * VOYA 5: Apr 1982. A realistic fictionalized account of the true story of Mary Ingles' captivity and wintertime escape from the Shawnee in 1755. For mature students.

Fur Trapping and Trade

986. Siegel, Beatrice. Fur Trappers and Traders: The Indians, the Pilgrims, and the Beaver. Walker, 1981. 64 p. ill. $9. Lib. ed. $9.
Gr 4-6. B 77: Apr 1 1981. B 83: Jun 15 1987. * SE 46: Apr 1982. SLJ 28: Dec 1981. A clear introduction to the economics of Plymouth Colony, which centered around the fur trade. The story unfolds in a highly illustrated question-and-answer format.

Immigration

987. Bailyn, Bernard. Voyagers to the West: A Passage in the Peopling of America on the Eve of the Revolution. Knopf, 1986. 704 p. ill. $30.
Adult. B 83: Oct 15 1986. * LJ 111: Nov 1 1986. Explains the migration patterns of families, single men, and indentured servants, providing many personal accounts and portraits.

Indentured Servants

988. van der Zee, John. Bound Over: Indentured Servitude and American Conscience. Simon & Schuster, 1985. 350 p. $18.
Adult. LJ 110: Aug 1985. Case studies of 31 individuals showing the political influence of this form of unfree labor.

Indentured Servants–Fiction

989. Avi. Encounter At Easton. Pantheon, 1980. 138 p. $7.
Gr 5+. B 76: Jun 15 1980. BC 33: Jul/Aug 1980. HB 56: Apr 1980. * SLJ 26: May 1980. Runaway indentured servants Robert and Elizabeth are tracked by a hired bully. Told through the alternating testimony of the major parties in a court investigation. Sequel to Night Journeys.

990. Avi. Night Journeys. Pantheon, 1979. 143 p. $7.
Gr 4-9. HB 55: Aug 1979. SLJ 25: Apr 1979. SE 44: Oct 1980. Two young indentured servants run away from their cruel employer. Prequel to Encounter at Eaton.

991. Bulla, Clyde Robert. Charlie's House. Crowell/Harper, 1983. 96 p. ill. $11.
Gr 3-6. B 79: Jun 15 1983. +- BC 36: Jul/Aug 1983. * SE 48: May 1984. SLJ 30: Sep 1983. Charlie encounters danger and adventure as an indentured servant and a runaway.

Indians of North America–Algonquin

992. Adams, Patricia. Story of Pocahontas, The. Dell/Yearling, 1987. 92 p. ill. Pb $3.
Gr 3-6. B 84: Mar 1 1988. Stresses Pocahontas' role as a peacemaker and food giver who helped keep the Jamestown colony alive.

993. D'Aulaire, Ingri. Pocahontas. Doubleday, 1978. 40 p. ill. $10.
Gr 1-4. Metzner [- B 43: Dec 15 1946. LJ 71: Dec 1 1946]. Colorful lithographs enhance the story which is told with simplicity and dignity, from Pocahontas' childhood to her royal reception in England.

994. Fritz, Jean. Double Life of Pocahontas, The. Putnam, 1983. 96 p. ill. $11.
Gr 4-8. B 80: Nov 1 1983. B 81: Apr 15 1985. B 82: Sep 15 1985. BC 37: Jan 1984. BR 2: Mar/Apr 1984. HB 59: Dec 1983. * SE 48: May 1984. Pocahontas' love for her own people and for the English colonists is told in this simple and colorful story.

995. Gleiter, Jan. Pocahontas. Raintree, 1984. 32 p. ill. $11. Pb $7.
Gr 2-6. +- SLJ 31: May 1985. A simple introduction to the exciting life of Pocahontas.

996. Jassem, Kate. Pocahontas, Girl of Jamestown. Troll, 1979. 48 p. ill. $5. Pb $2.
Gr 3-7. SLJ 26: Aug 1980. A high interest-low vocabulary biography, slightly fictionalized.

Indians of North America–Captives

997. Lenski, Lois. Indian Captive: The Story of Mary Jemison. Stokes, 1941. 269 p. ill. $13.
Gr 7-9. Metzner [B 38: Nov 15 1941. HB 17: Nov 1941. LJ 66: Nov 1 1941]. A true story based on the captivity of a 12-year-old girl who tried to adjust to Indian ways while retaining her hope for freedom.

Indians of North America–Fiction

998. Lederer, Paul Joseph. Manitou's Daughters. Signet, 1982. 283 p. Pb $3.
Gr 10+. * VOYA 6: Apr 1983. The love of an Oneida woman saved a Dutch captive and they sought to find peace as the British and French struggled for supremacy in the New World.

Indians of North America–Ottawa

999. Fleischer, Jane. Pontiac, Chief of the Ottawas. Troll, 1979. 48 p. ill. $5. Pb $2.
Gr 3-7. SLJ 26: Aug 1980. This high interest-low vocabulary biography of Pontiac includes some fictionalized dialogue and incidents.

Indians of North America–Pawtuxet

1000. Jassem, Kate. Squanto, the Pilgrim Adventure. Troll, 1979. 48 p. ill. $5. Pb $2.
Gr 3-7. SLJ 26: Aug 1980. This high interest-low vocabulary biography of Squanto is slightly fictionalized.

1001. Kessel, Joyce K. Squanto and the First Thanksgiving. (On My Own Books). Carolrhoda, 1983. 48 p. ill. $7.
Gr K-4. B 79: Mar 15 1984. * SE 48: May 1984. Squanto was captured by the English, sold as a slave, learned English, and was freed. He later befriended the Pilgrims and helped them survive the winter.

Jamestown

1002. Bridenbaugh, Carl. Jamestown, 1544-1699. Oxford University Press, 1980. 199 p. ill. $13.
Gr 9+. B 76: Mar 1 1980. LJ 105: Feb 15 1980. SLJ 27: Oct 1980. A reconstruction of the conditions at Jamestown, the first enduring English settlement, and the place where American democratic practice began.

Jamestown–Fiction

1003. Bulla, Clyde Robert. Lion to Guard Us, A. Crowell, 1981. 128 p. ill. $10.
Gr K-6. B 77: May 15 1981. +- BC 34: Jun 1981. HB 57: Aug 1981. * SE 46: Apr 1982. +- SLJ 27: May 1981. The Freebold youngsters flee London and join their father at Jamestown.

1004. O'Dell, Scott. Serpent Never Sleeps: A Novel of Jamestown and Pocohontas. Houghton, 1987. 227 p. ill. $16.
Gr 6-9. +- B 84: Nov 1 1987. BC 41: Sep 1987. +- SLJ 34: Sep 1987. +- VOYA 10: Oct 1987. Wearing a serpent ring to guard her from harm, Serena sets sail for Jamestown. A novel strong in grim reality and historical characters.

Jewish Americans

1005. Costabel, Eva Deutsch. Jews of New Amsterdam, The. Atheneum, 1988. 32 p. ill. $14.
Gr 2-4. B 85: Oct 1 1988. BC 42: Nov 1982. SLJ 35: Nov 1988. An Inquisition in Brazil caused many Jews to flee to New Amsterdam. This discusses the restrictions they faced in New York, their occupations, and social lives.

New Amsterdam

1006. Spier, Peter. Legend of New Amsterdam, The. Doubleday, 1979. 28 p. ill. $8.
Gr 5+. B 76: Sep 1 1979. B 79: Jun 1 1983. B 83: Mar 1 1987. BC 33: Nov 1979. HB 55 Oct 1979. SLJ 26: Oct 1979. In telling the legend of "Crazy Annie" the author presents an informative picture of life in New Amsterdam in the 1660s.

New Amsterdam–Fiction

1007. Lobel, Arnold. On the Day Peter Stuyvesant Sailed into Town. Harper, 1971. Unp. ill. $10.
Gr 1-3. B 83: Mar 1 1987. A story in rhyme of Peter Stuyvesant's efforts to make New Amsterdam into a model town. Delightful illustrations.

New Hampshire

1008. Fradin, Dennis B. New Hampshire Colony, The. (Thirteen Colonies). Childrens Press, 1988. 144 p. ill. $18.
Gr 4-7. B 84: May 15 1988. This introduction to the events and leaders of colonial New Hampshire includes numerous illustrations and a time line.

New York

1009. Fradin, Dennis B. New York Colony, The. (Thirteen Colonies). Childrens Press, 1988. 160 p. ill. $18.
Gr 4-7. B 85: Oct 1 1988. Numerous illustrations and a time line enchance this introduction to the events and leaders of colonial New York.

Pilgrims

1010. Brown, Margaret Wise. Homes in the Wilderness. Linnet Books, 1622, 1988. 77 p. ill. $16.
Gr 6+. BR 7: Sep/Oct 1988. Based on journal entries by William Bradford and others, this traces the Mayflower journey and explorations ashore, September 1620-March 1621. Includes drawings and glossary.

1011. Daugherty, James. Landing of the Pilgrims. (Landmark Books). Random House, 1950. 186 p. ill. Pb $4.
Gr 5-6. Metzner [B 47: Dec 1 1950]. The story of William Bradford, based on his writings. Tells of the Pilgrims' adventures and hardships with dry humor.

1012. Gruenbaum, Thelma. Before 1776: The Massachusetts Bay Colony from Founding to Revolution. Expressall, 1974. 38 p. Pb $4.
Gr 4-6. SE 45: Feb 1981. Emphasis is on everyday life, housing, clothing, and food, with brief information on government, education, and religion.

1013. Heaton, Vernon. Mayflower, The. Mayflower, 1980. 200 p. ill. $20.
Gr 9+. B 77: Dec 1 1980. LJ 105: Nov 1 1980. The personalities and events of the Pilgrims' voyage on the Mayflower and their first 10 years at Plymouth colony.

1014. Heimert, Alan. Puritans in America: A Narrative Anthology. Harvard University Press, 1985. 438 p. $25.
Gr 10+. HT 20: Feb 1987. Arranged chronologically, this collection of documents shows three generations of intellectual and spiritual development, agreement and disagreement, in New England. Includes introductory essays.

1015. Loeb, Robert H., Jr. Meet the Real Pilgrims: Everyday Life on Plimouth Plantation in 1627. Doubleday, 1979. 144 p. ill. $7.
Gr 4-6. +- BC 33: Dec 1979. * SE 44: Apr 1980. SLJ 26: Mar 1980. Loeb captures the lives, customs, and living conditions of the Pilgrims in a readable account that includes numerous photos of the reconstructed village of Plymouth.

1016. Sewall, Marcia. Pilgrims of Plimoth, The. Atheneum, 1986. 48 p. ill. $14.
Gr K-6. B 83: Sep 15 1986. HB 62: Nov/Dec 1986. * SE Apr/May 1987. * SLJ 33: Nov 1986. A first-person narrative of the early years of Plymouth colony.

1017. Siegel, Beatrice. New Look at the Pilgrims: Why They Came to America. Walker, 1987. 82 p. ill. $13.
Gr 3-7. B 83: Jun 15 1987. BR 6: Sep/Oct 1987. A question-and-answer format is used to discuss the

Pilgrims. Included are line drawings of Pilgrim leaders, clothing, ships, and tools.

1018. Smith, E. B. Coming of the Pilgrims: Told from Governor Bradford's Firsthand Account. Little, 1964. 60 p. ill. $12.
Gr 1-4. Metzner [HB 40: Apr 1964. LJ 89: Mar 15 1964]. Covers the persecution of the Pilgrims in England, their escape to Holland, their voyage to the New World, and the perils of their first year.

1019. Smith, E. B. Pilgrim Courage: From a Firsthand Account by Wm. Bradford, Governor of Plymouth Colony. Little, 1964. 108 p. ill. $7.
Gr 7-9. Metzner [B 58: Jun 1 1962. HB 38: Jun 1962. LJ 87: May 15 1962]. Selections from Bradford's accounts provide a dramatic picture of the persecutions of the Pilgrims, their voyage, and the troubles of the first settlers of Plymouth.

Pilgrims–Children

1020. DeLage, Ida. Pilgrim Children Come to Plymouth. (Beginning to Read History Book). Garrard, 1981. 48 p. ill. $7.
Gr 2-3. B 78: Nov 15 1981. SLJ 28: Dec 1981. The first year in the New World as seen by the children who came on the Mayflower.

1021. DeLage, Ida. Pilgrim Children on the Mayflower. (For Real Book). Garrard, 1980. 48 p. $7.
Gr 1-3. SLJ 27: Dec 1980. The adventures and difficulties of the children crossing the Atlantic on the Mayflower.

Pilgrims–Fiction

1022. Dillon, Ellis. Seekers, The. Scribner, 1986. 144 p. $13.
Gr 6-10. B 82: Jun 1 1982. BC 39: May 1986. * SE 51: Apr/May 1987. +- SLJ 32: May 1986. Andrew and Rebecca share the problems of the colony at Plymouth, and have mixed feelings about whether to remain or return to the Old Country.

1023. Wisler, G. Clifton. This New Land. (Walker's American History Series for Young People). Walker, 1987. 124 p. $14. Lib. ed. $15.
Gr 5-9. B 84: Mar 15 1988. +- BC 41: Nov 1987. BR 7: May/Jun 1988. SLJ 34: Nov 1987. The Pilgrim experience is seen through the eyes of 12-year-old Richard. Extensively researched, with graphic descriptions of the miseries faced that first year.

Pirates

1024. Ritchie, Robert C. Captain Kidd and the War against the Pirates. Harvard University Press, 1986. 298 p. $20.
Gr 9+. B 83: Oct 15 1986. A detailed and deglamourized portrait of pirates and pirating, that tells Kidd's story and shows how governments manipulated pirates in their own interest.

Public Officials

1025. Blackburn, Joyce. James Edward Oglethorpe. Dodd, 1983. 144 p. map. $9.
Gr 5-8. B 79: Jun 1 1983. A lively biography of the founder of Georgia.

Religious Leaders

1026. Rushing, Jane Gilmore. Covenant of Grace. Doubleday, 1982. 384 p. $17.
Gr 9+. B 78: Jun 1 1982. LJ 107: May 1 1982. This accurate and dramatic account of Anne Hutchinson's fight for religious freedom provides a good sense of life in colonial Massachusetts.

1027. Silverman, Kenneth. Life and Times of Cotton Mather, The. Harper, 1984. 408 p. ill. $29.
Adult. * B 80: Jan 1 1984. SE 49: May 1985. A witty biography that presents the gifted and intellectual Mather and his times.

1028. White, Florence M. Story of Junipero Serra, Brave Adventurer, The. Dell/Yearling, 1987. 86 p. ill. Pb $3.
Gr 3-6. B 84: Mar 1 1988. This introduction to Father Serra, who founded the first nine California missions is illustrated with pencil drawings.

Religious Leaders–Fiction

1029. Heidish, Marcy Moran. Witnesses: A Novel. Houghton, 1980. 235 p. $11.
Gr 9+. B 77: Sep 1 1980. LJ 105: Jul 1980. SLJ 27: Nov 1980. A biographical novel based on the life of Anne Hutchinson who struggled for religious freedom in Massachusetts in the 1630s. Based on primary sources.

Roanoke–Fiction

1030. Levitin, Sonia. Roanoke: A Novel of the Lost Colony. Atheneum, 1973. 213 p. $7.
Gr 6-9. B 70: Nov 15 1973. BC 27: Mar 1974. HB 49: Oct 1973. * LJ 98: Oct 15 1973. * SE 47: Apr 1983. The mystery of the Roanoke colony is examined in the story of William, a 16-year-old who befriended the Indians who were there.

Slaves and Slavery

1031. Davis, Thomas J. Rumor of Revolt: The "Great Negro Plot" in Colonial New York. Free Press, 1985. 321 p. $20.
Adult. LJ 110: Jun 15 1985. A detailed and lively examination of the white fear of a conspiracy to incite a slave revolt, and of the black resentment of slavery.

1032. Windley, Lathan A. Runaway Slave Advertisements: A Documentary History from the 1730s to 1790. Greenwood, 1983. 4 vol. $150.
Gr 10+. B 80: Feb 1 1984. A study of master-slave relationships, attitudes and behavior patterns.

Slaves and Slavery–Fiction

1033. Anderson, Joan. Williamsburg Household, A. Clarion, 1988. 46 p. ill. $16.
Gr 3-5. +- B 84: Aug 1988. +- BC 41: Jul 1988. SLJ 35: Sep 1988. Photos taken at colonial Williamburg are the backdrop for this story of colonial life from a slave's point of view.

1034. Howard, Ellen. When Daylight Comes. Atheneum, 1985. 210 p. $15.
Gr 5-9. +- BC 39: Oct 1985. SLJ 32: Nov 1985. Based on a slave rebellion in the Virgin Islands in 1733. Helen, the daughter of the Danish magistrate, is held captive by the liberated blacks and sees what it means to be a slave.

Social Life and Customs

1035. Demos, John. Little Commonwealth: Family Life in Plymouth Colony. Oxford University Press, 1970. 201 p. ill. $7.
Adult. SE 50: Apr/May 1986. Concerns family life and child rearing practices at Plymouth.

1036. Hawke, David Freeman. Everyday Life in Early America. (Everyday Life in America). Harper, 1988. 208 p. ill. $17. Pb $8.
Gr 9+. B 84: Dec 1 1987. Explores how the colonists used the available resources to make a better life that included both freedom and enough to eat.

1037. Hilton, Suzanne. World of Young George Washington, The. Walker, 1987. 106 p. ill. $13.
Gr 4-8. BR 6: May/June 1987. +- SLJ 33: Apr 1987. This entertaining view of pre-Revolutionary America, based on Washington's diaries and other writings of the period, includes a time line and illustrations.

1038. Madison, Arnold. How the Colonists Lived. McKay, 1981. 84 p. ill. $8.
Gr 5-8. B 77: Jul 1 1981. - SLJ 28: Feb 1982. A regional and chronological report on colonial life, including Jamestown, Pennsylvania, and New York. Discusses political events and cultural developments.

1039. Tunis, Edwin. Colonial Living. World, 1976. 155 p. ill. $19.
Gr 1+. Metzner [B 54: Oct 15 1957. HB 33: Dec 1957. LJ 82: Oct 15 1957]. SE 44: Oct 1980. A pictorial history of everyday life in seventeenth and eighteenth century America. Suitable for all ages.

1040. Tunis, Edwin. Frontier Living. World, 1976. 165 p. ill. $19.
Gr 5+. Metzner [B 58: Dec 15 1961. HB 38: Feb 1962. LJ 86: Dec 15 1961]. Text and drawings portray the manners and customs of the frontier family.

Social Life and Customs–Children

1041. Clarke, Amanda. Growing Up in Puritan Times. (Growing Up). Batsford, 1980. 72 p. ill. $13.
Gr 6-10. +- SLJ 27: Oct 1980. Provides an understanding of how children lived at both ends of the economic scale, and shows the negative aspects of life at the time.

1042. Earle, Alice M. Child Life in Colonial Days. Macmillan, 1899; reprinted by Corner House, 1975. 418 p. ill. $20.
Gr 6+. SE 50: Apr/May: 1986. Describes dress, toys, games, books, education, religious training, and discipline.

1043. Greven, Philip J., Jr. Protestant Temperament: Patterns of Child-Rearing, Religious Experience, and the Self in Early America. Knopf, 1977. 431 p. $15.
Adult. SE 50: Apr/May 1986. Discusses the relationship between adult religious attitudes and their discipline of children.

1044. Morgan, Edmund S. Puritan Family: Religion and Domestic Relations in Seventeenth Century New England. New ed., rev. and enlarged. Harper, 1966. 196 p. $6.
Adult. SE Apr/May: 1986. Discusses the early separation of Puritan parents from their children.

Social Life and Customs–Fiction

1045. Coleman, Terry. Thanksgiving. Simon & Schuster, 1981. 408 p. $15.
Gr 9+. B 78: Nov 1 1981. LJ 106: Nov 1 1981. SLJ 28: Feb 1982. The life of the Puritans is contrasted to that of the Dutch in New Amsterdam and the isolated fear-ridden life of the explorers, in a vivid account of the experiences of Wolsley Lowell and her children.

1046. Farber, Norma. Mercy Short: A Winter Journal, North Boston, 1692-93. Dutton, 1982. 139 p. $12.
Gr 7-10. BC 36: Jan 1983. HB 58: Dec 1982. Based on Cotton Mather's diary. Mercy, a victim of Indian captivity, resumes life in Boston soon after the Salem witch trials. She seeks Mather's help for release from the demons which she believes possess her.

1047. Field, Rachel. Calico Bush. Macmillan; Dell, 1931, 1973. 224 p. $13.
Gr 6-8. * SE Apr 1983. When the Sargents move to the wilderness of Maine, their bound-out servant, thirteen-year-old Maggie, must go too. They are all ill-prepared for the hardship and danger of frontier life.

1048. Forest, Heather. Baker's Dozen: A Colonial American Tale. Harcourt/Gulliver, 1988. 32 p. ill. $14.
Gr K-2. B 85: Sep 15 1988. BC 42: Oct 1988. Set in colonial New York state, this is the story of a baker who was cursed for being greedy until he began giving an extra cookie with each dozen purchased.

1049. Mitchell, Barbara. Tomahawks and Trombones. Carolrhoda, 1982. 56 p. ill. $6.
Gr 2-3. B 83: Mar 1 1987. BC 36: Oct 1982. SLJ 21: Jan 1983. The residents of Bethlehem, Pa. frightened away the hostile Iroquois by sounding the trombones they had brought to celebrate Christmas. Based on an actual event.

1050. Richter, Conrad. Light in the Forest. Knopf; Bantam, 1953. 117 p. $7.
Gr 7-8. * SE 47: Apr 1983. When a 15-year-old white boy, who had been raised by Indians since he was 4, is

reunited with his parents, he struggles with an unknown culture and its different values and expectations.

1051. Rossner, Judith. Emmeline. Simon & Schuster, 1980. 331 p. $13.
Gr 9+. - B 77: Sep 1 1980. LJ 105: Sep 1 1980. SLJ 27: Dec 1980. The tragedy of Emmeline, who worked in the Lowell, Massachusetts mills, is based on a true story. Presents a vivid description of working conditions and the conscience of the time.

Thanksgiving

1052. Anderson, Joan. First Thanksgiving Feast, The. Clarion/Houghton, 1984. 48 p. ill. $13.
Gr 2-6. * B 81: Dec 15 1984. HB 61: Mar/Apr 1985. * SE 49: Apr 1985. * SLJ 31: Dec 1984. A dramatized account, based on the writings of the people who were there. Unique photos, taken at a living history museum, work with the text to provide a sense of the individuality of both natives and settlers.

1053. Appelbaum, Diana Karter. Thanksgiving: An American Holiday, an American History. Facts on File, 1985. 305 p. ill. $16.
Gr 6+. B 81: Nov 1 1984. BR 4: May/Jun 1985. This account of the evolution of this uniquely American holiday includes photos, poems, and lyrics.

1054. Baldwin, Margaret. Thanksgiving. (First Book). Watts, 1983. 64 p. ill. $9.
Gr 4-6. B 79: Mar 1 1983. A dramatic retelling of the Thanksgiving story, suitable for reading aloud.

1055. Dalgliesh, Alice. Thanksgiving Story. Scribner, 1985. Unp. ill. $4.
Gr 1-3. Metzner [B 51: Nov 1 1954. * HB 30: Oct 1954]. The Pilgrim experience, from the sailing of the Mayflower to the Thanksgiving feast, through the eyes of one family.

1056. Kroll, Steven. Oh, What a Thanksgiving! Scholastic, 1988. 32 p. $13.
Gr K-3. B 85: Sep 15 1988. B 85: Oct 1 1988. +- SLJ 35: Sep 1988. David, who lives in the 1980s, imagines the first Thanksgiving.

1057. Roquitte, Ruth. Day of Thanksgiving, A. Dillon Press, 1981. 54 p. ill. $9.
Gr 1-3. B 78: Nov 15 1981. Explains the religious persecution that led the Pilgrims to the New World, and the other difficulties which led to their celebration of the first Thanksgiving.

Thanksgiving–Fiction

1058. Kroll, Steven. One Tough Turkey: A Thanksgiving Story. Holiday, 1982. 31 p. ill. $11.
Gr K-2. B 79: Oct 15 1982. BC 36: Dec 1982. SLJ 29: Oct 1982. When it is time for the first Thanksgiving, Solomon Turkey and his family try to convince the Pilgrims to feast on squash.

Virginia–History

1059. Fraden, Dennis B. Virginia Colony, The. Childrens Press, 1986. 158 p. ill. $11.
Gr 4-6. b 83: Apr 1 1987. SLJ 33: Aug 1987. A heavily illustrated volume that covers the Virginia colony from its beginning through the Revolution. Includes biographical sketches of prominent Virginians.

Witchcraft and Witches

1060. Karlsen, Carol F. Devil in the Shape of a Woman: Witchcraft in Colonial New England. Norton, 1987. 416 p. $23.
Gr 9+. B 84: Nov 1 1987. LJ 112: Nov 15 1987. This examination of the social and economic positions, and the mental and physical health of women accused of witchcraft, provides a different perspective on reasons that these individuals were persecuted.

1061. Petry, Ann. Tituba of Salem Village. Crowell, 1964. 248 p. $15.
Gr 6-9. Metzner [HB 41: Feb 1965. LJ 89: Sep 15 1964]. SE 47: Apr 1983. A slightly fictionalized biography of the slave Tituba who was accused of witchcraft.

1062. Clapp, Patricia. Witches' Children: A Story of Salem. Lothrop, 1982. 160 p. $9.
Gr 6+. B 78: May 15 1982. BC 35: Mar 1982. HB 58: Jun 1982. SLJ 28: Mar 1982. VOYA 5: Oct 1982. A convincing novel of the events of Salem, where proclaiming one's innocence amounted to a declaration of guilt.

1063. Roberts, Willo Davis. Elizabeth. Scholastic/Sunfire, 1984. 357 p. $3.
Gr 7+. B 81: Oct 1 1984. +- BC 38: Sep 1984. SLJ 31: Jan 1985. Elizabeth becomes deeply involved when her friend is accused of witchcraft.

1064. Smith, Claude Clayton. Stratford Devil, The. Walker, 1985. 192 p. $14.
Gr 6+. B 81: Dec 1 1984. BC 38: May 1985. HB 61: Sep/Oct 1985. SLJ 31: Mar 1985. * VOYA 8: Aug 1985. This novel about the trial and execution of a thoughtful and independent young woman accused of witchcraft is based on records from the Stratford, Connecticut area.

1065. Speare, Elizabeth G. Witch of Blackbird Pond. Houghton; Dell, 1958. 249 p. $13.
Gr 6-10. * SE 47 Apr 1983. Raised in easy-going Barbados, Kit finds adjustment to Puritan life difficult, since conformity is highly valued. After she befriends a Quaker outcast she finds herself accused of witchcraft.

Women

1066. Siegel, Beatrice. Basket Maker and the Spinner, The. Walker, 1987. 63 p. $11. Lib. ed. $12.
Gr 4-6. B 83: Aug 1987. BC 41: Sep 1987. This account of the daily lives of two women, one an Indian and one a colonist, clarifies their beliefs and responsibilities. Slightly fictionalized

1775-1783

United States–History–1775-1783

1067. Bliven, Bruce. American Revolution, 1760-1783. Random House, 1981. 159 p. ill. $7.
Gr 7-8. Metzner [B 55: Nov 1 1958]. Bliven covers causes, personalities, and events in this general introduction to the revolution.

1068. Holley, Erica. American Revolution, The. (Weighing Up the Evidence: How and Why). Dryad/David & Charles, 1986. 64 p. ill. $16.
Gr 7+. BR 6: Sep/Oct 1987. SLJ 33: Aug 1987. Short descriptions of events are enhanced by numerous illustrations, quotes from a variety of persons, and discussion questions. Presented from both the British and American points of view.

1069. Marrin, Albert. War for Independence, The. Atheneum, 1988. 288 p. ill. $16.
Gr 6+. * B 84: Jul 1988. BC 41: Apr 1988. * BR 7: Nov/Dec 1988. * SLJ 34: Jun/Jul 1988. * VOYA 11: Jun 1988. This useful overview, with numerous quotes, illustrations, and double-page maps of campaigns, provides a lively and thoughtful picture of the people who were willing to sacrifice comfort for freedom.

1070. Meltzer, Milton. American Revolutionaries: A History in Their Own Words. Harper/Crowell, 1987. 173 p. ill. $13.
Gr 6+. * B 83: Jun 1 1987. BC 40: Jun/Jul 1987. HB 63: Nov/Dec 1987. * SE 52: Apr/May 1988. * SLJ 33: Jun/Jul 1987. * VOYA 10: Oct 1987. Excerpts from the words of leaders and ordinary people, including soldiers, the indentured, immigrants, women, blacks, and prisoners.

1071. Middlekauff, Robert. Glorious Cause: The American Revolution, 1763-1789. (Oxford History of the United States). Oxford University Press, 1982. 544 p. ill. $25.
Gr 9+. B 78: May 1 1982. LJ 107: Mar 15 1982. Covers political and military history, the causes, campaigns, and results of the revolution, and the development of the new federal government. The first of a proposed 11-part series for the general reader.

1072. Morris, Richard B. American Revolution, The. (American History Topic Books). Lerner, 1985. 66 p. ill. $9.
Gr 4-6. B 82: Mar 1 1986. +- SLJ 32: Mar 1986. A revised edition of a standard introduction to the revolution.

1073. Tuchman, Barbara. First Salute, The. Knopf, 1988. 384 p. ill. $23.
Adult. B 84: Aug 1988. +- LJ 113: Sep 15 1988. Explores the military and diplomatic high points of the war, and emphasizes the relations of the new nation with Britain's European rivals.

American Loyalists

1074. Sabine, Lorenzo. Biographical Sketches of Loyalists of the American Revolution. 2nd ed. Genealogical Publishing Company, 1979. 2 v. $50.
Gr 9+. B 80: Jun 15 1984. Includes over 4400 entries. Some of the biographies are lengthy, but most are quite short.

Battles

1075. Birnbaum, Louis. Red Dawn at Lexington: "If They Mean to Have a War, Let It Begin Here!" Houghton, 1986. 385 p. ill. $19.
Gr 9+. B 82: Apr 15 1986. LJ 111: May 1 1986. SLJ 33: Nov 1986. This social, political, and military history of the Revolutionary War is based on primary documents and eyewitness accounts.

1076. Dwyer, William M. Day is Ours! November 1776-January 1777: An Inside View of the Battles of Trenton and Princeton. Viking, 1983. 403 p. $20.
Gr 11+. B 80: Nov 15 1983. LJ 108: Oct 15 1983. Using diaries, letters, and memoirs, Dwyer tells the story of the common soldiers on both sides of the famous battles of Trenton and Princeton that changed the course of the war.

1077. McPhillips, Martin. Battle of Trenton, The. (Turning Points in American History). Silver Burdett, 1985. 64 p. ill. $14.
Gr 4-6. B 82: Jan 15 1986. SLJ 32: Nov 1985. An introduction to the background of the war, an outline of the battle of Trenton, and a synopsis of the events of the following years.

1078. Stein, R. Conrad. Story of Lexington and Concord, The. (Cornerstones of Freedom). Childrens Press, 1983. 31 p. ill. $6.
Gr 3-6. +- B 79: Aug 1983. +- SLJ 30: Sep 1983. Covers the events that led to the famous battles at Lexington and Concord and the details of the day.

Battles–Fiction

1079. Fast, Howard. April Morning. Crown; Bantam, 1961, 1962. 184 p. $9. Pb $4.
Gr 6+. SE 47: Apr 1983. The battle of Lexington as seen by a young hero who survived the day.

Blacks–Fiction

1080. Collier, James Lincoln. War Comes to Willie Freeman. Delacorte; Dell, 1983. 192 p. $13. Pb $4.
Gr 4-8. B 79: Apr 1 1983. BC 36: Apr 1983. HB 59: Jun 1983. * SE 48: May 1984. SLJ 29: Apr 1983. * VOYA 6: Oct 1983. This gripping tale of survival and values concerns a free black girl whose father had been killed in the fighting. Disguised as a boy she searches for her mother. Historically accurate in fact and language.

Declaration of Independence

1081. Dalgliesh, Alice. Fourth of July Story, The. Scribner, 1956. 32 p. ill. $13.
Gr 3-4. Metzner [B 53: Sep 1 1956. HB 32: Oct 1956. LJ 81: Sep 15 1956]. The story of the writing of the Declaration of Independence.

Espionage and Spies

1082. Fritz, Jean. Traitor: The Case of Benedict Arnold. Putnam, 1981. 192 p. ill. $10.
Gr 4-9. B 78: Dec 15 1981. BC 35: Feb 1982. HB 57: Dec 1981. * SE 46: Apr 1982. * SLJ 28: Sep 1981. VOYA 4: Feb 1982. This psychological portrait of Arnold introduces the ambitious, brave, and complex man whose egotistical behavior led to tragedy.

1083. Hatch, Robert McConnell. Major John Andre: A Gallant in Spy's Clothing. Houghton, 1986. 332 p. ill. $18.
Gr 10+. B 82: Mar 1986. LJ 111: Feb 15 1986. This gripping story of the British intelligence chief who negotiated with Benedict Arnold shows the mistakes that resulted in tragedy for Andre and also presents a picture of the social life in occupied America.

Espionage and Spies–Fiction

1084. Epstein, Samuel. Change for a Penny. Coward, 1959. 254 p. ill. $7.
Gr 5-8. Metzner [B 56: Feb 1 1960. LJ 85: Feb 15 1960]. Tim must guide American soldiers and their whaleboats through the swamp to attack a British garrison.

1085. Roop, Peter. Buttons for General Washington. (On My Own Books). Carolrhoda, 1986. 48 p. ill. $9.
Gr 1-3. B 83: Dec 1 1986. +- BC 40: Dec 1986. +- SLJ 33: Dec 1986. * SE 51: Apr/May 1987. This story is based on incidents from the life of John Darragh, a Quaker who carried secrets to General Washington in coded buttons.

1086. Sherman, Dan. Traitor, The. Fine, 1987. 263 p. $18.
Gr 9+. B 83: Jun 1 1987. +- LJ 112: May 15 1987. A novel of espionage, politics, strategy, adventure, and treason.

Fiction

1087. Abel, Robert H. Freedom Dues. Dial, 1980. 404 p. $11.
Gr 9+. B 76: July 1 1980. +- LJ 105: July 1980. SLJ 27: Oct 1980. The story of a journalist from London whose thirst for news soon has him involved in revolutionary activity.

1088. Beatty, John. Who Comes to King's Mountain. Morrow, 1975. 287 p. $6.
Gr 8+. * B 72: Nov 1 1975. SE 44: Oct 1980. SLJ 22: Oct 1975. Alec, whose father is a loyalist and his grandfather a rebel, is pressed into service, first on one side and then the other. A vivid tale of conflicting loyalties set in South Carolina.

1089. Butters, Dorothy Gilman. Bells of Freedom, The. Peter Smith, 1984. 190 p. ill. $14.
Gr 9+. Metzner [HB 40: Feb 1964. LJ 88: Dec 15 1963]. HB 61: Sep/Oct 1985. Apprentice Jed witnesses action at Breed's Hill, Concord, and Dochester Heights.

1090. Cavanna, Betty. Ruffles and Drums. Morrow, 1975. 222 p. ill. $12.
Gr 6-8. SE 47: Apr 1983. The men are gone to war and Sarah and her mother struggle to run the farm alone. When they are forced to nurse an injured British officer too, Sarah must face the reality of war.

1091. Cheney, Cora. Christmas Tree Hessian. Holt, 1976. 160 p. ill. Pb $4.
Gr 4-6. Metzner [* LJ 82: Nov 15 1957]. This family story, full of action and humor, is set in Newport, Rhode Island, 1776-1777.

1092. Collier, James Lincoln. Bloody Country, The. Scholastic, 1976, 1985. 181 p. $3.
Gr 7-9. SE 47: Apr 1983. VOYA 8: Dec 1985. After a Connecticut Yankee boy settles in Pennsylvania he wonders why the concept of freedom applies to him but not to his father's slave.

1093. Collier, James Lincoln. My Brother Sam Is Dead. Four Winds; School Book Services, 1974; 1977. 240 p. 13. Pb $3.
Gr 6-9. B 83: Apr 15 1987. SE 47: Apr 1983. The story of a family split by the war, some becoming rebels, others remaining loyal to the crown.

1094. Cornwell, Bernard. Redcoat. Viking, 1988. 403 p. $18.
Gr 9+. B 84: Jan 1 1988. +- BR 7: Nov/Dec 1988. LJ 112: Dec 1987. Philadelphia's divided loyalties are illustrated through this story about redcoat Sam Gilpin, rebel Jonathan Becket, and his sister, Martha. The reality of war is contrasted with the gaity of Loyalist society.

1095. Cover, Arthur Byron. American Revolutionary. Bantam, 1985. 125 p. $3.
Gr 5-9. SLJ 32: Jan 1986. VOYA 9: Aug/Oct 1986. A time machine allows the young reader to participate in the Revolution.

1096. DeFord, Deborah H. Enemy among Them, An. Houghton, 1987. 208 p. $14.
Gr 6-9. B 84: Nov 15 1987. BC 41: Sep 1987. +- SLJ 34: Sep 1987. VOYA 10: Oct 1987. This story about a family of rebel German American colonists and their growing friendship with a wounded Hessian provides good detail on colonial life.

1097. Forbes, Esther. Johnny Tremain. Houghton; Dell, 1943; 1973. 272 p. Pb $3.
Gr 6+. SE 47: Apr 1983. This story of the adventures of a young Boston apprentice during the exciting days leading up to the Revolutionary War is a classic work first published in 1943.

1098. Lawrence, Mildred. Touchmark. Harcourt, 1975. 184 p. ill. $8.
Gr 6-8. SE 44: Oct 1980. Abigail is apprenticed to a pewterer as a servant and companion to his invalid

daughter. The two girls become involved in the revolution.

1099. Leckie, Robert. Forged in Blood. (Americans at War). Signet, 1982. 370 p. Pb $3.
Gr 10+. VOYA 5: Aug 1982. This story of the Gill family provides a good sense of the times in a skillful blend of history and fiction.

1100. Lowrey, Janette S. Six Silver Spoons. (I Can Read History Book). Harper, 1971. 64 p. ill. $10.
Gr 1-2. B 68: Dec 1 1971. B 83: Mar 1 1987. BC 25: Dec 1971. LJ 96: Dec 15 1971. Two children are able to give their mother a birthday present of six silver spoons made by Paul Revere because a warmhearted British soldier helps them smuggle the spoons across enemy lines.

1101. Marko, Katherine McGlade. Away to Fundy Bay. (Walker's American History Series for Young People). Walker, 1985. 145 p. $12. Lib. ed. $12.
Gr 5-9. B 82: Nov 15 1985. SLJ 32: Oct 1985. VOYA 8: Oct 1985. This exciting story, set in Nova Scotia during the Revolutionary War, deals with spies and counterspies and the fear of press gangs. Both Tory and Rebel views are presented.

1102. O'Dell, Scott. Sarah Bishop. Houghton, 1980. 184 p. $9.
Gr 5-9. B 76: May 1 1980. * BC 33: Jun 1980. HB 56: Apr 1980. * SLJ 26: May 1980. Sarah's family, divided between rebel and Tory, died in the Revolution. Fearful, she fled to a wilderness cave and tried to fend for herself. Based on real events.

1103. Pope, E. M. Sherwood Ring. Houghton, 1985. 366 p. ill. Pb $2.
Gr 9+. Metzner [B 54: Jun 1 1958. HB: 34 Apr 1958. +- LJ 83: Jul 1958]. While visiting her ancestral home Peggy meets family ghosts who were involved in the Revolution and solves a mystery.

1104. Rinaldi, Ann. Time Enough for Drums. Holiday, 1986. 249 p. $13.
Gr 6-10. B 82: May 1 1986. BC 39: May 1986. SLJ 32: May 1986. Jemima grows from a spoiled girl to a mature woman during the Revolution.

1105. Wibberley, Leonard. John Treegate's Musket. Farrar, 1959. 188 p. Pb $4.
Gr 4-9. Metzner [B 56: Nov 15 1959. HB 35: Dec 1959. LJ 84: Sep 15 1959]. HB 62: Sep/Oct 1986. One of a classic series on the adventures of the Treegate family at the time of the Revolution. Other titles in the series include Peter Treegate's War, Treegate's Raiders, Leopard's Prey, and The Last Battle.

Foreign Policy–France

1106. Alsop, Susan Mary. Yankees at the Court: First Americans in Paris. Doubleday, 1982. 312 p. ill. $18.
Adult. LJ 107: Apr 1 1982. A lively and reliable account of the efforts of Silas Deane, Benjamin Franklin, Arthur Lee, and John Adams to obtain financial and military assistance from the French government during the Revolution.

Frontier and Pioneer Life–Fiction

1107. Monjo, F.N. Indian Summer. Harper, 1969. 62 p. Pb $3.
Gr 1-3. B 83: Mar 1 1987. LJ 93: Nov 15 1968. There is suspenseful action in this story set on the Kentucky frontier. Father is away fighting the Revolutionary War and a pioneer family must protect itself against the Indians.

Immigration, Mexican–Fiction

1108. Gray, Genevieve. How Far, Filipe? (I Can Read History Book). Harper, 1978. 64 p. ill. $9.
Gr K-3. B 83: Mar 1 1987. BC 31: Jul 1978. SLJ 24: May 1978. Filipe and his beloved burro Filomena are the focus of this story of hardships and joys, based on the true story of migrants to California from Mexico in 1775 under the leadership of Col. Bautista de Anza.

Jewish Americans

1109. Schwartz, Laurens R. Jews and the American Revolution. McFarland, 1987. 20 p. $20.
Gr 10+. +- BR 6: Sep/Oct 1987. - VOYA 11: Apr 1988. A detailed account of the role Haym Solomon and other Jews played in the Revolution.

Military History

1110. Ford, Barbara. Underwater Dig: The Excavation of a Revolutionary War Privateer. Morrow, 1982. 154 p. ill. $8.
Gr 5-9. B 79: Jan 15 1983. HB 59: Feb 1983. SLJ 29: Jan 1983. The "Defense" was a Revolutionary War privateer that sank in 1779 with 100 men aboard. In the 1970s it was raised and restored. This study clarifies how these ships were built.

1111. Stein, R. Conrad. Story of Valley Forge, The. (Cornerstones of Freedom). Childrens Press, 1985. 31 p. ill. $7.
Gr 3-6. +- B 82: Nov 1 1985. SLJ 32: Mar 1986. An engaging introduction to the dire straits of the undersupplied Continental forces at Valley Forge.

1112. Wright, Robert K. Continental Army, The. Army Center of Military History, 1984. 451 p. ill. $15.
Adult. B 81: Mar 15 1985. This account of the birth and development of the American army emphasizes the influence of 18th-century military theorists and includes lineages of every permanent unit of the Continental Army, grouped by states.

Military History–Fiction

1113. Edwards, Sally. George Midgett's War. Scribner, 1985. 144 p. $13.
Gr 4-8. B 81: Jul 1985. SE 50: Apr/May 1986. George and his father smuggle precious supplies to Washington's army at Valley Forge. A story based on actual events.

1114. Haugaard, Erik Christian. Boy's Will, A. Houghton, 1983. 41 p. ill. $9.

Gr 4-7. +- BC 37: Jan 1984. HB 59: Dec 1983. SLJ 30: Feb 1984. A brave Irish boy risks his grandfather's wrath to warn John Paul Jones of a British ambush.

Military Personnel

1115. Bernier, Olivier. Lafayette: Hero of Two Worlds. Dutton, 1983. 320 p. ill. $20.
Adult. +- LJ 108: Nov 1 1983. This readable biography of Lafayette emphasizes his involvement in the American and French Revolutions.

1116. Brandt, Keith. John Paul Jones: Hero of the Seas. Troll, 1983. 48 p. ill. $7. Pb $2.
Gr 3-5. B 80: Sep 1 1983. +- SLJ 30: Oct 1983. This introduction to John Paul Jones emphasizes his youth.

1117. Carmer, Carl. Boy Drummer of Vincennes, The. Harvey House, 1972. Unp. ill. $4.
Gr 3-8. SE 44: Oct 1980. This dramatic poem about the march of George Rogers Clark and his men is enhanced by vivid illustrations.

1118. Clinton, Susan. Story of the Green Mountain Boys, The. (Cornerstones of Freedom). Childrens Press, 1988. 32 p. ill. $11.
Gr 3-6. B 84: May 15 1988. Ethan Allen led the rowdy Green Mountain Boys who became a valued regiment of the Continental Army. Includes illustrations and maps.

1119. Haley, Gale. Jack Jouett's Ride. Viking, 1973. 30 p. ill. $6.
Gr 1-3. B 70: Nov 15 1973. B 83: Mar 1 1987. BC 27: Feb 1974. LJ 98: Nov 15 1973. A simple story of "the Paul Revere of the South" who rode to warn Jefferson and other patriots that the King's Green Dragoons were on the way to capture them.

1120. Holbrook, Stewart. America's Ethan Allen. Houghton, 1949. 96 p. Pb $4.
Gr 4-6. Metzner [B 46: Oct 15 1949. +- HB 25: Nov 1949. LJ 74: Dec 1 1949]. B 82: Sep 15 1985. The dramatic story of the leader of the Green Mountain Boys.

1121. Mollo, John. Uniforms of the American Revolution. Sterling, 1985. 228 p. ill. Pb $7.
Gr 9+. SLJ 32: Nov 1985. Color plates show British, French, German, American, and Indian uniforms plus weapons and flags. The text summarizes the organization of the armies and the conditions under which the uniforms were worn.

1122. Nelson, Paul David. Anthony Wayne: Soldier of the Early Republic. Indiana University Press, 1985. 368 p. ill. $23.
Gr 9+. B 82: Jan 1 1986. LJ 110: Sep 15 1985. A thorough biography of the energetic and charismatic Wayne who led his troops to many victories against the Indians and the British and did much to develop the American army following the Revolution.

Military Personnel–Fiction

1123. Avi. Fighting Ground, The. Lippincott, 1984. 157 p. Lib. ed. $12.
Gr 4-8. B 80: Jun 1 1984. * BC 37: Jun 1984. HB 60: Jun 1984. * SE 49: Apr 1985. SLJ 31: Sep 1984. *

VOYA 7: Feb 1985. * VOYA 8: Dec 1985. The realities of war shatter Jonathan's romantic notions of being a soldier.

1124. Benchley, Nathaniel. George, the Drummer Boy. Harper, 1977. 61 p. ill. $9.
Gr 1-3. B 83: Mar 1 1987. B 73: May 15 1977. BC 31: Sep 1977. An action-filled introduction to the Revolution told through the experiences of a British drummer boy.

1125. Fast, Howard. Hessian, The. Morrow; Dell, 1972, 1980. 192 p. $6.
Gr 7+. SE 47: Apr 1983. A young Hessian soldier seeks aid and safety in a Connecticut town after his regiment is annihilated.

Military Personnel–Women

1126. McGovern, Ann. Secret Soldier: The Story of Deborah Sampson. Scholastic, 1977. Unp. ill. $2.
Gr 4-6. B 82: Sep 15 1985. B 84: Oct 15 1987. The biography of a woman who disguised herself as a man and joined the fight for freedom.

1127. Stevens, Bryna. Deborah Sampson Goes to War. Carolrhoda, 1984. 48 p. ill. $8.
Gr 2-4. +- BC 38: Sep 1984. SLJ 31: Dec 1984. Disguised as a man, Deborah Sampson enlisted as a soldier. This straightforward biography provides a strong sense of time and place.

Politics

1128. Carter, Alden R. Colonies in Revolt. (First Book). Watts, 1988. 96 p. ill. $11.
Gr 6-9. B 85: Dec 1 1988. SLJ 35: Nov 1988. Describes how British colonial policy led to discontent and ends with the battles of Lexington and Concord.

Public Officials

1129. Benjamin Franklin's "Good House:" The Story of Franklin Court, Independence National Historical Park, Philadelphia, Pennsylvania. (National Park Service Handbook). National Park Service, 1982. 64 p. ill. Pb $4.
Gr 9+. B 79: Nov 15 1982. The story of Franklin's home and the family who lived there. This handbook is number 114 of the series.

1130. Aliki. Many Lives of Benjamin Franklin, The. Prentice-Hall, 1977. Unp. ill. $7.
Gr 1-3. B 82: Sep 15 1985. An introduction to the multitalented Franklin.

1131. Bakeless, John. Signers of the Declaration. Houghton, 1969. 300 p. $20. Pb $5.
Gr 9+. B 80: Jun 15 1984. Lengthy essays on the 56 patriots who signed the Declaration of Independence, arranged by states. Includes facsimiles of all signatures.

1132. Clark, Ronald W. Benjamin Franklin. Random House, 1983. 480 p. ill. $23.
Gr 10+. B 79: Dec 15 1982. LJ 108: Jan 15 1983. A mature examination of the life of the quintessential American philosopher-inventor-statesman.

1133. Cousins, Margaret. Ben Franklin of Old Philadelphia. (Landmark Books). Random House, 1952, 1981. 184 p. ill. Pb $3.
Gr 7-8. Metzner [B 49: Jan 1 1953]. A lively account of Franklin's life as inventor, editor, and statesman.

1134. D'Aulaire, Ingri. Benjamin Franklin. Doubleday, 1950. 48 p. ill. $12.
Gr 1-4. Metzner [B 47: Dec 1 1950. LJ 75: Nov 15 1950]. A humorous picture-biography with decorative borders containing Poor Richard's proverbs.

1135. Forbes, Esther. America's Paul Revere. Houghton, 1946. 48 p. ill. $9. Pb $3.
Gr 4-6. Metzner [+- B 43: Nov 15 1946. * HB 22: Nov 1946. LJ 71: Dec 15 1946]. B 82: Sep 15 1985. This sound biography is full of little-known facts supported by excellent illustrations.

1136. Fowler, William M. Baron of Beacon Hill: A Biography of John Hancock. Houghton, 1980. 366 p. ill. $15.
Gr 9+. B 76: Jan 15 1980. LJ 104: Dec 1 1979. The president of the Second Continental Congress was generous in the use of his money to support the Revolution and was "a symbol of moderation and decency."

1137. Franklin, Benjamin. Writings. Library of America, 1987. 1605 p. $30.
Gr 9+. LJ 112: Oct 15 1987. A selection of Franklin's writings, with amplifying notes and index.

1138. Fritz, Jean. What's the Big Idea, Ben Franklin? Putnam/Coward-McCann, 1976. 48 p. ill. $10. Pb $5.
Gr 3-6. B 82: Sep 15 1985. A lively and humorous account of Franklin's life, suitable for reading aloud.

1139. Fritz, Jean. Where Was Patrick Henry on the 29th of May? Putnam/Coward-McCann, 1975. 48 p. ill. $10. Pb $5.
Gr 3-8. B 82: Sep 15 1985. SE 44: Oct 1980. A colorful and human biography of a man devoted to his country.

1140. Gleiter, Jan. Paul Revere. Raintree, 1986. 32 p. ill. $11. Pb $6.
Gr 2-4. SLJ 33: May 1987. Focuses on the early events of the Revolution, Revere's famous ride, and his work with John Hancock and Samuel Adams.

1141. Lee, Martin. Paul Revere. Watts, 1987. 95 p. ill. $10.
Gr 4-7. B 83: May 1 1987. +- SLJ 33: Apr 1987. Good basic coverage of Revere's youth, political activities, and business success.

1142. Mayer, Henry. Son of Thunder: Patrick Henry and the American Revolution. Watts, 1986. 529 p. $23.
Gr 9+. * BR 5: Sep/Oct 1986. * LJ 111: May 1 1986. SLJ 33: Sep 1986. Based on primary sources, a fascinating historical and political interpretation of Henry's life.

1143. Randall, Willard Sterne. Little Revenge: Benjamin Franklin and His Son. Little, 1984. 515 p. ill. $22.
Gr 10+. B 81: Nov 15 1984. LJ 109: Nov 1 1984. Relates the dramatic story of a father and son who chose opposite sides during the revolution.

1144. Reische, Diana. Patrick Henry. (First Book). Watts, 1987. 92 p. ill. $10.
Gr 4-7. B 83: May 1 1987. SLJ 33: Apr 1987. Includes many details and photos in a lively biography that provides a good background on the Revolutionary War.

1145. Sandak, Cass R. Benjamin Franklin. (First Book). Watts, 1986. 66 p. ill. $10.
Gr 5+. B 82: July 1986. BR 5: Nov/Dec 1986. SLJ 33: Sep 1986. A brief but clear coverage of the contributions of Franklin to the Revolution and to the development of the Constitution.

1146. Stevens, Bryna. Ben Franklin's Glass Armonica. (On My Own Books). Carolrhoda, 1983. 47 p. ill. $7.
Gr 2-4. B 79: Mar 15 1983. BC 36: Apr 1983. +- SLJ 29: Apr 1983. Illuminates one of Franklin's little-known inventions, a musical instrument made of spinning glass bowls.

1147. Wright, Esmond. Franklin of Philadelphia. Harvard University Press, 1986. 403 p. ill. $25.
Gr 10+. B 82: Mar 1986. * LJ 111: Mar 15 1986. This evolution of Franklin from "reluctant rebel" to "major engineer" of the peace provides a good sense of the times. Numerous quotes and illustrations explain Franklin as a private man and as a leader.

Public Officials–Fiction

1148. Graves, C. P. Paul Revere: Rider for Liberty. Garrard, 1964. 80 p. ill. $8.
Gr 3-5. Metzner. A simple and entertaining illustrated version of the Paul Revere story.

1149. Lawson, Robert. Ben and Me. Dell, 1973. 113 p. ill. Pb $3.
Gr 4-6. Metzner [B 36: Nov 15 1939. HB 15: Nov 1939. LJ 65: Feb 1 1940]. Amos the mouse reveals the truth that Franklin's maxims and inventions were inspired by him.

1150. Lawson, Robert. Mr. Revere and I. Little, 1982. 152 p. ill. Pb $2.
Gr 4-6. Metzner [B 50: Oct 15 1953. HB 29: Dec 1953. LJ 78: Oct 15 1953]. Revere's haughty British horse tells the story of their famous ride.

1151. Longfellow, Henry Wadsworth. Paul Revere's Ride. Greenwillow, 1985. Unp. ill. $12. Lib. ed. $12.
Gr 2-4. B 81: Mar 1 1985. BC 38: May 1985. HB 61: May/Jun 1985. SLJ 31: Aug 1985. A picture edition of the classic poem.

Slaves and Slavery

1152. Berlin, Ira. Slavery and Freedom in the Age of the American Revolution. (Blacks in the New World). University of Illinois Press, 1986. 314 p. Pb $11.
Gr 10+. +- BR 6: Sep/Oct 1987. Ten essays provide a picture of black life during and after the Revolution.

Slaves and Slavery–Fiction

1153. Collier, James Lincoln. Jump Ship to Freedom. Delacorte, 1981. 198 p. $10.
Gr 6-10. B 78: Oct 1 1981. BC 35: Oct 1981. HB 58: Feb 1982. * SE 46: Apr 1982. SLJ 28: Oct 1981. VOYA 5: June 1982. A story of high adventure in which Daniel tries to retrieve the stolen papers that gave freedom to his father, a former slave who fought in the Revolutionary War.

1154. Collier, James Lincoln. Who Is Carrie? Delacorte, 1984. 160 p. $15.
Gr 5-9. B 80: Apr 1 1984. +- BC 37: May 1984. +- BR 3: Jan/Feb 1985. * SLJ 30: May 1984. VOYA 7: Jun 1984. Kitchen slave Carrie searches for her heritage.

Social Life and Customs–Fiction

1155. Quackenbush, Robert M. Pop! Goes the Weasel and Yankee Doodle. Lippincott, 1976. Unp. ill. $11.
Gr K-3. B 72: Feb 15 1976. B 83: Mar 1 1987. SLJ 22: May 1976. Using the two title songs as a basis, the author contrasts scenes of New York in 1776 to New York today.

1156. Rappaport, Doreen. Boston Coffee Party, The. (I Can Read Book). Harper, 1988. 63 p. ill. $10. Lib. ed. $11.
Gr K-3. B 84: Apr 1 1988. BC 41: Feb 1988. HB 64: Sep/Oct 1988. SLJ 35: May 1988. Based on an actual event. A greedy coffee merchant is set upon by angry women and forced to surrender his hoard. An action-filled story.

Wit and Humor

1157. Adler, David A. Remember Betsy Floss and Other Colonial American Riddles. Holiday, 1987. 64 p. ill. $10.
Gr 2-6. B 84: Sep 15 1987. SLJ 34: Dec 1987. Delightful riddles to familiarize young readers with the founding fathers.

Women

1158. De Pauw, Linda G. Founding Mothers: Women of America in the Revolutionary Era. Houghton, 1975. 228 p. ill. $7.
Gr 6+. B 81: Jul 1985. De Pauw presents a lively account of the previously untold stories of women of all races and social classes who were soldiers, spies, couriers, and political activists.

Women–Biographies

1159. Anticaglia, Elizabeth. Heroines of '76. Walker, 1975. 111 p. ill. $7.
Gr 3-7. BC 29: Feb 1976. SLJ 22: Nov 1975. SE 44: Oct 1980. Slightly fictionalized biographies of 14 women whose involvement in the Revolution included espionage and soldiering.

1783-1815

United States–History–1783-1815

1160. Carter, Alden R. Birth of a Republic. (First Book). Watts, 1988. 96 p. ill. $11.
Gr 4-9. B 85: Dec 1 1988. +- SLJ 35: Nov 1988. Briefly describes the end of the Revolutionary War, the peace treaty, the failures of the Articles of Confederation, and the writing and ratification of the Constitution.

Articles of Confederation

1161. Morris, Richard B. Forging of the Union, 1781-1789. (New American Nation Series). Harper, 1987. 464 p. ill. $25.
Gr 9+. * B 83: Apr 15 1987. LJ 112: Apr 15 1987. Examines the years under the Articles of Confederation and those events that led to the adoption of the Constitution.

Authors

1162. Latham, J. L. Carry On, Mr. Bowditch. Houghton, 1973. 251 p. ill. $13. Pb $6.
Gr 7-9. Metzner [HB 31: Oct 1955. * LJ 80: Nov 15 1955]. A lively biography of a mathematician, sailor, and author, who wrote the classic American Practical Navigator before he was 30.

Blacks–Biographies

1163. Yates, Elizabeth. Amos Fortune, Free Man. Aladdin, 1967. 181 p. ill. $13.
Gr 6-9. Metzner [B 46: May 1 1950. * LJ 75: Apr 15, Jun 15 1950]. An introduction to the life of Amos Fortune, an ex-slave who became a public benefactor and an honored citizen.

California

1164. Barton, Bruce Walter. Tree at the Center of the World: A Story of the California Missions. Ross-Erikson, 1980. 321 p. ill. $20. Pb $10.
Gr 9+. B 76: Nov 15 1980. Examines 21 mission settlements and the changes brought about by priests, brothers, and the soldiers who accompanied them.

Constitution

1165. Anti-Federalist Papers and the Constitutional Covention Debates, The. New American Library/Mentor, 1986. 406 p. Pb $5.
Gr 10+. VOYA 10: Apr 1987. A collection of writings by leaders who favored a less powerful central government than that proposed in the new Constitution.

1166. Federalist Papers, The. Bantam, 1982. 477 p. Pb $3.

Gr 9+. VOYA 10: Apr 1987. A collection of the writings of leaders who favored the proposed Constitution and a strong federal government.

1167. Framing of the Federal Constituion, The. (National Park Services Handbook). National Park Service, 1986. 112 p. ill. Pb $5.
Gr 10+. B 83: Jan 15 1987. Describes the men and events surrounding the creation of the Constitution. Includes reproductions of the original text and the amendments. Number 103 in the series.

1168. Barbash, Fred. Founding: A Dramatic Account of the Writing of the Constitution. Linden, 1987. 247 p. $19.
Gr 9+. B 83: May 15, June 1 1987. LJ 112: Jul 1987. An excellent short account of the deliberations and political considerations of the convention enlivened by details and dialogue based on Madison's copious notes.

1169. Bernstein, Richard B. Are We to Be a Nation? Harvard University Press, 1987. 342 p. ill. $35. Pb $14.
Gr 9+. B 83: Apr 1, Jun 1 1987. LJ 112: Mar 1 1987. A profusely illustrated overview of the stormy years under the Articles of Confederation and the struggle to implement the new Constitution.

1170. Bowen, Catherine Drinker. Miracle at Philadelphia: The Story of the Constitutional Convention, May to September 1787. Little, 1986. 346 p. ill. $19. Pb $9.
Gr 10+. B 83: Jun 1 1987. BR 6: Sep/Oct 1987. Based on diaries, newspapers, and letters, this lively and authentic daily account of the Constitutional Convention portrays the disagreements and frustrations of the delegates and clarifies their personalities.

1171. Collier, Christopher. Decision in Philadelphia: The Constitutional Convention of 1787. Random House and Reader's Digest; dist. by McGraw, 1986. 331 p. $20.
Adult. BR 6: Sep/Oct 1987. LJ 111: May 1 1986. Traces the major issues and personalities of the convention in a popular history based on recent scholarship.

1172. Colman, Warren. Bill of Rights, The. (New True Book). Childrens Press, 1987. 45 p. ill. $12.
Gr 1-4. B 84: Nov 1 1987. SLJ 34: Dec 1987. A straightforward discussion of the first 10 amendments enlivened by illustrations and charts.

1173. Colman, Warren. Constitution, The. (New True Book). Childrens Press, 1987. 45 p. ill. $12.
Gr 2-4. B 84: Nov 1 1987. SLJ 34: Dec 1987. A straightforward coverage of the conception, writing, and ratification of the Constitution, written in simple terms and enlivened by illustrations and charts.

1174. Fritz, Jean. Shh! We're Writing the Constitution. Putnam, 1987. 64 p. ill. $13. Pb $6.
Gr 4-7. * B 83: Jun 1 1987. * BC 40: Jul/Aug 1987. HB 63: Jul/Aug 1987. * SE 52: Apr/May 1988. SLJ 33: Aug 1987. In delightful authoritative detail Fritz explores the differences among the delegates and explains the necessary compromises.

1175. Hauptly, Denis J. Convention of Delegates: The Creation of the Constitution. Atheneum, 1987. 111 p. $13.
Gr 5-9. B 83: Mar 1 1987. HB 63: Jul/Aug 1987. +- SLJ 33: Apr 1987. VOYA 10: Apr 1987. Emphasizes the lives of the leaders of the Constitutional Convention and shows how their experiences shaped their attitudes toward the major issues.

1176. Levy, Elizabeth. If You Were There when They Signed the Constitution. (If You Lived Series). Scholastic, 1987. 79 p. ill. Pb $3.
Gr 2-5. B 84: Sep 15 1987. +- SLJ 34: Nov 1987. Uses a question-and-answer format to present information about the writing of the Constitution.

1177. Lomask, Milton. Spirit of 1787: The Making of Our Constitution. Farrar, 1980. 213 p. $10.
Gr 7+. B 77: Oct 1 1980. BR 6: Sep/Oct 1987. HB 56: Dec 1980. SLJ 27: Jan 1981. A lively account of the arguments, compromises, and outright fights that eventually led to the adoption of the Constitution.

1178. Maestro, Betsy. More Perfect Union: The Story of Our Constitution. Lothrop, 1987. 48 p. ill. $13. Lib. ed. $13
Gr 2-4. B 84: Sep 1 1987. BC 41: Oct 1987. HB 63: Jul/Aug 1987. Clearly and simply explains the need for a stronger government than the Articles of Confederation, the compromises needed to design and ratify the Constitution, and the need for the Bill of Rights.

1179. McPhillips, Martin. Constitutional Convention, The. (Turning Points in American History). Silver Burdett, 1985. 63 p. ill. $14.
Gr 5-7. B 82: May 1 1986. BR 6: Sep/Oct 1987. Concentrates on the deliberations and points of view of the major figures.

1181. Morris, Richard B. Constitution, The. (American History Topic Books). Rev. ed. Lerner, 1985. 69 p. ill. $9.
Gr 4-6. B 82: Mar 1 1986. +- SLJ 32: Mar 1986. Morris' introduction to the Constitution includes comments on the voting rights of women, slaves, Indians and the propertyless. Revised edition.

1182. Morris, Richard B. Founding of the Republic, The. (American History Topic Books). Rev. ed. Lerner, 1985. 64 p. ill. $9.
Gr 4-7. B 82: Mar 1 1986. SLJ 33: Sep 1986. A basic introduction that clarifies the voting status of minorities when the Constitution was adopted.

1183. Morris, Richard B. Witnesses at the Creation: Hamilton, Madison, Jay and the Constitution. Holt, 1985. 279 p. $17.
Gr 9+. B 82: Jan 1 1986. BR 5: May/Jun 1986. * LJ 110: Sep 1 1985. +- VOYA 9: Apr 1986. Focuses on the condition and events that precipitated the writing of the Federalist papers.

1184. Peters, William. More Perfect Union: The Men and Events That Made the Constitution. Crown, 1987. 294 p. $20.
Gr 9+. B 83: Jan 1 1987. * LJ 112: Mar 15 1987. SLJ 34: Oct 1987. An effective use of the proceedings of

the Convention to tell the story of the summer of 1787, the causes of the Convention, and its results.

1185. Pole, J. R. American Constitution, For and Against: The Federalist and Anti-Federalist Papers. Hill and Wang, 1987. 308 p. $20. Pb $8.
Gr 9+. B 83: Mar 1 1987. These selections from the Federalist papers and anti-Federalist writings are intended to clarify the arguments, promote discussion of the issues, and underscore the importance of open discussion of disagreements.

1186. Sgroi, Peter. This Constitution. (First Book). Watts, 1986. 90 p. $10.
Gr 7+. B 82: Jul 1986. BC 40: Sep 1986. +- SLJ 33: Jan 1987. VOYA 9: Dec 1986. A clear introduction to the people and issues behind the creation of this revolutionary document.

1187. Williams, Selma R. Fifty-Five Fathers: The Story of the Constitutional Convention. Dodd, 1970, 1987. 179 p. ill. $12. Pb $5.
Gr 5+. B 83: Mar 1 1987. BR 6: Sep/Oct 1987. A lively narrative of the events that showed a need for the Constitutional Convention and an account of the convention and the events that followed.

Constitution–Fiction

1188. Anderson, Joan. 1787: A Novel. Harcourt/Gulliver, 1987. 208 p. ill. $15.
Gr 6+. +- B 83: May 1 1987. * SE 52: Apr/May 1988. * VOYA 10: Dec 1987. While serving as James Madison's aide 18-year-old Jared Mifflin becomes acquainted with the persons and the issues involved in writing the Constitution.

1189. Blair, Cynthia. Freedom to Dream. Fawcett Juniper, 1987. 139 p. Pb $3.
Gr 7+. * VOYA 10: Oct 1987. Modern-day Katy finds herself transported back to Philadelphia during the writing of the Constitution.

Explorers–Fiction

1190. Kunstler, James Howard. Embarrassment of Riches, An. Doubleday, 1985. 274 p. $16.
Adult. +- B 81: May 15 1985. LJ 110: Jun 1 1985. Samuel and his uncle are sent by President Jefferson to explore the wilderness between the Ohio River and the Gulf of Mexico.

Frontier and Pioneer Life–Children

1191. Anderson, Joan. Pioneer Children of Appalachia. Houghton/Clarion, 1986. 48 p. ill. $14.
Gr 2-7. B 83: Nov 1 1986. +- BC 40: Dec 1986. HB 63: Jan/Feb 1987. * SE 51: Apr/May 1987. SLJ 33: Nov 1986. A photo-essay on life in early 19th-century Appalachia. Photos from the museum at Fort New Salem clarify domestic chores and the necessity for thriftiness.

Frontier and Pioneer Life–Fiction

1192. Fritz, Jean. Cabin Faced West, The. Coward, 1958. 124 p. ill. $9.
Gr 4-7. Metzner [B54: Apr 1 1958. HB 34: Jun 1958. LJ 83: Apr 15 1958]. A homesick little girl on the Pennsylvania frontier enjoys a visit from General Washington.

1193. Herring, Reuben. Fire in the Canebrake. Broadman, 1980. 228 p. $7.
Gr 6+. SLJ 27: Feb 1981. A Kentucky pioneer feels called to become a traveling preacher in an unusual novel that provides interesting information on religious life on the frontier.

1194. Meadowcroft, E. L. By Wagon and Flatboat. Crowell, 1938. 170 p. ill. $12.
Gr 4-7. Metzner [+- B35: Dec 15 1938. HB 15: Jan 1939]. Two families travel by Conestoga and flatboat from Philadelphia to a new home in Losantiville (Cincinnati).

1195. Sanders, Scott R. Bad Man Ballad. Bradbury; dist. by Macmillan, 1986. 241 p. $14.
Gr 7+. B 83: Oct 1 1986. SLJ 33: Oct 1986. Is the 8-foot-tall wild man a fearsome savage or an innocent giant?

1196. Steele, William O. Lone Hunt. Harcourt, 1976. 176 p. ill. Pb $2.
Gr 4-6. Metzner [B 53: Dec 1 1956]. When Yance is allowed to join the men in the hunt he determines to bring in a buffalo or die trying.

Immigration, Irish–Fiction

1197. Rowe, Jack. Brandywine. Watts, 1984. 394 p. $16.
Gr 10+. B 80: Apr 1 1984. VOYA 7: Feb 1985. There is hardship, conflict, and lots of romance in this novel about Irish American "powdermen" at early DuPont chemical plants.

Indentured Servants–Fiction

1198. Lenski, Lois. Bound Girl of Cobble Hill. Lippincott, 1937. 291 p. ill. $17.
Gr 7-9. Metzner [B 35: Nov 1 1938. +- HB 14: Nov 1938. LJ 63: Nov 1938]. This story of an indentured girl in 1789 Connecticut presents a picture of the manners and customs of village life.

Indians of North America–Creek

1199. Chapman, George. Chief William McIntosh: A Man of Two Worlds. Cherokee Publishing Co., 1988. 151 p. ill. Pb $14.
Gr 10+. B 85: Sep 1 1988. LJ 113: Oct 15 1988. Following the Revolutionary War there was great pressure on the Creek Indians to leave their land in the southeast. McIntosh, a Creek chief, wanted to move his people west but was murdered by rebellious tribesmen.

Indians of North America–Fiction

1200. Kavanagh, P. G. Rebel for Good. Bodley Head; dist. by Merrimack, 1985. 189 p. Map. $12.
Gr 7+. B 81: Apr 15 1985. SLJ 32: Oct 1985. This adventure includes authentic detail of the efforts of

Tecumseh, a Shawnee leader, to develop a confederacy of Indian tribes.

1201. O'Dell, Scott. Streams to the River, River to the Sea: A Novel of Sacagawea. Houghton, 1986. 177 p. $15.
Gr 5+. B 82: Mar 15 1986. BC 39: Apr 1986. BR 5: Sep/Oct 1986. HB 62: Sep 1986. * SE 51: Apr 1987. SLJ 32: May 1986. VOYA 9: Jun 1986. Sacajawea, a Shoshone Indian, emerges as a flesh-and-blood person in this account of her early life and her adventure as guide and interpreter to the Lewis and Clark expedition.

Indians of North America–Shawnee

1202. Fleischer, Jane. Tecumseh, Shawnee War Chief. Troll, 1979. 48 p. ill. $5. Pb $2.
Gr 3-7. SLJ 26: Aug 1980. This high interest-low vocabulary biography of Tecumseh includes some fictionalized dialogue and incidents.

Indians of North America–Shoshone

1203. Clark, Ella Elizabeth. Sacagawea of the Lewis and Clark Expedition. University of California Press, 1980. 171 p. map. $11.
Gr 9+. B 77: Sep 1 1980. - LJ 105: Mar 1 1980. Clark carefully examined the explorer's journals and concluded that Sacagawea's legend is inaccurate, but that her actual contributions were considerable.

1204. Jassem, Kate. Sacajawea, Wilderness Guide. Troll, 1979. 48 p. ill. $5. Pb $2.
Gr 3-7. +- BC 33: Nov 1979. SLJ 26: Aug 1980. This high interest-low vocabulary biography of Sacajawea is slightly fictionalized.

Inventions and Inventors

1205. Philip, Cynthia Owen. Robert Fulton: A Biography. Watts, 1985. 384 p. $16.
Gr 9+. B 82: Sep 15 1985. +-BR 5: May/Jun 1986. LJ 110: Aug 1985. This colorful account of the artist and inventor who symbolizes America's role in the technological revolution provides good detail on Fulton's life and the temper of the times.

1206. Quackenbush, Robert M. Watt Got You Started, Mr. Fulton? A Story of James Watt and Robert Fulton. (Inventors). Prentice-Hall, 1982. 32 p. ill. $8.
Gr 4-5. B 78: May 1 1982. +- SLJ 29: Mar 1983. Introduces the basics of the lives of James Watt and Robert Fulton. Fulton used Watt's steam engine as the basis of his steamboat.

Lewis and Clark Expedition

1207. Blumberg, Rhoda. Incredible Journey of Lewis and Clark. Lothrop, 1987. 143 p. ill. $15.
Gr 5-8. * B 84: Jan 1 1988. * BC 41: Jan 1988. HB 64: Mar/Apr 1988. * SE 52: Apr/May 1988. SLJ 34: Dec 1987. A comprehensive chronicle of the expedition that was sent to chart the land and document the people, plants, animals, and geography of the land from the Mississippi to the Pacific.

1208. Hawke, David Freeman. Those Tremendous Mountains: The Story of the Lewis and Clark Expedition. Norton, 1980. 273 p. ill. $13.
Gr 9+. B 76: May 1 1980. LJ 105: Feb 15 1980. SLJ 27: Sep 1980. Jefferson's plans for the expedition, the careful preparation by its leaders, and the remarkable four-year trip, are all covered in a lively account based on primary sources.

1209. McGrath, Patrick. Lewis and Clark Expedition, The. (Turning Points in American History). Silver Burdett, 1985. 64 p. ill. $14. Lib. ed. $11.
Gr 5-8. B 82: May 1 1986. BC 39: Jun 1986. Reveals Jefferson's intent for the expedition, the personalities of the expedition members, and the highlights of this history-making adventure.

Lewis and Clark Expedition–Fiction

1210. Bohner, Charles. Bold Journey: West with Lewis and Clark. Houghton, 1985. 171 p. map. $12.
Gr 5-9. B 82: Sep 1 1985. +- BC 39: Oct 1985. BR 4: Sep/Oct 1985. HB 61: Sep/Oct 1985. SE 50: Apr/May 1986. SLJ 32: Sep 1985. * VOYA 8: Oct 1985. Action centers around Hugh McNeal, the youngest and least known member of the expedition.

Louisiana Purchase

1211. Phelan, Mary Kay. Story of the Louisiana Purchase, The. Crowell, 1979. 149 p. ill. $8. Lib. ed. $8.
Gr 3-8. B 76: Dec 15 1979. BC 33: Feb 1980. HB 56: Feb 1980. * SLJ 26: Apr 1980. A vivid picture of the power struggle that involved Jefferson, Napolean, and others in the negotiations for the huge territory that became the Louisiana Purchase.

1212. Tallant, Robert. Louisiana Purchase. (Landmark Books). Random House, 1952. 183 p. ill. $6.
Gr 5-6. Metzner [LJ 77: Oct 1 1952]. Explains the role of the Louisiana Purchase in the security and growth of the United States.

Military History

1213. Fowler, William M. Jack Tars and Commodores: The American Navy, 1783-1815. Houghton, 1984. 310 p. ill. $18.
Gr 10+. B 80: Jun 1 1984. LJ 109: Jul 1984. A lively account of the heyday of U.S. military sailing history, including combat, logistics, policy, politics, and diplomacy.

National Anthem

1214. Spier, Peter. Star-Spangled Banner. Doubleday, 1973. 52 p. ill. $12.
Gr 5-8. B 83: Mar 1 1987. Recreates the scene that led to the writing of the national anthem and explains its meaning today.

Pioneers–Biographies

1215. Brandt, Keith. Daniel Boone: Frontier Adventures. Troll, 1983. 48 p. ill. $7. Pb $2.

Gr 3-4. B 80: Sep 1 1983. +- SLJ 30: Oct 1983. A fictionalized biography that emphasizes Boone's youth.

1216. Gleiter, Jan. Daniel Boone. Raintree, 1984. 32 p. ill. $11. Pb $7.
Gr 2-6. SLJ 31: May 1985. Boone's love for the wilderness comes through in this brief biography.

1217. Hargrove, Jim. Daniel Boone: Pioneer Trailblazer. (People of Distinction Biographies). Childrens Press, 1985. 124 p. ill. $9.
Gr 5-7. +- SLJ 32: Mar 1986. The clear text presents a balanced picture of Boone's life.

1218. White, S. E. Daniel Boone: Wilderness Scout. Doubleday, 1922, 1976. 308 p. ill. $15.
Gr 7+. Metzner [B 19: Dec 1922]. In an inspiring account of Boone's difficult life, and his adventures with frontiersmen and Indians, White shows the character development of a man who was still trapping furs in Yellowstone at age 80.

Pioneers–Biographies–Fiction

1219. Chambers, Catherine E. Daniel Boone and the Wilderness Road. (Adventures in Frontier America). Troll, 1984. 32 p. ill. $9. Pb $2.
Gr 5-8. +- BR 3: Jan/Feb 1985. +- SLJ 31: Feb 1985. Grandpa Halliday tells his grandchildren about his experiences when he went exploring with Daniel Boone and helped in the settling of Boonesborough, Kentucky.

Pirates–Fiction

1120. Dewey, Ariane. Laffite the Pirate. Greenwillow, 1985. 48 p. ill. $12. Lib. ed. $12.
Gr K-4. B 82: Sep 15 1985. SLJ 32: Nov 1985. A tall-tale adventure based on the life of the legendary pirate.

Politics

1221. Paine, Thomas. Paine and Jefferson on Liberty. (Milestones of Thought). Ungar; dist. by Harper, 1988. 160 p. Pb $8.
Gr 9+. B 84: Aug 1988. A collection of highly quoted works. Jefferson's works include letters to Madison and the Bill for Establishing Freedom of Religion in Virginia. Paine's works include Common Sense and extracts from Rights of Man.

Presidents and Their Families–Adams, John

1222. Akers, Charles W. Abigail Adams: An American Woman. (Library of American Biography). Little, 1980. 173 p. ill. $10.
Gr 9+. B 76: Feb 1 1980. HB 56: Jun 1980. HT 14: Feb 1982. LJ 104: Dec 1 1979. SLJ 26: Apr 1980. Strong-minded and independent, Abigail Adams lamented the new nation's lack of concern for women and pressed for educational opportunities for girls and women. Based on her correspondence.

1223. Brill, Marlene Targ. John Adams: Second President of the United States. (Encyclopedia of Presidents). Childrens Press, 1986. 98 p. ill. $11.

Gr 4-6. B 83: Mar 15 1987. SLJ 33: May 1987. A clearly written biography enlivened by quotes, personal details, and historic context that show Adams' strengths and weaknesses.

1224. Levin, Phyllis Lee. Abigail Adams. St. Martin's, 1987. 492 p. ill. $25.
Gr 9+. B 83: Mar 15 1987. +- LJ 112: Mar 15 1987. A thorough and well-written biography which shows Abigail Adams to have been an active participant in the events of her time.

1225. Santrey, Laurence. John Adams: Brave Patriot. (Easy Biographies Series). Troll, 1986. 48 p. ill. $9. Pb $2.
Gr 3-8. SLJ 33: Sep 1986. This introduction to the life of John Adams emphasizes his youth.

1226. Stefoff, Rebecca. John Adams: Second President of the United States. (Presidents of the United States). Garrett Educational Corp., 1988. 118 p. ill. $13.
Gr 7-9. SLJ 35: Sep 1988. Anecdotes, background material, and illustrations enhance this useful introduction to the life of John Adams.

1227. Withey, Lynne. Dearest Friend: A Life of Abigail Adams. Free Press, 1981. 615 p. $20.
Gr 9+. B 78: Sep 15 1981. LJ 106: Sep 15 1981. Chronicles Abigail Adams' personal life, her contribution to her husband's career, and highlights the momentous events of the time.

Presidents and Their Families–Jefferson

1228. Adler, David A. Thomas Jefferson: Father of Our Democracy: A First Biography. Holiday, 1987. 48 p. ill. $13.
Gr 2-5. B 84: Nov 1 1987. +- BC 41: Jan 1988. +- SLJ 35: May 1988. An articulate and clearly organized biography that makes Jefferson, his strengths, weaknesses, and great accomplishments come alive for the young reader. Includes a chronology.

1229. Bober, Natalie S. Thomas Jefferson: Man on a Mountain. Atheneum, 1988. 235 p. $15.
Gr 7+. B 85: Jan 15 1989. * SLJ 35: Nov 1988. VOYA 11: Oct 1988. This readable biography that shows Jefferson's impressive achievements and complex personality is based on his writings, quotations from contemporaries, documents, and historical data.

1230. Bottorff, William. Thomas Jefferson. (Twayne's U.S. Authors Series). Twayne, 1979. 162 p. $9.
Gr 9+. SLJ 26: Jan 1980. Following a brief biography, Jefferson's writings are examined in order to determine his ideas and attitudes on such subjects as the arts, education, idealism, philosophy, politics, race, revolution, science, and style.

1231. Cunningham, Noble E. In Pursuit of Reason: The Life of Thomas Jefferson. (Southern Biography Series). Louisiana State University Press, 1987. 432 p. ill. $25.
Adult. * B 83: May 1 1987. * LJ 112: May 1 1987. For advanced students, a highly recommended biography that covers Jefferson the man, his politics, presidency, and times.

1232. Fisher, Leonard Everett. Monticello. Holiday, 1988. 64 p. ill. $13.
Gr 4-9. * B 84: Jun 1 1988. BC 41: Jun 1988. SLJ 34: Jun 1988. Monticello was designed by Jefferson and is full of his gadgets. The sense of history is enhanced by the numerous photos and drawings.

1233. Hargrove, Jim. Thomas Jefferson: Third President of the United States. (Encyclopedia of Presidents). Childrens Press, 1986. 98 p. ill. $11.
Gr 4-6. B 83: Mar 15 1987. SLJ 33: May 1987. Crisp writing, anecdotes, and illustrations enhance this biography that places Jefferson in historic context and shows his strengths and weaknesses.

1234. Hilton, Suzanne. World of Young Thomas Jefferson, The. Walker, 1986. 92 p. ill. $14. Lib. ed. $14.
Gr 6-8. BC 39: Jul/Aug 1986. SLJ 32: Aug 1986. This slightly fictionalized biography which emphasizes Jefferson's youth shows the development of his philosophy and provides insight into the social life of the times.

1235. Monjo, F.N. Grand Papa and Ellen Aroon. Holt, 1974. 58 p. ill. $6.
Gr 4-8. SE 44: Oct 1980. An account of Jefferson and his family, as seen through the eyes of his nine-year-old granddaughter, Ellen.

1236. Patterson, Charles. Thomas Jefferson. (First Book). Watts, 1987. 95 p. ill. $10.
Gr 5-8. B 83: May 15 1987. SLJ 33: Jun/Jul 1987. A short, well-organized biography that also includes a great deal of information about historic events that occurred during Jefferson's lifetime.

1237. Sabin, Francene. Young Thomas Jefferson. (Easy Biographies Series). Troll, 1986. 48 p. ill. $9. Pb $2.
Gr 3-8. SLJ 33: Sep 1986. This introduction to the life of Thomas Jefferson emphasizes his youth.

Presidents and Their Families—Madison

1238. Banfield, Susan. James Madison. (First Book). Watts, 1986. 72 p. ill. $10.
Gr 6-10. B 82: Dec 1 1986. BR 5: Nov/Dec 1986. SLJ 33: Nov 1986. Covers Madison's youth and clarifies his role as statesman, diplomat, shaper of the Constitution, and president.

1239. Clinton, Susan. James Madison: Fourth President of the United States. (Encyclopedia of Presidents). Childrens Press, 1986. 98 p. ill. $11.
Gr 4-6. B 83: Mar 15 1987. SLJ 33: May 1987. Anecdotes and illustrations enliven the crisp text which covers Madison's life, his successes and failures. A chronology of U.S. history places him in context.

1240. Leavell, J. Perry. James Madison. (World Leaders Past and Present Series). Chelsea House, 1988. 112 p. ill. $17.
Gr 7-10. B 84: Jul 1988. * BR 7: Sep/Oct 1988. * VOYA 11: Oct 1988. An objective and well-written text and extensive illustrations cover the career of the fourth president whose greatest accomplishment was his constitutional leadership.

1241. Riemer, Neil. James Madison: Creating the American Constitution. (Congressional Quarterly). Congressional Quarterly, 1986. 203 p. Pb $12.
Gr 11+. BR 6: May/Jun 1987. Focuses on Madison's leadership in the development of the Constitution and the Federalist Papers. For advanced students.

1242. Rutland, Robert A. James Madison and the Search for Nationhood. Library of Congress, 1981. 174 p. ill. $18.
Gr 11+. B 78: Mar 15 1982. B 84: Sep 1 1987. This richly illustrated book covers Madison's contributions to American life. It was published in connection with the opening of the new James Madison Memorial Building of the Library of Congress.

1243. Rutland, Robert A. James Madison: The Founding Father. Macmillan, 1987. 271 p. $20.
Gr 9+. B 84: Sep 1 1987. Madison's critical leadership role in the formation of the new nation is clearly presented and his performance as president is explained in terms of his beliefs about the proper role of the president.

Presidents and Their Families—Madison—Fiction

1244. Wilson, Dorothy Clarke. Queen Dolley: A Biographical Novel of the Life and Times of Dolley Madison. Doubleday, 1987. 373 p. $18.
Gr 10+. LJ 112: Jan 1987. Quotations enhance this fictional biography of the charming Dolley.

Presidents and Their Families—Washington

1245. Adler, David A. George Washington: Father of Our Country: A First Biography. Holiday, 1988. 48 p. ill. $13.
Gr 2-5. +- B 85: Dec 1 1988. SLJ 35: Nov 1988. An accurate and simply written biography that uses quotes to help establish Washington's character and provide good background on the times.

1246. Bourne, Miriam Anne. Uncle George Washington and Harriot's Guitar. Putnam/Coward-McCann, 1983. 64 p. ill. $9.
Gr 3-6. +- B 79: Jul 1983. B 82: Sept 15 1985. +- BC 36: Jun 1983. SLJ 29: Aug 1983. A biography of Washington's niece, Harriot, based on family letters.

1247. Brandt, Keith. George Washington. (Venture Into Reading Series). Troll, 1985. 29 p. ill. $8. Pb $2.
Gr 3-5. +- SLJ 32: Mar 1986. This brief biography of Washington is set in large print and enhanced by full-color illustrations.

1248. Bruns, Roger. George Washington. (World Leaders Past and Present Series). Chelsea House, 1987. 116 p. ill. $17.
Gr 7+. B 83: Mar 1 1987. SLJ 33: May 1987. A readable, highly illustrated biography that shows Washington's human side and his development as a leader. Strengthened by numerous quotes.

1249. Ferling, John E. First of Men: A Life of George Washington. University of Tennessee Press, 1988. 584 p. $40.
Adult. * LJ 113: Aug 1988. In this outstanding biography Ferling looks for reasons for Washington's personal and political successes by examining his personality and character.

1250. Fleming, Thomas. First in Their Hearts: A Biography of George Washington. Walker, 1984. 136 p. ill. $12.
Gr 7-9. B 81: Apr 1 1985. A well-documented biography that covers Washington's life from age 11.

1251. Foster, Genevieve. George Washington's World. Scribner, 1941. 348 p. maps. $15.
Gr 5-9. Metzner [B 38: Nov 1 1941. HB 17: Sep 1941. LJ 66: Sep 15 1941]. Describes the cultural and political world in which Washington grew to manhood.

1252. Higginbotham, Don. George Washington and the American Military Tradition. (Mercer University, Macon, Ga., Lamar Memorial Lectures). University of Georgia Press, 1985. 200 p. $17.
Adult. LJ 110: Dec 1985. Explains the basis for Washington's subordination of the military to civilian leadership and his sensitivity to the social values of the new nation. This is number 27 in the lecture series.

1253. Judson, C. I. George Washington. (Beginning to Read Book). Follett, 1951, 1961. 29 p. ill. Pb $2.
Gr 3-6. Metzner. This well-rounded biography of Washington from age eight stresses the youthful habits that were to form the character that made possible his distinguished public career. Provides a good sense of the times.

1254. Kent, Zachary. George Washington. (Encyclopedia of Presidents). Childrens Press, 1986. 98 p. ill. $11.
Gr 4-6. B 83: Mar 15 1987. SLJ 33: May 1987. Places Washington in historic context and shows his strengths and weaknesses. Includes numerous anecdotes, illustrations, and a chronology.

1255. Ketchum, Richard M. World of George Washington, The. American Heritage/Harmony, 1984. 275 p. ill. Pb $16.
Gr 7+. * BR 3: Mar/Apr 1985. The narrative and numerous illustrations make the colonial world come alive and reveal Washington to be a warm person.

1256. McGowen, Tom. George Washington. (First Book). Watts, 1986. 64 p. ill. $10.
Gr 5+. B 82: Jun 15 1986. * BR 5: Nov/Dec 1986. Emphasizes Washington's leadership qualities as a military leader and his unwilling elevation to the presidency.

1257. Meltzer, Milton. George Washington and the Birth of Our Nation. Watts, 1986. 188 p. ill. $13.
Gr 7+. * B 83: Nov 15 1986. BC 40: Dec 1986. BR 5: Jan/Feb 1987. HB 63:Mar/Apr 1987. * SE 51: Apr/May 1987. SLJ 33: Dec 1986. Covers Washington's private and public lives. Includes etchings, maps, and paintings.

1258. Nordham, George Washington. George Washington's Religious Faith. Adams Press, 1986. 62 p. Pb $8.
Gr 7+. BR 6: Nov/Dec 1987. This examination of Washington's religious beliefs also clarifies his diligence in assuring tolerance for all religions.

1259. Schwartz, Barry. George Washington: The Making of an American Symbol. Free Press, 1987. 242 p. ill. $23.
Gr 9+. B 83: Jul 1987. LJ 112: Sep 1 1987. A unique perspective on Washington's moral character and self-deprecating leadership that led to his position as a national hero when the nation desperately needed a leader.

1260. Smith, Kathie Billigslea. George Washington. (Great Americans Series). Messner, 1987. Unp. ill. $8. Pb $3.
Gr 2-5. SLJ 33: Jun/Jul 1987. Important events are highlighted by double-page sketches in this presentation of Washington's personal and political life.

Presidents and Their Families–Washington–Fiction

1261. Blair, Anne Denton. Hurrah for Arthur! A Mount Vernon Birthday Party. Seven Locks Press, 1983. 56 p. ill. $12.
Gr 2-5. SLJ 30: Sep 1983. A mouse-guided tour of Mount Vernon, suitable for reading aloud.

1262. Wilson, Dorothy Clarke. Lady Washington: A Biographical Novel about America's First First Lady. Doubleday, 1984. 376 p. $17.
Gr 9+. B 80: Jun 15 1984. LJ 109: May 15 1984. Colorful detail on the life of the attractive and wealthy widow who encouraged the general and first president.

Public Officials

1263. Bradbury, Pamela. Men of the Constitution. (Great Americans Series). Messner, 1987. Unp. ill. $8. Pb $3.
Gr 2-4. SLJ 34: Mar 1988. This biography of the men involved in writing the Constitution shows the sacrifices they made and the need for secrecy in their deliberation.

1264. Keller, Mollie. Alexander Hamilton. (First Book). Watts, 1986. 72 p. ill. $10.
Gr 5-7. B 83: Sep 1 1986. BC 40: Jan 1987. BR 5: Nov/Dec 1986. SLJ 33: Feb 1987. Hamilton was a poor boy who rose to become an important national leader. This biography deals with his personal and political life.

1265. McGee, Dorothy Horton. Framers of the Constitution. Dodd, 1968, 1987. 394 p. $14.
Gr 7+. B 83: Mar 1 1987. * BR 6: Sep/Oct 1987. Includes biographical sketches of the 55 delegates who framed the Constitution, a chronology of events, 1775-1791, and a summary of the adoption of the Articles of Confederation and the Constitution.

Ships and Shipping

1266. Gruppe, Henry E. Frigates, The. (Seafarers). Time-Life; dist. by Silver Burdett, 1980. 176 p. ill. $11.

Adult. LJ 105: Jan 15 1980. This explanation of the importance of frigates in asserting the power of the nation is enlivened by contemporary pictures and anecdotes.

Ships and Shipping–Fiction

1267. Cabral, Olga. So Proudly She Sailed: Tales of Old Ironsides. Houghton, 1981. 170 p. ill. $9.
Gr 5-9. B 78: Jan 1 1982. *SE 46: Apr 1982. SLJ 28: Jan 1982. In addition to her famous battles in the War of 1812, "Old Ironsides" went on naturalistic expeditions and controlled pirates. This blend of fact and fiction gives a glimpse of national life, 1797-1879.

Slaves and Slavery–Fiction

1268. Alderman, Clifford Lindsey. Rum, Slaves and Molasses. Macmillan, 1972. 127 p. ill. $5.
Gr 7+. B 69: Mar 1 1973. LJ 98: Mar 15 1973. SE 44: Oct 1980. Describes in vivid detail how slaves were captured and sold in exchange for West Indies' molasses that was brought to New England and made into rum that was sold at great profit, creating wealthy New England traders.

1269. Beyer, Audrey W. Dark Venture. Knopf, 1968. 205 p. $5.
Gr 6-10. SE 47: Apr 1983. The human story of the slave trade in the 18th century.

Social Life and Customs

1270. Hilton, Suzanne. We the People: The Way We Were 1783-1793. Westminster, 1981. 205 p. ill. $13.
Gr 6-9. B 78: Mar 1 1982. HB 58: Feb 1982. * SE 46: Apr 1982. SLJ 28: Feb 1982. Anecdotes and personal accounts which reveal home life, education, holidays, courtship and marriage, medical care, and other aspects of post-Revolutionary social history.

1271. Smith, Barbara Clark. After the Revolution: The Smithsonian History of Everyday Life in the 18th Century. Pantheon/National Museum of American History, 1985. 214 p. ill. $25.
Gr 9+. B 82: Nov 1 1985. BR 5: May/Jun 1986. * LJ 110: Nov 1 1985. SLJ 32: Apr 1986. VOYA 9: Jun 1986. This recreation of everyday life in post-Revolutionary America includes numerous illustrations. It provides a social history in the context of political and technological change.

Social Life and Customs–Fiction

1272. Greene, Jacqueline Dembar. Leveller, The. Walker, 1984. 117 p. $13.
Gr 5+. B 80: Jul 1984. - BC 37: Apr 1984. BR 3: Sep/Oct 1984. +- HB 60: Aug 1984. +- SLJ 30: Apr 1984. In a Massachusetts town, Tom Cook took from the rich and gave to the poor. Some thought him a child of

the devil, others thought of him as the Leveller. Based on fact.

Transportation

1273. Dohan, Mary Helen. Mr. Roosevelt's Steamboat. Dodd, 1981. 194 p. ill. $11.
Gr 9+. + LJ 106: Oct 15 1981. SLJ 28: Jan 1982. In 1811 Nicolas Roosevelt built a steamboat to Fulton's design and, with his family, made the first steamboat trip down the Mississippi, facing hostile rivermen, Indians, earthquake, fire, and a fickle river channel.

1274. St. George, Judith. Amazing Voyage of the New Orleans, The. Putnam, 1980. 62 p. $7.
Gr 4-8. B 77: May 1 1980. HB 56: Aug 1980. SLJ 26: Aug 1980. Nicholas Roosevelt, with his wife and newborn son, survived eqrthquake, flood, and Indian attacks as they brought the first steamboat down the Mississippi and changed the course of history.

Tripolitan War, 1801-1805

1275. Stein, R. Conrad. Story of the Barbary Pirates, The. (Cornerstones of Freedom). Childrens Press, 1982. 31 p. ill. $6.
Gr 4-6. B 79: Feb 15 1983. SLJ 29: Mar 1983. Explains how the new U.S. government stopped threats to its shipping.

War of 1812

1276. Marrin, Albert. 1812: The War Nobody Won. Atheneum, 1985. 175 p. ill. $13.
Gr 5-9. B 81: Aug 1985. HB 61: Sep/Oct 1985. SE 50: Apr/May 1986. SLJ 32: Sep 1985. This lively account of the causes and events of the war, told with many anecdotes and intriguing details, clarifies the everyday life and bravery of soldiers and sailors, white and black.

1277. Mitchell, Barbara. Cornstalks and Cannonballs. (On My Own Books). Carolrhoda, 1980. 46 p. ill. $5.
Gr 1-3. * B 76: May 15 1980. +- BC 34: Nov 1980. SLJ 26: May 1980. In 1812 the town of Lewes, Delaware, used a combination of luck and courage to drive away a British warship. Based on fact and legend.

1278. Morris, Richard B. War of 1812, The. (American History Topic Books). Lerner, 1985. 65 p. ill. $9.
Gr 4-7. B 82: Mar 1 1986. SLJ 33: Sep 1986. A simple introduction to the causes and events of the "second war for independence."

XYZ Affair

1279. Stinchcombe, William. XYZ Affair, The. (Contributions in American History). Greenwood, 1981. 216 p. ill. $24.
Adult. LJ 106: Mar 1 1981. The first book completely devoted to the XYZ affair is detailed but readable, covering the politics and personalities involved.

1815-1861

United States–History–1815-1861

1280. Smith, Page. Nation Comes of Age: A People's History of the Ante-bellum Years. (People's History of the United States). McGraw-Hill, 1981. 1231 p. $25.
Gr 9+. B 78: Jan 1 1982. LJ 106: Apr 1 1981. A lively history, based on diaries. Covers national growth and expansion and the development of regional differences because of slavery. Volume 4 of the series.

Blacks

1281. Johnson, Michael P. Black Masters: A Free Family of Color in the Old South. Norton, 1984. 418 p. ill. $23.
Adult. * LJ 109: Sep 1 1984. The struggle and success of black Americans in the antebellum South, and the range of racial relations during and after slavery told through the story of William Ellison and his family.

Blacks–Biographies

1282. Ferris, Jeri. Go Free or Die: A Story About Harriet Tubman. (Carolrhoda Creative Minds Book). Carolrhoda, 1988. 56 p. ill. $10.
Gr 3-6. B 84: Mar 1 1988. +- SLJ 34: Mar 1988. A clear account of Tubman's work with the Underground Railroad that resulted in freedom for over three hundred slaves.

1283. Walker, Juliet E. K. Free Frank: A Black Pioneer on the Antebellum Frontier. University Press of Kentucky, 1983. 240 p. ill. $20.
Adult. * LJ 108: Sep 15 1983. Demonstrates the ingenuity of a remarkable slave who bought freedom for himself and his family and became a successful landholder in Illinois.

California–Gold Rush

1284. Holliday, J. S. World Rushed In: The California Gold Rush Experience. Simon & Schuster, 1981. 559 p. ill. $17.
Gr 9+. B 78: Dec 15 1981. * LJ 106: Nov 15 1981. SLJ 28: Apr 1982. Portrays the day-to-day experience of the miners and their outlook on life. Based on an unpublished diary.

1285. Jackson, Donald Dale. Gold Dust: The Story of the Forty-Niners. Knopf; dist. by Random, 1980. 384 p. ill. $14.
Gr 9+. * B 76: May 1 1980. LJ 107: Mar 15 1980. Masses of contemporary information and personal details about this national mania presented in a well-organized and engrossing style.

1286. Stein, R. Conrad. Story of the Gold at Sutter's Mill, The. (Cornerstones of Freedom). Childrens Press, 1981. 31 p. ill. $6.
Gr 3-5. +- B 78: Feb 15 1982. SLJ 28: Mar 1982. A straightforward account, enlivened by anecdotes and quotes.

California–Gold Rush–Fiction

1287. Bristow, Gwen. Golden Dreams. Lippincott, 1980. 224 p. maps. $12.
Gr 9+. B 76: May 1 1980. +- LJ 105: May 1 1980. +- SLJ 27: Sep 1980. A saga of real-life figures whose lives were changed by the discovery at Sutter's Mill.

1288. Chambers, Catherine E. California Gold Rush: Search for Treasure. (Adventures in Frontier America). Troll, 1984. 32 p. ill. $9. Pb $2.
Gr 3-6. +- BC 38: Oct 1984. +- BR 3: Jan/Feb 1985. SLJ 31: Feb 1985. Through the experiences of one young boy the reader sees the life of the times. Historical fiction at a low reading level.

1289. Kelley, Leo P. Morgan. Doubleday, 1986. 192 p. $13.
Gr 10+. +- LJ 111: Jul 1986. An innocent Connecticut farm boy sets out for the California Gold Rush fields.

1290. Lasky, Kathryn. Beyond the Divide. Macmillan; Dell, 1983. 264 p. $12.
Gr 4-8. * B 79: Jul 1983. BC 36: Jun 1983. * SE 48: May 1984. SLJ 30: Sep 1983. * VOYA 6: Oct 1983. Shunned by their community, an Amish girl and her father join the rush to the California gold fields. Based on true-life accounts.

1291. Searls, Hank. Blood Song. Villard; dist. by Random House, 1984. 335 p. maps. $16.
Gr 9+. B 80: May 1 1984. +- BR 3: Jan/Feb 1985. SLJ 31: Jan 1985. * VOYA 7: Feb 1985. High suspense, romance, and history that comes alive as Bunkie follows her great-grandfather's route to the California Gold Rush.

Educators–Women

1292. Kaufman, Polly Welts. Women Teachers on the Frontier. Yale University Press, 1984. 270 p. $23.
Gr 10+. SLJ 30: Aug 1984. HT 19: Nov 1985. Based on the writings of women who taught in the frontier schools, 1846-1856.

Entertainers

1293. Cross, Helen Reeder. Real Tom Thumb, The. Four Winds, 1980. 92 p. $9.
Gr 4-7. +- B 77: Feb 1 1981. BC 34: Mar 1981. HB 57: Feb 1981. +- SLJ 28: Sep 1981. Cross uses numerous quotations in telling the story of Tom Thumb, a witty, intelligent, and dignified entertainer, and of his friend and promoter, P. T. Barnum.

Fiction

1294. Donahue, Marilyn Cram. Valley in Between. (Walker's American History Series for Young People). Walker, 1987. 203 p. $15. Lib. ed. $16.
Gr 6-10. +- B 84: Nov 1 1987. BC 41: Oct 1987. BR 7: May/Jun 1988. +- SLJ 34: Nov 1987. VOYA 10: Dec 1987. Good historical detail in this sequel to

Straight Along a Crooked Road. Emmie tests her self-reliance amid the tensions of the coming Civil War and the devisiveness of a growing community.

Firearms

1295. Garavaglia, Louis A. Firearms of the American West, 1803-1865. University of New Mexico Press, 1984. 402 p. ill. $35.
Adult. LJ 109: Oct 1 1984. This first of a two-volume study on the use and development of firearms covers their history, 1803-1865. Photos.

1296. Garavaglia, Louis A. Firearms of the American West, 1866-1894. University of New Mexico Press, 1985. 413 p. ill. $40.
Adult. LJ 111: Feb 1 1986. This second of a two-volume study discusses the firearms used in the last half of the 19th century. Includes over five hundred photos.

Foreign Policy–Japan

1297. Blumberg, Rhoda. Commodore Perry in the Land of the Shogun. Lothrop, 1985. 144 p. $13.
Gr 5-8. * B 82: Nov 1 1985. * BC 38: Jul/Aug 1985. * HB 61: Sep/Oct 1985. * SE 50: Apr/May 1986. * SLJ 32: Oct 1985. This story of Perry's voyage explains its economic importance and is sensitive to cultural differences. Based on primary sources.

Foreign Policy–Latin America

1298. Brown, Charles H. Agents of Manifest Destiny: The Lives and Times of the Filibusters. University of North Carolina Press, 1980. 525 p. ill. $25.
Gr 9+. * LJ 105: Jan 15 1980. For advanced readers, a lively account of the businessmen, expansionists, and politicans who actively tried to expand U.S. interests in Mexico, Cuba, and Central America.

Frontier and Pioneer Life

1299. Laycock, George. How the Settlers Lived. McKay. 1980. 113 p. ill. $9.
Gr 4-6. B 77: Sep 1 1980. +- SLJ 27: Mar 1981. This brief outline of the daily lives of 19th-century pioneers includes information on hunting, starting crops, clothing, hygiene, recreation, and the construction of shelter.

1300. McFarland, Gerald. Scattered People: An American Family Moves West. Pantheon, 1985. 235 p. ill. $20.
Gr 9+. B 81: Aug 1985. LJ 110: Sep 15 1985. Five families move west, sharing dreams, disappointments, and hardships. Rich in detail and based on the experiences of the author's ancestors.

1301. Mondy, Robert William. Pioneers and Preachers: Stories of the Old Frontier. Nelson-Hall, 1980. 268 p. ill. $22. Pb $11.
Gr 9+. B 76: Apr 1 1980. LJ 105: Mar 15 1980. SLJ 26: May 1980. Covers the basics of food, shelter, health care, trade, religion, sex, marriage, travel, humor, superstition, table manners, and the importance of neighbors as the frontier moved westward.

Frontier and Pioneer Life–Fiction

1302. Altsheler, J. A. Texan Scouts, The. Appleton, 1913, 1985. 355 p. $19.
Gr 7+. Metzner [B 9: Jun 1913]. Sequel to Texan Star. Continues the adventures of Ned Fulton through the fall of the Alamo and his escape on a schooner bound for New Orleans.

1303. Altsheler, J. A. Texan Star, The. Appleton, 1985. 371 p. $19.
Gr 7+. Metzner. Ned Fulton excapes from a prison in Mexico City and returns to Texas where he helps in the fight for independence.

1304. Altsheler, J. A. Texan Triumph, The. Appleton, 1985. 356 p. $19.
Gr 7+. Metzner [B 10: Feb 1914]. The dramatic story of Ned Fulton's adventures in the San Jacinto campaign that led to Texas' independence.

1305. Anderson, Joan. Joshua's Westward Journal. Morrow, 1987. 48 p. ill. $13. Lib. ed. $13.
Gr 3-7. +- B 84: Dec 15 1987. HB 63: Nov/Dec 1987. +- SLJ 34: Oct 1987. This sequel to Glorious Fourth at Prairietown continues the saga of the Carpenter family as it moves west. Photos are from the Living History Farms in Iowa and the Conner Prairie Pioneer Settlement in Indiana.

1306. Blos, Joan W. Brothers of the Heart: A Story of the Old Northwest, 1837-1838. Scribner, 1985. 162 p. $13.
Gr 4-9. +- B 82: Dec 15 1985. BC 39: Jan 1986. * SE 50: Apr/May 1986. +- SLJ 32: Jan 1986. * VOYA 9: Apr 1986. When Shem is lost during a storm on the Michigan frontier, an Indian woman teaches him survival skills and self-esteem. Based on excerpts and letters.

1307. Booky, Albert R. Son of Manitou. Sunstone, 1987. 152 p. Pb $11.
Gr 6+. * BR 6: Jan/Feb 1988. An accurate and involving story about four persons who discovered their interdependence as they went west.

1308. Chambers, Catherine E. Frontier Dream: Life on the Great Plains. (Adventures in Frontier America). Troll, 1984. 32 p. ill. $9. Pb $2.
Gr 5-8. +- BR 3: Jan/Feb 1985. +- SLJ 31: Jan 1985. A Scandinavian family struggles to make a home on the Dakota plains.

1309. Chambers, Catherine E. Frontier Farmer: Kansas Adventures. (Adventures in Frontier America). Troll, 1984. 32 p. ill. $9. Pb $2.
Gr 5-8. +- BR 3: Jan/Feb 1985. +- SLJ 31: Jan 1985. The efforts of a boy and his mother to prove their claim to a Kansas homestead.

1310. Chambers, Catherine E. Log Cabin Home: Pioneers in the Wilderness. (Adventures in Frontier America). Troll, 1984. 32 p. ill. $9. Pb $2.
Gr 5-8. +- BR 3: Jan/Feb 1985. +- SLJ 31: Feb 1985. The Craley family looks for a new home in the Kentucky hills.

1311. Chambers, Catherine E. Texas Roundup: Life on the Range. (Adventures in Frontier America). Troll, 1984. 32 p. ill. $9. Pb $2.
Gr 5-8. +- BR 3: Jan-Feb 1985. SLJ 31: Feb 1985. Covers everyday life, cattle roundups, dependence on neighbors, and the hardships and joys of life on the Texas frontier.

1312. Conrad, Pamela. Prairie Songs. Harper, 1985. 176 p. ill. $12. Lib. ed. $11.
Gr 4-9. +- B 82: Sep 1 1985. BC 39: Sep 1985. HB 62: Jan/Feb 1986. * SE 50: Apr/May 1986. * SLJ 32: Oct 1985. VOYA 8: Dec 1985. Louisa loves the beauty of the Nebraska prairie and takes its hardships in stride. She befriends the wife of the new doctor from New York City who finds the loneliness of the harsh prairie life more than she can bear.

1313. Field, R. L. Hitty, Her First Hundred Years. Macmillan, 1969. 207 p. ill. $13.
Gr 4-6. Metzner [B 26: Dec 1929]. The changes in American country life as seen through the memoirs of a remarkable doll.

1314. Kirby, Susan E. Ike and Porker. Houghton, 1983. 145 p. $9.
Gr 4-6. +- BC 37: Feb 1984. HB 59: Dec 1983. SLJ 30: Feb 1984. In this realistic picture of life on an Illinois farm in 1837, Ike tries to convince his father that he can be responsible.

1315. Mead, Robert Douglas. Heartland. Doubleday, 1986. 635 p. $23.
Gr 9+. B 82: Mar 15 1986. +- LJ 111: Feb 1 1986. Based on the history of the author's family and of the state of Kansas. The protagonist settles in the new state, hunts buffalo, trades with Indians, and invests in land, railroads, and banks.

1316. Minshull, Evelyn. Cornhusk Doll, The. Herald Press, 1987. 69 p. ill. $15.
Gr 1-4. +- B 83: Aug 1987. SLJ 34: Oct 1987. The trap that had been set for a bear crushed the foot of a passing Indian. Despite the efforts of Mary's family to help him and his daughter the Indian remained distrustful and angry.

1317. Nixon, Joan Lowery. If You Say So, Claude. Warne, 1980. 48 p. ill. $10.
Gr 1-4. B 83: Mar 1 1987. The story of a pioneer couple looking for a new home in the wild west.

1318. Shaw, Janet. Kirsten Saves the Day: A Summer Story. (American Girls Collection). Pleasant, 1988. 67 p. ill. $13. Pb $6.
Gr 3-5. B 85: Sep 15 1988. +- SLJ 35: Oct 1988. After a frightening experience Kirsten grows up a little in this story set in Minnesota in 1854. An appendix provides added information on the clothing, conditions, and customs of the time.

1319. Wallin, Luke. In the Shadow of the Wind. Bradbury, 1984. 216 p. $12.
Gr 7+. +- B 80: Jul 1984. BC 38: Oct 1984. BR 3: Mar/Apr 1985. HB 60: Sep 1984. * SE 49: Apr 1985. SLJ 31: Sep 1984. VOYA 7: Feb 1985. Cultural and territorial conflict result when white settlers with black slaves take over Indian lands in the 1830s.

1320. Wisler, S. Clifton. Raid, The. Dutton, 1985. 120 p. $12.
Gr 5-9. B 82: Feb 15 1986. +- BC 39: Nov 1985. BR 5: May/Jun 1986. +- SLJ 32: Dec 1985. Based on an actual event. Lige tries to protect the cattle on the Texas frontier while he copes with grief and guilt over the brother who was kidnapped by the Indians. Set in 1860.

1321. Yates, Elizabeth. Carolina's Courage. Dutton, 1964. 94 p. ill. $3.
Gr 3-6. SE 44: Oct 1980. Behind their oxen, a family moves from New Hampshire to Nebraska. We see the story through the eyes of Carolina, whose sacrifice of her doll assures their safety.

Frontier and Pioneer Life–Women

1322. Luchetti, Cathy. Women of the West. Antelope Island Press, 1982. 240 p. ill. $25.
Gr 7+. HT 20: Nov 1986. LJ 107: Oct 1 1982. * VOYA 6: Aug 1983. Based on letters and journals of 11 ordinary women, including minority women, who faced loneliness, heavy workloads, illness, and death on the journey west and in their frontier homes. Includes photos.

1323. Riley, Glenda. Frontierswomen: The Iowa Experience. Iowa State University Press, 1981. 211 p. $19.
Adult. LJ 106: Sep 15 1981. A clear and well organized study of the critical role played by ordinary women in the settlement of the West.

Fur Trapping and Trade

1324. Batman, Richard. American Ecclesiastes: The Stories of James Pattie. Harcourt, 1985. 328 p. ill. $23.
Adult. B 81: Jan 15 1985. LJ 110: Feb 1 1985. An objective record of Pattie, a fur trapper in the early 19th century West, whose famed reminiscences are examined.

1325. McClung, Robert M. True Adventures of Grizzly Adams, The. Morrow, 1985. 200 p. ill. $11.
Gr 5-7. B 82: Feb 1 1986. +- BC 39: Dec 85. SLJ 32: Nov 1985. VOYA 8: Dec 1985. A typical frontier hunter–loyal, courageous, occasionally cruel and a liar– Adams loved freedom, but captured animals.

Fur Trapping and Trade–Fiction

1326. Kherdian, David. Bridger: The Story of a Mountain Man. Greenwillow, 1987. 160 p. $12.
Gr 7-10. B 83: Mar 15 1987. +- BC 40: Apr 1987. BR 6: May/Jun 1987. +- SLJ 33: Apr 1987. +- VOYA 10: Jun 1987. Covers two years of Bridger's adventures as a trapper and explorer, including his discovery of the Great Salt Lake in 1824.

1327. McCord, Christian. Across the Shining Mountains. (Frontier Library). Jameson Books; dist. by Kampmann, 1986. 450 p. $16.
Gr 10+. LJ 111: Sep 1 1986. Based on primary sources, a realistic account of a fur trading post in Oregon.

1328. Schultz, J. W. Quest of the Fish-Dog Skin. Houghton; Beaufort Books, 1913, 1985. 218 p. ill. Pb $8.
Gr 6-9. Metzner [B 10: Oct 1913]. Describes the journey of two boys, one white and one Indian, across the mountains in 1861. The Fish-dog skin is the term used for seal skin. The 1985 Beaufort Books reprint contains 139 pages.

Holidays, Patriotic

1329. Anderson, Joan. Glorious Fourth at Prairietown, The. Morrow, 1986. 48 p. ill. $11. Lib. ed. $11.
Gr 2-7. B 82: May 1 1986. BC 39: Apr 1986. HB 62: May/Jun 1986. SLJ 32: May 1986. An Indiana Independence Day celebration, as seen through the eyes of young Joshua. Provides a convincing picture of the time.

Illinois

1330. Stein, R. Conrad. Story of the Chicago Fire, The. (Cornerstones of Freedom). Childrens Press, 1982. 31 p. ill. $6.
Gr 3-6. +- B 78: Jul 1982. +- BC 36: Nov 1982. SLJ 29: Sep 1982. Clarifies the causes of the fire and its high physical and economic toll.

Immigration, British

1331. Blumenthal, Shirley. Coming to America: Immigrants from the British Isles. Delacorte, 1980. 184 p. ill. $10. Pb $3.
Gr 7+. B 77: Oct 15 1980. B 81: Jul 1985. BC 34: Mar 1981. * SE 45: Apr 1981. SLJ 27: Jan 1981. - VOYA 4: Apr 1981. Documents reasons why the British, Welsh, Irish, and Scotch emigrated and their contributions to their new country.

Immigration–Fiction

1332. Cummings, Betty Sue. Now, Ameriky. Atheneum, 1979. 175 p. $9.
Gr 4-9. +- BC 33: Feb 1980. HB 55: Oct 1979. * SE 44: Apr 1980. * SE 47: Apr 1983. +- SLJ 26: Nov 1979. The potato famine forces Brigid to come to America to raise passage money for the rest of her family still in Ireland.

1333. De Mejo, Oscar. Forty-Niner, The. Harper, 1985. 46 p. ill. $12. Lib. ed. $12.
Gr K-4. BC 38: Jul/Aug 1985. SLJ 31: Aug 1985. A Scottish immigrant has many adventures, including gold mining.

1334. Shaw, Janet. Happy Birthday Kirsten! (American Girls Collection). Pleasant, 1987. 58 p. ill. $13. Pb $6.
Gr 3-5. B 84: Apr 1 1988. SLJ 35: May 1988. Since the birth of her baby sister 10-year-old Kirsten, a new immigrant from Sweden, has done many of the household chores, and she eagerly awaits her birthday when she will have the day off and a party.

1335. Shaw, Janet. Kirsten Learns a Lesson: A School Story. (American Girls Collection). Pleasant, 1986. 69 p. ill. $13. Pb $5.
Gr 2-5. B 83: Dec 1 1986. In 1854 Kirsten and her family moved from Sweden to Minnesota. A simple and appealing story of the immigrant experience and of common experiences shared by all growing girls.

1336. Shaw, Janet. Kirsten's Surprise: A Christmas Story. (American Girls Collection). Pleasant, 1986. 62 p. ill. $13. Pb $5.
Gr 2-5. B 83: Dec 1 1986. Kirsten fears that an American Christmas can never be as wonderful as one in Sweden.

1337. Shaw, Janet. Meet Kirsten: An American Girl. (American Girls Collection). Pleasant, 1986. 59 p. ill. $13. Pb $5.
Gr 2-5. B 83: Dec 1 1986. SLJ 33: Nov 1986. A young Swedish girl adjusts to life on the Minnesota plains.

Indians of North America

1338. Hofsinde, Robert. Indian Warriors and Their Weapons. Morrow, 1965. 96 p. ill. $11.
Gr 3-7. Metzner [HB 41: Jun 1965. LJ 90: Apr 15 1965]. Describes Indian weapons, war dress, and fighting techniques of tribes from the Northeast, Midwest, Southwest, and Rocky Mountain areas.

1339. O'Dell, Scott. Island of the Blue Dolphins. Houghton, 1960. 184 p. $10.
Gr 4-8. B 84: Mar 1 1988. * B 56: Apr 1 1960. * HB 36: Apr 1960. * LJ 85: Apr 15 1960. From 1835 to 1853 a young Indian woman who survived a tragedy lived alone on a remote California island. A classic work.

Indians of North America–Captives–Fiction

1340. Hotze, Sollace. Circle Unbroken, A. Clarion, 1988. 224 p. $14.
Gr 6-10. B 85: Sep 1 1988. B 85: Nov 1 1988. +- BC 42: Oct 1988. A captive of the Dakotas from age 10 to 17, Rachel is forced to return to her father who expects her to give up Dakota ways.

1341. Jones, Douglas C. Season of Yellow Leaf. Holt, 1983. 323 p. $16.
Gr 10+. LJ 108: Oct 1 1983. SLJ 30: Nov 1983. Life on the west Texas plains in the years before the Civil War, as seen through the eyes of a white girl who is captured by the Comanche.

Indians of North America–Cherokee

1342. Agnew, Brad. Fort Gibson: Terminal on the Trail of Tears. University of Oklahoma Press, 1980. 274 p. ill. $15.
Adult. LJ 105: Jun 1 1980. Covers the forced removal of the Cherokee nation from their homes in the Southeast to Oklahoma and the aftermath of this tragedy. Includes valuable illustrations and maps.

1343. Ehle, John. Trail of Tears: The Rise and Fall of the Cherokee Nation. Doubleday/Anchor, 1988. 480 p. ill. $20.
Gr 9+. B 85: Nov 15 1988. LJ 113: Oct 1 1988. Although the Cherokee adopted the values of white society, educated their children, spoke English, and developed farms, they were forced to leave their homes and move west. A powerful account based on primary sources.

1344. Foreman, Grant. Sequoyah. University of Oklahoma Press, 1985. 85 p. ill. $4.
Adult. SE 49: May 1985. Reveals the dignity and patience of a great Native American leader who tried to preserve the Indian way of life.

1345. Oppenheim, Joanne. Sequoyah, Cherokee Hero. Troll, 1979. 48 p. ill. $5. Pb $2.
Gr 3-7. BC 33: Nov 1979. SLJ 26: Aug 1980. A high interest-low vocabulary biography, slightly fictionalized.

Indians of North America–Fiction

1346. Eckert, Allan W. Johnny Logan: Shawnee Spy. Little, 1983. 192 p. $13.
Gr 9+. B 80: Sep 1 1983. LJ 108: Oct 15 1983. A novel based on the life of Spemica Lawba (Johnny Logan), the first Indian to be buried with military honors. Provides a vivid picture of frontier history and Shawnee culture.

1347. Price, Joan. Truth Is a Bright Star. Celestial Arts, 1982 143 p. Pb $8.
Gr 5-8. +- BR 1: Nov/Dec 1982. SLJ 29: Nov 1982. VOYA 5: Dec 1982. In the 1830s 13 Hopi children and a young woman were kidnapped by Spanish soldiers and sold into slavery. Based on historic events.

1348. Wisler, G. Clifton. Buffalo Moon. Dutton/Lodestar, 1984. 105 p. $11.
Gr 6-9. B 80: Jun 15 1984. - BC 38: Oct 1984. +- SLJ 31: Nov 1984. VOYA 8: Jun 1985. Unable to accept his father's plans for his future, Willie meets the rugged test of manhood when friendly Comanches invite him to live up to their ways. Prequel to Thunder on the Tennessee.

Indians of North America–Sauk

1349. Oppenheim, Joanne. Black Hawk, Frontier Warrior. Troll, 1979. 48 p. ill. $5. Pb $2.
Gr 3-7. SLJ 26: Aug 1980. A high interest-low vocabulary biography, slightly fictionalized.

Indians of North America–Seminole

1350. Oppenheim, Joanne. Oseceola, Seminole Warrior. Troll, 1979. 48 p. ill. $5. Pb $2.
Gr 3-7. SLJ 26: Aug 1980. A high interest-low vocabulary biography, slightly fictionalized.

Indians of North America–Wars

1351. Hargrove, Jim. Story of the Black Hawk War, The. (Cornerstones of Freedom). Childrens Press, 1986. 31 p. ill. $10.

Gr 3-5. B 82: Jul 1986. - SLJ 33: Jan 1987. Covers the war from the point of view of the Sauk and Fox tribes.

Inventions and Inventors

1352. McCall, Edith. Mississippi Steamboatman. (Walker's American History Series for Young People). Walker, 1986. 115 p. $12.
Gr 5-9. +- BC 39: Mar 1986. BR 5: May/Jun 1986. SLJ 32: Mar 1986. VOYA 9: Apr 1986. About the inventor of the first steamboat that could travel up the Mississippi and Ohio rivers.

1353. Quackenbush, Robert M. Oh, What an Awful Mess! A Story of Charles Goodyear. Prentice-Hall, 1980. 32 p. ill. $8.
Gr 3-4. B 77: Dec 15 1980. +- BC 34: Feb 1981. - SLJ 27: Feb 1981. A humorous look at Goodyear's troubles as he tried to make rubber into a useful product.

Journalists

1354. Maxwell, Alice. Virago! The Story of Anne Newport Royall. McFarland, 1985. 305 p. $20.
Gr 11+. BR 5: May/Jun 1986. Royall was an early investigative journalist who challenged corruption and incompetence. For advanced students.

Judicial Branch and Judges

1355. Stites, Francis N. John Marshall: Defender of the Constitution. (Library of American Biography). Little, 1981. 181 p. $12. Pb $5.
Gr 8+. +- BC 34: May 1981. HB 57: Jun 1981. LJ 105: Dec 1 1980. SLJ 27: Mar 1981. VOYA 4: Apr 1981. An interesting study of the chief justice who established the power of the Supreme Court. Reviews landmark cases.

Labor Unions and Laborers–Fiction

1356. Lord, Athena V. Spirit to Ride the Whirlwind, A. Macmillan, 1981. 205 p. $11.
Gr 4-8. +- B 78: Jan 15 1982. BC 35: Jan 1982. HB 58: Feb 1982. SLJ 28: Nov 1981. * VOYA 5: Jun 1982. At age 12 Binnie went to work in the Massachusetts textile mills where most of the workers were women. Longer hours and lower pay eventually led to her involvement in a dramatic strike. Based on real events.

1357. Marzollo, Jean. Halfway Down Paddy Lane. Dial; Scholastic, 1981, 1984. 165 p. $10. Pb $3.
Gr 7+. B 77: May 1981. +- SLJ 27: May 1981. VOYA 4: Dec 1981. VOYA 8: Jun 1985. A vivid depiction of the life of Irish Catholic factory workers, told through the eyes of 20th-century Kate who finds herself transported back to 1850 New England.

Labor Unions and Laborers–Women

1358. Selden, Bernice. Mill Girls: Lucy Larcom, Harriet Hanson Robinson and Sarah G. Bagley. Atheneum, 1983. 200 p. ill. $11.

Gr 5+. BC 37: Dec 1983. * SE 48: May 1984. +- SLJ 30: Jan 1984. VOYA 7: Jun 1984. Life at the beginning of the Industrial Revolution, and its impact on women and society in general.

Mormons

1359. Mormon Trail: A Study Report. Heritage Conservation and Recreation Service, 1978. 91 p. ill. Pb $4.
Gr 9+. B 76: May 15 1980. Describes the Mormon Trail and associated scenic, historical, recreational, and cultural areas.

1360. Brown, Joseph E. Mormon Trek West, The. Doubleday, 1980. 184 p. ill. $35.
Gr 9+. B 76: Apr 15 1980. LJ 105: Apr 1 1980. Traces the Mormon journey from Illinois to Utah in search of religious freedom.

1361. Jones, Helen. Over the Mormon Trail. Childrens Press, 1963, 1980. 128 p. ill. $11.
Gr 3-6. Metzner. An introduction to the Mormon trek west and the difficulties they faced.

1362. Williams, Barbara. Brigham Young and Me, Clarissa. Doubleday, 1978. 80 p. $7.
Gr 10+. B 75: Oct 15 1978. SE 44: Oct 1980. SLJ 25: Nov 1978. Brigham Young's fifty-first child tells the story of her family.

Nevada–Silver Rush–Fiction

1363. Mooser, Stephen. Orphan Jeb at the Massacree. Knopf, 1984. 87 p. ill. $10.
Gr 5-8. +- B 80: Mar 1 1984. HB 60: Aug 1984. +- SLJ 30: Apr 1984. Abandoned during the 1859-1861 Silver Rush, Jed sets out for Virginia City to find his father.

Overland Journeys to the Pacific

1364. Bloch, Louis M., Jr. Overland to California in 1859: A Guide for Wagon Train Travelers. Bloch, 1983. 64 p. ill. $10.
Gr 5+. B 80: Oct 15 1983. BC 37: Dec 1983. SLJ 30: Jan 1984. Selections from actual guides used by wagon train travelers.

1365. Gorsline, Marie. Pioneers, The. Random House, 1982. 32 p. ill. Lib. ed. $5. Pb $2.
Gr 3-5. +- BC 36: Nov 1982. General information on the westward movement with emphasis on the Oregon Trail.

Overland Journeys to the Pacific–Fiction

1366. Arntson, H. E. Caravan to Oregon. Binfords, 1957. 200 p. ill. $5.
Gr 7-9. Metzner. A story of the journey west by wagon train.

1367. Chambers, Catherine E. Wagons West: Off to Oregon. (Adventures in Frontier America). Troll, 1984. 32 p. ill. $9. Pb $2.

Gr 5-8. +- BR 3: Jan/Feb 1985. +- SLJ 31: Jan 1985. Describes a wagon train journey from Missouri to Oregon. Drawings portray details of daily life.

1368. Coerr, Eleanor. Josefina Story Quilt, The. (I Can Read Book). Harper, 1986. 64 p. ill. $9. Lib. ed. $10.
Gr 1-3. B 82: Mar 15 1986. B 83: Mar 1 1987. BC 39: May 1986. HB 62: Jul/Aug 1986. * SE 51 Apr/May 1987. SLJ 32: May 1986. On her quilt patches Faith records the events of the westward journey, including the adventures of her mischievous hen, Josefina.

1369. Donahue, Marilyn Cram. Straight along a Crooked Road. (Walker's American History Series for Young People). Walker, 1985. 188 p. $13.
Gr 6-9. B 82: Jan 15 1986. BC 39: Nov 1985. SLJ 32: Oct 1985. VOYA 8: Feb 1986. A realistic portrayal of the small events in the overland journeys of most westward migrants.

1370. Harvey, Brett. Cassie's Journey: Going West in the 1860s. Holiday, 1988. 40 p. ill. $13.
Gr 2-5. B 84: May 15 1988. BC 41: Jul 1988. HB 64: Jul/Aug 1988. +- SLJ 34: Aug 1988. This warm picturebook story of a family going to California by wagon train is told by a little girl, using a diary format. Based on actual diaries.

1371. Murrow, Liza Ketchum. West against the Wind. Holiday, 1987. 232 p. map. $14.
Gr 6-9. B 84: Jan 15 1988. BC 41: Dec 1987. HB 64: Jan/Feb 1988. * SLJ 34: Dec 1987. Abby Parker joins a wagon train so she can look for her father in the California gold fields. Morrow's story presents a realistic picture of the brutal journey, told from Abby's point of view.

1372. Parkman, Francis. Oregon Trail. Several editions available, 1849, 1969. Paging varies. maps. $30. Pb $2.
Gr 7+. Metzner. The classic tale of the overland journey to the Pacific by wagon train, based on Parkman's journals. A major work.

1373. Ross, Ann T. Pilgrimage, The. Macmillan, 1987. 304 p. $18.
Gr 10+. LJ 112: Jul 1987. Emma Louise, a courageous and outspoken 12-year-old, and her beautiful sister are a part of the Donner party (1846) and the Whitman mission.

1374. Shub, Elizabeth. White Stallion, The. (Greenwillow Read-Alone Books). Greenwillow, 1982. 46 p. ill. $7. Lib. ed. $7.
Gr 1-3. B 79: Oct 1 1982. B 83: Mar 1 1987. HB 58: Dec 1982. Little Gretchen fell asleep as she was riding on an old mare that was following the wagon train. No one noticed when the mare wandered off to join a herd of wild horses. Based on a real event.

1375. Taylor, Theodore. Walking Up a Rainbow. Delacorte, 1986. 275 p. $15.
Gr 6+. B 82: Jun 15 1986. BC 39: May 1986. BR 5: Mar/Apr 1987. +- SLJ 32: Aug 1986. VOYA 9: Jun 1986. A feisty 14-year-old Iowa orphan engages drovers to help her take 2000 sheep to the California gold fields where she hopes to sell them to pay her father's debts.

Overland Journeys to the Pacific–Women

1376. Schlissel, Lillian. Women's Diaries of the Westward Journey. (Studies in the Life of Women). Schocken, 1982. 262 p. $17. Pb $9.
Gr 9+. B 78: Feb 1 1982. * BR 1: Nov/Dec 1982. HT 20: Nov 1986. LJ 107: Apr 15 1982. SLJ 29: Sep 1982. Examines the covered wagon journey as experienced by women, 1840-1870.

Pioneers–Biographies

1377. Gleiter, Jan. Johnny Appleseed. Raintree, 1986. 32 p. ill. $11. Pb $7.
Gr 2-4. SLJ 33: May 1987. Colorful illustrations enhance the familiar story of John Chapman's trek across the Ohio Valley to plant apple trees.

1378. Gleiter, Jan. Kit Carson. Raintree, 1987. 32 p. ill. $11. Pb $7.
Gr 3-5. +- SLJ 34: Oct 1987. An accurate introduction to the exciting life of a pioneer explorer.

1379. Guild, Thelma S. Kit Carson: A Pattern for Heroes. University of Nebraska Press, 1984. 362 p. ill. $19.
Gr 10+. B 81: Oct 1 1984. LJ 109: Aug 1984. A solid and readable biography of the mountain man, guide, officer, and Indian agent.

1380. Santrey, Laurence. Davy Crockett: Young Pioneer. Troll, 1983. 45 p. ill. $7. Pb $2.
Gr 3-5. B 80: Sep 1 1983. +- SLJ 30: Oct 1983. A slightly fictionalized biography, emphasizing Crockett's youth.

Pioneers–Biographies–Fiction

1381. McCall, Edith. Message from the Mountains. (Walker's American History Series for Young People). Walker, 1985. 122 p. map. $12.
Gr 6-9. BC 39: Dec 1985. SLJ 32: Nov 1985. VOYA 8: Dec 1985. A fictionalized but accurate account of young Kit Carson and his friend Jim, growing up in Franklin, Missouri in 1826.

Presidency and the Executive Branch–Cabinet, Agencies, etc.

1382. McCall, Edith. Mail Riders: Paul Revere to Pony Express. Childrens Press, 1961, 1980. 125 p. ill. $11.
Gr 3-8. Metzner. Introduces the people and processes that moved the mail in our early history.

1383. Stein, R. Conrad. Story of the Pony Express, The. (Cornerstones of Freedom). Childrens Press, 1981. 31 p. ill. $6.
Gr 3-5. +- B 78: Feb 15 1982. SLJ 28: Mar 1982. A straightforward account, enlivened by anecdotes and quotes.

Presidents and Their Families–Adams, John Quincy

1384. Kent, Zachary. John Qunicy Adams: Sixth President of the United States. (Encyclopedia of Presidents). Childrens Press, 1987. 98 p. ill. $15.
Gr 4-8. B 84: Oct 15 1987. SLJ 34: Jan 1988. Covers Adams' 50 years of public service as ambassador, senator, president, and member of the House. Easy to read, with many illustrations quotations, and a chronology.

1385. Shepherd, Jack. Cannibals of the Heart: A Personal Biography of Louisa Catherine and John Quincy Adams. McGraw-Hill, 1981. 438 p. $15.
Gr 10+. B 77: Dec 1 1980. LJ 106: Jan 15 1981. Told primarily from Louisa's point of view, this biography covers the career of John Quincy Adams, but also clarifies the role of women in the 19th century.

Presidents and Their Families–Buchanan

1386. Shelley, Mary Virginia. Harriet Lane: First Lady of the White House. Sutter House, 1980. 48 p. ill. $7.
Gr 3-6. +- SLJ 27: Apr 1981. Covers the contributions of Lane, who served as first lady for her uncle, James Buchanan.

Presidents and Their Families–Fillmore

1387. Casey, Jane Clark. Millard Fillmore: Thirteenth President of the United States. (Encyclopedia of Presidents). Childrens Press, 1988. 100 p. ill. $15.
Gr 4-7. B 84: Aug 1988. A well-rounded biography that includes photos and a chronology.

Presidents and Their Families–Harrison

1388. Fitz-Gerald, Christine Maloney. William Henry Harrison. (Encyclopedia of Presidents). Childrens Press, 1988. 100 p. ill. $15.
Gr 4-7. B 84: May 15 1988. A well-rounded biography that includes photos and a chronology.

Presidents and Their Families–Jackson

1389. Osinski, Alice. Andrew Jackson: Seventh President of the United States. (Encyclopedia of Presidents). Childrens Press, 1987. 98 p. ill. $15.
Gr 4-7. B 84: Oct 15 1987. SLJ 34: Jan 1988. A competent biography of a man of tireless energy, a lawyer, judge, general and president, who believed in states rights and the common people.

1390. Quackenbush, Robert M. Who Let Muddy Boots into the White House? A Story of Andrew Jackson. Prentice-Hall, 1986. 36 p. ill. $12.
Gr 3-6. B 83: Nov 15 1986. BC 40: Sep 1986. SLJ 33: Jan 1987. A humorous, highly illustrated biography.

1391. Remini, Robert V. Andrew Jackson and the Course of American Democracy, 1833-1845. Harper, 1984. 672 p. $28.

Adult. B 80: Mar 1 1984. LJ 109: May 1 1984. SE 49: May 1985. Third and final volume of an authoritative biography.

1392. Sabin, Louis. Andrew Jackson: Frontier Patriot. (Easy Biographies Series). Troll, 1986. 48 p. ill. $9. Pb $2.
Gr 2-5. SLJ 33: Sep 1986. Emphasizes Jackson's youth and major contributions.

1393. Stefoff, Rebecca. Andrew Jackson: Seventh President of the United States. (Presidents of the United States). Garrett Educational Corp., 1988. 119 p. ill. $13.
Gr 5-7. * BR 7: Nov/Dec 1988. SLJ 35: Sep 1988. Anecdotes, background material, and illustrations enhance this useful introduction to Jackson.

Presidents and Their Families–Jackson–Fiction

1394. Davis, Louise Littleton. Snowball Fight in the White House. Westminster, 1974. 63 p. ill. $4.
Gr 3-4. BC 28: Nov 1974. SE 44: Oct 1980. Describes a Christmas party in the Jackson White House. Based on the writings of Mary Donelson.

Presidents and Their Families–Monroe

1395. Bains, Rae. James Monroe: Young Patriot. (Easy Biographies Series). Troll, 1986. 48 p. ill. $9. Pb $2.
Gr 2-5. SLJ 33: Sep 1986. Emphasizes Monroe's youth.

1396. Fitz-Gerald, Christine Maloney. James Monroe: Fifth President of the United States. (Encyclopedia of Presidents). Childrens Press, 1987. 98 p. ill. $15.
Gr 4-8. B 84: Oct 15 1987. SLJ 34: Jan 1988. Covers Monroe's 43 years of public service as soldier, diplomat, governor of Virginia, U.S. senator, secretary of state, secretary of war, and two terms as president. Includes photos, letters, and news articles.

Presidents and Their Families–Polk

1397. Lillegard, Dee. James K. Polk: Eleventh President of the United States. (Encyclopedia of Presidents). Childrens Press, 1988. 100 p. ill. $15.
Gr 4-7. B 84: Aug 1988. A readable biography which includes a chronology that places Polk in the context of U.S. history. Illustrated by photos and engravings.

Presidents and Their Families–Taylor

1398. Kent, Zachary. Zachary Taylor: Twelfth President of the United States. (Encyclopedia of Presidents). Childrens Press, 1988. 100 p. ill. $15.
Gr 4-7. B 84: Aug 1988. A readable biography which includes a chronology that places Taylor in the context of U.S. history. Illustrated by photos and engravings.

Presidents and Their Families–Tyler

1399. Lillegard, Dee. John Tyler. (Encyclopedia of Presidents). Childrens Press, 1988. 100 p. ill. $15.

Gr 4-7. B 84: May 15 1988. A readable biography which includes a chronology that places Tyler in the context of U.S. history. Illustrated by photos and engravings.

Presidents and Their Families–Van Buren

1400. Hargrove, Jim. Martin Van Buren. (Encyclopedia of Presidents). Childrens Press, 1988. 100 p. ill. $15.
Gr 4-7. B 84: May 15 1988. A well-rounded biography that includes photos and a chronology.

Public Officials

1401. Fritz, Jean. Make Way for Sam Houston. Putnam, 1986. 109 p. ill. $13. Pb $5.
Gr 4-8. * B 82: Jun 1 1986. BC 39: May 1986. HB 62: May/Jun 1986. * SLJ 32: May 1986. VOYA 9: Jun 1986. A lively account, with details and quotations. Houston was president of the Republic, as well as governor and senator of the state of Texas.

1402. Webb, W.P. Story of the Texas Rangers, The. Grosset, 1971. 160 p. ill. $13.
Gr 7+. Metzner [* LJ 82: May 15 1957]. An authoritative and readable account of the Texas Rangers, written for students by an expert on Texas and the Texas Rangers. Illustrated.

Reformers

1403. DeGering, Etta. Gallaudet: Friend of the Deaf. McKay, 1982. 192 p. ill. $6.
Gr 6-8. Metzner [HB 41: Apr 1965. LJ 89: Sep 15 1964]. This biography of an advocate of a normal life and education for the deaf is well researched and moves quickly.

1404. Neimark, Anne E. Deaf Child Listened: Thomas Gallaudet, Pioneer in American Education. Morrow, 1983. 116 p. $8.
Gr 6-9. B 79: Aug 1983. BC 36: Jun 1983. * SE 48: May 1984. SLJ 30: Sep 1983. Based on letters and diaries. Society believed that the deaf were also retarded, but a shy man sought ways for them to communicate and receive education.

1405. Stewart, James Brewer. Wendell Phillips: Liberty's Hero. Louisiana State University Press, 1986. 350 p. ill. $35.
Adult. LJ 111: Jul 1986. A leading abolitionist, Phillips also fought for free labor, women's rights, and black suffrage.

Reformers–Black

1406. Huggins, Nathan Irvin. Slave and Citizen: The Life of Frederick Douglass. (Library of American Biography). Little, 1980. 194 p. $10. Pb $5.
Gr 9+. B 76: Apr 1 1980. HT 15: Feb 1982. LJ 105: Mar 15 1980. An insightful examination of Douglass' life, and of the complexities of abolitionist thought and black freedom.

1407. McKissack, Patricia. Frederick Douglass: The Black Lion. (People of Distinction Biographies). Childrens Press, 1987. 136 p. ill. $12.
Gr 4-6. B 84: Nov 1 1987. A balanced biography that presents the high points and tragedies in the life of this accomplished leader in the anti-slavery movement.

1408. Miller, Douglas T. Frederick Douglass and the Fight for Freedom. (Makers of America). Facts on File, 1988. 152 p. ill. $16.
Gr 7+. B 85: Nov 1 1988. * SLJ 35: Oct 1988. This balanced and fast-paced biography includes numerous quotes from Douglass' writings, and covers his experience as a slave, abolitionist leader, and author.

1409. Russell, Sharman Apt. Frederick Douglass. (Black Americans of Achievement). Chelsea House, 1987. 110 p. ill. $17.
Gr 6-10. B 84: Feb 1 1988. SLJ 34: Jun/Jul 1988. This useful biography, based on Douglass' writings, covers his personal and political life. Includes photos.

1410. Santrey, Laurence. Young Frederick Douglass: Fight for Freedom. Troll, 1983. 48 p. ill. $7. Pb $2.
Gr 3-5. B 80: Sep 1 1983. +- SLJ 30: Oct 1983. A slightly fictionalized biography of Douglass emphasizing his youth.

Reformers–Women

1411. Scott, John Anthony. Woman against Slavery: The Story of Harriet Beecher Stowe. Crowell, 1978. 169 p. $8.
Gr 10+. B 74: May 1 1978. HB 54: Aug 1978. SE 44: Oct 1980. Shows the influence of family and friends on Stowe's involvement in the anti-slavery movement.

1412. Slater, Abby. In Search of Margaret Fuller. Delacorte, 1978. 215 p. $8.
Gr 7+. B 74: Apr 1 1978. SE 44: Oct 1980. A brilliant, ambitious writer and reformer, Fuller worked tirelessly in social causes of the early 19th century.

Santa Fe Trail

1413. Simmons, Mark. Along the Santa Fe Trail. University of New Mexico Press, 1986. 184 p. ill. $30. Pb $20.
Gr 10+. * BR 5: Mar/Apr 1987. The author recreates the hardships of the wagon train journey on the Santa Fe Trail. Carefully researched and supported by excellent photos.

Santa Fe Trail–Fiction

1414. Holling, H. C. Tree in the Trail. Houghton, 1942. 63 p. ill. $16.
Gr 4-7. Metzner [- B 39: Jan 15 1943. HB 19: Jan 1943. LJ 68: Jan 15 1943]. The story of a symbolic landmark along the Santa Fe Trail.

Ships and Shipping

1415. Stein, R. Conrad. Story of Mississippi Steamboats, The. (Cornerstones of Freedom). Childrens Press, 1987. 30 p. ill. $10.

Gr 3-6. B 84: Oct 15 1987. BC 41: Dec 1987. +- SLJ 34: Jan 1988. An introduction to the glamour and danger of steamboat travel and to the challenges of being a steamboat pilot.

1416. Stein, R. Conrad. Story of the Clipper Ships, The. (Cornerstones of Freedom). Childrens Press, 1981. 31 p. ill. $6.
Gr 3-4. SLJ 28: Mar 1982. Clarifies the importance of shipping to the history and economic development of the U.S. through interesting detail. Slightly fictionalized.

1417. Whipple, A. B. C., & Time-Life Books. Clipper Ships, The. (Seafarers). Time-Life; dist. by Silver Burdett, 1980. 176 p. ill. $11.
Gr 9+. LJ 105: Jul 1980. Combines fact and lore in a readable book with numerous photos.

Ships and Shipping–Fiction

1418. Lewis, Thomas P. Clipper Ship. (I Can Read History Book). Harper, 1978. 64 p. ill. $9.
Gr 1-3. B 83: Mar 1 1987. HB 54: Aug 1978. +- SLJ 25: Sep 1978. The experiences of actual clipper ship passengers are told in this story of the Murdock family on their way to the California gold fields.

1419. Stevenson, Janet. Departure. Harcourt, 1985. 280 p. $18.
Adult. B 81: Apr 15 1985. * LJ 110: Apr 1 1985. In 1851 the sailing captain's wife finds herself the only one able to navigate their way across the Pacific.

Slaves and Slavery

1420. Bisson, Terry. Nat Turner. (Black Americans of Achievement). Chelsea House, 1988. 111 p. ill. $17.
Gr 7-10. B 84: Aug 1988. This biography of the man who led a slave rebellion in 1831 shows the horrors of slavery and the results of the ill-fated rebellion.

1421. Blockson, Charles. Underground Railroad, The. Prentice-Hall, 1987. 260 p. $19.
Gr 9+. B 84: Nov 1 1987. LJ 112: Nov 15 1987. First-person accounts of 47 blacks who survived the dangers of the Underground Railroad.

1422. Hamilton, Virginia. Anthony Burns: The Defeat and Triumph of a Fugitive Slave. Knopf, 1988. 193 p. $12.
Gr 7+. +- B 84: Jun 1 1988. BC 41: Jun 1988. * HB 64: Sep/Oct 1988. VOYA 11: Oct 1988. The gripping biography of a slave who escaped to freedom but was returned to slavery under the Fugitive Slave Act. He taught himself to read and write, obtained freedom, and realized his dream of becoming a preacher.

1423. Stein, R. Conrad. Story of the Underground Railroad, The. (Cornerstones of Freedom). Childrens Press, 1981. 31 p. ill. $6.
Gr 3-5. +- B 78: Feb 15 1982. SLJ 28: Mar 1982. A straightforward account, enlivened by anecdotes and quotes.

Slaves and Slavery–Fiction

1424. Cheatham, K. Follis. Bring Home the Ghost. Harcourt, 1980. 288 p. $9.
Gr 9+. BC 34: Jan 1981. HB 57: Feb 1981. SLJ 27: Nov 1980. VOYA 3: Feb 1981. After his father's death, Tolin, the son of the plantation owner, and his slave Jason head west. Jason is set free but is in danger from bounty hunters. A strong story with vivid characterizations.

1425. Clark, Margaret Goff. Freedom Crossing. Scholastic, 1980. 164 p. Pb $2.
Gr 5-7. +- SLJ 27: Nov 1980. Laura understands why her relatives regard slavery as an economic necessity and is troubled by her family's involvement with the Underground Railroad.

1426. Fox, Paula. Slave Dancer. Bradbury; Dell, 1973, 1975. 127 p. $12. Pb $3.
Gr 5-8. B 80: Sep 1 1983. SE 47: Apr 1983. Kidnapped by the crew of a slave ship, a 13-year-old boy discovers that he is to play music for the exercise periods of the human cargo. A realistic and moving novel.

1427. Franchere, Ruth. Hannah Herself. Crowell, 1977. 176 p. Pb $2.
Gr 6-8. SE 47: Apr 1983. Metzner. [HB 40: Apr 1964. LJ 89: Mar 15 1964.] Hannah's brother-in-law is accused of harboring runaway slaves at his 1830s rural Illinois boarding school.

1428. Fritz, Jean. Brady. Coward, 1960. 223 p. ill. $8.
Gr 4-8. Metzner [B 57: Jan 15 1961. HB 36: Dec 1960. LJ 85: Sep 15 1960]. A boy learns to keep a secret about the Underground Railroad.

1429. Howe, Fanny. White Slave, The. Avon, 1980. 309 p. Pb $5.
Gr 9+. SLJ 27: Sep 1980. Based on the true story of an illegitimate white boy who was raised as the son of a slave.

1430. Lester, Julius. This Strange New Feeling. Dial, 1982. 151 p. $11.
Gr 6+. B 78: Apr 15 1982. BC 35: May 1982. HB 58: Aug 1982. * SE 47: Apr 1983. SLJ 28: Apr 1982. VOYA 5: Oct 1982. The love stories of three slave couples and their struggles for freedom. Based on true stories.

1431. Stowe, Harriet Beecher. Uncle Tom's Cabin. Available in several editions, 1847. 480 p. $15. Pb $3.
Gr 6+. Metzner. A significant abolitionist document, this novel delineates the horrible conditions of slavery.

1432. Turner, Ann. Nettie's Trip South. Macmillan, 1987. 30 p. ill. $12.
Gr 3-6. B 83: Aug 1987. HB 63: Jul/Aug 1987. SLJ 33: Aug 1987. A vivid story of a 10-year-old girl who visited in the South and saw slavery as it really was.

Slaves and Slavery–Women

1433. Bains, Rae. Harriet Tubman: The Road to Freedom. Troll, 1982. 48 p. ill. $7. Pb $2.
Gr 3-6. B 82: Sep 15 1985. A brief introduction to the many faceted life of Tubman, who escaped from slavery and led others to freedom by way of the Underground Railroad. Enhanced by full-page drawings.

1434. Petry, Ann. Harriet Tubman: Conductor on the Underground Railroad. Doubleday, 1980. 247 p. Pb $2.
Gr 7-11. Metzner [HB 31: Oct 1955. * LJ 80: Sep 15 1955]. A well-written objective biography that notes the childhood influences that made Harriet into a crusader who led over 300 slaves to freedom.

1435. White, Deborah Gray. Ar'n't I a Woman? Female Slaves in the Plantation South. Norton, 1985. 182 p. $19.
Gr 9+. B 82: Nov 15 1985. +- LJ 110: Nov 15 1985. Debunks the Mammy and Jezebel myths and examines the degrading plight of slave women who suffered from both racism and sexism. Also explores the slave woman's daily life, occupations, role, and friendships.

Social Life and Customs

1436. Anderson, Joan. Christmas on the Prairie. Clarion; dist. by Ticknor & Fields, 1985. 44 p. ill. $14.
Gr 2-5. B 82: Nov 15 1985. BC 39: Nov 1985. +- BR 4: Mar/Apr 1986. SE 50: Apr/May 1986. SLJ 32: Dec 1985. Photographed at the Conner Prairie Pioneer Settlement near Noblesville, Indiana, this shows Christmas as it was celebrated in Indiana in the early 1800s.

1437. Costabel, Eva Deutsch. New England Village, A. Atheneum, 1983. 48 p. ill. $12.
Gr K-6. BC 37: Sep 1983. * SE 48: May 1984. SLJ 29: Apr 1983. Drawings and text present life in New England in the 19th century.

1438. dePaola, Tomie. Early American Christmas. Holiday, 1987. 32 p. ill. $15.
Gr K-3. * B 84: Sep 1 1987. +- BC 41: Nov 1987. HB 63: Nov/Dec 1987. * SE 52: Apr/May 1988. SLJ 34: Oct 1987. Shows the growth of Christmas customs among early Americans. Illustrated by the author.

1439. Henry, Joanne Landers. Log Cabin in the Woods: A True Story about a Pioneer Boy. Macmillan/Four Winds, 1988. 60 p. ill. $13.
Gr 3-6. +- B 84: Jul 1988. SLJ 34: Aug 1988. A month-by-month account of the life of a frontier family, based on the memoirs of 11-year-old Oliver who assumed almost adult responsibilities. Suitable for reading aloud to younger students.

1440. Smith, Daniel Black. Inside the Great House: Planter Family Life in Eighteenth-Century Chesapeake Society. Cornell University Press, 1980. 368 p. ill. $25.
Adult. SE 50: Apr/May 1986. This study of plantation family life in the Chesapeake area examines the relationships between parents and children.

Social Life and Customs–Children

1441. Censer, Jane Turner. North Carolina Planters and Their Children, 1800-1860. Louisiana State University Press, 1984. 361 p. $20.
Adult. LJ 109: Apr 1 1984. SE 50: Apr/May 1986. Traces one generation of planters from childhood through adulthood.

1442. Longmate, Elizabeth. Children at Work, 1830-1885. (Then and There Series). Longman, 1981. 96 p. ill. Pb $5.
Gr 7+. SE 46: May 1982. The realities of child labor on farms, and in mines, factories, and domestic service.

Social Life and Customs–Fiction

1443. Blos, Joan W. Gathering of Days: A New England Girl's Journal, 1830-1832. Scribner, 1979. 144 p. $8.
Gr 5-7. B 76: Dec 1979. BC 33: Apr 1980. HB 56: Apr 1980. * SE 44: Apr 1980. SLJ 26: Nov 1979. Written as a journal, and based on records from New Hampshire communities, this records Catherine's thirteenth year in which her best friend dies, her father remarries, and she breaks the law by assisting a runaway slave.

1444. Chambers, Catherine E. Flatboats on the Ohio. (Adventures in Frontier America). Troll, 1984. 32 p. ill. $9. Pb $2.
Gr 5-8. +- BR 3: Jan/Feb 1985. +- SLJ Feb 1985. The Craley family moves from Virginia to Kentucky searching for a new home.

1445. Chambers, Catherine E. Frontier Village: A Town Is Born. (Adventures in Frontier America). Troll, 1984. 32 p. ill. $9. Pb $2.
Gr 5-8. +- BR 3: Jan/Feb 1985. +- SLJ 31: Jan 1985. Follows the development of a small Wisconsin town over a four-year period.

1446. Chambers, Catherine E. Indiana Days: Life in a Frontier Town. (Adventures in Frontier America). Troll, 1985. 32 p. ill. $9. Pb $2.
Gr 5-8. +- BR 3: Jan/Feb 1985. SLJ 31: Feb 1985. In telling the story of Kristi, who must leave the Iowa frontier to be educated in Indiana, the author presents a clear picture of life in the 1840s.

1447. Levin, Betty. Keeping-Room, The. Greenwillow, 1981 256 p. $9.
Gr 6+. B 77: Jan 1 1981. BC 34: Apr 1981. HB 57: Apr 1981. * SE 46: Apr 1982. SLJ 27 May 1981. VOYA 4: Aug 1981. Hal's research leads to the discovery of the bones of Hannah, who died in 1838. A complex and well-written story, full of detail of 19th-century life.

1448. Nixon, Joan Lowery. Caught in the Act. (Orphan Train Quartet Series). Bantam, 1988. 160 p. $14.
Gr 4-8. +- B 84: Jun 1 1988. +- BC 41: Apr 1988. * BR 6: Mar/Apr 1988. HB 64: Mar/Apr 1988. +- SLJ 34: Aug 1988. +- VOYA 11: Aug 1988. Eleven-year-old Mike was one of the orphans sent from New York City to work on a Missouri farm to earn his living. Suspected of dishonesty and mistreated, he ran away to find his sister, Marta. Second in the series.

1449. Nixon, Joan Lowery. Family Apart, A. (Orphan Train Quartet Series). Bantam, 1987. 176 p. $14.
Gr 4-8. B 84: Sep 15 1987. +- BC 41: Oct 1987. BR 6: Nov/Dec 1987. HB 64: Mar/Apr 1988. SLJ 34: Nov 1987. * VOYA 10: Oct 1987. Based on the work of the Children's Aid Society that sent over 100,000 New York orphans to homes in the west, this is the story of Frances whose Missouri adoptive family was involved with the Underground Railroad.

1450. Nixon, Joan Lowery. In the Face of Danger. (Orphan Train Quartet Series). Bantam, 1988. 151 p. $14.
Gr 5-8. * BR 7: Nov/Dec 1988. VOYA 11: Dec 1988. Twelve-year-old Megan tries to adjust to life on the Kansas prairie with her new foster parents. They are kind to her, but she can't help feeling that she causes bad luck, just as the gypsy said.

1451. Olson, Arielle North. Lighthouse Keeper's Daughter. Little, 1987. 32 p. ill. $15.
Gr K-3. B 84: Dec 1 1987. BC 41: Nov 1987. HB 64: Jan 1988. SLJ 34: Oct 1987. A fictionalized account of a young girl who kept the lighthouse lamps burning during a lengthy storm while her father was away. Based on a real event.

1452. Roop, Peter. Keep the Lights Burning, Abbie. (On My Own Books). Carolrhoda, 1985. 40 p. ill. $9.
Gr 1-3. * B 82: Jan 15 1986. B 83: Mar 1 1987. +- BC 39: Jan 1986. SLJ 32: May 1986. Based on the true story of young Abbie's efforts, during a terrible four-week storm, to keep the lighthouse oil lamps burning, and care for her sisters and bedridden mother.

1453. Twain, Mark. Adventures of Huckleberry Finn. Available in several editions, 1884. Paging varies. Price varies by edition.
Gr 6+. Metzner. Huck Finn runs away with an escaped slave and makes a long trip on a raft down the Mississippi River.

Technology and Civilization

1454. Macaulay, David. Mill. Houghton, 1983. 128 p. ill. $15.
Gr 4+. * B 80: Oct 1 1983. * BC 37: Nov 1983. BR 2: Jan/Feb 1984. HB 59: Dec 1983. * SE 48: May 1984. * SLJ 30: Oct 1983. Magnificent details of the construction of a Rhode Island spinning mill. Provides excellent information on 19th-century technology, in addition to social and political history. Suitable for all ages.

Texas

1455. Fisher, Leonard Everett. Alamo, The. Holiday, 1987. 64 p. ill. $13.
Gr 4-8. B 83: May 15 1987. BC 40: Jun 1987. HB 63: Jul/Aug 1987. * SLJ 33: Jun/Jul 1987. A concise explanation of the reasons why the Texans wanted independence from Mexico and an account of the tragedy at the Alamo and the events that followed.

1456. Kerr, Rita. Juan Seguin: A Hero of Texas. Eakin Press, 1985. 54 p. $7.
Gr 4-6. +- SLJ 32: Mar 1986. This Hispanic hero befriended Americans in their efforts to free Texas from Mexico.

1457. Stein, R. Conrad. Story of the Lone Star Republic, The. (Cornerstones of Freedom). Childrens Press, 1988. 32 p. ill. $12.
Gr 3-8. B 84: Aug 1988. SLJ 35: Sep 1988. Traces Texas history from the battle of the Alamo to statehood.

Texas–Fiction

1458. King, C. Richard. Birthday in Texas, A. Shoal Creek, 1980. 60 p. ill. $7.
Gr 3-5. +- SLJ 28: Mar 1982. The life of Catherine, a 10-year-old Texan, is disrupted by the War for Independence when her father goes to fight and Santa Anna's troops attack the plantation.

1459. Milligan, Bryce. With the Wind, Kevin Dolan: A Novel of Ireland and Texas. Corona, 1987. 193 p. ill. $16.
Gr 5-7. B 83: Aug 1987. +- SLJ 34: Sep 1987. Leaving Ireland in the 1830s, Kevin and Tom moved to Texas where they settled in the new territory. The story closes on the eve of the Texas revolution.

Transportation

1460. Boyer, Edward. River and Canal. Holiday, 1986. 48 p. ill. $12.
Gr 5-8. B 82: Jul 1986. BC 39: May 1986. HB 62: Jul 1986. SLJ 33: Sep 1986. An introduction to the design, construction, and operation of canals in the eastern U.S.

1461. Kytle, Elizabeth. Home on the Canal. Seven Locks, 1983. 244 p. ill. $15.
Adult. LJ 108: Mar 15 1983. An informal and affectionate history of the Chesapeake and Ohio Canal. Based on interviews with canal workers.

1462. McCall, Edith. Pioneers on Early Waterways: Davey Crockett to Mark Twain. Childrens Press, 1961, 1980. 127 p. ill. $11.
Gr 3-8. Metzner. Explains the importance of waterways in the westward movement.

1463. McCall, Edith. Steamboats to the West. Childrens Press, 1959, 1980. 43 p. ill. $11.
Gr 3-7. Metzner. An illustrated introduction to the role of steamboats in our history.

1464. Rickard, Graham. Canals. (Topics). Watts/Bookwright Press, 1988. 32 p. ill. $11.
Gr 2-5. B 84: Apr 15 1988. Traces the development of canal systems and explains how they work. Includes large photos, charts, period artwork, and a glossary.

1465. St. George, Judith. Brooklyn Bridge: They Said It Couldn't Be Built. Putnam, 1982. 126 p. ill. $11.
Gr 4-9. B 78: Aug 1982. B 81: Jul 1985. HB 58: Aug 1982. * SE 47: Apr 1983. Tells in equal parts of biography, history, engineering, and sociology, the fascinating story of the struggles and tragedy involved in building the bridge.

1466. Stein, R. Conrad. Story of the Erie Canal, The. (Cornerstones of Freedom). Childrens Press, 1985. 31 p. ill. $7.
Gr 3-6. +- B 82: Nov 1 1985. +- SLJ 32: Mar 1986. Explains the need for the canal and shows the details of construction.

1467. Zeck, Pam. Mississippi Sternwheelers. Carolrhoda, 1982. 32 p. ill. $7.
Gr 3-5. B 78: Aug 1982. The beginning of sternwheelers, the people who ran them, their use by early settlers, and a look at vacation steamboats in use today.

Whaling

1468. Fisher, Leonard Everett. Death of Evening Star: The Diary of a Young New England Whaler. Doubleday, 1972. 125 p. ill. $4.
Gr 5-8. B 69: Oct 15 1972. BC 26: Jun 1973. * SE 47: Apr 1983. An engrossing tale of the excitement, cruelty, and bloodiness of life on a whaler in the 1840s.

1469. Stein, R. Conrad. Story of the New England Whalers. (Cornerstones of Freedom). Childrens Press, 1982. 31 p. ill. $6.
Gr 3-6. B 78: Jul 82. SLJ 29: Sep 1982. Explains the economic significance of whaling and the living conditions aboard ship.

Women

1470. Lipsett, Linda Otto. Remember Me: Women and Their Friendship Quilts. Quilt Digest Press, 1985. 135 p. ill. $30. Pb $20.
Gr 9+. B 82: Jan 15 1986. LJ 111: Jan 1986. Using oral history and family records, the author covers the lives of seven 19th-century New England women. Includes color plates of their quilts.

1471. Stansell, Christine. City of Women: Sex and Class in New York, 1789-1860. Knopf, 1986. 320 p. $30.
Adult. * LJ 111: Nov 1 1986. A look at family and street life, factory and house work, innocent pleasure and vice, in pre-Civil War New York.

Women–Biographies

1472. Jakes, John. Susanna of the Alamo: A True Story. Harcourt, 1986. 30 p. ill. $14.
Gr 2-6. * B 82: Jun 15 1986. BC 39: Jun 1986. * SE 51: Apr/May 1987. SLJ 32: Aug 1986. Susanna Dickinson, a survivor of the Alamo, was sent by General Santa Anna to inform Sam Houston of the outcome.

1861-1865

United States–History–1861-1865

1473.   Civil War: Soldiers and Civilians. (Social Issues Resources Series). Social Issues Resources Series, Inc., 1982. Boxed unit. ill. $30.
Gr 9+.   BR 1: Sep/Oct 1982.   Facsimile copies of documents from the Civil War, including letters, maps, and handbills.   Includes teacher's guide.   Useful for study and display.

1474.   Batty, Peter. Divided Union: The Story of the Great American War, 1861-65.   Salem; dist. by Merrimack Publishers' Circle, 1987. 224 p. ill. $25.
Gr 9+.   LJ 112: Dec 1987.   SLJ 34: Mar 1988.   Batty describes the major battles and the conditions of the war in a work that includes numerous attractive illustrations.

1475.   Bowman, John S. Civil War Almanac, The. Facts on File, 1983. 400 p. ill. $20.
Gr 10+.   LJ 108: Sep 1 1983.   Includes a daily chronology, biographies, photos and other illustrations, plus information on weapons and naval warfare.

1476.   Catton, Bruce. Reflections on the Civil War. Doubleday, 1981. 246 p. ill. $16.
Gr 9+.   B 78: Nov 1 1981.   LJ 106: Sep 15 1981.   The noted Civil War historian summarized the causes, significance, and ramifications of the war as they related to personal lives and to national history.   The illustrations are from a sketchbook kept by a Union private.

1477.   Davis, William C. End of an Era, The. (Image of War, 1861-1865). Doubleday, 1984. 496 p. ill. $40.
Gr 10+.   LJ 109: Nov 1 1984.   This last of a six-volume set is an excellent photo-essay that clarifies the fundamental transformation affected by the war.

1478.   Donovan, Timothy H. American Civil War, The. (West Point Military History Series). Avery, 1987. 260 p. ill. $25. Pb $18.
Gr 9+. +- B 83: Dec 15 1986.   LJ 111: Dec 1986. Covers the social, political, and economic aspects of the war.   Designed for use by West Point Cadets.

1479.   Faust, Patricia L. Historical Times Illustrated Encyclopedia of the Civil War. Harper, 1986. 850 p. ill. $40.
Gr 9+.   B 83: Mar 15 1987.   Covers military leaders and events as well as political, diplomatic, social and economic issues.   Includes nearly 1000 illustrations of over 2000 entries.   Cross references.

1480.   Garrison, Webb. Treasury of Civil War Tales, A. Rutledge Hill Press; dist. by Word Books, 1988. 224 p. ill. $15.
Gr 9+.   B 85: Oct 15 1988.   Chronologically arranged anecdotes drawn from history and legend concerning events before, during, and after the war.

1481.   McPherson, James M. Ordeal by Fire: The Civil War and Reconstruction. Knopf, 1982. 694 p. ill. $30.
Gr 9+.   B 78: May 1 1982.   LJ 107: Feb 15 1982.   A balanced examination of the origins, battles, and results of the war.

1482.   Smith, Page. Trial by Fire: A People's History of the Civil War and Reconstruction. (People's History of the United States). McGraw-Hill, 1982. 1056 p. $30.
Gr 9+.   B 78: Jul 1982.   LJ 107: Sep 1 1982.   Smith based this fresh account of the war and its aftermath on the diaries and private writing of leaders and of ordinary citizens.

1483.   Straubing, Harold Elk. Civil War Eyewitness Reports. Shoe String/Archon, 1985. 264 p. ill. $25.
Gr 9+.   B 81: Apr 1 1985.   LJ 110: Apr 15 1985. Reports on the lives of varied persons affected by the Civil War, including a pro-Union woman living in the South, a conscientious objector, and an American Indian, in addition to accounts of battles.

Battles

1484.   Vicksburg and the Opening of the Mississippi River, 1862-63: A History and Guide Prepared for Vicksburg National Military Park, Mississippi. (National Park Service Handbook Series). National Park Serice, 1986. 79 p. ill. Pb $4.
Gr 9+.   B 83: Jan 15 1987.   This useful guide for visitors to the Vicksburg National Military Park describes the 14-month battle there.   Includes maps and illustrations. Handbook no. 137 of the series.

1485.   Catton, Bruce. Stillness at Appomattox. Doubleday; Pocket/Washington Square Press, 1953. 512 p. $17. Pb $5.
Gr 9+.   B 82: Jan 1 1986.   Traces the Army of the Potomac from early 1864 to April 1865 and through the campaign at Appomatox.

1486.   Coffey, Vincent J. Battle of Gettysburg, The. (Turning Points in American History). Silver Burdett, 1985. 64 p. ill. $14.
Gr 4-6.   B 82: Jan 15 1986.   This account of the daily happenings at Gettysburg includes maps and photos.

1487.   Kent, Zachary. Story of Sherman's March to the Sea, The. (Cornerstones of Freedom). Childrens Press, 1987. 31 p. ill. $10.
Gr 3-6.   B 84: Oct 15 1987. +- SLJ 34: Jan 1988. Shows the reasons for, and results of, Sherman's belief that "the more awful you can make war the sooner it will be over."

1488.   McDonough, James L. Chattanooga: A Death Grip on the Confederacy.   University of Tennessee Press, 1984. 300 p. $20.
Gr 11+.   LJ 109: Oct 1 1984.   A highly detailed and readable account of a complex campaign.

1489.   Sears, Stephen W. Landscape Turned Red: The Battle of Antietam.   Popular Library, 1985. 484 p. ill. $4.
Gr 10+.   VOYA 8: Oct 1985.   This extensively detailed account of the battle includes photos and excerpts from diaries and memoirs.

Battles–Fiction

1490. Altsheler, J. A. Guns of Shiloh, The. Appleton, 1914, 1976. 335 p. ill. Lib. ed. $19.
Gr 7+. Metzner. A story of the great western campaign. Complement to Guns of Bull Run.

1491. Altsheler, J. A. Rock of Chickamauga, The. Appleton, 1915, 1976. 328 p. ill. $19.
Gr 7+. Metzner. A story of the western crisis.

1492. Altsheler, J. A. Scouts of Stonewall, The. Appleton, 1914, 1985. 351 p. $20.
Gr 7+. Metzner [* B 11: Nov 1914]. Prequel to Star of Gettysburg. Henry Kenton is an aide on the staff of Stonewall Jackson. Provides detail of the Virginia campaign, told from the southern point of view.

1493. Altsheler, J. A. Shades of the Wilderness, The. Appleton, 1916, 1951. 311 p. Lib. ed. $19.
Gr 7+. Metzner [B 12: Jul 1916]. Sequel to Star of Gettysburg. Provides a striking portrait of Lee and other southern leaders as they retreat from the loss at Gettysburg. Through Henry Kenton the reader sees the war from the southern side.

1494. Altsheler, J. A. Star of Gettysburg, The. Appleton, 1915, 1976. 370 p. Lib. ed. $20.
Gr 7+. Metzner [+- B 11: Jun 1915]. Sequel to The Scouts of Stonewall. Henry Kenton is part of the Confederate forces and sees action at Gettysburg.

1495. Altsheler, J. A. Sword of Antietam, The. Appleton, 1916, 1985. 338 p. ill. Lib. ed. $20.
Gr 7+. Metzner. A story of the nation's crisis.

1496. Altsheler, J. A. Tree of Appomattox, The. Appleton, 1916, 1951. 321 p. ill. $19.
Gr 7+. Metzner. A story of the close of the Civil War.

1497. Perez, N. A. Slopes of War, The. Houghton, 1984. 224 p. $11.
Gr 4-8. B 80: May 15 1984. BC 37: Jul/Aug 1984. BR 3: Sep/Oct 1984. HB 60: Jun 1984. * SE 49: Apr 1985. +- SLJ 31: Sep 1984. The tragedy of war, portrayed in this story of the first four days of the Battle of Gettysburg.

Biographies

1498. Sifakis, Stewart. Who Was Who in the Civil War. Facts on File, 1988. 600 p. ill. $45.
Gr 9+. B 85: Oct 1 1988. +- LJ 113: July 1988. Includes over 2500 artists, diplomats, nurses, photographers, physicians, politicians, spies, high rank military officers, and others. Covers the life of the biographee before, during, and after the war. Illustrated.

Confederate States of America

1499. Cannon, Devereaux D. Flags of the Confederacy: An Illustrated History. St. Luke's/Broadfoot Pub., 1988. 91 p. ill. $30. Pb $10.
Gr 9+. B 84: Jun 15 1988. +- SLJ 34: Aug 1988. Charts the development of the 72 flags connected with the Confederacy. The story of the flags clarifies the inability of the Confederates to unite.

1500. Clark, James C. Last Train South. McFarland, 1984. 164 p. $18.
Gr 9+. BR 4: Sep/Oct 1985. A lively account of the end of the Confederacy that examines the war from the Southern perspective.

Confederate States of America–Biographies

1501. Wakelyn, Jon L. Biographical Dictionary of the Confederacy. Greenwood, 1977 601 p. $45.
Gr 9+. B 74: July 15 1978. B 80: Jun 15 1984. Includes 650 biographical entries, a three-page chronology, and a bibliography.

Espionage and Spies

1502. Brandt, Nat. Man Who Tried to Burn New York, The. Syracuse University Press, 1986. 285 p. ill. $20.
Gr 11+. * LJ 111: Aug 1986. The story of a little-known plot to destroy New York in retaliation for Sherman's march to the sea.

1503. Reit, Seymour. Behind Rebel Lines: The Incredible Story of Emma Edmonds, Civil War Spy. Harcourt Brace Jovanovich/Gulliver, 1988. 106 p. $13.
Gr 4-8. B 84: Mar 1 1988. +- BC 41: Mar 1988. +- SLJ 34: Mar 1988. A fictionalized biography of the woman who adopted many disguises and made 11 trips into the South as a spy.

Espionage and Spies–Fiction

1504. Batchelor, John Calvin. American Falls. Norton, 1985. 574 p. ill. $17
Adult. B 82: Nov 1 1985. * LJ 110: Sep 15 1985. Based on fact, this tale of espionage also explores the complexity of the issues that brought about the war.

1505. Burchard, Peter. Deserter: A Spy Story of the Civil War. Crowell, 1973. 95 p. $5.
Gr 7+. SE 44: Oct 1980. Based on the adventures of Levi Blair who, pretending to be a Union deserter, served on a Confederate ship as a spy.

Fiction

1506. Beatty, Patricia. Charley Skedaddle. Morrow, 1987. 186 p. $12.
Gr 5-8. B 84: Nov 15 1987. * BC 41: Oct 1987. BR 6: Nov/Dec 1987. HB 63: Nov/Dec 1987. * SE 52: Apr/May 1988. SLJ 34: Nov 1987. VOYA 10: Dec 1987. A tough Bowery boy, caught in the horror of battle, runs away. Given shelter by a cranky backwoods woman, he faces new challenges with courage and regains his self-respect.

1507. Beatty, Patricia. Turn Homeward, Hannalee. Morrow, 1984. 205 p. $11.
Gr 4-9. B 81: Nov 1 1984. BC 38: Nov 1984. * BR 3: Nov/Dec 1984. HB 60: Nov/Dec 1984. * SE 49: Apr 1985. SLJ 31: Jan 1985. VOYA 7: Feb 1985. The life of a 12-year-old Georgia mill worker is greatly changed by the war. Based on a historical incident.

1508. Brenner, Barbara. Saving the President: What if Lincoln Had Lived? (What If Mystery). Messner, 1988. 90 p. ill. $10.
Gr 4-8. +- BC 41: May 1988. +- SLJ 34: May 1988. A sculptress who is doing a bust of Lincoln uncovers the assassination plot and acts in time to save the president. The focus of the book is on the fictional heroine.

1509. Brown, Dee Alexander. Conspiracy of Knaves. Holt, 1987. 392 p. $18.
Gr 9+. B 83: Oct 1 1986. LJ 112: Jan 1987. A light-hearted novel of a bumbling attempt to turn the tide of the war by taking over Chicago.

1510. Clapp, Patricia. Tamarack Tree: A Novel of the Siege of Vicksburg. Lothrop, 1986. 214 p. $11.
Gr 7-10. +- B 83: Nov 15 1986. BC 40: Nov 1986. BR 5: Jan/Feb 1987. HB 62: Sep/Oct 1986. SLJ 33: Oct 1986. VOYA 9: Feb 1987. An English immigrant is torn between her affection for her Southern friends and her abhorrence of slavery.

1511. Climo, Shirley. Month of Seven Days, A. Harper/Crowell, 1987. 153 p. $13. Lib. ed. $13.
Gr 5-7. +- B 84: Dec 1 1987. +- BC 41: Oct 1987. SLJ 34: Dec 1987. Zoe helps her mother cook for the demanding Yankees who have taken over their Georgia home, but when she learns that the Yankee captain is superstitious Zoe tries to frighten him away.

1512. Hiser, Berniece T. Adventure of Charley and His Wheat-Straw Hat: A Memorat. Dodd, 1986. 32 p. ill. $13.
Gr 1-3. B 83: Nov 1 1986. HB 63: Jan/Feb 1987. * SE 51: Apr/May 1987. A picture book story of Charles, who accidentally became a hero. Based on a true story and suitable for reading aloud.

1513. Hunt, Irene. Across Five Aprils. Follett; Grosset and Dunlap; Ace, 1964; 1978. 192 p. Pb $3.
Gr 6-9. SE 47: Apr 1983. The extraordinary story of the happenings on a farm in southern Illinois across the five Aprils of the war. Action centers around Jethro, the youngest, left to run the farm as the other men go to war.

1514. Jones, Douglas C. Elkhorn Tavern. Holt, 1980. 311 p. map. $13.
Gr 9+. B 77: Oct 1 1980. LJ 105: Sep 1 1980. SLJ 27: Jan 1981. VOYA 3: Dec 1980. This story is based on actual events and people. It presents the turmoil of a family caught up in the Civil War.

1515. Safire, William. Freedom. Doubleday, 1987. 1123 p. ill. $25.
Adult. +- B 83: Jun 15 1987. * LJ 112: Aug 1987. A detailed novel of the 20 months preceding the Emancipation Proclamation.

1516. Shore, Laura Jan. Sacred Moon Tree: Being the True Account of the Trials and Adventures of Phoebe Sands in the Great War Between the States, 1861-1865. Bradbury, 1986. 224 p. $14.
Gr 6-8. +- B 82: Jun 1 1986. BC 39: Jul/Aug 1986. +- SLJ 33: Nov 1986. VOYA 9: Dec 1986. With a Northern father and a Southern mother, Phoebe grows up in a nation divided by war.

1517. Smith, William Ferguson. Rival Lovers: A Story of the War Between the States. Peachtree, 1980. 186 p. $10.
Gr 8+. +- SLJ 27: Mar 1981. Orginally published in 1877, this is an autobiographical novel of a young man's experience in the war, written in the style and vocabulary of the day.

1518. Yep, Laurence. Mark Twain Murders. Four Winds, 1982. 151 p. $9.
Gr 6-9. B 79: Sep 1 1982. BC 38: Dec 1984. SLJ 28: May 1982. VOYA 5: Oct 1982. A young Mark Twain, working as a reporter, uncovers a Confederate plot to rob the San Francisco mint and discredit President Lincoln. Provides humor, salty characters, and a good sense of the time.

1519. Yep, Laurence. Tom Sawyer Fires, The. Morrow, 1984. 143 p. $11.
Gr 5-9. B 81: Oct 1 1984. +- BC 38: Dec 1984. - BR 3: Nov/Dec 1984. SLJ 31: Nov 1984. VOYA 7: Feb 1985. A teenage street urchin works with reporter Mark Twain and fireman Tom Sawyer to stop sabotage. This action-adventure set in San Francisco during the war incorporates Twain-style humor.

Frontier and Pioneer Life–Fiction

1520. Beatty, Patricia. Wait for Me, Watch for Me, Eula Bee. Morrow, 1978. 221 p. $13.
Gr 6-10. SE 47: Apr 1983. The only survivors of a Comanche attack, Lewallen and his four-year-old sister live with the Indians, but he is determined to escape. Provides rich detail of Texas life.

1521. Wisler, G. Clifton. Winter of the Wolf. Elsevier/Nelson, 1981. 124 p. $8.
Gr 5-10. B 77: Dec 1 1980. HB 57: Apr 1981. * SE 47: Apr 1983. SLJ 27: Jan 1981. VOYA 4: Dec 1981. A 14-year-old Texas boy and his Indian friend hunt a silver wolf purported to be a devil.

Inventions and Inventors

1522. Burnett, C. B. Captain John Ericsson: Father of the "Monitor." Vanguard, 1960. 255 p. $7.
Gr 6-10. Metzner [B 57: May 15 1961. LJ 86: Feb 15 1961]. This account of Ericsson's life highlights his extraordinary engineering abilities including the revolutionary design of the ironclad "Monitor."

Kansas–Fiction

1523. Woodrell, David. Woe to Live On. Holt, 1987. 214 p. $17.
Gr 9+. * VOYA 10: Dec 1987. The bloody story of the guerilla bands who fought for control of Kansas is told in vivid detail through the experiences of Jake, age 16.

Medical Personnel

1524. Clara Barton. (National Park Service Handbook). National Park Service, 1981. 79 p. ill. Pb $4.

Gr 9+. B 78: Sep 15 1981. A chronology, a biography, and a guide to the Clara Barton National Historic site. This is number 110 of the series.

1525. Boylston, Helen. Clara Barton, Founder of the American Red Cross. Random House, 1955. 182 p. ill. $8.
Gr 5-6. Metzner [LJ 80: Oct 15 1955]. Biography of a pioneer nurse who served in the Civil War and founded the American Red Cross.

1526. Bull, Angela. Florence Nightingale. (Profiles). Hamish Hamilton; dist. by David & Charles, 1985. 60 p. ill. $9.
Gr 4-6. SLJ 32: Apr 1986. A detailed and balanced biography which makes clear the price to be paid by a lonely crusader.

1527. Hamilton, Leni. Clara Barton. (American Women of Achievement). Chelsea House, 1987. 111 p. ill. $17.
Gr 5-10. B 84: Nov 1 1987. Presents the skills Barton employed as an administrator, lobbyist, educator, nurse, and feminist, in order to found the American Red Cross.

1528. Kent, Zachary. Story of Clara Barton, The. (Cornerstones of Freedom). Childrens Press, 1987. 30 p. ill. $10.
Gr 3-6. B 84: Oct 15 1987. SLJ 34: Jan 1988. Shows Barton's independence and determination as a teacher, a nurse to the Civil War wounded, and the founder of the Red Cross.

1529. Rose, M. C. Clara Barton, Soldier of Mercy. Garrard, 1960. 80 p. ill. $7.
Gr 2-5. Metzner. Barton worked to supply the needs of the injured during the Civil War. Following this she founded the American Red Cross. This illustrated biography introduces Barton to young readers.

Military History

1530. Cowles, Calvin D. Official Military Atlas of the Civil War: Reprint of the 1891 Edition. Arno and Crown, 1978. 350 p. ill. $48.
Gr 10+. B 76: Jun 15 1980. For comprehensive collections, official military records of the Union and Confederacy. Includes 821 maps, 106 engravings, and 209 drawings.

1531. Frassanito, William A. Grant and Lee: The Virginia Campaigns, 1864-1865. Scribner, 1983. 448 p. ill. $25.
Adult. LJ 108: May 1 1983. A thorough analysis of the photographic record of the battles of the war. For extensive collections.

1532. Hattaway, Herman. How the North Won: A Military History of the Civil War. University of Illinois Press, 1983. 762 p. ill. $25.
Gr 9+. B 79: Apr 15 1983. Presents in understandable terms the major battles and generals, military training, tactics, and administration, and the economic mobilization of the nation.

1533. Kent, Zachary. Story of the Surrender at Appomattox Court House, The. (Cornerstones of Freedom). Childrens Press, 1988. 32 p. ill. $11.
Gr 3-5. B 84: May 15 1988. An engrossing analysis of the war and the final surrender of Lee to Grant on April 9, 1865. Includes historical illustrations.

1534. McDonough, James L. War So Terrible: Sherman and Atlanta. Norton, 1987. 329 p. ill. $20.
Gr 9+. B 84: Oct 1 1987. LJ 112: Oct 15 1987. A detailed account of the Atlanta campaign that provides insight into Atlanta society and Sherman's ability. Also compares fact with the fiction of Mitchell's Gone with the Wind.

1535. Paludan, Philip Shaw. Victims: A True Story of the Civil War. University of Tennessee Press, 1981. 145 p. $11.
Gr 11+. LJ 106: Aug 1981. In January 1863, 13 suspected Union guerillas were removed from a Confederate jail and massacred. Paludan examines this and other atrocities and the nature of guerilla warfare.

Military History–Fiction

1536. Davis, Paxton. Three Days. Atheneum, 1980. 90 p. $8.
Gr 7+. +- HB 56: Apr 1980. SLJ 27: Sep 1980. The battle of Gettysburg is seen through the eyes of Robert E. Lee and a 19-year-old Confederate soldier in this novelized character study.

1537. Keneally, Thomas. Confederates. Harper, 1980. 427 p. $13.
Gr 9+. B 77: Oct 1 1980. LJ 105: Sep 1 1980. SLJ 27: Dec 1980. For mature readers, a gripping look at the tragedy of war, with explicit battle scenes and realistic character development.

Military Personnel

1538. Cornish, Dudley Taylor. Lincoln's Lee: The Life of Samuel Phillips Lee, U.S. Navy, 1812-1897. University of Kansas Press, 1986. 256 p. ill. $30.
Adult. LJ 111: Aug 1986. Lee was a leader in the Union naval forces. His biography provides insight into the development of the U.S. Navy.

1539. Davis, Burke. Sherman's March. Random House, 1980. 329 p. ill. $13.
Gr 9+. B 76: May 15 1980. LJ 105: May 15 1980. SLJ 27: Oct 1980. This examination of Sherman's personality and the effects of his infamous march through the South also includes stories of other persons involved in, or affected by, the march.

1540. DeGrummond, L. Y. Jeb Stuart. Lippincott, 1962, 1979. 160 p. ill. Pb $5.
Gr 5-7. Metzner. An illustrated introduction to the colorful life and leadership of the Confederate general that Lee called "the eyes of the army."

1541. Fleming, Thomas. Band of Brothers: West Point in the Civil War. Walker, 1988. 94 p. ill. $14. Lib. ed. $15.

Gr 6-9. B 84: Feb 1 1988. +- SLJ 34: Feb 1988. +- VOYA 11: Apr 1988. An anecdotal account of some of the men who attended West Point and then found themselves providing leadership on opposite sides during the Civil War.

1542. Haythornthwaite, Philip. Uniforms of the American Civil War. Blandford Press, 1985. 192 p. ill. $7.
Gr 9+. SLJ 32: Nov 1985. Illustrates and describes over 150 Confederate and Union uniforms, and describes all types of armaments.

1543. Mitchell, Reid. Civil War Soldiers. Viking, 1988. 259 p. $25.
Gr 10+. B 84: Aug 1988. * LJ 113: Sep 15: 1988. Extensive quotes are combined with narrative to show the views of Union and Confederate citizen-soldiers. Topics include the politics of the war, the soldiers' fears, and their reactions to battle and imprisonment.

1544. Ramage, James A. Rebel Raider: The Life of General John Hunt Morgan. University Press of Kentucky, 1986. 328 p. ill. $25.
Adult. LJ 111: Jul 1986. A detailed narrative of a Confederate hero, whom Ramage compares to a modern guerilla fighter. For comprehensive collections.

1545. Smith, Gene. Lee and Grant: A Dual Biography. McGraw-Hill, 1984. 400 p. $18.
Adult. B 80: Jun 1 1984. LJ 109: Jun 1 1984. SE 49: May 1985. A revealing comparison of Lee and Grant.

1546. Thomas, Emory M. Bold Dragoon: The Life of J. E. B. Stuart. Harper, 1986. 354 p. ill. $20.
Gr 9+. B 82: Apr 1 1986. LJ 111: Sep 1 1986. An account of the general's military career and his perception of himself as a romantic cavalier-warrior.

1547. Warner, Ezra J. Generals in Blue: Lives of the Union Commanders. Louisiana State University Press, 1964. 679 p. ill. $25.
Gr 9+. B 80: Jun 15 1984. This carefully documented work provides biographical sketches of Union generals and a listing of brigadier generals and majors. It also lists campaigns and battles, and is illustrated.

1548. Weidhorn, Manfred. Robert E. Lee. Atheneum, 1988. 149 p. ill. $15.
Gr 5+. * B 84: Mar 1 1988. BC 41: May 1988. BR 7: Sep/Oct 1988. * SLJ 34: Jun/Jul 1988. VOYA 11: Aug 1988. Explores the personality and tactics of the Confederate general whose genius prolonged the Civil War beyond reasonable expectations.

1549. Windrow, Martin. Civil War Rifleman, The. (Soldier Through the Ages). Watts, 1986. 32 p. ill. $11.
Gr 4-10. B 82: Mar 15 1986. BR 5: Jan/Feb 1987. * SE 51: Apr/May 1987. SLJ 33: Nov 1986. Examines the place of the individual soldier in the context of the war, including training, dress, weapons, strategy, and tactics.

Military Personnel–Black–Fiction

1550. Hansen, Joyce. Which Way Freedom? (Walker's American History Series for Young People). Walker, 1986. 120 p. $13. Lib. ed. $13.
Gr 6-9. B 82: Aug 1986. BC 39: Jun 1986. * SE 51: Apr/May 1987. SLJ 32: Aug 1986. * VOYA 10: Apr 1987. The story of a former slave who served as a private in the 13th Tennessee Battalion.

Military Personnel–Fiction

1551. Jones, Douglas C. Barefoot Brigade. Holt, 1982. 313 p. $16.
Gr 7-9. B 78: Jul 1982. LJ 107: Sep 1 1982. SLJ 29: Oct 1982. VOYA 6: Feb 1983. With careful attention to detail the author tells the unauthorized story of a Confederate infantry regiment. The courage and tragedy of the common soldier comes through.

1552. Wisler, G. Clifton. Thunder on the Tennessee. Lodestar, 1983. 153 p. $11.
Gr 7-10. B 79: May 15 1983. +- BC 37: Feb 1984. SLJ 30: Sep 1983. Details of the war abound in this story of Willie and his father.

Politics

1553. Kent, Zachary. Story of the Election of Abraham Lincoln, The. (Cornerstones of Freedom). Childrens Press, 1986. 30 p. ill. $10.
Gr 3-5. B 82: Jul 1986. - SLJ 33: Jan 1987. A brief look at the national crisis surrounding Lincoln's election.

Presidents and Their Families

1554. Van der Heuvel, Gerry. Crowns of Thorns and Glory: Mary Todd Lincoln and Varina Howell Davis: The Two First Ladies of the Civil War. Dutton, 1988. 352 p. ill. $20.
Gr 10+. B 84: Jun 15 1988. LJ 113: Jul 1988. A unique dual biography which parallels the lives of the only concurrent first ladies in U.S. history.

Presidents and Their Families–Lincoln

1555. Bains, Rae. Abraham Lincoln. (Venture Into Reading Series). Troll, 1985. 30 p. ill. $8. Pb $2.
Gr 3-5. SLJ 32: Mar 1986. Lincoln is warmly portrayed in this simply-told biography that covers his unhappy youth and shows his development into a man of compassion. Full-color illustrations and large print.

1556. Bishop, Jim. Day Lincoln Was Shot, The. Harper, 1964. 304 p. ill. $5.
Gr 9+. B 82: Jan 1 1986. A dramatic reconstruction of the events surrounding the assassination.

1557. Cavanah, Frances. Abe Lincoln Gets His Chance. Rand McNally, 1959. 92 p. ill. $2.
Gr 4-6. Metzner [+- B 55: Jun 15 1959. LJ 84: Mar 15 1959]. A somewhat fictionalized account of Lincoln's life up to his election as president.

1558. Colver, Anne. Abraham Lincoln: For the People. (Discovery Series). Garrard, 1960. 78 p. ill. $7.
Gr 2-5. Metzner. An illustrated introduction to Lincoln's life and accomplishments.

1559. Cremaschi, Gabriella. Abraham Lincoln. (Why They Became Famous). Silver Burdett, 1985. 64 p. ill. $14. Pb $7.
Gr 4-7. BR 4: Jan/Feb 1986. This short, easy-to-read, highly illustrated biography includes a chronology.

1560. D'Aulaire, Ingri. Abraham Lincoln. Doubleday, 1939, 1957. unp. ill. $13. Pb $9.
Gr 1-4. Metzner [B 35: May 1 1939. HB 15: May 1939. * LJ 64: May 1 1939]. A brief but well-rounded biography highlighted by humorous lithographs.

1561. Davis, Burke. Mr. Lincoln's Whiskers. Coward, 1979. Unp. ill. $7.
Gr 3-6. SE 44: Oct 1980. The true story of a little girl's letter that caused the president to grow a beard.

1562. Frazier, Carl. Lincoln Country in Pictures, The. Hastings, 1963. unp. ill. $7.
Gr 4-8. Metzner [LJ 89: Jan 15 1964]. Descriptive captions enhance these photos of the places where Lincoln lived and the things he might have used.

1563. Freedman, Russell. Lincoln: A Photobiography. Clarion, 1987. 150 p. ill. $16.
Gr 4-10. * B 84: Dec 15 1987. * BC 41: Jan 1988. HB 64: Mar 1988. * SE 52: Apr/May 1988. * SLJ 34: Dec 1987. An outstanding photobiography that reveals the man behind the myth, his attitudes toward slavery, and numerous quotes from his work. The photos also provide a clear picture of the realities of the war.

1564. Hanchett, William. Lincoln Murder Conspiracies, The. University of Illinois Press, 1983. 304 p. ill. $17.
Gr 10+. * BR 5: Mar/Apr 1987. LJ 108: Oct 1 1983. Examines the truths and half-truths surrounding the Lincoln murder.

1565. Handlin, Oscar. Abraham Lincoln and the Union. Atlantic Monthly Press; dist. by Little, Brown, 1980. 190 p. $11.
Gr 9+. B 76: Jul 1 1980. LJ 105: Sep 1 1980. A thoughtful portrait of the president who was driven by his desire to ensure personal freedoms, preserve the Union, achieve equality for all, and serve God.

1566. Kent, Zachary. Story of Ford's Theater and the Death of Lincoln, The. (Cornerstones of Freedom). Childrens Press, 1988. 32 p. ill. $11.
Gr 3-5. B 84: May 15 1988. A compelling analysis of Lincoln's last day. Includes numerous photos.

1567. Kigel, Richard. Frontier Years of Abe Lincoln: In the Words of His Friends and Family. Walker, 1986. 227 p. $16.
Gr 7+. B 83: Mar 15 1987. * BR 5: Mar/Apr 1987. SLJ 33: Jan 1987. +- VOYA 9: Feb 1987. Based on quotations from interviews with Lincoln's friends and acquaintances shortly after his death, this colorful portrait humanizes the president.

1568. Kolpas, Norman. Abraham Lincoln. (Great Leaders Series). McGraw-Hill, 1981. 69 p. ill. $8.
Gr 6-9. B 78: Nov 15 1981. SLJ 28: Mar 1982. Reveals Lincoln as a product of his time which rewarded perseverance over hardship.

1569. Kunhardt, Philip B., Jr. New Birth of Freedom: Lincoln at Gettysburg. Little, 1983. 224 p. ill. $20.
Gr 9+. B 80: Jan 15 1984. LJ 108: Nov 15 1983. Explains why and how Lincoln wrote and delivered his famous speech.

1570. Metzger, Larry. Abraham Lincoln. (First Book). Watts, 1987. 93 p. ill. $10.
Gr 5-8. B 83: May 15 1987. SLJ 33: Jun/Jul 1987. This introduction to Lincoln clarifies his changing perspective on slavery.

1571. Mitgang, Herbert. Fiery Trial: A Life of Lincoln. Viking, 1974, 1979. 207 p. ill. $8.
Gr 7+. B 70: Jul 1 1974. SE 44: Oct 1980. Explores Lincoln's personal and political life, and his beliefs. Uses numerous quotes.

1572. Neely, Mark E., Jr. Abraham Lincoln Encyclopedia, The. McGraw-Hill, 1982. 356 p. ill. $45.
Adult. B 78: Feb 1 1982. LJ 107: Feb 15 1982. LJ 107: May 15 1982. Information on Lincoln, on the political and social atmosphere of the time, and on significant people and events.

1573. Reck, W. Emerson. A. Lincoln: His Last 24 Hours. McFarland, 1987. 232 p. ill. $20.
Gr 9+. B 83: Aug 1987. BR 6: Nov/Dec 1987. SLJ 34: Nov 1987. VOYA 10: Dec 1987. This detailed account of the president's last day includes photos of persons he saw that day and other illustrations. An appendix recounts some of the still unsolved mysteries surrounding the assassination.

1574. Sandburg, Carl. Abe Lincoln Grows Up. Harcourt, 1985. 222 p. ill. $15.
Gr 7-11. B 82: Oct. 1 1985. HB 61: Sep/Oct 1985. VOYA 8: Dec 1985. Metzner. [B 25: Nov 1928]. This contains the early chapters from Sandburg's two-volume biography.

1575. Smith, Kathie Billingslea. Abraham Lincoln. (Great Americans Series). Messner, 1987. Unp. ill. $8. Pb $3.
Gr 2-5. SLJ 33: Jun/Jul 1987. This introductory overview of Lincoln's personal and political life has important events highlighted by double page sketches.

Presidents and Their Families–Lincoln–Fiction

1576. O'Toole, George. Cosgrove Report: Being the Private Inquiry of a Pinkerton Detective Into the Death of President Lincoln. Rawson; dist. by Atheneum, 1979. 424 p. $13.
Gr 9+. B 76: Jan 15 1980. LJ 104: Nov 15 1979. Intriguing fiction, as a 20th-century detective seeks to verify a report that John Wilkes Boothe did not die in that barn in Virginia.

1577. Vidal, Gore. Lincoln: A Novel. Random House, 1984. 657 p. $20.
Adult. B 80: Apr 15 1984. LJ 109: Jun 1 1984. SE 49: May 1985. This highly acclaimed novel shows Lincoln's rise to greatness. Detailed and factual, with well-developed characterizations of all major figures.

1578. Walters, Helen B. No Luck for Lincoln. Abingdon, 1981. 160 p. ill. $8.
Gr 3-6. SLJ 28: Nov 1981. This fictionalized biography of Lincoln's youth includes a chronology and bibliography.

Public Officials

1579. Ballard, Michael B. Long Shadow: Jefferson Davis and the Final Days of the Confederacy. University Press of Mississippi, 1986. 215 p. ill. $23.
Adult. B 83: Oct 15 1986. LJ 111: Nov 15 1986. Concentrates on the final months of the Confederacy, and analyzes the significance to the nation of Davis' assuming the role of martyr to a lost cause. Suitable for extensive collections.

Reformers

1580. Graham, Lorenz B. John Brown: A Cry for Freedom. Crowell, 1980. 180 p. ill. $10. Lib. ed. $10.
Gr 5-10. B 77: Feb 15 1981. +- HT 15: Aug 1982. SLJ 27: Jan 1981. VOYA 9: Feb 1987. Reveals that the "fierce and righteous anger" of Brown's anti-slavery activities had a significant impact on history. Captures the temper of the time and the complexity of the man.

1581. Kent, Zachary. Story of John Brown's Raid on Harper's Ferry, The. (Cornerstones of Freedom). Childrens Press, 1988. 32 p. ill. $12.
Gr 4-8. B 84: Aug 1988. SLJ 35: Sep 1988. Using many quotes Kent clearly presents the causes of the Civil War in this account of the ill-fated raid by abolitionist Brown.

1582. Scott, John Anthony. John Brown of Harper's Ferry. (Makers of America). Facts on File, 1988. 184 p. ill. $15.
Gr 7+. +- B 84: Feb 1 1988. BR 7: Nov/Dec 1988. SLJ 35: May 1988. +- VOYA 11: Aug 1988. Presents a full picture of the events leading up to Brown's anti-slavery terrorist activities and the resulting tragedy.

Ships and Shipping

1583. Stein, R. Conrad. Story of the Monitor and the Merrimac, The. (Cornerstones of Freedom). Childrens Press, 1983. 31 p. ill. $6.
Gr 4+. B 79: Aug 83. SLJ 30: Sep 1983. Colorful details add spice to the familiar story.

Ships and Shipping–Fiction

1584. O'Dell, Scott. 290, The. Houghton, 1976. 118 p. $7.

Gr 6-8. * SE 47: Apr 1983. The story of a famous Confederate raiding ship that was responsible for sinking 69 Yankee ships.

Slaves and Slavery–Fiction

1585. Tolliver, Ruby C. Muddy Banks. (Chapparal Books). Texas Christian University Press, 1987. 151 p. Map. $15.
Gr 5-8. SLJ 34: Dec 1987. VOYA 11: Apr 1988. After escaping from a Confederate ship a slave seeks refuge on the muddy Texas shoreline. He finds help and friendship, and becomes involved in a critical battle.

1586. Walker, Margaret. Jubilee. Houghton; Bantam, 1966. 432 p. $16. Pb $4.
Gr 9+. B 81: Jul 1985. Through the life of Vyry, a slave woman, we see slavery, the war, and emancipation. A novel rich in details of Southern life and the relationships between blacks and whites.

Social Life and Customs–Fiction

1587. Alcott, Louisa May. Little Women. Messner, 1982. 561 p. ill. $15. Lib. ed. $15.
Gr 5-9. B 79: Feb 15 1983. The classic story of the March girls, whose mother struggled to raise them while their father was on duty with the Union army, provides a sentimental picture of warm family life.

1588. Kassem, Lou. Listen for Rachel. Macmillan, 1986. 159 p. $12.
Gr 7-10. B 83: Nov 15 1986. * SE 51: Apr/May 1987. Rachel learns the ways of folk medicine in the Tennessee mountains as the war divides families.

1589. Plain, Belva. Crescent City. Delacorte; dist. by Doubleday, 1984. 428 p. $17.
Gr 10+. B 80: Jul 1984. LJ 109: Aug 1984. An immigrant Jewish woman and her brother are caught up in the conflicts of tradition, abolition, and slavery.

1590. Rinaldi, Ann. Last Silk Dress, The. Holiday, 1988. 209 p. $16.
Gr 6-10. B 84: Jun 15 1988. BC 41: Jun 1988. +- SLJ 34: May 1988. VOYA 11: Dec 1988. Fourteen-year-old Susan is an ardent Confederate and helps collect silk dresses to make an observation balloon. Through the story she gradually comes to understand the evils of slavery.

Women–Fiction

1591. McSherry, Frank. Civil War Women: American Women Shaped by Conflict in Stories by Alcott, Chopin, Welty, and Others. August House, 1988. 208 p. Pb $9.
Gr 10+. B 84: Jul 1988. LJ 113: Aug 1988. SLJ 35: Sep 1988. Ten short stories explore the Civil War experience of women, both northern and southern.

1865-1900

United States–History–1865-1900

1592. Cashman, Sean Dennis. America in the Gilded Age: From the Death of Lincoln to the Rise of Theodore Roosevelt. New York University Press; dist.by Columbia Univ. Press, 1984. 384 p. ill. $28. Pb $12.
Adult. LJ 108: Dec 15 1983. Examines economics, labor, immigration, inventions, railroads, industry, and the robber barons, as they combined to create modern America.

1593. Painter, Nell Irvin. Standing at Armageddon: The United States, 1877-1919. Norton, 1987. 378 p. ill. $23.
Gr 9+. B 84: Sep 1 1987. LJ 112: Sep 15 1987. An introduction to the Gilded Age and the Progressive Era, with attention to minorities, laboring classes, and the elite. Covers political, social, and economic history.

1594. Smith, Page. Rise of Industrial America: A People's History of the Post-Reconstruction Era. (People's History of the United States). McGraw-Hill, 1984. 1008 p. $30.
Gr 10+. B 80: Mar 15 1984. Covers the settling of the Far West, the subjugation of the Indians, the rise of industry and labor problems, new immigrants, and the debate over Darwin's theory. This is volume 6 of the series.

Alaska

1595. Clinton, Susan. Story of Seward's Folly, The. (Cornerstones of Freedom). Childrens Press, 1987. 30 p. ill. $10.
Gr 3-6. B 84: Oct 15 1987. SLJ 34: Jan 1988. A colorful account of the controversy surrounding U.S. acquisition of Alaska for two cents an acre.

Alaska–Gold Rush

1596. Wells, E. Hazard. Magnificence and Misery: A Firsthand Account of the 1897 Klondike Gold Rush. Doubleday, 1984. 272 p. ill. $18.
Gr 10+. LJ 109: Jul 1984. Wells was a reporter who covered the Gold Rush. His photos, dispatches, and journals provide a fascinating account.

Authors

1597. Quackenbush, Robert M. Mark Twain? What Kind of Name Is That? A Story of Samuel Langhorne Clemens. Prentice-Hall, 1984. 32 p. ill. $11.
Gr 2-6. B 80: May 1 1984. B 82: Sep 15 1985. SLJ 30: Aug 1984. A humorous look at the many occupations of this noted author provides a glimpse of life at that time.

Balloons–Fiction

1598. Coerr, Eleanor. Big Balloon Race, The. (I Can Read Book). Harper, 1981, 1984. 62 p. ill. $8. Pb $3.
Gr 1-2. HB 61: Jan/Feb 1985. SLJ 28: Dec 1981. Based on the adventures of the Myers family, famous for their contributions to the art and science of ballooning.

Blacks–Biographies

1599. Franklin, John Hope. George Washington Williams: A Biography. University of Chicago Press, 1985. 347 p. ill. $25.
Gr 9+. B 82: Oct 15 1985. * LJ 110: Oct 15 1985. Williams was a Civil War soldier, a pastor, editor, lawyer, legislator, and historian.

Blacks–Fiction

1600. Brenner, Barbara. Wagon Wheels. (I Can Read History Book). Harper, 1977. 64 p. ill. Pb $3.
Gr 1-4. B 74: May 15 1978. * B 83: Mar 1 1987. BC 32: Oct 1987. SLJ 25: Sep 1978. A simply told story based on the true experiences of a black family who moved to a dugout in Kansas and faced cold, starvation, and Indians.

1601. Hurmence, Belinda. Tancy. Clarion; dist. by Ticknor & Fields, 1984. 203 p. $12.
Gr 6+. B 80: May 15 1984. BC 37: Jun 1984. BR 3: Sep/Oct 1984. * SE 49: Apr 1985. SLJ 31: Sep 1984. VOYA 7: Oct 1984. House slave Tancy suffers sexual assault and then fear of the unknown after emancipation.

1602. Irwin, Hadley. I Be Somebody. Atheneum, 1984. 170 p. $12.
Gr 4-6. +- BC 38: Sep 1984. Based on a true story of a black family who moved from Oklahoma to Canada following the Civil War.

1603. Morrison, Toni. Beloved. Knopf, 1987. 275 p. $11.
Gr 9+. B 83: Jul 1987. * LJ 112: Sep 1 1987. SLJ 34: Jan 1988. * VOYA 11: Dec 1988. The searing memoirs of a former slave who, as a slave, had run away. When her capture was imminent, she murdered her infant daughter to prevent the child's capture.

Blacks–Women

1604. Lewis, Selma. Angel of Beale Street: A Biography of Julia Ann Hooks, The. St. Luke's, 1986. 318 p. $20.
Gr 7+. BR 5: May/Jun 1986. LJ 111: Apr 15 1986. Hooks was a black educator, activist, and philanthropist. This volume tells of her life from 1851-1892.

Business and Business People

1605. Boardman, Fon W., Jr. America and the Robber Barons: 1865 to 1913. Walck: McKay, 1979. 152 p. $9.
Gr 7+. SLJ 26: Feb 1980. Blends biography and the history of our economic development. Covers Vanderbilt, Gould, Rockefeller, Carnegie, and 11 other business leaders in the context of the time.

1606. Hawke, David Freeman. John D.: The Founding Father. Harper, 1980. 250 p. ill. $10.
Gr 9+. LJ 105: May 1 1980. An objective coverage of the Rockefeller success story.

Constitution

1607. Stein, R. Conrad. Story of the Nineteenth Amendment, The. (Cornerstones of Freedom). Childrens Press, 1982. 31 p. ill. $9. Pb $3.
Gr 4-6. B 79: Feb 15 1983. B 81: Sep 15 1984. SLJ 29: Mar 1983. An overview of the women's suffrage movement highlighting the work of Elizabeth Cady Stanton and Susan B. Anthony.

Cowhands

1608. Freedman, Russell. Cowboys of the Wild West. Clarion; dist. by Ticknor & Fields, 1985. 103 p. ill. $15.
Gr 4+. * B 81: Dec 15 1985. BC 39: Dec 1985. HB 60: Feb 1984. HB 62: Mar/Apr 1986. SE 50: Apr/May 1986. * SLJ 32: Dec 1985. Explores the familiar mix of fact and fiction that make up the cowboy legend. Includes photos.

1609. Gorsline, Marie. Cowboys. (Random House Picturebook). Random House, 1980. 32 p. ill. Lib. ed. $4. Pb $2.
Gr 3-4. B 76: Apr 15 1980. Explains how the need for cattle drives led to the existance of cowboys, and highlights the famous and infamous. Numerous illustrations.

1610. James, Will. Lone Cowboy: My Life Story. Scribner, 1930, 1985. 431 p. ill. $29.
Gr 7-10. Metzner [B 27: Nov 1930]. James' autobiography in cowboy vernacular. Tells of trapping, riding, and cowpunching, and James' development as an artist of the West.

1611. Taylor, Lonn. American Cowboy, The. Harper, 1983. 228 p. ill. $50.
Gr 10+. LJ 108: Dec 1 1983. An authoritative examination of who the cowboy was and what he came to represent. Highly illustrated. Compiled from a catalog of an exhibition by Cornelia and Michael Bessie.

Cowhands–Fiction

1612. Hancock, Sibyl. Old Blue. Putnam, 1980. Unp. ill. $7.
Gr 1-4. B 77: Jan 15 1981. B 83: Mar 1 1987. SLJ 27: Dec 1980. An action-filled story about Davy and his friend, Old Blue, the lead steer on a cattle drive north. A historic note gives added information about cattle drives from Texas to Kansas and the real Old Blue.

1613. James, Will. Will James' Book of Cowboy Stories. Scribner, 1951. 242 p. ill. $20.
Gr 5+. Metzner [B 47: Jul 1 1951. HB 27: Jul 1951. LJ 76: Jun 15 1951]. A collection of authentic and vivid stories about cowboys and horses, enhanced by James' drawings.

Cowhands–Women

1614. Jordan, Teresa. Cowgirls: Women of the American West. Doubleday, 1982. 352 p. ill. $20.
Gr 10+. B 79: Sep 15 1982. LJ 107: Aug 1982. SLJ 29: Dec 1982. This account of the hardships and joys of women who did equal work with the men on the land during the 19th and early 20th centuries is based on diaries, newspaper articles, songs, poetry, and interviews.

Crime and Criminals

1615. Baldwin, Margaret. Wanted! Frank & Jesse James: The Real Story. Messner, 1981. 192 p. $11.
Gr 7-10. B 78: Jan 1 1982. VOYA 5: Aug 1982. This colorful and factual biography of Frank and Jesse James conveys the flavor of the time.

1616. Cline, Don. Alias Billy the Kid, The Man Behind the Legend. Sunstone, 1986. 145 p. ill. $13.
Gr 7+. B 82: Feb 1 1986. * BR 5: Nov/Dec 1986. This carefully researched work reveals the common murderer who hid behind a charming personality.

1617. Hansen, Ron. Assassination of Jesse James by the Coward Robert Ford, The. Knopf, 1983. 320 p. $15.
Adult. LJ 108: Sep 1 1983. Examines the complexities of James' personality, how Ford came to assassinate his idol, and the American obsession with the famous.

1618. Hartman, Mary. Bald Knobbers. Pelican, 1988. 224 p. $15. Pb $9.
Gr 10+. +- BR 7: Sep/Oct 1988. Detailed information on the Bald Knobbers, a vigilante group that started out to bring law and order to the Ozarks, and later used extreme violence against all who disagreed with them.

1619. O'Neal, Bill. Encyclopedia of Western Gunfighters. University of Oklahoma Press, 1979. 386 p. ill. $25.
Gr 10+. B 76: Jun 1 1980. - LJ 104: May 1 1979. A readable reference work that provides brief biographical information on over 250 gunfighters and the details of nearly 600 gunfights.

1620. Patterson, Richard. Train Robbery: The Birth, Flowering and Decline of a Notorious Western Enterprise. Johnson, 1981. 239 p. ill. Pb $8.
Gr 9+. B 78: Dec 15 1981. LJ 106: Sep 1 1981. Covers all the known train robbers and their techniques. Includes photos.

Education

1621. Loeper, John J. Going to School in 1876. Atheneum, 1984. 96 p. ill. $10.
Gr 4-8. B 80: May 1 1984. BC 37: May 1984. * SE 49: Apr 1985. SLJ 30: Aug 1984. Describes schools, books, lessons, teachers, clothes, and pastimes, as well as the typical experiences of several children.

Entertainers

1622. Buffalo Bill and the Wild West. Brooklyn Museum of Art; dist. by University of Pittsburgh, 1981. 96 p. ill. Pb $12.
Gr 9+. B 78: Apr 1 1982. A pictorial chronicle of the life of Buffalo Bill Cody, his Wild West Show, and the West, as seen by contemporary artists.

1623. Alderman, Clifford Lindsey. Annie Oakley and the World of Her Time. Macmillan, 1979. 112 p. ill. $9.
Gr 4-6. B 75: Apr 15 1979. * SE 44: Apr 1980. SLJ 25: Apr 1979. This biography of a talented and independent woman provides accurate information on life at that time.

1624. Gleiter, Jan. Annie Oakley. Raintree, 1986. 32 p. ill. $11. Pb $7.
Gr 2-4. SLJ 33: May 1987. This simple introduction to Annie Oakley and other noted figures of the Old West is made appealing by the use of fictionalized dialogue.

1625. Quackenbush, Robert M. Who's That Girl with the Gun? A Story of Annie Oakley. Prentice-Hall, 1988. 36 p. ill. $12.
Gr 3-5. B 84: Feb 1 1988. BC 41: Mar 1988. SLJ 34: Mar 1988. A sprightly biography of the mistreated orphan who grew to world fame as a sharpshooter.

1626. Sayers, Isabelle S. Annie Oakley and Buffalo Bill's Wild West. Dover, 1981. 89 p. ill. Pb $5.
Gr 9+. B 78: Apr 1 1982. SLJ 28: Dec 1981. A unique chronicle of the famous female sharpshooter. Includes handbills, posters, and numerous rare photos.

1627. Yost, Nellis Snyder. Buffalo Bill: His Family, Friends, Fame, Failures, and Fortunes. Swallow, 1980. 500 p. ill. $18.
Gr 9+. * B 76: May 1 1980. LJ 105: Mar 15 1980. An authentic biography of Buffalo Bill Cody, the famed Pony Express rider, scout, and entertainer.

Entertainers–Fiction

1628. Heidish, Marcy. Secret Annie Oakley, The. New American Library, 1983. 240 p. $15.
Gr 9+. B 79: Apr 1 1983. LJ 108: Mar 1 1983. A well-researched and moving novel based on the known facts of the life of Annie Oakley, a mistreated child who grew into a strong and independent woman.

Fiction

1629. Beatty, Patricia. Be Ever Hopeful, Hannalee. Morrow, 1988. 212 p. $12.
Gr 5-8. SLJ 35: Oct 1988. VOYA 11: Dec 1988. After Hannalee's brother Davey returns from the Civil War without an arm the family moves to Atlanta to find work, but tragedy strikes when Davey is accused of murder. Sequel to Turn Home Hannalee.

1630. Beatty, Patricia. Melinda Takes a Hand. Morrow, 1983. 189 p. $10.
Gr 4-7. B 80: Nov 15 1983. BC 37: Jan 1984. HB 59: Dec 1983. SLJ 30: Jan 1984. Details of time and place are abundant in this lighthearted story of the 1893 visit of Sarah Jane and Melinda to a small Colorado town.

1631. Brown, Diana. Hand of a Woman, The. St. Martin's, 1984. 528 p. $17.
Gr 9+. B 81: Sep 1 1984. A young woman studies medicine and faces bigotry and hatred.

1632. Brown, Irene Bennett. Before the Lark. Atheneum, 1982. 191 p. $11.
Gr 5-7. B 79: Oct 15 1982. +- BC 36: Jan 1983. +- SLJ 29: Jan 1983. Kansas, 1888. Josey and her grandmother attempt to run the farm deserted by Josey's father.

1633. Burchard, Peter. Digger: A Novel. Putnam, 1980. 154 p. $9.
Gr 5-9. B 77: Jan 15 1981. BC 34: Mar 1981. SLJ 27: Jan 1981. Based on actual events in Boss Tweed's corrupt New York, 1871. A newspaper boy investigating arson becomes involved in gang warfare.

1634. Butler, Beverly. My Sister's Keeper. Dodd, 1980. 220 p. $7.
Gr 6-10. +- B 76: May 1 1980. * SE 45: Apr 1981. +- SLJ 26: Apr 1980. This historically accurate account of the 1871 forest fire that devastated northern Wisconsin is the background for the story of Mary James, a vain, flirtatious girl who matured during the ordeal.

1635. Fleming, Thomas. Spoils of War, The. Putnam, 1985. 556 p. $19.
Adult. B 81: Feb 15 1985. +- LJ 110: Feb 15 1985. Good characterization highlights this novel of romance that provides an authentic social and political history of the Reconstruction period. Set in the South and in New York City.

1636. Harris, Marilyn. American Eden. Doubleday, 1987. 591 p. $19.
Gr 10+. B 83: Jan 15 1987. LJ 112: Apr 1 1987. Burke's progressive social beliefs during the Reconstruction lead to the kidnapping of his daughter. Good characterizations and high adventure in an authentic story of the Old South. The sixth of the Eden series.

1637. Hoguet, Susan Ramsey. Solomon Grundy. Dutton, 1986. 32 p. ill. $12.
Gr K-3. * B 82: Apr 15 1986. BC 39: Jul/Aug 1986. * HB 62: Sep/Oct 1986. SLJ 32: May 1986. A double-page watercolor spread depicts the fictional life of Solomon Grundy (1836-1910) who sold pies to raise money for the Statue of Liberty.

1638. Jones, Douglas C. Roman. Holt, 1986. 387 p. $17.
Gr 9+. B 82: Jun 15 1986. +- LJ 111: Jun 15 1986. SLJ 33: Oct 1986. VOYA 9: Aug/Oct 1986. An epic adventure in which Roman explores life in Kansas and the West. A sequel to Elkhorn Tavern.

1639. Lasky, Kathryn. Bone Wars, The. Morrow, 1988. 394 p. $12.
Gr 7+. B 85: Nov 15 1988. * SLJ 35: Nov 1988. Thad Longworth serves as a scout for paleontologists who

wish to find dinosaur bones in the Montana badlands in this action-filled saga of the American West in the 1870s.

1640. Moeri, Louise. Save Queen of Sheba. Elsevier/Dutton, 1981. 116 p. $9.
Gr 4-8. * B 77: May 15 1981. BC 35: Sep 1981. HB 57: Oct 1981. SLJ 27: May 1981. Survivors of a Sioux attack, the boy King David, and his spoiled sister, Queen of Sheba, try to reach their parents who are in an advance party. Both of their points of view are expressed in this taut survival story.

Frontier and Pioneer Life

1641. Fradin, Dennis B. Pioneers. (New True Book). Childrens Press, 1984. 45 p. ill. $8.
Gr 1-4. B 81: Mar 1 1985. SLJ 31: Apr 1985. Examines who the pioneers were, why they went, their hardships, and their impact on our nation.

1642. Hoy, Jim. Plains Folk: A Commonplace of the Great Plains. University of Oklahoma Press, 1987. 190 p. ill. $18.
Gr 10+. B 83: Aug 1987. +- LJ 112: Sep 1 1987. Based on journals, diaries, and other writings of 19th-century plains dwellers, primarily Kansans. Includes essays on farm life, games, and stories.

1643. Reedstrom, Ernest Lisle. Historic Dress of the Old West. Blandford Press; dist. by Sterling, 1987. 160 p. ill. $20.
Gr 10+. B 83: Jun 1 1987. Describes the clothes and weapons of cowboys, Indians, soldiers, miners, outlaws, gamblers, and other citizens of the Old West.

1644. Silliman, Eugene Lee. We Seized Our Rifles: Recollections of the Montana Frontier. Mountain Press, 1982. 214 p. ill. $15. Pb $8.
Gr 9+. B 78: May 1 1982. Covers the adventures of a buffalo hunter, a mountain man, soldiers, and others. Based on primary sources.

Frontier and Pioneer Life–Fiction

1645. Alter, Judith MacBain. Luke and the Van Zandt County War. Texas Christian University Press; dist. by Sundance, 1984. 131 p. ill. $11.
Gr 5-9. B 81: Feb 1 1985. HB 61: Mar/Apr 1985. SLJ 31: Mar 1985. A story of action and drama in post-Civil War Texas.

1646. Altsheler, J. A. Horsemen of the Plains. Macmillan, 1910, 1976. 390 p. $21.
Gr 7+. Metzner. When Omaha was a frontier town and the West was a battleground for Indians and white men, Bob and a band of veteran trappers faced danger and high adventure as they hunted furs in the Rocky Mountains.

1647. Brink, Carol. Magical Melons: More Stories about Caddie Woodlawn. Macmillan, 1967. 193 p. ill. $4.
Gr 4-6. Metzner [B 41: Dec 15 1944. LJ 69: Dec 15 1944]. Old favorite stories of a girl's life on the Wisconsin frontier.

1648. Cooke, John Byrne. Snowblind Moon, The. Simon & Schuster, 1985. 687 p. $19.
Adult. B 81: Feb 15 1985. LJ 110: Feb 1 1985. Mountain men, wagon train scouts, cattle ranchers, and Chinese immigrants are all a part of this novel set in Wyoming in 1876.

1649. Gipson, Fred. Old Yeller. Harper, 1964. 158 p. ill. $14. Lib. ed. $14.
Gr 5+. Metzner [HB 32: Oct 1956. LJ 81: Jul 1956]. The classic story of a boy and his dog on the Texas plains in in the 1860s.

1650. Gipson, Fred. Savage Sam. Harper, 1976. 214 p. ill. $3.
Gr 5+. Metzner [+- B 58: Apr 1 1962. +- HB 38: Apr 1962. LJ 87: Feb 15 1962]. In this sequel to Old Yeller, pioneer children are captured by Apache raiders on the Texas frontier.

1651. Harvey, Brett. My Prairie Year: Based on the Diary of Elenore Plaisted. Holiday, 1986. 40 p. ill. $12.
Gr K-6. B 83: Nov 1 1986. BC 40: Dec 1986. HB 63: Jan/Feb 1987. * SE 51 Apr/May 1987. SLJ 33: Nov 1986. A picture book based on the diary of the author's grandmother.

1652. Lawlor, Laurie. Addie across the Prairie. Albert Whitman, 1986. 128 p. ill. $9.
Gr 3-5. B 82: Aug 1986. SLJ 33: Oct 1986. Nine-year-old Addie learns bravery as she deals with life on the prairie.

1653. Lyon, George Ella. Regular Rolling Noah, A. Bradbury, 1986. Unp. ill. $14.
Gr K-3. B 83: Sep 1 1986. * SLJ 33: Nov 1986. A first-person account of a move from Kentucky to Canada by train, taking all the livestock. A humorous story with charming illustrations which provide detail of the preparations and the great adventure.

1654. MacLachlan, Patricia. Sarah, Plain and Tall. Harper, 1986. 64 p. ill. Pb $9.
Gr 4-6. B 81: May 1 1985. BC 38: May 1985. HB 61: Sep/Oct 1985. * SE 50: Apr/May 1986. SLJ 31: May 1985. Sarah, plain and tall, answers a newspaper ad for a wife. Anna and Caleb hope their gentle new mother will come to love the prairie as much as she loved the sea. A Newberry winner.

1655. Oke, Janette. Love's Long Journey. Bethany, 1982. 207 p. Pb $5.
Gr 7-9. VOYA 6: Apr 1983. In this sequel to Love Comes Softly and Love's Enduring Promise, a young couple goes west by wagon train to establish a cattle ranch.

1656. Purdy, Carol. Iva Dunnit and the Big Wind. Dial; dist. by Dutton, 1985. 32 p. ill. $12. Lib. ed. $13.
Gr K-3. * B 82: Nov 1 1985. B 83: Mar 1 1987. BC 39: Feb 1986. HB 62: Mar/Apr 1986. +- SLJ 32: Nov 1985. A hilarious tale in which Iva and her six children hold out against fire, wolves, and horse thieves, but a tornado is almost too much.

1657. Roderus, Frank. Duster. Christian University Press, 1986. 265 p. $15.

Gr 6-8. * VOYA 11: Apr 1988. An authentic and action-filled story of a Texas boy who, at age 16, must join a cattle drive in order to save the family farm.

1658. Talbot, Charlene Joy. Sodbuster Venture, The. Atheneum, 1982. 194 p. $11.
Gr 4-8. B 78: Apr 15 1982. +- BC 35: Mar 1982. HB 58: Jun 1982. SLJ 78: Aug 1982. VOYA 5: Aug 1982. On a homestead in central Kansas two young women struggle against a blizzard, insects, and an unfriendly neighbor. A rich account, full of action, with well-drawn characters.

1659. Turner, Ann. Dakota Dugout. Macmillan, 1985. 32 p. ill. $11.
Gr K-3. B 82: Dec 1 1985. B 83: Mar 1 1987. +- BC 39: Oct 1985. HB 62: Jan/Feb 1986. +- SLJ 32: Nov 1985. Black-and-white drawings illustrate a young wife's life in a sod house on the prairie in the last century.

1660. Turner, Ann. Third Girl from the Left. Macmillan, 1986. 180 p. $11.
Gr 7+. B 82: Jun 1 1986. BC 39: Jun 1986. HB 62: Sep/Oct 1986. * SE: Apr/May 1987. SLJ 32: Aug 1986. VOYA 9: Aug/Oct 1986. Sarah faces life as a mail order bride in Montana.

1661. Walter, Mildred Pitts. Justin and the Best Biscuits in the World. Lothrop, 1986. 122 p. $12.
Gr 3-6. B 83: Oct 15 1986. SLJ 33: Nov 1986. A humorous and warm story of a black family. Unable to get along at home, Justin visits his grandfather's ranch and learns to accept responsibility. Details of ranch life, rodeos, and black cowboys will appeal to readers.

1662. Wheeler, Richard S. Winter Grass. Walker, 1983. 211 p. $13.
Gr 10+. B 80: Sep 1 1983. LJ 108: Oct 15 1983. SLJ 30: Feb 1984. VOYA 7: Jun 1984. Hard times on a Montana ranch, as Putnam faces drought, cattle disease, and battles over barbed wire.

1663. Wilder, Laura I. Little House in the Big Woods. Harper, 1932, 1953. 237 p. ill. $13.
Gr 5+. Metzner [B 29: Jun 1932]. A delightful story of life in a Wisconsin log cabin, with its cold winter days, problems with wild animals, social gatherings, and family fun.

1664. Wilder, Laura I. Little House on the Prairie. Harper, 1935, 1953. 334 p. ill. $13.
Gr 5+. Metzner [B 32: Oct 1935. HB 11: Nov 1935]. This leisurely story, rich in local color, finds the family homesteading Kansas prairie land. Sequel to Little House in the Big Woods.

1665. Wilder, Laura I. Long Winter, The. Harper, 1940, 1953. 334 p. ill. $13.
Gr 5+. Metzner [B 37: Dec 1 1940. HB 17: Jan 1941. LJ 65: Dec 15 1940]. In the Dakota Territory, 1880-81, the family endures blizzards, low supplies, and other hardships. An autobiographical novel.

1666. Wilder, Laura I. On the Banks of Plum Creek. Harper, 1937, 1953. 338 p. ill. $13.
Gr 5+. Metzner [B 34: Nov 15 1937. HB 13: Nov 1937. LJ 62: Nov 1 1937]. In the third in this series,

a little girl experiences hardships in pioneering Minnesota wheat country. Provides a strong sense of family relationships and pioneer spirit.

1667. Williams, Jeanne. Lady of No Man's Land. St. Martin's, 1988. 416 p. $20.
Gr 9+. B 85: Oct 15 1988. Swedish immigrant Kirsten and her sister arrive in Dodge City where Kirsten hopes to make a living as a traveling seamstress. Based on family recollections, this novel is full of historic detail.

Frontier and Pioneer Life–Women

1668. Jeffrey, Julie Roy. Frontier Women: The Trans-Mississippi West, 1840-1880. Hill and Wang, 1979. 240 p. Pb $6.
Gr 11+. HT 13: May 1980. For advanced students, a detailed study which clarifies the contrast between the image of pioneer life and its reality.

1669. Stratton, Joanna. Pioneer Women: Voices from the Kansas Frontier. Simon & Schuster, 1981. 329 p. ill. $17.
Gr 7+. B 77: Mar 15 1981. BR 1: Nov/Dec 1982. LJ 106: Mar 1 1981. SLJ 28: Oct 1981. Based on letters and photos of Kansas pioneer women and organized by such topics as the journey, settlement, daily life, problems with nature, relations with Indians, and social life.

Immigration

1670. Beard, A. E. S. Our Foreign Born Citizens. Crowell, 1922, 1968. 308 p. $15.
Gr 7+. Metzner [B 19: Dec 1922]. Biographical sketches of 34 immigrants who made great contributions to their new homeland, including Audubon, Bell, Bok, Ericcson, Carnegie, Muir, Pulitzer, Riis, and Tesla.

1671. Blumenthal, Shirley. Coming to America: Immigrants from Eastern Europe. Delacorte, 1981. 258 p. ill. $12.
Gr 7+. B 78: Jan 1 1982. BC 35: Mar 1982. SLJ 29: Nov 1982. VOYA 5: Jun 1982. A graphic portrayal of the struggles of eight million new Americans who came from Russia, Poland, Latvia, Hungary, and other parts of Eastern Europe between 1870 and 1924.

Immigration–Children

1672. Freedman, Russell. Immigrant Kids. Dutton, 1980. 72 p. ill. $12.
Gr 4-7. B 77: Oct 1 1980. B 81: Jul 1985. BC 34: Dec 1980. * SE 45: Apr 1981. SLJ 27: Oct 1980. A photographic essay on the lives of children who immigrated.

Immigration–Fiction

1673. Angell, Judie. One-Way to Ansonia. Bradbury; dist. by Macmillan, 1985. 183 p. $12.
Gr 5-10. B 82: Jan 1 1986. +- BC 33: Nov 1985. HB 62: Mar/Apr 1986. +- SLJ 32: Dec 1985. VOYA 8: Feb 1986. Young immigrant Rose works back-breakingly hard, yet she holds on to her dreams of education and a home with trees. For better readers.

1674. Fahrmann, Willi. Long Journey of Lukas B., The. Bradbury; dist. by Macmillan, 1985. 280 p. $13.
Gr 6+. B 81: Jun 15 1985; Jul 1985. BC 39: Sep 1985. SE 50: Apr/May 1986. SLJ 32: Sep 1985. VOYA 8: Dec 1985. A young German immigrant in the post-Civil War South learns carpentry and the complexities of family love.

1675. Lehmann, Linda. Tilli's New World. Elsevier/Nelson, 1981. 154 p. $10.
Gr 4-7. BC 35: Jan 1982. HB 58: Feb 1982. * SE 46: Apr 1982. SLJ 28: Nov 1981. Based on the experience of the author's mother, this is a realistic portrayal of the immigrant experience on a Missouri farm.

1676. Levinson, Riki. Watch the Stars Come Out. Dutton, 1985. 32 p. ill. $13.
Gr K-3. * B 82: Oct 15 1985. BC 39: Dec 1985. SE 50: Apr/May 1986. SLJ 32: Dec 1985. A picture book of the immigrant experience.

1677. Pellowski, Anne. First Farm in the Valley: Anna's Story. Philomel, 1982. 191 p. ill. $10.
Gr 3-5. B 79: Mar 1 1983. +- BC 36: Mar 1983. HB 59: Feb 1983. +- SLJ 29: May 1983. As more immigrants come from Poland, U.S. born Anna hears their stories about the old country and wishes she could go there. Fourth of a series.

1678. Pellowski, Anne. Stairstep Farm: Anna Rose's Story. Philomel, 1981. 176 p. $10.
Gr 4-7. +- B 78: Jan 15 1982. +- BC 35: Jan 1982. HB 58: Apr 1982. SLJ 28: Mar 1982. Daily happenings in the life of Anna Rose and her family of Polish immigrant farmers. Second of a series.

1679. Sandin, Joan. Long Way to a New Land, The. (I Can Read History Book). Harper, 1981. 64 p. ill. $8. Lib. ed. $8.
Gr K-3. B 81: Jul 1985. BC 35: Mar 1982. HB 58: Feb 1982. * SE 46: Apr 1982. SLJ 28: Dec 1981. To escape famine, the Erik family embarks on a frightening journey from their Swedish homeland to America. Realistic and effective.

1680. Talbot, Charlene Joy. Orphan for Nebraska, An. Atheneum, 1979. 208 p. $8.
Gr 4-8. B 75: Mar 15 1979. BC 32: May 1979. * SE 44: Apr 1980; Oct 1980. Orphaned Irish immigrant Kevin O'Rourke joins a group of other children who go to Nebraska for adoption and is apprenticed in a print shop. Based on actual events.

Indians of North America

1681. Brown, Dee Alexander. Bury My Heart at Wounded Knee: An Indian History of the American West. Holt; Pocket/Washington Square Press, 1971. 480 p. $18. Pb $5.
Gr 9+. * B 80: Oct 15 1983. B 82: Jan 1 1986. Examines the battles, massacres, and broken treaties of the Indian struggle from 1860 to 1890 in a gripping chronicle. Based on primary sources.

1682. McLuhan, T. C. Dream Tracks: The Railroad and the American Indian, 1890-1930. Abrams, 1985. 208 p. ill. $38.

Gr 10+. B 82: Dec 15 1985. LJ 111: Feb 15 1986. Examines 150 photos of various Indian tribes used by the Santa Fe Railway to promote tourism, creating the stylized myth of the noble savage.

Indians of North America–Apache

1683. Ball, Eve. Indeh: An Apache Odyssey. Brigham Young University Press, 1980. 326 p. ill. $20.
Adult. LJ 105: Jul 1980. An oral history of their nation told by the last Apaches to live free before confinement on a reservation. Based on 30 years of interviews.

Indians of North America–Biographies

1684. Freedman, Russell. Indian Chiefs. Holiday, 1987. 151 p. ill. $16.
Gr 6+. * B 83: May 1 1987. BC 40: May 1987. * HB 63: Jul/Aug 1987. * SE 52: Apr/May 1988. * SLJ 33: May 1987. * VOYA 10: Aug/Sep 1987. A thoughtful narrative of the lives of six Indian chiefs: Red Cloud, Santana, Quanah Parker, Washakie, Joseph, and Sitting Bull.

Indians of North America–Comanche

1685. Hilts, Len. Quanah Parker. Gulliver/Harcourt, 1987. 160 p. maps. $13.
Gr 5-9. +- BC 41: Oct 1987. * SE 52: Apr/May 1988. +- SLJ 34: Jan 1988. Fictionalized dialogue is used in this well-researched biography of the chief who led Comanche resistance, and, after defeat in 1875, led their assimilation.

Indians of North America–Fiction

1686. Altsheler, J. A. Great Sioux Trail, The. Appleton, 1918, 1976. 340 p. $19.
Gr 7+. Metzner [* B 15: Oct 1918]. Will Clark is captured by the Sioux and spends the winter learning their ways. The story presents the Indian point of view about being forced from their land.

1687. Gall, Grant. Apache: The Long Ride Home. Sunstone, 1988. 112 p. Pb $10.
Gr 7+. * BR 7: Sep/Oct 1988. As a child Pedro was captured and raised by the Apache. He tells the story of the Apache struggle to survive the encroaching white settlement.

1688. Goble, Paul. Death of the Iron Horse. Macmillan/Bradbury, 1987. 32 p. ill. $13.
Gr 1-3. B 84: May 1 1988. BC 40: Apr 1987. HB 63: May/Jun 1987. SLJ 33: May 1987. Cheyenne Indians attempted to stop the white man's westward movement by ambushing a train. This story is based on an 1867 incident.

1689. Highwater, Jamake. Ceremony of Innocence, The. Harper, 1985. 192 p. $11.
Gr 8+. * B 81: May 15 1985. B 82: Oct 1 1985. BC 38: May 1985. SLJ 31: Apr 1985. * VOYA 8: Aug 1985. Amana is forced into the white man's world in order to survive, but she yearns to return to the old culture. Part two of the Ghost Horse Cycle.

1690. Highwater, Jamake. Eyes of Darkness. Lothrop, 1985. 176 p. $13.
Gr 6+. B 82: Oct 15 1985. BC 39: Dec 1985. BR 4: Jan/Feb 1986. * SE 50: Apr/May 1986. +- SLJ 32: Nov 1985. VOYA 8: Feb 1986. A novel based on the life of C. A. Eastman, Sioux Indian physician and writer.

1691. Highwater, Jamake. Legend Days. Harper, 1984. 160 p. $13. Lib. ed. $11.
Gr 8-10. B 80: Jul 1984. B 81: Apr 15 1985. BC 37: Jun 1984. * BR 3: Sep 1984. HB 60: Jun 1984. VOYA 7: Aug 1984. An Indian girl sees smallpox and the disappearance of the buffalo destroy her people. This tragic and violent Part One of the Ghost Horse Cycle presents a detailed picture of daily life and an inspiring heroine.

1692. Jones, Douglas C. Arrest Sitting Bull. Scribner, 1977. 253 p. $9.
Gr 9+. B 74: Oct 1 1977. LJ 102: Aug 1977. SE 47: Apr 1983. This story of the last days of Sitting Bull, leader of the Sioux nation, effectively shows how conflicts of personalities and beliefs can cause unforeseen tragedy.

1693. Jones, Douglas C. Gone the Dreams and Dancing. Holt, 1984. 323 p. $16.
Gr 10+. +- VOYA 8: Jun 1985. A Civil War veteran narrates this story of the decline of the Comanche nation.

1694. Jones, Weyman. Edge of Two Worlds. Dial, 1968. 160 p. ill. $8.
Gr 5-8. B 81: Apr 15 1985. The survivor of a wagon train massacre meets Sequoyah who developed a written language for the Cherokee nation.

1695. Lampman, Evelyn Sibley. White Captives. Atheneum, 1975. 192 p. $7.
Gr 6-8. +- B 81: Apr 15 1985. A harsh but realistic story of sisters held captive by Apaches and Mojave Indians.

1696. Lederer, Paul Joseph. Cheyenne Dreams. (Indian Heritage Series). New American Library, 1985. 319 p. $4.
Gr 7+. VOYA 8: Feb 1986. Provides a good view of the Indian perspective of the relationships between Indians and the whites during the mid-19th century.

1697. Sanford, John A. Song of the Meadowlark: An American Indian and the Nez Perce War. Harper, 1986. 320 p. $17.
Gr 10+. B 82: May 1 1986. LJ 111: May 1 1986. This novel acquaints the reader with the culture and leaders of the Nez Perce nation, as it tells of their 1700 mile trek to Canada to escape the U.S. Army.

1698. Welch, James. Fools Crow. Viking, 1986. 391 p. ill. $19.
Gr 9+. LJ 111: Oct 15 1986. VOYA 10: Aug/Sep 1987. Describes the coming of age of Fools Crow, a Blackfoot Indian, and his efforts to retain his culture and religion in the face of white man's encroachment.

Indians of North America–Navaho

1699. O'Dell, Scott. Sing Down the Moon. Houghton; Dell, 1970. 148 p. $12. Pb $3.

Gr 5-8. B 81: Apr 15 1985. SE 47: Apr 1983. A first-person story about Navaho life in the mid-1800s.

Indians of North America–Nez Perce

1700. Gidley, M. With One Sky Above Us: Life on an Indian Reservation at the Turn of the Century. Putnam, 1979. 159 p. ill. $15.
Gr 9+. B 76: Jan 1 1980. LJ 104: Dec 15 1979. SLJ 26: Feb 1980. The photographer, Edward H. Latham, was a physician at the Colville Reservation in Washington state in the late 19th century. Gidley's text clarifies the injustices of the reservation system.

1701. Jassem, Kate. Chief Joseph, Leader of Destiny. Troll, 1979. 48 p. ill. $5. Pb $2.
Gr 3-7. SLJ 26: Aug 1980. This high interest-low vocabulary biography of the Nez Perce chief who led his people on a 1000 mile retreat in 1877 is slightly fictionalized.

1702. Pollock, Dean. Joseph, Chief of the Nez Perce. Binfords, 1950. 184 p. ill. $6.
Gr 5-8. Metzner [B 47: Sep 15 1950]. A stirring account of the brilliant and peaceful Chief Joseph who led his people's heroic retreat across 1500 miles of mountain wilderness in 1877.

Indians of North America–Omaha

1703. Brown, Marion Marsh. Homeward the Arrow's Flight. Abingdon, 1980. 175 p. ill. $8.
Gr 4-6. B 77: Oct 15 1980. BC 34: Nov 1980. * SE 45: Apr 1981. SLJ 28: Sep 1981. VOYA 3: Feb 1981. A fictionalized biography of the first Indian woman to become a physician.

Indians of North America–Paiute

1704. Boring, Mel. Wovoka. (Story of an American Indian). Dillon Press, 1981. 72 p. ill. $7.
Gr 4-7. +- SLJ 28: Nov 1981. In 1887 a Paiute named Wovoka has a vision that Jesus would come again as an Indian and restore prosperity. The resultant religious fervor eventually led to the massacre at Wounded Knee.

1705. Canfield, Gae Whitney. Sarah Winnemucca of the Northern Paiutes. University of Oklahoma Press, 1983. 295 p. ill. $20.
Adult. B 79: Aug 1983. LJ 108: Apr 1 1983. Canfield presents Winnemucca's account of her life and the views of her critics, and places them in context. The result is a sympathetic biography of this 19th-century Indian activist.

1706. Kloss, Doris. Sarah Winnemucca. (Story of an American Indian). Dillon Press, 1981. 78 p. $8.
Gr 6-8. B 78: Sep 15 1981. B 81: Apr 15 1985. The daughter and granddaughter of Paiute chiefs was named chief for defending her people's rights.

1707. Morrison, Dorothy Nafus. Chief Sarah: Sarah Winnemucca's Fight for Indian Rights. Atheneum, 1980. 170 p. ill. $10.
Gr 9+. B 76: Jul 15 1980. BC 34: Feb 1981. * SE 45: Apr 1981. SLJ 27: Nov 1980. Winnemucca was a

noted speaker who fought against the corrupt Bureau of Indian Affairs. Based on newspaper accounts, official documents, and her autobiography, the first by an American Indian to be published in English.

Indians of North America–Sioux

1708. Anderson, Gary Clayton. Little Crow: Spokesman for the Sioux. Minnesota Historical Society, 1986. 259 p. ill. $20.
Gr 9+. B 83: Nov 1 1986. Although he had opposed war, Little Crow was called upon to lead the Sioux in a war of self-preservation.

1709. Fleischer, Jane. Sitting Bull, Warrior of the Sioux. Troll, 1979. 48 p. ill. $5. Pb $2.
Gr 3-7. SLJ 26: Aug 1980. A high interest-low vocabulary biography with some fictionalized dialogue and incidents.

1710. Forman, James D. Life and Death of Yellow Bird, The. Farrar, 1973. 224 p. $11.
Gr 6-9. B 81: Apr 15 1985. The life of an Indian seer who died at Wounded Knee.

1711. Hook, Jason. Sitting Bull and the Plains Indians. (Life and Times). Bookwright Press; dist. by Watts, 1987. 61 p. ill. $12.
Gr 4-8. SLJ 33: Aug 1987. A brief biography of Sitting Bull is followed by a summary of the history and customs of the Plains Indians.

1712. Kadlecek, Edward. To Kill an Eagle: Indian Views on the Death of Crazy Horse. Johnson, 1981. 170 p. ill. Pb $8.
Gr 9+. B 78: Apr 1 1982. New information on Crazy Horse and his people, based on interviews with Sioux friends.

1713. Lee, Betsy. Charles Eastman. (Story of an American Indian). Dillon Press, 1979. 62 p. ill. Lib. ed. $6.
Gr 6-8. B 76: May 15 1980. Although he was educated as a physician in white schools, Eastman became a noted author, lecturer, and defender of Native American rights who struggled to keep the Sioux culture alive.

Indians of North America–Wars

1714. Benchley, Nathaniel. Only Earth and Sky Last Forever. Harper; Scholastic Book Services, 1972, 1973. 204 p. Pb $3.
Gr 7-10. SE 47: Apr 1983. A young Indian tells the realistic tale of the white man's war with the Cheyenne and Sioux in the 1870s. Sometimes sad, sometimes funny, but realistic.

1715. Marrin, Albert. War Clouds in the West: Indians and Cavalrymen, 1860-1890. Atheneum, 1984. 224 p. ill. $15.
Gr 6+. B 81: Jan 15 1985; Apr 15 1985. HB 61: Mar/Apr 1985. SLJ 31: Mar 1985. Marrin chronicles the final Indian military resistance to white encroachment and presents historical and cultural perspectives on the struggle for the West.

1716. McGaw, Jessie Brewer. Chief Red Horse Tells about Custer: The Battle of the Little Bighorn, an Eyewitness Account Told in Indian Sign Language. Elsevier/Nelson, 1981. unp. ill. $9.
Gr 4-8. SLJ 28: Dec 1981. Following the Battle of Little Bighorn, a Sioux warrior told the story to an army surgeon in sign language. Using sketches made by that surgeon, McGaw relates the stark and dramatic events.

1717. Stein, R. Conrad. Story of the Little Bighorn, The. (Cornerstones of Freedom). Childrens Press, 1983. 30 p. $7.
Gr 3-6. B 80: Jan 15 1984. SLJ 30: Apr 1984. Stein presents the Indian point of view on the causes for the hostility that led to the tragedy at Little Bighorn.

1718. Stein, R. Conrad. Story of Wounded Knee, The. (Cornerstones of Freedom). Childrens Press, 1983. 30 p. $7.
Gr 3-6. B 80: Jan 15 1984. SLJ 30: Apr 1984. This sequel to Story of Little Bighorn continues the story of Indian-white relations from the Indian point of view.

Inventions and Inventors

1719. Anderson, Norman D. Ferris Wheels. Pantheon, 1983. 56 p. ill. $11. Lib. ed. $11.
Gr 4-8. B 80: Feb 15 1984. BC 37: Mar 1984. BR 2: Mar/Apr 1984. HB 60: Apr 1984. SLJ 30: Apr 1984. Traces the history of the Ferris wheel, with emphasis on the wheel built by George Ferris for the 1893 Columbia Exposition. That wheel was 250 feet in diameter with space for 1440 passengers.

1720. Cousins, Margaret. Story of Thomas Alva Edison, The. Random House, 1981. 160 p. ill. Pb $4.
Gr 5-8. B 82: Sep 15 1985. This account of Edison's work emphasizes how he has influenced our culture.

1721. Greene, Carol. Thomas Alva Edison: Bringer of Light. Childrens Press, 1985. 128 p. ill. $9.
Gr 5-7. B 82: Dec 15 1985. This lively biography of Edison chronicles his childhood, his development as an inventor, and the obsession with his work that led to family problems as well as his successes.

1722. Lampton, Christopher. Thomas Alva Edison. (First Book). Watts, 1988. 96 p. ill. $10.
Gr 4-7. B 84: Mar 15 1988. +- BC 41: May 1988. +- SLJ 34: Apr 1988. A brisk, highly illustrated biography that includes numerous quotes and Edison's drawings. Emphasis is on Edison's work.

1723. Mitchell, Barbara. Click! A Story about George Eastman. (Carolrhoda Creative Minds Book). Carolrhoda, 1986. 56 p. ill. $9.
Gr 3-6. SLJ 33: Sep 1986. A lively biography of the founder of the Eastman Kodak Company.

1724. Mitchell, Barbara. Shoes for Everyone: A Story about Jan Matzeliger. (Carolrhoda Creative Minds Book). Carolrhoda, 1986. 63 p. ill. $9.
Gr 3-6. B 82: Aug 1986. BC 39: Jul/Aug 1986. SLJ 33: Sep 1986. Black inventor Jan Ernst Matzeliger immigrated to the U.S. from Dutch Guiana and designed a machine that revolutionized the shoe industry.

1725. Quackenbush, Robert M. Ahoy! Ahoy! Are You There? A Story of Alexander Graham Bell. Prentice-Hall, 1981. 36 p. ill. $8.
Gr 3-5. B 78: Jan 1 1982. +- SLJ Sep 1982. A brisk, upbeat biography of the inventor of the telephone, who was a teacher of the deaf.

1726. Sabin, Louis. Thomas Alva Edison: Young Inventor. Troll, 1983. 48 p. ill. $7. Pb $2.
Gr 3-5. B 80: Sep 1 1983. A slightly fictionalized biography that shows that Edison was a boy who learned best outside the classroom.

1727. Tessendorf, K. C. Look Out! Here Comes the Stanley Steamer. Atheneum, 1984. 58 p. ill. $12.
Gr 3-6. B 80: May 15 1984. +- BC 37: Apr 1984. SLJ 30: Aug 1984. This story of the twin brothers who developed the Stanley Steamer includes information about the operation of the car.

Labor Unions and Laborers

1728. Stein, R. Conrad. Story of the Pullman Strike, The. (Cornerstones of Freedom). Childrens Press, 1982. 31 p. ill. $6.
Gr 3-6. +- B 78: Jul 1982. +- SLJ 29: Sep 1982. The importance of this 1894 strike is clarified by straightforward text.

Labor Unions and Laborers–Children

1729. Bethell, Jean. Three Cheers for Mother Jones! Holt, 1980 48 p. ill. $7.
Gr K-3. B 77: Dec 15 1980. * SE 45: Apr 1981. +- SLJ 27: Dec 1980. A 10-year-old participant recounts Mother Jones' famous children's march which demonstrated the plight of child laborers.

Labor Unions and Laborers–Fiction

1730. Rappaport, Doreen. Trouble at the Mines. Harper/Crowell, 1987. 85 p. ill. $12.
Gr 3-5. B 83: May 1 1987. BC 40: Mar 1987. HB 63: Mar/Apr 1987. - SLJ 33: Apr 1987. The story of the 1898 Pennsylvania coal miner's strike, led by union organizer Mother Jones, is told through the experiences of Rosie and her family. Based on newspaper accounts.

Medical Personnel

1731. Steelsmith, Shari. Elizabeth Blackwell: The Story of the First Woman Doctor. Parenting Press, 1987. 24 p. ill. Pb $6.
Gr K-3. +- BC 40: Jun 1987. +- SLJ 33: Aug 1987. A fictionalized first-person account of the struggle of Elizabeth Blackwell to become the first woman doctor.

1732. Wilson, Dorothy Clarke. I Will Be a Doctor!: The Story of America's First Woman Physician. Abingdon, 1983. 160 p. Pb $7.
Gr 4-8. B 80: Dec 1 1983. SLJ 30: Feb 1984. An informative and descriptive biography of our first woman physician.

Military Personnel

1733. Custer, Elizabeth. Boots and Saddles: Or, Life in the Dakota with General Custer. Harper, 1885, 1977. 315 p. Lib. ed. $17.
Gr 7-9. Metzner. This memoir by General George Custer's wife deals with their life in the Dakota territory in the 1870s just prior to the Battle of Little Bighorn.

1734. Frost, Lawrence A. Custer Legends. Bowling Green University Popular Press, 1981. 251 p. ill. $20. Pb $10.
Gr 9+. B 78: Nov 1 1981. This clarification of the Custer story refutes unfounded stories and is full of unusual details.

1735. Utley, Robert M. Cavalier in Buckskin: George Armstrong Custer and the Western Military Frontier. University of Oklahoma Press, 1988. 248 p. ill. $20.
Gr 9+. * B 85: Oct 15 1988. This biography examines the Custer myths and presents a fair picture of a complex man. It also shows how government policy led to the tragedy at Little Bighorn.

Minnesota

1736. Finsand, Mary Jane. Town That Moved, The. (On My Own Books). Carolrhoda, 1983. 48 p. ill. $7.
Gr K-4. B 79: Apr 15 1983. SE 48: May 1984. SLJ 21: May 1983. A true story about Hibbing, Minnesota, where a tornado revealed a rich iron ore vein and the people decided to move the whole town.

1737. Swenson, Grace. From the Ashes. Croixside Press, 1979. 246 p. Pb $11.
Gr 7+. SE 44: Oct 1980. The story of the 1894 fire in Hinkley, Minnesota, and the rebuilding of the town.

Photographers

1738. Hoobler, Dorothy. Photographing the Frontier. Putnam, 1980. 192 p. ill. $10.
Gr 7+. B 76: Apr 1 1980. +- BC 33: Jun 1980. SLJ 26: Aug 1980. Topically arranged anecdotes of, and photos by, those who made a photographic record of the American frontier.

Presidents and Their Families–Cleveland

1739. Collins, David R. Grover Cleveland: 22nd and 24th President of the United States. (Presidents of the United States). Garrett Educational Corp., 1988. 119 p. ill. $13.
Gr 7-9. SLJ 35: Sep 1988. This introduction to Cleveland and his times includes anecdotes, background information, and illustrations.

Presidents and Their Families–Garfield

1740. Lillegard, Dee. James A. Garfield. (Encyclopedia of Presidents). Childrens Press, 1988. 100 p. ill. $15.
Gr 4-7. B 84: May 15 1988. A readable biography which includes a chronology that places Garfield in the context of U.S. history. Illustrated by photos and engravings.

1741. McElroy, Richard L. James A. Garfield: His Life and Times. Daring Press, 1986. 128 p. ill. $22. Pb $10.
Gr 7+. B 83: Dec 15 1986. LJ 111: Dec 1986. Although he served only six months as president, Garfield was noted as an educator, minister, major general and politician. This pictorial biography clarifies the values of the age.

Presidents and Their Families–Grant

1742. Falkof, Lucille. Ulysses S. Grant: 18th President of the United States. (Presidents of the United States). Garrett Educational Corp., 1988. 124 p. ill. $13.
Gr 6-9. SLJ 35: Oct 1988. Emphasizes Grant's military career and family life.

Public Officials

1743. DeArment, Robert K. Bat Masterson: The Man and the Legend. University of Oklahoma Press, 1979. 441 p. ill. $15.
Gr 9+. B 76: May 15 1980. Separates fact from legend and documents Masterson's years as buffalo hunter, Indian scout, peace officer, gambler, and newspaperman.

1744. Horan, James David. Authentic Wild West: The Lawmen. (Authentic Wild West Series). Crown, 1980. 309 p. ill. $16.
Gr 9+. B 77: Dec 15 1980. LJ 105: Oct 15 1980. SLJ 27: Jan 1981. The last of a trilogy on the people of the west. Covers Bat Masterson, Wyatt Earp, Jesse James, Theodore Roosevelt, and others. The author offers new facts and debunks old legends.

1745. Lavash, Donald R. Sheriff William Brady: Tragic Hero of the Lincoln County War. (Western Legacy Series). Sunstone, 1986. 128 p. Pb $11.
Gr 7+. BR 5: Nov/Dec 1986. An Irish immigrant, Brady was a military leader, served in the Territorial House of Representatives, and was a noted New Mexico sheriff.

1746. Richards, Colin. Sheriff Pat Garrett's Last Days. (Western Legacy Series). Sunstone, 1986. 95 p. $9.
Gr 7+. BR 5: Nov/Dec 1986. Information on New Mexico at the turn of the century, on western law, order, and politics, as well as on Sheriff Pat Garrett.

Reconstruction

1747. Sterling, Dorothy. Trouble They Seen: Black People Tell the Story of the Reconstruction. Doubleday, 1976. 491 p. ill. $10.
Gr 7+. B 81: Sep 15 1984. From speeches, letters, oral history, and newspaper articles, Sterling presents the black view of Reconstruction.

Reformers–Black

1748. Claflin, Edward Beecher. Sojourner Truth and the Struggle for Freedom. (Henry Steele Commager's Americans). Barron's, 1987. 153 p. map. Pb $5.

Gr 4-6. SLJ 34: Mar 1988. Covers Truth's involvement in the abolitionist movement, the Underground Railroad, women's rights, and lobbying activities.

1749. Ferris, Jeri. Walking the Road to Freedom: A Story about Sojourner Truth. (Carolrhoda Creative Minds Book). Carolrhoda, 1988. 64 p. ill. $10.
Gr 3-6. B 84: Mar 1 1988. +- SLJ 34: Mar 1988. A clear and sensitive account of the life of Sojourner Truth who secured her freedom from slavery and was an active abolitionist and worker for women's rights.

1750. Krass, Peter. Sojourner Truth. Chelsea House, 1988. 110 p. ill. $17.
Gr 7+. +- B 85: Oct 1 1988. This biography integrates Truth's personal life with the events of the times and shows her work as an abolitionist and feminist. Includes numerous photos and a chronology.

1751. Lindstrom, Aletha Jane. Sojourner Truth: Slave, Abolitionist, Fighter for Women's Rights. Messner, 1980. 124 p. ill. $8.
Gr 5-7. +- BC 34: Oct 1980. * SE 45: Apr 1981. Presents the major events of the life of Sojourner Truth. Uses fictionalized dialogue.

1752. Ortiz, Victoria. Sojourner Truth, A Self-Made Woman. Lippincott; Harper, 1974. 160 p. ill. $13.
Gr 6-9. B 70: Jul 15 1974. B 81: Sep 15 1984. SE 44: Oct 1980. This former slave became a spokesperson for abolition and women's rights. Ortiz covers the events that shaped Sojourner's work, and includes quotes that illustrate her wit and wisdom.

Reformers–Fiction

1753. Clarke, Mary Stetson. Bloomers and Ballots: Elizabeth Cady Stanton and Women's Rights. Viking, 1972. 223 p. $7.
Gr 7-9. SE 46: Oct 1982. A fictionalized biography of the first president of the National Woman Suffrage Association.

1754. Jacobs, William Jay. Mother, Aunt Susan, and Me: The First Fight for Women's Rights. Harper/Crowell, 1979. 61 p. ill. $8.
Gr 4-8. B 81: Sep 15 1984. * SE 44: Apr 1980. Stanton's daughter tells of the struggle for human rights by Elizabeth Cady Stanton and Susan B. Anthony in a vivid historical novel.

Reformers–Women

1755. Bacon, Margaret Hope. Valiant Friend: The Life of Lucretia Mott. Walker, 1980. 246 p. ill. $15.
Gr 9+. B 76: May 15 1980. LJ 105: May 1 1980. Examines Mott's Quaker upbringing and her work for human rights, including the abolition of slavery and women's suffrage.

1756. Banner, Lois W. Elizabeth Cady Stanton: A Radical for Woman's Rights. (Library of American Biography). Little, 1980. 173 p. ill. $10.
Gr 9+. B 76: Jan 15 1980. HT 15: Feb 1982. LJ 104: Dec 15 1979. SLJ 25: Apr 1980. An analytical portrayal

of how a woman, born to a well-to-do family, became a tireless reformer who worked for the rights of all women.

1757. Barry, Kathleen. Susan B. Anthony: A Biography of a Singular Feminist. New York University Press; dist.by Columbia Univ. Press, 1988. 416 p. ill. $28.
Gr 10+. B 85: Sep 15 1988. LJ 113: Oct 1 1988. A readable and personal biography of Susan B. Anthony who, in her 20s, decided to devote her life to social justice.

1758. Bordin, Ruth. Frances Willard: A Biography. University of North Carolina Press, 1986. 294 p. ill. $25.
Adult. LJ 111: Nov 15 1986. Based on primary sources, this biography of Willard shows her to be a leader of the temperance movement whose ideas of womanliness and domesticity were ahead of her time.

1759. Cooper, Ilene. Susan B. Anthony. (Impact Biography). Watts, 1984. 128 p. $11.
Gr 5+. B 80: May 1 1984. B 81: Sep 15 1984. B 82: Sep 15 1985. SLJ 30: Aug 1984. A comprehensive and insightful biography of one of the first leaders in the campaign for women's rights.

1760. Levinson, Nancy Smiler. First Women Who Spoke Out. (Contributions of Women). Dillon Press, 1983. 126 p. ill. $9.
Gr 5-9. B 79: Jun 1 1983. SLJ 29: Aug 1983. VOYA 6: Aug 1983. The lives and achievements of early feminists, Sarah and Angelina Grimke, Lucretia Mott, Sojourner Truth, Elizabeth Cady Stanton, Susan B. Anthony and Lucy Stone.

1761. Morrison, Dorothy. Ladies Were Not Expected: Abigail Scott Duniway and Women's Rights. Atheneum, 1977. 158 p. ill. $7.
Gr 5-7. B 81: Sep 15 1984. A biography of an Oregon crusader for women's right to vote. Based on primary sources and richly illustrated.

Social Life and Customs

1762. Barth, Gunther. City People: The Rise of Modern City Culture in Nineteenth-Century America. Oxford University Press, 1980. 289 p. ill. $20.
Gr 9+. LJ 105: Sep 15 1980. SLJ 27: Mar 1981. Examines life in the big city, including apartment buildings, the metropolitan press, department stores, ball parks, and vaudeville. An informative view of the urbanization of America.

1763. Bettmann, Otto L. Good Old Days–They Were Terrible, The. Random House, 1974. 207 p. Pb $7.
Gr 9+. SE 64: May 1982. This survey of life in 19th-century America covers rural life, work, crime, food, health, education, and leisure.

1764. Cable, Mary. Blizzard of '88, The. Atheneum, 1988. 197 p. $20.
Gr 9+. B 84: Feb 1 1988. LJ 113: Jan 1988. VOYA 11: Oct 1988. A realistic account of life at the time is presented in this account of people, ordinary and wealthy, urban and rural, who struggled to survive a crippling five-day blizzard in 1888.

1765. Hilton, Suzanne. Way It Was–1876, The. Westminster, 1975. 216 p. ill. $7.
Gr 8+. SE 44: Oct 1980. Facts about everyday life are illustrated with prints and photos.

1766. Wellikoff, Alan. American Historical Supply Catalogue: A Nineteenth-Century Sourcebook. Schocken, 1984. 256 p. ill. Pb $17.
Gr 10+. LJ 110: Feb 1 1985. A catalog of 19th-century Americana reproduced from old molds and patterns. Items range from cigar store Indians to Gatling guns. Includes history, descriptions, prices, and illustrations.

Social Life and Customs–Children

1767. Freedman, Russell. Children of the Wild West. Clarion/Ticknor & Fields, 1983. 112 p. ill. $13.
Gr 3-8. * B 80: Dec 15 1983. BC 37: Apr 1984. HB 60: Feb 1984. * SE 48: May 1984. * SLJ 30: Jan 1984. A photographic essay on the experiences and expectations of white children on the westward journey and how they lived on the frontier, and of the lives of Indian children during a time of upheaval in their culture.

Social Life and Customs–Fiction

1768. Beatty, Patricia. Something to Shout About. Morrow, 1976. 254 p. $7. Lib. ed. $6.
Gr 7-8. * SE 47: Apr 1983. A group of women decide that if their Montana town can build a new jail and courthouse, then a refurbished chicken coop is not adequate for a school. Humorous, and based on a true incident.

1769. Beatty, Patricia. That's One Ornery Orphan. Morrow, 1980. 222 p. $8.
Gr 7-9. B 76: May 1 1980. +- BC 34: Sep 1980. HB 56: Aug 1980. SLJ 26: Aug 1980. VOYA 3: Aug 1980. Orphaned Hollie, a 13-year-old Texan, is addicted to telling whoppers and has difficulty finding a new home. Good information on orphans and the times.

1770. Calvert, Patricia. Snowbird, The. Scribner; New American Library, 1980. 146 p. $9. Pb $2
Gr 6-9. B 77: Nov 15 1980. +- BC 34: Feb 1984. * BR 1: Jan/Feb 1983. HB 62: Apr 1981. * SE 47: Apr 1983. SLJ 27: Mar 1981. VOYA 4: Apr 1981. Orphaned Willie and her brother move from Tennessee to the Dakota Territory to live with relatives. A new colt helps them adjust, and Willie comes to admire her independent aunt. A good character study.

1771. Dreiser, Theodore. Sister Carrie. Doubleday; New American Library, 1900, 1962. 557 p. $4.
Gr 11+. SE 46: Oct 1982. In 1889, 18-year-old Carrie leaves her hometown. She flaunts convention and becomes a material success, but happiness eludes her.

1772. Emerson, Kathy Lynn. Julia's Mending. Orchard/Watts, 1987. 135 p. $12. Lib. ed. $12.
Gr 4-8. BC 41: Sep 1987. SLJ 34: Oct 1987. In this authentic picture of 19th-century childhood on a farm in upper New York state, Julia, a spoiled 12-year-old, goes to the farm to live with cousins while her missionary parents are in China.

1773. Johnston, Tony. Quilt Story, The. Putnam, 1985. 28 p. ill. $13. Pb $5.
Gr K-2. * B 81: Aug 1985. B 83: Mar 1 1987. SLJ 32: Sep 1985. Abigail's quilt is her comfort as her pioneer family moves west. Years later another little girl finds it comforting in the same way.

1774. Yolen, Jane. Gift of Sarah Barker, The. Viking, 1981. 156 p. $10.
Gr 6+. B 77: May 1981. BC 35: Dec 1981. HB 57: Aug 1981. +- SLJ 28: Oct 1981. Because of their love for each other, Sarah and Abel are expelled from their Shaker community.

Social Life and Customs–Women

1775. Green, Harvey. Light of the Home: An Intimate View of the Lives of Women in Victorian America. Pantheon, 1983. 256 p. ill. $19.
Gr 10+. B 79: Jun 1 1983. LJ 108: May 15 1983. An enjoyable portrait of daily life and customs–courtship, manners, clothes, hygiene, medicine, interior decoration, housekeeping, and recreation.

Spanish American War

1776. Kent, Zachary. Story of the Sinking of the Battleship Maine, The. (Cornerstones of Freedom). Childrens Press, 1988. 32 p. ill. $12.
Gr 4-8. B 84: Aug 1988. SLJ 35: Sep 1988. Kent shows the emotional and political climate in the U.S. and Cuba (then a Spanish possession) that made it possible for the U.S. to go to war with Spain although there was little real evidence of Spanish wrongdoing.

1777. Trask, David F. War with Spain in 1898, The. (Wars of the United States). Macmillan, 1981. 634 p. maps. $30.
Gr 9+. B 78: Sep 1 1981. LJ 106: May 1 1981. Exciting battle scenes and an examination of the political and geographical ramifications of the war are a part of this exciting history.

Statue of Liberty

1778. Bell, James B. In Search of Liberty: The Story of the Statue of Liberty and Ellis Island. Doubleday, 1984. 128 p. ill. $25. Pb $11.
Gr 9+. B 81: Oct 1 1984. LJ 109: Aug 1984. Photographs and period drawings highlight this account of the Lady, Ellis Island and the liberties they symbolize. Vital statistics appended.

1779. Blanchet, Christian. Statue of Liberty: The First Hundred Years. American Heritage; dist. by Houghton, 1985. 192 p. ill. $30.
Gr 9+. B 82: Nov 1 1985. LJ 110: Nov 15 1985. Over 350 illustrations accompany a definitive text that covers the construction of the statue and its international significance.

1780. Burchard, Sue. Statue of Liberty: Birth to Rebirth. Harcourt, 1985. 199 p. ill. $13.
Gr 5+. B 82: Dec 1 1985. HB 62: Jan/Feb 1986. SLJ 32: Dec 1985. VOYA 9: Aug/Oct 1986. A thorough examination of the history, maintenance, renovation, and importance of the statue in American life.

1781. Coerr, Eleanor. Lady with a Torch: How the Statue of Liberty Was Born. Harper, 1986. 84 p. $11. Lib. ed. $11.
Gr 2-4. B 82: Jun 15 1986. BC 40: Sep 1986. SLJ 33: Sep 1986. A factual but fictionalized story of the Lady and her designer, Frederic Bartholdi.

1782. Fisher, Leonard Everett. Statue of Liberty, The. Holiday, 1985. 64 p. ill. $13.
Gr 4-9. B 82: Oct 1 1985. BC 39: Dec 1985. HB 62: Jan/Feb 1986. SE 50: Apr/May 1986. SLJ 32: Dec 1985. Attractive illustrations highlight the traditional story that places the building of the statue in its historic and social context.

1783. Forte, Joseph. Story of the Statue of Liberty, The. Holt, 1986. Unp. ill. $16.
Gr K-5. SLJ 33: Sep 1986. Covers Bartholdi's life and the construction of the statue. Pop-ups, fold-outs, cutouts, and string movements make this book unique.

1784. Fox, Mary Virginia. Statue of Liberty, The. Simon & Schuster/Messner, 1985. 64 p. ill. $7. Lib. ed. $10.
Gr 3-6. +- B 82: Dec 1 1985. SLJ 32: Apr 1986. Includes numerous color and b/w photos with a readable factual account.

1785. Fox, Nancy Jo. Liberties With Liberty: The Fascinating History of America's Proudest Symbol. Dutton/Museum of American Folk Art, 1986. 72 p. ill. $23. Pb $15.
Gr 9+. B 83: Sep 1 1986. Includes folk art, cartoons, primitive art, domestic and commercial art, all about the statue and its place in our lives.

1786. George, Michael. Statue of Liberty, The. Abrams, 1985. 56 p. ill. $15.
Gr 6+. B 81: Jun 15 1985. * VOYA 8: Dec 1985. A photographic essay on Miss Liberty and on conditions in France and the U.S. at the time of her creation.

1787. Grumet, Michael. Images of Liberty. Arbor House, 1986. 137 p. ill. $13.
Gr 10+. +- VOYA 9: Aug/Oct 1986. Anecdotes and pictures of all types of images of the Statue of Liberty, including posters, paintings, sculptures, ads, and replicas, enliven this short history.

1788. Hargrove, Jim. Gateway to Freedom: The Story of the Statue of Liberty and Ellis Island. Childrens Press, 1986. 111 p. ill. $13.
Gr 3-6. SLJ 33: May 1987. A lively introduction to 19th-century immigration and the building of the statue, highly illustrated with photos and cartoons.

1789. Harris, Jonathan. Statue for America: The First 100 Years of the Statue of Liberty. Macmillan/Four Winds, 1985. 225 p. ill. $15.
Gr 6+. B 82: Dec 1 1985. BR 5: Nov/Dec 1986. HB 62: Jan/Feb 1986. SLJ 32: Apr 1986. VOYA 9: Aug/Oct 1986. Emphasis is on the financial and legal problems of construction. Includes numerous anecdotes concerning events that have occurred near the statue.

1790. Haskins, James. Statue of Liberty: America's Proud Lady. Lerner, 1986. 48 p. ill. $9.
Gr 2-7. B 82: Mar 1 1986. HB 62: May/Jun 1986. +- SLJ 32: Apr 1986. This overview for middle-graders covers the history, construction, and rejuvenation of the statue, and discusses her meaning to Americans of all races.

1791. Krensky, Stephen. Maiden Voyage: The Story of the Statue of Liberty. Atheneum, 1985. 53 p. ill. $11.
Gr 2-5. +- B 82: Dec 1 1985. HB 62: Jan/Feb 1986. SLJ 32: Dec 1985. An account of the design and construction of the statue and her meaning to the world.

1792. Levinson, Nancy Smiler. I Lift My Lamp: Emma Lazarus and the Statue of Liberty. (Jewish Biography Series). Dutton/Lodestar, 1986. 128 p. ill. $14.
Gr 5-8. B 82: Aug 1986. +- BC 39: Mar 1986. HB 62: May/Jun 1986. SLJ 32: May 1986. These highlights of the Miss Liberty story, and the life of the woman who wrote the inspirational words at the base, present a clear picture of American life in the last half of the 19th century.

1793. Maestro, Betsy. Story of the Statue of Liberty, The. Lothrop, 1986. 39 p. ill. $13. Lib. ed. $13.
Gr K-3. B 82: Mar 1 1986. BC 39: Apr 1986. HB 62: May/Jun 1986. * SLJ 32: Apr 1986. An overview of the building of the Lady. Includes statistics and chronology.

1794. Mercer, Charles. Statue of Liberty. Putnam, 1985. 96 p. $8.
Gr 4+. B 81: Aug 1985. HB 62: Jan/Feb 1986. +- SLJ 32: Sep 1985. VOYA 8: Dec 1985. This revised version of the 1979 edition includes information on the restoration project.

1795. Shapiro, Mary J. Gateway to Liberty: The Story of the Statue of Liberty and Ellis Island. Random House/Vintage, 1986. 276 p. ill. $15.
Gr 7+. * B 83: Sep 1 1986. BR 5: Nov/Dec 1986. LJ 111: Jun 1 1986. Based on primary sources, with over 200 illustrations. Emphasizes the immigrant experience.

1796. Shapiro, Mary J. How They Built the Statue of Liberty. Random House, 1985. 61 p. ill. $10. Lib. ed. $10.
Gr 4-9. * B 82: Dec 1 1985. BC 39: Dec 1985. HB 62: Jan/Feb 1986. * SE 50: Apr/May 1986. * SLJ 32: Dec 1985. Detailed pencil sketches explain the detail of construction and provide perspective.

1797. Shapiro, William E. Statue of Liberty, The. (First Book). Watts, 1985. 66 p. ill. $10.
Gr 4-9. B 82: Dec 1 1985. BC 39: Dec 1985. BR 5: May/Jun 1986. SLJ 32: Dec 1985. Includes historic photos and covers the reasons for this gift from France, its construction, the story of Ellis Island, and the centennial restoration.

1798. Spiering, Frank. Bearer of a Million Dreams: The Biography of the Statue of Liberty. Jameson Books; dist. by Kampmann, 1986. 224 p. ill. $17.
Gr 9+. B 82: Jul 1986. +- LJ 111: Jul 1986. An account based on the writings of Bartholdi, the designer of the statue.

Statue of Liberty–Fiction

1799. Eger, Jeffrey. Statue in the Harbor: A Story of Two Apprentices. Silver Burdett, 1986. 128 p. ill. $8. Pb $5.
Gr 3-7. +- BR 5: May/June 1986. SLJ 32: May 1986. A 10-year-old apprentice coppersmith assists in building the Statue of Liberty.

Technology and Civilization

1800. Greenhill, Ralph. Engineer's Witness. Godine, 1985. 214 p. ill. $35.
Adult. B 81: Jun 15 1985. LJ 110: Jun 15 1985. Photos of industrial engineering works of the last half of the 19th century, including bridges, tunnels, subways, and factories.

Transportation

1801. Gordon, John Steele. Scarlet Woman of Wall Street: Jay Gould, Jim Fisk, Cornelius Vanderbilt, and the Erie Railway Wars. Weidenfeld & Nicolson, 1988. 418 p. ill. $23.
Adult. B 84: Jul 1988. * LJ 113: Aug 1988. A fascinating study of the development of Wall Street as a center for international financial dealing and of the market manipulations that surrounded the development of railroads.

1802. Nathan, A. G. Building of the First Transcontinental Railroad. (Landmark Books). Random House, 1950. 180 p. ill. $2.
Gr 5-6. Metzner [B 47: Nov 15 1950]. An informative account of the personalities and problems involved in spanning our continent by railroad. Large print.

1803. Williams, John Hoyt. Great and Shining Road: The Epic Story of the Transcontinental Railroad. Times Books, 1988. 331 p. map. $23.
Gr 9+. B 84: Apr 15 1988. LJ 113: Apr 1 1988. The awe-inspiring story of the determination and technology that combined to make it possible to cross the mountains and desert of the American West.

West, The

1804. Flanagan, Mike. Out West. Abrams, 1987. 207 p. ill. $28.
Gr 9+. B 83: May 15 1987. An attractive compilation of articles on the West that originally appeared in the Denver Post, arranged by theme and accompanied by over 100 photos.

West, The–Fiction

1805. Tuska, Jon. American West in Fiction. New American Library, 1982. 400 p. $4.
Gr 6+. B 78: Jun 1 1982. VOYA 5: Oct 1982. Twenty short stories on the American West by Twain, Harte, Cather, Grey, and others.

Women

1806. Clinton, Catherine. Other Civil War, The: American Women in the Nineteenth Century. (American Century Series). Hill and Wang, 1984. 272 p. $17. Pb $8.
Gr 9+. B 80: May 1 1984. LJ 109: Apr 1 1984. Surveys women's complex struggle for rights, the temperance and anti-slavery movements, and the influence of the Civil War.

1807. Culley, Margo. Day at a Time, A. Feminist Press, 1985. 346 p. $30. Pb $13.
Gr 11+. B 82: Feb 15 1986. LJ 111: Feb 15 1986. Diary excerpts tell how women struggled to cope with infant death, sickness, old age, murder, and other experiences.

1808. Western Writers of America. Women Who Made the West, The. Doubleday, 1980. 252 p. $11.
Gr 9+. B 77: Sep 1 1980. LJ 105: Jun 1 1980. Stories about 18 ordinary women who contributed to the settling of the West, including businesswomen, reformers, healers, and homemakers.

Women–Biographies

1809. Farnsworth, Martha. Plains Woman: The Diary of Mary Farnsworth, 1882-1922. Indiana University Press, 1985. 352 p. ill. $28.

Gr 10+. * LJ 110: Oct 15 1985. This biography includes much detail about life on the plains.

1810. Herr, Pamela. Jessie Benton Fremont: A Biography. Watts, 1987. 406 p. $25.
Gr 9+. B 83: Feb 1 1987. * LJ 112: Mar 1 1987. A well-researched biography of a brilliant and spirited woman who served as her famous husband's ghost writer, press agent, and chief of staff. When his career collapsed she supported the family by writing.

1811. Morrison, Dorothy Nafus. Under a Strong Wind: The Adventures of Jesse Benton Fremont. Atheneum, 1983. 176 p. ill. $11.
Gr 6-10. B 80: Oct 15 1983. B 82: Sep 15 1985. HB 59: Oct 1983. * SE 48: May 1984. SLJ 30: Nov 1983. With her explorer husband, Jesse Fremont participated in the opening of the West and the formation of the Republican Party.

Women–Fiction

1812. Haruf, Kent. Tie That Binds, The. Holt, 1984. 246 p. $13.
Gr 10+. * BR 3: Mar/Apr 1985. VOYA 8: Jun 1985. For over 50 years Edith was driven by duty to her demanding family. A realistic novel of life on a Colorado homestead for mature readers.

1900-1939

United States–History–1900-1939

1813. 1920s, The. National Archives/Social Issues Resources Series, Inc., 1986. 69 items, boxed. ill. $35.
Gr 7+. BR 1: Sep/Oct 1982. BR 5: Sep/Oct 1986. A boxed set of primary sources on the politics, economics, and culture of the 1920s, with a teacher's guide. Suitable to supplement individual or group study. Includes letters, photos, maps, and news clippings.

1814. Great Depression and the New Deal, The. (Social Issues Resources Series). Social Issues Resources Series, Inc., 1982. Boxed unit. ill. $30.
Gr 9+. BR 1: Sep/Oct 1982. Includes letters, news clippings, photos, and other primary sources to clarify political, social, economic, and cultural events of the time.

1815. Alexander, Mary. Progressive Years 1898-1917, The. (Social Issues Resources Series). Social Issues Resources Series, Inc., 1982. 40 documents. ill. $30.
Gr 7+. BR 2: May/Jun 1983. Photographs, documents, and exercises to supplement a study of the political, economic, and social aspects of the times.

1816. Klingaman, William. 1919: The Year Our World Began. St. Martin's, 1987. 673 p. ill. $28.
Gr 9+. B 83: Aug 1987. LJ 112: Aug 1987. An anecdotal chronicle of social and political events of 1919, with emphasis on personalities, from Babe Ruth to Woodrow Wilson and his doomed efforts to achieve international cooperation.

1817. Sandler, Martin W. This Was America. Little, 1980. 271 p. ill. $20.

Gr 9+. +- B 77: Dec 1 1980. A photo essay of life at the turn of the century.

1818. Smith, Page. America Enters the World: v.7: A People's History of the Progressive Era and World War I. (People's History of the United States). McGraw-Hill, 1985. 1148 p. ill. $33.
Gr 10+. B 81: Nov 15 1984. Covers the labor movement and the growth of U.S. international relations. This is volume 7 of the series.

1819. Smith, Page. Redeeming the Time: A People's History of the 1920s and the New Deal. (People's History of the United States). McGraw-Hill, 1986. 1232 p. ill. $35.
Gr 10+. +- LJ 111: Nov 1 1986. This overview of the New Deal, literature, music, foreign policy, medicine, and other aspects of life in the '20s and '30s, is volume 8 of the series.

1820. Wilson, Edmund. Thirties: From Notebooks and Diaries of the Period. Farrar, 1980. 740 p. ill. $18.
Adult. B 76: Jun 15 1980. LJ 105: Jun 15 1980. Wilson traveled across the country as a reporter during the Depression. Here he presents a personal view of the time.

Airplanes and Pilots

1821. Howard, Fred. Wilbur and Orville: A Biography of the Wright Brothers. Knopf, 1987. 560 p. ill. $25.
Gr 9+. B 83: Jun 1 1987. LJ 112: Aug 1987. This lively definitive biography explains how the Wright brothers built on the work of their precursors, and makes

clear what they achieved before, during, and after, the 1903 flight.

1822. Lindbergh, Charles. Spirit of St. Louis, The. Scribner, o.p.; Avon, 1953. 544 p. Pb $6.
Gr 7+. B 82: Jan 1 1986. B 82: Mar 1 1986. This epic and spell-binding account of the first solo transatlantic flight, 1927, is told by the pilot, who interweaves his earlier flying experience.

1823. McKay, Ernest A. World to Conquer: The Epic Story of the First Around-the-World Flight. Arco, 1981. 201 p. ill. $13.
Gr 9+. B 77: Jul 1 1981. SLJ 28: Aug 1982. In 1924 four young Americans spent 175 days encircling the globe. The details of the planning of the trip are provided, along with photos and an extensive bibliography.

1824. Sabin, Louis. Wilbur and Orville Wright: The Flight to Adventure. Troll, 1983. 48 p. ill. $7. Pb $2.
Gr 3-5. B 80: Sep 1 1983. A slightly fictionalized biography of the Wright brothers that emphasizes the experiences of their youth.

1825. Stein, R. Conrad. Story of the Flight at Kitty Hawk, The. (Cornerstones of Freedom). Childrens Press, 1981. 31 p. ill. $6.
Gr 3-5. +- B 78: Feb 15 1982. SLJ 28: Mar 1982. Anecdotes and quotes enliven the straightforward text. Slightly fictionalized.

Airplanes and Pilots—Women

1826. Brown, Fern G. Amelia Earhart Takes Off. Albert Whitman, 1985. 61 p. ill. $10.
Gr 3-8. B 82: Mar 1 1986. +- SLJ 32: Mar 1986. This account of Earhart's life and disappearance includes anecdotes and photographs.

1827. Chadwick, Roxane. Amelia Earhart: Aviation Pioneer. (Achievers). Lerner, 1987. 56 p. ill. $8. Pb $5.
Gr 4-6. B 83: Jun 15 1987. BC 40: Jun 1987. SLJ 33: Aug 1987. A complete biography that emphasizes Earhart's youthful independence and ingenuity, and presents the varied theories on her disappearance.

1828. Chadwick, Roxane. Anne Morrow Lindbergh: Pilot and Poet. (Achievers). Lerner, 1987. 56 p. ill. $8. Pb $5.
Gr 4-6. +- B 83: Jun 15 1987. BC 40: Jun 1987. SLJ 33: Aug 1987. Covers Lindbergh's work as a navigator, radio operator, and co-pilot for her famous husband, in addition to the kidnapping and murder of her son and the family's exile in England.

1829. Lauber, Patricia. Lost Star: The Story of Amelia Earhart. Scholastic, 1988. 72 p. ill. $11.
Gr 5-7. B 85: Oct 1 1988. A gripping biography of the noted flyer who coped with the difficulties of her life by becoming free and independent. Includes photos.

1830. Loomis, Vincent V. Amelia Earhart. Random House, 1985. 155 p. $17.
Gr 9+. B 81: Jul 1985. LJ 110: Jul 1985. Loomis investigates the possibility that Earhart crashed in the Mar-

shall Islands and was captured by the Japanese prior to World War II.

1831. Pearce, Carol A. Amelia Earhart. (Makers of America). Facts on File, 1988. 169 p. ill. $15.
Gr 6+. +- B 84: Jul 1988. * BR 7: Sep/Oct 1988. +- SLJ 34: May 1988. +- VOYA 11: Aug 1988. An overview of Earhart's life that covers the problems of her childhood, her love of flying, her accomplishments, and theories concerning her death.

1832. Randolph, Blythe. Amelia Earhart. (Impact Biography). Watts, 1987. 128 p. ill. $12.
Gr 7-9. B 83: May 15 1987. BC 40: May 1987. +- BR 6: Nov/Dec 1987. SLJ 33: Jun/Jul 1987. * VOYA 10: Sep 1987. Earhart's charisma, independent spirit, and intelligence are shown in this biography that is made more realistic by well-captioned photos and maps of her important flights.

1833. Sabin, Francene. Amelia Earhart: Adventure in the Sky. Troll, 1983. 48 p. ill. $7. Pb $2.
Gr 3-5. B 80: Sep 1 1983. +- SLJ 30: Oct 1983. A slightly fictionalized biography that emphasizes Earhart's youth as a free-thinking and independent girl.

1834. Shore, Nancy. Amelia Earhart. (American Women of Achievement). Chelsea House, 1987. 111 p. ill. $17.
Gr 4-9. B 84: Sep 1 1987. Emphasis is on Earhart's flying accomplishments. The text is accompanied by an abundance of good photos.

Appalachia—Fiction

1835. Lee, Mildred. People Therein, The. Houghton/Clarion, 1980. 271 p. $11. Pb $2.
Gr 7-10. B 82: Mar 1 1986. BC 34: Jan 1981. HB 57: Feb 1981. SLJ 27: Oct 1980. +- VOYA 3: Dec 1980. A perceptive and leisurely story of life in the Smokey Mountains at the turn of the century in which crippled Lanthy and Drew, a naturalist from Boston, fall in love. Strong characterization and sense of place.

1836. Marshall, Catherine. Christy. McGraw-Hill; Avon, 1967. 496 p. $15. Pb $4.
Gr 7+. B 82: Mar 1 1986. A teacher in 1912 Appalachia shares the hard times of her students and their families.

Artists

1837. Kurelek, William. Prairie Boy's Winter, A. Houghton/Sandpiper, 1984. 46 p. ill. $5.
Gr 3+. HB 61: May/Jun 1985. A collection of nostalgic paintings and affectionate remembrances of the author/illustrator's boyhood in a prairie farming community. Suitable for all ages.

1838. O'Kelley, Mattie Lou. From the Hills of Georgia: An Autobiography in Paintings. Atlantic Monthly Press; dist. by Little, Brown, 1983. 32 p. ill. $15.
Gr K+. * B 80: Dec 15 1983. B 82: Sep 15 1985. BC 37: Jan 1984. HB 60: Feb 1984. SLJ 30: Jan 1984. A noted artist shares her memories of childhood in rural Georgia in the early 1900s through 28 detailed paintings with text, all depicting daily life. Suitable for all ages.

Authors

1839. Fritz, Jean. Homesick: My Own Story. Putnam, 1982. 136 p. ill. $11. Pb $3.
Gr 5+. * B 79: Sep 1 1982. B 82: Mar 1 1986. * BC 35: Jul/Aug 1982. SLJ 29: Sep 1982. A slightly fictionalized version of Fritz' youth. Raised in China to the age of 12, she came to the U.S. and found in her peers little understanding of China and the Chinese.

1840. Meltzer, Milton. Starting from Home: A Writer's Beginnings. Viking, 1988. 128 p. ill. $14.
Gr 7+. * B 84: Aug 1988. BC 42: Sep 1988. HB 64: Sep/Oct 1988. * SLJ 35: Sep 1988. Meltzer, a noted author grew up in a poor Jewish immigrant family in Massachusetts during the '20s and '30s. These warm memories of family and friends include candid remarks about anti-Semitism.

1841. Stevenson, James. When I Was Nine. Greenwillow, 1986. unp. ill. $12.
Gr K-3. B 82: Jun 15 1986. +- BC 40: Sep 1986. HB 62: Jul/Aug 1986. SLJ 32: Aug 1986. In a warm reminiscence the author details his daily life during a summer in the '30s when things were simpler but people were just the same. Illustrated with free-form watercolors.

Authors–Black

1842. Angelou, Maya. I Know Why the Caged Bird Sings. Random House; Bantam, 1970. 281 p. $15. Pb $4.
Gr 9+. B 82: Mar 1 1986. In telling of her Depression childhood in rural Arkansas, the author shows how, in spite of a racist society, her loving family helped her to grow up strong.

1843. Hughes, Langston. Big Sea, The. Knopf, o.p.; Hill & Wang, 1940. 335 p. Pb $9.
Gr 8+. B 82: Mar 1 1986. The author's memories of growing up in 1920s Harlem.

1844. Wright, Richard. Black Boy. Harper, 1945. 228 p. $17. Pb $4.
Gr 8+. B 82: Mar 1 1986. Describes the author's struggle to survive the poverty and brutal racism of the South.

Blacks–Fiction

1845. Baldwin, James. Go Tell It on the Mountain. Dial/Doubleday; Dell, 1953. 256 p. $14. Pb $5.
Gr 9+. B 82: Mar 1 1986. SE 46: Oct 1982. In Harlem during the 1930s a boy struggles with his religious awakening.

1846. Sebestyen, Ouida. Words By Heart. Atlantic Monthly Press; dist. by Little, Brown, 1979. 162 p. $13. Pb $3.
Gr 7-10. B 82: Mar 1 1986. HB 62: May/Jun 1986. A black family faces violence when they move into a small western town in 1910.

1847. Taylor, Mildred D. Friendship, The. Dial; dist. by Dutton, 1987. 53 p. ill. $12. Lib. ed. $12.

Gr 3-7. B 84: Dec 15 1987. BC 41: Dec 1987. HB 64: Jan/Feb 1988. * SE 52: Apr/May 1988. * SLJ 34: Jan 1988. A short and bitter story. After the black boy, Tom, saved his life John swore lifelong friendship. Then as adults John insisted that Tom call him "mistah" as was the custom, but Tom insisted on the promise.

1848. Taylor, Mildred D. Let the Circle Be Unbroken. Dial; dist. by Dutton; Bantam, 1981. 339 p. $13. Pb $3.
Gr 6+. B 78: Dec 1 1981. B 81: Sep 15 1984. BC 35: Dec 1981. HB 58: Apr 1982. * SE 46: Apr 1982. SLJ 28: Dec 1981. VOYA 5: June 1982. Cassie and her loving family continue to suffer from prejudice and the Depression in a powerful novel that tells of the effect of a black woman's decision to register to vote. Sequel to Roll of Thunder, Hear My Cry.

1849. Taylor, Mildred D. Roll of Thunder, Hear My Cry. Dial; Bantam, 1976. 276 p. $14. Pb $3.
Gr 7-10. B 82: Mar 1 1986. * SE 47: Apr 1983. A loving black family faces racism during the Depression.

Blacks–Women

1850. Brooks, Sara. You May Plow Here: The Narrative of Sara Brooks. Norton, 1986. 212 p. $13.
Gr 9+. B 82: Jan 15 1986. LJ 111: Jan 1986. Brooks tells her story of growing up in rural Alabama and of her life as a domestic in Cleveland.

Business and Business People

1851. Aird, H. B. Henry Ford, Boy with Ideas. (Childhood of Famous Americans Series). Bobbs-Merrill, 1960. 192 p. ill. $6.
Gr 3-7. Metzner [LJ 85: Apr 15 1960]. The emphasis is on Ford's childhood in this fictionalized biography.

1852. Gelderman, Carol. Henry Ford: The Wayward Capitalist. Dial, 1981. 416 p. ill. $15.
Gr 9+. +- B 77: Feb 1 1981. LJ 106: Feb 1 1981. Details the unusual life of the mechanical genius who led the way to worker benefits but opposed unions. Based on extensive research.

1853. Harris, Jacqueline L. Henry Ford. (Impact Biography). Watts, 1984. 116 p. ill. $9.
Gr 6-10. B 80: May 15 1984. +- BR 3: Nov/Dec 1984. SLJ 30: Aug 1984. VOYA 7: Dec 1984. Clarifies Ford's role in the growth of technology, shows the development of the Industrial Revolution, and explores Ford's creative and eccentric personality.

1854. Lacey, Robert. Ford: The Men and the Machine. Little, 1986. 778 p. ill. $25.
Gr 9+. B 82: Jul 1986. LJ 111: Sep 1 1986. A detailed but lively history of the man, the car, and the dynasty.

1855. Miller, Russell. House of Getty, The. Holt, 1986. 362 p. ill. $18.
Gr 10+. LJ 111: May 1 1986. This account of the personal and business exploits of the billionaire Getty is suitable for advanced students.

1856. Mitchell, Barbara. We'll Race You, Henry: A Story about Henry Ford. (Carolrhoda Creative Minds Book). Carolrhoda, 1986. 56 p. ill. $9.
Gr 3-6. +- B 82: Aug 1986. SLJ 33: Sep 1986. Slightly fictionalized stories about Ford's early experiences that led to his success.

California

1857. Levine, Ellen. If You Lived at the Time of the Great San Francisco Earthquake. (If You Lived Series). Scholastic, 1987. 63 p. ill. Pb $3.
Gr 3-6. +- SLJ 34: Oct 1987. Uses a question-and-answer format with quotes and anecdotes to help the young reader understand the violence of this earthquake.

1858. Pelta, Kathy. Bridging the Golden Gate. Lerner, 1987. 96 p. ill. $11. Pb $5.
Gr 4-8. B 83: Apr 15 1987. +- BC 40: May 1987. * SE 52: Apr/May 1987. SLJ 33: May 1987. This celebration of the 50th anniversary of the Golden Gate Bridge focuses on the vision of its builder who accomplished what others believed to be impossible. Includes photos and drawings.

1859. Stein, R. Conrad. Story of the San Francisco Earthquake, The. (Cornerstones of Freedom). Childrens Press, 1983. 31 p. ill. $7.
Gr 3-6. B 80: Jan 15 1986. SLJ 30: Apr 1984. The story of the earthquake, with abundant detail and good illustrations.

Chinese Americans–Fiction

1860. Howard, Ellen. Her Own Song. Atheneum, 1988. 192 p. $13.
Gr 4-7. B 85: Dec 1 1988. +- BC 42: Nov 1988. Millie knew that she was Chinese and had been adopted by a loving white family, but it took an accident for her to learn the truth about her birth. Based on a true story.

1861. Yep, Laurence. Dragonwings. Harper, 1975. 256 p. $12.
Gr 8+. SE 44: Oct 1980. Turn-of-the-century San Francisco is seen through Asian eyes in this story of a Chinese immigrant who built and flew a biplane in 1909. A unique historical novel based on a real incident.

Civil Rights

1862. Russell, Francis. Sacco and Vanzetti: The Case Resolved. Harper, 1986. 242 p. $17.
Gr 10+. B 82: Mar 1 1986. LJ 111: Mar 1 1986. Russell presents a riveting examination of the hard evidence and finds that Vanzetti was innocent, but Sacco was guilty. He provides a valuable legal and historical perspective for the advanced student.

Conscientious Objectors

1863. Moore, Howard W. Plowing My Own Furrow. Norton, 1985. 195 p. ill. $13.
Gr 9+. B 81: Apr 15 1985. LJ 110: Apr 15 1985. Moore was a pacifist and conscientious objector during World War I and faced brutal internment.

Cowhands

1864. Lanning, Jim. Texas Cowboys: Memories of the Early Days. Texas A&M University Press, 1984. 240 p. ill. $16.
Gr 10+. LJ 109: Jul 1984. An anthology of first-person accounts given by Texas cowboys to members of the Federal Writer's Project in the 1930s.

Crime and Criminals

1865. Treherne, John. Strange History of Bonnie and Clyde, The. Stein & Day, 1985. 263 p. ill. $17.
Adult. B 81: Jun 1 1985. LJ 110: Jun 1 1985. Explores the various folk myths that surrounded this criminal duo, and divulges the amazing facts of the crime wave that caught the public fancy.

Depression

1866. Agee, James. Let Us Now Praise Famous Men. Houghton, 1941. 496 p. ill. $20. Pb $12.
Gr 8+. B 82: Mar 1 1986. A photo-documentary of the lives of three Alabama sharecropper families during the Depression.

1867. Galbraith, John Kenneth. Great Crash, 1929, The. 50th anniversary ed. Houghton, 1979. 206 p. $11.
Gr 9+. B 76: Feb 1 1980. This new edition of Galbraith's witty and brief lesson on speculation makes clear that at some point an economic boom must collapse. He also explains the causes for the fantastic gains and devastating losses.

1868. Garraty, John A. Great Depression: An Inquiry Into the Causes, Course, and Consequences of the Worldwide Depression of the 1930s as Seen by Contemporaries in the Light of History. Harcourt, 1986. 254 p. $18.
Gr 10+. * LJ 111: Sep 1 1986. This examination of the Depression from a world perspective clarifies the ways in which many different nations reacted to the tragedy. Emphasis is on western nations.

1869. Glassman, Bruce. Crash of '29 and the New Deal, The. (Turning Points in American History). Silver Burdett, 1986. 63 p. ill. $14. Pb $6.
Gr 5-9. B 82: Aug 1986. BC 40: Nov 1986. SLJ 33: Dec 1986. Traces the crash and the recovery efforts of the New Deal. Includes a glossary and abundant illustrations.

1870. Low, Ann Marie. Dust Bowl Diary. University of Nebraska Press, 1984. 188 p. $18.
Gr 10+. * LJ 109: Dec 1984. LJ 110: Jan 1985. Memoirs of growing up on a North Dakota farm during the Depression.

1871. McElvaine, Robert S. Great Depression: America, 1929-1941. Times Books; dist. by Harper, 1984. 416 p. ill. $19.
Gr 10+. B 80: Jan 1 1984. * LJ 108: Dec 1 1983. SE 49: May 1985. Through portrayals of well-known and ordinary people, and comparisons of Depression events to more recent ones, McElvaine's treatment of everyday life and values is effective.

1872. Stein, R. Conrad. Story of the Great Depression, The. (Cornerstones of Freedom). Childrens Press, 1985. 31 p. ill. $10.
Gr 3-5. B 82: Mar 15 1986. +- SLJ 32: Mar 1986. A simple introduction to the causes and effects of the Depression.

1873. Terkel, Studs. Hard Times. Pantheon; Washington Square Press; Avon, 1970; 1975. 462 p. $17. Pb $6.
Gr 8+. B 82: Mar 1 1986. SE 46: Oct 1982. Oral histories of the famous and obscure evoke the Depression experience.

Depression–Fiction

1874. Aaron, Chester. Lackawanna. Lippincott, 1986. 224 p. $12. Lib. ed. $12.
Gr 6+. +- B 82: Feb 15 1986. BC 39: Apr 1986. *BR 5: Sep/Oct 1986. SLJ 32: Apr 1986. * VOYA 9: Jun 1986. Six orphaned or abandoned kids make their own family unit to face the harsh realities of the Depression.

1875. Ames, Mildred. Dancing Madness, The. Delacorte, 1980. 144 p. $9.
Gr 7-10. +- B 77: Oct 15 1980. B 82: Mar 1 1986. HB 57: Feb 1981. When Sue Ellen fails to fulfill her stagestruck mother's dream by winning a marathon dance contest she commits suicide, and leaves 12-year-old Mary to deal with the tragedy.

1876. Anderson, Edward. Hungry Men. Penguin, 1935, 1985. 275 p. Pb $7.
Gr 9+. B 81: Apr 15 1985. B 82: Mar 1 1986. The author's experiences as a hobo add to the authenticity of this grimly realistic novel of life on the road during the Depression. First published in 1935.

1877. Bess, Clayton. Tracks. Houghton, 1986. 159 p. $13.
Gr 7-10. B 82: Mar 1 1986. BC 39: Apr 1986. * SE 51: Apr/May 1987. SLJ 32: Aug 1986. * VOYA 9: Jun 1986. A rich novel of the travels of two brothers who see bigotry, murder, and the struggles of the dispossessed.

1878. Cannon, Bettie. Bellsong for Sarah Raines, A. Scribner, 1987. 184 p. $13.
Gr 7+. * B 83: Jul 1987. +- BC 40: Jun 1987. * BR 6: Nov/Dec 1987. SLJ 33: Jun/Jul 1987. VOYA 10: Jun 1987. After her grandfather's suicide, Sarah and her mother moved in with relatives in the Kentucky mountains. A good story about Appalachian life at the time.

1879. Capote, Truman. Thanksgiving Visitor, The. Random House, 1968. 63 p. $15.
Gr 7+. B 82: Mar 1 1986. An autobiographical short story about Buddy, who visits his elderly cousin at Thanksgiving.

1880. Clifford, Eth. Man Who Sang in the Dark, The. Houghton, 1987. 112 p. ill. $13.
Gr 3-7. B 84: Dec 15 1987. BC 41: Oct 1987. HB 63: Nov/Dec 1987. SLJ 34: Oct 1987. +- VOYA 10: Feb 1988. A warm extended family develops when Leah, Daniel and their widowed mother rent an apartment from a poor elderly couple whose blind nephew lives downstairs.

1881. Colman, Hila. Ellie's Inheritance. Morrow, 1979. 190 p. $7. Lib. ed. $7.
Gr 4-8. * B 76: Nov 15 1979. BC 33: Mar 1980. HB 56: Feb 1980. * SE 44: Apr 1980. +- SLJ Dec 1979. VOYA 3: Jun 1980. Eileen, raised in luxury, must learn the skills necessary to earn a living. Her sturdy character helps her to meet this challenge and mature in a time of changing social values.

1882. Corcoran, Barbara. Sky Is Falling, The. Atheneum/Jean Karl, 1988. 190 p. $14.
Gr 7-10. B 85: Sep 15 1988. SLJ 35: Sep 1988. VOYA 11: Oct 1988. Annah's pleasant life is shattered when her father loses his job and she is sent to live with her aunt in New Hampshire.

1883. Cross, Helen Reeder. Isabella Mine. Lothrop, 1982. 147 p. ill. $10.
Gr 5-6. +- B 78: Mar 15 1982. +- BC 35: Jun 1982. - SLJ 28: Apr 1982. A story of family and friends in a Tennessee mining town.

1884. Doctorow, E. L. World's Fair. Random House, 1985. 338 p. $18.
Gr 9+. B 82: Sep 15 1985. * LJ 110: Oct 15 1985. Growing up in New York City during the Depression.

1885. Edwards, Pat. Nelda. Houghton, 1987. 178 p. $13.
Gr 6-9. BR 6: Sep/Oct 1987. HB 63: May/Jun 1987. SLJ 33: May 1987. VOYA 10: Aug/Sep 1987. Nelda is a child of Mississippi migrant workers. When her dreams of becoming rich may come true she finds her beliefs tested. This story has strong characterizations and provides a sense of the time.

1886. Fante, John. 1933 Was a Bad Year. Black Sparrow, 1985. 127 p. $14. Pb $9.
Gr 9+. B 82: Feb 1 1986. The autobiographical novel of an immigrant's son who grew up in a small Colorado town during the Depression.

1887. Huffaker, Clair. One Time I Saw Morning Come Home: A Remembrance. Simon & Schuster, 1974. 319 p. $9.
Gr 8+. B 82: Mar 1 1986. The author tells a fictionalized story of his parents' courtship in Utah during the Depression.

1888. Hunt, Irene. No Promises in the Wind. Follett; Ace, 1970; 1971. 224 p. Pb $3.
Gr 5+. SE 47: Apr 1983. Two boys leave home to seek work during the Depression.

1889. Huntington, Lee Pennock. Maybe a Miracle. Coward, 1984. 93 p. ill. $10.
Gr 2-6. B 81: Oct 1 1984. +- BC 37: Jul/Aug 1984. HB 60: Sep/Oct 1984. SLJ 31: Oct 1984. A minister's daughter learns that God may answer prayer in unexpected ways. Set in a small town during the Depression.

1890. Klass, Sheila Solomon. Nobody Knows Me in Miami. Scribner, 1981. 149 p. $10.

Gr 4-6. B 78: Sep 1 1981. BC 35: Nov 1981. In 1937, a Jewish girl from Brooklyn must decide whether to stay with her poor parents or live with wealthy relatives in Miami.

1891. Lyon, George Ella. Borrowed Children. Watts/Orchard, 1988. 154 p. $13. Lib. ed. $13.
Gr 6-9. * B 84: Feb 15 1988. BC 41: Mar 1988. HB 64: May/Jun 1988. * VOYA 11: Jun 1988. A lyrically written coming-of-age story about Mandy who assumed family responsibilities when the birth of another child left her mother very ill.

1892. Marshall, Catherine. Julie. McGraw-Hill, 1984. 364 p. $16.
Gr 9+. SLJ 31: Jan 1985. VOYA 7: Feb 1985. A story of growing up in a flood-prone Pennsylvania town during the Depression.

1893. Mazer, Harry. Cave Under the City. Crowell, 1986. 152 p. $12.
Gr 5-8. B 83: Oct 15 1986. BC 40: Jan 1987. HB 63: Mar/Apr 1987. SLJ 33: Dec 1986. VOYA 9: Dec 1986. Tolley (age 12) and Bubber (age 6) flee to the streets rather than be sent to a children's shelter, and care for themselves with wit and endurance. A harsh but credible story.

1894. Mills, Claudia. What about Annie? (Walker's American History Series for Young People). Walker, 1985. 68 p. $10.
Gr 5-8. B 82: Sep 1 1985. +- BC 38: May 1985. SLJ 31: May 1985. A vivid picture of the stresses of severe economic depression on a Baltimore family of six girls whose father is unemployed.

1895. Olsen, Violet. Growing Season, The. Atheneum, 1982. 228 p. $11.
Gr 5-7. BC 36: Sep 1982. SLJ 29: Sep 1982. This simple story of life on an Iowa farm has good characterization and excellent detail of time and place.

1896. Peck, Robert Newton. Hallapoosa. Walker, 1988. 215 p. $17.
Gr 9+. * BR 7: Nov/Dec 1988. * VOYA 11: Dec 1988. Rich characterization brings to life Uncle Hiram, the tragic Glory, Vestavia, the feisty black housekeeper, and the crude and cruel Crickers in a suspenseful tale with mature themes, set in Hallapoosa, Florida.

1897. Peck, Robert Newton. Spanish Hoof. Knopf, 1985. 181 p. $12.
Gr 6+. B 81: Apr 15 1985. BR 4: Sep/Oct 1985. SE 50: Apr/May 1986. - SLJ 31: May 1985. VOYA 8: Oct 1985. Life on Spanish Hoof cattle ranch in Florida is made difficult by hard economic times, cattle disease, and overwork. Harry struggles to help her mother and learns the value of sacrifice.

1898. Potter, Marian. Blatherskite. Morrow, 1980. 190 p. $7. Lib. ed. $7.
Gr 4-6. +- SLJ 27: Nov 1980. These adventures of warmhearted ten-year-old Maureen, who talked so much that she neglected her chores and irritated others, present a good picture of rural life at the time.

1899. Potter, Marian. Chance Wild Apple, A. Morrow, 1982. 224 p. $10.
Gr 4-6. B 78: Mar 1 1982. HB 58: Jun 1982. * SE 47: Apr 1983. SLJ 28: Aug 1982. Details of everyday farm life in rural Missouri come through in this delightful story of the chatterbox Maureen who is jealous of her talented cousin, Skeets.

1900. Simon, Kate. Wider World: Portraits in an Adolescence. Harper, 1986. 192 p. $15. Pb $7.
Gr 11+. B 82: Feb 1 Mar 1 1986. LJ 111: Feb 15 1986. A Jewish adolescent matures in Depression-time New York.

1901. Slaatten, Evelyn. Good, the Bad, and the Rest of Us, The. Morrow, 1980. 192 p. $8. Lib. ed. $8.
Gr 3-6. +- BC 34: Mar 1981. SLJ 27: Sep 1980. A nostalgic look at the troubles and joys of family life during the Depression.

1902. Smith, Betty. Tree Grows in Brooklyn, A. Harper, 1947. 443 p. $13. Pb $4.
Gr 9+. B 82: Mar 1 1986. A story of family life in Brooklyn during the Depression.

1903. Steinbeck, John. Grapes of Wrath, The. Viking; Penguin, 1939. 619 p. $20. Pb $4.
Gr 8+. B 82: Mar 1 1986. Desperate "Okies" travel to California hoping to find work as migrant laborers during the Depression.

1904. Stolz, Mary. Ivy Larkin. Harcourt, 1986. 200 p. $14.
Gr 7-9. * B 83: Nov 1 1986. BC 40: Jan 1987. +- SLJ 33: Dec 1986. Ivy and her family struggle with the hardships caused by unemployment and the necessity of moving to a new neighborhood. Masterful characterizations.

1905. Thrasher, Crystal. Dark Didn't Catch Me, The. Atheneum, 1975, 1979. 182 p. Pb $3.
Gr 6-10. * SE 47: Apr 1983. Seely's family moves to the Indiana hills so her father can find work. Amid the difficulties of the Depression, Seely does a lot of growing up. Prequel to Between the Dark and Daylight.

1906. Thrasher, Crystal. End of a Dark Road. Atheneum, 1982. 192 p. $11.
Gr 4-8. B 79: Sep 1 1982. BC 36: Nov 1982. HB 58: Oct 1982. * SE 47: Apr 1983. SLJ 29: Sep 1982. Sophomore Seeley Robinson and her family face her father's unemployment and death. Their struggle rings true in this sequel to Between Dark and Daylight and Julie's Summer.

1907. Thrasher, Crystal. Julie's Summer. Atheneum, 1981. 263 p. $12.
Gr 7+. B 78: Oct 1 1981. BC 35: Jan 1982. HB 58: Feb 1982. SLJ 28: Oct 1981. VOYA 5: Jun 1982. Julie Robinson is pursued by gossip and suspicion in a small Indiana town, but she works hard to achieve her dream of becoming a teacher. Sequel to The Dark and the Daylight.

1908. Thrasher, Crystal. Taste of Daylight, A. Atheneum, 1984. 177 p. $13.

Gr 7-10. * B 81: Sep 15 1984. * B 82: Mar 1 1986. BC 38: Oct 1984. HB 60: Sep/Oct 1984. The last of five volumes on the struggles and growth of an affectionate and courageous family from the Indiana hills.

1909. Whitmore, Arvella. You're a Real Hero, Amanda. Houghton, 1985. 184 p. $13.
Gr 6-8. B 82: Dec 15 1985. BC 39: Feb 1982. VOYA 8: Feb 1986. This fascinating story presents excellent characterization and sense of time and place (Kansas, 1931). A fifth grader's pet rooster is kidnapped and her idol, unwed and pregnant, faces the moral outrage of the town.

Educators

1910. McKissack, Patricia C. Mary McLeod Bethune: A Great American Educator. (People of Distinction Biographies). Childrens Press, 1985. 111 p. ill. $12.
Gr 4-8. B 82: Apr 15 1986. SLJ 32: Mar 1986. Photographs, letters and a time line add to the value of this warm biography of the noted black educator.

1911. Meltzer, Milton. Mary McLeod Bethune: Voice of Black Hope. (Women of Our Time). Viking, 1987. 58 p. ill. $10.
Gr 4-7. B 83: Mar 15 1987. BC 40: May 1987. +- SLJ 33: Mar 1987. This brief but effective biography of the noted black educator describes her accomplishments and the times of which she was a part.

Entertainers

1912. Campbell, Chester W. Will Rogers (The Story of an American Indian). Dillon Press, 1979. 78 p. ill. Lib. ed. $6.
Gr 6-8. B 76: Mar 15 1980. A simple biography of the cowboy, wanderer, and showman who was able to poke fun at powerful people and get them to laugh with him.

1913. Greenfield, Eloise. Paul Robeson. Crowell, 1975. 33 p. ill. $5.
Gr 2-6. B 83: Apr 15 1987. BC 29: Jan 1976. SLJ 22: Sep 1975. An easy-to-read biography of an outstanding musician whose career was undercut by his crusade for justice and freedom.

Explorers

1914. Gilman, Michael. Matthew Henson. (Black Americans of Achievement). Chelsea House, 1988. 112 p. ill. $17.
Gr 5-10. B 84: Jun 15 1988. BC 42: Oct 1988. SLJ 34: Apr 1988. Henson served as first assistant to Peary in the search for the North Pole but never received the honor due him because America was not ready for a black hero.

1915. Gleiter, Jan. Matthew Henson. (Stories Series). Raintree, 1988. 32 p. ill. $12. Pb $7.
Gr 3-6. +- SLJ 35: Oct 1988. Tells the story of Henson's exploration of the Arctic with Peary.

1916. Olds, Elizabeth. Women of the Four Winds. Houghton, 1985. 263 p. ill. $18. Pb $9.

Gr 9+. * B 82: Oct 1 1985. LJ 110: Sep 1 1985. Introduces four women explorers: D. J. Akeley (Africa); M. Harrison (Persia); L. A. Boyd (Arctic); A. S. Peck (South America). Akeley was also an anthropologist, Harrison was a spy, and Peck was a mountaineer.

Fiction

1917. Adkins, Jan. Storm without Rain, A. Little, 1983. 179 p. $11.
Gr 7+. B 79: Apr 15 1983. HB 59: Aug 1983. John travels through time to Penikese Island, 1904, where he meets his great-great-grandfather. Provides a strong sense of place with good imagery and characterization.

1918. Belland, F. W. True Sea, The. Holt, 1984. 289 p. $16.
Gr 10+. +- LJ 109: May 15 1984. VOYA 7: Dec 1984. World War I as seen by Arlis Coleman, a boy growing up in the Florida Keys.

1919. Brown, Irene Bennett. Morning Glory Afternoon. Atheneum, 1981. 219 p. $10.
Gr 6+. +- B 77: Mar 15 1981. - BC 34: Jul/Aug 1981. +- SLJ 28: Nov 1981. Jessamyn is involved in violence by the Ku Klux Klan in a small Kansas town in 1924.

1920. Byrd, Elizabeth. I'll Get By. Viking, 1981. 196 p. $10.
Gr 7+. B 77: Jun 1 1981. BC 34: May 1981. HB 57: Aug 1981. SLJ 27: May 1981. VOYA 4: Oct 1981. An episodic story set in New York in the 1920s, this provides a strong sense of time and place. Fifteen-year-old Julie is studying to become an actress; she is deeply troubled by her parents' separation.

1921. Cameron, Eleanor. Private Worlds of Julia Redfern, The. Dutton, 1988. 218 p. $14.
Gr 6-8. +- BR 7: Nov/Dec 1988. * VOYA 11: Dec 1988. Following the death of her father in World War I, Julia, age 15, adjusts to family changes and the problems of being a teenager.

1922. Cameron, Eleanor. That Julia Redfern. Dutton, 1982. 124 p. $10.
Gr 4-7. B 79: Oct 1 1982. BC 36: Sep 1982. HB 58: Dec 1982. SLJ 29: Sep 1982. Recaps Julia's childhood just at the close of World War I. Prequel to A Room Made of Windows and Julia and the Hand of God.

1923. Carey, Mary. Place For Allie, A. Dodd, 1985. 250 p. $13.
Gr 5-8. B 82: Jan 1 1986. BC 39: Dec 1985. SLJ 32: Feb 1986. In this glimpse of life at the turn of the century, a widow and her children try to make a new life in Boston.

1924. Doctorow, E. L. Ragtime. Random House; Bantam, 1975. 270 p. $13. Pb $5.
Gr 9+. B 72: Sep 1 1975. B 82: Mar 1 1986. The famous and infamous of turn-of-the-century U.S. mingle with a fictional family.

1925. Dubus, Elizabeth Nell. Where Love Rules. Putnam, 1985. 414 p. $18.

Adult. B 81: Jun 15 1985. LJ 110: Jul 1985. Louisiana politics in the 1920s and '30s provide the setting for a romantic family saga.

1926. Fitzgerald, F. Scott. Great Gatsby, The. Scribner, 1925. 182 p. $20. Pb $4.
Gr 10+. B 82: Mar 1 1986. Exposes the shallowness of the Jazz Age of the 1920s as young Gatsby seeks love and acceptance.

1927. Froehlich, Margaret. Reasons to Stay. Houghton, 1986. 181 p. $13.
Gr 6-9. +- BC 40: Dec 1986. BR 5: Mar/Apr 1987. HB 63: Jan/Feb 1987. +- SLJ 33: Dec 1986. VOYA 9: Dec 1986. Set in 1906. Babe searches to find the truth of her parentage in this story of poverty and abuse.

1928. Hemingway, Ernest. For Whom the Bell Tolls. Scribner, 1940. 482 p. $15. Pb $6.
Gr 10+. B 82: Mar 1 1986. An American sees courage and sacrifice in the Spanish Civil War.

1929. Naylor, Phyllis Reynolds. Maudie in the Middle. Atheneum, 1988. 158 p. ill. $14.
Gr 3-5. * B 84: Apr 1 1988. +- BC 41: May 1988. SLJ 34: May 1988. As one of seven children Maudie resents the lack of special attention, so she determines to be especially good, with mixed results. A realistic look at life at the turn of the century.

1930. Newcomb, Kerry. Ghosts of Elkhorn, The. Viking, 1982. 261 p. $13.
Gr 9+. LJ 107: Jan 15 1982. SLJ 28: May 1982. VOYA 5: Oct 1982. An old man, a relic of the wild West, befriends a couple hiding from a gangster. The old man's conversations with the ghost of a friend he betrayed provide a humorous and poignant picture of the West.

1931. Parini, Jay. Patch Boys, The. Holt, 1986. 218 p. $16.
Gr 10+. BR 6: Nov/Dec 1987. LJ 111: Nov 1 1986. VOYA 9: Dec 1986. A realistic story of growing up in a 1925 Pennsylvania mining town.

1932. Ross, Rhea Beth. Bet's On, Lizzie Bingman! Houghton, 1988. 186 p. $13.
Gr 6-10. B 84: Jun 1 1988. +- BC 41: Jun 1988. BR 7: Sep/Oct 1988. +- SLJ 34: Apr 1988. Fourteen-year-old Lizzie bets her chauvinistic brothers that she can go through the whole summer without their help. Set in a small Missouri town, 1914.

1933. Snyder, Zilpha Keatley. And Condors Danced. Delacorte, 1987. 211 p. $15.
Gr 4-7. B 84: Oct 1 1987. +- BC 41: Nov 1987. BR 6: Jan/Feb 1988. HB 64: Jan/Feb 1988. SLJ 34: Dec 1987. VOYA 10: Dec 1987. In California, 1907, eleven-year-old Carly records in her journal the events of her life, her mother's illness and a family feud. Provides a good sense of time and place.

1934. Tripp, Valerie. Samantha Saves the Day: A Summer Story. (American Girls Collection). Pleasant, 1988. 65 p. ill. $13. Pb $6.
Gr 3-6. B 85: Sep 15 1988. +- SLJ 35: Oct 1988. After a frightening experience Samantha grows up a little in

this story set in the Adirondacks in 1904. An appendix provides information on the clothing, conditions, and customs of the time.

1935. Vidal, Gore. Empire. Random House, 1987. 474 p. $23.
Gr 10+. B 83: May 15 1987. * LJ 112: Jul 1987. Encompasses the major political events of the late 19th and early 20th centuries, from the Spanish American War through the stormy presidency of Theodore Roosevelt. Well-researched with good characterizations.

1936. Wiegand, Roberta. Year of the Comet, The. Bradbury, 1984. 133 p. $10.
Gr 4-7. B 81: Dec 1 1984. +- BC 38: Nov 1984. HB 60: Nov/Dec 1984. Sarah believed that 1910, the year of Halley's Comet, would bring great changes in her life. Vignettes of family life in a Nebraska town and Sarah's maturing show that her beliefs came true.

Florida

1937. Rinhart, Floyd. Victorian Florida: America's Last Frontier. Peachtree, 1986. 208 p. ill. $30.
Gr 10+. LJ 111: Sep 15 1986. A pictorial chronology of what early tourists saw in Florida.

Frontier and Pioneer Life

1938. Borland, Hal. High Wide and Lonesome: Growing Up on the Colorado Frontier. Hall, 1984. 270 p. Pb $7.
Gr 7-10. BR 3: Mar/Apr 1985. Drought, blizzards, rattlesnakes, and illness challenge a family homesteading on the Colorado plains.

1939. Burt, Nathaniel. Jackson Hole Journal. University of Oklahoma Press, 1983. 232 p. ill. $17.
Gr 10+. LJ 108: Aug 1983. A memoir of growing up in Wyoming.

1940. Nelson, Paula M. After the West Was Won: Homesteaders and Town-Builders in South Dakota. University of Iowa Press, 1986. 219 p. ill. $23.
Adult. LJ 111: Dec 1986. Explores the life of a homesteader on the dry plains of South Dakota. Based on primary sources.

1941. Strait, Treva Adams. Price of Free Land, The. Lippincott, 1979. 96 p. ill. $9. Lib. ed. $9.
Gr 5-7. BC 33: Feb 1980. * SE 44: Apr 1980. The story of the author's family who pioneered on the Nebraska plain.

Frontier and Pioneer Life–Fiction

1942. Baylor, Byrd. Best Town in the World, The. Scribner, 1983. 32 p. ill. $12.
Gr 1-8. +- BC 37: Apr 1984. HB 50: Feb 1984. * SE 48: May 1984. SLJ 30: Mar 1984. A nostalgic picture book of small town life in Texas where things were "just exactly as they ought to be." Gentle humor with full-page watercolors.

1943. Beatty, Patricia. Behave Yourself, Bethany Brant. Morrow, 1986. 192 p. $12.

Gr 5-7. B 83: Nov 1 1986. BC 40: Oct 1986. * BR 5: Jan/Feb 1987. HB 63: Jan/Feb 1987. * VOYA 9: Feb 1987. Bethany, a feisty preacher's daughter, struggles with life on the Texas frontier.

1944. Beatty, Patricia. Eight Mules from Monterey. Morrow, 1982. 224 p. $9.
Gr 5-8. B 78: Mar 1 1982. +- BC 35: Mar 1982. HB 58: Aug 1982. * SE 47: Apr 1983. * VOYA 5: Aug 1982. Based in part on the true story of a Monterey, California, librarian who established libraries in saloons, general stores, or wherever there were readers. Includes high adventure and humor.

1945. Callaway, Kathy. Bloodroot Flower, The. Knopf, 1982. 198 p. $10.
Gr 4-8. B 79: Oct 15 1982. +- BC 36: Nov 1982. * SE 47: Apr 1983. - SLJ 29: Nov 1982. VOYA 6: Feb 1983. Growing up in the Minnesota north woods at the turn of the century.

Immigration

1946. Jastrow, Marie. Looking Back: The American Dream through Immigrant Eyes, 1907-1918. Norton, 1986. 202 p. ill. $16.
Gr 9+. B 82: Jun 15 1986. +- LJ 111: Jul 1986. A brief memoir of the immigration of the author and her parents and their first decade in the U.S.

Immigration, Jewish

1947. Bernstein, Burton. Family Matters: Sam, Jennie, and the Kids. Summit, 1982. 200 p. $15.
Gr 9+. B 78: Jul 1982. LJ 107: Jul 1982. A delightful, thoughtful biography of the immigrant Bernstein family, including their brilliant children, Leonard, Burton, and Shirley.

1948. Fisher, Leonard Everett. Russian Farewell, A. Four Winds, 1980. 133 p. ill. $10.
Gr 6-8. B 77: Feb 15 1981. BC 34: May 1981. * SE 45: Apr 1981. SLJ 27: Jan 1981. Suffering persecution and property loss in Czarist Russia, the Shapiro family sought refuge in the U.S. Effective drawings enhance the dramatic story.

1949. Meckler, Brenda Weisberg. Papa Was a Farmer. Algonquin, 1988. 318 p. ill. $16.
Gr 9+. B 84: Aug 1988. A delightful account of the struggle of the author's family following their 1904 arrival in the U.S. from Russia.

Immigration, Jewish–Fiction

1950. Cohen, Barbara. Gooseberries to Oranges. Lothrop, 1982. 32 p. ill. $12.
Gr 1-3. B 79: Sep 15 1982. B 83: Mar 1 1987. +- BC 40: Jan 1983. HB 58: Oct 1982. +- SLJ 29: Oct 1982. Just after World War I, eight-year-old Fanny must leave her war-torn home in Russia and cross the ocean to join her father in America. Based on experiences of the author's ancestors.

1951. Harvey, Brett. Immigrant Girl: Becky of Eldridge Street. Holiday, 1987. 40 p. ill. $12.

Gr 2-4. B 83: Apr 15 1987. BC 40: May 1987. SLJ 33: May 1987. Ten-year-old Becky tells the story of her Jewish Russian immigrant family who live in a New York tenement. Provides a good sense of time, place, and living conditions. Includes a glossary.

1952. Mark, Michael. Toba at the Hands of a Thief. Bradbury, 1985. 144 p. $12.
Gr 7+. B 81: May 15 1985. BC 39: Sep 1985. SLJ 31: Aug 1985. VOYA 8: Feb 1986. This realistic story portrays the conflicts felt by Toba, a young Jewish girl, as she prepares to leave Poland to join her sister in America. Provides vivid descriptions and good characterization.

Immigration, Mexican

1953. Galarza, Ernesto. Barrio Boy. University of Notre Dame Press, 1971. 228 p. $5.
Gr 9+. B 81: Jun 15 1985. A Mexican family escapes the 1910 revolution and settles in California.

Immigration–Fiction

1954. Berman, Chaim. Patriarch, The. St. Martin's, 1981. 424 p. $15.
Gr 9+. LJ 106: May 1 1981. SLJ 28: Sep 1981. A realistic saga of a Russian Jewish family who came to the U.S. at the turn of the century.

1955. Cummings, Rebecca. Kaisa Kilponen: Two Stories. Coyote Love Press; dist. by Maine Writers/Pub. Alliance, 1985. 48 p. ill. Pb $5.
Gr 9+. B 82: Sep 1 1985. Two charming stories about Finnish immigrants.

1956. Evernden, Margery. Dream Keeper, The. Lothrop, 1985. 173 p. $11.
Gr 5-8. BC 39: Jan 1986. +- SLJ 32: Dec 1985. +- VOYA 8: Feb 1986. Modern-day Becka finds tapes that tell the dramatic story of her Jewish immigrant great-grandmother whose family fled from Russian army conscription.

1957. Geras, Adele. Voyage. Atheneum, 1983. 193 p. $11.
Gr 6-10. +- B 79: Mar 1 1983. +- BC 36: Jun 1983. HB 59: Aug 1983. SLJ 29: May 1983. +- VOYA 6: Dec 1983. A collection of the thoughts of people, chiefly Jews, fleeing persecution and poverty and seeking homes in the New World.

1958. Janus, Christopher G. Miss 4th of July, Goodbye. Sheffield Books; dist. by Lake View Press, 1986. 223 p. $15.
Gr 9+. B 82: Jan 15 1986. Based on his sister's letters, Janus tells the story of a 16-year-old Greek immigrant who came to West Virginia in 1917.

1959. Lasky, Kathryn. Night Journey, The. Warne, 1981. 150 p. ill. $9.
Gr 4-8. * B 78: Nov 15 1981. BC 35: Dec 1981. +- HB 58: Apr 1982. * SE 46: Apr 1982. SLJ 28: Jan 1982. Nana Sashie tells the story of her Jewish family's harrowing escape from Czarist Russia when she was nine.

1960. Roth, Henry. Call It Sleep. Cooper Square; Avon/Bard, 1934. 599 p. $20. Pb $4.
Gr 10+. B 82: Mar 1 1986. A Jewish boy and his mother adjust to life in the New World, but the father is enraged by their immigrant life.

1961. Sendak, Philip. In Grandpa's House. Harper, 1985. 42 p. ill. $10. Lib. ed. $10.
Gr 3-7. HB 62: Jan/Feb 1986. The art of Maurice Sendak illustrates a story told by his father, a Jewish immigrant who wished to share his values with his son.

Indians of North America–Algonquin

1962. Kazimiroff, Theodore L. Last Algonquin, The. Walker, 1982. 197 p. $13.
Gr 8+. B 78: Jul 1982. BR 1: Jan/Feb 1983. LJ 107: Jul 1982. VOYA 5: Dec 1982. On his deathbed, Joseph Two-Trees told his story to the author's father. Recommended for insight into Indian culture, character, and treatment by the white community.

Indians of North America–Fiction

1963. Borland, Hal. When the Legends Die. Lippincott; Bantam Books, 1972. 288 p. $4.
Gr 9+. SE 46: Oct 1982. A Ute Indian boy, raised in traditional ways, is taken away and "civilized" against his will. He becomes a bronc-buster with a murderous riding style.

1964. Erdrich, Louise. Tracks. Holt, 1988. 226 p. $18.
Gr 9+. * B 84: Jul 1988. * LJ 113: Sep 1 1988. This rich tale of Chippewa Indians struggling against white encroachment and internal division begins in 1912.

1965. La Farge, Oliver. Laughing Boy. Houghton; several paperback editions available, 1929. 259 p. $13. Pb ca. $5.
Gr 9+. B 82: Mar 1 1986. The love story of Laughing Boy, who retains Navaho values, and Slim Girl, who had adopted ideas of the whites.

1966. Thayer, Marjorie. Climbing Sun: The Story of a Hopi Indian Boy. Dodd, 1980. 96 p. ill. $7.
Gr 4-6. BC 34: Apr 1981. +- SLJ 27: Nov 1980. To continue his education an 11-year-old Hopi boy is sent to the Sherman Indian Institute where he must learn the ways of a different culture. Set in the 1920s, and based on reminiscences.

Indians of North America–Yahi

1967. Kroeber, Theodore Krob. Ishi, Last of His Tribe. Houghton/Parnasus Press, Bantam, 1964. 224 p. $8. Pb $3.
Gr 5-8. B 81: Apr 15 1985. SE 46: Oct 1982. The moving story of Ishi, a Yahi Indian, who was the last survivor of his tribe.

1968. Meyer, Kathleen Allan. Ishi. (Story of an American Indian). Dillon Press, 1980. 70 p. ill. Lib. ed. $6.
Gr 4-7. B 77: Sep 15 1980. B 82: Sep 15 1985. BC 34: Dec 1980. SLJ 27: March 1981. A compelling photo-illustrated story of the last Yahi Indian whose peaceful tribe slowly died after hiding from warring tribes and white civilization for generations.

Inventions and Inventors

1969. Mitchell, Barbara. Pocketful of Goobers: A Story about George Washington Carver. (Carolrhoda Creative Minds Book). Carolrhoda, 1986. 64 p. ill. $9.
Gr 3-6. +- B 82: Aug 1986. SLJ 33: Sep 1986. Slightly fictionalized stories about Carver's research and his struggle against racism.

Japanese Americans–Fiction

1970. Uchida, Yoshiko. Best Bad Thing, The. Atheneum, 1983. 116 p. $10.
Gr 4-7. B 80: Sep 15 1983. BC 37: Oct 1983. HB 59: Oct 1983. * SE 48: May 1984. SLJ 30 Nov 1983. Sequel to A Jar of Dreams. Rinko goes to help eccentric Mrs. Hata, and is intrigued by the mysterious old man who lives in the barn.

1971. Uchida, Yoshiko. Happiest Ending, The. Atheneum, 1985. 111 p. $11.
Gr 4-8. B 82: Nov 1 1985. BC 39: Oct 1985. SE 50: Apr/May 1986. SLJ 32: Nov 1985. The arranged marriage of her friend, according to Japanese custom, is upsetting to 12-year-old Rinko, but she tries to understand adult problems and not make hasty judgments.

1972. Uchida, Yoshiko. Jar of Dreams, A. Atheneum, 1981. 132 p. $10.
Gr 3-8. B 78: Oct 15 1981. BC 35: Sep 1981. HB 57: Dec 1981. * SE 46: Apr 1982. SLJ 27: Aug 1981. A Japanese-American family suffers prejudice and economic hard times during the Depression.

Jewish Americans–Fiction

1973. Herman, Ben. Rhapsody in Blue of Mickey Klein, The. Stemmer House, 1981. 143 p. $9.
Gr 7+. HB 58: Feb 1982. A uniquely human story of growing up Jewish in a Maryland steel town in the '30s, as Mickey deals with his hopes, fears, fantasies, racism, and emerging sexuality.

1974. Moskowitz, Faye. Leak in the Heart: Tales from a Woman's Life. Godine, 1985. 224 p. $15.
Gr 9+. B 81: May 1 1985. B 82: Mar 1 1986. LJ 110: May 1 1985. A collection of autobiographical stories about growing up Jewish in the 1930s and '40s in a small town in Michigan.

1975. Potok, Chaim. Davita's Harp. Knopf, 1985. 371 p. $17.
Gr 9+. B 81: Dec 15 1984. BR 4: Sep/Oct 1985. * LJ 110: Feb 15 1985. * VOYA 8: Aug 1985. Her politically active parents are concerned with the Spanish Civil War and the impending World War II as Davita grows to maturity.

1976. Schiffman, Ruth. Turning the Corner. Dial, 1981. 192 p. $10.
Gr 7+. +- B 78: Sep 1 1981. +- BC 35: Dec 1981. HB 57: Dec 1981. * SE 46: Apr 1982. +- SLJ 28: Feb

1982. VOYA 5: Apr 1982. An affectionate Jewish family suffers discrimination and economic hardship during the Depression. Set in Forgetown, Pa., and centers around 18-year-old Rebecca.

Journalists

1977. Baker, Russell. Growing Up. Congdon & Weed, 1982. 278 p. $15.
Gr 12+. B 79: Sep 15 1982. BR 2: Nov/Dec 1983. HB 59: Feb 1983. LJ 107: Oct 1982. SE 48: Dec 1982. This account of growing up fatherless in rural Virginia during the Depression is a memoir by a feature writer for the New York Times Magazine.

1978. Brady, Kathleen. Ida Tarbell: Portrait of a Muckraker. Seaview/Putnam, 1984. 272 p. $18.
Gr 9+. B 80: Aug 1984. LJ 109: Sep 1 1984. The biography of a high-principled woman whose life was devoted to her efforts to expose the power of big business trusts.

1979. Paradis, Adrian A. Ida M. Tarbell: Pioneer Woman Journalist and Biographer. (People of Distinction Biographies). Childrens Press, 1985. 120 p. ill. $12.
Gr 6-8. +- B 82: Mar 15 1986. SLJ 32: Mar 1986. The story of a pioneer journalist and biographer whose exposure of the Standard Oil trust led to its dissolution.

Judicial Branch and Judges

1980. Gross, David C. Justice for All the People: Louis D. Brandeis. (Jewish Biography Series). Dutton/Lodestar, 1987. 116 p. ill. $14.
Gr 5-9. B 83: May 1 1987. +- BC 40: May 1987. SLJ 33: Aug 1987. Explores the life of the Supreme Court justice who was an ardent champion of fair labor laws to benefit women and children and an active Zionist.

1981. Paper, Lewis J. Brandeis: A New Biography of One of America's Truly Great Supreme Court Justices. Prentice-Hall, 1983. 448 p. ill. $19.
Adult. LJ 108: Sep 1 1983. Justice Brandeis served on the Supreme Court, 1916-1939, and as a presidential advisor who worked for the safety of the Jews during World War II. This thorough biography covers his private and public lives.

1982. Peterson, Helen Stone. Oliver Wendell Holmes: Soldier, Lawyer, Supreme Court Justice. Fox Hills Press, 1979. 91 p. ill. $8. Lib. ed. $8.
Gr 3-6. +- B 76: Nov 15 1979. +- BC 34: Nov 1980. HB 57: Feb 1981. SLJ 26: Feb 1980. Abundant quotations and photos enliven this concise biography of the "great dissenter."

1983. Urofsky, Melvin I. Louis D. Brandeis and the Progressive Tradition. (Library of American Biography). Little, 1981. 183 p. $12.
Gr 9+. LJ 105: Dec 15 1980. SLJ 27: May 1981. A clear exposition of Brandeis' contribution to jurisprudence and to civic and industrial reform.

Kansas

1984. Ikenberry, Larry. Kansas Past: A Photographic Essay of the Great Plains of Western Kansas. Cascade Photographics, 1979. 117 p. ill. $13. Pb $8.
Gr 9+. B 76: May 15 1980. Historic commentary and a map of the Smoky Hill Trail accompany 100 black-and-white photos of Kansas and its people at the turn of the century.

Ku Klux Klan–Fiction

1985. Hooks, William H. Circle of Fire. Atheneum, 1982. 138 p. $10.
Gr 4-8. * B 79: Sep 1 1982. BC 36: Oct 1982. HB 58: Oct 1982. * SE Apr 1983. VOYA 6: Feb 1983. An 11-year-old white boy and his two black friends seek to protect a band of wandering Irish tinkers from the Ku Klux Klan. Set in North Carolina circa 1925.

Labor Unions and Laborers

1986. Bird, Stewart. Solidarity Forever: An Oral History of the IWW. Lake Preview Press, 1985. 247 p. ill. $30. Pb $10.
Adult. B 82: Sep 1 1985. LJ 110: Aug 1985. A colorful oral history of the labor union that was ahead of its time (1905-1922) in its commitment to economic equality, social justice, and civil liberties, and in its stand against racism and sexism.

1987. Carlson, Peter. Roughneck: The Life and Times of "Big Bill" Haywood. Norton, 1983. 352 p. $18.
Gr 9+. B 79: May 1 1983. LJ 108: Mar 15 1983. Events and conditions turned the quiet Haywood into a radical labor unionizer who founded the International Workers of the World.

1988. Gompers, Samuel. Seventy Years of Life and Labor: An Autobiography. ILR Press, 1984. 296 p. ill. $25. Pb $9.
Adult. B 81: Sep 1 1984. LJ 109: Dec 1984. This carefully abridged version of the 1925 original presents a balanced view of a fascinating and important union leader who strove for equity in union politics.

1989. Tripp, Anne Huber. I.W.W. and the Paterson Silk Strike of 1913, The. University of Illinois Press, 1987. 432 p. ill. $30.
Adult. LJ 112: Oct 15 1987. This overview shows the way the International Workers of the World union was organized, introduces its leaders, and details those events that led to nearly total defeat for the union.

Labor Unions and Laborers–Fiction

1990. Giardina, Denise. Storming Heaven. Norton, 1987. 277 p. $17.
Gr 9+. B 83: Jun 15 1987. LJ 112: Jul 1987. A powerful novel based on a 1921 armed confrontation between 10,000 United Mine Workers and the mine owners which eventually involved the U.S. Army.

1991. Hendershot, Judith. In Coal Country. Knopf, 1987. 40 p. ill. $14. Lib. ed. $14.
Gr 1-4. * B 83: Apr 1 1987. B 84: May 1 1988. BC 40: Jun 1987. HB 63: May 1987. SE 52: Apr 1988. SLJ 33: May 1987. A quiet memoir of growing up in a coal mining town in the 1930s, enriched by photos and charcoal drawings.

1992. Herrick, William. That's Life: A Fiction. New Directions; dist. by Norton, 1985. 228 p. $18. Pb $9.
Gr 9+. B 81: Jul 1985. Stories of a Jewish family involved with the labor union movement in the 1930s.

1993. Mays, Lucinda. Other Shore, The. Atheneum, 1979. 223 p. $9.
Gr 7-10. B 81: July 1985. +- BC 33: Mar 1980. * SE 44: Apr 1980. - SLJ 26: Nov 1979. Gabriella and her Italian immigrant family live in Manhattan during the early 1900s. Her father is involved in the labor movement and Gabriella observes the infamous Triangle Shirtwaist fire.

1994. Perez, N. A. Breaker. Houghton, 1988. 207 p. $14.
Gr 6-9. B 84: Jul 1988. +- BC 41: Jul/Aug 1988. * BR 7: Nov/Dec 1988. SLJ 34: Aug 1988. Set in a Pennsylvania coal mining town in 1902, this tells of the struggle to organize unions and the tensions between the Irish Catholic community and the new Polish immigrants.

1995. Sachs, Marilyn. Call Me Ruth. Doubleday, 1982. 128 p. $12. Lib. ed. $13.
Gr 4-8. B 79: Sep 1 1982. BC 36: Nov 1982. HB 58: Oct 1982. SLJ 29: Oct 1982. As Jewish Rifka and her widowed mother adjust to American life, Rifka (Ruth) becomes an enthusiastic student and her shy mother becomes involved in a labor dispute. Provides a good sense of time and place.

1996. Sebestyen, Ouida. On Fire. Atlantic Monthly Press; dist. by Little, Brown, 1985. 207 p. $13.
Gr 7+. B 81: May 15 1985. BC 39: Sept 1985. HB 61: Jul/Aug 1985. SLJ 31: Apr 1985. * VOYA 8: Aug 1985. A dramatic story of class struggle as unions develop and management seeks to break the strike.

1997. Sherburne, James. Poor Boy and a Long Way from Home. Houghton, 1984. 361 p. $15.
Gr 9+. B 80: Jul 1984. LJ 109: Jul 1984. SLJ 31: Jan 1985. Glen's 1909 travels acquaint him with the radical labor movement, the Tong War, the movie industry and his own sexuality.

1998. Skurzynski, Gloria. Tempering, The. Clarion; dist. by Ticknor & Fields, 1983. 178 p. $11.
Gr 7-10. B 79: Apr 1 1983. B 82: Mar 1 1986. BC 36: Jun 1983. BR 2: Nov/Dec 1983. HB 59: Aug 1983. VOYA 6: Aug 1983. The ethnic customs and working-class characters evoke the time and place in this story of three young men growing up in a 1911 Pennsylvania steel town.

Panama Canal

1999. Markun, Patricia Maloney. Panama Canal. (First Book). Rev. ed. Watts, 1979. 66 p. ill. $6.
Gr 3-5. B 76: Oct 15 1979. SLJ 26: Apr 1980. This update of Markun's 1959 edition covers the history of the Canal, its economic importance, the future of the Panama Canal Commission, and a typical journey through the locks.

2000. Stein, R. Conrad. Story of the Panama Canal, The. (Cornerstones of Freedom). Childrens Press, 1982. 31 p. ill. $6.
Gr 4-6. B 79: Feb 15 1983. B 82: Dec 1 1985. Explains the importance of the canal and the enormity of the engineering and medical problems that had to be solved.

Photographers

2001. Haskins, James. James Van DerZee: The Picture-Takin' Man. Dodd, 1979. 256 p. ill. $9.
Gr 7+. B 80: Aug 1984. B 82: Mar 1 1986. * SE 44: Apr 1980. Van DerZee grew up in Harlem. As a noted photographer he became acquainted with many black celebrities.

2002. Meltzer, Milton. Dorothea Lange: Life through the Camera. (Women of Our Time). Viking, 1985. 57 p. ill. $10.
Gr 4-8. * B 81: Aug 1985. B 82: Sep 15 1985. BC 39: Oct 1985. HB 62: Sep/Oct 1986. SLJ 32: Sep 1985. The life of a famous photographer of the poor during the Depression.

2003. Ohrn, Karin Becker. Dorothea Lange and the Documentary Tradition. Louisiana State University Press, 1980. 277 p. ill. $28.
Gr 9+. B 77: Sep 1 1980. LJ 105: Apr 15 1980. A chronological treatment, emphasizing Lange's documentation of rural poverty and her efforts to become a humane photographer who could reach people everywhere.

Polish Americans–Fiction

2004. Pellowski, Anne. Winding Valley Farm: Annie's Story. Philomel, 1982. 192 p. ill. $10.
Gr 3-6. B 78: Aug 1982. HB 58: Aug 1982. * SE 47: Apr 1983. SLJ 29: Sep 1982. The third in a series about the author's Polish-American family includes details of farming and Polish customs that provide a strong sense of time and place.

Presidency and the Executive Branch

2005. Clements, Kendrick A. Woodrow Wilson, World Statesman. (Twayne's Twentieth Century American Biography Series). Twayne, 1987. 288 p. ill. $25. Pb $11.
Gr 9+. SLJ 34: May 1988. A well-documented and easy-to-read account of Wilson's efforts to define the U.S. as a global power.

2006. Davis, Kenneth S. FDR: The New Deal Years, 1933-1937. Random House, 1986. 739 p. $23.
Adult. B 83: Sep 1 1986. LJ 111: Sep 15 1986. One of a multipart work, this volume treats FDR's first term and his political response to the Depression.

2007. Ferrell, Robert H. Woodrow Wilson and World War I, 1917-1921. Harper, 1985. 336 p. ill. $18. Pb $10.
Gr 9+. B 81: Feb 15 1985. +- LJ 110: Apr 1 1985. Covers the presidency and Wilson's leadership during and after World War I.

Presidents and Their Families–Hoover

2008. Clinton, Susan. Herbert Hoover: Thirty-first President of the United States. (Encyclopedia of Presidents). Childrens Press, 1988. 100 p. ill. $15.
Gr 4-7. B 84: Aug 1988. A well-rounded biography that includes photos and a chronology.

2009. Hilton, Suzanne. World of Young Herbert Hoover, The. Walker, 1987. 103 p. ill. $13. Lib. ed. $14.
Gr 4-8. +- BC 41: Oct 1987. SLJ 34: Jan 1988. Anecdotes enliven this clearly written account of the Quaker youth who served as congressman and our thirty-first president. Includes a chronology.

Presidents and Their Families–Roosevelt, Theodore

2010. Felsenthal, Carol. Alice Roosevelt Longworth. Putnam, 1988. 304 p. ill. $22.
Gr 10+. * LJ 113: Feb 15 1988. A fascinating biography of the outrageous daughter of Theodore Roosevelt. She was a noted Washington hostess and friend to several generations of politicians.

2011. Force, Eden. Theodore Roosevelt. (First Book). Watts, 1987. 94 p. ill. $10.
Gr 5-8. B 83: May 15 1987. SLJ 33: Jun/Jul 1987. A solid and well-rounded introduction that includes photos and reproductions of documents.

2012. Kent, Zachary. Theodore Roosevelt: Twenty-Sixth President of the United States. (Encyclopedia of Presidents). Childrens Press, 1988. 100 p. ill. $15.
Gr 4-8. B 84: Aug 1988. SLJ 35: Oct 1988. A lively biography, presented with numerous quotes, photos, and a chronology that places Roosevelt in the context of his time.

2013. Longworth, Alice Roosevelt. Mrs. L: Conversations with Alice Roosevelt Longworth. Doubleday, 1981. 203 p. ill. $20.
Gr 10+. B 78: Sep 1 1981. LJ 106: Aug 1981. A lively oral history by the witty daughter of Theodore Roosevelt. Numerous photos enhance this narrative which comments on the many political figures she knew during her 96 years.

2014. McCullough, David G. Mornings on Horseback. Simon & Schuster, 1981. 447 p. $20.
Gr 9+. B 77: Apr 15 1981. HB 58: Feb 1982. LJ 106: May 15 1981. SLJ 28: Oct 1981. Based on primary sources, the story of the transformation of an asthmatic little boy into a vigorous, flamboyant, young politician at age 28.

2015. Morris, Sylvia Jukes. Edith Kermit Roosevelt: Portrait of a First Lady. Coward, 1980. 512 p. ill. $17.

Adult. B 76: Jul 1 1980. HB 56: Oct 1980. LJ 105: Jul 1980. This charming and well documented biography clarifies the role of this successful first lady, and also provides much information on her famous husband, Theodore.

2016. Sabin, Louis. Teddy Roosevelt: Rough Rider. (Easy Biographies Series). Troll, 1986. 48 p. ill. $9. Pb $2.
Gr 3-8. SLJ 33: Sep 1986. Emphasis is on Roosevelt's youth.

2017. Stefoff, Rebecca. Theodore Roosevelt: 26th President of the United States. (Presidents of the United States). Garrett Educational Corp., 1988. 121 p. ill. $13.
Gr 7-9. SLJ 35: Sep 1988. Anecdotes, background material, and illustrations enhance this useful introduction to Roosevelt's private and political life.

Presidents and Their Families–Roosevelt, Theodore–Fiction

2018. Schorr, Mark. Bully! St. Martin's, 1985. 196 p. $13.
Gr 9+. B 82: Sep 15 1985. In this romp, Roosevelt infiltrates a secret society which threatens to undermine his presidency.

Presidents and Their Families–Wilson

2019. Leavell, J. Perry. Woodrow Wilson. (World Leaders Past and Present Series). Chelsea House, 1986. 116 p. ill. $17.
Gr 6-10. B 83: Mar 1 1987. SLJ 33: May 1987. A straightforward and readable biography, with many quotes and statistics. The coverage of pivotal events in Wilson's administration presents a clear picture of the times.

Prohibition–Fiction

2020. Avi. Shadrach's Crossing. Pantheon, 1983. 148 p. $11. Lib. ed. $11.
Gr 4-8. B 79: Apr 15 1983. BC 36: Jun 1983. HB 59: Aug 1983. SLJ 29: Aug 1983. Shad's family lives on an island terrorized by smugglers during Prohibition, and he seeks to free them from the hopelessness of this situation. High adventure.

2021. Peck, Robert Newton. Justice Lion. Little, 1981. 264 p. $10.
Gr 8+. B 77: Feb 1 1981. * SE 46: Apr 1982. SLJ 27: Mar 1981. VOYA 4: Aug 1981. In 1923 Vermont, Prohibition is not considered seriously until a federal agent forces the issue. In the trial that follows the issues of right and wrong, loyalty, and the law, must be decided by each citizen.

Public Officials

2022. Ashby, LeRoy. William Jennings Bryan: Champion of Democracy. (Twayne's Twentieth Century American Biography Series). Twayne, 1987. 245 p. ill. $25. Pb $11.

Gr 9+. B 83: Jul 1987. SLJ 34: Jan 1988. An effective biography of a presidential contender and Secretary of State who fought for small-town values and greater democracy for the common people.

2023. Kamen, Gloria. Fiorello: His Honor, the Little Flower. Atheneum, 1981. 60 p. ill. $9.
Gr 3-6. B 78: Nov 15 1981. BC 35: Jan 1982. SLJ 28: Feb 1982. * SE 46: Apr 1982. The life story of New York City's nationally known mayor (1933-1945).

Public Officials–Women

2024. White, Florence M. First Woman in Congress: Jeannette Rankin. Messner, 1980. 96 p. ill. $8.
Gr 4-6. * SE 45: Apr 1981. As a representative of Montana, Rankin was the first woman in Congress. She alone voted against U.S. participation in both World Wars.

Reformers–Black

2025. Hanley, Sally. A. Philip Randolph. Chelsea House, 1988. 112 p. ill. $17.
Gr 5-9. B 85: Oct 1 1988. Randolph led the first successful black union and later became a civil rights activist whose non-violent tactics inspired Martin Luther King, Jr.

2026. Lawler, Mary. Marcus Garvey: Black Nationalist Leader. (Black Americans of Achievement). Chelsea House, 1987. 110 p. ill. $17.
Gr 6+. B 84: Dec 1 1987. +- SLJ 34: Apr 1988. VOYA 11: Oct 1988. A profusely illustrated biography of the founder of the Universal Negro Improvement Association, who attempted to secure an independent African homeland for all blacks.

Reformers–Women

2027. Hoy, Linda. Emmeline Pankhurst. (Profiles). Hamish Hamilton; dist. by David & Charles, 1985. 64 p. ill. $9.
Gr 4-6. SLJ 32: Apr 1986. A revealing biography of a leading worker for women's civil rights.

2028. Kittredge, Mary. Jane Addams. (American Women of Achievement). Chelsea House, 1988. 111 p. ill. $17.
Gr 6-10. B 84: Jun 15 1988. An engrossing biography of the woman who founded Hull House in an effort to provide decent housing for oppressed immigrants. Illustrated with photos and etchings.

2029. Kudlinski, Kathleen V. Juliette Gordon Low: America's First Girl Scout. Viking, 1988. 64 p. ill. $11.
Gr 3-6. B 85: Nov 15 1988. BC 42: Oct 1988. A simply-written biography about a woman who devoted her life to establish the Girl Scouts in order to help girls learn to be free and responsible.

2030. Meigs, Cornelia. Jane Addams, Pioneer for Social Justice. Little, 1970. 274 p. ill. $10.
Gr 7+. B 83: Apr 15 1987. LJ 95: Jun 15 1970. A biography of the founder of Hull House in Chicago, a

refuge for the desperately poor. For her leadership in social work she received the Nobel Peace Prize in 1931.

2031. Topalian, Elyse. Margaret Sanger. (Impact Biography). Watts, 1984. 128 p. $10.
Gr 7+. B 80: Jun 15 1984. BC 37: Jul/Aug 1984. * SE 49: Apr 1985. SLJ 31: Sep 1984. * VOYA 8: Apr 1985. An exciting biography of the woman who pioneered the birth control movement in the United States.

2032. Van Voris, Jacqueline. Carrie Chapman Catt: A Public Life. Feminist Press, 1987. 307 p. ill. $25.
Gr 9+. B 84: Jan 15 1988. A significant biography of the woman who directed the passage of women's suffrage, founded the League of Women Voters, kept her privacy, and carefully maintained the middle ground between conservatives and radicals.

2033. Wepman, Dennis. Helen Keller. (American Women of Achievement). Chelsea House, 1987. 111 p. ill. $17.
Gr 6-10. B 83: Aug 1987. SLJ 34: Sep 1987. This succinct biography includes many quotes from Keller's writing and by those who knew her. Numerous photos.

Ships and Shipping

2034. Ballard, Robert D. Discovery of the Titanic, The. Warner/Madison Press, 1987. 230 p. ill. $30.
Gr 6+. B 84: Dec 1 1987. * BR 6: Mar/Apr 1988. LJ 113: Jan 1988. * VOYA 11: Apr 1988. A detailed account of the search for the Titanic and what was found in the wreckage, written by the Frenchman who organized the effort.

2035. Davie, Michael. Titanic: The Death and Life of a Legend. Knopf, 1987. 272 p. ill. $20.
Gr 9+. B 83: Jun 1 1987. LJ 112: Jul 1987. This sound, well-researched account examines the accident, including the inadequate number of lifeboats, the captain's role, why certain passengers found safety in lifeboats, and why the lookouts lacked binoculars.

2036. Donnelly, Judy. Titanic: Lost...and Found. (Step into Reading). Random House, 1987. 47 p. ill. $6. Pb $3.
Gr 2-4. B 83: Jun 1 1987. SLJ 33: Jun/Jul 1987. Donnelly describes the Titanic and the tragedy, and explains the long-lasting safety measures which resulted. An appealing book.

2037. Dudman, John. Sinking of the Titanic, The. Bookwright Press; dist. by Watts, 1988. 32 p. ill. $11.
Gr 3-6. SLJ 34: Aug 1988. Tells the story of the Titanic and describes the discovery of the wreck through photos and color drawings and a simple text.

2038. Hartford, John. Steamboat in a Cornfield. Crown, 1986. 40 p. ill. $11.
Gr 3-7. B 83: Jan 15 1987. HB 63: Mar/Apr 1987. * SE 51: Apr/May 1987. SLJ 33: Mar 1987. The true story of a steamboat that ran aground in a cornfield during a flood. Newspaper accounts and photos add to the fascinating account.

2039. Lord, Walter. Night Lives On, The. Morrow, 1986. 256 p. ill. $16.
Gr 9+. B: 82 Aug 1986. BR 5: Jan/Feb 1987. LJ 111: Aug 1986. A companion to the author's "A Night to Remember," with more information on the Titanic disaster.

2040. Rust, Claude. Burning of the General Slocum, The. Elsevier/Nelson, 1981. 148 p. ill. $11.
Gr 7+. B 78: Sep 1 1981. +- BC 35: Oct 1981. SLJ 28: Sep 1981. VOYA 4: Oct 1981. Recounts the tragic loss of over 1000 passengers because corruption made the General Slocum, its crew, and its lifeboats unsafe.

2041. Sloan, Frank. Titanic. (First Book). Watts, 1987. 88 p. ill. $10.
Gr 4-7. B 84: Jan 1 1988. BC 41: Dec 1987. BR 6: Jan/Feb 1988. SLJ 34: Dec 1987. Covers the story of the Titanic from its design to the discovery of its wreckage. Includes photos, diagrams, trivia, and glossary.

2042. Smith, E. Boyd. Seashore Book, The. Houghton, 1985. 56 p. ill. $13.
Gr 2-4. B 81: Jun 1 1985. HB 61: Jul/Aug 1985. SE 50: Apr/May 1986. A handsome look at New England shipbuilding and recollections about life at sea. Originally printed in 1912.

2043. Wade, Wyn. Titanic: End of a Dream, The. Rawson Wade, 1979. 338 p. ill. $14.
Gr 9+. SLJ 26: Feb 1980. Combines flashbacks by survivors with information from Senate hearings concerning the Titanic tragedy.

Social Life and Customs

2044. Bosetti, Noel. Turn of the Century, The. (Events of Yesteryear). Silver Burdett, 1987. 69 p. ill. $15.
Gr 7+. * BR 6: Jan/Feb 1988. +- SLJ 34: Dec 1987. Shows the effects of new technology and contrasts the lives of the middle class with the lives of factory and mine workers.

2045. Fisher, Andrea. Let Us Now Praise Famous Women: Women Photographers for the U.S Government, 1935-1944. Pandora; dist. by Methuen, 1987. 160 p. ill. Pb $17.
Gr 9+. +- B 84: Jan 1 1988. HT 21: Aug 1988. SLJ 34: Feb 1988. A photographic record of American life from 1935 to 1940, with essays putting the photos in their social context. Features the work of noted female photographers.

2046. Hall, Donald. Ox-Cart Man. Viking, 1979. 40 p. ill. $9.
Gr K-2. B 76: Dec 15 1979. B 83: Mar 1 1987. BC 33: Feb 1980. HB 56: Feb 1980. SLJ 26: Oct 1979. * SE 44: Apr 1980. A simple story of the annual cycle of plant and harvest on a turn-of-the-century New England farm.

2047. Hastings, Scott E. Goodbye Highland Yankee: Stories of a North Country Boyhood. Chelsea Green, 1988. 166 p. $18.
Gr 9+. B 85: Sep 15 1988. A witty memoir of growing up on a Vermont farm.

2048. Katz, William Loren. Making Our Way. Dial, 1975. 170 p. $7.
Gr 7+. SE 44: Oct 1980. Fourteen first-person accounts of the lives of the poor and powerless at the turn of the century.

2049. Marquis, Alice G. Hopes and Ashes: The Birth of Modern Times, 1929-1939. Free Press, 1986. 261 p. $23.
Adult. B 83: Dec 15 1986. LJ 111: Dec 1986. An overview of how our culture was shaped by new technology, modern art, the Depression and the impending World War.

2050. Miller, Frederic. Still Philadelphia: A Photographic History, 1890-1940. Temple University Press, 1983. 290 p. ill. $25.
Gr 10+. LJ 108: Jul 1983. Using hundreds of photos, the authors show the turbulent changes to Philadelphia brought about by massive immigration, automobiles, and industrialization.

2051. Scott, Lynn H. Covered Wagon: And Other Adventures. University of Nebraska Press, 1987. 135 p. ill. $13.
Gr 6+. SLJ 34: May 1988. Because of the father's ill health, from 1906 to 1923 the Scott family moved by wagon and train to Nebraska, Wyoming, Oregon, California, and back to Nebraska twice. This is an anecdotal story of their adventures.

2052. Smith, E. Boyd. Farm Book, The. Houghton, 1982. 55 p. ill. $13.
Gr 2-8. B 79: Jan 1 1983. * HB 58: Dec 1982. * SE 47: Apr 1983. SLJ 29: Dec 1982. This reproduction of a 1910 book gives a view of turn-of-the-century New England farm life. Watercolor illustrations.

Social Life and Customs–Children

2053. Nasaw, David. Children of the City: At Work and at Play. Anchor/Doubleday, 1985. 312 p. ill. $19.
Adult. SE 50: Apr/May 1986. Presents the daily activities of working-class children who lived in American cities between 1900 and 1929.

2054. Nasaw, David. Children of the City: How Our Grandparents Grew Up. Anchor/Doubleday, 1985. 203 p. ill. $19.
Adult. * LJ 110: Mar 15 1985. Explains how the children of immigrants became urban Americans in the tenements of the early 20th century.

Social Life and Customs–Fiction

2055. Adler, Susan S. Meet Samantha: An American Girl. (American Girls Collection). Pleasant, 1986. 61 p. ill. $13. Pb $5.
Gr 2-5. B 83: Dec 1 1986. SLJ 33: Nov 1986. Orphaned Samantha lives with her wealthy grandfather (1904). As she observes the lives around her she seeks to define her own values.

2056. Adler, Susan S. Samantha Learns a Lesson: A School Story. (American Girls Collection). Pleasant, 1986. 61 p. ill. $13. Pb $5.

Gr 2-5. B 83: Dec 1 1986. Samantha, a wealthy orphan, learns that her fine clothes are made at a factory that exploits child labor.

2057. Bell, W. Bruce. Little Dab of Color, A. Lothrop, 1980. 192 p. $8. Lib. ed. $8.
Gr 3-7. B 77: Dec 15 1980. HB 57: Feb 1981. SLJ 27: Sep 1980. VOYA 3: Feb 1981. Episodic stories of growing up in 1914, based on the author's recollections. Good for reading aloud.

2058. Bradbury, Ray. Dandelion Wine. Doubleday, o.p./Knopf; Bantam, 1957. 269 p. $15. Pb $3.
Gr 9+. B 82: Mar 1 1986. During one summer in a midwestern town Douglas Spaulding, age 12, perceives the marvels of life and the realities of death and loss.

2059. Burch, Robert. Ida Early Comes Over the Mountain. Viking, 1980. 145 p. $9.
Gr 4-6. B 77: Dec 15 1980. BC 34: Dec 1980. HB 56: Dec 1980. * SE 45: Apr 1981. SLJ 27: Oct 1980. In rural Georgia, Mr. Sutton hires Ida Early to care for his motherless children. Ida isn't much of a housekeeper, but she is understanding, humorous, and a teller of tall tales.

2060. Burns, Olive Ann. Cold Sassy Tree. Ticknor & Fields; dist. by Houghton, 1984. 391 p. $17.
Gr 9+. B 81: Oct 15 1984. B 82: Mar 1 1986. +- BR 3: Jan/Feb 1985. LJ 109: Oct 15 1984. SLJ 31: Feb 1985. Cold Sassy, Georgia, 1906. With the help of his beautiful young Yankee wife, Rucker Blakeslee brings the first auto dealership and other modern ways to a rural town.

2061. Chaikin, Miriam. Finders Weepers. Harper, 1980. 120 p. ill. $9. Lib. ed. $9.
Gr 3-7. B 77: Nov 15 1980. BC 34: Feb 1981. HB 57: Feb 1981. SLJ 27: Sep 1980. Molly finds, and keeps, a gold ring that she knows belongs to a Jewish refugee. As the holy holidays approach, Molly's conscience bothers her. Set in Brooklyn, late 1930s. Sequel to I Should Worry, I Should Care.

2062. Delton, Judy. Kitty from the Start. Houghton, 1987. 141 p. $13.
Gr 3-6. B 83: Apr 1 1987. HB 63: May/Jun 1987. SLJ 33: May 1987. Prequel to Kitty in the Middle. As a third grader Kitty moves to a different Catholic school and finds herself torn between her new friends, one mischievous and one determined to be perfect.

2063. Edmonds, Walter D. Bert Breen's Barn. Little, 1975. 270 p. $15.
Gr 7-9. SE 44: Oct 1980. In upstate New York at the turn of the century a courageous young boy is determined to raise a barn on the family farm. An excellent character study.

2064. Ellison, Lucile Watkins. Butter on Both Sides. Scribner, 1979. 150 p. $8.
Gr 4-7. +- BC 33: Mar 1980. HB 56: Apr 1980. SLJ 26: Mar 1980. An autobiographical novel of fond recollections of life on an Alabama farm in the 1900s.

2065. Hamilton, Virginia. Willie Bea and the Time the Martians Landed. Greenwillow, 1983. 224 p. $12.

Gr 4-9. B 80: Nov 1 1983. BC 37: Nov 1983. BR 2: Mar/Apr 1984. HB 60: Feb 1984. * SE 48: May 1984. SLJ 30: Dec 1983. VOYA 7: Aug 1984. The story of a black family whose life is affected by the 1938 Halloween broadcast of Orson Welles' "War of the Worlds."

2066. Homola, Priscilla. Willow Whistle, The. Dodd, 1983. 109 p. ill. $9.
Gr 5-7. +- BC 37: Jan 1984. BR 2: Jan/Feb 1984. SLJ 30: Dec 1983. On the South Dakota prairie at the turn of the century Annie's stern father forbids her budding romance.

2067. Howard, Ellen. Circle of Giving. Atheneum, 1984. 99 p. $10.
Gr 4-6. +- B 80: May 15 1984. +- BC 37: Apr 1984. +- SLJ 30: Aug 1984. In the 1920s the Sloan family moved to Los Angeles. A neighbor child with cerebral palsy is the focus of the action. Based on a true story.

2068. Isadora, Rachel. Jesse and Abe. Greenwillow, 1981. 32 p. ill. $8.
Gr K-4. B 77: Mar 1 1981. BC 34: Jun 1981. SE 46: Apr 1982. SLJ 27: Mar 1981. Jesse visits his grandfather, a doorman at a vaudeville theater in the 1920s.

2069. Johnston, Norma. Nice Girl Like You, A. Atheneum, 1980. 222 p. $10.
Gr 7+. B 78: Mar 15 1980. +- BC 33: Jul/Aug 1980. HB 56: Jun 1980. SLJ 26: May 1980. VOYA 3: Aug 1980. The Bronx, 1917. Saranne is involved in high school activities, her mother is a sufragette. A good character study, providing a sense of time and place as the U.S. becomes involved in World War I.

2070. Kirkpatrick, Doris. Honey in the Rock. Elsevier/Nelson, 1979. 218 p. $9.
Gr 8+. +- BC 33: Nov 1979. SE 44: Oct 1980. There are good character studies, humor, suspense, and a few sad moments in this story of a backward Vermont town that becomes modernized.

2071. Lee, Harper. To Kill a Mockingbird. Harper; Warner, 1960. 284 p. $16. Pb $4.
Gr 10+. B 81: Jul 1985. An attorney is condemned by town racists for defending a black man.

2072. Levinson, Riki. I Go with My Family to Grandma's. Dutton, 1986. 32 p. ill. $11.
Gr K-3. +- BC 40: Oct 1986. HB 62: Nov/Dec 1986. * SE 51: Apr/May 1987. SLJ 33: Oct 1986. At the turn of the century five little girls visit Grandma in Brooklyn. Lively illustrations enhance this bit of social history.

2073. McCall, Edith. Better Than a Brother. (Walker's American History Series for Young People). Walker, 1988. 144 p. ill. $14. Lib. ed. $15.
Gr 4-8. +- B 84: Jul 1988. +- BC 41: May 1988. BR 7: Sep/Oct 1988. SLJ 34: May 1988. A good sense of time and place is provided in this story set on the shore of a Wisconsin lake at the turn of the century. Based on the experiences of the author's grandmother.

2074. Meyer, Carolyn. Summer I Learned about Life, The. Atheneum, 1983. 198 p. $12.

Gr 7+. B 80: Oct 1 1983. +- BC 37: Oct 1983. HB 60: Feb 1984. * VOYA 7: Jun 1984. In 1928 15-year-old Teddie's mother is training her to be a model young lady, but she wants to become an aviatrix. A humorous examination of societal traditions.

2075. Miles, Betty. I Would if I Could. Knopf, 1982. 120 p. $9.
Gr 3-6. B 78: Mar 15 1982. BC 58: Jun 1982. SLJ 28: Apr 1982. In a small town in Ohio in the late 1930s, Patty learns to ride a bicycle, there is a polio scare, and a stranger might be a spy. A simple timeless tale.

2076. Peck, Robert Newton. Day No Pigs Would Die, A. Knopf; Dell, 1972. 144 p. $14. Pb $3.
Gr 7+. B 82: Mar 1 1986. Rob faces the death of his father and the loss of his pet pig. An autobiographical novel about a Shaker family set in 1920s Vermont.

2077. Perez, N. A. One Special Year. Houghton, 1985. 200 p. $13.
Gr 6-9. B 81: Jun 15 1985. BR 4: Sep/Oct 1985. SLJ 31: Aug 1985. Social and political events in New York state at the turn of the century and family troubles contribute to the personal growth of Jen McAlister.

2078. Rogers, Paul. From Me to You. Watts/Orchard, 1988. 30 p. ill. $13.
Gr K-3. B 84: Feb 15 1988. BC 41: May 1988. HB 64: Sep/Oct 1988. +- SLJ 34: Apr 1988. Grandmother tells the story of her growing up in a nostalgic verse story.

2079. Rosenblum, Richard. My Block. Atheneum, 1988. 32 p. ill. $12.
Gr K-2. B 85: Oct 15 1988. This fond reminiscence of childhood in 1930s Brooklyn introduces the coal truck driver, ice man, scissors grinder, candy man, and others.

2080. Rylant, Cynthia. When I Was Young in the Mountains. Dutton, 1982. 31 p. ill. $10.
Gr 5-7. B 78: Apr 15 1982. BC 35: Apr 1982. HB 58: Jun 1982. SLJ 28: May 1982. Reminiscences of childhood in Appalachia, as two children and their grandparents live a simple life in a four-room house.

2081. Saunders, Susan. Fish Fry. Viking, 1982. 32 p. $13.
Gr K-3. B 79: Dec 1 1982. * SE 47: Apr 1983. SLJ 29: Sep 1982. In this story of an annual catfish picnic, readers learn about life in the east Texas piney woods in 1912.

2082. Schur, Maxine Rose. Samantha's Surprise: A Christmas Story. (American Girls Collection). Pleasant, 1986. 66 p. ill. $13. Pb $5.
Gr 2-5. B 83: Dec 1 1986. Orphaned Samantha learns to appreciate her grandmother's values while retaining her own beliefs.

2083. Sinclair, Upton. Jungle, The. New American Library/Signet, 1906. 352 p. $2.
Gr 9+. B 82: Mar 1 1986. An expose of the filthy Chicago stockyards at the turn of the century.

2084. Stover, Marjorie. Patrick and the Great Molasses Explosion. Dillon Press, 1985. 35 p. ill. $9.

Gr 1-3. SLJ 33: Aug 1986. Based on a real event. When Patrick comes home sticky from head to toe, his mother won't believe that the storage tank exploded and the street is full of molasses.

2085. Terris, Susan. Nell's Quilt. Farrar, 1987. 162 p. $13.
Gr 7+. B 84: Nov 1 1987. +- BC 41: Nov 1987. SLJ 34: Nov 1987. VOYA 10: Feb 1988. Expected to marry the man her parents have chosen, Nell's attempts at delay involve embroidering a quilt. Her depression leads to anorexia and near death, but she then chooses life–under her own control.

2086. Tripp, Valerie. Happy Birthday, Samantha! (American Girls Collection). Pleasant, 1987. 62 p. ill. $13. Pb $6.
Gr 2-5. +- B 84: Apr 1 1988. SLJ 35: May 1988. In 1904 New York, Samantha celebrates her birthday. A chase after a mischievous puppy ends at a suffragette meeting.

Storms–Fiction

2087. Nelson, Theresa. Devil Storm. Watts/Orchard/Richard Jackson, 1987. 212 p. $13. Lib. ed. $13.
Gr 4-8. B 84: Dec 1 1987. +- BC 41: Sep 1987. BR 6: Jan/Feb 1988. * HB 63: Nov/Dec 1987. SLJ 33: Jun/Jul 1987. VOYA 10: Feb 1988. A remarkable picture of Texas small-town life, language, superstition, and prejudice at the time of a devastating hurricane that killed over 6000 persons.

Technology and Civilization

2088. Clinton, Patrick. Story of the Empire State Building, The. (Cornerstones of Freedom). Childrens Press, 1988. 30 p. ill. $11.
Gr 3-6. B 84: May 15 1988. Explains how the design of a safe elevator system and new construction technology made skyscrapers possible and changed the development of modern cities. Includes numerous photos.

Transportation

2089. Smith, E. Boyd. Railroad Book, The. Houghton, 1983. 56 p. ill. $13.
Gr K-8. B 80: Feb 1 1984. HB 60: Feb 1984. * SE 48: May 1984. A grand view of American railroads in a beautifully illustrated book originally published in 1913.

2090. Wamsley, James S. American Ingenuity: Henry Ford Museum and Greenfield Village. Abrams, 1985. 223 p. ill. $38.
Gr 9+. B 81: Jul 1985. LJ 110: Jul 1985. A visual history of U.S. transportation and other aspects of early 20th-century American life.

Transportation–Fiction

2091. Baker, Betty. Great Desert Race, The. Macmillan, 1980. 144 p. $9.

Gr 6-8. BC 34: Oct 1980. SLJ 27: Nov 1980. Two 16-year-old girls are the driving team for a steam powered automobile in the 1908 race from Los Angeles to Phoenix in this humorous story based on the events of a real race.

2092. Weitzman, David. Superpower: The Making of a Steam Locomotive. Godine, 1987. 107 p. ill. $20.
Gr 6+. +- SLJ 34: Jan 1988. In depicting the detail of the construction of a steam locomotive, Weitzman also conveys the sense of pride, tradition, and community that prevailed in Lima, Ohio, in the 1920s.

West, The

2093. Strickland, Ron. River Pigs and Cayuses: Oral Histories from the Pacific Northwest. Lexikos, 1984. 224 p. ill. $12.
Adult. B 81: Jan 15 1985. LJ 110: Feb 1 1985. A wide range of ethnic occupational groups provide oral histories of the west in the early 20th century.

Women

2094. Brown, Dorothy M. Setting a Course: American Women in the 1920s. (Amercian Women in the Twentieth Century). Twayne, 1987. 328 p. ill. $19. Pb $10.
Gr 9+. B 83: Jan 1 1987. LJ 112: Feb 1 1987. Shows the evolving role of women between World War I and the Depression.

Women–Biographies

2095. Douglas, George H. Women of the 20s. Saybrook; dist. by Norton, 1986. 230 p. $17.
Gr 9+. B 82: Jun 15 1986. Includes Aimee Semple McPherson, Amelia Earhart, Martha Graham, Edna St. Vincent Millay, Dorothy Parker, and Anita Loos.

2096. Hendricks, Cecilia Hennel. Letters from Honeyhill: A Woman's View of Homesteading, 1914-1931. Pruett, 1986. 500 p. ill. $20.
Gr 10+. B 83: Sep 15 1986. LJ 111: Sep 15 1986. Hendricks tells of her homesteading experiences and of her political activities in Wyoming. She was a friend of governor Nellie Ross.

2097. Peavy, Linda. Women Who Changed Things. Scribner, 1983. 188 p. $13.
Gr 6+. B 79: Apr 1 1983. BR 2: Nov/Dec 1983. SLJ 30: Oct 1983. VOYA 6: Dec 1983. These biographies are of nine relatively unknown women who changed the lives of others. They include reformers, educators, politicians, journalists, and explorers.

Women–Fiction

2098. Bolton, Carole. Never Jam Today. Atheneum/Aladdin, 1971. 241 p. Pb $1.
Gr 7-9. B 81: Sep 15 1984. The struggle for women's suffrage upsets 17-year-old Maddy's ordered life.

2099. Constant, Alberta Wilson. Does Anybody Care about Lou Emma Miller? Harper/Crowell, 1979. 278 p. $11.

Gr 5-8. B 81: Sep 15 1984. Sophomore Lou Emma helps elect Kansas' first woman mayor.

2100. Hunt, Irene. Claws of a Young Century. Scribner, 1980. 292 p. $10.
Gr 7+. B 76: Jun 15 1980. +- BC 33: Jul/Aug 1980. +- HB 56: Oct 1980. +- SLJ 26: Aug 1980. This novel that depicts the struggle for women's rights as seen through the story of Ellen Archer captures the turbulence of the times.

2101. Mays, Lucinda. Candle and the Mirror, The. Atheneum, 1982. 182 p. $10.
Gr 7-9. +- BC 36: Oct 1982. SE 47: Apr 1983. A fictionalized biography of Anne Simmons, a career nurse, whose mother was a labor organizer and social reformer.

World War, 1914-1918

2102. Barnett, Correlli. Great War, The. Putnam, 1980. 192 p. ill. $20.
Gr 9+. SLJ 26: Aug 1980. An objective photo-history that includes an analysis of strategy, covers all areas of the war, and discusses the impact of the war on social change. This reprint of a British title does not emphasize U.S. activity.

2103. Everett, Susanne. World War I: An Illustrated History. Rand McNally, 1980. 256 p. ill. $20.
Gr 9+. LJ 106: Feb 15 1981. The land war is emphasized in this overview that coveys the drudgery and terror of war. There is a chapter each on sea and air battles.

2104. Marrin, Albert. Yanks Are Coming: The United States in the First World War. Atheneum, 1986. 175 p. ill. $15.
Gr 7-10. B 83: Oct 15 1986. BC 40: Nov 1986. +- SLJ 33: Feb 1987. VOYA 10: June 1987. A comprehensive look at the battles, the homefront, and the propaganda. Includes photos and maps.

2105. Mee, Charles L. End of Order: Versailles 1919. Elsevier-Dutton, 1980. 301 p. $16.
Gr 9+. B 77: Jan 1 1981. LJ 105: Nov 1 1980. Explores the personal and political reasons why the leaders at Versailles were unable to restore order from the chaos following World War I.

2106. Pimlott, John. First World War, The. (Conflict in the 20th Century). Watts, 1986. 62 p. ill. $12.
Gr 6-9. B 83: Jan 15 1987. SLJ 33: Apr 1987. Covers causes, battles, strategies, and personalities. Includes maps and a chronology.

2107. Snyder, Louis Leo. World War I. (First Book). Rev. ed. Watts, 1981. 90 p. ill. $8.
Gr 4-7. B 78: Jan 1 1982. SLJ 28: Mar 1982. This simple presentation of the causes, major events, personalities, peace process, and costs of the war, includes photos, quotes, and a glossary.

2108. Stokesbury, James L. Short History of World War I, A. Morrow, 1981. 370 p. maps. $14.

Gr 9+. B 77: Jan 15 1981. LJ 106: Feb 1 1981. This vigorous overview of the war covers all the battles and clarifies the problems of the leaders on both sides.

2109. Terraine, John. To Win a War: 1918, the Year of Victory. Doubleday, 1981. 268 p. ill. $15.
Adult. LJ 106: Aug 1981. A deft analysis of the major personalities and the political aspects of the war.

2110. Vansittart, Peter. Voices from the Great War. Watts, 1984. 303 p. $15.
Gr 10+. B 80: Mar 14 1984. SLJ 31: Jan 1985. VOYA 7: Dec 1984. Quotes from patriots, idealists, politicians, and pacifists, concerning the harsh realities of combat.

2111. Weintraub, Stanley. Stillness Heard Round the World: The End of the Great War: November 1918. Dutton, 1985. 448 p. ill. $20.
Gr 10+. B 81: Jul 1985. LJ 110: Aug 1985. Blends memoirs and eyewitness accounts of the end of the fighting and tells how the news of peace was greeted by civilians.

World War, 1914-1918–Aerial Operations and Aircraft

2112. Bowen, Ezra. Knights of the Air. Time-Life; dist. by Silver Burdett, 1980. 192 p. ill. $11.
Gr 9+. LJ 105: May 1 1980. Examines the changing role of airplanes in the war, their glamour, and the terrible toll of eager young fliers.

2113. Maynard, Christopher. Aces: Pilots and Planes of World War I. (Wings: The Conquest of the Air). Watts, 1987. 32 p. ill. $11.
Gr 4-8. B 84: Jan 1 1988. BR 6: Jan/Feb 1988. SLJ 34: Apr 1988. A visual history of air warfare and air heroes in World War I.

2114. Nordhoff, C. B. Falcons of France: A Tale of Youth and Air. Little, 1929. 332 p. $31.
Gr 7-9. Metzner [B 26: Nov 1929]. A picture of the experiences of the Lafayette Flying Corps during their service in France during World War I.

2115. Stein, R. Conrad. Story of the Lafayette Escadrille, The. (Cornerstones of Freedom). Childrens Press, 1983. 31 p. ill. $6.
Gr 4-6. B 79: Aug 1983. SLJ 30: Sep 1983. The story of a unique group of fighter pilots, French and American, who wrote the first pages of aviation combat history.

World War, 1914-1918–Fiction

2116. Hemingway, Ernest. Farewell to Arms, A. Scribner, 1929. 336 p. $15. Pb $5.
Gr 10+. B 82: Mar 1 1986. An American ambulance driver sees the horror of World War I.

2117. Rostkowski, Margaret I. After the Dancing Days. Harper, 1986. 221 p. $14. Lib. ed. $14.
Gr 6-9. * B 83: Oct 15 1986. BC 40: Jan 1987. HB 63: Jan/Feb 1987. VOYA 10: Apr 1987. As Annie visits the patients at the veterans hospital where her father is a physician she comes to terms with the horrors of war.

2118. Voigt, Cynthia. Tree by Leaf. Atheneum, 1988. 192 p. $14.
Gr 6-10. B 84: Apr 1 1988. +- BC 41: Apr 1988. * BR 7: Sep/Oct 1988. +- HB 64: May/Jun 1988. +- SLJ 34: May 1988. VOYA 11: Aug 1988. When her father went to the war against her grandfather's wishes, Clothilde and her family were forced to leave their luxurious home. When her father returned seriously injured, the whole family suffered.

World War, 1914-1918–Military Personnel

2119. Colby, C. B. Fighting Gear of World War I: Equipment and Weapons of the American Doughboy. Coward, 1961. 48 p. ill. $7.
Gr 4-8. Metzner. An illustrated guide to the equipment and weapons used by military personnel during World War I.

2120. Tames, Richard. Great War, The. (Living through History). Batsford; dist. by David & Charles, 1984. 71 p. ill. $15.
Gr 7+. SLJ 31: Feb 1985. Tells the story of the war through biographies, with numerous quotes, photos, maps, drawings, and advertisements.

World War, 1914-1918–Poetry

2121. Lewis, Claudia. Long Ago in Oregon. (Great Disasters). Harper, 1987. 53 p. ill. $12. Lib. ed. $12.
Gr 3-8. B 83: Jul 1987. BC 40: May 1987. * SE 52: Apr/May 1988. SLJ 34: Sep 1987. Memories of childhood in the 1910s, written in appealing free verse, enhanced by pencil drawings. Covers typical growing-up concerns in addition to poems about the impact of World War I on the family.

1939-1945

United States–History–1939-1945

2122. Baudot, Marcel. Historical Encyclopedia of World War II, The. Facts On File, 1980. 548 p. ill. $25.
Gr 9+. +- B 78: Sep 15 1981. +- LJ 106: Feb 15 1981. Approximately 900 articles on events and people, alphabetically arranged. Also includes a chronology and numerous photos, charts, and diagrams. Originally published in France.

2123. Hart, Jeffrey. From This Moment On: America in 1940. Crown, 1987. 352 p. $20.
Gr 9+. B 83: Apr 1 1987. +- LJ Jun 15 1987. A nostalgic view of the U.S. and its notable persons on the eve of World War II.

2124. Hills, C.A.R. Second World War, The. (Living Through History). Batsford; dist. by David & Charles, 1986. 72 p. ill. $17.
Gr 7+. SLJ 33: Nov 1986. A look at the war through the eyes of leaders, fighters, civilians, and victims.

2125. Masson, Philippe. Second World War: A Photographic History. Larousse; dist. by Dutton, 1985. 335 p. ill. $30.
Gr 10+. LJ 110: Sep 1 1985. From the archives of the combatants 650 photos were chosen, arranged alphabetically by subject, and provided with extensive explanatory captions.

2126. McCombs, Don. World War II Super Facts. Warner, 1983. 659 p. Pb $4.
Gr 9+. B 79: Jul 1983. LJ 108: Jun 15 1983. An alphabetic arrangement of World War II trivia useful for browsing and reference.

2127. Messenger, Charles. Second World War, The. (Conflict in the 20th Century). Watts, 1987. 62 p. ill. $13.
Gr 6-10. B 83: Jun 15 1987. * BR 6: Sep/Oct 1987. SLJ 33: Jun/Jul 1987. A clear and well-organized overview and analysis of the events of the war and its results.

2128. Pierre, Michel. Second World War. (Events of Yesteryear). Silver Burdett, 1987. 69 p. ill. $15.
Gr 7+. BR 6: Jan/Feb 1988. +- SLJ 34: Dec 1987. An overview of the war is presented with detailed maps and news clippings. A special section highlights cultural events and key persons of the time.

2129. Snyder, Louis Leo. World War II. (First Book). Watts, 1981. 90 p. ill. $8.
Gr 4-6. B 78: Jan 1 1982. SLJ 28: Mar 1982. A simple presentation of the causes, major events, personalities, peace process, and costs of the war, with photos, quotes, and a glossary.

2130. Sullivan, George. Strange But True Stories of World War II. Walker, 1983. 100 p. $11.
Gr 6-9. B 80: Sep 15 1983. SLJ 30: Dec 1983. Accounts of eleven episodes that helped change the course of the war. Fascinating reading, suitable for reluctant readers.

2131. Terkel, Studs. Good War: An Oral History of World War II. Pantheon, 1984. 589 p. $20.
Gr 10+. B 80: Aug 1984. BR 4: May/Jun 1985. * LJ 109: Sep 1 1984. LJ 110: Jan 1985. SE 49: May 1985. SLJ 31: Mar 1985. An oral history of 100 people affected by World War II.

2132. Weinberg, Gerhard. World in the Balance: Behind the Scenes of World War II. (Tauber Institute Series, No. 1) University Press of New England, 1981. 165 p. Pb $6.
Gr 10+. B 78: Mar 15 1982. HT 17: Nov 1983. A series of six interwoven essays examining the causes of the war, its global nature, Hitler's attitude toward America, and the German resistance movement. For extensive collections.

2133. Wootton, Angela M. Second World War, The. Larousse, 1985. 334 p. ill. $30.
Gr 9+. B 82: Sep 1 1985. A pictorial encyclopedia, with brief text, on most aspects of the war. Includes maps.

2134. Young, Peter. World Almanac Book of World War II, The. Prentice-Hall, 1981. 613 p. ill. $17.

Gr 9+. B 78: Nov 15 1981. B 79: Sep 1 1982. +- LJ 106 Dec 1 1981. Comprehensive coverage, with brief descriptions, on an enormous number of topics. Includes a detailed chronology, a section on weapons and equipment, and a section of biographies.

2135. Young, Peter. World Almanac of World War II: The Complete and Comprehensive Documentary of World War II. 1st rev. ed. World Almanac; dist. by Ballantine, 1986. 514 p. ill. Pb $15.
Gr 9+. +- B 83: Jan 15 1987. SLJ 33: May 1987. Similar to the 1981 edition with minor corrections and additions.

Airplanes and Pilots

2136. Blair, Clay. Ridgway's Paratroopers: The American Airborne in World War II. Dial; dist. by Doubleday, 1985. 600 p. ill. $25.
Adult. B 81: Aug 1985. LJ 110: Sep 1 1985. A clearly written biography of Ridgway and a comprehensive history of American airborne troops in World War II.

2137. Comer, John. Combat Crew. Texian Press, 1986. 267 p. ill. $17.
Gr 9+. B 83: Dec 15 1986. Memoirs of a B-17 flight engineer/gunner who flew 75 missions.

2138. Dunn, William R. Fighter Pilot: The First American Ace of World War II. University Press of Kentucky, 1982. 272 p. ill. $18.
Adult. B 79: Jan 15 1983. LJ 107: Oct 1 1982. For aviation buffs and extensive collections, the lively reminiscences of a much-decorated veteran of the air wars over Europe and Asia.

2139. Gaffney, Timothy R. Chuck Yeager: First Man to Fly Faster Than Sound. (People of Distinction Biographies). Childrens Press, 1986. 126 p. ill. $9.
Gr 4-8. B 83: Feb 1 1987. SLJ 33: Feb 1987. Yeager was a pilot in World War II and Vietnam, and was the first to break the sound barrier. This biography includes a time line of the history of aviation.

2140. Glines, Carrol V. Doolittle Raid: America's Daring First Strike Against Japan. Crown/Orion, 1988. 247 p. $18.
Gr 9+. B 85: Oct 1 1988. +- LJ 113: Oct 15 1988. This sound account of the 1942 raid on Japan includes interviews with members of the bombing crews.

2141. Hoyt, Edwin P. McCampbell's Heroes. Avon, 1983. 272 p. $4.
Gr 7+. VOYA 7: Feb 1985. An account of the fighter pilots from the carrier Essex in the battle of the Pacific.

2142. Jackson, Robert. Bomber! Famous Bomber Missions of World War II. St. Martin's, 1980. 157 p. $9.
Gr 9+. B 76: May 1 1980. An episodic approach to significant bomber missions written in an animated narrative style.

2143. Levinson, Nancy Smiler. Chuck Yeager: The Man Who Broke the Sound Barrier. Walker, 1988. 133 p. ill. $14. Lib. ed. $15.
Gr 5-8. B 84: Aug 1988. +- BR 7: Sep/Oct 1988. SLJ 35: May 1988. +- VOYA 11: Aug 1988. This lively

biography emphasizes Yeager's years as a test pilot. Extensively researched, this work includes photos and a glossary.

2144. Marrin, Albert. Airman's War: World War II in the Sky. Atheneum, 1982. 213 p. ill. $12.
Gr 6-9. B 79: Dec 15 1982. * SE 47: Apr 1983. SLJ 29: Nov 1982. * SE 47: Apr 1983. A look at Allied and Axis airpower in the European and Pacific theaters. A well-researched and appealing presentation.

2145. Maynard, Christopher. Air Battles: Air Combat in World War II. (Wings: Conquest of the Air). Watts, 1987. 32 p. ill. $11.
Gr 4-8. B 84: Jan 1 1988. BR 6: Jan/Feb 1988. SLJ 34: Apr 1988. Explains the vital role of the air force and the pressure to develop new technology to achieve air superiority. Also covers major air battles, strategies, and major planes.

2146. Muirhead, John. Those Who Fall. Random House, 1987. 290 p. ill. $19.
Gr 9+. * B 83: Jan 1 1987. LJ 112: Jan 1987. The author was a bomber pilot who was shot down and imprisoned. An outstanding memoir.

2147. Munson, Kenneth George. American Aircraft of World War II in Color. Blandford Press; dist. by Sterling, 1982. 160 p. ill. $16.
Gr 9+. B 78: May 15 1982. A sound, basic guide with good photos of all types of World War II aircraft, including those used for training and transport.

2148. O'Leary, Michael. United States Naval Fighters of World War II in Action. (In Action). Poole, Dorset, Blandford Press; dist. by Sterling, 1980. 160 p. ill. $18. Lib. ed. $15.
Gr 9+. B 78: Mar 1 1982. Presents action photos with descriptive captions. Emphasis is on the Bearcat, Buffalo, Corsair, Hellcat, Tigercat, and Wildcat. Covers technical detail.

2149. Samson, Jack. Chennault. Doubleday, 1987. 343 p. ill. $20.
Gr 9+. B 84: Oct 1 1987. LJ 112: Nov 15 1987. Traces the career of the man who led the Flying Tigers in the Asian theater. The author of this thoroughly researched work served under Chennault.

2150. Schultz, Duane. Doolittle Raid, The. St. Martin's, 1988. 352 p. $19.
Gr 9+. B 85: Oct 1 1988. LJ 113: Oct 15 1988. A readable fast-moving account of the Doolittle raid on Tokyo, April 1942. A capsule biography of Doolittle is included.

2151. Schultz, Duane. Maverick War: Chennault and the Flying Tigers. St. Martin's, 1987. 368 p. ill. $19.
Gr 9+. B 83: Jun 15 1987. LJ 112: Jun 1 1987. A complete account of the Flying Tigers and their leader Claire Chennault. These volunteers, working with outdated equipment, were extraordinarily effective in covert operations.

2152. Smith, Peter C. Dive Bombers in Action. Blandford Press; dist. by Sterling, 1988. 160 p. ill. $30.

Gr 9+. B 85: Oct 15 1988. Emphasis is on the dive bombers of World War II. Well-researched, readable, and highly illustrated.

2153. Sweeney, James B. Famous Aviators of World War II. Watts, 1987. 94 p. ill. $10.
Gr 4-8. B 83: May 1 1987. BR 6: Nov/Dec 1987. SLJ 34: Sep 1987. Brief biographies of five flying aces: Claire Chennault, Jimmy Doolittle, Curtis LeMay, Carl Spaatz, and Emmett (Rosie) O'Donneell.

2154. Toland, John. Flying Tigers, The. Random House, 1963, 1979. 172 p. ill. Pb $3.
Gr 6-8. Metzner [LJ 89: Jan 15 1964]. The story of volunteer American pilots and mechanics, led by Claire Chenault, who tried to help China's fight against the Japanese.

2155. Yeager, Chuck. Yeager: An Autobiography. Bantam, 1985. 342 p. ill. $18.
Adult. B 81: May 1 1985. LJ 110: Sep 15 1985. SLJ 32: Nov 1985. Yeager, a World War II fighter pilot hero who was shot down over occupied France, went on to break the sound barrier and make aviation history.

Airplanes and Pilots–Fiction

2156. Ferry, Charles. Raspberry One. Houghton, 1983. 224 p. $9.
Gr 7+. B 79: May 15 1983. HB 59: Jun 1983. * SLJ 30: Sep 1983. VOYA 7: Apr 1984. This novel of two young airmen depicts their training, their experiences in battle, and how they deal with their injuries and the deaths of friends. Strong characterization and description.

2157. Green, Wayne L. Allegiance. Crown, 1983. 320 p. $15.
Gr 9+. B 79: Apr 1 1983. LJ 108: Mar 15 1983. Based on an actual incident. A downed U.S. pilot is sheltered by a Japanese doctor who had been educated in the U.S.

Battles

2158. Archer, Jules. Jungle Fighters: A GI Correspondent's Experiences in the New Guinea Campaign. Messner, 1985. 224 p. ill. $10.
Gr 7+. B 81: Feb 1 1985. * SLJ 31: Aug 1985. This vivid description of the Pacific conflict on land, told by a noted author who was there, includes numerous photos.

2159. Bliven, Bruce. From Pearl Harbor to Okinawa: The War in the Pacific: 1941-1945. (Landmark Books). Random House, 1960. 192 p. ill. $7.
Gr 7-8. Metzner [* B 57: Jan 1 1961]. In this account of all the major land and sea battles in the Pacific, Bliven shows the horrors faced by the military personnel and their courage and heroism. Includes photos and maps.

2160. Bliven, Bruce. Story of D-Day: June 6 1944. (Landmark Books). Random House, 1956, 1981. 180 p. ill. $7.
Gr 7-8. Metzner [B 53: Jan 1 1957]. A dramatic hour-by-hour account of American operations on D-Day.

2161. Breuer, William B. Operation Dragoon: The Allied Invasion of the South of France. Presidio, 1987. 280 p. ill. $18.
Adult. B 84: Sep 1 1987. LJ 112: Sep 15 1987. Breuer focuses on the first day of the controversial Allied invasion of southern France in August 1944, and places it in the context of the total war effort.

2162. Breuer, William B. Retaking the Philippines: America's Return to Corregidor and Bataan, July 1944-March 1945. St. Martin's, 1986. 336 p. ill. $19.
Gr 9+. B 83: Nov 15 1986. LJ 111: Nov 15 1986. A full-scale account of the battle in the Philippines.

2163. Crookenden, Napier. Battle of the Bulge 1944. Scribner, 1980. 160 p. ill. $18.
Gr 9+. B 77: Nov 15 1980. Charts the course of the battle through captioned contemporary photos from American, British, and German archives.

2164. Dank, Milton. D-Day. (Turning Points of World War II). Watts, 1984. 106 p. ill. $10.
Gr 6+. B 81: Dec 15 1984. BR 4: Sep/Oct 1985. SLJ 31: Mar 1985. VOYA 8: Apr 1985. This excellent overview of the largest amphibious military operation in history includes photos and maps.

2165. Flanagan, E.M. Corregidor—The Rock Force Assault, February 1945. Presidio, 1988. 316 p. $19.
Gr 9+. B 84: Feb 1 1988. Following a brief presentation of the pre-1941 history of Corregidor is a readable account of its fall to the Japanese and its subsequent recapture by the Americans.

2166. Hammel, Eric. Guadalcanal: Decision at Sea: The Naval Battle of Guadalcanal, November 13-15, 1942. Crown, 1988. 496 p. $25.
Gr 9+. B 85: Oct 15 1988. A meticulous reconstruction of the details of the air and naval battles at Guadalcanal.

2167. Hammel, Eric. Guadalcanal: The Carrier Battles: The Pivotal Aircraft Carrier Battles of the Eastern Solomons and Santa Cruz. Crown, 1987. 512 p. ill. $25.
Gr 9+. B 83: Jul 1987. This exciting account of one of the bloodiest and most crucial campaigns of the Pacific war shows the role of carriers and the emergence of U.S. naval air superiority.

2168. Hapgood, David. Monte Cassino. Congdon & Weed; dist. by St. Martins, 1984. 320 p. ill. $18.
Adult. B 80: Mar 15 1984. LJ 109: Mar 1 1984. SE 49: May 1985. A well-researched but controversial account of the battle that resulted in the destruction of Monte Cassino, an artistic and religious treasure in northern Italy.

2169. Harris, Nathaniel. Pearl Harbor. (Day That Made History). Batsford; dist. by David & Charles, 1986. 64 p. ill. $15.
Gr 6-10. * BR 6: Sep/Oct 1987. +- SLJ 34: Sep 1987. Emphasis is on the actual events of December 7, 1941, with a brief explanation of its causes.

2170. Hastings, Max. Overlord: D-Day and the Battle for Normandy. Simon & Schuster, 1984. 355 p. ill. $18.

Gr 9+. B 80: Jun 15 1984. LJ 109: Jun 1 1984. Following a brief analysis of the war situation at the time is a vivid picture of the difficulties of the British and American troops in their efforts to take Normandy Beach from superior German forces.

2171. Hoyt, Edwin P. Invasion Before Normandy: The Secret Battle of Slapton Sands. Stein & Day, 1985. 252 p. ill. $19.
Gr 9+. B 81: May 15 1985. Covers the preparations for D-Day, the disputes among the Allies, and their plans to deceive the Germans, as well as a full-scale account of the Battle of Slapton Sands in which two American troop ships were sunk.

2172. Lee, Robert Edward. Victory at Guadalcanal. Presidio, 1981. 268 p. ill. $15.
Gr 9+. LJ 106: Aug 1981. A blend of ground, naval, and air action into a lively day-by-day narrative.

2173. MacDonald, Charles B. Time For Trumpets, A. Morrow, 1984. 715 p. ill. $20.
Adult. B 81: Oct 1 1984. LJ 109: Oct 15 1984. This coverage of the battle of Bastogne from strategy to the battlefield is also a tribute to the human side of the battle.

2174. Macdonald, John. Great Battles of World War II. Macmillan, 1986. 200 p. ill. $35.
Gr 10+. B 83: Nov 15 1986. LJ 111: Nov 15 1986. Provides detail on twenty-six land, sea, and air battles of World War II.

2175. Marrin, Albert. Overlord: D-Day and the Invasion of Europe. Atheneum, 1982. 177 p. ill. $13.
Gr 6-9. B 79: Feb 1 1983. HB 55: Dec 1982. SLJ 29: Nov 1982. A action-filled and readable overview of the planning and the events of D-Day enhanced by excellent black-and-white photos.

2176. McGowen, Tom. Midway and Guadalcanal. (Turning Points of World War II). Watts, 1984. 104 p. ill. $10.
Gr 7+. B 81: Dec 15 1984. BR 4: Sep/Oct 1985. SLJ 31: Mar 1985. VOYA 8: Apr 1985. The actions of famous leaders and of common soldiers interwoven in exciting detail.

2177. Miller, Marilyn. D-Day. (Turning Points in American History). Silver Burdett, 1987. 64 p. ill. $15. Pb $6.
Gr 5-8. B 83: Jul 1987. +- BR 6: Sep/Oct 1987. +- SLJ 33: Aug 1987. Presents the successes and tragedies of this massive invasion. Enriched by numerous maps and illustrations.

2178. Prange, Gordon W. December 7, 1941: The Day the Japanese Attacked Pearl Harbor. McGraw-Hill, 1987. 477 p. ill. $23.
Gr 9+. B 84: Oct 15 1987. * LJ 112: Oct 15 1987. A detailed account of the attack on Pearl Harbor based on eyewitness accounts. Focuses on Japanese attackers as well as on American defenders.

2179. Prange, Gordon W. Miracle at Midway. McGraw-Hill, 1982. 455 p. ill. $20.

Gr 9+. B 79: Oct 1 1982. * LJ 107: Nov 1 1982. Offers a good view of the strategies and errors of both sides and the turns of fate that affected the outcome.

2180. Ross, Bill D. Iwo Jima: Legacy of Valor. Vanguard, 1985. 336 p. ill. $23.
Adult. * LJ 110: Mar 15 1985. In 36 days of ferocious fighting (over 28,000 American casualties) the Marines took strategic Iwo Jima from the Japanese. A gripping and accurate book.

2181. Ryan, Cornelius. Longest Day: June 6, 1944. Simon & Schuster, 1959. 350 p. Pb $4.
Gr 9+. B 56: Dec 15 1959. B 82: Jan 1 1986. +- LJ 84: Nov 15 1959. A reconstruction of the events of D-Day, based on interviews with hundreds of military personnel on both sides.

2182. Shapiro, William E. Pearl Harbor. (Turning Points of World War II). Watts, 1984. 103 p. ill. $10.
Gr 6+. B 81: Dec 15 1984. BR 4: Sep/Oct 1985. SLJ 31: Mar 1985. VOYA 7: Feb 1985. Covers the events that led up to the attack, describes the events of the day, and explains its results.

2183. Skipper, G.C. Battle of Leyte Gulf. (World At War). Childrens Press, 1981. 45 p. ill. $6.
Gr 3-6. B 77: Jul 1981. SLJ 28: Sep 1981. This slightly fictionalized presentation of the highlights of the battle is suitable for reluctant readers. It includes numerous photos with captions.

2184. Skipper, G.C. Battle of Midway. (World at War). Childrens Press, 1980. 45 p. ill. $6.
Gr 3-7. B 77: Feb 1 1981. +- SLJ 27: Mar 1981. This slightly fictionalized presentation of the highlights of the battle is suitable for reluctant readers. It includes numerous photos with captions.

2185. Skipper, G.C. Battle of the Coral Sea. (World at War). Childrens Press, 1981. 45 p. ill. $6.
Gr 3-7. B 77: Jul 1981. +- SLJ 28: Sep 1981. This slightly fictionalized presentation of the highlights of the battle is suitable for reluctant readers. It includes numerous captioned photos.

2186. Skipper, G.C. Invasion of Sicily. (World at War). Childrens Press, 1981. 48 p. ill. $6.
Gr 3-7. B 77: Jul 1981. +- SLJ 28: Sep 1981. This slightly fictionalized presentation of the highlights of the invasion includes numerous photos with captions. It is suitable for reluctant readers.

2187. Skipper, G.C. Pearl Harbor. (World at War). Childrens Press, 1983. 48 p. ill. $7.
Gr 4-8. B 80: Feb 15 1984. +- SLJ 30: Apr 1984. A concise presentation of the causes of the attack on Pearl Harbor and its results that includes photos and maps.

2188. Stein, R. Conrad. Battle of Guadalcanal. (World at War). Childrens Press, 1983. 48 p. ill. $7.
Gr 3-5. B 79: Aug 1983. +- SLJ 30: Nov 1983. A simplified account of the six-month battle.

2189. Stein, R. Conrad. Battle of Okinawa. (World at War). Childrens Press, 1985. 45 p. ill. $11.

Gr 4-6. B 82: Mar 1 1986. An introduction to the encounter between the American fleet and Japanese kamikaze pilots.

2190. Stein, R. Conrad. Road to Rome. (World at War). Childrens Press, 1984. 48 p. ill. $8.
Gr 4-6. B 81: May 1 1985. SLJ 31: Apr 1985. Briefly covers the battles at Anzio, Salerno, and Cassino, and the liberation of Rome.

2191. Taylor, Theodore. Battle Off Midway Island, The. (Great Sea Battles of World War II). Avon, 1981. 141 p. ill. Pb $3.
Gr 6+. B 78: Dec 1 1981. SLJ 28: May 1982. A vivid account of the battle with an assessment of the causes for this victory that was crucial to the Allies. This is number one in the series.

2192. Tregaskis, Richard. Guadalcanal Diary. (Landmark Books). Random House, 1943, 1955. 180 p. ill. Pb $3.
Gr 7-8. Metzner [B 39: Feb 1 1943. LJ 68: Jan 1 1943]. A day-by-day account of the landing of the American marines on Guadalcanal as told by an accomplished journalist who was there. Illustrated with photographs.

2193. Vedder, James S. Surgeon on Iwo: Up Front With the 27th Marines. Presidio, 1984. 257 p. ill. $16.
Gr 9+. B 80: Aug 1984. LJ 109: Oct 15 1984. This day-to-day account of the activities of the marines at Iwo Jima is a blend of tragedy and humor.

2194. Wheeler, Richard S. Iwo. Lippincott, 1980. 288 p. ill. $13.
Gr 9+. B 76: May 1 1980. LJ 105: Apr 15 1980. A veteran of the battle of Iwo Jima presents a vivid and gory account reconstructed from war records, correspondence, and interviews with survivors.

Concentration Camps

2195. Abzug, Robert H. Inside the Vicious Heart: Americans and the Liberation of Nazi Concentration Camps. Oxford University Press, 1985. 192 p. ill. $17.
Adult. LJ 110: May 15 1985. Text and photos record the reactions of eyewitnesses to the horrors found when the concentration camps were liberated.

Equipment and Supplies

2196. Colby, C. B. Fighting Gear of World War II: Equipment and Weapons of the American G.I. Coward, 1961. 48 p. ill. $7.
Gr 4-8. Metzner. An illustrated guide to the equipment and weapons used by American military personnel during the war.

Espionage and Spies

2197. Aline, Countess of Romanones. Spy Wore Red: My Adventures As an Undercover Agent in World War II. Random House, 1987. 277 p. $19.
Gr 9+. B 83: May 15 1987. +- LJ 112: May 15 1987. The true story of a 20-year-old model who became a U.S. spy.

2198. Dunlop, Richard. Donovan: America's Master Spy. Rand McNally, 1982. 576 p. ill. $20.
Gr 9+. B 79: Oct 1 1982. LJ 107: Dec 1 1982. An anecdotal history of the founder of the OSS (Office of Strategic Services). Donovan led the OSS during the war, and was responsible for the creation of the Central Intelligence Agency.

2199. Marrin, Albert. Secret Armies: Spies, Counterspies and Saboteurs in World War II. Atheneum, 1985. 239 p. ill. $14.
Gr 7+. B 82: Oct 1 1985. HB 62: Mar/Apr 1986. SLJ 32: Apr 1986. Covers the work of intelligence agents, resistance fighters, code breakers, and assassins. Numerous photos.

2200. Pape, Richard. Boldness Be My Friend. St. Martin's, 1985. 420 p. maps. $17.
Gr 9+. B 82: Sep 15 1985. SLJ 32: Dec 1985. A fascinating account of the author's espionage activities, his three years behind enemy lines, and the horrors he saw.

2201. Pujol, Juan. Operation GARBO: The Personal Story of the Most Successful Double Agent of World War II. Random House, 1986. 224 p. ill. $18.
Gr 10+. B 83: Sep 15 1986. LJ 111: Sep 15 1986. For comprehensive collections, the story of an agent who for three years successfully sent misinformation to the Germans.

2202. West, Nigel. Thread of Deceit: Espionage Myths of World War II. Random House, 1985. 172 p. ill. $17.
Adult. B 81: Mar 15 1985. LJ 110: Mar 15 1985. In times of tragedy, fact may become confused by myth. West examines the myths of World War II, including the idea that Roosevelt and Churchill had prior knowledge of the attack at Pearl Harbor.

Evacuation of Civilians

2203. Bailey, Anthony. America, Lost & Found. Random House, 1981. 152 p. $10.
Gr 9+. B 77: Mar 1 1981. HB 58: Feb 1982. LJ 106: Feb 15 1981. At age seven the author was brought from war-torn Britain to safety in Ohio. He recounts his experience of having a family on both sides of the Atlantic.

Fiction

2204. Campbell, Barbara. Girl Called Bob and a Horse Called Yoki, A. Dial, 1982. 167 p. $10. Lib. ed. $10.
Gr 4-6. +- B 78: Aug 1982. BC 35: Mar 1982. HB 58: Aug 1982. SLJ 28: Apr 1982. Bob is approaching her confirmation and is upset about her part in the theft of a horse in an effort to keep him from a glue factory. Set in St Louis during the war.

2205. Chalker, Jack L. Devil's Voyage: A Novel About Treachery, Heroism, Sharks and The Bomb. Doubleday, 1981. 328 p. $12.
Gr 9+. B 77: Feb 15 1981. +- LJ 106: Mar 15 1981. Based on the tragic sinking of the ship that had carried the atomic bomb to its launch site, this describes the secrecy surrounding the voyage and the horrors suffered by the survivors.

2206. Greene, Bette. Summer of My German Soldier. Dial; Bantam, 1973; 1974. 230 p. $10.
Gr 7-10. B 82: Feb 1 1986. * SE 47: Apr 1983. A Jewish American girl who lives in the South befriends an escaped German POW and is alienated from her family.

2207. Kaminsky, Stuart M. Fala Factor, The. St. Martin's, 1984. 182 p. $12.
Gr 9+. B 80: Jul 1984. An amusing mystery as Toby Peters helps an anxious Eleanor Roosevelt who believes that an imposter has replaced the President's beloved Scottie, Fala.

2208. Kaminsky, Stuart M. Smart Moves. St. Martin's, 1987. 212 p. $16.
Gr 9+. B 83: Mar 1 1987. Lots of atmosphere in a fun story as private-eye Toby Peters tries to protect Albert Einstein from a Nazi plot.

2209. Kerr, M.E. Gentlehands. Harper; Bantam, 1978, 1979. 144 p. $13. Pb $3.
Gr 9+. SE 47: Apr 1983. Buddy, who used his elegant and sophisticated grandfather to impress the wealthy Skye Pennington, found his world crumbling as evidence accumulated that this cultured man was a wanted Nazi war criminal.

2210. Leffland, Ella. Rumors of Peace. Harper; Fawcett, 1979; 1980. 389 p. $11.
Gr 9+. HB 56: Feb 1980. * SE 47: Apr 1983. A ten-year-old California trapeze artist, Suse, becomes preoccupied with the war and its victims. Through her reading and experiences she achieves a mature understanding of the moral issues involved.

2211. Lisle, Janet Taylor. Sirens and Spies. Bradbury; dist. by Macmillan, 1985. 169 p. $12.
Gr 7+. * B 81: May 15 1985. B 82: Oct 1 1985. BC 38: Jun 1985. HB 61: Sep/Oct 1985. * SLJ 31: Aug 1985. VOYA 8: Dec 1985. Music teacher, Miss Fitch, reveals her life during World War II which led to accusation of collaboration.

2212. Nathanson, E.M. Dirty Distant War, A. Viking, 1987. 484 p. $20.
Gr 10+. BR 6: Mar/Apr 1988. LJ 112: Aug 1987. SLJ 34: Apr 1988. VOYA 11: Apr 1988. Late in the war in southeast Asia, the Dirty Dozen are to destroy arms before the Japanese can get them and assist any enemy of the Japanese, including Vietnamese guerrillas. Full of action and political intrigue.

2213. Piercy, Marge. Gone to Soldiers. Summit, 1987. 703 p. $20.
Gr 9+. +- B 83: Mar 1 1987. * LJ 112: Apr 1 1987. SLJ 34: Oct 1987. A powerful episodic novel of the war as seen through the varied lives of several characters who fought the war away from the front lines: in offices, oil fields, the merchant marine, the Resistance, and elsewhere.

2214. Smith, Doris Buchanan. Salted Lemons. Four Winds, 1980. 233 p. $10.
Gr 3-7. B 77: Dec 1 1980. BC 34: Mar 1981. HB 57: Feb 1981. SLJ 27: Feb 1981. When Darby's family moves to Atlanta, her suffering from bigotry because she

is a Yankee is similar to that suffered by her Japanese American friend, Yoko.

2215. Toland, John. Gods of War. Doubleday, 1985. 600 p. $18. Pb $5.
Gr 9+. B 81: Feb 1 1985. * LJ 110: Apr 1 1985. Two families related by marriage, one American and one Japanese, experience all aspects of the war.

2216. Wouk, Herman. Caine Mutiny, The. Doubleday, 1954. 494 p. $18. Pb $6.
Gr 10+. B 47: Apr 15 1951. B 84: Jul 1988. * LJ 76: Mar 15 1951. The story of Willie Keith's career from midshippman to captain of a minesweeper reveals how men are tested and developed under war conditions.

Immigration–Fiction

2217. Lord, Athena V. Today's Special: Z.A.P. and Zoe. Macmillan, 1984. 150 p. ill. $11.
Gr 4-7. BC 38: Jan 1985. HB 61: Jan/Feb 1985. SLJ 31: Jan 1985. VOYA 8: Jun 1985. The adventures of a lively 11-year-old Greek immigrant, flecked with references to problems of immigrants, Greek mythology and culture.

Japanese Americans

2218. Armor, John. Manzanar. Times Books, 1988. 192 p. ill. $25.
Gr 9+. B 85: Nov 1 1988. * LJ 113: Nov 1 1988. Photos by Ansel Adams add a powerful component to the text that documents the lives of the Japanese Americans who were interned at Manzanar.

2219. Davis, Daniel S. Behind Barbed Wire: The Imprisonment of Japanese Americans During World II. Dutton, 1982. 166 p. ill. $13.
Gr 5+. B 78: Apr 15 1982. BC 36: Jan 1983. BR 1: Nov/Dec 1982. HB 58: Jun 1982. * SE 47: Apr 1983. * SLJ 28: Aug 1982. Examines the political, economic, and sociological factors which led to internment, its effects on Japanese Americans, and the question of whether this could happen again. Suitable for a wide range of readers.

2220. Gesensway, Deborah. Beyond Words: Images from America's Concentration Camps. Cornell University Press, 1987. 176 p. ill. $25.
Gr 10+. LJ 112: May 1 1987. Japanese Americans who were interned in camps in the U.S. during World War II provide an oral history and over 75 art works about their experiences.

2221. Houston, Jeanne Wakatsuki. Farewell to Manzanar: A True Story of Japanese American Experience During and After World War II. Bantam, 1974. 177 p. Pb $3.
Gr 7+. SE 46: Oct 1982. Deals with the psychological aspects of being Japanese in California during the war.

2222. Tateishi, John. And Justice for All. Random House, 1984. 259 p. ill. $19.
Gr 9+. B 80: Jun 1 1984. BR 3: Jan/Feb 1985. SLJ 31: Feb 1985. VOYA 7: Dec 1984. Interviews with Japanese Americans who were forced to leave their homes and jobs to live in internment camps.

2223. Uchida, Yoshiko. Desert Exile: The Uprooting of a Japanese-American Family. University of Washington Press, 1984. 170 p. ill. $9.
Gr 7+. VOYA 8: Jun 1985. These experiences of one Japanese American family in a relocation camp are told with dignity and enhanced by photos and original poetry.

2224. Uchida, Yoshiko. Journey to Topaz: A Story of the Japanese-American Evacuation. Creative Arts, 1971, 1985. 149 p. ill. Pb $6.
Gr 4-7. HB 47: Dec 1971. HB 61: Sep/Oct 1985. This moving story of 11-year-old Yuki, and her mother and brother who were interned in a Japanese relocation camp during the war, is told from the point of view of the little girl.

Japanese Americans–Fiction

2225. Garrigue, Sheila. Eternal Spring of Mr. Ito, The. Bradbury, 1985. 163 p. $12.
Gr 4-9. +- B 82: Dec 15 1985. * BC 39: Dec 1985. HB 62: Jan/Feb 1986. SE 50: Apr/May 1986. SLJ 32: Nov 1985. VOYA 8: Feb 1986. Sara's friendship with Mr. Ito, the family gardener, extends through his internment during the war.

Jewish Americans–Fiction

2226. Levoy, Myron. Alan and Naomi. Harper; Dell, 1977, 1979. 192 p. $13. Pb $3.
Gr 5-9. * B 74: Feb 15 1978. BC 31: Jun 1978. HB 53: Dec 1977. SE 47: Apr 1983. SLJ 24: Nov 1977. A skillful and compassionate evocation of Nazi horror, its affect on survivors, and the price of personal responsibility.

Journalists

2227. MacVane, John. On the Air in World War II. Morrow, 1979. 384 p. ill. $13.
Gr 9+. B 76: Apr 1 1980. LJ 105: Feb 15 1980. MacVane, a radio journalist, covered combat and interviewed leaders in the European theater. Here he recounts historic events and his personal experiences.

2228. Pyle, Ernie. Ernie's War: The Best of Ernie Pyle's World War II Dispatches. Random House, 1986. 480 p. ill. $20.
Gr 9+. B 83: Sep 1 1986. * BR 5: Mar/Apr 1987. * LJ 111: Sep 1 1986. SLJ 33: Dec 1986. Pyle. a Pulitzer Prize winning journalist, wrote about the foot soldiers of W.W. II. Editor David Nichols presents the best of Pyle's popular and readable essays, chronologically arranged, and a brief biography. Photos.

Military History

2229. Baron, Richard. Raid! The Untold Story of Patton's Secret Mission. Putnam, 1981. 283 p. maps. $13.
Gr 9+. B 78: Sep 1 1981. LJ 106: Aug 1981. SLJ 28: Oct 1981. Describes a failed secret operation, ordered

by Patton, intended to rescue American prisoners of war held 60 miles behind enemy lines.

2230. Benford, Timothy B. World War II Quiz and Fact Book, The. Harper, 1982. 224 p. ill. $13. Pb $8.
Gr 9+. LJ 107: Oct 1 1982. A trivia book to delight all World War II buffs.

2231. Breuer, William B. Devil Boats: The PT War Against Japan. Presidio, 1987. 236 p. ill. $17.
Gr 9+. +- B 83: Oct 15 1986. Describes the heroic achievements of PT crews in fragile craft who made a major impact on the outcome of the war.

2232. Costello, John. Pacific War, The. Rawson; dist. by Atheneum, 1981. 768 p. ill. $25.
Gr 9+. B 78: Dec 1 1981. LJ 106: Dec 1 1981. Charts the long-term causes of the war with Japan, analyzes the role of military intelligence, and examines the battles.

2233. Dolan, Edward. Victory in Europe. Watts, 1988. 159 p. ill. $13.
Gr 7+. BR 7: Sep/Oct 1988. SLJ 34: Jun/Jul 1988. - VOYA 11: Aug 1988. Dolan focuses on the military actions of the last six months of the war in Europe.

2234. Forty, George. United States Tanks of World War II in Action. Blandford Press; dist. by Sterling, 1983. 160 p. ill. $17.
Adult. B 80: Nov 1 1983. +- BR 2: Mar/Apr 1984. This introduction to the U.S. armored forces has first-person accounts of tank warfare and abundant photos and illustrations of tanks, plus specifications and comparisons of tanks. Uses a technical vocabulary.

2235. Galantin, I.J. Take Her Deep! A Submarine Against Japan in World War II. Algonquin, 1987. 352 p. ill. $18.
Gr 10+. B 84: Oct 1 1987. LJ 112: Oct 15 1987. The U.S.S. Halibut was a submarine that sank seven Japanese ships. This is her story, told by her captain.

2236. Goralski, Robert. Oil and War: How the Deadly Struggle for Fuel in WW II Meant Victory or Defeat. Morrow, 1987. 320 p. ill. $18.
Adult. B 83: Jun 15 1987. LJ 112: Jul 1987. Examines World War II from the point of view of the availability of oil supplies and shows how this affected Axis and Allied strategy.

2237. Hamilton, John. War at Sea, 1939-1945. Blandford Press; dist. by Sterling, 1986. 272 p. ill. $50.
Gr 9+. * B 82: Aug 1986. LJ 111: Sep 1 1986. Lavishly illustrated with paintings and maps, this is a detailed and entertaining account of every naval battle from early U-Boat raids to the end of the war.

2238. Hough, Richard. Longest Battle: The War at Sea. Morrow, 1987. 371 p. ill. $20.
Gr 11+. B 83: Apr 1 1987. +- LJ 112: May 1 1987. This one-volume overview of the naval battles of the war emphasizes the American navy but also covers the German, British, and Japanese operations.

2239. Hoyt, Edwin P. Closing the Circle: War in the Pacific, 1945. Van Nostrand, 1982. 192 p. ill. $15.

Adult. LJ 107: Jul 1982. A synthesis of the decisions and events of the concluding days of the war.

2240. Hoyt, Edwin P. U-Boat Wars, The. Arbor House, 1984. 222 p. $20.
Gr 10+. B 81: Nov 1 1984. LJ 109: Oct 15 1984. These highlights of the complex 6-year campaign between Allied naval forces and German submarines, make clear the determination of the U-boat crews and the enormous effort required for the Allies to win.

2241. Johnson, Frank, D. United States PT Boats of World War II in Action. (In Action). Poole, Dorset, Blandford Press; dist. by Sterling, 1980. 160 p. ill. $15.
Gr 9+. B 78: Mar 1 1982. Johnson highlights the development, production, and combat operation of the controversial torpedo boats of World War II. Both photos and text are indexed.

2242. Leckie, Robert. Delivered from Evil: The Saga of World War II. Harper, 1987. 768 p. ill. $30.
Gr 9+. B 84: Oct 1 1987. LJ 112: Sep 1 1987. This one-volume history of the war covers battle tactics, generalship, and memoirs of both Axis and Allied soldiers. It conveys the reality of the conflict with personal stories and deft use of detail.

2243. Leckie, Robert. Story of World War II, The. Random House, 1964. 193 p. ill. $9.
Gr 6-10. Metzner [* LJ 89: Dec 15 1964]. A one-volume overview of the war, from the rise of Hitler to the surrender of Japan, enhanced by 15 maps and over 100 photos.

2244. Lowder, Hughston E. Batfish: The Champion "Submarine-Killer" Submarine of World War II. Prentice-Hall, 1980. 240 p. ill. $11.
Gr 9+. LJ 105: Jul 1980. The day-by-day drama of life aboard a Pacific Fleet submarine that destroyed 14 ships, including 3 other submarines.

2245. Macksey, Kenneth. Military Errors of World War Two. Arms and Armour; dist. by Sterling, 1987. 252 p. ill. $20.
Gr 9+. B 84: Nov 1 1987. Macksey compares the leadership of the Allied and Axis heads of state and concludes that the flexibility allowed to the military by Roosevelt and Churchill contributed significantly to Allied success.

2246. Marrin, Albert. Victory in the Pacific. Atheneum, 1983. 217 p. $13.
Gr 5+. B 79: Jun 15 1983. BR 3: May/Jun 1984. HB 59: Apr 1983. VOYA 6: Oct 1983. Commentary, photos, maps and diagrams, and a chronology, provide a simply written overview of the war in the Pacific theater.

2247. McKay, Ernest A. Carrier Strike Force: Pacific Air Combat in World War II. Messner, 1981. 191 p. ill. $10.
Gr 7-10. SLJ 28: Feb 1982. VOYA 5: Apr 1982. Traces the development of aircraft carriers and their impact on the war.

2248. Morrison, Wilbur H. Above and Beyond: 1941-1945. St. Martin's, 1983. 336 p. ill. $17.

Gr 9+. LJ 108: Feb 15 1983. SLJ 30: Sep 1983. This account of the role of aircraft carrier airpower in the Pacific Theater includes tactics and pilot's-eye anecdotes of the fighting.

2249. Powell, Geoffrey. Devil's Birthday, The. Watts, 1985. 276 p. $19.
Gr 10+. B 81: Apr 15 1985. VOYA 8: Oct 1985. A detailed examination of a major Allied defeat which resulted when thousands of British and American troops were parachuted into Holland in September, 1944.

2250. Schaffer, Ronald. Wings of Judgment: American Bombing in World War II. Oxford University Press, 1985. 265 p. $19.
Adult. B 82: Sep 15 1985. LJ 110: Oct 1 1985. A scholarly examination of the military and moral implications of strategic bombing.

2251. Schultz, Duane. Last Battle Station: The Story of the U.S.S. Houston. St. Martin's, 1985. 320 p. ill. $16.
Gr 9+. B 81: Feb 1 1985. LJ 110: Feb 1 1985. Schultz tells the story of the Houston, from her days as flagship to her sinking, and of her crew who became prisoners of war.

2252. Shapiro, Milton J. Tank Command: General George S. Patton's 4th Armored Division. McKay, 1979. 58 p. ill. $7.
Gr 6-8. +- SLJ 26: Feb 1980. A simple, realistic, overview of the maneuvers of Patton's tank corps in 1944. Numerous photos.

2253. Shapiro, Milton J. Undersea Raiders: U.S. Submarines in World War II. McKay, 1979. 56 p. ill. $7.
Gr 7+. SLJ 26: Mar 1980. A short photo-filled account of the major Pacific battles involving submarines. Suitable for reluctant readers.

2254. Skipper, G.C. Submarines in the Pacific. (World at War). Childrens Press, 1980. 46 p. ill. $6.
Gr 3-7. B 77: Feb 1 1981. +- SLJ 27: Mar 1981. This slightly fictionalized presentation of the highlights of submarine activities in the Pacific includes numerous photos. It is suitable for reluctant readers.

Military History–Fiction

2255. Collenette, Eric J. Ninety Feet to the Sun: A Sea Novel of World War II. Walker, 1986. 192 p. $16.
Gr 10+. LJ 111: Apr 15 1986. High adventure in a submarine off the coast of Norway in the early days of the war.

2256. Follett, James. Churchill's Gold. Houghton, 1981. 218 p. $10.
Gr 9+. B 77: Jul 1 1981. - LJ 106: Jun 15 1981. The rousing adventure of a U.S. whaling captain who is involved in an elaborate scheme to transport British gold from Africa.

Military Personnel

2257. Bradley, Omar N. General's Life, A. Simon & Schuster, 1983. 540 p. ill. $20.

Adult. B 79: Jan 1 1983. LJ 108: Feb 1 1983. A well-researched authorized biography of Bradley's experiences and influence on the Allied High Command. Written with collaborator Clay Blair and completed after Bradley's death.

2258. Casewit, Curtis W. Saga of the Mountain Soldiers: The Story of the 10th Mountain Division. Messner, 1981. 159 p. ill. $10.
Gr 6-10. B 78: May 15 1982. SLJ 28: Feb 1982. * VOYA 5: Jun 1982. An account of the training and battlefield experience of the elite mountaineering division that destroyed the entrenched German army in Italy during the last months of the war. Based on primary sources.

2259. Coffey, Thomas M. Hap: The Story of the U.S. Air Force and the Man Who Built It, General Henry "Hap" Arnold. Viking, 1982. 389 p. ill. $25.
Gr 9+. * B 79: Sep 15 1982. +- LJ 107: Sep 15 1982. A balanced look at the personal life and military career of the man who served during the war as Chief of Staff of the U.S. Army Air Force.

2260. Devaney, John. Blood and Guts: The True Story of General George S. Patton. Messner, 1982. 96 p. ill. $10.
Gr 4-6. B 82: Sep 15 1985. Many photos add appeal to this biography of the controversial Patton.

2261. Eisenhower, David. Eisenhower: At War, 1943-1945. Random House, 1986. 950 p. ill. $30.
Gr 10+. B 82: Jul 1986. LJ 111: Sep 15 1986. A detailed look at Eisenhower as a key figure in the overthrow of the Nazi regime, able to deal with the complexities of coalition warfare. The first of a proposed three-volume work.

2262. Irving, David. War Between the Generals: Inside the Allied High Command. Congdon & Lattes; dist. by St. Martin's, 1981. 384 p. ill. $18.
Gr 11+. LJ 106: Mar 1 1981. An unusual social history of the struggles of the British and American generals to gain position and power over one another while they were directing the war against Germany.

2263. James, D. Clayton. Time for Giants: Politics of the American High Command In World War II. Watts, 1987. 317 p. $20.
Gr 9+. B 84: Oct 1 1987. * BR 7: May/Jun 1988. LJ 112: Oct 1 1987. SLJ 34: Jun/Jul 1988. Profiles 18 generals and admirals, explains how each prepared himself politically and militarily for career advancement, and describes the contributions of each leader. Includes many anecdotes.

2264. Kennett, Lee. G.I.: The American Soldier in World War II. Scribner, 1987. 261 p. $21.
Gr 9+. B 83: Mar 15 1987. LJ 112: Mar 1 1987. An overview of the experiences of the American citizen-soldier, primarily draftees, from basic training through combat. Lively and anecdotal, this also includes polls and data suitable for reports.

2265. Leary, William M. We Shall Return: MacArthur's Commanders and the Defeat of Japan,

1942-1945. University Press of Kentucky, 1988. 320 p. ill. $25.
Gr 10+. LJ 113: Jul 1988. Biographies of MacArthur's senior generals and admirals, including Generals Blamey, Krueger, Kenney, Eichelberger, and Whitehead, and Admirals Kinkaid and Barbey.

2266. Mosley, Leonard. Marshall: Hero for Our Times. Hearst, 1982. 570 p. ill. $19.
Adult. B 78: Jun 1 1982. LJ 107: Aug 1982. A balanced study of the personal and professional life of the Army Chief of Staff who later became an influential Secretary of State.

2267. Parton, James. Air Force Spoken Here: General Ira Eaker and the Command of the Air. Adler; dist. by Harper, 1986. 557 p. ill. $25.
Gr 10+. B 83: Oct 15 1986. LJ 111: Oct 15 1986. General Eaker led the U.S. Air Force in England and championed daylight bombing of German industry. He was a modest but brilliant leader.

2268. Potter, E. B. Bull Halsey. Naval Institute, 1985. 400 p. ill. $20.
Adult. B 82: Oct 15 1985. LJ 110: Nov 1 1985. An objective biography of the colorful and cantankerous admiral who led the U.S. victory in the Pacific.

2269. Schultz, Duane. Hero of Bataan: The Story of General Wainwright. St. Martin's, 1981. 512 p. ill. $20.
Gr 9+. +- B 78: Dec 1 1981. LJ 106: Oct 15 1981. SLJ 28: Apr 1982. This full-scale biography of the general who surrendered Bataan and Corregidor also discusses the fall of the Philippines and MacArthur's part in events.

2270. Shapiro, Milton J. Ranger Battalion: American Rangers in World War II. Messner, 1979. 191 p. maps. $8.
Gr 7+. +- B 76: Jan 15 1980. SLJ 26: Feb 1980. Traces the activities of the Rangers, whose role was to carry out difficult commando assignments requiring exceptional courage and skill.

2271. Stein, R. Conrad. Nisei Regiment. (World at War). Childrens Press, 1985. 47 p. ill. $11.
Gr 4-6. B 82: Mar 1 1986. The Japanese American Nisei Regiment fought for the Allies even though their families were in internment camps in the U.S.

2272. Sweeney, James B. Army Leaders of World War II. (First Book). Watts, 1984. 82 p. ill. $9.
Gr 4-6. B 81: Jan 15 1985. SLJ 31: Dec 1984. Covers Eisenhower, Marshall, MacArthur, Patton, and Arnold in mini-biographies.

2273. Windrow, Martin. World War II GI, The. (Soldier Through the Ages). Watts, 1986. 32 p. ill. $12.
Gr 5-7. B 83: Jan 15 1987. * SE 51: Apr/May 1987. An overview of the experiences of the average GI, including uniforms, training, weapons, boredom, discomfort, and death. Includes glossary.

Military Personnel–Black

2274. Hargrove, Hondon. Buffalo Soldiers in Italy: Black Americans in World War II. McFarland, 1985. 199 p. $19.
Gr 7+. BR 4: Sep/Oct 1985. Presents the origin and traditions of the only black division to fight in World War II. For advanced readers.

Military Personnel–Black–Personal Narratives

2275. Downey, Bill. Uncle Sam Must Be Losing the War. Strawberry Hill, 1982. 224 p. ill. Pb $8.
Adult. LJ 107: Dec 1 1982. Memoirs of a black World War II enlisted marine.

Military Personnel–Fiction

2276. Boyd, William Young. Gentle Infantryman, The. St. Martin's, 1985. 372 p. $16.
Gr 9+. B 81: May 1 1985. LJ 110: May 1 1985. The story of an 18-year-old draftee who became a soldier in the last days of World War II.

2277. Mazer, Harry. Last Mission, The. Delacorte; Dell, 1979; 1981. 182 p. $8.
Gr 7-10. B 80: Oct 15 1983. B 84: Jul 1988. BC 33: Mar 1980. HB 56: Feb 1980. * SE 47: Apr 1983. Enlisting by using his brother's birth certificate, 15-year-old Jack, a would-be hero, becomes a tough, tired, veteran who believes "War is one stupid thing after another." Based on the author's experiences.

2278. Shepard, Jim. Paper Doll. Knopf, 1986. 231 p. $16.
Gr 9+. B 83: Oct 15 1986. BR 5: Mar/Apr 1987. +- LJ 111: Nov 15 1986. * VOYA 10: Apr 1987. The young and inexperienced crew of the "Paper Doll", a B-17 Flying Fortress, face tension and tedium as they prepare for their first big mission.

Military Personnel–Personal Narratives

2279. Berry, Henry. Semper Fi, Mac: Living Memories of the U.S. Marines in World War II. Arbor House, 1982. 375 p. ill. $16.
Adult. B 79: Oct 1 1982. LJ 107: Sep 15 1982. These interviews with veterans of the Pacific campaigns include good combat yarns and anecdotes.

2280. Hoyt, Edwin P. GI's War: The Story of American Soldiers in Europe in World War II. McGraw-Hill, 1988. 603 p. ill. $25.
Gr 9+. B 84: May 15 1988. LJ 113: Jun 15 1988. A simple presentation of the matter-of-fact attitude of many GIs toward their experiences. Based on letters and interviews.

2281. Leinbaugh, Harold P. Men of Company K: The Autobiography of a World War II Rifle Company. Morrow, 1985. 320 p. $19.

Adult. B 82: Nov 15 1985. LJ 110: Dec 1985. An account of the wartime and post-war experiences of men who saw over 100 days of combat, including the Battle of the Bulge, told in the words of the survivors.

2282. Lidz, Richard. Many Kinds of Courage: An Oral History of World War II. Putnam, 1980. 266 p. $10.
Gr 7+. * B 76: Jun 15 1980. LJ 105: Jun 15 1980. SLJ 26: May 1980. First person accounts from participants at Dunkirk, the Battle of Britain, Pearl Harbor, Corregidor, Normandy, Auschwitz, Hiroshima, and other areas, linked by an effective and easily understood synopsis of the war.

2283. Mason, John T. Pacific War Remembered: An Oral History Collection. Naval Institute, 1986. 344 p. ill. $25.
Gr 9+. B 82: May 1 1986. LJ 111: May 15 1986. Twenty-eight naval officers of all ranks provide candid descriptions of their experiences, including decision-making and action under fire. The editor provides summaries of events and biographies to provide context.

2284. Mason, Theodore. Battleship Sailor. Naval Institute, 1982. 271 p. ill. $15.
Adult. B 79: Oct 15 1982. LJ 107: Sep 1 1982. For extensive collections, the vivid and accurate memoir of an enlisted man on the "California," which was sunk at Pearl Harbor.

2285. Newby, Leroy W. Target Ploesti: View from a Bombsight. Presidio, 1983. 326 p. $16.
Adult. LJ 108: Aug 1983. The author flew 50 missions during World War II and provides a vivid narrative of his experiences.

2286. Phibbs, Brendan. Other Side of Time: A Combat Surgeon in World War II. Little, 1987. 352 p. $18.
Adult. * B 83: May 15 1987. LJ 112: May 15 1987. Frank anecdotes about the author's experiences as a surgeon in the European theater.

2287. Tapert, Annette. Lines of Battle: Letters from U.S. Servicemen, 1941-45. Times Books, 1987. 297 p. ill. $20.
Gr 9+. B 83: May 15 1987. * BR 6: Sep/Oct 1987. LJ 112: May 1 1987. SLJ 34: Oct 1987. A collection of letters from U.S. servicemen of all ranks. Some of the letters were written shortly before the death of the writer. Arranged chronologically.

2288. Winston, Keith. V-Mail: Letters of a World War II Combat Medic. Algonquin, 1985. 310 p. ill. $15.
Gr 9+. B 82: Nov 1 1985. LJ 110: Sep 15 1985. SLJ 32: Apr 1986. These letters of a combat medic to his family offer rare insight into the GI's view of the world.

Nuclear Warfare

2289. Chisholm, Anne. Faces of Hiroshima: A Report. Jonathan Cape; dist. by Merrimack Publishers' Circle, 1986. 182 p. Pb $10.
Gr 9+. * B 82: Feb 15 1986. An account of 25 Japanese girls, victims of atomic burns, who come to the U.S. for treatment, and of those who helped them.

2290. Goldman, Peter. End of the World That Was: Six Lives in the Atomic Age. Dutton; New American Library, 1986. 144 p. $17. Pb $7.
Gr 9+. +- B 82: Apr 15 1986. LJ 111: May 15 1986. Focuses on six persons affected by the A-bombing of Hiroshima, three whose job it was to prepare and drop the bomb, and three victims of it. An effective reminder of the effect of the bomb on all persons.

2291. Jones, Vincent C. Manhattan: The Army and the Atomic Bomb. (U.S. Army in W.W.II. Special Studies. Center of Military History). Center of Military History, U.S. Army, 1985. 412 p. ill. $21.
Gr 9+. B 82: Nov 15 1985. Explores the role of the army in administering the top secret Manhattan Project. This is CMH publication 11-10 in the Special Studies series.

2292. Kurzman, Dan. Day of the Bomb: Countdown to Hiroshima. McGraw-Hill, 1985. 546 p. $20.
Gr 9+. B 81: Oct 1 1985. +- LJ 110: Dec 1985. An account of the events and people in the United States and Japan affected by the atomic bomb.

2293. MacPherson, Malcolm C. Time Bomb: Fermi, Heisenberg, and the Race for the Atomic Bomb. Dutton, 1986. 316 p. $19.
Gr 7+. B 82: Jun 15 1986. LJ 111: May 15 1986. * VOYA 9: Aug/Oct 1986. A vivid history of the race to produce the atomic bomb, and a profile of the amoral world of a physicist.

2294. Stein, R. Conrad. Hiroshima. (World at War). Childrens Press, 1982. 48 p. ill. $3.
Gr 4-6. B 79: Feb 15 1983. B 80: Mar 15 1984. An account of the Manhattan Project and events leading up to the bombing of Hiroshima and Nagasaki.

2295. Wyden, Peter. Day One: Before Hiroshima and After. Warner, 1985. 415 p. $4.
Gr 10+. B 81: Oct 1 1984. B 82: Jan 1 1986. LJ 109: Nov 1 1984. VOYA 8: Dec 1985. Wyden shows how the decision to use the bomb affected scientists, government and military leaders, common soldiers, and the Japanese people.

Nuclear Warfare–Fiction

2296. Bograd, Larry. Los Alamos Light. Farrar, Straus, Giroux, 1983. 168 p. $11.
Gr 7+. B 80: Oct 15 1983. B 80: Mar 15 1984. SLJ 30: Nov 1983. * VOYA 7: Apr 1984. Maggie's father is a scientist engaged in top secret research on the atomic bomb.

Nuremberg Trial

2297. Tusa, Ann. Nuremberg Trial, The. Atheneum, 1984. 519 p. ill. $23.
Gr 9+. B 81: Dec 1 1984. +- LJ 109: Oct 1 1984. A detailed account of court debates, deliberations, and verdicts, with attention to the defendants' wartime activities and their participation in the trial.

Pacifists

2298. Wetzel, Donald. Pacifist: Or, My War and Louis Lepke. Permanent Press, 1986. 209 p. $18.
Gr 9+. +- B 82: Aug 1986. An angry condemnation of war by a pacifist who was imprisoned and abused during World War II.

Politics

2299. Brinkley, David. Washington Goes to War. Knopf, 1988. 286 p. $19.
Gr 10+. B 84: Mar 1 1988. * LJ 113: Apr 1 1988. An insider's account of the transformation of Washington from a sleepy town to the power center of the free world during World War II. Includes anecdotal, witty, and revealing accounts of the nation's leaders.

Presidency and the Executive Branch

2300. Larrabee, Eric. Commander in Chief: Franklin Delano Roosevelt, His Lieutenants, and Their War. Harper, 1987. 715 p. ill. $25.
Adult. B 83: Mar 1 1987. * LJ 112: May 1 1987. For advanced students, a sophisticated examination of Roosevelt's leadership skills and day-by-day direction of the armed forces.

Presidents and Their Families–Roosevelt, Franklin Delano

2301. Alsop, Joseph. FDR, 1882-1945: A Centenary Remembrance. Viking, 1982. 255 p. ill. $25. Pb $4.
Gr 9+. B 78: Oct 1 1981. LJ 107: Jan 15 1982. A photo-memoir by a noted journalist who is a Roosevelt relative and was frequently at the White House. Includes anecdotes and comments on the president's character and personality.

2302. Devaney, John. Franklin Delano Roosevelt, President. (First Book). Walker, 1987. 78 p. ill. $13.
Gr 5+. B 84: Jan 1 1988. SLJ 34: Jan 1988. VOYA 10: Dec 1987. An easy-to-read, photo-filled overview of Roosevelt's life, his political successes, and his personal strengths and weaknesses.

2303. Faber, Doris. Eleanor Roosevelt: First Lady of the World. (Women of Our Time). Viking/Kestrel, 1985. 58 p. $10.
Gr 4-8. +- B 82: Sep 1 1985. HB 61: Sep/Oct 1985. HB 62: Sep/Oct 1986. SLJ 31: Aug 1985. A brief introduction to the first lady, with emphasis on the years when her husband served as governor and president.

2304. Feinberg, Barbara Silberdick. Franklin D. Roosevelt, Gallant President. Lothrop, 1981. 94 p. ill. $11. Lib. ed. $11.
Gr 3-7. B 77: Jun 1981. B 82: Sep 15 1985. SLJ 28: Dec 1981. This brief biography makes the significance of FDR's contributions to U.S. history understandable. It covers his personal and political life and includes numerous photos.

2305. Gallagher, Hugh Gregory. FDR's Splendid Deception. Dodd, 1985. 250 p. ill. $17.
Gr 9+. B 81: Apr 15 1985. +- LJ 110: May 1 1985. SLJ 32: Sep 1985. VOYA 8: Oct 1985. FDR, with the discreet cooperation of others, carefully devised elaborate schemes to conceal his paralysis from the public.

2306. Goldberg, Richard Thayer. Making of Franklin D. Roosevelt: Triumph Over Disability. Abt. Dee, 1981. 242 p. ill. $17.
Gr 9+. LJ 107: Apr 1 1982. SLJ 28: May 1982. Examines how Roosevelt's life and his presidency were influenced by his physical disability.

2307. Graham, Otis L. Franklin D. Roosevelt: His Life and Times: An Encyclopedic View. (G.K. Hall Presidential Encyclopedia Series). Hall, 1985. 472 p. ill. $28.
Gr 9+. B 81: May 1 1985. LJ 110: May 1 1985. An encyclopedic presentation of 321 topical and biographical entries on all aspects of FDR's public and private life.

2308. Hacker, Jeffrey H. Franklin D. Roosevelt. (Impact Biography). Watts, 1983. 119 p. ill. $9.
Gr 7+. +- B 79: Jul 1983. SLJ 30: Sep 1983. An overview of Roosevelt's life and his administration, clarifying how he could be simultaneously loved and hated by his contemporaries. Includes full-page photos.

2309. Hickok, Lorena A. Eleanor Roosevelt: Reluctant First Lady. Dodd, 1980. 176 p. ill. $9.
Gr 9+. B 76: Jun 1 1980. The author was a confidant of Eleanor Roosevelt for over 30 years and presents a readable and sympathetic account of her life.

2310. Jacobs, William Jay. Eleanor Roosevelt: A Life of Happiness and Tears. Coward, 1983. 108 p. ill. $11.
Gr 5-8. B 80: Feb 15 1984. * BR 2: Mar/Apr 1984. +- SLJ 30: Feb 1984. A brief but well-rounded biography that covers Eleanor Roosevelt's youth as well as her adult years. Enhanced by photos.

2311. Lash, Joseph P. Eleanor and Franklin: The Story of Their Relationship Based on Eleanor Roosevelt's Private Papers. Norton; New American Library/Signet, 1971. 765 p. ill. $16. Pb $5.
Adult. B 82: Jan 1 1986. Emphasis is on Eleanor Roosevelt's role as wife, mother, and first lady.

2312. Lash, Joseph P. Life Was Meant To Be Lived: A Centenary Portrait of Eleanor Roosevelt. Norton, 1984. 163 p. ill. $25.
Adult. B 81: Oct 1 1984. * LJ 109: Oct 1 1984. SE 49: May 1985. This tribute to Eleanor Roosevelt includes 130 photos.

2313. Lash, Joseph P. World of Love: Eleanor Roosevelt and Her Friends, 1943-1962. Doubleday, 1984. 578 p. ill. $25.
Gr 10+. B 81: Oct 1 1984. * LJ 109: Oct 1 1984. Eleanor Roosevelt's friendships are portrayed through letters sent and received.

2314. McAuley, Karen. Eleanor Roosevelt. (World Leaders Past and Present Series). Chelsea House, 1986. 116 p. ill. $17.

Gr 6-10. B 83: Mar 15 1987. SLJ 33: May 1987. A straightforward biography that notes Eleanor Roosevelt's problems and achievements. Includes numerous photos.

2315. Miller, Nathan. FDR: An Intimate History. Doubleday, 1983. 552 p. ill. $23.
Gr 9+. B 79: Jan 15 1983. * LJ 108: Jan 1 1983. Covers FDR's entire life, giving equal treatment to the pre-presidential years, to the New Deal years, and to the war. This shows a "prismatic" president who presented different images to different people.

2316. Osinski, Alice. Franklin D. Roosevelt. (Encyclopedia of Presidents). Childrens Press, 1988. 100 p. ill. $15.
Gr 4-7. B 84: May 14 1988. This readable biography is illustrated by photos and engravings and includes a chronology that places Roosevelt in the context of U.S. history.

2317. Roosevelt, Eleanor. Autobiography of Eleanor Roosevelt, The. Hall, 1984. 454 p. Pb $10.
Gr 7+. * BR 3: Mar/Apr 1985. SE 48: Nov/Dec 1984. A one-volume personal narrative that provides warm glimpses into the life of Eleanor Roosevelt.

2318. Roosevelt, Elliot. Eleanor Roosevelt, With Love: A Centenary Remembrance. Dutton/Lodestar, 1984. 176 p. $13.
Gr 7-10. B 81: Dec 15 1984. BC 38: Feb 1985. SE 49: Apr 1985. - SLJ 31: Nov 1984. Focuses on Eleanor Roosevelt's personal and public life during the White House years and later.

2319. Scharf, Lois. Eleanor Roosevelt: First Lady of American Liberalism. (Twayne's Twentieth-Century American Biography). Twayne, 1987. 202 p. ill. $25. Pb $11.
Gr 9+. B 84: Dec 1 1987. BR 7: May/Jun 1988. LJ 112: Nov 15 1987. SLJ 34: Jan 1988. A lively biography that emphasizes Eleanor Roosevelt's maturation into a compassionate person and a significant political leader.

2320. Whitney, Sharon. Eleanor Roosevelt. (Impact Biography). Watts, 1982. 118 p. ill. $9.
Gr 6+. B 79: Jan 1 1983. * SE 47: Apr 1983. SLJ 30: Sep 1983. Shows Eleanor Roosevelt's personality, personal growth, and the many different and difficult roles which she assumed.

Prisoners of War

2321. Charles, H. Robert. Last Man Out. Eakin, 1988. 232 p. ill. $17.
Adult. * LJ 113: May 15 1988. The author was a Japanese prisoner who helped build their railroad through the jungles of Thailand and Burma. This memoir concentrates on a Dutch physician whose efforts saved the lives of many prisoners.

2322. Durand, Arthur A. Stalag Luft III: The Secret Story. Louisiana State University Press, 1988. 399 p. $30.
Gr 9+. B 84: May 1 1988. LJ 113: Jun 1 1988. This fascinating and well-researched chronicle of life in a German POW camp that housed over 10,000 prisoners

shows the prisoners' heroic struggle to provide for their needs and help the war effort.

2323. Grashio, Samuel C. Return to Freedom: The War Memoirs of Col. Samuel C. Grashio USAF (Ret.). MCN Press, 1982. 177 p. ill. $15.
Adult. LJ 108: Jan 1 1983. An affecting, low-key autobiography that details the author's imprisonment in, and escape from, a Japanese prisoner-of-war camp.

2324. Kerr, E. Bartlett. Surrender and Survival: The Experience of American POWs in the Pacicic, 1941-1945. Morrow, 1985. 424 p. $19.
Adult. B 82: Sep 1 1985. LJ 110: Aug 1985. A comprehensive history of the Americans who were Japanese prisoners of war. Clarifies the cultural and economic reasons behind the brutality of their treatment.

2325. Knox, Donald. Death March: The Survivors of Bataan. Harcourt, 1981. 534 p. ill. $20.
Adult. B 78: Dec 15 1981. LJ 106: Dec 15 1981. Recollections of survivors of the Death March, covering every service branch, and including men and women, some who escaped to join guerrilla forces, and some who collaborated with the Japanese.

2326. Lawton, Manny. Some Survived. Algonquin, 1984. 295 p. ill. $17.
Adult. B 81: Oct 1 1984. LJ 110: Feb 1 1985. A survivor of the fall of Bataan, the "Hell Ship" which transported prisoners to Japan, and a Japanese prison camp, tells his incredible story.

2327. Stein, R. Conrad. Prisoners of War. (World at War). Childrens Press, 1987. 45 p. ill. $8.
Gr 4-7. BC 41: Nov 1987. SLJ 34: Feb 1988. Compares the treatment received by prisoners of the Russians, Germans, Americans, and Japanese. Includes photos.

Prisoners of War–Fiction

2328. Boulle, Pierre. Bridge over the River Kwai, The. Vanguard, 1954. 224 p. $12.
Gr 10+. B 81: Jul 1985. A British Colonel drives prisoners of the Japanese to build a railroad bridge and resists its destruction by the British.

Public Officials

2329. McJimsey, George. Harry Hopkins: Ally of the Poor and Defender of Democracy. Harvard University Press, 1987. 467 p. ill. $25.
Adult. B 83: Mar 15 1987. LJ 112: Apr 15 1987. A detailed and readable biography of Hopkins who served Roosevelt as federal relief administrator, political strategist, defense expert, cabinet member, and friend.

Racism

2330. Dower, John. War Without Mercy: Race and Power in the Pacific War. Pantheon, 1986. 317 p. $23.
Adult. B 82: May 15 1986. * LJ 111: Apr 1 1986. This fresh insight into the Pacific war examines the racist stereotypes that dominated the way each side thought about the other.

Refugees

2331. Gruber, Ruth. Haven: The Unknown Story of FDR and 1000 World War II Refugees. Coward, 1983. 336 p. $16.
Gr 10+. B 79: Aug 1983. LJ 108: Jun 1 1983. Gruber was a U.S. government agent, sent to bring 1000 Italian refugees, mostly Jewish, to the United States and to help them settle here.

Scientists

2332. Kunetka, James W. Oppenheimer: The Years at Risk. Prentice-Hall, 1982. 292 p. ill. $16.
Gr 9+. +- B 79: Feb 1 1983. LJ 108: Feb 15 1983. Covers Oppenheimer's accomplishments (director of the laboratory that developed the atomic bomb and head of the Atomic Energy Commission) and his persecution during the McCarthy era.

Social Life and Customs

2333. Hall, Carolyn. Forties in Vogue, The. Harmony; Crown, 1985. 160 p. ill. $25.
Gr 9+. B 82: Jan 15 1986. LJ 111: Jan 1986. A photographic account of how the upper class was affected by the war.

2334. Harris, Mark Jonathan. Homefront: America During World War II. Putnam, 1984. 256 p. ill. $18. Pb $9.
Gr 6+. B 80: Mar 1 1984. LJ 109: Feb 15 1984. SLJ 30: Aug 1984. VOYA 7: Feb 1985. An oral history based on the recollections of Americans on the homefront, covering topics such as women workers in the factories, internment of U.S. citizens, racism, wartime romance, and other effects of the war.

2335. Kennett, Lee. For the Duration: The United States Goes to War, Pearl Harbor-1942. Scribner, 1985. 256 p. ill. $16.
Gr 9+. B 81: Feb 15 1985. +- LJ 110: Feb 1 1985. An overview of the homefront as it responded to Pearl Harbor and prepared for war.

2336. Lawson, Don. Album of World War II Home Fronts, An. (Picture Albums Series). Watts, 1980. 90 p. ill. $8.
Gr 7+. B 76: Jun 1 1980. SLJ 27: Mar 1981. A photographic essay which surveys what life was like for noncombatants in Europe, Asia, and the U.S. Covers food shortages, spies, blackmarket, working women, and the treatment of minorities.

2337. Stein, R. Conrad. Home Front, The. (World At War). Childrens Press, 1986. 47 p. ill. $11.
Gr 4-8. B 83: Mar 15 1987. SLJ 33: May 1987. An overview of life in the U.S. during the war, including how it affected women, children, and minorities.

Social Life and Customs–Fiction

2338. Brooks, Jerome. Make Me a Hero. Dutton, 1980. 152 p. $9.
Gr 6-9. * B 76: May 1 1980. BC 34: Sep 1980. SLJ 26: Aug 1980. Young Jake's parents are worried about his brothers who are in the service and do not see his need for their approval. A good evocation of a Chicago neighborhood during the war.

2339. Chaikin, Miriam. Lower, Higher, You're a Liar! Harper, 1984. 128 p. ill. $12. Lib ed. $12.
Gr 4-6. +- B 80: Jul 1984. BC 38: Sep 1984. SLJ 30: Aug 1984. Molly, a Jewish girl growing up in Brooklyn during World War II, tries various ways to deal with the bully who took Estelle's bracelet.

2340. Ferry, Charles. One More Time! Houghton, 1985. 171 p. $12.
Gr 7+. B 81: May 15 1985. BC 39: Sep 1985. BR 4: Sep/Oct 1985. +- SLJ 31: Aug 1985. +- VOYA 8: Aug 1985. Evokes the flavor of big band music at its peak and the trepidation of a nation at war.

2341. Lowry, Lois. Autumn Street. Houghton, 1980. 195 p. $7.
Gr 5-7. * B 76: Apr 15 1980. BC 34: Nov 1980. HB 56: Aug 1980. SLJ 26: Apr 1980. VOYA 3: Oct 1980. When her father goes to the war Elizabeth's family moves to Pennsylvania to live with grandparents. An unforgettable story of growing up during the 1940s.

2342. Rosenblum, Richard. My Sister's Wedding. Morrow, 1987. 32 p. ill. $11.
Gr K-3. * SE 52: Apr/May 1988. SLJ 33: Aug 1987. Introduces the social customs of the 1940s, the turmoil of life on the homefront. Jewish wedding customs are conveyed in the story and drawings.

2343. Todd, Leonard. Best Kept Secret of the War, The. Knopf, 1984. 165 p. $10. Lib. ed. $10.
Gr 5-8. B 81: Sep 1 1984. BC 37: May 1984. +- SLJ 30: May 1984. This vivid picture of small-town southern life centers on 10-year old Cam whose father is off fighting the war.

2344. Tripp, Valerie. Happy Birthday Molly! (American Girls Collection). Pleasant, 1987. 65 p. ill. $13. Pb $6.
Gr 2-5. B 84: Apr 1 1988. SLJ 35: May 1988. In 1944 Molly shared her birthday party with a girl from London who had been evacuated during the blitz. This easy-to-read story has colorful illustrations and believable characters.

2345. Tripp, Valerie. Meet Mollie: An American Girl. (American Girls Collection). Pleasant, 1986. 58 p. ill. $13. Pb $5.
Gr 2-5. B 83: Dec 1 1986. SLJ 33: Nov 1986. The story of an American girl whose father is serving overseas as a physician. Focus is on the changes in everyday life because of the war.

2346. Tripp, Valerie. Molly Learns a Lesson: A School Story. (American Girls Collection). Pleasant, 1986. 67 p. ill. $13. Pb $5.
Gr 2-4. B 83: Dec 1 1986. A family story of everyday life during the war, as Molly yearns for her father who is a doctor serving in England.

2347. Tripp, Valerie. Molly Saves the Day: A Summer Story. (American Girls Collection). Pleasant, 1988. 69 p. ill. $13. Pb $6.

Gr 3-6. B 85: Sep 15 1988. +- SLJ 35: Oct 1988. In this story set in 1944, Molly attends summer camp. A frightening experience causes her to grow up a little. An appendix provides information on the clothes, customs, and conditions of the time.

2348. Tripp, Valerie. Molly's Surprise: A Christmas Story. (American Girls Collection). Pleasant, 1986. 64 p. ill. $13. Pb $5.
Gr 2-4. B 83: Dec 1 1986. A warm story of family life during the war.

Women

2349. Campbell, D'Ann. Women at War With America: Private Lives in a Patriotic Era. Harvard University Press, 1984. 310 p. $20.
Adult. LJ 109: Dec 1984. A lively history of women during the war, covering the many roles they filled and the problems they faced.

2350. Frank, Miriam. Life and Times of Rosie the Riveter: The Story of Three Million Working Women During World War II. Clarity Productions, 1982. 112 p. ill. Pb $9.
Gr 9+. B 78: Jul 1982. LJ 107: Sep 1 1982. An attempt to de-romanticize the prevailing view of women workers during World War II. Based on interviews, autobiography, and other sources.

2351. Gluck, Sherna Berger. Rosie the Riveter Revisited: Women, the War, and Social Change. Twayne, 1987. 228 p. $20.
Adult. B 83: May 1 1987. LJ 112: May 15 1987. Lively and informative oral histories of ten women who successfully worked in aircraft factories but were replaced by returning soldiers.

2352. Honey, Maureen. Creating Rosie the Riveter: Class, Gender, and Propaganda During World War II. University of Massachusetts Press, 1984. 265 p. ill. $20.
Gr 10+. LJ 109: Nov 15 1984. Analyzes the social pressures that caused women to respond to the need for all types of workers during the war and then return to a dependent role in the home once the war was over.

1945-1961

United States—History—1945-1961

2353. Arnold, Eve. Fifties: Photographs of America. Pantheon, 1985. 175 p. ill. $30. Pb $15.
Gr 9+. B 81: Aug 1985. LJ 110: Jul 1985. Photos document the social, political, and artistic culture of the U.S. during the 1950s.

2354. Carter, Paul A. Another Part of the Fifties. Columbia University Press, 1983. 320 p. ill. $20.
Adult. B 79: Jul 1983. * LJ 108: Jul 1983. Carter's re-examination of the 1950s challenges common myth. He examines politics, foreign affairs, and social life, and provides a new perspective.

2355. Diggins, John Patrick. Proud Decades: America in War and in Peace, 1941-1960. Norton, 1988. 330 p. ill. $20.
Gr 9+. B 85: Sep 15 1988. LJ 113: Oct 1 1988. Discusses the Cold War, U.S. foreign policy, politics, and popular culture during the two decades when the U.S. emerged as a superpower.

2356. Gilbert, James. Another Chance: Postwar America, 1945-1968. Temple University Press, 1982. 307 p. ill. $18.
Gr 9+. LJ 107: Apr 1 1982. SE 46: Oct 1982. SLJ 28: Aug 1982. An effective synthesis of the social, political, economic, and cultural changes in post-World War II society. Covers important persons and changes in the presidency.

2357. Goldman, Eric Frederick. Crucial Decade—And After: America 1945-1960. Random/Vintage, 1956, 1961. 298 p. Pb $5.
Adult. B 85: Oct 1 1988. B 53: Sep 15 1956. LJ 81: Aug 1956. A lively commentary on American persons, events, and attitudes in the decade following World War II, a decade that greatly influenced later domestic and foreign policies.

2358. Merritt, Jeffrey D. Day by Day: The Fifties. Facts On File, 1979. 1015 p. ill. $65.
Gr 9+. +- B 77: Jan 1 1981. Includes charts of world and national affairs divided into 10 categories, a summary for each year of the decade, and photos. Useful as a supplement for other sources and to trace obscure events.

2359. O'Neil, Doris. Life: The Second Decade, 1946-1955. Graphic Society; dist. by Little, Brown, 1984. 224 p. ill. $30.
Gr 9+. B 81: Mar 1 1985. LJ 110: Mar 15 1985. SE 49: May 1985. Dramatic photos of the post-World War II years.

2360. Oakley, J. Ronald. God's Country: America in the Fifties. Dembner Books; dist. by Norton, 1986. 495 p. $25.
Gr 9+. B 82: May 1 1986. LJ 111: May 1 1986. An overview of the culture and politics of the transitional '50s.

Airplanes and Pilots

2361. McDonald, John J. Howard Hughes and the Spruce Goose. (Modern Aviation Series). TAB Books, 1981. 160 p. ill. Pb $7.
Gr 9+. B 78: May 1, May 15 1982. The story of the largest airplane in the world and its creator.

Airplanes and Pilots—Women

2362. Cochran, Jacqueline. Jackie Cochran: An Autobiography. Bantam, 1987. 355 p. ill. $19.
Gr 9+. B 83: Aug 1987. LJ 112: Aug 1987. Cochran set more speed, distance, and altitude records than any other woman aviator. This insightful autobiography clarifies her mark on aviation history.

Authors

2363. Hentoff, Nat. Boston Boy. Knopf, 1986. 192 p. $16.
Gr 9+. * B 82: Apr 15 1986. LJ 111: Mar 15 1986. A colorful memoir of the Boston youth of a foremost novelist, civil libertarian, and jazz critic.

Blacks–Biographies

2364. Brown, Claude. Manchild in the Promised Land. New American Library, 1971. 415 p. Pb $4.
Gr 10+. SE 46: Oct 1982. For mature students, the autobiography of a young black man growing up in Harlem.

2365. Parker, Robert. Capitol Hill in Black and White. Dodd, 1986. 256 p. ill. $17.
Gr 10+. LJ 111: May 1 1986. As chauffeur for LBJ and headwaiter in the Senate dining room, Parker observed behind-the-scenes Washington for 30 years.

Blacks–Fiction

2366. Thomas, Joyce Carol. Marked by Fire. Avon, 1982. 160 p. Pb $3.
Gr 7+. B 78: Feb 15 1982. SLJ 28: Mar 1982. VOYA 5: Aug 1982. This unusual story of a black girl growing up in rural Oklahoma is strengthened by powerful characterizations.

Chinese Americans–Fiction

2367. Namioka, Lensey. Who's Hu? Vanguard, 1981. 185 p. $9.
Gr 7+. B 77: Jun 1981. SLJ 28: Feb 1982. A humorous novel about Emma Hu as she tries to reconcile her culture and mathematical abilities with the prevailing view of an American teenage girl in the '50s.

Civil Rights–Fiction

2368. Marger, Mary Ann. Justice at Peachtree. Elsevier/Nelson, 1980. 140 p. $8.
Gr 6-9. +- BC 34: Feb 1981. +- SLJ 27: Jan 1981. A convincing picture of the ferment of change in the South during the 1950s is seen in this story of a high school senior who becomes aware of political and social inequity based on race.

2369. Shange, Ntozake. Betsey Brown. St. Martin's, 1985. 207 p. $13.
Gr 10+. B 81: Mar 1 1985. * LJ 110: May 15 1985. SLJ 32: Dec 1985. * VOYA 8: Oct 1985. Ordinary adolescent problems are added to the stress Betsey faces during forced school integration.

2370. Walter, Mildred Pitts. Girl on the Outside, The. Lothrop, 1982. 148 p. $10.
Gr 6-10. B 79: Sep 1 1982. BC 36: Nov 1982. * SE 47: Apr 1983. SLJ 29: Jan 1983. Tells of the emotions and experiences of a white girl and a black girl who worked to promote desegregation. Based on a 1957 Little Rock incident.

Congress and the Legislative Branch

2371. Reedy, George E. U.S. Senate, The. Crown, 1986. 224 p. $17.
Gr 10+. B 83: Oct 15 1986. LJ 111: Nov 1 1986. Explains the workings of the Senate and presents an analysis of its achievements in the 1950s.

Entertainers

2372. Patterson, Charles. Marian Anderson. Watts, 1988. 159 p. ill. $13.
Gr 6+. +- B 85: Dec 15 1988. +- BC 42: Nov 1988. A clear account of Anderson's struggle against racial prejudice as she rose to international acclaim as a singer.

2373. Tedards, Anne. Marian Anderson. (American Women of Achievement). Chelsea House, 1987. 112 p. ill. $17.
Gr 6-10. B 84: Feb 1 1988. SLJ 34: Apr 1988. Provides the historic setting for Anderson's outstanding musical career during which she broke many racial barriers. Includes illustrations and photos.

Espionage and Spies

2374. Beschloss, Michael R. MAYDAY: Eisenhower, Krushchev, and the U-2 Affair. Harper, 1986. 402 p. $20.
Gr 9+. B 82: Feb 1 1986. LJ 111: May 15 1986. When a CIA U-2 spy plane was shot down over the U.S.S.R. in 1960 the dream of detente was shattered.

2375. Lamphere, Robert J. FBI-KGB War: A Special Agent's Story. Random House, 1986. 352 p. ill. $19.
Adult. LJ 111: Jun 1 1986. A memoir of an FBI agent whose career was devoted to foiling post-war Soviet espionage in the U.S.

Fiction

2376. Bauer, Marion Dane. Rain of Fire. Clarion/Ticknor & Fields, 1983. 153 p. $11.
Gr 5-8. * B 80: Sep 15 1983. BC 37: Nov 1983. +- SLJ 30: Feb 1984. A veteran's young brother responds to his pacifist views but then has trouble with the neighborhood bully.

2377. Boutis, Victoria. Looking Out. Four Winds, 1988. 139 p. $12.
Gr 5-9. +- BC 41: Apr 1988. - SLJ 34: Jun/Jul 1988. +- VOYA 11: Aug 1988. Ellen's parents are communists–a dangerous belief during the McCarthy era–and she must keep their secret even though their political activities cause them to neglect her.

2378. Doctorow, E. L. Book of Daniel, The. Fawcett, 1971. 303 p. $10.
Gr 10+. B 85: Oct 1 1988. LJ 96: Jun 15 1971. The son of parents condemned to death for stealing atomic secrets for the Russians attempts to discover the truth. This portrayal of the Cold War fears of the '50s is based on the Rosenberg case.

Foreign Policy

2379. Pimlott, John. Cold War, The. (Conflict in the 20th Century). Watts, 1987. 62 p. ill. $13.
Gr 6+. B 83: Jun 15 1987. * BR 6: Sep/Oct 1987. SLJ 33: Aug 1987. This overview traces the events of the Cold War from the Soviet invasion of Hungary to 1986. Includes charts, maps, and glossary.

Foreign Policy–Japan

2380. Schaller, Michael. American Occupation of Japan: The Origins of the Cold War in Asia. Oxford University Press, 1985. 384 p. $23.
Adult. LJ 110: Nov 1 1985. A clear presentation of the development of Japan's international role following the war.

Foreign Policy–Vietnam

2381. Gardner, Lloyd C. Approaching Vietnam: From World War II through Dienbienphu, 1941-1954. Norton, 1988. 425 p. $23.
Gr 10+. B 84: May 1 1988. LJ 112: May 15 1988. Focuses on U.S. and British policies that supported the French as a bulwark against communism in Southeast Asia, eventually leading to the French defeat at Dienbienphu and more involvement in the area by the U.S.

2382. Kahin, George McT. Intervention: How America Became Involved in Vietnam. Knopf, 1986. 537 p. $25.
Adult. B 82: Apr 15 1986. LJ 111: Apr 1 1986. Chronicles U.S. involvement in Vietnam, 1945-1966, indicating points at which the U.S. had opportunities to pull out. For advanced students.

2383. Prados, John. Sky Would Fall: Operation Vulture; the U.S. Bombing Mission, Indochina, 1954. Dial, 1983. 288 p. $18.
Gr 9+. LJ 108: Jun 1 1983. An account of the tragic French involvement in Vietnam and of how the U.S. became involved.

2384. Spector, Ronald H. Advice and Support: The Early Years of the U.S. Army in Vietnam, 1941-1960. Center of Military History, U.S. Army/Free Press, 1983. 391 p. ill. $18. Pb $11.
Gr 9+. B 80: Mar 15 1984. Traces U.S. involvement in Vietnam from World War II to 1960.

Immigration

2385. Ryan, Allan A. Quiet Neighbors: Prosecuting Nazi War Criminals in America. Harcourt, 1984. 372 p. ill. $16.
Gr 9+. B 81: Nov 1 1984. LJ 109: Dec 1984. The shocking story of the thousands of Nazi war criminals who came legally to the U.S. following the war.

Immigration, Chinese–Fiction

2386. Chao, Evelina. Gates of Grace. Warner, 1985. 372 p. $16.
Gr 9+. B 82: Sep 15 1985. Realism, intrigue, and romance in the lives of Chinese immigrants.

2387. Lord, Bette Bao. In the Year of the Boar and Jackie Robinson. Harper, 1984. 169 p. ill. $10. Lib. ed. $10.
Gr 3-6. B 81: Dec 1 1984. BC 38: Oct 1984. HB 60: Sep/Oct 1984. * SE 49: Apr 1985. SLJ 31: Dec 1984. A warm and humorous story of a Chinese American girl learning the culture of her new country while she retains her pride in being Chinese. Based partly on the author's experience as an immigrant.

Indians of North America

2388. Fixico, Donald L. Termination and Relocation: Federal Indian Policy, 1945-1960. University of New Mexico Press, 1986. 268 p. $28.
Gr 9+. * BR 6: Sep/Oct 1987. A detailed account of legal actions that threaten Indian culture. From 1945-1960 over 12,000 Indians and a million acres were affected by these laws.

Inventions and Inventors

2389. Rashke, Richard. Stormy Genius: The Life of Aviation's Maverick, Bill Lear. Houghton, 1985. 402 p. ill. $19.
Gr 10+. LJ 110: Nov 1 1985. Lear designed light-duty jet aircraft, jet engines, airplane instruments, sound recording systems and more. His life was productive but controversial.

Japanese Americans–Fiction

2390. Uchida, Yoshiko. Journey Home. Atheneum, 1978. 131 p. ill. $8.
Gr 6-8. SE 44: Oct 1980. Shows the difficulties of Japanese Americans trying to pick up the pieces of their lives after they are released from internment camps. Sequel to Journey to Lopez.

Jewish Americans–Fiction

2391. Ascher, Carol. Flood, The. Crossing Press, 1987. 191 p. $17.
Gr 9+. B 83: Apr 15 1987. +- LJ 112: May 15 1987. The daughter of Jewish refugees, Eva finds her values tested when her parents offer refuge from a terrible flood to an anti-Semitic family, and when her black friends are affected by school integration.

2392. Lelchuk, Alan. On Home Ground. Harcourt/Gulliver, 1987. 72 p. ill. $10.
Gr 5-9. B 84: Jan 1 1988. BC 41: Oct 1987. * SE 52: Apr/May 1988. SLJ 34: Dec 1987. A subtle story of 10-year-old Aaron who understands the struggles of his idol, Jackie Robinson, and his friend, a wounded veteran, but cannot understand the problems of his immigrant father.

Journalists

2393. Daniel, Clifton. Lords, Ladies and Gentlemen: A Memoir. Arbor House, 1984. 256 p. ill. $18.
Gr 10+. B 80: Aug 1984. LJ 109: Jul 1984. Daniel, a journalist, and husband to Margaret Truman, presents

anecdotes concerning the famous people and events of the 1940s.

2394. May, Antoinette. Witness to War: A Biography of Marguerite Higgins. Beaufort, 1983. 128 p. ill. $18.
Gr 9+. B 80: Nov 1 1983. +- LJ 108: Dec 1 1983. As a journalist, Higgins covered the liberation of Buchenwald and Dachau, the Nuremburg trials, and the Berlin airlift, as well as the Korean and Vietnamese Wars.

2395. Sperber, A. M. Murrow: His Life and Times. Freundlich Books; dist. by Scribner, 1986. 608 p. ill. $23.
Gr 10+. B 82: Apr 1986. LJ 111: Jul 1986. An exhaustive and powerful biography of a journalist who fought for free dissemination of information.

Korean War, 1950-1953

2396. Alexander, Bevin. Korea: The First War We Lost. Hippocrene, 1986. 558 p. ill. $25.
Adult. B 82: Jun 1 1986. LJ 111: Jun 15 1986. Covers the political and military aspects of the war.

2397. Berry, Henry. Hey, Mac, Where Ya Been? Living Memories of the U.S. Marines in the Korean War. St. Martin's, 1988. 368 p. ill. $23.
Gr 9+. +- B 84: May 15 1988. LJ 113: Jun 1 1988. The vivid reminiscences of 60 Marines of all rank, including one of the first black Marines. Covers all phases of the war.

2398. Fincher, Ernest Barksdale. War in Korea, The. (First Book). Watts, 1981. 64 p. ill. $8.
Gr 5-9. B 78: Oct 1 1981. SLJ 28: Mar 1982. Summarizes causes, results, major events, and personalities of the Korean War, and provides an overview of U.S.-Korean relations, viewed as a part of the Cold War. Includes anecdotes, quotes, and numerous photos.

2399. Gardella, Lawrence. Sing a Song to Jenny Next. Dutton, 1981. 246 p. $14.
Gr 9+. LJ 106: Dec 1 1981. VOYA 5: Apr 1982. A realistic account of six men who were dropped into China in the early days of the Korean conflict. They did not know that their mission was so dangerous that no plans were made to recover them.

2400. Hastings, Max. Korean War, The. Simon & Schuster, 1987. 364 p. ill. $23.
Gr 9+. B 84: Oct 15 1987. B 85: Oct 1 1988. LJ 112: Dec 1987. An overview of the political and military aspects of the war, including a section on the Chinese view.

2401. Hopkins, William B. One Bugle No Drums: The Marines at Chosin Reservoir. Algonquin, 1986. 274 p. ill. $16.
Adult. LJ 111: Aug 1986. This account of U.S. Marines battling both the Chinese and sub-zero weather includes other observations on the war.

2402. Stokesbury, James L. Short History of the Korean War, A. Morrow, 1988. 348 p. ill. $19.
Gr 9+. B 85: Sep 1 1988. * LJ 113: Sep 1 1988. A concise, clearly-written, and balanced analysis of the war.

Korean War, 1950-1953–Fiction

2403. Michener, James. Bridges at Toko-ri. Random House, 1953. 146 p. Pb $3.
Gr 9+. B 50: Sep 1 1953. B 85: Oct 1 1988. HB 29: Dec 1953. LJ 78: Jul 1953. A short vivid novel covering a few days of action during the Korean War when American fliers had to destroy four heavily defended bridges.

Labor Unions and Laborers–Women

2404. Byerly, Victoria. Hard Times Cotton Mill Girls: Womanhood and Poverty in the South. ILR Press, 1987. 220 p. ill. $26. Pb $10.
Gr 11+. B 83: Dec 15 1986. LJ 111: Dec 1986. A series of oral histories of women, black and white, who worked in the North Carolina cotton mills.

Migrant Labor–Fiction

2405. Lenski, Lois. Judy's Journey. Lippincott, 1947. 212 p. ill. $13.
Gr 4-6. Metzner [B 44: Sep 1 1947. HB 23: Sep 1947. LJ 72: Aug 1947]. An authentic picture of migrant laborers in the 1940s.

Military History

2406. Stevens, George. Victory in Europe: D-Day to V-E Day. Little, 1985. 192 p. ill. $25.
Adult. LJ 110: Jul 1985. This photo-essay on the end of the war includes 200 color photos taken by Stevens after D-Day.

Military Personnel

2407. Herbert, Anthony B. Herbert–the Making of a Soldier. Hippocrene, 1982. 189 p. ill. $15.
Gr 9+. B 79: Sep 15 1982. LJ 107: Sep 1 1982. The experiences of an American soldier during the Korean War.

2408. Smith, Robert. MacArthur in Korea: The Naked Emperor. Simon & Schuster, 1982. 256 p. $17.
Gr 9+. HT 16: Nov 1982. +- LJ 107: Feb 15 1982. The author praises MacArthur's military and administrative skills and his courage. He also reveals the general's arrogance, recklessness, and ambition, in this introduction to the conclusion of the Korean War.

Photographers

2409. Daffron, Carolyn. Margaret Bourke-White. (American Women of Achievement). Chelsea House, 1988. 112 p. ill. $17.
Gr 6+. B 84: May 1 1988. * BR 7: May/Jun 1988. SLJ 34: Aug 1988. A candid account of the career and personal life of the renowned photographer of the Depression and World War II who also recorded events in Russia, South Africa, India, and Korea. Numerous photos.

2410. Goldberg, Vicki. Margaret Bourke-White. Harper, 1986. 448 p. ill. $25.

Gr 9+. B 82: May 15 1986. LJ 111: Jun 1 1986. Bourke-White photographed steel mills, bombing raids on Germany, and Ghandi, as Life magazine's star photographer.

2411. Iverson, Genie. Margaret Bourke-White: News Photographer. Creative Education; dist. by Childrens Press, 1980. 31 p. ill. Lib. ed. $6.
Gr 3-4. B 77: Feb 1 1981. An introduction to the famous woman photographer for Fortune and Life magazines. Bourke-White was noted for her coverage of World War II, and for U.S. and international industrial photography.

2412. Siegel, Beatrice. Eye on the World: Margaret Bourke-White, Photographer. Warne, 1980. 124 p. ill. $9.
Gr 6-10. B 77: Sep 1 1980. BC 34: Oct 1980. HB 56: Aug 1980. * SE 45: Apr 1981. SLJ 27: Sep 1980. This pioneer woman photographer achieved fame for her photos of industry, of World War II, and of most of the major events since. Includes photos.

Politics

2413. Chambers, Whittaker. Witness. Random; Regnery, 1952. 808 p. $15. Pb $11.
Adult. B 85: Oct 1 1988. B 48: Jun 1 1952. LJ 77: May 15 1952. A powerful autobiography of an ex-Communist who became an important figure in the Cold War.

Presidency and the Executive Branch

2414. Donovan, Robert J. Tumultuous Years: The Presidency of Harry S. Truman, 1949-1953. Norton, 1982. 640 p. ill. $20.
Adult. LJ 107: Aug 1982. Detailed coverage of the Truman presidency and the political figures of his time. Over one-third of the book is on the Korean War.

2415. McCoy, Donald R. Presidency of Harry S. Truman, The. (American Presidency Series). University of Kansas Press, 1984. 360 p. $25. Pb $15.
Gr 10+. LJ 109: Aug 1984. A readable examination of the Truman presidency, showing the evolution of foreign and domestic affairs.

2416. Richardson, Elmo. Presidency of Dwight D. Eisenhower, The. (American Presidency Series). University of Kansas Press, 1979. 218 p. $12.
Gr 10+. HT 13: Feb 1980. A balanced overview of Eisenhower's strengths and weaknesses as president.

2417. Williams, Herbert Lee. Newspaperman's President, The. Nelson-Hall, 1984. 208 p. $23.
Adult. LJ 110: Feb 1 1985. This analysis of Truman's relations with the press presents a human portrait of a feisty and outspoken president.

Presidents and Their Families–Eisenhower

2418. Ambrose, Stephen E. Eisenhower. Vol. 1: Soldier, General of the Army, President-Elect, 1890-1952. Simon & Schuster, 1983. 640 p. $20.
Adult. B 80: Sep 1 1983. * LJ 108: Sep 1 1983. The first of a two-volume work, this focuses on Eisenhower's personal life, his activities during World War II, and his early political career.

2419. Ambrose, Stephen E. Eisenhower. Vol. 2: The President. Simon & Schuster, 1984. 752 p. ill. $25.
Adult. B 81: Sep 15 1984. LJ 109: Sep 15 1984. SE 49: May 1985. Ambrose lauds Eisenhower's abilities as a peacemaker in this biography which covers 1953-1961. Based on recent research.

2420. Brendon, Piers. Ike: His Life and Times. Harper, 1986. 480 p. ill. $20.
Gr 9+. B 83: Sep 15 1986. +- LJ 111: Sep 15 1986. A rare perspective on, and critical examination of, the military and political Eisenhower.

2421. Burk, Robert F. Dwight D. Eisenhower: Hero and Politician. (Twayne's Twentieth Century American Biography Series). Twayne, 1986. 232 p. ill. $19. Pb $10.
Gr 9+. B 82: Aug 1986. HT 21: Aug 1988. LJ 111: Oct 1 1986. VOYA 10: Apr 1987. This biography integrates Eisenhower's military and political careers and emphasizes his individualism, sense of responsibility, and personal values. This is number two in the series.

2422. Hargrove, Jim. Dwight D. Eisenhower: Thirty-Fourth President of the United States. (Encyclopedia of Presidents). Childrens Press, 1987. 98 p. ill. $15.
Gr 4-7. B 84: Dec 15 1987. +- SLJ 34: Dec 1987. Explores how Eisenhower's popularity as a military leader enabled him to become president. Includes highlights of his life, quotes, and anecdotes.

2423. Sandberg, Peter Lars. Dwight D. Eisenhower. (World Leaders Past and Present Series). Chelsea House, 1986. 116 p. ill. $16.
Gr 8+. SLJ 33: Nov 1986. A warm and humanizing biography.

2424. Van Steenwyk, Elizabeth. Dwight David Eisenhower, President. (Presidential Biography Series). Walker, 1987. 128 p. $13.
Gr 5+. B 83: May 15 1987. BR 6: Nov/Dec 1987. SLJ 33: May 1987. This chronological presentation is enlivened by quotes and anecdotes. It emphasizes Eisenhower's military and political career.

Presidents and Their Families–Truman

2425. Ferrell, Robert H. Truman: A Centenary Remembrance. Viking, 1984. 256 p. ill. $25.
Gr 9+. B 80: Apr 1 1984. LJ 109: May 1 1984. A pictorial tribute to the 33rd President.

2426. Hargrove, Jim. Harry S. Truman. (Encyclopedia of Presidents). Childrens Press, 1987. 98 p. ill. $15.
Gr 4-7. B 84: Dec 15 1987. +- SLJ 34: Dec 1987. These highlights from the life of the honest and independent Missouri senator who became president are enlivened by quotes and anecdotes.

2427. Leavell, J. Perry. Harry S. Truman. (World Leaders Past and Present Series). Chelsea House, 1987. 112 p. ill. $17.

Gr 7+. B 84: Jan 15 1988. SLJ 34: Feb 1988. A lively, balanced, and well-researched biography of the no-nonsense president from Missouri. Includes photos.

2428. Miller, Merle. Plain Speaking: An Oral Biography of Harry S. Truman. Berkley Pub.; dist. by Putnam, 1974. 448 p. $10. Pb $5.
Gr 9+. B 85: Oct 1 1988. LJ 99: Feb 15 1974. This oral history, based on interviews with Truman and his acquaintances, covers his political ideas, his personal conduct, and shows his independent spirit.

2429. Robbins, Jhan. Bess and Harry: An American Love Story. Putnam, 1980. 204 p. ill. $11.
Gr 9+. B 77: Sep 15 1980. - LJ 105: Sep 15 1980. Based on interviews with political figures, friends, and acquaintances.

2430. Truman, Harry S. Dear Bess: The Letters from Harry to Bess Truman, 1910-1959. Norton, 1983. 593 p. ill. $20.
Adult. LJ 108: Nov 1 1983. When they were apart Truman wrote to his wife almost daily. These selected letters reveal his prejudices, worries, political tactics, and his insight into national and international events.

2431. Truman, Margaret. Bess W. Truman. Macmillan, 1986. 480 p. ill. $20.
Gr 9+. B 82: Mar 1 1986. LJ 111: Apr 1 1986. This exploration of the life of Bess Truman clarifies the development of her strong and independent character.

Public Officials

2432. Champagne, Anthony. Congressman Sam Rayburn. Rutgers University Press, 1984. 228 p. $20.
Gr 10+. HT 19: Aug 1986. A concise study of the life of Rayburn, who served as a member of the House of Representatives from 1913 to 1961 and was Speaker for 17 years.

2433. Church, F. Forrester. Father and Son: A Personal Biography of Senator Frank Church of Idaho by His Son. Harper, 1985. 208 p. ill. $19.
Gr 9+. B 82: Nov 1 1985. LJ 110: Oct 15 1985. An unusual dual biography of the senator and his son, a Unitarian minister.

2434. Ingalls, Robert P. Point of Order: A Profile of Senator Joe McCarthy. Putnam, 1981. 159 p. ill. $10.
Gr 7+. B 78: Jan 15 1982. BC 35: Feb 1982. * SE 46: Apr 1982. SLJ 28: Mar 1982. The anti-communist hysteria of the 1950s and Senator McCarthy's role are portrayed.

2435. Schapsmeier, Edward L. Dirksen of Illinois: Senatorial Statesman. University of Illinois Press, 1984. 296 p. $20.
Adult. LJ 110: Jan 1985. Covers the political career of the minority leader in the Senate during the Kennedy and Johnson administrations. A lively biography of a unique statesman.

Reformers–Black

2436. Wilkins, Roy. Standing Fast: The Autobiography of Roy Wilkins. Viking, 1982. 343 p. ill. $16.

Gr 9+. B 78: Jun 1 1982. LJ 107: Jul 1982. Through the story of his life, Wilkins gives an overview of the development of the NAACP and the civil rights movement.

Social Life and Customs

2437. Drake, Nicholas. Fifties in Vogue, The. Holt, 1987. 160 p. ill. $25.
Gr 9+. B 83: May 1 1987. SLJ 33: Jun/Jul 1987. Presents the life of the rich and famous in the '50s.

2438. Hine, Thomas. Populuxe: The Look and Life of America in the '50s and '60s from Tailfins and TV Dinners to Barbie Dolls and Fallout Shelters. Knopf, 1986. 192 p. ill. $30.
Gr 9+. B 83: Nov 1 1986. Examines the popular culture of the 1950s and '60s and its underlying optimism.

2439. May, Elaine Tyler. Homeward Bound: American Families in the Cold War Era. Basic Books, 1988. 320 p. ill. $21.
Gr 9+. B 85: Sep 15 1988. LJ 113: Sep 15 1988. Explores the efforts of American families to find personal happiness amidst the fears and tensions of the Cold War.

2440. O'Neill, William L. American High: The Years of Confidence, 1945-1960. Free Press, 1987. 309 p. $20.
Gr 10+. LJ 111: Dec 1986. This history of the post-war U.S. centers on those events that laid the foundation for social reforms in the decades to follow.

Social Life and Customs–Children

2441. Harris, Alex. World Unsuspected: Portraits of Southern Childhood. (Lyndhurst Series on the South). University of North Carolina Press, 1987. 237 p. ill. $17.
Gr 10+. B 84: Sep 15 1987. BR 6: Nov/Dec 1987. LJ 112: Sep 1 1987. Twelve southern writers have each written an essay on a childhood memory, some funny, some sad, but each reflecting a child's life in the South, 1945-1960.

Social Life and Customs–Fiction

2442. Delton, Judy. Kitty in High School. Houghton, 1984. 114 p. $11.
Gr 4-7. B 80: Aug 1984. +- BC 37: Jul/Aug 1984. HB 60: Sep/Oct 1984. +- SLJ 31: Sep 1984. These adventures of friends in a 1940s Catholic high school recreate a time when adolescence was an unsophisticated and enjoyable time. Sequel to Kitty in the Middle.

2443. Herman, Charlotte. Millie Cooper, 3B. Dutton, 1985. 73 p. $10.
Gr 2-4. * B 81: Apr 1 1985. BC 38: Jun 1985. HB 61: Jul/Aug 1985. SLJ 31: Aug 1985. The adventures of third grader Millie give a delightful sense of time and place–1946, Chicago, the week before Thanksgiving.

2444. Knowles, John. Peace Breaks Out. Bantam, 1982. 178 p. Pb $3.
Gr 7+. * BR 2: May/Jun 1983. Pete Hallam, a wounded veteran, returns to New Hampshire to teach, and finds

that World War II is being reenacted in the microcosm of Devon High School.

2445. New, Michael. Year of the Apple, The. Addison-Wesley, 1980. 96 p. ill. $8.
Gr 5-7. * SE 45: Apr 1981. +- SLJ 27: Mar 1981. A reminiscence of boyhood in the 1950s.

2446. Savitz, Harriet May. Summer's End. Signet, 1984. 159 p. $3.
Gr 7+. SLJ 32: Sep 1985. * VOYA 8: Jun 1985. Postwar life in the United States, including problems of Holocaust survivors.

2447. Steiner, Barbara. Tessa. Morrow, 1988. 208 p. $12.
Gr 6-9. B 84: Apr 15 1988. +- BC 41: Apr 1988. HB 64: Nov/Dec 1988. SLJ 34: Mar 1988. In this story of growing up in rural Alabama in 1946 Tessa must cope with her own adolescence, her parents' divorce, and the racial attitudes that separate her from her black friend.

Women–Biographies

2448. Kaldin, Eugenia. Mothers and More: American Women in the 1950s. Hall, 1984. 260 p. $16. Pb $7.
Gr 10+. +- HT 20: Nov 1986. Includes encyclopedic coverage of individual women and information on discrimination and other forces of the 1950s that led to the feminist movement of the '60s.

1961-

United States–History–1961-

2449. Archer, Jules. Incredible Sixties: The Stormy Years That Changed America. Harcourt, 1986. 159 p. ill. $16.
Gr 7+. B 82: May 15 1986. B 84: Sep 1 1987. +- BC 40: Sep 1986. * SLJ 33: Sep 1986. * VOYA 10: Apr 1987. Provides chapters on politics, music, art, science, economics, religion, and social issues. The final chapter relates the 1960s to the mid-'80s. Numerous photos.

2450. Bohmbach, Dwight. What's Right With America: 1986, A Handbook for Americans. 3rd ed. Bantam, 1986. 336 p. $4.
Gr 9+. B 82: Jun 1 1986. The trends and general state of life in the U.S.

2451. Emmens, Carol A. Album of the Sixties, An. Watts, 1981. 90 p. ill. $9.
Gr 5-9. B 77: Apr 15 1981. - SLJ 28: Feb 1982. A photo essay of the political, social, and cultural landmarks of the decade.

2452. Evans, Harold. Eyewitness: 25 Years through World Press Photos. Morrow, 1981. 192 p. ill. $20.
Gr 9+. SLJ 28: Apr 1982. Photos of world events 1956-1980. Excellent for browsing and curricular support.

2453. Haskins, James. 60s Reader, The. Viking, 1988. 244 p. ill. $14.
Gr 7+. * B 85: Sep 1 1988. BC 42: Oct 1988. BR 7: Nov/Dec 1988. * SLJ 34: Aug 1988. A smooth synthesis sets the background for brief biographies and excerpts from critical speeches, articles, documents, and songs. Together they present a balanced picture of the decade and its impact.

2454. Hoobler, Dorothy. Album of the Seventies, An. (Picture Albums Series). Watts, 1981. 90 p. ill. $9.
Gr 6+. B 78: Oct 15 1981. SLJ 28: Mar 1982. An overview of the Nixon years and the social changes of the 1970s. Arranged topically.

2455. Morrison, Joan. From Camelot to Kent State: The Sixties Experience in the Words of Those Who Lived It. Times Books, 1987. 338 p. ill. Pb $13.
Gr 9+. B 84: Nov 1 1987. An oral history that allows persons who were outspoken popular leaders during the 1960s to reflect on how those years affected their lives.

2456. Parker, Thomas. Day By Day: The Sixties. Facts on File, 1983. 2 vol. $90.
Gr 9+. B 81: Dec 1 1984. A chronology of specific events and an overview of the times. Indexed.

2457. Steinbeck, John. Travels with Charley. Bantam, 1962. 275 p. $4.
Gr 10+. * B 58: Jul 1 1962. LJ 87: Jun 15 1962. SE 46: Oct 1982. Steinbeck, with his poodle Charley, made a journey across America and recorded his reactions to the people and the land in this unique book.

Antinuclear Movement

2458. Bentley, Judith. Nuclear Freeze Movement, The. Watts, 1984. 128 p. ill. $10.
Gr 7+. B 81: Sep 1 1984. * BR 3: Sep/Oct 1984. SE 49: Apr 1985. +- SLJ Aug 1984. A comprehensive treatment of the history and growth of the movement, written by an advocate of the cause.

2459. Kome, Penney. Peace: A Dream Unfolding. Sierra Club; dist. by Random, 1986. 256 p. ill. $35. Pb $19.
Gr 9+. B 83: Jan 1 1987. * BR 5: Mar/Apr 1987. SLJ 33: Apr 1987. An anthology of writings and artworks on the subject of peace from many cultures throughout history. Also covers the effects of nuclear blasts, the arms race, and the international peace movement.

Artists

2460. Bober, Natalie S. Breaking Tradition: The Story of Louise Nevelson. Atheneum, 1984. 176 p. ill. $13.
Gr 7+. B 80: Apr 15 1984. BC 37: May 1984. HB 60: Apr 1984. * SE 49: Apr 1985. SLJ 30: Aug 1984. VOYA 7: Feb 1985. This is a readable account of the experiences of a Russian immigrant girl who struggled to become a recognized artist.

Assassination

2461. Goode, Stephen. Assassination! Kennedy, King, Kennedy. Watts, 1979. 175 p. ill. $7.
Gr 7-8. * SE 44: Apr 1980. Examines the evidence and the theories surrounding the three assassinations.

Astronauts

2462. Challengers: The Inspiring Life Stories of the Seven Brave Astronauts of Shuttle Mission 51-L. Pocket Books, 1986. 191 p. ill. Pb $4.
Gr 9+. +- B 82: Jun 1 1986. Includes one chapter on each of the Challenger crew members, and an account of the explosion. Written by the staff of the Washington Post.

2463. Bond, Peter. Heroes in Space: From Gagarin to Challenger. Basil Blackwell, 1987. 467 p. ill. $25.
Gr 9+. B 84: Oct 1 1987. LJ 112: Jun 15 1987. Focuses on the American and Soviet astronauts, 1957-1986, and how they dealt with the many stresses they faced.

2464. Cassutt, Michael. Who's Who in Space: The First 25 Years. Hall, 1987. 311 p. ill. $35.
Gr 7+. B 83: June 15 1987. SLJ 34: May 1988. Information on all astronauts from all nations through July 1986. Emphasis is on their aerospace accomplishments rather than on the personal lives of the biographees.

2465. Cohen, Daniel. Heroes of the Challenger. Archway, 1986. 119 p. ill. Pb $3.
Gr 4-8. B 83: Sep 15 1986. SLJ 33: Sep 1986. A simple, factual account of the Challenger tragedy.

2466. Haskins, James. Space Challenger: The Story of Guion Bluford. Carolrhoda, 1984. 64 p. ill. $9.
Gr K-7. B 81: Sep 1 1984. SE 49: Apr 1985. SLJ 31: Oct 1984. The story of the first black American in space.

2467. Van Riper, Frank. Glenn: The Astronaut Who Would Be President. Empire Books; dist. by Harper, 1983. 360 p. ill. $14.
Gr 9+. B 80: Dec 15 1983. +- LJ 108: Dec 1 1983. A well-researched, even-handed biography of John Glenn, winner of over 20 medals during World War II and the Korean War, the first American to orbit the earth, and a senator from Ohio.

2468. Westman, Paul. Alan Shepard: First American in Space. (Taking Part Books). Dillon Press, 1979. 48 p. ill. $6.
Gr 3-6. +- SLJ 26: Jan 1980. A slightly fictionalized biography.

2469. Westman, Paul. Frank Borman: To the Moon and Back. (Taking Part Books). Dillon Press, 1981. 48 p. ill. $7.
Gr 3-5. B 78: Apr 15 1982. SLJ 28: Apr 1982. Emphasis is on Borman's fascination with flight from his youth through his Apollo VIII flight around the moon. Includes photos.

2470. Westman, Paul. John Young, Space Shuttle Commander. (Taking Part Books). Dillon Press, 1981. 56 p. ill. $7.
Gr 3-5. +- B 78: Mar 1 1982. SLJ 28: Apr 1982. These highlights of Young's career include NASA photos.

2471. Westman, Paul. Neil Armstrong: Space Pioneer. (Achievers). Lerner, 1980. 64 p. ill. Lib. ed. $6.
Gr 3-5. B 77: Feb 15 1981. +- SLJ 27: Jan 1981. A simple biography that makes clear Armstrong's contribution to the team which first landed on the moon. Includes photos and a chart of information on space flights.

2472. Wolfe, Tom. Right Stuff, The. Farrar; Bantam, 1979. 436 p. $16. Pb $5.
Gr 9+. B 84: Sep 1 1987. LJ 104: Oct 15 1979. This story of the early years of the space program emphasizes the selection and training of the astronauts.

Astronauts–Women

2473. Behrens, June. Sally Ride, Astronaut: An American First. Childrens Press, 1984. 32 p. ill. Pb $3.
Gr 3-6. B 82: Sep 15 1985. A large-print, highly illustrated biography of America's first woman astronaut.

2474. Billings, Charlene W. Christa McAuliffe: Pioneer Space Teacher. Enslow, 1986. 64 p. $12.
Gr 4-8. B 83: Dec 1 1986. * BR 5: Mar/Apr 1987. SLJ 33: Dec 1986. +- VOYA 9: Aug/Oct 1986. A chronology of the events leading to the Challenger disaster.

2475. Blacknall, Carolyn. Sally Ride: America's First Woman in Space. (Taking Part Books). Dillon Press, 1984. 78 p. ill. $9.
Gr 4-6. B 81: Feb 15 1985. SLJ 31: Mar 1985. An introductory biography enhanced by lively anecdotes and good photos.

2476. Fox, Mary Virginia. Women Astronauts: Aboard the Shuttle. Rev. ed. Messner, 1988. 135 p. ill. $11. Pb $6.
Gr 4-9. B 84: Jun 1 1988. Includes biographies of eight women astronauts and information on their training.

2477. Fox, Mary Virginia. Women Astronauts: Aboard the Shuttle. Messner, 1984. 159 p. ill. $10.
Gr 5-10. B 81: Mar 15 1985. BC 38: May 1985. SLJ 31: Feb 1985. Explores the backgrounds of all women astronauts and provides a glimpse of life aboard the shuttle.

2478. Hohler, Robert T. I Touch the Future ... : The Story of Christa McAuliffe. Random House, 1986. 224 p. ill. $17.
Gr 9+. B 83: Nov 1 1986. LJ 111: Dec 1986. SLJ 33: May 1987. VOYA 10: Aug/Sep 1987. Based on primary sources and written by a journalist from McAuliffe's hometown.

2479. O'Connor, Karen. Sally Ride and the New Astronauts: Scientists in Space. Watts, 1983. 88 p. ill. $9.
Gr 5+. B 79: Jun 1 1983. +- BC 36: Jul/Aug 1983. - BR 2: Jan/Feb 1984. SLJ 29: Aug 1983. Chapters on many aspects of the NASA program and a chapter on Sally Ride.

2480. Ride, Sally. To Space and Back. Lothrop, 1986. 96 p. ill. $15.
Gr 3-7. * B 83: Nov 1 1986. Ride provides a description of everyday life aboard the space shuttle and an account of her own reactions to space flight.

Authors–Black

2481. Angelou, Maya. All God's Children Need Traveling Shoes. Random House, 1986. 208 p. $16.
Gr 10+. B 82: Feb 1 1986. * BR 5: Nov/Dec 1986. LJ 111: Mar 15 1986. SLJ 32: Aug 1986. +- VOYA 9: Aug/Oct 1986. This continuation of Angelou's biographical series covers her years in Ghana in the early 1960s.

2482. Angelou, Maya. Heart of a Woman, The. Random House, 1981. 272 p. $13.
Gr 9+. B 78: Sep 1 1981. LJ 106: Oct 1 1981. SLJ 28: Dec 1981. VOYA 5: Apr 1982. Covers Angelou's experiences in the civil rights movement, her recollections of Martin Luther King, Malcolm X, James Baldwin, and others, and her personal life during this hectic time.

Blacks

2483. Jackson, Florence. Blacks in America, 1954-1979. Watts, 1980. 89 p. ill. $7.
Gr 7+. SLJ 28: Oct 1981. This continuation of the author's series on black history and culture examines the people and events of the civil rights movement and the effort to gain recognition for black theater, dance, music, and literature.

2484. Kennedy, Theodore R. You Gotta Deal with It: Black Family Relations in a Southern Community. Oxford University Press, 1980. 215 p. map. $13.
Gr 9+. B 76: Mar 15 1980. LJ 105: May 1 1980. Through interviews the author reveals what it is like to be poor and black in the South after a decade of civil rights reform. Based on the author's 1972 Ph.D. dissertation.

2485. Thomas, Arthur E. Like It Is: Arthur E. Thomas Interviews Leaders on Black America. Dutton, 1981. 169 p. $11. Pb $7.
Gr 9+. SLJ 28: Oct 1981. The host of the television series "Like It Is" presents interviews which touch on historical and current events. Includes brief biographies of interviewees, including Rosa Parks, Julian Bond, and Maya Angelou.

2486. X, Malcolm. End of White World Supremacy, The. Arbor House, 1971, 1986. 148 p. Pb $6.
Gr 7+. BR 5: Mar/Apr 1987. * VOYA 10: Jun 1987. Includes four powerful speeches that clarify the beliefs of the Black Muslims of the 1960s. The introduction to each speech places it in context.

Blacks–Biographies

2487. Who's Who among Black Americans, 1980-81. 3rd ed. Who's Who among Black Americans Publishing Company, 1981. 1006 p. $50.
Gr 9+. B 80: Jun 15 1984. This frequently revised reference work covers 16,000 persons.

2488. Matney, William C. Who's Who among Black Americans, 1988. 5th ed. Educational Communications, 1988. 870 p. $104.
Adult. B 84: Apr 1 1988. VOYA 11: Apr 1988. Includes living black Americans who have "accomplished some conspicuous achievement." Listed by occupation and state of residence.

2489. Monroe, Sylvester. Brothers: A Story of Courage and Survival against the Odds of Today's Society. Morrow, 1988. 288 p. ill. $19.
Gr 9+. * B 84: Jun 1 1988. LJ 113: Aug 1988. A collective biography of 12 young black men who grew up in a Chicago ghetto.

Blacks–Women

2490. Roberts, Naurice. Barbara Jordan: The Great Lady from Texas. (Picture-Story Biographies). Childrens Press, 1984. 32 p. ill. $11.
Gr 2-6. B 80: Aug 1984. B 82: Sep 15 1985. SLJ 31: Sep 1984. Highlights of Jordan's life and political career.

Business and Business People

2491. Abodaher, David. Iacocca. Macmillan, 1982. 288 p. ill. $15.
Gr 9+. LJ 107: Dec 1 1982. This stimulating biography of the man who led both Ford and Chrysler includes an excellent history of both corporations.

2492. Iacocca, Lee. Iacocca: An Autobiography. Bantam, 1984. 368 p. $10. Pb $5.
Adult. B 81: Dec 1 1984. LJ 110: Jan; Mar 1 1985. SE 49: May 1985. A candid memoir by the son of Italian immigrants who rose to become the head of Ford Motor Company and the Chrysler Corporation.

Civil Rights

2493. Bullard, Pamela. Hardest Lesson: Personal Accounts of a Desegregation Crisis. Little, 1980. 223 p. $9.
Gr 6+. B 76: Feb 15 1980. LJ 105: Apr 1 1980. SLJ 26: May 1980. The frank and balanced narrative is based on interviews with hundreds of persons affected in various ways by the integration crisis.

2494. Cagin, Seth. We Are Not Afraid: The Story of Goodman, Schwerner, and Chaney and the Civil Rights Campaign for Mississippi. Macmillan, 1988. 320 p. ill. $19.
Adult. * LJ 113: May 1 1988. An exhaustive and eloquent account of the civil rights movement of the early 1960s, centering around the murders of three civil rights workers.

2495. Forman, James D. Freedom's Blood. Watts, 1979. 114 p. ill. $7.
Gr 7-8. SE 44: Apr 1980. Reconstructs the June 1964 weekend which culminated in the murder of three civil rights activists in rural Mississippi.

2496. Hamlin, David. Nazi/Skokie Conflict: A Civil Liberties Battle. Beacon Press, 1981. 184 p. $13.
Gr 9+. B 77: Jan 15 1981. LJ 106: Jan 1 1981. SLJ 27: Apr 1981. VOYA 4: Jun 1981. This clarifies the issues in the civil rights legal battle that occurred when a group of Nazis held a rally in Skokie, Illinois, which has a large Jewish population.

2497. King, Martin Luther, Jr. Stride Toward Freedom: The Montgomery Story. Harper, 1958. 230 p. ill. $14. Gr 9+. B 82: Jan 1 1986. The first nonviolent strike against segregation in the South as described by its leader.

2498. Miller, Marilyn. Bridge at Selma, The. (Turning Points in American History). Silver Burdett, 1985. 64 p. ill. $14. Gr 5+. B 82: Nov 1 1985. BC 39: Sep 1985. BR 4: Jan/Feb 1986. SLJ 32: Dec 1985. * VOYA 8: Oct 1985. A crisp and well-organized presentation of the 1965 confrontation between civil rights marchers and the police in Selma, Alabama, that eventually led to the passage of the Voting Rights Act.

2499. Stein, R. Conrad. Story of the Montgomery Bus Boycott, The. (Cornerstones of Freedom). Childrens Press, 1986. 31 p. ill. $10. Gr 3-5. B 82: Jul 1986. SLJ 33: Jan 1987. Chronicles the beginning of the civil rights movement.

2500. Webb, Sheyann. Selma, Lord, Selma. University of Alabama Press; Quill/Morrow, 1980. 147 p. ill. $10. Pb $5. Gr 7+. B 84: Sep 1 1987. BC 33: Jun 80. LJ 105: Jul 1980. SLJ 27: May 1981. A moving account of the experiences of two girls, eight and nine years old, who were caught up in the civil rights movement.

2501. Whalen, Charles. Longest Debate: A Legislative History of the 1964 Civil Rights Act. Seven Locks Press, 1985. 340 p. ill. $16. Adult. LJ 110: Mar 1 1985. This exploration of the political maneuverings necessary to pass this controversial legislation is also a valuable account of the complexity of congressional battles.

2502. Williams, Juan. Eyes On the Prize: America's Civil Rights Years, 1954-1965. Viking, 1987. 397 p. ill. $25. Gr 9+. B 83: Nov 15 1986. B 84: Sep 1 1987. * BR 6: Sep/Oct 1987. SLJ 33: Aug 1987. * VOYA Aug/Sep 1987. A balanced, detailed, and objective account of the civil rights movement. Each chapter explores a major event in civil rights history.

Civil Rights–Fiction

2503. Schotter, Roni. Northern Fried Chicken. Philomel, 1983. 144 p. $11. Gr 7+. B 80: Nov 1 1983. +- BC 37: Feb 1984. +- BR 3: May/Jun 1984. HB 60: Feb 1984. SLJ 30: Dec 1983. VOYA 7: Jun 1984. Portrays racial prejudice and the civil rights movement of the early 1960s through the experiences of Betsy, a shy girl who believes in equality.

2504. Wilkinson, Brenda. Not Separate, Not Equal. Harper, 1987. 152 p. $13. Gr 6-10. +- BC 41: Nov 1987. - BR 6: Mar 1988. SLJ 34: Apr 1988. Malene is one of six black students chosen to integrate a white high school.

Congress and the Legislative Branch

2505. Cohn, Mary W. Congress and the Nation, Vol. VI, 1981-1984: A Review of Government and Politics. (Congressional Quarterly). Congressional Quarterly, 1985. 1162 p. ill. $110. Gr 9+. B 82: Jun 15 1986. A comprehensive review of legislative, political, and presidential activities during the first term of the Reagan administration.

2506. Lammers, Nancy. Powers of Congress. (Congressional Quarterly). 2nd ed. Congressional Quarterly, 1982. 380 p. Pb $9. Gr 7+. BR 2: Sep/Oct 1983. Traces the increased use of congressional powers in areas formerly controlled by the president. Divided into eight chapters for easy use.

2507. Miller, James A. Running in Place: Life Inside the Modern Senate. Simon & Schuster, 1986. 193 p. $18. Gr 11+. B 82: Apr 15 1986. LJ 111: May 15 1986. A typical week in the life of three senators and their aides.

Conscientious Objectors

2508. Moore, Joy Hofacker. Ted Studebaker: A Man Who Loved Peace. Herald Press, 1987. 40 p. ill. Pb $10. Gr 2-4. +- SLJ 33: Aug 1987. A simple biography of a man whose conscience would not allow him to fight in Vietnam, but he went there to serve as an agriculturalist and was killed by the Viet Cong.

Constitution

2509. Lewis, Anthony. Gideon's Trumpet. Random House/Vintage, 1964. 262 p. Pb $3. Gr 9+. B 82: Jan 1 1986. An account of the case which led the Supreme Court to decide that all defendants are entitled to counsel.

2510. Mansbridge, Jane J. Why We Lost the ERA. University of Chicago Press, 1986. 327 p. $35. Pb $10. Gr 9+. B 83: Sep 15 1986. LJ 111: Dec 1986. A clear analysis and historical perspective of the ERA, related legislation and court decisions, amplified by tables and notes.

2511. Murchland, Bernard. Voices in America: Bicentennial Conversations. Prakken, 1987. 253 p. Pb $20. Gr 10+. +- BR 6: Nov/Dec 1987. Interviews with 16 public figures concerning the Constitution in relation to current social issues.

2512. Rogers, Donald J. Press Versus Government: Constitutional Issues. Messner, 1986. 121 p. ill. $11. Gr 5-8. * B 83: Mar 15 1987. * SLJ 33: May 1987. A balanced and thought-provoking examination of important cases and shifting public opinion concerning freedom of the press.

2513. Steiner, Gilbert Y. Constitutional Inequality: The Political Fortunes of the Equal Rights Amendment. Brookings Institution, 1985. 113 p. $23. Pb $9.
Adult. LJ 110: Sep 1 1985. Surveys the history of the equal rights movement since 1848, but emphasizes the effort, since 1970, to pass an equal rights amendment to the Constitution.

2514. Whitney, Sharon. Equal Rights Amendment: The History and the Movement. Watts, 1984. 102 p. $10.
Gr 6+. B 81: Jan 1 1985. BC 38: Apr 1985. BR 3: Mar/Apr 1985. SLJ 31: Dec 1984. VOYA 7: Feb 1985. Background information about the women's rights movement and the support for, and opposition to, an equal rights amendment.

Crime and Criminals

2515. Harris, Jonathan. Super Mafia. Messner, 1984. 192 p. ill. $10.
Gr 7+. B 81: Sep 15 1984. SLJ 31: Dec 1984. Describes the power of organized crime and how it affects modern life.

2516. MacGillis, Donald. Crime in America: The ABC Report. Chilton, 1983. 216 p. $15. Pb $11.
Gr 9+. B 80: Nov 1 1983. * BR 3: May/Jun 1984. LJ 108: Dec 1 1983. Examines the causes of crime in the 1980s in the context of America's history of criminal violence.

Espionage and Spies

2517. Barron, John. Breaking the Ring. Houghton, 1987. 224 p. $18.
Gr 10+. B 83: Mar 15 1987. LJ 112: Apr 1 1987. A frightening and engrossing account of the espionage activities of the Walker family spy ring.

2518. Campbell, Duncan. Secret Service. (Issues–Issues–Issues). Gloucester; dist. by Watts, 1988. 32 p. ill. $11.
Gr 4-9. B 84: Jun 15 1988. +- BC 41: Jun 1988. BR 7: Sep/Oct 1988. Explains the purposes for gaining economic, political, and military information about other countries, how the information is gathered, and the problems this causes.

2519. Hersh, Seymour M. Target Is Destroyed: What Really Happened to Flight 007 and What America Knew About It. Random House, 1986. 282 p. $18.
Gr 9+. B 83: Oct 1 1986. LJ 111: Dec 1986. Hersh blames technical and human error in the KAL 007 incident in which a Korean passenger plane was shot down because the Soviets thought it was a U.S. spy plane.

2520. Johnson, R. W. Shootdown: Flight 007 and the American Connection. Viking, 1986. 323 p. ill. $19.
Adult. B 82: Jul 1986. LJ 111: Jun 15 1986. An evaluation of the various hypotheses covering the mysteries around KAL 007, and a consideration of whether this Korean passenger plane was involved in U.S. espionage when it was shot down by the Soviets.

2521. Kneece, Jack. Family Treason: The Walker Spy Case. Stein & Day, 1986. 240 p. ill. $18.
Gr 9+. B 83: Jan 1 1987. John Walker, his brother and son, all naval personnel, spied for the Soviets beginning in the 1960s. This recounts their activities, personalities, and the damage they did.

Fiction

2522. Cooney, Ellen. Small-Town Girl. Houghton, 1983. 188 p. $10.
Gr 5-9. B 79: Apr 1 1983. +- BC 36: Mar 1983. SLJ 30: Sep 1983. A story of growing up Catholic during the unsettled 1960s.

2523. Paulsen, Gary. Crossing, The. Orchard/Watts, 1987. 114 p. $12.
Gr 7+. BC 41: Sep 1987. BR 6: Jan/Feb 1988. HB 63: Nov/Dec 1987. SLJ 34: Nov 1987. +- VOYA 10: Oct 1987. The story of an orphaned Mexican boy desperately seeking to get into the U.S. and an American soldier desperately trying to escape memories of Vietnam.

Foreign Policy

2524. Quest for Peace, The: Principle United States and Documents Relating to the Arab-Israeli Peace Process, 1967-1983. Department of State, 1983. 134 p. Pb $4.
Gr 10+. B 80: May 15 1984. The text of principal public statements and documents relating to U.S. involvement in the Arab-Israeli dispute since the 1967 war, arranged chronologically by topics.

2525. Brown, Seyom. Crises of Power: An Interpretation of United States Foreign Policy During the Kissinger Years. Columbia University Press, 1979. 170 p. $11.
Gr 9+. B 76: Feb 15 1980. +- LJ 104: Dec 1 1979. A balanced assessment of Kissinger's achievements and failures during the Nixon and Ford administrations.

2526. Brzezinski, Zbigniew. In Quest of National Security. Westview Press, 1988. 232 p. $34.
Adult. LJ 113: Oct 1 1988. An anthology of articles and speeches by the author, discussing U.S. foreign policy from 1977 to 1988. Brzezinski was National Security Advisor during the Carter administration.

2527. Brzezinski, Zbigniew. Power and Principle: Memoirs of the National Security Advisor, 1977-1981. Farrar, 1983. 573 p. ill. $23.
Adult. B 79: Mar 15 1983. LJ 100: Apr 15 1983. The author's memoirs provide an articulate account of U.S. foreign policy during the Carter administration.

2528. Hersh, Seymour M. Price of Power: Kissinger in the Nixon White House. Summit; dist. by Simon & Schuster, 1983. 698 p. $20.
Adult. * LJ 108: Aug 1983. Examines foreign policy during the Nixon administration.

2529. Kissinger, Henry. White House Years. Little, 1979. 1521 p. ill. $23.
Gr 9+. B 76: Jan 15 1980. LJ 104: Dec 1 1979. In this first volume of his memoirs Kissinger explains the

diplomatic problems of Nixon's first term from his view-point as national security advisor.

2530. Kissinger, Henry. Years of Upheaval. Little, 1982. 1283 p. ill. $25.
Gr 9+. B 78: Apr 15 1982. LJ 107: Jun 1 1982. This second volume of Kissinger's memoirs covers Nixon's second term and shows how U.S. foreign policy was affected by Watergate.

2531. Linowitz, Sol M. Making of a Public Man, The. Little, 1985. 288 p. $20.
Adult. B 82: Oct 1 1985. LJ 110: Sep 15 1985. In the first part of his memoir the former chairman of the board discusses the early history of the Xerox Corporation. The second part details his work as ambassador/negotiator for presidents Johnson and Carter.

2532. Nixon, Richard M. Real Peace. Little, 1984. 107 p. $13.
Gr 10+. B 80: Jan 15 1984. +- LJ 109: Mar 1 1984. The former president speaks on the foreign policy of the Reagan administration.

2533. Reddleman, Marlow. U.S. Foreign Policy, Vol. 55, No. 3. Wilson, 1983. 214 p. Pb $7.
Gr 9+. * BR 3: Sep/Oct 1984. An overview of U.S. foreign policy during the first Reagan administration as seen through speeches, book excerpts, and articles.

2534. Vance, Cyrus R. Hard Choices: Four Critical Years in America's Foreign Policy. Simon & Schuster, 1983. 320 p. $18.
Adult. B 79: Apr 15 1983. LJ 108: May 15 1983. An even-handed analysis of the successes and failures of the foreign policy of the Carter administration.

2535. Wofsy, Leon. Before the Point of No Return: An Exchange of Views on The Cold War, The Reagan Doctrine, and What Is To Come. Monthly Review Press, 1986. 160 p. $24. Pb $8.
Gr 9+. * B 83: Dec 1 1986. Examines the nature and history of the Cold War and U.S. policy during the Reagan administration.

Foreign Policy–Caribbean

2536. Carroll, Raymond. Caribbean: Issues in U.S. Relations. (Impact Book). Watts, 1984. 104 p. map. $10.
Gr 6+. +- B 81: Dec 1 1984. SLJ 31: May 1985. VOYA 8: Apr 1985. An examination of the history, economics, and politics of the Caribbean area and the reasons for U.S. involvement there. Includes a map.

Foreign Policy–Central America

2537. Bender, David L. Central America: Opposing Viewpoints. (Opposing Viewpoints Series). Greenhaven, 1984. 244 p. $12. Pb $6.
Gr 10+. B 80: Jan 15 1985. B 81: Jan 15 1985. SLJ 32: Dec 1985. VOYA 8: Apr 1985. Includes a chronology of historical events 1812-1984 that involve Central America and the U.S., a balanced selection of articles on all sides of the issue, a list of organizations, and a bibliography.

2538. Cheney, Glenn Alan. Revolution in Central America. Watts, 1984. 90 p. $10.
Gr 7+. SLJ 30: Aug 1984. SLJ 32: Dec 1985. VOYA 7: Dec 1984. An evaluation of the historic problems of the area and the current U.S.-U.S.S.R. struggle for dominance.

Foreign Policy–Granada

2539. Gilmore, William C. Grenada Intervention, The. Facts on File, 1984. 116 p. $15.
Gr 9+. BR 4: May/Jun 1985. The history of Grenada and an examination of the 1983 United States intervention.

Foreign Policy–Iran

2540. Christopher, Warren. American Hostages in Iran: The Conduct of a Crisis. Yale University Press, 1985. 448 p. ill. $25.
Adult. B 81: Jun 1 1985. LJ 110: May 1 1985. An account of the Iran hostage crisis written by the negotiators.

2541. Follett, Ken. On Wings of Eagles. Hall; NAL/Signet, 1984. 664 p. $17. Pb $5.
Gr 9+. B 80: Sep 15 1983. LJ 108: Aug 1983. SE 49: May 1985. Describes the rescue of two American prisoners of the Ayatollah Khomeni by a group of private American citizens.

2542. Ledeen, Michael. Debacle: The American Failure in Iran. Knopf; dist. by Random, 1981. 320 p. $15.
Gr 9+. B 77: Mar 1 1981. LJ 106: Apr 1 1981. Examines U.S. relations with the Shah and the failure to protect U.S. interests when the revolution was inevitable. Discusses the implications of these experiences for future foreign policy.

2543. McFadden, Robert D. No Hiding Place: The New York Times Inside Report on the Hostage Crisis. Times Books, 1981. 320 p. $16.
Gr 9+. B 28: Oct 1 1981. LJ 106: Nov 1 1981. This overview, written from the perspective of the U.S hostages in Iran, includes essays on other important aspects of the crisis.

2544. Queen, Richard. Inside and Out: Hostage to Iran, Hostage to Myself. Putnam, 1981. 286 p. ill. $14.
Gr 9+. B 78: Oct 1 1981. +- LJ 106: Nov 15 1981. An intimate, day-to-day portrait of Queen's experience as a captive, and his view of the fall of the embassy where he served as a member of the diplomatic corps.

2545. Rubin, Barry M. Paved with Good Intentions: The American Experience and Iran. Oxford University Press, 1980. 448 p. ill. $18.
Gr 9+. B 77: Nov 1 1980. LJ 105: Nov 1 1980. A balanced examination of U.S.-Iran relations 1930-1980.

2546. Salinger, Pierre. America Held Hostage: The Secret Negotiations. Doubleday, 1981. 360 p. ill. $17.
Gr 9+. B 78: Oct 1 1981. LJ 106: Nov 15 1981. Details the delicate behind-the-scenes negotiations of the Iran hostage crisis 1979-1981.

2547. Scott, Charles W. Pieces of the Game: The Human Drama of Americans Held Hostage in Iran. Peachtree, 1984. 407 p. ill. $15.
Gr 9+. +- B 80: May 15 1984. LJ 109: Mar 1 1984. The author, who was sent to Iran as chief of the Army mission, was one of the hostages. He tells of the beatings and solitary confinement he suffered because his captors were certain that he was a CIA agent.

2548. Weir, Ben. Hostage Bound, Hostage Free. Westminster, 1987. 274 p. map. $13.
Gr 9+. B 83: May 1 1987. The personal story of Weir's captivity and his efforts to get the government to do more to help other hostages.

2549. Wells, Tim. 444 Days: The Hostages Remember. Harcourt, 1985. 435 p. $20.
Gr 9+. B 82: Nov 1 1985. LJ 110: Nov 15 1985. An oral history by the Americans who were hostages in Iran.

Foreign Policy–Lebanon

2550. Petit, Michael. Peacekeepers at War: A Marine's Account of the Beirut Catastrophe. Faber & Faber; dist. by Harper, 1986. 230 p. $18.
Gr 9+. B 82: May 1 1986. LJ 111: May 1 1986. A private's eye view of the experiences of a peacekeeping force that was the target of a suicide bomb attack in Lebanon in 1983.

Foreign Policy–Mexico

2551. Reynolds, Clark W. U.S.-Mexico Relations: Economic and Social Aspects. Stanford University Press, 1983. 392 p. $25.
Adult. LJ 108: Oct 1 1983. Deals with issues such as migration, agriculture, national security, trade, and other economic and social topics.

2552. Ribaroff, Margaret Flesher. Mexico and the United States Today: Issues between Neighbors. (Impact Book). Watts, 1985. 104 p. ill. $11.
Gr 6+. B 81: Aug 1985. +- SLJ 32: Sep 1985. +- VOYA 8: Oct 1985. Provides both U.S. and Mexican views on topics that create tension between them, including trade relations, illegal immigrants, and political changes in Central America.

Foreign Policy–U.S.S.R.

2553. Luttwak, Edward N. On the Meaning of Victory. Simon & Schuster, 1986. 320 p. $19.
Gr 9+. B 82: Apr 15 1986. LJ 111: Jun 1 1986. Essays on the recent history of U.S.-U.S.S.R. balance of power.

2554. Cohen, Stephen. Sovieticus: American Perceptions and Soviet Realities. Norton, 1985. 154 p. $13.
Gr 9+. B 81: Jun 15 1985. LJ 110: Jun 1 1985. A collection of the author's columns on the U.S.S.R. that have appeared in Nation magazine, divided into sections on U.S. media bias, Soviet leaders from Stalin to Gorbachev, Soviet dissidents, and the Cold War.

2555. Gaddis, John Lewis. Long Peace: Inquiries into the History of the Cold War. Oxford University Press, 1987. 352 p. $25.

Adult. B 83: Aug 1987. LJ 112: Oct 15 1987. Eight essays examine how the U.S. and U.S.S.R. have managed to avoid war for the past 40 years of the Cold War.

2556. Podhoretz, Norman. Present Danger: Do We Have the Will to Reverse the Decline of American Power. Simon & Schuster, 1980. 109 p. $8.
Gr 10+. B 76: Jul 15 1980. LJ 105: Sep 15 1980. SE 45: Mar 1981. The author analyzes the foreign affairs of the 1970s and argues in favor of hard-line policy toward the Soviet Union.

Historic Sites

2557. Reflections on the Wall: The Vietnam Veterans Memorial. Stackpole, 1987. 160 p. ill. $17.
Gr 9+. B 83: Jul 1987. A photo-essay that focuses on veterans, families, and friends who have come to the memorial in remembrance of those lost. Compiled by the Smithsonian Institute.

2558. Ashabranner, Brent. Always to Remember: The Vietnam Veterans Memorial. Dodd, 1988. 40 p. ill. $13.
Gr 6-10. * B 84: Jun 15 1988. BC 42: Sep 1988. SLJ 35: Oct 1988. Following a brief history of the Vietnam War is the moving story of the development of the memorial, its design, and its meaning to the families of those who served and to the nation.

2559. Lopes, Sal. Wall: Images and Offerings from the Vietnam Veterans Memorial. Collins; dist. by Harper, 1987. 127 p. ill. $25.
Gr 9+. B 84: Nov 15 1987. LJ 112: Nov 15 1987. Stunning and poignant photos of many who have visited the memorial, with a background essay.

2560. Palmer, Laura. Shrapnel in the Heart: Letters and Remembrances from the Vietnam Memorial. Random House, 1987. 256 p. ill. $18.
Gr 7+. B 84: Nov 15 1987. * LJ 112: Dec 1987. SLJ 34: Mar 1988. VOYA 11: Apr 1988. Palmer examined letters and other memorabilia left at the Vietnam Veterans Memorial and interviewed 28 of the survivors who left them, to provide a eulogy of the young men who died.

Immigration

2561. Ashabranner, Brent. New Americans: Changing Patterns in U.S. Immigration. Dodd, 1983. 212 p. ill. $14.
Gr 6+. B 79: Aug 1983. BR 2: Nov/Dec 1983. * SE 48: May 1984. SE 50: Mar 1986. - SLJ 29: Aug 1983. Surveys the reasons for recent immigration, the cultural contributions of the new citizens, the problems faced by immigrants and U.S. governing bodies, and controversial immigration policies.

2562. Bentley, Judith. American Immigration Today: Pressures, Problems, Policies. Messner, 1981. 190 p. ill. $11. Pb $5.
Gr 7+. B 78: Nov 1 1981. * SE 46: Apr 1982. SE 50: Mar 1986. Discusses the problems of recent im-

migrants, the ambivalent feelings of Americans toward them, and the inconsistencies of U.S. policy.

2563.   Day, Carol Olsen. New Immigrants, The. (Impact Book). Watts, 1985. 120 p. $11.
Gr 6+. B 81: May 15 1985. BR 4: Jan/Feb 1986. SLJ 31: Aug 1985. VOYA 8: Oct 1985. Covers the problems of the U.S. government and the new Vietnamese, Mexican, Soviet Jewish, and other immigrants, including legal and illegal immigrants, in a well-written overview that examines legislation.

2564.   Haines, David W. Refugees in the United States: A Reference Guide. Greenwood, 1985. 243 p. $40.
Gr 9+. B 82: Apr 1 1986. A comprehensive examination of the refugee program and the problems faced by refugees as they integrate into society, followed by a survey of the ethnic groups that make up the 1.5 million refugees of the past 25 years.

2565.   Kessner, Thomas. Today's Immigrants, Their Stories: A New Look at the Newest Americans. Oxford University Press, 1981. 282 p. ill. $16.
Gr 9+. B 78: Sep 15 1981. +- LJ 106: Oct 1 1981. Interviews with immigrants, background information on their reasons for coming, and the problems they face. Includes immigrants from China, Greece, Indochina, Italy, Korea, Peru, the Soviet Union, and elsewhere.

2566.   Maidens, Melinda. Immigration: New Americans, Old Questions. Facts on File, 1981. 190 p. ill. $20.
Gr 9+. B 78: Apr 1 1982. Presents a wide diversity of political and moral opinion on new immigration. Clippings from articles on events and legislation represent all 50 states and the District of Columbia.

2567.   Rosenberg, Maxine B. Making a New Home in America. Lothrop, 1986. 48 p. ill. $11. Lib. ed. $11.
Gr 1-6. B 82: Mar 1 1986. B 83: Oct 1 1986. BC 39: Apr 1986. HB 62: Jul/Aug 1986. SLJ 32: Aug 1986. Four new immigrant children, from Japan, Cuba, Guyana, and India, learn about life in the U.S.

2568.   Santoli, Al. New Americans: An Oral History: Immigrants and Refugees in the U.S. Today. Viking, 1988. 385 p. $20.
Gr 9+. B 85: Sep 15 1988. LJ 113: Nov 15 1988. Narratives by 18 new immigrants from around the world provide insight into their experience, their perception of the U.S., and the impact of immigration on American life.

Immigration, Asian

2569.   Success of Asian Americans: Fact or Fiction? (Clearinghouse Publication). Commission on Civil Rights, 1980. 28 p. ill. One copy free.
Gr 10+. B 77: Dec 15 1980. Challenges the stereotype of the economic success of new Asian immigrants with current information on their economic, educational, and occupational status. Number 64 of the series.

Immigration, Guatemalan

2570.   Ashabranner, Brent. Children of the Maya: A Guatemalan Indian Odyssey. Dodd, 1986. 54 p. ill. $13.
Gr 5-9. * B 82: May 1 1986. B 83: Jun 15 1987. * BC 39: Jul 1986. HB 62: Sep 1986. HB 63: Nov 1987. * SE 51: Apr 1987. * SLJ 32: Aug 1986. Recounts in their own words the lives of Guatemalan refugees who fled to the U.S. to escape military conflict. Informal photos document their experiences.

Immigration, Jewish

2571.   Bernstein, Joanne. Dmitry: A Young Soviet Immigrant. Houghton/Clarion Books/Tichnor & Fields, 1981. 80 p. ill. $11.
Gr 3-8. +- B 78: Jan 1 1982. B 81: Jul 1985. HB 58: Feb 1982. * SE 46: Apr 1982. +- SLJ 28: Jan 1982. A photographic essay of the experiences, good and bad, of a new Jewish American citizen.

Immigration, Mexican

2572.   Beatty, Patricia. Lupita Manana. Morrow, 1981. 192 p. $9. Lib. ed. $9.
Gr 3-8. +- B 77: May 1 1981. - BC 34: Apr 1981. HB 57: Jun 1981. * SE 46: Apr 1982. - SLJ 27: Apr 1981. An authentic picture of the obstacles faced by an illegal immigrant from Mexico.

Immigration, Soviet

2573.   Aksyonov, Vassily. In Search of Melancholy Baby. Random House, 1987. 229 p. $16.
Gr 10+. B 83: May 15 1987. LJ 112: Jul 1987. A warm, perceptive, and funny book about the author's experiences as a new American.

2574.   Golyakhovsky, Vladimir. Price of Freedom: A Russian Doctor Emigrates to America. Dutton, 1986. 343 p. $20.
Gr 10+. B 83: Sep 15 1986. LJ 111: Sep 15 1986. The experiences of a Russian physician and his family as they learn a new language, new skills, and a new culture.

2575.   Karlowich, Robert A. Young Defector. Messner, 1983. 64 p. ill. $9.
Gr 4-7. B 79: Feb 15 1983. SLJ 29: Aug 1983. The story of 12-year-old Walter Polovchak who chose to remain in the U.S. when his parents returned to the U.S.S.R.

2576.   Polovchak, Walter. Freedom's Child: A Teenager's Courageous True Story of Fleeing His Parents–And the Sovier Union–To Live in the United States. Random House, 1988. 246 p. ill. $18.
Gr 9+. B 84: Feb 1 1988. BR 7: May/Jun 1988. +- LJ 113: Apr 1 1988. VOYA 11: Aug 1988. When his parents decided to return to the U.S.S.R., a 12-year-old boy chose to remain in the U.S. and requested political asylum, creating an international legal battle.

Immigration, Vietnamese

2577. Haskins, James. New Americans: Vietnamese Boat People. Enslow, 1980. 64 p. ill. $11.
Gr 5-8. B 83: Oct 1 1986. VOYA 3: Feb 1981. The conditions which caused the Vietnamese to emigrate and the conditions they found upon arrival.

2578. Rutledge, Paul. Vietnamese in America, The. (In America Series). Lerner, 1987. 63 p. ill. $8. Pb $4.
Gr 4-7. B 84: Sep 1 1987. BC 41: Sep 1987. SLJ 34: Sep 1987. Following a brief history of the Vietnamese War is an explanation of the problems of the many refugees who came to the U.S. and their efforts to overcome cultural conflicts.

2579. Stanek, Muriel. We Came from Vietnam. Albert Whitman, 1985. 46 p. ill. $10.
Gr 4-6. B 82: Nov 1 1985. +- BC 39: Nov 1985. SLJ 32: Dec 1985. Introduces the Nguyan family, tells why they left Vietnam, and shows their efforts to adjust to their new home. Includes photos and a brief glossary of Vietnamese terms and names.

Immigration–Children

2580. Ashabranner, Brent. Into a Strange Land: Unaccompanied Refugee Youth in America. Dodd, 1987. 120 p. ill. $13.
Gr 5-10. * B 83: Jul 1987. BC 41: Sep 1987. * BR 6: Nov 1987. HB 63: Jul 1987. * SE 52: Apr 1988. * SLJ 33: Jun 1987. * VOYA 10: Oct 1987. A moving examination of the plight of Asian and Latin American children who are sent to the U.S. alone. Many of these political refugees know little English. All suffer from culture shock.

Immigration–Fiction

2581. Blue, Rose. Cold Rain on the Water. McGraw, 1979. 123 p. $8.
Gr 7-9. * SE 44: Apr 1980. - SLJ 26: Sep 1979. A Jewish family, new immigrants from Russia, have difficulty adjusting to a different culture.

Indians of North America–Fiction

2582. Rogers, Jean. Goodbye, My Island. Greenwillow, 1983 96 p. ill. $9.
Gr 4-6. B 79: Apr 15 1983. BC 37: Sep 1983. HB 59: Aug 1983. SE 48: May 1984. SLJ 29: Apr 1983. An authentic novel about Eskimo life after World War II that includes details of Eskimo life and shows the pain of a people caught between two cultures.

Japanese Americans–Fiction

2583. Irwin, Hadley. Kim/Kimi. Macmillan, 1987. 208 p. $13.
Gr 7-10. B 83: Mar 15 1987. +- BC 40: Mar 1987. +- BR 6: Nov/Dec 1987. SLJ 33: May 1987. VOYA 10: Jun 1987. Kim's Japanese father died before her birth and now, at 16, she lives with her Caucasian mother and stepfather but yearns to understand her "Japaneseness."

Journalists

2584. Broder, David S. Behind the Front Page: A Candid Look at How the News Is Made. Simon & Schuster, 1987. 339 p. $19.
Gr 9+. * B 83: Apr 15 1987. LJ 112: May 1 1987. SLJ 34: Sep 1987. Shows the changes in the relations between the White House and the press since Eisenhower.

2585. Buchanan, Patrick J. Right from the Beginning. Little, 1988. 400 p. ill. $19.
Gr 9+. B 84: Apr 15 1988. +- LJ 113: Jun 1 1988. A leading conservative columnist reminisces about his youth, his political activity, and the development of his personal and political beliefs.

2586. Daniloff, Nicholas. Two Lives, One Russia. Houghton, 1988. 299 p. $20.
Gr 9+. B 85: Sep 15 1988. U.S. journalist Daniloff, working in Moscow, was arrested as a spy. This memoir of his experiences also discusses the experiences of his grandfather who was sent to Siberia for anti-Czarist activities.

2587. Martin, John Bartlow. It Seems Like Only Yesterday: Memoirs of Writing, Presidential Politics, and Diplomatic Life. Morrow, 1986. 384 p. $20.
Adult. LJ 111: Sep 1 1986. Includes the personal and professional recollections of a journalist who was active in the Kennedy and Johnson campaigns and served as U.S. ambassador to the Dominican Republic.

2588. Nagorski, Andrew. Reluctant Farewell. Holt, 1985. 291 p. $17.
Adult. B 82: Dec 1 1985. LJ 110: Dec 1985. Newsweek magazine's Moscow bureau chief shares his experiences with the Soviet people and their government.

2589. Westman, Paul. Walter Cronkite; The Most Trusted Man in America. (Taking Part Books). Dillon Press, 1980. 47 p. ill. $7.
Gr 3-4. +- BC 34: Jan 81. SLJ 27: Nov 1980. A simple biography that describes Cronkite's work and association with the events and the famous people of the time.

2590. White, William S. Making of a Journalist, The. University Press of Kentucky, 1986. 264 p. ill. $22.
Adult. B 83: Sep 1 1986. LJ 111: Sep 1 1986. An insider's view of the Kennedy and Johnson administrations and other political events, along with personal biographical data.

Judicial Branch and Judges

2591. Bentley, Judith. Justice Sandra Day O'Connor. Messner, 1983. 125 p. ill. $10.
Gr 6-8. B 80: Jan 15 1984. SLJ 30: Feb 1984. VOYA 7: Jun 1984 Emphasizes O'Connor's adult life as attorney, judge, and Supreme Court justice. Includes quotes from family and friends and from her speeches and writing.

2592. Fox, Mary Virginia. Justice Sandra Day O'Connor. Enslow, 1983. 96 p. ill. $13.

Gr 5-9. B 79: Apr 1 1983. VOYA 6: Jun 1983. An introduction to the life of the first woman Supreme Court justice, enhanced by quotes from acquaintances and colleagues.

2593. Friedman, Leon. Supreme Court, The. (Know Your Government). Chelsea House, 1987. 92 p. ill. $13. Gr 6-9. B 83: Jun 1 1987. SLJ 33: Jun/Jul 1987. Covers Supreme Court history, organization, daily work, and pivotal court cases. Numerous photos.

2594. Goode, Stephen. Controversial Court: Supreme Court Influences on American Life. Messner, 1982. 192 p. ill. $10. Gr 7+. * B 78: May 1 1982. * VOYA 6: Feb 1983. Compares the Warren and Burger courts and their responses to controversial issues. Clarifies "judicial activism" and "judicial restraint."

2595. O'Brien, David M. Storm Center: The Supreme Court in American Politics. Norton, 1986. 321 p. ill. $19. Gr 9+. B 82: Jun 15 1986. LJ 111: Jul 1986. A first-rate primer for those seeking to understand the modern Supreme Court.

2596. Rierden, Anne B. Reshaping the Supreme Court: New Justices, New Directions. Watts, 1988. 128 p. ill. $12. Gr 8+. B 85: Sep 15 1988. +- BR 7: Sep/Oct 1988. Covers the Burger and Rehnquist courts, explains judicial restraint and activism, and provides information on the justices.

2597. Witt, Elder. Different Justice: Reagan and the Supreme Court. (Congressional Quarterly). Congressional Quarterly, 1986. 208 p. ill. Pb $12. Gr 9+. * BR 5: Nov/Dec 1986. An overview of the Court which focuses on Reagan's attempt to make it more conservative.

2598. Woods, Harold. Equal Justice: A Biography of Sandra Day O'Connor. (Reaching Out). Dillon Press, 1985. 127 p. ill. $10. Gr 6-8. +- B 82: Nov 1 1985. +- BR 4: Jan/Feb 1986. SLJ 32: Sep 1985. This biography includes numerous quotes from O'Connor's writings and clarifies her political philosophy. Includes photographs of the justice and of the Day and O'Connor families.

2599. Woodward, Bob. Brethren: Inside the Supreme Court. Simon & Schuster, 1980. 467 p. ill. $14. Gr 9+. B 76: Feb 15 1980. LJ 105: Feb 15 1980. Investigates the work and personalities of the Court from 1969 to 1975.

Ku Klux Klan

2600. Thompson, Jerry. My Life in the Klan: A True Story by the First Investigative Reporter to Infiltrate the Ku Klux Klan. Putnam, 1982. 320 p. $15. Gr 9+. B 78: Jun 15 1982. LJ 107: Jun 15 1982. Thompson infiltrated the Klan for 16 months (1979-80), and presents an accurate but disturbing account of racism and violence.

Labor Unions and Laborers

2601. Employment in America. (Congressional Quarterly). Congressional Quarterly, 1983. 208 p. $10. Gr 9+. BR 2: Jan/Feb 1984. Changes in the labor force and employment trends since World War II, including automation, foreign competition and regulations.

2602. Huck, Gary. Bye! American: The Labor Cartoons. Charles H. Kerr, 1987. 111 p. ill. $20. Pb $9. Gr 9+. B 84: Sep 1 1987. A collection of forceful labor cartoons and puns by editorial cartoonists whose work appears in over 100 union newspapers.

Massachusetts

2603. Lukas, J. Anthony. Common Ground. Knopf, 1985. 672 p. maps. $20. Adult. B 81: Jun 15 1985. * LJ 110: Aug 1985. The politics of neighborhoods and communities in Boston, focusing on three families, black, Irish, and WASP.

Mexican Americans

2604. Ashabranner, Brent. Vanishing Border: A Photographic Journey along Our Frontier with Mexico. Dodd, 1987. 175 p. ill. $15. Gr 6+. B 84: Feb 1 1988. BC 41: Mar 1988. * SE 52: Apr/May 1988. SLJ 34: Feb 1988. The problems of the border, illegal aliens, smuggling, and poverty are told through interviews, supported by facts, statistics, and photos.

2605. Hall, Douglas Kent. Border: Life on the Line. Abbeville Press, 1988. 249 p. ill. $35. Gr 9+. B 85: Sep 1 1988. +- LJ 113: Oct 1 1988. A photographer's insightful personal view of life on the border where two distinct cultures meet.

2606. Langley, Lester D. MexAmerica: Two Countries, One Future. Crown, 1988. 312 p. $20. Gr 9+. LJ 113: Jul 1988. VOYA 11: Oct 1988. An insightful analysis of the obstacles to the mutually beneficial settlement of Mexicans in several U.S. cities, including Chicago, Houston, San Diego, Los Angeles, San Antonio, Kansas City, and Denver.

Migrant Labor

2607. Ashabranner, Brent. Dark Harvest: Migrant Farmworkers in America. Dodd, 1985. 160 p. ill. $15. Gr 7+. +- B 82: Sep 1 1985. BC 39: Dec 1985. * BR 5: Sep/Oct 1986. HB 62: Mar/Apr 1986. SE 50: Apr/May 1986. SLJ 32: Dec 1985. A powerful collection of oral histories that document the tragedy of migrant laborers who suffer from wretched working and living conditions, disease, child labor, and inadequate education.

Military History

2608. Miller, D. M. O. Balance of Military Power: An Illustrated Assessment Comparing the Weapons and Capabilities of NATO and the Warsaw Pact. St. Martin's, 1982. 208 p. ill. $25.

Gr 9+. LJ 107: Mar 15 1982. SLJ 28: Apr 1982. Over 400 photos, charts, and tables accompany a somewhat technical text that compares NATO and Soviet bloc military strength.

2609. Tobias, Sheila. What Kinds of Guns Are They Buying for Your Butter? A Beginner's Guide to Defense, Weaponary, and Military Spending. Morrow, 1982. 474 p. $14.
Gr 9+. B 79: Oct 15 1982. This layman's guide to the history of military equipment and strategy provides clear descriptions of modern weaponry and includes statistics, technical details, costs, and informative notes.

Military Personnel

2610. Coffey, Thomas M. Iron Eagle: The Turbulent Life of General Curtis LeMay. Crown, 1986. 480 p. $19.
Gr 10+. B 82: Jun 1 1986. LJ 111: Jul 1986. A biography of Curtis LeMay who led innovative bombing programs during W.W. II, developed the Strategic Air Command, guided the Air Force into the space age, and served as Air Force chief of staff (1961-1965).

Nuclear Power

2611. Stephens, Mark. Three Mile Island: The Hour by Hour Account of What Really Happened. Random House, 1981. 245 p. $12.
Gr 9+. B 77: Nov 1 1980. LJ 106: Jan 1 1981. SLJ 27: May 1981. VOYA 4: Jun 1981. An hour-by-hour account that records the events, the confusion among the regulatory agencies, and the reactions of politicians, when a potentially deadly accident occurred at the nuclear power plant at Three Mile Island.

Nuclear Warfare

2612. Powaski, Ronald E. March to Armageddon: The United States and the Nuclear Arms Race, 1939 to the Present. Oxford University Press, 1987. 304 p. $20.
Gr 9+. B 83: Jun 15 1987. LJ 112: Sep 1 1987. A thorough and well-written review of the nuclear arms race since 1945.

2613. Smoke, Richard. Think about Nuclear Arms Control: Understanding the Arms Race. (Think Series). Walker, 1988. 176 p. ill. $15. Pb $6.
Gr 9+. * SLJ 34: May 1988. Provides a historic perspective on nuclear arms control, information on both sides of the issue, supporting documents, and an analysis of future prospects. Spine title: Nuclear Arms Control.

Nuclear Waste

2614. Barlett, Donald L. Forevermore: Nuclear Waste in America. Norton, 1985. 316 p. ill. $18.
Gr 9+. B 81: Apr 1 1985. LJ 110: Mar 1 1985. A well-documented and readable history of 30 years of failure to deal with the dangers of nuclear waste.

Peace Corps

2615. Fitzgerald, Merni Ingrassia. Peace Corps Today, The. Dodd, 1986. 128 p. ill. $12.
Gr 5-7. B 82: Jun 1 1986. BC 40: Sep 1986. SLJ 33: Sep 1986. This introduction to Peace Corps history includes recollections by volunteers and information on the selection and training process. Photos provide a sense of the widely varied experiences of Peace Corps workers.

2616. Redmon, Coates. Come as You Are: The Peace Corps Story. Harcourt, 1986. 414 p. ill. $23.
Gr 10+. B 83: Oct 1 1986. +- LJ 111: Oct 15 1986. A first-person account of the early years of the Peace Corps.

2617. Rice, Gerard. Bold Experiment: JFK'S Peace Corps. University of Notre Dame Press, 1985. 342 p. $16.
Adult. LJ 110: Nov 1 1985. A clear account of the origins and structure of the Peace Corps and the training of early volunteers.

2618. Viorst, Milton. Making a Difference: The Peace Corps at Twenty-Five. Weidenfield & Nicolson, 1986. 218 p. $17.
Gr 9+. B 83: Oct 1 1986. LJ 111: Nov 1 1986. Essays, letters and comments by individuals involved in the formative years of the Peace Corps.

Politics

2619. Choosing the President, 1984. Nick Lyons Books; dist. by Schocken, 1984. 112 p. Pb $6.
Gr 9+. B 80: Mar 15 1984. BR 3: Sep 1984. SLJ 30: Apr 1984. * VOYA 7: Oct 1984. Describes the election process, political action committees, and the pros and cons of the electoral college. Updated each election year. Sponsored by the League of Women Voters Educational Fund.

2620. Historic Documents of 1978: Cumulative Index 1974-1978. (Congressional Quarterly). Congressional Quarterly, 1979. 965 p. $39.
Gr 10+. B 76: May 1 1980. Includes selected letters and reports from President Carter, excerpts from Supreme Court decisions, the Camp David accords and other international documents, plus the index for Historic Documents volumes 1974-1978.

2621. Historic Documents of 1982. (Congressional Quarterly). Congressional Quarterly, 1983. 1021 p. $57.
Gr 10+. BR 3: May/Jun 1984. Provides background information on the major events of the year including Supreme Court decisions, a report on Soviet agriculture, and the State of the Union address.

2622. Presidential Campaign, 1976, The; Vol. 3, the Debates. Congress. House. Committee on House Administration, 1979. 285 p. $5.

Gr 10+. B 76: Jan 15 1980. Includes transcripts of the debates between Gerald Ford and Jimmy Carter, FCC decisions on equal time and financing, and comments by the press.

2623. Barone, Michael. Almanac of American Politics: The President, the Senators, the Representatives, the Govenors: Their Records and Election Results, Their States and Districts, 1984. National Journal, 1983. 1402 p. $38. Pb $25.
Gr 9+. B 80: Aug 1984. The broad coverage of this biannual serial includes information on topics such as campaign financing, political action committees, power politics, and state and federal elected officials.

2624. Bornstein, Jerry. Neo-Nazis: The Threat of the Hitler Cult. Messner, 1986. 132 p. $11.
Gr 7+. B 83: Jan 15 1987. +- SLJ 33: Feb 1987. Traces the history of American Naziism, describes personalities, tactics, and ties with other extremist groups, and discusses Nazi terrorist tactics.

2625. Brookhiser, Richard. Outside Story: How Democrats and Republicans Re-elected Reagan. Doubleday, 1986. 298 p. $17.
Adult. LJ 111: Jun 1 1986. A thorough analysis of the causes of the 1984 Reagan landslide.

2626. Brooks, Charles. Best Editorial Cartoons of the Year: 1988 Edition. Pelican, 1988. 160 p. Pb $10.
Gr 7+. B 84: Jun 1 1988. BR 7: Sep/Oct 1988. Political cartoons of 1987, covering the stock market, TV evangelists, political figures, Canada, and other major topics. Includes information on the cartoonists and major awards.

2627. Drew, Elizabeth. Campaign Journal: The Political Events of 1983-1984. Macmillan, 1985. 352 p. $18.
Adult. B 81: Jan 1 1985. LJ 110: Apr 15 1985. The Mondale-Reagan campaign seen through selected typical events.

2628. Duke, Paul. Beyond Reagan: The Politics of Upheaval. Warner, 1986. 338 p. Pb $10.
Gr 10+. LJ 111: Jun 1 1986. These essays are based on the Washington Week in Review television programs broadcast during the Reagan administration and cover politics, defense, fundamentalism, and terrorism.

2629. Ervin, Sam J. Whole Truth: The Watergate Conspiracy. Random House, 1981. 311 p. $15.
Adult. LJ 106: Jan 15 1981. A clear account of the Watergate conspiracy by the senator who chaired the investigative committee.

2630. Feiffer, Jules. Ronald Reagan in Movie America: A Jules Feiffer Production. Andrews and Mc-Meel, 1988. 127 p. ill. Pb $8.
Gr 9+. B 84: Jul 1988. Political cartoonist Feiffer looses barbs at the Reagan administration, liberals, the media, and others.

2631. Finch, Phillip. God, Guts, and Guns: A Close Look at the Radical Right. Seaview/Putnam, 1983. 240 p. $16.

Adult. +- LJ 108: Mar 1 1983. An introduction to numerous extreme right-wing groups, including the KKK, John Birch Society, and Nazis.

2632. Graber, Doris A. Mass Media and American Politics. (Congressional Quarterly). Congressional Quarterly, 1980. 304 p. $7.
Gr 9+. SLJ 27: Sep 1980. This thorough treatment of the impact of media coverage on the perceptions of voters, individual privacy, and crises, also discusses the unevenness of foreign coverage and alternative media.

2633. Henry, William. Visions of America: How We Saw the 1984 Election. Atlantic Monthly Press, 1985. 275 p. $18.
Adult. B 81: Aug 1985. LJ 110: Oct 15 1985. This exploration of how the voters saw the election, and the impact of the electronic media, includes interviews with campaign leaders.

2634. Keefe, William. Parties, Politics, and Public Policy in America. (Congressional Quarterly). 5th ed. Congressional Quarterly, 1988. 300 p. Pb $15.
Gr 9+. BR 7: May/Jun 1988. Explores the currently weak condition of American political parties and the role they play in the political process. Includes tables and graphs.

2635. O'Connor, Patricia Ann. Iran-Contra Puzzle, The. (Congressional Quarterly). Congressional Quarterly, 1987. 495 p. $30.
Gr 9+. BR 7: Sep/Oct 1988. An overview is followed by information on the investigation and the struggle between the executive and legislative branches. Includes character sketches, a chronology, testimony, and documents.

2636. Polsby, Nelson W. Presidential Elections: Strategies of American Electoral Politics. 5th ed. Scribner, 1980. 300 p. $13. Pb $7.
Gr 9+. B 76: May 1 1980. For advanced readers, this covers the battle for the presidency, including financing, the campaign and convention, interest groups, political parties, and recent reforms.

2637. Reston, James. Reston's Washington. Macmillan, 1986. 256 p. $18.
Gr 10+. LJ 111: Oct 1 1986. A thoughtful personal look, by one of America's most noted journalists, at nine topics including the presidency, the press, and U.S. culture since 1967.

2638. Seib, Philip. Who's In Charge? How the Media Shape News and Politicians Win Votes. Taylor, 1988. 174 p. $15.
Gr 7+. B 84: May 15 1988. LJ 113: Jun 1 1988. Discusses the relationship between politics and the media since the 1970s and the responsibilities of the media in a democracy.

2639. Smith, Curt. Long Time Gone: The Years of Turmoil Remembered. Icarus; dist. by Harper, 1982. 239 p. ill. $16.
Gr 9+. B 79: Mar 1 1983. LJ 107: Nov 1 1982. Examines 1969-1973 by means of interviews with leaders of the cataclysmic time, including Richard Nixon, Billy Graham, George Wallace, Julian Bond, and others.

2640. Spero, Robert. Duping of the American Voter: Dishonesty and Deception in Presidential Television and Advertising. Lippincott, 1980. 256 p. $13.
Gr 9+. B 76: Jul 1 1980. LJ 105: Jul 1980. Lambastes politicians for manipulating the media, reveals dishonesty in past campaigns, and suggests resolutions for change.

2641. Taylor, L. B. New Right, The. (Impact Book). Watts, 1981. 88 p. $8.
Gr 7-9. B 78: Dec 15 1981. * SE 46: Apr 1982. Examines the evolution of new conservative groups and their beliefs, and compares these to the beliefs of more liberal groups.

2642. Tower, John. Tower Commission Report: The Full Text of the President's Special Review Board. Bantam/Times Books, 1987. 550 p. Pb $6.
Gr 9+. B 83: May 15 1987. The complete report of the Tower Commission that explored the Iran-Contra affair.

2643. Trager, Oliver. Iran-Contra Arms Scandal, The. (Editorials on File Book.) Facts on File, 1988. 224 p. $25.
Gr 9+. +- BR 7: Sep/Oct 1988. A wide range of opinions is represented in this collection of editorials and political cartoons. A summary of events introduces each episode. Includes a chronology.

2644. Udall, Morris K. Too Funny to Be President. Holt, 1988. 249 p. $18.
Gr 10+. LJ 112: Dec 1987. VOYA 11: Jun 1988. A delightful book of political humor, written by the man chosen in 1984 as the most effective and respected member of Congress.

2645. Wayne, Stephen J. Road to the White House: The Politics of Presidential Elections. St. Martin's, 1980. 269 p. ill. $11. Pb $6.
Gr 9+. B 77: Sep 1 1980. Analyzes contemporary presidential electoral politics, the electoral college, campaign financing, and the impact of the media.

2646. White, Theodore H. Making of the President. Atheneum, 1969. 459 p. maps. $10.
Gr 10+. B 84: Sep 1 1987. LJ 94: Sep 15 1969. Chronicles the people, events, and issues of the election of 1968, including the Chicago riots at the Democratic convention and the assassination of Robert Kennedy.

Presidency and the Executive Branch

2647. President Reagan. (Congressional Quarterly). Congressional Quarterly, 1981. 123 p. ill. $8.
Gr 9+. B 77: Jul 1 1981. LJ 106: Jul 1981. SLJ 28: Nov 1981. Profiles Reagan's career and covers his vice-president, cabinet, White House staff, and his liaison on Capitol Hill.

2648. Barrett, Laurence I. Gambling with History: Ronald Reagan in the White House. Doubleday, 1983. 552 p. ill. $20.
Gr 9+. B 79: Jun 15 1983. LJ 108: Jun 1 1983. Examines the first years of the Reagan presidency.

2649. Bernstein, Carl. All the President's Men. Simon & Schuster; Warner, 1974. 349 p. Pb $5.
Gr 9+. B 82: Jan 1 1986. The investigation that precipitated the Watergate scandal.

2650. Block, Herbert. Herblock Through the Looking Glass. Norton, 1984. 256 p. ill. $13.
Gr 9+. B 81: Nov 15 1984. Herblock's cartoons cover Reagan's fiscal policy, cabinet, defense strategy, civil rights policies, etc.

2651. Bornet, Vaughn Davis. Presidency of Lyndon B. Johnson, The. (American Presidency Series). University of Kansas Press, 1983. 432 p. $25. Pb $15.
Adult. LJ 108: Oct 1 1983. This subject approach to the Johnson presidency examines the Great Society, Vietnam, Johnson's health, relations with the media, and other topics.

2652. Campling, Elizabeth. Kennedy. (World Leaders in Context). Batsford, 1980. 96 p. $15.
Gr 7+. SLJ 27: Apr 1981. A balanced account of the Kennedy presidency written by a British author.

2653. Carter, Jimmy. Keeping Faith: Memoirs of a President. Bantam, 1982. 622 p. ill. $23.
Gr 9+. B 79: Nov 15 1982. LJ 107: Dec 15 1982. Carter presents his view of the major domestic and foreign problems of his administration.

2654. Cook, Fred J. Crimes of Watergate, The. Watts, 1981. 183 p. ill. $9.
Gr 7+. +- B 78: Nov 15 1981. BC 35: Apr 1982. SLJ 28: Aug 1982. This clear summary uses quotes liberally and introduces the major personalities involved in the Watergate affair.

2655. Green, Mark. Reagan's Reign of Error: The Instant Nostalgia Edition. Pantheon, 1987. 176 p. ill. Pb $7.
Gr 9+. B 84: Feb 1 1988. Catalogs Reagan's misstatements on foreign policy, defense, economics, social programs, energy, justice, and other topics, presents the facts, and argues for truth in government.

2656. Jordan, Hamilton. Crisis: The Last Year of the Carter Presidency. Putnam, 1982. 431 p. ill. $17.
Gr 9+. B 79: Oct 15 1982. LJ 107: Dec 1 1982. For the advanced student, a balanced examination of the hostage crisis and the difficult reelection campaign of 1980.

2657. Killian, James. Sputnik, Scientists, and Eisenhower. MIT Press, 1977. 315 p. $33. Pb $10.
Adult. B 85: Oct 1 1988. LJ 103: Jan 15 1978. The author served as science advisor to President Eisenhower. This covers the beginning of the U.S. space program, the development of the ICBM, and the opening of arms control talks with the U.S.S.R.

2658. King, Anthony. Both Ends of the Avenue: The Presidency, the Executive Branch, and Congress in the 1980's. American Enterprise Institute, 1983. 272 p. $17. Pb $9.
Adult. LJ 108: Sep 15 1983. Nine essays on changes in congressional-presidential relationships from Kennedy

through Reagan, and on presidential management style and negotiating skills.

2659. Mollenhoff, Clark R. President Who Failed: Carter Out of Control. Free Press, 1980. 264 p. $11.
Gr 9+. B 76: Apr 15 1980. LJ 105: Jul 1980. Mollenhoff analyzes the policies and performance of the Carter administration and finds them unsatisfactory.

2660. Pierpoint, Robert. At the White House: Assignments to Six Presidents. Putnam, 1981. 240 p. ill. $12.
Gr 9+. B 78: Sep 1 1981. LJ 106: Jul 1981. These memoirs of a CBS White House reporter convey the flavor of the different administrations and the successes and failures of presidential coverage.

2661. Randall, Marta. John F. Kennedy. (World Leaders Past and Present Series). Chelsea House, 1987. 112 p. ill. $17.
Gr 9+. B 84: Jan 15 1988. BR 7: Sep/Oct 1988. * VOYA 11: Oct 1988. Photos on every page, numerous quotes, and a chronology highlight this work that emphasizes the major issues of the Kennedy presidency.

2662. Schlesinger, Arthur M., Jr. Thousand Days: John F. Kennedy in the White House. Fawcett, 1965. 1087 p. Pb $4.
Gr 11+. B 84: Sep 1 1987. LJ 90: Nov 1965. LJ 90: Nov 1 1965. A detailed chronicle of Kennedy's nomination, campaign, inauguration, and administration, including the glory and the problems.

Presidency and the Executive Branch–Cabinet, Agencies, etc.

2663. McGehee, Ralph W. Deadly Deceits: My 25 Years in the CIA. Sheridan Square, 1983. 231 p. $15. Pb $8.
Gr 9+. B 79: Apr 15 1983. LJ 108: Apr 1 1983. A controversial examination of the CIA as it has been, and as it is in the 1980s, with recommendations for change.

Presidents and Their Families

2664. Bruce, Preston. From the Door of the White House. Lothrop, 1984. 176 p. $11.
Gr 6+. B 81: Dec 15 1984. +- BC 38: Dec 1984. SE 49: Apr 1985. SLJ 31: Jan 1985. The autobiography of a White House doorman provides a sympathetic view of presidents Eisenhower through Ford and their families.

2665. Gardner, Gerald. All the Presidents' Wits: The Power of Presidential Humor. Morrow, 1986. 300 p. ill. $16.
Gr 9+. B 83: Sep 1 1986. LJ 111: Sep 1 1986. Anecdotes and humor illustrate the personalities and approaches to humor of recent presidents.

2666. Kellerman, Barbara. All the President's Kin. Free Press, 1981. 345 p. $15.
Gr 10+. LJ 106: Jul 1981. Examines the roles of various family members and their impact on the presidency, from Kennedy through Carter.

2667. Smith, Elizabeth Simpson. Five First Ladies: A Look into the Lives of Nancy Reagan, Rosalynn Carter, Betty Ford, Pat Nixon, and Lady Bird Johnson. Walker, 1986. 128 p. ill. $13.
Gr 5+. +- BC 40: Dec 1986. BR 5: Jan/Feb 1987. A brief and easy-to-read introduction that presents the backgrounds and duties of the first ladies.

Presidents and Their Families–Bush

2668. Bush, George. Looking Forward. Doubleday, 1987. 257 p. ill. $19.
Gr 9+. B 84: Oct 1 1987. LJ 112: Oct 1 1987. SLJ 34: Mar 1988. Anecdotal memoirs of Bush's experiences as a Navy pilot, Texas oil man, representative to the U.N. and China, director of the CIA, and vice-president.

2669. King, Nicholas. George Bush: A Biography. Dodd, 1980. 146 p. ill. $8. Pb $6.
Gr 10+. +- LJ 105: Nov 1 1980. A superficial overview of Bush's accomplishments before his 1980 vice-presidential candidacy.

Presidents and Their Families–Carter

2670. Carter, Rosalynn. First Lady from Plains. Houghton, 1984. 357 p. ill. $18.
Gr 10+. +- B 80: Apr 1 1984. +- LJ 109: May 1 1984. The former first lady speaks out on the Carter administration.

2671. Glad, Betty. Jimmy Carter: In Search of the Great White House. Norton, 1980. 546 p. $20.
Gr 9+. B 77: Sep 15 1980. Analyzes Carter's personal life and political career, examining his personal strengths and weaknesses, and those of his administration.

2672. Smith, Betsy Covington. Jimmy Carter, President. Walker, 1986. 124 p. ill. $13.
Gr 5-10. B 83: Feb 15 1987. SLJ 33: Dec 1986. A balanced, anecdotal portrayal of Carter's personal and political life.

Presidents and Their Families–Ford

2673. Randolph, Sallie G. Gerald R. Ford, President. (Presidential Biography Series). Walker, 1987. 120 p. ill. $13. Lib. ed. $14.
Gr 4-9. B 83: Jul 1987. BR 6: Nov/Dec 1987. +- SLJ 33: Aug 1987. Based on Ford's recollections, enlivened by quotes, anecdotes, and photos.

Presidents and Their Families–Johnson

2674. Conkin, Paul K. Big Daddy from the Pedernales: Lyndon B. Johnson. (Twayne's Twentieth Century American Biography Series). Twayne, 1986. 312 p. ill. $20. Pb $10.
Gr 9+. HT 21: Aug 1988. LJ 111: Oct 1 1986. SLJ 33: May 1987. This balanced treatment of Johnson's life and career is the first in the series.

2675. Devaney, John. Lyndon Baines Johnson, President. (Presidential Biography Series). Walker, 1986. 94 p. ill. $13. Lib. ed. $13.
Gr 5-10. B 83: Sep 1 1986. SLJ 33: Nov 1986. Emphasizes Johnson's capacity for political scheming and

his high ambition. Includes photos and anecdotes on his relations with other national leaders.

2676. Hargrove, Jim. Lyndon B. Johnson. (Encyclopedia of Presidents). Childrens Press, 1988. 100 p. ill. $15.
Gr 4-7. B 84: May 15 1988. This well-rounded biography of Lyndon B. Johnson includes photos and a chronology.

2677. Kaye, Tony. Lyndon B. Johnson. (World Leaders Past and Present Series). Chelsea House, 1987. 112 p. ill. $17.
Gr 5-10. B 84: Jan 15 1988. SLJ 34: Apr 1988. A balanced biography, with numerous photos and quotes, showing Johnson's successes as a senator, his Great Society program, and the devastating effects of the Vietnamese War on his presidency.

2678. Miller, Merle. Lyndon: An Oral Biography. Putnam, 1980. 637 p. $18.
Gr 9+. B 77: Sep 1 1980. * LJ 105: Sep 1 1980. Based on comments from family, friends, and associates, this biography captures Johnson's attributes and flaws.

2679. Reedy, George E. Lyndon Johnson: A Memoir. Andrews & McMeel, 1982. 176 p. $13.
Adult. LJ 107: Nov 1 1982. Johnson's press secretary (1964-1965) provides a negative personal view of the president, balanced by his admiration of Johnson's political expertise.

Presidents and Their Families–Kennedy

2680. Collier, Peter. Kennedys: An American Drama. Summit, 1984. 576 p. ill. $21.
Gr 9+. B 80: Aug 1984. LJ 109: Sep 15 1984. SE 49: May 1985. A popular coverage of Kennedy family history that emphasizes their competitiveness, ambition, and their serious problems.

2681. Falkof, Lucille. John F. Kennedy: Thirty-Fifth President of the United States. (Presidents of the United States). Garrett Educational Corp., 1988. 119 p. ill. $13.
Gr 6-9. * BR 7: Nov/Dec 1988. +- SLJ 35: Oct 1988. Emphasizes Kennedy's background and personal life, with enough information about historic issues and events to place him in context.

2682. Gadney, Reg. Kennedy. Holt, 1983. 176 p. ill. $23.
Gr 9+. SLJ 30: Feb 1984. The balanced account of Kennedy's personal life enhanced by a collection of well-coordinated photos.

2683. Goodwin, Doris Kearns. Fitzgeralds and the Kennedys, The. Simon & Schuster, 1987. 864 p. ill. $23.
Adult. B 83: Dec 15 1986. * LJ 112: Feb 15 1987. A clear and balanced treatment of the ambitions, glories, and tragedies of the Fitzgeralds and the Kennedys.

2684. Hurt, Henry. Reasonable Doubt: An Investigation into the Assassination of John F. Kennedy. Holt, 1985. 531 p. $19.

Gr 9+. B 82: Nov 15 1985. SLJ 32: Aug 1986. A well-researched synthesis of previous writing on the assassination.

2685. Kent, Zachary. John F. Kennedy: Thirty-Fifth President of the United States. (Encyclopedia of Presidents). Childrens Press, 1987. 99 p. ill. $15.
Gr 4-9. B 84: Dec 15 1987. SLJ 34: Dec 1987. A balanced text covers Kennedy's successes and failures. Easy to read, highly illustrated, with a chronology and numerous quotations.

2686. Langley, Andrew. John F. Kennedy. (Great Lives). Bookwright Press; dist. by Watts, 1986. 31 p. ill. $10.
Gr 4-7. SLJ 33: Aug 1986. Focuses on Kennedy's achievements. The photos make this suitable for browsers as well as for those needing facts.

2687. MacNeil, Robert. Way We Were: 1963: The Year Kennedy Was Shot. Carrol & Graf, 1988. 256 p. ill. $40.
Gr 9+. B 85: Oct 1 1988. The emphasis is on JFK himself, but this highly illustrated volume also covers the people, politics, and culture of the U.S. in 1963.

2688. Manchester, William. One Brief Shining Moment: Remembering Kennedy. Little, 1983. 280 p. ill. $25.
Gr 10+. B 84: Sep 1 1987. LJ 109: Feb 15 1984. Written by a friend, this memoir covers Kennedy's personal and political life, his relationship with his vice-president, Lyndon Johnson, and his assassination.

2689. Martin, Ralph G. Hero for Our Time: An Intimate Story of the Kennedy Years. Macmillan, 1983. 608 p. ill. $20.
Gr 9+. B 79: Jul 1983. LJ 108: Aug 1983. Using quotes from interviews, reminiscences, witticisms, and anecdotes, Martin provides a picture of the Kennedy era and family.

2690. Mills, Judie. John F. Kennedy. Watts, 1988. 384 p. ill. $15.
Gr 9+. B 84: Jun 15 1988. * BC 41: Jun 1988. - BR 7: Sep/Oct 1988. * SLJ 34: May 1988. VOYA 11: Aug 1988. A thorough and balanced coverage of Kennedy's youth, early political career, and presidency.

2691. Parmet, Herbert S. Jack: The Struggles of John F. Kennedy. Dial, 1980. 704 p. ill. $15.
Adult. LJ 105: May 15 1980. A balanced biography of JFK's pre-presidential years.

2692. Parmet, Herbert S. JFK: The Presidency of John F. Kennedy. Dial, 1983. 608 p. ill. $20.
Adult. B 79: Jan 15 1983. +- LJ 108: Feb 1 1983. Examines the major events of the Kennedy presidency, but the emphasis is on Kennedy's personality and private life.

2693. Sheed, Wilfrid. Kennedy Legacy, The. Viking, 1988. 210 p. ill. $25.
Gr 9+. +- B 84: May 1 1988. LJ 113: Sep 15 1988. This memorial to the Kennedy legend is enhanced by numerous photos by J.F.K.'s official photographer.

2694. Smith, Kathie Billingslea. John F. Kennedy. (Great Americans Series). Messner, 1987. Unp. ill. $8. Pb $3.
Gr 2-4. SLJ 34: Mar 1988. An easy-to-read overview of Kennedy's life that shows his early interest in reading and in world events.

2695. Stein, R. Conrad. Story of the Assassination of John F. Kennedy, The. (Cornerstones of Freedom). Childrens Press, 1985. 31 p. ill. $10.
Gr 3-5. B 82: Mar 15 1986. SLJ 32: Mar 1986. Faithfully relates the events of the Dallas tragedy.

2696. Tregaskis, Richard. John F. Kennedy and PT-109. (Landmark Books). Random House, 1962. 192 p. ill. $6.
Gr 7-8. Metzner [B 58: Apr 15 1962. LJ 87: Apr 15 1962]. Explains the important role of the PT boat in the South Pacific and shows Kennedy's heroism when his PT boat was sunk.

Presidents and Their Families–Nixon

2697. Ambrose, Stephen E. Nixon: The Education of a Politician, 1913-1962. Simon & Schuster, 1987. 695 p. ill. $23.
Adult. B 83: Feb 15 1987. * LJ May 1 1987. LJ 113: Jan 1988. The first of two projected volumes that reconsider Nixon's career in historical context. This volume thoroughly covers his pre-presidential years.

2698. Anson, Robert Sam. Exile: The Unquiet Oblivion of Richard M. Nixon. Simon & Schuster, 1984. 360 p. $18.
Adult. B 80: Jun 1 1984. LJ 109: Aug 1984. Examines Nixon's life since his resignation.

2699. Hargrove, Jim. Richard M. Nixon: The Thirty-Seventh President. (People of Distinction Biographies) Childrens Press, 1985. 128 p. ill. $9.
Gr 5-7. B 82: Nov 1 1985. An even-handed biography for young readers.

2700. Lillegard, Dee. Richard Nixon: Thirty-Seventh President of the United States. (Encyclopedia of Presidents). Childrens Press, 1988. 100 p. ill. $15.
Gr 4-7. B 84: Aug 1988. +- SLJ 35: Oct 1988. This biography of Richard Nixon covers his personal life and political career. It includes photos and a chronology.

2701. Ripley, C. Peter. Richard Nixon. (World Leaders Past and Present Series). Chelsea House, 1987. 112 p. ill. $17.
Gr 9+. B 84: Dec 1 1987. BR 7: May/Jun 1988. SLJ 34: Dec 1987. A thoughtful analysis of Nixon's history of abuse of power through his political life, and of his success in foreign relations.

Presidents and Their Families–Reagan

2702. Behrens, June. Ronald Reagan: An All American. Childrens Press, 1981. 32 p. ill. $7.
Gr 2-4. +- SLJ 28: Mar 1982. A simple biography through Reagan's first inauguration as president. Includes numerous photos.

2703. Boyarsky, Bill. Ronald Reagan: His Life and Rise to the Presidency. Random House, 1981. 205 p. $13.
Gr 9+. B 77: Jun 1981. +- LJ 106: Sep 15 1981. Chronicles the Reagan career through his 1980 candidacy for president.

2704. Cannon, Lou. Reagan. Putnam, 1982. 432 p. $18.
Gr 9+. B 78: Aug 1982. * LJ 107: Oct 1 1982. This critical but sympathetic biography of Reagan's political and personal life through the first year of his presidency provides insight into Reagan's political philosophy.

2705. Edwards, Anne. Early Reagan. Morrow, 1987. 448 p. ill. $22.
Gr 9+. B 83: May 1 1987. LJ 112: Jul 1987. An impartial account of Reagan's personal and political life through 1966. Anecdotal, with lively episodes on many of the notable figures in Reagan's life.

2706. Fox, Mary Virginia. Mister President: The Story of Ronald Reagan. Rev. ed. Enslow, 1986. 160 p. ill. $14.
Gr 4-8. B 83: Nov 1 1986. BR 5: Mar/Apr 1987. +- SLJ 33: Dec 1986. Updates the 1982 edition.

2707. Fox, Mary Virginia. Mister President: The Story of Ronald Reagan. Enslow, 1982. 128 p. ill. $9.
Gr 6-8. +- B 78: May 15 1982. BR 1: Jan/Feb 1983. SLJ 29: Sep 1982. VOYA 5: Aug 1982. An overview of Reagan's life through his election as president.

2708. Friedman, Stanley P. Ronald Reagan: His Life Story in Pictures. Dodd, 1986. 159 p. ill. Pb $13.
Gr 9+. B 83: Nov 15 1986. - BR 5: Mar/Apr 1987. A wealth of photos on the life and careers of the president.

2709. Lawson, Don. Picture Life of Ronald Reagan, The. Rev. ed. Watts, 1984. 48 p. ill. $10.
Gr 2-5. B 77: Jun 1981. B 82: Sep 15 1985. SLJ 32: Sep 1985. An introductory photographic essay of Reagan's life from childhood through his first term as president.

2710. Lawson, Don. Picture Life of Ronald Reagan. Watts, 1981. 48 p. ill. $7.
Gr 3-5. B 77: Jun 1981. SLJ 27: Aug 1981. An introductory photographic essay of the president's life.

2711. Leamer, Laurence. Make-Believe: The Story of Nancy & Ronald Reagan. Harper, 1983. 416 p. ill. $15.
Adult. B 79: May 1 1983. LJ 108: May 1 1983. A detailed biography, covering the personalities of Nancy and Ronald Reagan, the complexities of their lives, and information on the first lady's influence on the president.

2712. Smith, Hedrick. Reagan the Man, the President. Macmillan, 1981. 186 p. ill. $10.
Gr 9+. B 77: Mar 15 1981. LJ 106: Mar 15 1981. An examination of Reagan's personal and political performance, style, and judgment up to the time of his election as president.

2713. Sullivan, George. Ronald Reagan. Messner, 1985. 126 p. ill. $10.

Gr 5-7. B 82: Mar 15 1986. SLJ 32: Jan 1986. This introductory biography that covers Reagan's first administration includes a chapter devoted to Reagan's critics, and is illustrated with well-selected photos.

2714. Wallace, Chris. First Lady: A Portrait of Nancy Reagan. St. Martin's, 1986. 160 p. ill. $23.
Gr 9+. B 83: Sep 1 1986. LJ 111: Oct 1 1986. Based on interviews with President and Mrs. Reagan, their family, friends, and staff.

2715. Wills, Gary. Reagan's America: Innocents at Home. Doubleday, 1987. 451 p. ill. $20.
Gr 10+. B 83: Dec 1 1986. LJ 112: Feb 1 1987. Emphasis is on the persons, experiences, and institutions that molded the Reagan personality and political values. A revealing and provocative analysis.

Public Officials

2716. Political Profiles: The Kennedy Years; The Nixon/Ford Years; The Eisenhower Years; The Johnson Years; The Truman Years; The Carter Years. Facts on File, 1982. 5 vol. $195.
Gr 9+. B 80: Jun 15 1984. Covers the elected and appointed officials and leaders of each administration.

2717. David, Lester. Bobby Kennedy: The Making of a Folk Hero. Dodd, 1986. 416 p. ill. $20.
Gr 9+. B 83: Sep 1 1986. BR 6: Nov/Dec 1987. A balanced overview of Kennedy's career and his influence during his brother's presidential administration.

2718. Deaver, Michael. Behind the Scenes: In Which the Author Talks about Ronald and Nancy Reagan...and Himself. Bantam, 1988. 288 p. ill. $13.
Adult. B 84: Dec 1 1987. LJ 113: Feb 1 1988. Deaver's account of his life in Washington, that led to his indictment for influence peddling, is rich in personal stories about Nancy and Ronald Reagan, whom he has known since the 1960s.

2719. Dole, Robert. Doles: Unlimited Partners. Simon & Schuster, 1988. 272 p. $20.
Gr 9+. B 84: Jan 15 1988. LJ 113: Mar 15 1988. This joint autobiography has alternating chapters by the senator and his wife, Elizabeth, who served as Secretary of Transportation under Reagan and as Secretary of Labor under Bush.

2720. Ehrenhalt, Alan. Politics in America: Members of Congress in Washington and at Home, 1982. (Congressional Quarterly). Congressional Quarterly, 1981. 1382 p. ill. $30.
Gr 9+. B 80: Jun 15 1984. Profiles of U.S. congressmen, 1980-1982, tables of committee memberships, key votes, etc.

2721. Furgurson, Ernest B. Hard Right: The Rise of Jesse Helms. Norton, 1986. 302 p. $19.
Gr 10+. LJ 111: Dec 1986. SLJ 33: May 1987. The political career and beliefs of the North Carolina senator who was a spokesman for the ultra-conservative New Right and known as "Senator No."

2722. Gillies, John. Senor Alcade: A Biography of Henry Cisneros. (People in Focus Book). Dillon Press, 1988. 127 p. ill. $12.
Gr 5-9. B 84: Aug 1988. +- BC 41: Jul 1988. SLJ 35: Sep 1988. Cisneros is the first Hispanic mayor of a major U.S. city (San Antonio). This biography includes many family photos and quotes.

2723. Hayden, Tom. Reunion: A Memoir. Random House, 1988. 518 p. ill. $23.
Gr 9+. B 84: Apr 15 1988. * LJ 113: Jun 15 1988. Hayden's biography explores the major events of the '60s, in many of which he participated, including the anti-war and civil rights demonstrations, and follows this with his analysis of those events as he sees them now.

2724. Hilton, Stanley G. Bob Dole: American Political Phoenix. Contemporary Books, 1988. 256 p. ill. $19.
Adult. LJ 113: Jul 1988. Hilton, a former Dole aide, interprets the senator's personality and political ambitions in light of Dole's background and experiences.

2725. Israel, Fred L. Henry Kissinger. (World Leaders Past and Present Series). Chelsea House, 1986. 116 p. ill. $17.
Gr 6+. B 83: Feb 1 1987. SLJ 33: Mar 1987. This balanced biography traces Kissinger's rise as a foreign policy expert, his work as Nixon's secretary of state and his contributions to other administrations. Numerous photos.

2726. Kennedy, Robert. Robert Kennedy: In His Own Words: The Unpublished Recollections of the Kennedy Years. Bantam, 1988. 528 p. ill. $23.
Gr 10+. BR 7: Nov/Dec 1988. LJ 113: Aug 1988. Includes interviews with Kennedy and his remarks concerning public events in which he participated.

2727. Kenney, Charles. Dukakis: An American Odyssey. Houghton, 1988. 248 p. $17.
Gr 9+. B 84: May 1 1988. LJ 113: Apr 15 1988. A balanced biography of the Massachusetts governor and 1988 Democratic presidential candidate. Based primarily on interviews with supporters and adversaries.

2728. Lewis, Finlay. Mondale: Portrait of an American Politician. Harper, 1980. 304 p. $11.
Gr 9+. B 76: Mar 15 1980. Covers the political career of this U.S. senator and vice-president.

2729. Liddy, G. Gordon. Will: The Autobiography of G. Gordon Liddy. St. Martin's, 1980. 374 p. ill. $14.
Gr 9+. B 76: Jul 1 1980. +- LJ 105: Jun 15 1980. Liddy's autobiography shows his self-righteous attitude and the moral and political values that resulted in his becoming a Watergate co-conspirator.

2730. McElvaine, Robert S. Mario Cuomo. Scribner, 1988. 288 p. $16.
Gr 9+. B 84: May 1 1988. The author presents a lauditory biography of the New York governor.

2731. O'Neill, Tip. Man of the House: The Life and Political Memoirs of Speaker Tip O'Neill. Random House, 1987. 416 p. ill. $20.

Gr 9+. B 83: Aug 1987. * LJ 112: Oct 15 1987. Entertaining recollections and apocryphal stories of O'Neill's acquaintances and experiences.

2732. Roberts, Naurice. Harold Washington: Mayor with a Vision. (Picture-Story Biographies). Childrens Press, 1988. 32 p. ill. $11.
Gr 2-5. +- B 84: Aug 1988. SLJ 35: Sep 1988. A simple introduction to the life and political career of the Chicago mayor.

2733. Roberts, Naurice. Henry Cisneros: Mexican-American Mayor. (Picture-Story Biographies). Childrens Press, 1986. 30 p. ill. $11.
Gr 2-4. B 82: Jul 1986. B 83: Jun 15 1987. SLJ 33: Oct 1986. This short biography of the first Mexican American to be elected mayor of a major American city includes illustrations and a chronology.

2734. Schneider, Tom. Walter Mondale: Serving All the People. (Taking Part Books). Dillon Press, 1984. 63 p. ill. $9.
Gr 4-7. B 81: May 1 1985. +- SLJ 31: Aug 1985. Covers Mondale's early life and career through his nomination for the presidency in 1984.

2735. Westman, Paul. Hubert H. Humphrey: The Politics of Joy. (Taking Part Books). Dillon Press, 1979. 48 p. ill. $6.
Gr 3-6. SLJ 26: Jan 1980. A slightly fictionalized biography of this senator, vice-president, and 1968 Democratic presidential candidate.

Public Officials–Black

2736. Haskins, James. Andrew Young: Man with a Mission. Lothrop, 1979. 192 p. $8.
Gr 4-8. * SE 44: Apr 1980. The biography of a privileged black man who used his abilities to help others.

2737. Jakoubek, Robert E. Adam Clayton Powell, Jr. Chelsea House, 1988. 112 p. ill. $17.
Gr 7+. B 85: Oct 1 1988. VOYA 11: Dec 1988. A candid biography of Powell's career as a preacher, militant anti-racist, and congressman for over 20 years.

2738. Roberts, Naurice. Andrew Young: Freedom Fighter. (Picture-Story Biographies). Childrens Press, 1983. 31 p. ill. $7.
Gr 2-4. +- B 80: Feb 1 1984. SLJ 30: Apr 1984. A short biography of the black politician who was a civil rights worker, served in the Carter administration, and became mayor of Atlanta, Georgia.

Public Officials–Women

2739. Ferraro, Geraldine A. Ferraro: My Story. Bantam, 1985. 352 p. ill. $18. Pb $18.
Gr 9+. B 82: Nov 1 1985. LJ 111: Jan 1986. Ferraro, the first woman to be nominated for vice-president by a major political party, tells her side of the 1984 campaign.

2740. Haskins, James. Fighting Shirley Chisholm. Dial, 1975. 211 p. $6.
Gr 7+. SE 44: Oct 1980. In 1972 Chisholm was elected as the first black woman to serve in the House.

2741. Haskins, James. Shirley Temple Black: Actress to Ambassador. Viking, 1988. 57 p. ill. $11.
Gr 4-6. B 85: Sep 15 1988. BC 42: Nov 1988. This biography emphasizes the youth of the child movie star who became a diplomat.

2742. Lawson, Don. Geraldine Ferraro. Messner, 1985. 64 p. ill. $10.
Gr 6+. B 81: Jul 1985. BR 5: May/Jun 1986. SLJ 32: Sep 1985. Covers Ferraro from her childhood through her 1984 race for the vice-presidency of the United States.

2743. Stineman, Esther. American Political Women: Contemporary and Historical Profiles. Libraries Unlimited, 1980. 228 p. $20.
Gr 9+. SLJ 27: Apr 1981. Sixty biographical sketches of contemporary female office holders.

2744. Williams, Barbara. Breakthrough: Women in Politics. Walker, 1979. 186 p. ill. $10.
Gr 7+. BC 33: Feb 1980. * SE 44: Apr 1980. SLJ 27: Oct 1980. A chapter on the history of women in U.S. politics is followed by profiles of seven women who have achieved political importance, including senators, representatives, governors, and mayors.

Puerto Rican Americans–Fiction

2745. Mohr, Nicholasa. Going Home. Dial, 1986. 192 p. $12. Lib. ed. $12.
Gr 3-7. B 82: Jul 1986. BC 39: May 1986. HB 62: Sep/Oct 1986. SLJ 32: Aug 1986. Felita, a young New Yorker, is of Puerto Rican ancestry and faces prejudice because of this. Then, on a visit to Puerto Rico she faces prejudice because she is an American.

2746. Rivera, Edward. Family Installments: Memories of Growing Up Hispanic. Morrow, 1982. 300 p. $14.
Gr 9+. B 79: Oct 1 1982. LJ 107: Sep 1 1982. An autobiographical novel concerning the coming of age of a Puerto Rican American boy in New York. Told with humor, pride, and style.

Racism–Fiction

2747. Baldwin, James. Evidence of Things Not Seen. Holt, 1985. 144 p. $12.
Gr 10+. +- B 82: Oct 1 1985. - LJ 110: Dec 1985. * VOYA 9: Apr 1986. A novel which explores racism in modern America; based on the conviction of Wayne Williams, convicted of the murder of 28 black children.

Reformers

2748. King, Mary. Freedom Song: A Personal Story of the 1960s Civil Right Movement. Morrow, 1987. 450 p. $20.
Gr 9+. B 83: Jun 1 1987. LJ 112: Jul 1987. A vivid memoir of King's experiences as a white member of the Student Nonviolent Coordinating Committee that led the integration movement of the 1960s.

2749. Roberts, Naurice. Cesar Chavez and La Causa. (Picture-Story Biographies). Childrens Press, 1986. 31 p. ill. $11.

Gr 2-5. B 82: July 1986. B 83: Jun 15 1987. B 84: Feb 1 1988. SLJ 33: Oct 1 1986. An easy-to-read and straightforward biography of the founder of the United Farm Workers, a labor union for migrant workers.

Reformers–Black

2750. Chaplik, Dorothy. Up with Hope: A Biography of Jesse Jackson. (People in Focus Book). Dillon Press, 1986. 126 p. ill. $11.
Gr 5-9. B 83: Jan 1 1987. BC 40: Mar 1987. SLJ 33: Feb 1987. This well-rounded biography covers Jackson's personal life as well as his civil rights and political careers through his first presidential bid.

2751. Farmer, James. Lay Bare the Heart: An Autobiography of the Civil Rights Movement. Arbor House, 1985. 347 p. $18.
Gr 9+. B 81: Mar 1 1985. LJ 110: Mar 1 1984. Farmer founded the Congress of Racial Equality which favored nonviolent demonstrations to overcome discrimination.

2752. Halliburton, Warren J. Picture Life of Jesse Jackson, The. Rev. ed. Watts, 1984. 48 p. ill. $10.
Gr 2-5. B 80: Aug 1984. - SLJ 30: Aug 1984. This update of the 1973 edition concludes before Jackson's 1984 presidential campaign.

2753. Kosof, Anna. Jesse Jackson. Watts, 1987. 112 p. ill. $12.
Gr 6+. B 84: Jan 1 1988. * BR 6: Jan/Feb 1988. SLJ 34: Jan 1988. VOYA 11: Jun 1988. Quotes Jackson, his supporters and opponents, and includes the author's observations. Presents Jackson's personal and political life and his impact on U.S. politics to 1987. Includes photos.

2754. Landess, Thomas H. Jesse Jackson and the Politics of Race. Jameson Books; dist. by Kampmann, 1985. 300 p. $18.
Adult. B 82: Nov 1 1985. LJ 111: Jan 1986. A harsh but realistic portrait of Jackson and his beliefs.

2755. Reynolds, Barbara. Jesse Jackson: America's David. JFS Associates, 1985. 489 p. ill. $18.
Gr 9+. B 82: Nov 1 1985. Examines Jackson's political activities and his strengths and weaknesses as a leader.

2756. Stone, Eddie. Jesse Jackson. Holloway, 1979, 1984. 249 p. $3.
Gr 7+. VOYA 7: Dec 1984. A biography that presents Jackson's personal and political life and his strengths and limitations.

2757. Westman, Paul. Jesse Jackson: I Am Somebody. (Taking Part Books). Dillon Press, 1981. 47 p. ill. $7.
Gr 3-6. B 77: Mar 15 1981. BC 34: May 1981. SLJ 28: Nov 1981. A straightforward, simple biography of Jackson's youth and involvement with various civil rights organizations.

2758. White, C. C. No Quittin' Sense. University of Texas Press, 1969. 216 p. $6.
Gr 10+. SE 4: May 1982. Based on interviews with Charley White, an 80-year-old preacher who conducted a one-man war on poverty and worked for harmonious race relations.

Reformers–King

2759. Adler, David A. Martin Luther King, Jr.: Free at Last. Holiday, 1986. 48 p. ill. $12. Pb $5.
Gr 2-6. * B 83: Nov 15 1986. HB 63: Mar/Apr 1987. SE 51: Apr/May 1987. - SLJ 33: Oct 1986. A chronology of the major dates in King's life is followed by a simple, realistic, and highly illustrated text.

2760. Bennett, Lerone. What Manner of Man: A Biography of Martin Luther King, Jr. Johnson, 1964. 227 p. ill. $13.
Gr 9+. B 82: Jan 1 1986. B 84: Sep 1 1987. An objective portrayal of King's role as a leader of the civil rights movement.

2761. Clayton, Ed. Martin Luther King: The Peaceful Warrior. Prentice-Hall; Pocket/Archway, 1964. 80 p. Pb $2.
Gr 4-6. B 82: Sep 15 1985. Metzner. Key events of King's life.

2762. Davidson, Margaret. I Have a Dream: The Story of Martin Luther King. Scholastic, 1986. 127 p. ill. Pb $3.
Gr 2-4. +- SLJ 33: Nov 1986. Covers King's life from his boyhood through his assassination. Includes numerous photos.

2763. Faber, Doris. Martin Luther King, Jr. Messner, 1986. 125 p. ill. $10.
Gr 6+. +- B 82: Aug 1986. SLJ 32: Aug 1986. A concise, simply written, and moving account of King's life from the childhood experience that acquainted him with segregation through his death. Provides a sense of the times.

2764. Garrow, David J. Bearing the Cross: Martin Luther King, Jr., and the Southern Christian Conference, 1955-1968. Morrow, 1986. 2 vol. $20.
Adult. * LJ 111: Nov 15 1986. A biography of King that shows him to be a less-than-heroic person who, when leadership was thrust upon him, rose to meet the need.

2765. Garrow, David J. F.B.I. and Martin Luther King, Jr., The. Norton, 1981. 320 p. $16.
Gr 9+. LJ 106: Dec 1 1981. SLJ 28: Jan 1982. Examines the FBI surveillance of King in historical context and explains how such abuse of power could occur.

2766. Harris, Jacqueline L. Martin Luther King, Jr. (Impact Biography). Watts, 1983. 128 p. ill. $11.
Gr 7+. +- B 79: Jun 15 1983. B 81: Sep 15 1984. Provides introductory information on King's public career.

2767. Hunter, Nigel. Martin Luther King, Jr. (Great Lives). Bookwright Press; dist. by Watts, 1985. 32 p. ill. $10.
Gr 2-5. +- BC 39: Mar 1986. +- SLJ 32: Mar 1986. This introduction to King's life includes a chronology and glossary.

2768. King, Coretta Scott. Words of Martin Luther King, Jr. Newmarket, 1983. 112 p. $10.

Gr 6+. LJ 108: Dec 1 1983. VOYA 9: Feb 1987. A collection of quotes from King's writings in addition to a brief biography.

2769. Lowery, Linda. Martin Luther King Day. (On My Own Books). Carolrhoda, 1987. 56 p. ill. $9. Pb $5.

Gr 2-4. B 83: Apr 1 1987. SLJ 33: Jun/Jul 1987. A simply-written biography that tells why and how we celebrate King's birthday.

2770. McKissack, Patricia. Martin Luther King, Jr.: A Man to Remember. (People of Distinction Biographies). Childrens Press, 1984. 128 p. ill. $9.

Gr 5-7. B 81: Sep 1 1984. SLJ 31: Oct 1984. Traces King's life and the challenges he faced when his policy of nonviolence did not seem to achieve the purposes of the civil rights movement.

2771. Milton, Joyce. Marching to Freedom: The Story of Martin Luther King, Jr. Dell/Yearling, 1987. 92 p. ill. Pb $3.

Gr 3-7. +- B 83: Jun 15 1987. BR 6: May 1987. SLJ 34: Oct 1987. A balanced, well-written and easy-to-read biography that presents the difficulties of organizing massive demonstrations. The Birmingham Children's Crusade is highlighted.

2772. Oates, Stephen. Let the Trumpet Sound: The Life of Martin Luther King. Harper; New American Library, 1982, 1985. 562 p. ill. $15.

Gr 10+. B 78: May 1 1982. +- LJ 107: Jul 1982. VOYA 8: June 1985. Traces the evolution of King's religious and racial doctrines, belief in nonviolence, and involvement in the civil rights movement.

2773. Pyatt, Sherman E. Martin Luther King, Jr: An Annotated Bibliography. (Bibliographies and Indexes in Afro-American and African Studies). Greenwood, 1986. 154 p. $30.

Gr 9+. B 83: Jan 1 1987. A thorough bibliography arranged by such categories as biographies, awards, philosophy, marches and demonstrations, FBI, writings, and assassination. Number 12 in the series.

2774. Richardson, Nigel. Martin Luther King. (Profiles). Hamish Hamilton; dist. by David & Charles, 1983. 63 p. ill. $8.

Gr 4-8. BR 2: Jan/Feb 1984. - SLJ 30: Oct 1983. An objective and straightforward biography by a British author.

2775. Schulke, Flip. King Remembered. Norton; Pocket, 1986. 288 p. ill. $17. Pb $8.

Gr 9+. B 82: Jan 1 1986. LJ 111: Feb 15 1986. A survey of King's life and accomplishments.

2776. Schulke, Flip. Martin Luther King, Jr.: A Documentary...Montgomery to Memphis. Norton, 1976. 224 p. ill. $20. Pb $10.

Gr 9+. B 80: Oct 15 1983. B 72: Jun 1 1976. SLJ 22: May 1976. Interviews, photos, and examples of King's sermons and writings effectively profile his work for racial integration.

2777. Smith, Kathie Billingslea. Martin Luther King, Jr. (Great Americans Series). Messner, 1987. Unp. ill. $8. Pb $3.

Gr 2-5. SLJ 33: Jun/Jul 1987. This introductory overview of King's work for civil rights and world peace is highlighted by photos and double-page illustrations.

2778. Washington, James M. Testament of Hope: The Essential Writings of Martin Luther King, Jr. Harper, 1986. 676 p. $23.

Gr 9+. B 82: Mar 1 1986. LJ 111: Apr 1 1986. SLJ 32: Aug 1986. This anthology of sermons, speeches, interviews, essays, and book excerpts is arranged chronologically within broad topics. It is a balanced collection that reflects King's goals and philosophy.

2779. Witherspoon, William Roger. Martin Luther King, Jr.: To the Mountaintop. Doubleday, 1985. 256 p. ill. $25.

Gr 9+. B 82: Dec 15 1985. LJ 110: Dec 1985. Concentrates on King's public life.

Reformers–Women

2780. Cantarow, Ellen. Moving the Mountain: Women Working for Social Change. (Women's Lives/Women's Work). Feminist Press, 1980. 166 p. ill. $5.

Gr 9+. LJ 105: May 1 1980. SLJ 26: May 1980. Powerful biographies of Ella Baker, civil rights leader; Jessie Lopez de la Cruz, who supports the rights of farm workers; and Florence Luscomb, who is active in peace and civil rights works.

2781. Meltzer, Milton. Betty Friedan: A Voice for Women's Rights. (Women of Our Time). Viking/Kestrel, 1985. 64 p. ill. $10.

Gr 4-8. B 82: Oct 15 1985. BC 39: Feb 1986. SLJ 32: Dec 1985. Introduces the first president of the National Organization for Women.

Religious Leaders

2782. Harrell, David Edwin. Pat Robertson: A Personal, Religious, and Political Portrait. Harper, 1988. 192 p. ill. $16.

Gr 9+. B 84: Jan 1 1988. LJ 113: Apr 1 1988. An objective biography that discusses Robertson's political ideas but emphasizes his religious views.

Royalty

2783. Bradford, Sarah. Princess Grace. Stein & Day, 1984. 272 p. ill. $18.

Gr 9+. +- B 80: Apr 1 1984. LJ 109: May 15 1984. This biography of Grace Kelly, who grew up in Philadelphia, became a movie star, and married the Prince of Monaco, covers the glamour and the difficulties of her life. Includes a filmography.

2784. Englund, Steven. Grace of Monaco: An Interpretive Biography. Doubleday, 1984. 336 p. ill. $18.

Gr 9+. B 81: Apr 1 1984. B 82: Dec 1 1985. A psychological biography that includes engrossing detail of the life of the American socialite and movie star who became the wife of Prince Rainier of Monaco. Also includes a history of the principality of Monaco.

2785. Spada, James. Grace: The Secret Lives of a Princess. Doubleday/Dolphin, 1987. 338 p. ill. $18.
Gr 10+. B 83: Apr 1 1987. LJ 112: May 1 1987. A well-researched account of the life of the American actress who became the Princess of Monaco.

Social Life and Customs

2786. Carver, Richard. One Day USA: A Self-Portrait of America's Cities. Abrams, 1986. 256 p. ill. $35.
Gr 10+. B 83: Oct 15 1986. +- LJ 111: Nov 15 1986. From local photo contests held across the nation, the editors chose representative photos of contemporary American life.

2787. Cohen, David. Day in the Life of America, A. Collins, 1986. 272 p. ill. $40.
Gr 9+. LJ 111: Nov 15 1986. Top photographers present snapshots of this extraordinary country on one ordinary day.

2788. Fyson, Nance Lui. Through the Year in the USA. (Through the Year in...). Batsford, 1982. 72 p. ill. $15.
Gr 6+. BR 1: Nov/Dec 1982. SLJ 29: Mar 1983. A unique look at national, regional, and ethnic group customs and holidays through the eyes of a first generation American. Includes photos, lists, charts, and terms.

2789. Gitlin, Todd. Sixties: Years of Hope, Days of Rage. Bantam, 1987. 512 p. $20.
Gr 9+. +- B 84: Nov 1 1987. A thoughtful examination of the complex events and movements of the 1960s, why they developed, and what they accomplished.

2790. Greene, Bob. Be True to Your School: A Diary of 1964. Atheneum, 1987. 320 p. $19.
Gr 10+. B 83: Feb 15 1987. LJ 112: Apr 15 1987. The author wanted to be a reporter, so for practice he kept this remarkable journal of his growing up in the late 1960s and early 1970s. A good chronicle of the time.

2791. Liu Zongren. Two Years in the Melting Pot. China Books and Periodicals, 1984. 208 p. $9.
Gr 10+. LJ 109: Nov 1 1984. SE 50: Feb 1986. Following his visit to the U.S. in 1980, Liu, a Chinese journalist, wrote this candid account of the difficulties of cross-cultural adjustment.

2792. McConnell, Malcolm. Stepping Over: Personal Encounters with Young Extremists. Reader's Digest Association; dist. by Random, 1984. 358 p. $18.
Gr 10+. B 80: Mar 1 1984. +- VOYA 7: Oct 1984. Explores the shattered lives of 10 once-promising young adults, victims of the social disruption of the 1960s and '70s.

2793. Warhol, Andy. America. Harper, 1985. 224 p. ill. Pb $16.
Gr 9+. LJ 111: Feb 15 1986. Photos of contemporary American life with comments by the noted artist.

2794. Wright, Lawrence. In the New World: Growing Up with America, 1960-1984. Knopf, 1988. 328 p. $19.

Gr 10+. B 84: Dec 15 1987. LJ 113: Jan 1988. Wright was a boy growing up in Dallas at the time of the Kennedy assassination. This is the story of Wright's personal and political coming of age.

Social Life and Customs–Fiction

2795. Barry, Lynda. Good Times Are Killing Me, The. Real Comet Press, 1988. 120 p. ill. $17.
Gr 9+. * B 85: Oct 1 1988. Seventh-grader Edna tells how it was to grow up in a racially mixed neighborhood in the late 1960s.

Social Policy

2796. American Millstone: An Examination of the Nation's Permanent Underclass. Contemporary Books, 1986. 307 p. ill. Pb $9.
Gr 9+. B 83: Dec 1 1986. Examines the causes of poverty and the lives of the poor.

2797. Meltzer, Milton. Poverty in America. Morrow, 1986. 125 p. $12.
Gr 6-9. B 82: Aug 1986. BC 39: Apr 1986. BR 5: Sep/Oct 1986. HB 62: May/Jun 1986. * SLJ 32: Aug 1986. VOYA 9: Aug/Oct 1986. The historical causes, effects, and social ramifications of poverty.

2798. Murray, Charles. Losing Ground: American Social Policy, 1950-1980. Basic Books, 1984. 323 p. $24.
Adult. SE 49: May 1985. Examines the history and possible negative results of social programs intended to help minorities and the poor.

2799. Rosenbaum, Robert. Public Issues Handbook: A Guide for the Concerned Citizen. Greenwood, 1983. 409 p. $35.
Gr 10+. B 80: Jan 15 1984. Essays on public policy issues, including civil liberties, education, poverty, and welfare. Includes background and opposing opinions.

Space Flight

2800. U.S.-Soviet Cooperation in Space: A Technical Memorandum. Congress. Office of Technology Assessment, 1985. 123 p. ill. Pb $5.
Adult. LJ 110: Nov 15 1985. The history and status of U.S. and Soviet cooperation in space.

2801. Allen, Joseph P. Entering Space: An Astronaut's Odyssey. Stewart, Tabori & Chang; dist. by Workman, 1984. 223 p. ill. $25.
Adult. LJ 110: Feb 1; Mar 1 1985. A realistic personal account of a space shuttle mission, from liftoff through touchdown. Photo-filled.

2802. Baker, David. Conquest: A History of Space Achievements From Science Fiction to the Shuttle. Salem; dist. by Merrimack Publisher's Circle, 1985. 191 p. ill. Pb $13.
Gr 10+. LJ 110: Apr 1 1985. VOYA 8: Oct 1985. This easily understood text that emphasizes 1963-1983 is enhanced by outstanding photos. Lists and tables of data are included.

2803. Berger, Melvin. Space Shots, Shuttles and Satellites. Putnam, 1984. 80 p. ill. $8.
Gr 5-8. B 80: Apr 15 1984. SLJ 30: May 1984. +-
VOYA 7: Jun 1984. A brief history of the space effort.

2804. DeWaard, E. John. History of NASA: America's Voyage to the Stars. Exeter Books; dist. by Bookthrift, 1984. 192 p. ill. $13.
Gr 9+. B 81: Mar 15 1985. Introduces each of the astronauts and describes the spacecraft and their missions. The text is accessible and is illustrated by outstanding color photos.

2805. Furniss, Tim. Man in Space. (Today's World Series). Batsford, 1981. 72 p. ill. $15.
Gr 7+. SLJ 28: Jan 1982. A British author discusses international involvement in the "space race" and clarifies how the U.S.-U.S.S.R. competition to be first on the moon jeopardized public understanding of the value of space exploration.

2806. Hallion, Richard P. Apollo: Ten Years Since Tranquility Base. Smithsonian Institution Press, 1979. 174 p. $18. Pb 7.
Gr 9+. SLJ 26: Mar 1980. A collection of essays stressing the cultural and political aspects of the space program.

2807. Lewis, Richard S. Challenger: The Final Voyage. Columbia University Press, 1988. 249 p. ill. $30.
Gr 9+. B 84: May 15 1988. LJ 113: Apr 1 1988. A clear and balanced account of the Challenger disaster and recommendations for fixing the shuttle hardware.

2808. McCarter, James. Space Shuttle Disaster, The. (Great Disasters). Bookwright Press; dist. by Watts, 1988. 32 p. ill. $11.
Gr 3-6. B 85: Jan 15 1989. SLJ 35: Nov 1988. Following a brief history of the shuttle and a description of life on board, McCarter explains the technological causes for the tragedy.

2809. Newton, David. U.S. and Soviet Space Programs. Watts, 1988. 141 p. $13.
Gr 7+. B 85: Oct 1 1988. * BR 7: Sep/Oct 1988. *
VOYA 11: Oct 1988. This balanced history of the space race compares U.S. and U.S.S.R. goals, methods, and accomplishments.

2810. Osman, Tony. Space History. St. Martin's, 1983. 217 p. ill. $17.
Gr 9+. B 80: Dec 15 1983. +- LJ 10: Dec 15 1983. A history of the race for space, with abundant information on the technology involved.

2811. Smith, Howard E. Daring the Unknown: A History of NASA. Harcourt/Gulliver, 1987. 179 p. ill. $15.
Gr 5-9. +- B 84: Jan 15 1988. SLJ 34: Jan 1988. A dramatic presentation of the achievements of NASA plus information on the astronauts. Numerous photos.

2812. Stein, R. Conrad. Story of Apollo 11, The. (Cornerstones of Freedom). Childrens Press, 1985. 31 p. ill. $7.

Gr 3-5. B 82: Mar 15 1986. SLJ 32: Mar 1986. The story of the first moon landing and the competition for space.

2813. Stern, Alan. U.S. Space Program after Challenger: Where Are We Going? (Impact Book). Watts, 1987. 128 p. ill. $12.
Gr 7+. +- B 84: Feb 15 1988. +- SLJ 34: Mar 1988. * VOYA 11: Jun 1988. Describes in detail the development of the U.S. space program through the Challenger accident and considers suggested alternatives for its future. Includes numerous quotes of diverse opinion.

2814. Vogt, Gregory. Twenty-Fifth Anniversary Album of NASA, A. Watts, 1983. 96 p. ill. Lib. ed. $10. Pb $5.
Gr 4-8. B 80: Dec 1 1983. BR 3: May/Jun 1984. SLJ 70: Dec 1983. This documentary of aeronautics and space travel from the Wright Brothers to the U.S. space program also covers the U.S.-Russian rivalry for superiority in space. Oversize format with numerous photos.

Technology and Civilization

2815. Rogers, Everett M. Silicon Valley Fever: The Growth of High Technology Culture. Basic Books, 1984. 302 p. $20.
Adult. SE 49: May 1985. Discusses the growth of Silicon Valley, a center of the development of microcomputers in Northern California, and the companies which created it.

Vietnamese War

2816. Anzenberger, Joseph F. Combat Art of the Vietnam War. McFarland, 1986. 133 p. ill. $30.
Gr 10+. B 83: Jan 15 1987. BR 5: Mar/Apr 1987. Insight into the Vietnam experience is provided through an examination of the lives of the artists who recorded all aspects of the war.

2817. Beckett, Brian. Illustrated History of the Vietnam War, The. W. H. Smith, 1985. 263 p. ill. $15.
Gr 10+. LJ 111: Feb 1 1986. A photographic overview of the war.

2818. Bender, David L. Vietnam War: Opposing Viewpoints. (Opposing Viewpoints Series). Greenhaven, 1984. 214 p. ill. $12. Pb $6.
Gr 9+. B 81: Jan 1 1985. SLJ 31: Mar 1985. VOYA 8: Aug 1985. Includes a chronology of U.S. involvement in Vietnam since 1930, articles about U.S. involvement in the war, and writings on the effect of the war on U.S. society.

2819. Boettcher, Thomas D. Vietnam: The Valor and the Sorrow: From the Home Front to the Front Lines in Words and Pictures. Little, 1985. 495 p. ill. $28. Pb $15.
Gr 9+. * B 81: Jul 1985. B 82: Jan 15 1986. B 84: Sep 1 1987. LJ 110: Jun 15 1985. Explains the events that led to U.S. involvement in Vietnam, with photos of U.S. and Vietnamese life during the war.

2820. Bonds, Ray. Vietnam War: The Illustrated History of the Conflict in Southeast Asia. Rev. ed. Crown, 1983. 261 p. ill. $20.
Gr 9+. B 80: Nov 1 1983. This revised comprehensive assemblage of facts and illustrations on the war includes a chapter on political and military developments in Southeast Asia 1979-1982.

2821. Bowman, John S. Vietnam War: An Almanac. World Almanac; dist. by Ballantine, 1985. 512 p. ill. $25.
Adult. B 82: Jun 1 1986. * LJ 110: Oct 1 1985. A chronology of the history of the Vietnamese War, with detail that clarifies the causes of American involvement and the complexities and distortions that caused so much confusion in the U.S.

2822. Brown, Ashley. Green Berets: U.S. Special Forces from Vietnam to Delta Force. (Villard Military Series). Villard/Random House, 1986. 96 p. Pb $5.
Gr 9+. BR 5: Jan 1987. VOYA 10: Apr 1987. Traces the history of the Green Berets, with emphasis on their role in Vietnam. Includes a chronology.

2823. Edwards, Richard. Vietnam War, The. (Flashpoints). Rourke, 1987. 77 p. ill. $11.
Gr 7-10. SLJ 33: Aug 1987. An overview that presents changing events in the United States as well as the events of the war.

2824. Esper, George. Eyewitness History of the Vietnam War, 1961-1975, The. Villard; Ballantine, 1983. 208 p. ill. $20. Pb $10.
Gr 9+. B 80: Feb 1 1984. BR 3: Sep/Oct 1984. VOYA 7: Aug 1984. An overview, with anecdotes and abundant photographs.

2825. Fincher, Ernest Barksdale. Vietnam War, The. (Impact Book). Watts, 1980. 87 p. ill. Lib. ed. $7.
Gr 6+. * B 76: Apr 15 1980. B 83: Oct 1 1986. SLJ 27: Oct 1980. * SE 45: Apr 1981. A summary of Vietnamese history of foreign domination, the reasons for U.S. involvement in the war, the results of the war both in the U.S. and in Vietnam, and the plight of the boat people.

2826. FitzGerald, Frances. Fire in the Lake: The Vietnamese and the Americans in Vietnam. Atlantic Monthly Press; dist. by Little; Random, 1972. 491 p. ill. $15. Pb $5.
Gr 9+. B 82: Jan 1 1986. B 84: Sep 1 1987. A Pulitzer Prize winning history and analysis of U.S. involvement in Vietnam.

2827. Gettleman, Marvin E. Vietnam and America: A Documented History. Grove Press, 1985. 524 p. $30. Pb $12.
Adult. LJ 110: Dec 1985. Important documents and statements by leaders that explore all sides of the controversy surrounding the Vietnamese War are included in this convenient one-volume compilation that includes notes and introductions.

2828. Griffiths, John. Last Day in Saigon, The. (Day That Made History). Batsford; dist. by David & Charles, 1987. 64 p. ill. $15.

Gr 6-9. B 83: Jul 1987. BR 6: Sep/Oct 1987. - SLJ 34: Sep 1987. An outline of the war, details of the "last day," and the events that followed. Includes a European perspective on the war.

2829. Hammer, Ellen J. Death in November: America in Vietnam, 1963. Dutton, 1987. 400 p. ill. $23.
Gr 9+. B 83: Mar 15 1987. LJ 112: Apr 1 1987. Shows the gradual involvement of the U.S. in Vietnam that resulted in a puppet government that went against the beliefs of the Vietnamese people.

2830. Hauptly, Denis J. In Vietnam. Atheneum, 1985. 175 p. ill. $13.
Gr 6+. B 82: Sep 15 1985. BC 39: Feb 1986. HB 62: Jan/Feb 1986. SE 50: Apr/May 1986. +- SLJ 32: Dec 1985. VOYA 9: Apr 1986. Includes ancient to modern Vietnamese history, an overview of the war, and the issues surrounding the war.

2831. Jones, Bruce E. War without Windows: A True Account of a Young Army Officer Trapped in an Intelligence Cover-Up, Saigon, 1967-1968. Vanguard, 1988. 260 p. $19.
Gr 9+. B 84: Feb 15 1988. As an intelligence officer in Vietnam, Jones was involved in the attempt to misrepresent the strength of the Vietcong to Congress and the American people. Includes both military and personal history.

2832. Karnow, Stanley. Vietnam: A History. Viking, 1983. 669 p. $20.
Gr 10+. B 80: Sep 1 1983. LJ 108: Oct 1 1983. * VOYA 6: Feb 1984. VOYA 7: Feb 1985. A well-researched and complete account of Vietnamese history and how the U.S. become involved in a "war nobody won."

2833. Lawson, Don. Album of the Vietnam War, An. Watts, 1986. 87 p. ill. $13.
Gr 5+. B 82: Jun 15 1986. B 83: Oct 1 1986. BC 39: Jul/Aug 1986. * SE 51: Apr/May 1987. * SLJ 32: Aug 1986. A photo-essay on the war, the escape of the boat people, and the building of the war memorial.

2834. Lawson, Don. United States in the Vietnam War, The. (Young People's History of America's Wars Series). Crowell, 1981. 160 p. ill. $11.
Gr 6+. * B 77: Jul/Aug 1981. B 83: Oct 1 1986. +- BR 1: Jan/Feb 1983. * SE 46: Apr 1982. * SLJ 27: Apr 1981. This balanced commentary chronicles the gradual involvement of the U.S. and clarifies the human issues involved.

2835. Lawson, Don. War in Vietnam, The. (First Book). Watts, 1981. 83 p. ill. $8.
Gr 5-10. B 78: Dec 15 1981. BC 35: Dec 1981. SLJ 28: Mar 1982. Lawson presents the background of the war and discusses the causes and results of U.S. involvement in Vietnam.

2836. Mabie, Margot C. J. Vietnam: There and Here. Holt, 1985. 166 p. ill. $12.
Gr 6+. * B 81: May 1 1985. B 83: Oct 1 1986. BR 4: Sep/Oct 1985. HB 61: Nov/Dec 1985. +- SLJ 31: Aug 1985. VOYA 8: Oct 1985. The war, its causes, the tragedy of the boat people, and the problems of the Viet-

namese and the U.S. government caused by their immigration.

2837. Maclear, Michael. Ten Thousand Day War: Vietnam, 1945-1975. St. Martin's, 1981. 368 p. ill. $17.
Gr 9+. B 78: Jan 1 1982. +- LJ 107: Feb 15 1982. Based on interviews with soldiers, politicians, and civilians from all the nations involved in the complex 30-year drama.

2838. Olson, James S. Dictionary of the Vietnam War. Greenwood, 1988. 585 p. ill. $65.
Adult. B 84: May 1 1988. LJ 113: Mar 1 1988. A balanced one-volume dictionary that covers the places, events, battles, people, movies, and books concerned with the Vietnamese War.

2839. Summers, Harry G. Vietnam War Almanac. Facts on File, 1985. 414 p. ill. $25.
Gr 10+. B 82: Jun 1 1986. BR 7: May/June 1988. * LJ 111: Jan 1986. Brief articles on all aspects of the war, suitable for reference.

2840. Turley, William S. Second Indochina War: A Short Political and Military History, 1954-1975. New American Library, 1987. 252 p. ill. $5.
Gr 9+. VOYA 10: Sep 1987. Maps, charts, and other illustrations clarify this concise and clear chronology of the Vietnamese War, 1954-1975.

2841. Welsh, Douglas. History of the Vietnam War, The. Exeter Books; dist. by Bookthrift, 1984. 192 p. ill. $15.
Gr 9+. B 81: Jan 15 1985. A well-balanced and abundantly illustrated overview of the war.

2842. Willenson, Kim. Bad War: An Oral History of the Vietnam War. New American Library, 1987. 464 p. $19.
Gr 9+. B 83: Jun 15 1987. * LJ 112: Sep 1 1987. An oral history of the war from the widely varied points of view of American civilians, military personnel, anti-war activists, those in intelligence work, and a number of Vietnamese citizens.

2843. Williams, William Appleman. America in Vietnam: A Documentary History. Doubleday/Anchor, 1985. 288 p. $20. Pb $10.
Gr 10+. B 81: Feb 1 1985. HT 20: Feb 1987. LJ 110: Jan 1985. A valuable collection of primary materials, including official reports, interviews, documents and articles.

Vietnamese War–Aerial Operations and Aircraft

2844. United States Air Force in Southeast Asia, 1961-1973: An Illustrated Account. Rev. ed. Office of Air Force History, U.S. Air Force, 1984. 383 p. ill. $20.
Adult. B 81: Jul 1985. Presents information arranged chronologically and topically on the activities of the U.S. Air Force in Southeast Asia. Includes numerous color photos.

2845. Berry, F. Clifton. Strike Aircraft. (Illustrated History of the Vietnam War). Bantam, 1988. 157 p. ill. Pb $7.

Gr 9+. B 84: Apr 1 1988. A solid introduction to the air war in Vietnam.

2846. Chinnery, Phil. Air War in Vietnam. Exeter Books; dist. by Bookthrift, 1987. 192 p. ill. $13.
Gr 9+. B 84: Jan 1 1988. This attractive overview of the air war includes numerous color photos.

2847. Gurney, Gene. Vietnam: The War in the Air: A Pictorial History of the U.S. Air Forces in the Vietnam WAr: Air Force, Army, Navy, and Marines. Crown, 1984. 277 p. ill. $18.
Gr 9+. B 81: Aug 1985. LJ 110: Jul 1985. SLJ 31: Aug 1985. The background of the war, the development of air operations, military strategy, and the homecoming of the POW's.

Vietnamese War–Bibliographies

2848. Those Who Were There: Eyewitness Accounts of the War in Southeast Asia 1956-1975, & Aftermant; Annotated Bibliography of Books, Articles and Topical Magazines, Covering Writing Both Factual and Imaginative. (American Dust Series). Dustbooks, 1984. 297 p. $13.
Gr 10+. * LJ 109: Oct 15 1984. An annotated bibliography of books, articles, and topic-related magazines, covering writings both factual and imaginative. Number 15 in the series.

2849. Indochina Curriculum Group. Vietnam Era: A Guide to Teaching Resources. Indochina Curriculum Group, 1978. 105 p. Pb $5.
Gr 9+. SE 44: Oct 1980. An evaluative guide to books, films, and slide sets. Emphasis is on anti-establishment views of the war.

2850. Newman, John. Vietnam War Literature: An Annotated Bibliography of Imaginative Works About Americans Fighting in Vietnam. Scarecrow, 1982. 117 p. $10.
Gr 9+. B 80: Nov 1 1983. An annotated bibliography of novels, short stories, poetry, drama, humor and cartoons dealing with the Vietnam War and returning veterans.

2851. Peake, Louis A. United States in the Vietnam War, 1954-1975: A Selected, Annotated Bibliography. (Wars of the United States). Garland, 1986. 406 p. $49.
Gr 10+. B 83: Sep 1 1986. Arranged by 10 broad categories, this wide-ranging annotated bibliography includes works partisan to all sides. Number four in the series.

Vietnamese War–Blacks–Personal Narratives

2852. Myers, Walter. Fallen Angels. Scholastic, 1988. 286 p. $13.
Gr 9+. B 84: Apr 15 1988. BC 41: Apr 1988. BR 7: Sep/Oct 1988. * HB 64: Jul/Aug 1988. * SLJ 34: Jun/Jul 1988. VOYA 11: Aug 1988. A tough and realistic account of the experiences of a young black American soldier in Vietnam who faced racism, terror, and boredom.

2853. Terry, Wallace. Bloods: An Oral History of the Vietnam War by Black Veterans. Random House, 1984. 311 p. ill. $18.
Gr 11+. * BR 4: May/Jun 1985. LJ 109: Sep 15 1984. SLJ 31: Aug 1985. VOYA 8: Apr 1985. Twenty black veterans speak candidly and explicitly of their experiences during and after the Vietnam War.

Vietnamese War–Fiction

2854. Anderson, Rachel. War Orphan, The. Oxford University Press; dist. by Merrimack, 1986. 256 p. $14.
Gr 7+. +- B 83: Sep 1 1986. +- BC 40: Oct 1986. BR 5: Sep/Oct 1986. - SLJ 33: Oct 1986. An English schoolboy learns about the war from Ha, a young Vietnamese war orphan.

2855. Anderson, Robert A. Cooks and Bakers: A Novel of the Vietnam War. Avon, 1982. 205 p. Pb $3.
Gr 9+. B 78: Jul 1982. VOYA 5: Oct 1982. Episodes in the life of a young Marine lieutenant during the Tet Offensive. Evocative action scenes show the nightmare of combat.

2856. Bograd, Larry. Travelers. Lippincott; dist. by Harper, 1986. 184 p. $12. Lib. ed. $12.
Gr 9+. * B 82: Mar 1 1986. +- BC 39: Jun 1986. VOYA 9: Jun 1986. Jack travels to meet his deceased father's Vietnamese war buddies. An upbeat seriocomic coming-of-age novel.

2857. Coleman, Charles. Sergeant Back Again. Harper, 1980. 237 p. $13.
Gr 9+. B 77: Jan 15 1981. LJ 105: Nov 1 1980. SLJ 27: Apr 1981. Probes the mental and physical trauma suffered by soldiers. A strong novel that follows one victim through his experiences in mental wards following a breakdown.

2858. Currey, Richard. Fatal Light. Dutton/Seymour Lawrence, 1988. 197 p. $17.
Gr 9+. B 84: Apr 1 1988. LJ 113: May 15 1988. The haunting story of a young man torn from a quiet home in middle America into the horror of combat.

2859. Degens, T. Friends. Viking, 1981. 161 p. $10.
Gr 5-7. +- BC 34: Jul/Aug 1981. - SLJ 27: May 1981. +- VOYA 3: Feb 1981. Nell faces problems common to many 11-year-olds who were growing up in the U.S. during the Vietnam War.

2860. Hahn, Mary Downing. December Stillness. Clarion, 1988. 181 p. $14.
Gr 5-9. B 85: Sep 1 1988. +- BC 42: Sep 1988. HB 64: Nov/Dec 1988. +- SLJ 35: Oct 1988. For a term paper, Kelly attempts to interview a bag man who is a mentally disturbed Vietnam veteran. After persistent efforts lead to his accidental death, she and her father visit the Vietnam Memorial.

2861. Martin, Ron. To Be Free. Vanguard, 1986. 256 p. $15.
Gr 10+. LJ 111: Jul 1986. Ramsey, a Marine POW in Vietnam, lived only for escape. Recommended as a classic tale of escape and survival.

2862. Mason, Bobbie Ann. In Country. Harper, 1985. 245 p. $16.
Gr 10+. B 81: Aug 1985. * LJ 110: Oct 1 1985. Sam's father died in Vietnam; her uncle may suffer from Agent Orange. A story of the impact of the 1960s on the culture of the '80s.

2863. Wolitzer, Meg. Caribou. Greenwillow, 1984. 176 p. $11.
Gr 4-8. BC 38: Dec 1984. - BR 3: Mar/Apr 1985. * SE 49: Apr 1985. SLJ 31: Jan 1985. VOYA 8: Apr 1985. When Becca's brother goes to Canada to avoid the Vietnamese War she questions her own beliefs and realizes the difficulties adults face in making choices.

Vietnamese War–Military Personnel

2864. Clements, Charles. Witness to War. Bantam, 1984. 366 p. $16.
Gr 10+. B 80: Jun 15 1984. LJ 109: Jun 15 1984. Clements' experiences in Vietnam led this son of a military family to an awakened social conscience and medical school. After becoming a Quaker he volunteered for civilian medical service in El Salvador.

2865. McConnell, Malcolm. Into the Mouth of the Cat: The Story of Lance Sijan, A Hero of Vietnam. Norton, 1984. 224 p. $14.
Gr 10+. B 81: Nov 1 1984. +- LJ 109: Nov 15 1984. Sijan, a Medal of Honor winner, died after surviving six weeks in the jungle and torture by his captors. A powerful story.

2866. Schneider, Donald K. Air Force Heroes in Vietnam. (USAF Southeast Asia Monograph Series). Office of Air Force History, U.S. Air Force, 1980. 86 p. ill. Pb $4.
Gr 10+. B 77: Dec 15 1980. Biographical information on 12 Air Force heroes who received the Medal of Honor. Also describes their aircraft and missions. This monograph is volume 7, number 9, of the series.

Vietnamese War–Naval Operations and Ships

2867. Mersky, Peter B. Naval Air War in Vietnam, The. Nautical and Aviation Publishing Company of America, 1981. 224 p. ill. $18.
Gr 9+. B 78: Oct 15 1981. Lavish photos enhance this analysis of Navy and Merchant Marine air operations in Vietnam 1964-1975.

Vietnamese War–Personal Narratives

2868. Brandon, Heather. Casualties: Death in Vietnam, Anguish and Survival in America. St. Martin's, 1984. 357 p. ill. $16.
Gr 10+. LJ 109: Nov 1 1984. Interviews with some of the family members who survived the 58,000 Vietnam casualties.

2869. Brennan, Matthew. Brennan's War: Vietnam, 1965-1969. Presidio, 1985. 272 p. ill. $18.

Adult. B 82: Sep 15 1985. LJ 110: Sep 15 1985. A memoir of a man who served three tours, rising from private to lieutenant.

2870. Broyles, William. Brothers in Arms: A Journey from War to Peace. Knopf, 1986. 283 p. $18.
Gr 9+. B 82: Jun 1 1986. * LJ 111: Jun 1 1986. A veteran's impressions of post-war Vietnam and his feelings toward his former enemies.

2871. Carhart, Tom. Offering, The. Morrow, 1987. 361 p. $18.
Gr 9+. B 83: Mar 1 1987. +- LJ 112: Mar 15 1987. Carhart's idealized notions about the glories of battle were soon changed by his experiences on the front line and as an advisor in Vietnam, 1967-1968.

2872. Clodfelter, Michael. Mad Minutes and Vietnam Months. McFarland, 1988. 235 p. Pb $16.
Gr 9+. +- BR 7: Sep/Oct 1988. The author was in Vietnam in 1965 and 1966, before the war became unpopular. His informative account includes his participation in atrocities.

2873. Donovan, David. Once a Warrior King: Memories of an Officer in Vietnam. McGraw; Ballantine, 1986. 320 p. Pb $4.
Gr 10+. * B 81: Jun 1 1985. LJ 110: Jun 1 1985. Using a pseudonym the author writes of his experiences as a military advisor in the Mekong Delta in 1969. Includes anecdotes and effective descriptions of his encounters with civilians and military persons.

2874. Edelman, Bernard. Dear America: Letters Home from Vietnam. Norton, 1985. 276 p. $14.
Adult. * LJ 110: Jun 1 1985. Following each letter is a short epilogue telling what happened to the soldier after he wrote the letter.

2875. Goldman, Peter. Charlie Company: What Vietnam Did to Us. Morrow; Ballantine, 1983. 358 p. Pb $4.
Adult. B 84: Sep 1 1987. LJ 108: Mar 1 1983. A memoir of the 365-day tour of duty in the jungles north of Saigon by 65 young American combat soldiers.

2876. MacPherson, Myra. Long Time Passing: Vietnam and the Haunted Generation. Doubleday, 1984. 672 p. $20.
Gr 10+. B 80: Apr 15 1984. +- LJ 109: May 15 1984. This forum for veterans of the Vietnamese War allows them to express how the war determined their later values.

2877. Mason, Robert C. Chickenhawk. Viking, 1983. 316 p. $18.
Adult. B 79: Jun 15 1983. * LJ 108: Jul 1983. As a helicopter pilot in Vietnam, Mason saw brutality on both sides. In this memoir he relates his wartime experiences and problems following his return.

2878. McDonough, James R. Platoon Leader. Presidio, 1985. 249 p. map. $16.
Gr 9+. B 81: May 15 1985. McDonald's narrative offers his perspective on the suffering of war and the responsibilities of a platoon leader.

2879. Santoli, Al. Everything We Had: An Oral History of the Vietnam War as Told by 33 American Soldiers Who Fought It. Random House, 1981. 265 p. ill. $13.
Gr 9+. B 80: Oct 15 1983. LJ 106: Apr 15 1981. SLJ 28: Sep 1981. Powerful personal accounts of the war by 33 veterans.

2880. Santoli, Al. To Bear Any Burden: The Vietnam War and Its Aftermath in the Words of Americans and Southeast Asians. Dutton, 1985. 373 p. ill. $18.
Gr 9+. +- B 81: Apr 15 1985. +- LJ 110: May 1 1985. SLJ 32: Sep 1985. Interviews provide a testimony to the ordeals of Americans and Southeast Asians during the war.

2881. Stockdale, Jim. In Love and War: The Story of a Family's Ordeal and Sacrifice During the Vietnam War. Harper, 1984. 512 p. ill. $19.
Gr 10+. LJ 109: Aug 1984. In alternate chapters a POW and his wife tell how they overcame adversity.

2882. Wilcox, Fred A. Waiting for an Army to Die: The Tragedy of Agent Orange. Random House, 1983. 222 p. $16. Pb $7.
Gr 8+. BR 2: Mar/Apr 1984. Interviews with veterans who believe their illnesses are caused by Agent Orange, a chemical defoliant used by the U.S. Army, and with officials who deny government responsibility.

2883. Zumwalt, Elmo, Jr. My Father, My Son. Macmillan, 1986. 222 p. ill. $19.
Gr 10+. B 83: Sep 1 1986. * LJ 111: Sep 15 1986. The real-life tragedy of the admiral who ordered the use of Agent Orange and his son who contracted cancer because of it.

Vietnamese War–Prisoners of War

2884. Brace, Ernest C. Code to Keep: The True Story of America's Longest-Held Civilian Prisoner of War in Vietnam. St. Martin's, 1988. 283 p. ill. $17.
Gr 9+. B 84: Jan 1 1988. LJ 113: Jan 1988. A moving account of the author's experience as America's longest-held civilian POW in Vietnam.

2885. Colvin, Rod. First Heroes: The POWs Left behind in Vietnam. Irvington, 1987. 411 p. ill. $20.
Gr 9+. B 83: Jun 15 1987. Based on the testimony of those who were there, Colvin makes a strong case for the continued existence of American MIAs and POWs in Vietnam.

Vietnamese War–Women

2886. Marshall, Kathryn. In the Combat Zone: A Oral History of American Women in Vietnam, 1966-1975. Little, 1987. 250 p. $18.
Gr 9+. B 83: Jan 15 1987. HT 21: Aug 1988. LJ 112: Jan 1987. A poignant and diverse collection of interviews with civilian and military women who served in Vietnam and suffered the same trauma as the men.

Vietnamese War–Women–Personal Narratives

2887. Borton, Lady. Sensing the Enemy: An American Woman among the Boat People of Vietnam. Doubleday/Dial, 1984. 192 p. ill. $15.
Gr 9+. B 80: Jun 1 1984. LJ 109: Apr 1 1984. Borton presents a very personal report of the six months she spent as a health advisor at a tiny island that housed over 70,000 refugees from Vietnam.

2888. Byrd, Barthy. Home Front: Women and Vietnam. Shameless Hussy, 1986. 68 p. Pb $9.
Gr 9+. B 83: Sep 1 1986. Discusses the effects of the war on nine Vietnamese and American women.

2889. Keenan, Barbara Mullen. Every Effort. St. Martin's, 1986. 351 p. $17.
Gr 9+. B 82: Jun 15 1986. LJ 111: Jun 15 1986. A first-person account of a woman's prolonged struggle to locate her MIA husband.

2890. Van Devanter, Lynda. Home before Morning: The Story of an Army Nurse in Vietnam. Beaufort, 1983. 320 p. $17.
Gr 10+. B 79: Mar 15 1983. LJ 108: Mar 1 1983. +- VOYA 6: Aug 1983. A vivid account of the experiences of an Army nurse in Vietnam.

2891. Walker, Keith. Piece of My Heart: The Stories of Twenty-Six American Women Who Served in Vietnam. Presidio, 1986. 337 p. ill. $18.
Adult. LJ 111: Feb 1 1986. An oral history of the devastating effect of the war on the lives of American women who were in Vietnam.

Violence

2892. Arnold, Terrell E. Think About Terrorism: The New Warfare. (Think Series). Walker, 1988. 153 p. ill. $15.
Gr 7+. - BC 41: Jul 1988. SLJ 35: Sep 1988. VOYA 11: Aug 1988. Using the journalistic technique, Arnold discusses the what, why, who, where, and when of international terrorism. Includes policy statements, glossary, bibliography, photos, and graphs.

2893. Dobson, Christopher. Never-Ending War: Terrorism in the 80's. Facts on File, 1987. 356 p. $19.
Gr 9+. SLJ 34: Oct 1987. A comprehensive examination of international terrorist groups of the 1980s.

2894. Dolan, Edward F. Youth Gangs. Messner, 1984. 144 p. $10.
Gr 5+. B 80: Mar 15 1984. BC 37: Jul/Aug 1984. SE 49: Jan 1985. +- SLJ 30: Aug 1984. VOYA 8: Apr 1985.
A brief history of how youth gangs have changed in recent decades, the reasons for the success of gangs, and efforts at control.

2895. Hyde, Margaret O. Terrorism: A Special Kind of Violence. Dodd, 1987. 92 p. $13.
Gr 9+. B 83: Apr 15 1987. +- BC 40: Jul 1987. SLJ 33: May 1987. Explores world terrorism from the U.S. perspective, examines the effect of terrorism on its victims, recounts efforts to curb terrorism.

2896. Martin, David C. Best Laid Plans: America's War against Terrorism. Harper, 1988. 416 p. $19.
Gr 9+. B 84: Jul 1988. A detailed and suspenseful account of highjacking and hostage incidents through the Carter and Reagan administrations.

Women

2897. Gibson, Anne. Women's Atlas of the United States, The. Facts on File, 1986. 248 p. maps. $35.
Gr 9+. B 83: May 1 1987. LJ 112: Apr 1 1987. Presents 145 maps on all aspects of the lives of U.S. women, based on census data.

2898. Gold, Maxine. Women Making History: Conversations with Fifteen New Yorkers. New York City Commission on the Status of Women, 1985. 149 p. ill. Pb $5.
Gr 9+. SLJ 32: Nov 1985. VOYA 8: Dec 1985. The dreams and accomplishments of women in medicine, business, sports, law, politics and the arts.

2899. Goldstein, Eleanor. Women, Volume 2. Social Issues Resources Series, Inc., 1982. 60 articles. $39.
Gr 8+. BR 1: Nov/Dec 1982. Sixty articles, mostly from popular periodicals, on all aspects of women's concerns during the 1970s, including ERA, single parenting, the elderly, and sexual harassment.

Women–Biographies

2900. Chellis, Marcia. Living with the Kennedys: The Joan Kennedy Story. Simon & Schuster, 1985. 240 p. ill. $18.
Adult. B 82: Oct 1 1985. LJ 110: Nov 15 1985. A multifaceted work of a woman triumphant over alcoholism and the pressures of life in a prominent political family.

2901. Uglow, Jennifer S. International Dictionary of Women's Biography, The. Continuum, 1983. 534 p. ill. $28.
Gr 9+. LJ 108: Mar 1 1983. Short biographies of 1500 women from all fields, with emphasis on those from North America, Europe, and the British Commonwealth.

Author Index

Aaron, Chester.
Lackawanna., 1874

Abel, Robert H.
Freedom Dues., 1087

Abodaher, David.
Iacocca., 2491

Abrahams, Peter.
View from Coyaba, The., 118

Abzug, Robert H.
Inside the Vicious Heart: Americans and the Liberation of Nazi ..., 2195

Adams, Alexander B.
Disputed Lands: A History of the American West., 877

Adams, Patricia.
Story of Pocahontas, The., 992

Adams, Russell L.
Great Negroes, Past and Present., 105

Adamson, Lynda G.
Reference Guide to Historical Fiction for Children and Young Adults, A., 240

Adkins, Jan.
Storm without Rain, A., 1917

Adler, David A.
George Washington: Father of Our Country: A First Biography., 1245
Martin Luther King, Jr.: Free at Last., 2759
Remember Betsy Floss and Other Colonial American Riddles., 1157
Thomas Jefferson: Father of Our Democracy: A First Biography., 1228

Adler, Mortimer J.
We Hold These Truths: Understanding the Ideas and Ideals of the..., 173

Adler, Susan S.
Meet Samantha: An American Girl., 2055
Samantha Learns a Lesson: A School Story., 2056

Agee, James.
Let Us Now Praise Famous Men., 1866

Agel, Jerome.
America At Random: Q & A., 4

Agnew, Brad.
Fort Gibson: Terminal on the Trail of Tears., 1342

Aird, H. B.
Henry Ford, Boy with Ideas., 1851

Akers, Charles W.
Abigail Adams: An American Woman., 1222

Aksyonov, Vassily.
In Search of Melancholy Baby., 2573

Albornoz, Miguel.
Hernando de Soto: Knight of the Americas., 925

Alcott, Louisa May.
Little Women., 1587

Alderman, Clifford Lindsey.
Annie Oakley and the World of Her Time., 1623
Rum, Slaves and Molasses., 1268

Alexander, Bevin.
Korea: The First War We Lost., 2396

Alexander, Mary.
Progressive Years 1898-1917, The., 1815

Aliki.
Many Lives of Benjamin Franklin, The., 1130

Aline, Countess of Romanones.
Spy Wore Red: My Adventures As an Undercover Agent in World War II., 2197

Allen, G. Freeman.
Railways: Past, Present & Future., 845

Allen, Joseph P.
Entering Space: An Astronaut's Odyssey., 2801

Allman, T. D.
Miami: City of the Future., 250

Alotta, Robert I.
Look at the Vice Presidency, A., 654

Alsop, Joseph.
FDR, 1882-1945: A Centenary Remembrance., 2301

Alsop, Susan Mary.
Yankees at the Court: First Americans in Paris., 1106

Alter, Judith MacBain.
Luke and the Van Zandt County War., 1645

Altsheler, J. A.
Border Watch, The., 970
Eyes of the Woods, The., 971
Forest Runners, The., 972
Free Rangers, The., 973
Great Sioux Trail, The., 1686
Guns of Shiloh, The., 1490
Horsemen of the Plains, 1646
Keepers of the Trail, The., 974
Riflemen of the Ohio, The., 975
Rock of Chickamauga, The., 1491
Scouts of Stonewall, The., 1492
Scouts of the Valley, The., 976
Shades of the Wilderness, The., 1493
Star of Gettysburg, The., 1494
Sword of Antietam, The., 1495
Texan Scouts, The., 1302
Texan Star, The., 1303
Texan Triumph, The., 1304
Tree of Appomattox, The., 1496
Young Trailers: A Story of Early Kentucky., 977

Alweis, Frank.
Our Social and Cultural History: American Studies., 281

Ambrose, Stephen E.
Eisenhower. Vol. 1: Soldier, General of the Army, President-Elect, 1890..., 2418
Eisenhower. Vol. 2: The President., 2419
Nixon: The Education of a Politician, 1913-1962., 2697

American Mothers Committee.
Mothers of Achievement in American History, 1776-1976., 915

Ames, Mildred.
Dancing Madness, The., 1875

Anderson, Edward.
Hungry Men., 1876

Anderson, Gary Clayton.
Little Crow: Spokesman for the Sioux., 1708

Anderson, Joan.
1787: A Novel., 1188
Christmas on the Prairie., 1436
First Thanksgiving Feast, The., 1052
Glorious Fourth at Prairietown, The., 1329
Joshua's Westward Journal., 1305
Pioneer Children of Appalachia., 1191
Williamsburg Household, A., 1033

Title Index

Subject Index

Tracks., 1964

Truth Is a Bright Star., 1347

Waterlily., 956

When the Legends Die., 1963

White Captives., 1695

Indians of North America–Hopi

Hopi, The., 416

Indians of North America–Mixed Bloods

Black Indians: A Hidden Heritage., 417

Indians of North America–Modoc

Modoc, The., 418

Indians of North America–Nanticoke

Nanticoke, The., 419

Indians of North America–Navaho

Here Come the Navaho: A History of the Largest Indian Tribe in the U.S., 422

Navaho, The., 421

Sing Down the Moon., 1699

Some People Are Indians., 420

Indians of North America–Nez Perce

Chief Joseph, Leader of Destiny., 1701

Joseph, Chief of the Nez Perce., 1702

With One Sky Above Us: Life on an Indian Reservation at the Turn of the..., 1700

Indians of North America–Omaha

Homeward the Arrow's Flight., 1703

Indians of North America–Ottawa

Pontiac, Chief of the Ottawas., 999

Indians of North America–Paiute

Chief Sarah: Sarah Winnemucca's Fight for Indian Rights., 1707

Sarah Winnemucca of the Northern Paiutes., 1705

Sarah Winnemucca., 1706

Wovoka., 1704

Indians of North America–Pawtuxet

Squanto and the First Thanksgiving., 1001

Squanto, the Pilgrim Adventure., 1000

Indians of North America–Potawatomi

Potawatomi, The., 423

Indians of North America–Pueblo

Native Americans: The Pueblos., 424

Pueblo, The., 425

Indians of North America–Sauk

Black Hawk, Frontier Warrior., 1349

Indians of North America–Seminole

Oseceola, Seminole Warrior., 1350

Seminole, The., 426

Indians of North America–Shawnee

Tecumseh, Shawnee War Chief., 1202

Indians of North America–Shoshone

Sacagawea of the Lewis and Clark Expedition., 1203

Sacajawea, Wilderness Guide., 1204

Indians of North America–Sioux

Brule: The Sioux People of the Rosebud., 427

Charles Eastman., 1713

Life and Death of Yellow Bird, The., 1710

Little Crow: Spokesman for the Sioux., 1708

Native Americans: The Sioux., 428

Sioux, The., 429

Sitting Bull and the Plains Indians., 1711

Sitting Bull, Warrior of the Sioux., 1709

To Kill an Eagle: Indian Views on the Death of Crazy Horse., 1712

Indians of North America–Wars

Chief Red Horse Tells about Custer: The Battle of the Little Bighorn,..., 1716

Fighting Indians of the West., 432

Indian Wars, The., 431

North American Indian Wars., 430

Only Earth and Sky Last Forever., 1714

Story of the Black Hawk War, The., 1351

Story of the Little Bighorn, The., 1717

Story of Wounded Knee, The., 1718

War Clouds in the West: Indians and Cavalrymen, 1860-1890., 1715

Indians of North America–Yahi

Ishi, Last of His Tribe., 1967

Ishi., 1968

Indians of North America–Yankton

Yankton Sioux, The., 433

Industrial Workers of the World

See Labor Unions and Laborers

Industry

See Business and Business People; Labor Unions and Laborers; Technology and Civilization; etc.

Inuit

See Indians of North America–Eskimo

Inventions and Inventors

Ahoy! Ahoy! Are You There? A Story of Alexander Graham Bell., 1725

Captain John Ericsson: Father of the "Monitor.", 1522

Click! A Story about George Eastman., 1723

Dreamers & Doers: Inventors Who Changed Our World., 439

Farm Combine, The., 438

Ferris Wheels., 1719

Light Bulb, The., 435

Look Out! Here Comes the Stanley Steamer., 1727

Mississippi Steamboatman., 1352

Oh, What an Awful Mess! A Story of Charles Goodyear., 1353

Pocketful of Goobers: A Story about George Washington Carver., 1969

Robert Fulton: A Biography., 1205

Rubber., 436

Sewing Machine, The., 440

Shoes for Everyone: A Story about Jan Matzeliger., 1724

Small Inventions That Make a Big Difference., 434

Steam Engine, The., 441

Stormy Genius: The Life of Aviation's Maverick, Bill Lear., 2389

Story of Thomas Alva Edison, The., 1720

Thomas Alva Edison., 1722

Thomas Alva Edison: Bringer of Light., 1721

Thomas Alva Edison: Young Inventor., 1726

Tractors: From Yesterday's Steam Wagons to Today's Turbocharged Giants., 437

Watt Got You Started, Mr. Fulton? A Story of James Watt and Robert Fulton., 1206

Iowa

Iowa., 442

Iowa: In Words and Pictures., 443

Irish Americans

Irish Americans, The., 444

Ishi

Ishi, Last of His Tribe., 1967

Ishi., 1968

Series Index

Grade Level Index

9–Adult